# INTENTIONALITY, COGNITION, AND MENTAL REPRESENTATION IN MEDIEVAL PHILOSOPHY

Medieval Philosophy
TEXTS AND STUDIES

SERIES EDITOR

Gyula Klima
*Fordham University*

EDITORIAL BOARD

Richard Cross
Brian Davies
Peter King
Brian Leftow
John Marenbon
Giorgio Pini
Robert Pasnau
Richard Taylor
Jack Zupko

# Intentionality, Cognition, and Mental Representation in Medieval Philosophy

Edited by
GYULA KLIMA

Fordham University Press • New York • 2015

Copyright © 2015 Fordham University Press

All rights reserved. No part of this publication may be reproduced, stored in a retrieval system, or transmitted in any form or by any means— electronic, mechanical, photocopy, recording, or any other—except for brief quotations in printed reviews, without the prior permission of the publisher.

Fordham University Press has no responsibility for the persistence or accuracy of URLs for external or third-party Internet websites referred to in this publication and does not guarantee that any content on such websites is, or will remain, accurate or appropriate.

Fordham University Press also publishes its books in a variety of electronic formats. Some content that appears in print may not be available in electronic books.

Visit us online at www.fordhampress.com.

Library of Congress Cataloging-in-Publication Data
Intentionality, cognition, and mental representation in medieval philosophy / edited by Gyula Klima.
    pages cm — (Medieval philosophy: texts and studies)
    Includes bibliographical references and index.
    ISBN 978-0-8232-6274-8 (cloth : alk. paper) — ISBN 978-0-8232-6275-5 (pbk. : alk. paper)
    1. Philosophy, Medieval. 2. Intentionality (Philosophy) 3. Cognition. 4. Representation (Philosophy) I. Klima, Gyula, editor.
    B721.I55 2015
    128.09'02—dc23
                        2014024865

Printed in the United States of America

17 16 15   5 4 3 2 1

First edition

CONTENTS

*Acknowledgments* xi

Introduction: Intentionality, Cognition, and Mental Representation in Medieval Philosophy
GYULA KLIMA 1

Concepts and Meaning in Medieval Philosophy
STEPHEN READ 9

Mental Language in Aquinas?
JOSHUA P. HOCHSCHILD 29

Causality and Cognition: An Interpretation of Henry of Ghent's *Quodlibet* V, q. 14
MARTIN PICKAVÉ 46

Two Models of Thinking: Thomas Aquinas and John Duns Scotus on Occurrent Thoughts
GIORGIO PINI 81

Thinking About Things: Singular Thought in the Middle Ages
PETER KING 104

Singular Terms and Vague Concepts in Late Medieval Mental Language Theory: Or, the Decline and Fall of Mental Language
HENRIK LAGERLUND 122

Act, Species, and Appearance: Peter Auriol on Intellectual Cognition and Consciousness
  RUSSELL L. FRIEDMAN  141

Ockham's Externalism
  CLAUDE PANACCIO  166

Was Adam Wodeham an Internalist or an Externalist?
  ELIZABETH KARGER  186

How Chatton Changed Ockham's Mind: William Ockham and Walter Chatton on Objects and Acts of Judgment
  SUSAN BROWER-TOLAND  204

The Nature of Intentional Objects in Nicholas of Autrecourt's Theory of Knowledge
  CHRISTOPHE GRELLARD  235

On the Several Senses of *"Intentio"* in Buridan
  JOHN ZUPKO  251

Mental Representation in Animals and Humans: Some Late Medieval Discussions
  OLAF PLUTA  273

The Intersubjective Sameness of Mental Concepts in Late Scholastic Thought
  STEPHAN MEIER-OESER  287

Mental Representations and Concepts in Medieval Philosophy
  GYULA KLIMA  323

*Bibliography* 339
*List of Contributors* 355
*Index* 357

ACKNOWLEDGMENTS

This volume has been too long in the making, so my first words of gratitude are due to the contributors, not only for their excellent contributions, but also for their unwavering patience, and in some cases their willingness to rework their contribution even multiple times to keep it up to date for its final appearance.

Besides the diligent cooperation of the contributors, this volume could not have materialized in its present form without Helen Tartar's passionate support for it, as well as for the series in which it finally appears. Her premature death was a shock that can be appeased only by carrying on her legacy.

I dedicate this book to my loving wife, Judit, and to my son, Greg, who had to endure the most during its protracted production.

INTENTIONALITY, COGNITION, AND MENTAL
REPRESENTATION IN MEDIEVAL PHILOSOPHY

# Introduction
## Intentionality, Cognition, and Mental Representation in Medieval Philosophy

GYULA KLIMA

It is supposed to be common knowledge in the history of ideas that one of the few medieval philosophical contributions preserved in modern philosophical thought is the idea that mental phenomena are distinguished from physical phenomena by their *intentionality*, their intrinsic directedness toward some object. As is usually the case with such commonplaces about the history of ideas, especially those concerning medieval ideas, this claim is not quite true. Medieval philosophers routinely described ordinary physical phenomena, such as reflections in mirrors or sounds in the air, as exhibiting intentionality, while they described what modern philosophers would take to be typically mental phenomena, such as sensation and imagination, as ordinary physical processes. Still, it is true that medieval philosophers would regard all acts of cognition as characterized by intentionality, on account of which all these acts are some sort of representations of their intended objects.[1]

The essays in this volume explore the intricacies and varieties of the conceptual relationships among intentionality, cognition, and mental representation as conceived by some of the greatest medieval philosophers, including Aquinas, Scotus, Ockham, and Buridan, and some of their lesser-known but in their own time just as influential contemporaries. The clarification of these conceptual connections sheds new light not only on the intriguing historical relationships between medieval and modern thought on these issues, but also on some fundamental questions in the philosophy of mind as it is conceived today.

The first essay, by Stephen Read, provides the ideal introduction to the exploration of these historical and conceptual connections by surveying the relationships between the psychology and logic of mental representations comparing some medieval doctrines with that of the recently very influential approach of Jerry Fodor. Fodor identifies five nonnegotiable constraints on any theory of concepts. These theses were all shared by the standard medieval theories of concepts.

---

1. For more on the differences between medieval and modern accounts of intentionality, see G. Klima, "Three Myths of Intentionality vs. Some Medieval Philosophers," *International Journal of Philosophical Studies* 21 (2013): 359–376.

However, those theories were cognitivist, in contrast with Fodor's: for medievals concepts are (mostly implicit, but explicable) definitions (*rationes*), a form of natural knowledge (an issue that I will take up in more detail in the closing essay). The medieval theories were formed under two influences, from Aristotle by way of Boethius, and from Augustine. The tension between them resulted in the Ockhamist notion of a natural language, concepts as signs. Thus conventional signs, spoken and written, signify things in the world by the mediation of concepts which themselves form a language of thought, signifying those things naturally by their representational similarity (to be distinguished from qualitative similarity, like the similarity of the shapes of two eggs). Indeed, later thinkers realized that everything signifies itself and what is like it naturally in a broad sense by means of the concept of its natural likeness.

Joshua Hochschild's essay takes up the issue of mental language—discussed by Read mostly in connection with later, nominalist authors—in connection with the thought of perhaps the most influential medieval thinker, Thomas Aquinas. Ockham is usually considered the first to hold a proper theory of mental language, but Aquinas is willing to call the concept, or the act of intellect by which something is understood, a *verbum mentis* or "mental word." In his essay, Hochschild explores the sense in which Aquinas regarded concepts as language-like. Along the way responding to arguments from John O'Callaghan that Aquinas's notion of the *verbum mentis* has no philosophical significance, Hochschild argues that Aquinas did regard thought as language-like, but that his understanding of concepts and their objects meant that his application of syntactic and semantic analysis to them did not and could not lead in the direction of theories of mental language as it was conceived by nominalist philosophers.

Although viewed from our modern perspective, given his influence even today, Aquinas can justifiably be regarded as the most influential medieval thinker, nevertheless, in Aquinas's own time, Henry of Ghent, Aquinas's formidable opponent on many issues, was at least as influential as Aquinas himself. Martin Pickavé's essay delves into the intricacies of Henry's theory of *intelligible species*, one of the centerpieces of Aquinas's theory of intellectual operations, and indeed, one of the central items in all medieval theorizing about human thought. Henry firmly denies that species are "impressed" in the intellect because in this way a species would be in the mind "as in a subject" (*ut in subiecto*), which cannot be the case for two main reasons. First, an "impressed species" would cause a natural change (*transformatio naturalis*) of its subject, but the intellect does not undergo this kind of real change when it understands. Second, the "impressed species" would be individualized by its subject, whence it would not be cognizable by the intellect, because the intellect is only directed toward something universal. Therefore, Henry concludes, a species (here, he talks about "expressed species") can only exist in the intellect "as in a cognizer" (*ut in cognoscente*). To deny this means having a wrong conception of the nature of the intellect. Thus, Henry draws a clear distinction between categorial being that things have outside the mind and mental being, the being of mental objects in the intellect. Therefore, his teaching plays an important role in the development of the theory of *esse obiectivum* that proved to be so important for fourteenth-century philosophers.

Another prominent critic of Aquinas's thought on many issues was the somewhat younger John Duns Scotus, the focus of the essay by Giorgio Pini. As Pini says, even though Scotus did not develop his account in direct opposition to Aquinas, a contrast between these two thinkers helps us to focus on some distinctive features of their respective approaches and on some characteristic moves they made to answer the question, "What is it to think?" Scotus agreed with Aquinas that, barring divine intervention, an intelligible species must be received in the intellect prior to the production of an occurrent thought about a thing's essence. Unlike Aquinas, however, Scotus argued that occurrent thoughts are qualities and not actions. This allowed him to reject the view held by Aquinas that the presence of the intelligible species in the intellect explains a thought's intentionality. Rather, Scotus claimed that a thought's intentionality is explained by a relation grounded in that thought and directed at its object.

Peter King discusses further refinements concerning the same predicament, focusing on the problem of singular thought. It should be clear from the foregoing that in the High Scholastic period, philosophers offered several competing analyses of intellective cognition in general. Yet, it is not clear whether they could give an adequate account of, say, Plato's thought of Socrates in particular. There are three problems associated with such types of cognition: (1) whether acts of thinking are able to single out individual things, akin to the modern problem of "singular thought"; (2) whether acts of thinking are able to identify the things they are about, roughly the issue of *de re* thought; (3) whether we know what thing an act of thinking about a thing is thinking about, a worry that involves internalism/externalism and consciousness of mental states. It turns out that the approaches to (1) and (3) wind up in conflict: from a naive theory as met with in Aquinas, the Scholastics wound up with an account of intuitive intellectual cognition combined with an externalist approach to thought—one of the reasons Ockham tried for an end-run around the problem by rejecting the "mentalist" series of questions in the first place. King's essay sketches out the historical development of these issues to see whether there is any way out of the thicket of these problems.

Henrik Lagerlund picks up historically where King's essay leaves off. He argues that, taken together, Buridan's attempt to supplement Ockham's theory of thought with a more plausible theory of cognition and his overall aim to give a psychologically more plausible account of human thinking radically change the Ockhamist theory. Although he stays true to the spirit of Ockham's theory, he modifies it in ways that leave no room for doubt that this is a quite different theory of thought. The differences are most clear in Ockham's and Buridan's respective views on singular terms and the corresponding singular concepts. To account for some problems associated with Ockham's theory of cognition, Buridan introduces "vague individuals" into the language of thought, the concepts expressible by a common term and a demonstrative pronoun, such as "this man." Lagerlund's essay takes a closer look at this kind of concept and shows how the introduction of such concepts ultimately changes the whole theory. It also argues that it is Buridan's theory that influences the long language-of-thought tradition that follows by tracing this theory of thought in the works of Nicholas Oresme, Marsilius of Inghen, Albert of Saxony, Peter of Ailly, and Gabriel Biel.

Buridan's key notion of singular thought was the idea that what accounts for the singularity of a singular act of cognition is the appearance of the object of thought to the cognizer as if it were in his view (*sicut in prospectu cognoscentis*), emphasizing the importance of the *content* of thought *as it appears to the cognizer*, in stark contrast to Ockham's causal account of the singularity of singular thought, let alone Aquinas's denial of the possibility of direct singular intellectual cognition (while allowing it indirectly, through a conversion to *phantasms*, the sensory representations of singulars *qua* singulars stored in sensory memory or the imagination).

A generation before Buridan, for the French Franciscan Peter Auriol, the focus of the essay by Russell Friedman, in any cognitive act, the object of cognition appears to the cognitive faculty in a special form of being, apparent being (*esse apparens*), which Auriol also calls *intentional being* (*esse intentionale*). Indeed, on Auriol's account, upon cognitive acquaintance the cognitive faculty "converts" the object of cognition into *apparent being*. Auriol argues that an apparent being is numerically identical with the thing itself, differing merely in a relational way—that is, because the thing is appearing to us. According to Auriol, Socrates of his very nature has two different ways of existing: in real being as extramental Socrates, and in apparent being as the object of the senses and intellect. Socrates as really existing and Socrates as cognized are so thoroughly identical that Auriol says whatever is predicated of the one can also be predicated of the other. Auriol's theory of cognition raises a host of questions about the role and the limitations of mental representation in theories of cognition. For instance, despite his claim that the thing as extramental and the thing as cognized are numerically identical, Auriol appears to be duplicating the world, having a thing on one plane of existence, and its representation on another plane, thus introducing at least the conceptual possibility of a "veil of perception," a possibility that is becoming ever more significant for the next generation of thinkers, working their way toward the early modern "chasm" between the phenomenal appearance of the object to the cognizer and its existence (or nonexistence) in itself.

It is this new conceptual possibility that receives a new theoretical foundation in Ockham's externalist semantics, cognitive psychology, and epistemology, the subject matter of Claude Panaccio's essay. Externalism, understood as the thesis that "meanings are not in the head," has come to the forefront of discussions in philosophy of language and mind in the past thirty years or so. And it has often been presented as a radically new approach in the history of philosophy. Panaccio's paper shows that there was an important externalist drive in William of Ockham's theory of language and mind in the fourteenth century. After distinguishing three different forms of externalism (linguistic externalism, mental content externalism and epistemic externalism), Panaccio argues that Ockham has a principled externalist stance on all three counts. One particularly important result of Panaccio's investigations is that Ockham's externalism critically hinges on his account of the semantic content of concepts as being causally determined, quite independently from what Panaccio calls the "perceptual schemata" enclosed in concepts. The latter are what the cognitive subject having the concept is aware of about the typical phenomenal appearance of the objects to which the concept applies, which helps the cognizer to recognize individuals falling under the concept as such, most of the time fairly reliably, but not infallibly. This separation of the semantic and phenomenal content of intellectual concepts is again moving in the direction of opening up the logical (and hence by divine omnipotence certainly realizable) possibility of the separation of the phenomenal content of subjective consciousness and the external reality this consciousness is normally supposed to be about, an issue of much recent discussion in the literature, to be taken up briefly again in the last essay.[2]

A rather different development can be detected in the thought of Ockham's younger contemporary, Adam Wodeham, whom Elizabeth Karger discusses in her essay. Adam Wodeham held, as did most of his contemporaries, that God could always have acted alone to cause the effect caused by a natural cause, while the essence of the thing caused would have remained the same. The essay intends to show how this assumption shaped Wodeham's theory of mind. More specifically, according to Wodeham, our thoughts are the thoughts they are, with the content they have, quite independently of the things existing in our environment, including those things, which, as a matter of fact, may have contributed to causing them. Rather, the content of each of our thoughts is fixed by a property intrinsic to the thought itself. Its content would therefore have been the same if God had acted alone to produce it in our mind. However, Karger concludes, this suggests that Wodeham's theory of mind should be regarded as internalist, rather than externalist.

Another key player of late medieval developments is Nicholas of Autrecourt, the focus of Christophe Grellard's essay. Its main aim is to elucidate the status of the objects of intentional acts in Nicholas of Autrecourt's epistemology. Autrecourt's description of the acts of knowing, feeling, thinking and other

---

2. For a thorough discussion of the related issues, see G. Klima and A. Hall, eds., *The Demonic Temptations of Medieval Nominalism* (Newcastle-upon-Tyne: Cambridge Scholars Publishers, 2011).

intentional acts relies on the Aristotelian conception of intentional identity between the knower and the known. Having presented this theory (especially using information given in the anonymous commentary of the manuscript Harley 3243 of the British Library), Grellard focuses on the problem of the nature of intentional objects. It seems that Autrecourt's conception evolved over time. In his early work, he is defending a kind of direct realism. The *apparentia* is the mental act that is isomorphic to the external object. But in his later work, toward the end of his academic teaching (that is, in the last part of *Exigit ordo*, and in the disputed question on vision), Autrecourt is espousing a theory close to *phenomenalism*, probably because of some Platonist influences: the object of knowledge on this conception is not the real being of the external thing, which is unknowable *in se*, but the *esse obiectivum* of the object in the mind.

The essays so far have focused on the intricacies of late medieval debates concerning the acts and objects of simple apprehension and only briefly touched on issues of the other two basic mental operations distinguished by Aristotle (in connection with the problems of interpreting medieval conceptions of a "mental language"), namely, judgment formation and reasoning. After covering these intricacies, the stage is set for delving into some details of late medieval analyses of these other operations, which is the focus of Susan Brower-Toland's essay. In particular, she discusses some intricate details of the development of Ockham's thought concerning the objects of acts of judgment, as prompted by his debates with his slightly younger contemporary, Walter Chatton. It is well known that Chatton is among the earliest and most vehement critics of Ockham's theory of judgment, but scholars have overlooked the role Chatton's criticisms play in shaping Ockham's final theory of judgment. Brower-Toland demonstrates not only that Ockham's most mature treatment of judgment contains revisions that resolve the problems Chatton identifies in Ockham's earlier theories, but also that these revisions ultimately bring his final account of objects of judgment surprisingly close to Chatton's own. Even so, she concludes, there remain significant differences between their respective analyses of the structure and intentionality of judicative states.

Jack Zupko offers a kind of "natural history" of the concept of intention in the great nominalist synthesis of John Buridan, meticulously contrasting Buridan's understanding of the term *intentio* in its various uses with that of his medieval forebears, as well as with our modern notion of intentionality. With respect to the latter, Zupko says, "it turns out that Brentano recovered only small part of what *intentio* meant for medieval philosophers and theologians, and missed the part they would have regarded as the most important." Intentionality cannot be "the mark of the mental" in any exclusive sense for Buridan because he attributes *intentiones* to brute animals and even to inanimate objects like fire, in which the term designates nonintellectual dispositions and various unrealized but entirely physical potentialities. In this sense, intentionality marks not only the mental, but also something much greater: the "true word" in Augustine's sense, that is, the intelligible structure of a world freely created by a provident God. Thus, as Zupko concludes, "fires and donkeys and men are all suffused with meaning, and what they signify is the rational hand of their creator."

While the previous essays almost exclusively focused on *mental* representation in the stricter medieval sense (meaning *intellectual* representation) especially in humans, Olaf Pluta's gives us a taste of the rich medieval literature on cognitive representation in animals, focusing on Buridan's treatment of the cognitive abilities of animals, by raising the question whether in some sense even animals think. During the Middle Ages, it was generally assumed that the capacity to form universal concepts is characteristic of and unique to human thinking. While animal souls were considered to be material forms, that is to say, educed from the potency of matter, the human intellective soul was taken to be immaterial and immortal. Thomas Aquinas used the ability to form universal concepts as the key argument in his demonstration that the human intellect is immaterial and hence immortal. Some medieval thinkers, however, did not share this common view. John Buridan, for example, argues against this opinion, which, as he says, is held by many contemporaries and nearly all ancient commentators (*multi et quasi omnes expositores antiqui*), against the opinion, that is, that the human intellect apprehends universally because it is immaterial and unextended. In two parallel and complementary texts from his *Questions on Aristotle's Physics* and *Questions on Aristotle's De anima* respectively, Buridan shows that the human intellect is capable of universal cognition even if we assume that it is a material form. According to his natural philosophy, the human intellect is taken to be a generated and corruptible material form, educed from the potency of matter and extended like matter just like the soul of animals—"like the soul of a cow or a dog." Consequently, Buridan holds that animals can likewise refer to things universally. Some higher species of animals such as dogs are even "capable of thinking in a logical way, albeit not in such a sophisticated and complete a way as man or ape." Referring to an example known since antiquity, Buridan argues that a dog is using logical reasoning— Buridan uses the terms *ratiocinari* and *syllogizare*—to determine which way to go when the dog comes to a three-way crossroads. According to Buridan, a syllogism is a simple mental act within the soul, even though it is a complex semantic structure. Such an act may easily be possible for animals, even though they cannot express it by means of language.

Stephan Meier-Oeser returns to intellectual representation in the context of even later developments in scholastic philosophy, focusing on the issue of intersubjective understanding. According to an important statement of Aristotle's *De Interpretatione*, mental concepts are the same for all men (*eaedem omnibus passiones animae sunt*). What does this mean? In what sense is it possible for concepts, as particular mental entities or acts of certain individuals, to be the same for all?[3] Late scholastic logic explored and discussed different interpretations and justifications of this statement which are closely connected to some systematic, fundamental epistemological and truth-theoretical issues, such as the simplicity of concepts, the intellect's infallibility regarding simple concepts or the existence of *veritas simplex*, that is, truth (or even falseness; Descartes's *falsitas materialis*) on the level of the so-called first mental operation or simple apprehension. The essay gives a survey of the main positions and central points of these debates from the fourteenth to the seventeenth century.

Finally, I provide a systematic survey of the main issues concerning scholastic theories of mental representation covered in the volume. I argue that basically two major approaches developed, determining two fundamentally different constructions of logical semantics and related theories in cognitive psychology and epistemology: the realist *via antiqua* and the nominalist *via moderna*, branching out under these names into separate schools or movements of thought over the last centuries of medieval scholasticism (the centuries covered by the previous essay). One of the main contentions of my essay is that what fundamentally separates these schools of thought is not so much their otherwise obvious factual (but not *in principle*) difference *in ontology*, as their different constructions of *logical semantics*: an "intensionalist" construction on the part of realists and an "extensionalist" one on the part of the nominalists. A further contention of the essay is that this difference is still not the most fundamental one, however, as it is still based on the two parties' different understanding of what concepts are. I conclude that, as evidenced by the foregoing essays, the new conceptions of concepts emerging with the *via moderna* open up the late medieval possibility of "Demon-skepticism," paving the way to the *epistemological* predicaments of early modern philosophy, still affecting many contemporary approaches in the field. It is primarily for this reason that the essays of the volume are not only contributions to our better understanding of history, but they are also contributions to a better understanding of our contemporary problems in the field.

---

3. For a discussion of the same issue in the context of Ockhamist nominalism, see G. Klima, "Ontological Reduction by Logical Analysis and the Primitive Vocabulary of Mentalese," *American Catholic Philosophical Quarterly* 86 (2012): 303–414.

# Concepts and Meaning in Medieval Philosophy

STEPHEN READ

The medieval theory of signification underpinned the theory of truth, which in turn fed into a theory of inference. The theory of signification describes generally how words relate to things and how propositions come to mean what they do. But this general description needs a further account of how a particular occurrence of a word in a particular proposition is related to which things in what way. Only then can one say what has to be the case for the proposition to be true, and so determine how truth is preserved in an inference.

For the medievals in whom I am interested, the signification of words and propositions was made possible by their link to concepts. Vocal signs are seen as imposed by custom as marks or signs for concepts, and written signs are in turn marks or signs for vocal signs, and so indirectly for concepts. Concepts, however, signify or conceive a range of objects naturally, not by any conventional imposition. Concepts are formed by abstraction from sensory cognition. These medieval thinkers inherited from Aristotle, and took further, an elaborate and rich theory of cognitive powers that drew from sensation the whole panoply of cognitive awareness. The common sense discovers shape, motion, and other aspects of cognition not present in each particular sense—separate experiences are needed to discern motion, and both sight and touch are needed to learn about shape or figure. An estimative or cogitative sense is needed to recognize the hostility of the wolf or the friendliness of the dog, qualities not immediately evident in sensation. Further composition and division is needed to create further concepts, and abstraction to understand generality. But they were empiricists, following Aristotle in believing that all knowledge is derived from the senses: "The mind is a *tabula rasa* on which nothing is at first written, but can be written" (*De Anima* 430a1). The innate powers of cognition were

---

This essay was delivered as the Brigitte Rosenkranz Memorial Lecture at UCLA in 2002, a series of annual lectures in memory of Brigitte Rosenkranz, who was a graduate student there. The paper is largely drawn from my contribution to the introduction to E. P. Bos and S. Read, *Concepts: The Treatises of Thomas of Cleves and Paul of Gelria* (Leuven: Peeters, 2001), with permission of Peeters Publishers. It also draws on passages in my article "How Is Material Supposition Possible," *Medieval Philosophy and Theology* 8 (1999): 1–20, with permission of Cambridge University Press.

manifold and considerable, but no more than is necessary to the empiricist project of obtaining all real knowledge through the senses.

Concepts, therefore, have a natural epistemological relation to the class of things that they signify. To call it "natural" means that the concept is linked by a lawlike causal connection to that of which it is a concept, that causal link being explained by the mind's cognitive abilities. Conventional signs, the signs of spoken and written language, in contrast, gain their signification only by being linked by custom and practice to those natural signs. They obtain their signification indirectly, in what Simon Blackburn called a "dog-legged" manner.[1] Their immediate signification, or what they are primarily attached or subordinate to, is the concept; thereby, their ultimate signification is the range of things to which the concept applies. John Buridan wrote, in the 1350s: "Categorematic words ... signify things by the mediation of their concepts, according to which concepts, or similar ones, they were imposed to signify. So we call the things conceived by those concepts 'ultimate significata' ... but the concepts we call 'immediate significata.'"[2]

## CONCEPTS IN MODERN PHILOSOPHY

What are concepts? Nowadays, just as in medieval times, it is common to identify them as constituents of mental propositions or thoughts. Many mental states have content. They consist in representing something as of some character. That content is specified by a proposition. Just as the sentence expressing that proposition has structure and consists of subsentential expressions, so it is claimed, propositions can be articulated into components. These propositions have a content that is structured and consists of concepts arranged in a certain conceptual structure, a mental language of concepts.

Concepts are hyperintensional. That is, the criteria of distinctness of concepts are stricter than necessary equivalence. For example, the concepts "triangle" and "trilateral" are necessarily equivalent—anything that is trilateral is necessarily triangular, and vice versa. Nonetheless, the concepts are distinct. What makes them distinct is that one can believe that the one applies to something without the other. Concepts map out the fine structure of beliefs.

The central opposition in theories of concepts is between those who treat concepts as mental particulars and those who treat them as abstract objects. What unites concepts is their content, and that content consists of a common conceptual structure. Without the mental acts of judging, believing, thinking,

---

1. Simon Blackburn, *Spreading the Word* (Oxford: Clarendon Press, 1984), 40.
2. Johannes Buridan, *Summulae de Dialectica*, tr. G. Klima (New Haven: Yale University Press, 2001), 253–254; cf. Buridan, *Summulae de Suppositionibus*, ed. R. van der Lecq (Nijmegen: Ingenium, 1998), 39: "dictiones categorematicae ... significant res aliquas mediantibus conceptibus earum, secundum quos conceptus vel similitudines impositae fuerunt ad significandum. Sic ergo res illas illis conceptibus conceptas vocamus ultimata significata in proposito. Illos autem conceptus vocamus significata immediata."

there would be no content, no abstract universal. The nominalist urges that concepts have no existence beyond our minds, yet is willing to treat them as a common medium for the articulation and expression of those thoughts. The realist, in contrast, claims priority for the common medium, construing the private thoughts as derivative therefrom.

On the common view, concepts are a kind of particular. They are not only mind-dependent but also private. We may suggest that different people can share the same concept, since they can think the same thought—that is, their thoughts can have the same content. But all these terms equivocate between a private and a public reference. Each of us has his or her own thoughts and beliefs, and we make our own judgments; we speak loosely when we say that we share and communicate these thoughts, that we can have the same beliefs, and that we make the same judgments.

The hardest question is how a concept is related to its instances, to objects. Again, the popular view grounds this relation in the elaboration of conceptual structure as a mental language. As a language, its constituents are signs, and a concept is related to its instances as a sign to what it signifies. Just as sentences and words are signs, so too mental propositions and concepts are signs, with their own special relation to those objects. What is that relation? Contemporary philosophy of mind is predominantly naturalistic, so that such relations are to be explained in terms of some natural relation, for example, a causal relation. Acquaintance with the object causes the formation of the concept, which then becomes a natural sign for it. An alternative theory claims that the atomic elements of the language of thought are, in some way, innate. Yet, that threatens to make their relation to objects mysterious and unanalyzable, or at least to require an explanation not grounded in experience. Less mysterious is the normal empiricist resort, which is to posit a faculty (innate) of abstraction, which responds to suitable input by eliciting the appropriate concept. Indeed, it is difficult to see how a naturalistic, for example, causal theory, can work without such an inborn ability.

Concepts play an explanatory role. Intentional explanation of a person's actions needs to relate those actions to the intentions and goals to which they are directed. To fill out the intentional nature of the explanation, those actions need to be described in terms that relate to the agent's beliefs and purposes. Thus, similar actions can result from dissimilar intents; and different actions can subserve similar purposes. The theory of content articulates this explanatory scheme into a language of the mind. The building blocks of this language are concepts.

Not only is this conceptual language the focus of contemporary research into cognitive science and philosophy of mind, but it was also the center of attention in philosophical thinking in the fourteenth century. There is a remarkable parallel indeed between contemporary concerns and theories and medieval conceptions. Perhaps this should not be remarkable—after all, the one preceded the other by some six centuries. But the chain of descent is tangled, and there is assuredly no direct influence of the one on the other. Some may argue that it illustrates the phenomenon of convergence on the truth, others that the same siren voices continue to lead the best thinkers astray.

In his book *Concepts*, Jerry Fodor presents five theses that together make up what he calls the Representative Theory of Mind, which is to form the bedrock of his theory of concepts.[3] Concepts are mental particulars with both causal powers and semantic content. The central task he presents is to reveal the link between these two aspects. The first thesis states:

1. Psychological explanation is typically nomic and is intentional through and through.

Those who deny this are those physicalists who believe that one day all will be stateable in the language of physics. The medieval conception was definitely on Fodor's side.

2. "Mental representations" are the primitive bearers of intentional content.

That is, the mental realm is prior to, and explanatory of, the vocal and written realm. The medievals would heartily agree.

3. Thinking is computation.

Fodor makes much here of Turing's analysis of the notion of effective computation. The crux seems to be, however, that Turing treated mental representations as symbols. We will see in §3 that this was the revolutionary insight of the thirteenth century that produced the flowering of semantic theory in the fourteenth century.

4. Meaning is information (more or less).

The intention is that semantic content follows (somehow) from causal relations, that the content of a concept is a result of its causal relationship to what falls under it. This is what the medievals articulated in their talk of cognitions "naturally signifying" those things which were included in them. Nor were they backward in describing the sensory and intellectual mechanisms by which the cognitions were formed, building on Aristotle's discussion in his *De Anima* and other biological works.

5. Whatever distinguishes coextensive concepts is ipso facto "in the head."

The medievals would agree: if the things signified are the same—where then can the difference lie? It must lie in the cognitions—"in the head." The cogni-

---

3. J. Fodor, *Concepts: Where Cognitive Science Went Wrong* (Oxford: Oxford University Press, 1998), especially 7 ff.

tions have different content, but any abstract notion of content is parasitic on the particular content of particular mental states. So Fodor shares an internalist conception with his medieval precursors.

Fodor's main target in his study is to show that concepts cannot be definitions, for no such concepts could be acquired—or at least, the primitive basis must be atomic and not definitional. He describes his preferred theory as informational atomism, where the concept $x$ is not constituted by reference to $x$s, but by reference to the response which we humans have to experience of $x$s. Here he departs radically not just from contemporary cognitive science—as he recognizes—but also from the medieval picture. For the medieval conception is through and through cognitivist: there is a mechanism by which we acquire the concept of $x$ by experience of $x$s. The medievals received this model from Aristotle. It is a classical, empiricist model. For it is worth recognizing that the contrast between empiricism and rationalism is really one of degree, not of kind. The former announces that all concepts are acquired, the latter that some are innate. But each has to modify its claim, the empiricist admitting that some "innate" capacity or mechanism (abstraction, induction or whatever) is needed in order to acquire concepts from experience; the rationalist that concepts are only latently there at birth, and their overt recognition is triggered by experience through an appropriate "innate" mechanism. The medievals then are seen as Aristotelians, interested in the mechanism of concept acquisition; Fodor as Platonist, interested in the trigger by which we respond to experience by producing certain concepts to which we are by our nature prone. Fodor describes his theory as explicitly "non-cognitivist": a concept $x$ is constituted not (as the definitional theory claims) by what $x$s have in common, but by our response to $x$s—how $x$s strike us. Only in this way, he believes, can one explain concept acquisition.

Medieval authors show their rejection of such a theory from the start: "First, we say that concepts are cognitions," writes Thomas of Cleves in the first paragraph of his treatise on *Concepts* of 1370 or thereabouts.[4] This is not just a pun: Concepts for the medievals really put us in touch with how things are, and they constitute a form of knowledge. Moreover, concepts are definitions. The main casualty of denying this, Fodor notes, is analytic connection. If each concept embraces others, either as parts in a literally combinatorial conception, or as constituted by its inferential connections with others, we have an immediate explanation of analytic connections as connections between concepts. On the other hand, if concepts are atomic, connections between them can only be inessential and by association—a position sympathetic to Quine's notorious rejection of analyticity.

---

4. See E. P. Bos and S. Read, *Concepts: The Treatises of Thomas of Cleves and Paul of Gelria* (Leuven: Peeters, 2001), 91: "Dicamus . . . primo quod conceptus sunt cognitiones."

In fact, both definitional and atomist theories of concepts admit both complex and unanalyzable concepts. Only a holistic theory—the "theory theory,"[5] as it has been called—can claim that every concept is decomposable. Fodor's so-called atomist theory includes molecular concepts like "white man," which conjoins the possibly atomic concepts "white" and "man." Conversely, the definitional theory cannot maintain that all concepts decompose further, on pain of a regress. The real difference between the two accounts lies in their account of concept acquisition and application: what is the link between the concept $x$ and $x$s? For Fodor, it is contingent and statistical; for the definitional theory, it is essential—causal and natural.

Thomas of Cleves devotes several pages to discussion of such analytic connections. His analysis suggests a compositional conception of concepts and signs. For example, "white man" is superior in signification to "man," for it includes it as part of its signification and so signifies more. But it is inferior to "man" inferentially (*in consequendo*), for if there is a white man there is a man, but not vice versa. Signs and concepts are constituted by their signification, which results in their inferential connections. But the inferential model, which in more recent times has displaced the compositional model as an articulation of the definitional theory, is not in evidence. It is the innate capacity to abstract that makes the compositional and definitional conception of concepts viable.

Thomas's treatment of concepts, a model of its time, is thus very different in its epistemological basis from Fodor's information-theoretic account. What they share, however, is also important and extensive. Concepts are mental particulars which provide categories for classification, and they can be composed into thoughts or propositions in such a way that the signification of the composite thought derives from that of its constituents. Concepts are—for us humans, at any rate—learned and public: we all learn them and share them. Fodor describes his five conditions on any theory of concepts as "non-negotiable" (23), so it is not too surprising, perhaps, that he shares them with Paul of Gelria and Thomas of Cleves. But it is important, for it shows how contemporary are the medievals' concerns, despite the six hundred years that separate us from them.

### THE BOETHIAN AND AUGUSTINIAN TRADITIONS

Our conception of concepts and content has, as described earlier, an ancestry in the semantic theories and epistemology of the Middle Ages, which in turn were inspired by a passage in Aristotle's *De Interpretatione* as interpreted by Boethius. Boethius translates Aristotle's remark at 16a3–4 as follows: "spoken [words] are signs (*notae*) of impressions (*passionum*) in the soul, and the written ones

---

5. Fodor, *Concepts*, 112 ff.

are those of the spoken ones;"⁶ and in his commentary he elaborates on the relation between written inscription (*litterae*), the spoken sound (*vox*), the thought or concept (*intellectus*) and the thing (*res*) as follows: "for thing, concept, sound and letter are four: the concept conceives the thing, spoken sounds are signs of the concept, and letters signify the sounds."⁷ That is, the letters (in writing) signify the spoken utterance, which in turn designates (a literary variant of "signify," perhaps, since in the Aristotelian passage they were both *notae*) the concept.⁸ The function of the concept is to act as an intermediary, relating word (spoken and written) and thing, for the concept is an effect or impression (*passio*) of the thing in the mind. So, if the word signifies the concept by some human conventional imposition, then on hearing the word, we will come naturally to think of the thing. For the mind forms a likeness (*similitudo*) of things by a natural capacity. Whereas different peoples, speaking different languages have different words, both written and spoken, the things and the concepts and likenesses by which they conceive them are the same. Boethius's translation of Aristotle continues: "and just as the letters are not the same, neither are the sounds. But they are signs of the same impressions for all, and those in turn are likenesses of the same things."⁹ Thus we inhabit the same world and conceive of it the same way, says Aristotle; but we speak (and so write) of it differently.

This is the dominant semantic scheme of the medieval period: words signify concepts, which are likenesses of things in the world. But there is a further suggestion, indeed, a rather different picture, present in Boethius that was fully elaborated only in the thirteenth and fourteenth centuries. A few pages later in his first commentary, Boethius writes: "for the spoken sound and the concept of the thing signify the same thing."¹⁰ The spoken sound signifies both the concept and the thing in the world. When we say "stone," we signify first the thought or concept of stone and secondarily the stone itself. But in his second commentary, Boethius draws back from this conception, declaring that "although sounds are names of things, but we don't use sounds in this way to signify things, but [to signify] those impressions of things in the soul which are within

---

6. Boethius, *Commentarii in librum Aristotelis Peri Hermeneias: Editio Prima*, ed. C. Meiser (Leipzig: Teubner, 1877), 36: "sunt ergo ea quae sunt in voce earum quae sunt in anima passionum notae et ea quae scribuntur eorum quae sunt in voce."

7. Ibid., 37: "cum igitur haec sint quattuor: res, intellectus, vox, littera, rem concipit intellectus, intellectum vero voces designant, ipsas vero voces litterae significant."

8. Cf. E. J. Ashworth, "Jacobus Naveros (fl. ca. 1533) on the question: 'Do spoken words signify concepts or things?'" in *Logos and Pragma*, ed. L. M. de Rijk and H. Braakhuis (Nijmegen: Ingenium, 1987), 208 n. 10.

9. Boethius, *Commentarii*, 36: "et quemadmodum nec litterae omnibus eaedem, sic nec voces eaedem. Quorum autem haec primorum notae, eaedem omnibus passiones animae et quorum hae similitudines, res etiam eaedem."

10. Boethius, *Commentarii*, 40: "vox enim et intellectum rei significat et ipsam rem."

us."[11] That is, although spoken sounds are names of things and are so by virtue of signifying (by convention) their corresponding concepts (*passiones animae*), the vocal utterance does not itself in any way signify the thing conceived. For Aristotle had not expressed it in that way.

Equally influential, however, if not more so, was a passage in Augustine's *De Doctrina Christiana*, where Augustine defines the sign: "for a sign is something that besides its image (*species*) which it impresses on the senses makes something else come into thought."[12] There is explicit reference to this definition in, for example, the *Commentary on Priscian Major* ascribed to Robert Kilwardby,[13] and an implicit one in William of Ockham's *Summa Logicae* I 1,[14] and many other places. However, the Augustinian account differs from Boethius' in two important respects. First, what is signified is the thing—as brought out by Augustine's examples: a footprint is a sign of a foot; and "cow" signifies cows (II x 15)—in both cases because the sign brings the object to mind. Secondly, the sign is required to act on the senses, whether visually, or aurally, or through one of the other senses (cf. II III 4).

The first of these differences takes further the idea that we saw Boethius toyed with in his first commentary, that names signify those things of which they are names. To be sure, they do so through the mediation of a concept or act of mind. That mental act is vital to Augustine's semiotics, but it is not itself signified by the sign. Rather, he speaks of the sign "showing" (*demonstrare*) what is in the mind: "Conventional signs are those which living things give to each other, in order to show . . . the acts of their soul (*motus animi*), or what they have sensed or thought."[15] The spoken and written word serves to convey from one mind to another these thoughts or emotions (*motus animi*). But in the Augustinian account, words signify what they name—the things we talk about.

The question, whether words signify concepts or things, came to the fore in the mid–thirteenth century. Roger Bacon speaks of a great debate on the

---

11. Boethius, *Commentarii in librum Aristotelis Peri Hermeneias: Editio Secunda*, ed. C. Meiser, Leipzig: Teubner, 1880), 41: "licet voces rerum nomina sint, tamen non idcirco utimur vocibus, ut res significemus, sed ut eas quae ex rebus nobis innatae sunt animae passiones."

12. Augustine, *De Doctrina Christiana*, ed. R. P. H. Green (Oxford: Clarendon Press, 1995), II I 1: "signum est enim res praeter speciem quam ingerit sensibus aliud aliquid ex se faciens in cogitationem venire."

13. K. M. Fredborg, N. J. Green-Pedersen, L. Nielsen, and J. Pinborg, "The Commentary on 'Priscianus Maior' Ascribed to Robert Kilwardby," *Cahiers de l'Institut du Moyen-Age Grec et Latin* 15 (1975): 1.

14. G. de Ockham, *Summa Logicae*, ed. P. Boehner, G. Gál, and S. F. Brown (St. Bonaventure, N.Y.: Franciscan Institute, 1974), 9.

15. Augustine, *De Doctrina Christiana*, ed. R. P. H. Green (Oxford: Clarendon Press, 1995), II II 3: "Data vero signa sunt quae sibi quaeque viventia invicem dant ad demonstrandos quantum possunt motus animi sui vel sensa aut intellecta quaelibet."

subject,[16] as does John Duns Scotus some years later.[17] Besides the authority of Aristotle via Boethius—and what Aristotle meant is open to interpretation—arguments on each side can be given. For example, if words signified things, would empty names not then become impossible?[18] On the other hand, when I say that Socrates runs, I mean that Socrates himself runs, not that some image or concept in the mind runs (or images running in the mind).[19] Bacon was only one among many, such as Peter of Auvergne, Peter of Cornwall, and ps-Kilwardby, to extend what is signified from concepts to things.[20]

In tandem with this change in what was signified (things, not concepts) went another, but this time one to which the Augustinian formula was antithetical, in its further requirement that the sign affect the senses in some way. If the word (spoken or written) signifies the thing by virtue of its connection to the concept, what is the right account of the connection of concept and thing? The big idea, which was to produce a huge theoretical development in the fourteenth century, was to suggest that the concept itself is a sign. This was the major original contribution of the thirteenth century, prefigured in Boethius but contrary to the Augustinian inheritance. For it goes directly against Augustine's suggestion that the concept is invoked as intermediary by the operation of the sign on the senses: concepts are insensible; but in the Boethian tradition, although the concept is what is signified by the spoken sound, there is a suggestion that it itself signifies. Boethius writes: "of which therefore there are these four: letters, sounds, concepts, things, and most closely and principally letters signify verbs and names. These in turn principally and truly designate concepts, but in the second place also things. Concepts however are significative only of things."[21]

The new conception of the signification of concepts is found as early as the *Logica* attributed to Lambert of Auxerre (c. 1240).[22] Ps-Kilwardby shows how to square the new conception with the Augustinian requirement. "Sign" can be taken in two ways, he says. In one way, it is material and sensible, and works

---

16. R. Bacon, *De Signis*, in K. M. Fredborg L. Nielsen and J. Pinborg, "An Inedited Part of Roger Bacon's *Opus maius: De signis*," *Traditio* 34 (1978): 132.

17. J. Duns Scotus, *Ordinatio*, ed. C. Balic, vol. 6 (Vatican City: Typis Polyglottis Vaticanis, 1963), 97 (I d 27 ad 1ᵃᵐ).

18. Kilwardby in Fredborg et al., "The Commentary on 'Priscianus Maior,'" 67 (§2.1.7) and 71 (§2.1.9).

19. Cf. Bacon, *De Signis*, 133.

20. See, e.g., Joel Biard, *Logique et Théorie du Signe au XIVᵉ Siècle* (Paris: Librairie Philosophique, 1989), 33 ff.

21. Boethius, *Commentarii: Editio Secunda*, 24: "cui igitur haec sint quattuor, litterae, voces, intellectus, res, proxime quidem et principaliter litterae verba nominaque significant. Haec vero principaliter quidem intellectus, secundo vero loco res quoque designant. Intellectus vero ipsi nihil aliud nisi rerum significativi sunt."

22. Lambert, *Logica (Summa Lamberti)*, ed. F. Alessio (Florence: La Nuova Italia, 1971), 205–6.

by its action on the senses. But in another way, we can think of it in abstraction from its sensible and material aspects—and this is the real subject of the science of signs.[23] This new departure found its greatest influence in the work of Scotus and Ockham. It also needs to be squared with Aristotle. Scotus writes: "the concept is a natural sign of its object (*De Interpretatione* ch. 1: impressions [in the soul] are signs of things and naturally so)."[24] Bacon says much the same: "not every sign is offered to the sense as the usual description of a sign supposes, but something is offered to the intellect alone, as Aristotle observed, who says that impressions in the soul are signs of things."[25] Perhaps misquotation is the only solution, for Aristotle goes on to say categorically that every name is so by convention, since no name is a name naturally: "I said, 'according to convention,' for nothing is naturally a name but only when it is a sign."[26] The way was now clear for Ockham to open his *Summa Logicae* with the words: "a concept-term is a concept or impression in the soul signifying or consignifying something naturally."[27] In doing so, he refers explicitly to Boethius and to Augustine.

### MENTAL LANGUAGE

The seeds were sown in Boethius's commentary on Aristotle; they were nurtured and developed in the thirteenth-century discussions of the sign; but the full theory of a language of concepts, a mental language, found its most famous (or notorious) exponent in the fourteenth century, namely, William of Ockham. A further inspiration for Ockham, and others, was Augustine's image, in his *De Trinitate*, of an inner language. For Ockham, this finally broke the most important link in the Aristotelian chain, that between spoken word and concept. Ockham no longer describes this as a link of signification. Rather, the spoken word is subordinated to the corresponding mental word, and the spoken proposition is subordinated to the mental proposition. The mental word is a concept, a mental item fitted for inclusion in a mental proposition. This is the primary language, what naturally has signification. The spoken word and spoken proposition pick up this signification derivatively and secondarily by corresponding

---

23. Fredborg et al., "The Commentary on 'Priscianus Maior,'" 4.
24. J. Duns Scotus, *Quaestiones subtillisimae super libros Metaphysicos Aristotelis*, lib. VI quaestio III (*Opera Omnia*, vol. 7. Paris: Vivès, 1893), 334a: "intellectio, ut est obiecti, est signum naturale eius (I. Peri Hermeneias: 'passiones sunt notae rerum' et hoc naturaliter)."
25. Bacon attributes the doctrine to Aristotle, too: "non omne signum offertur sensui ut vulgata descriptio signi supponit, sed aliquod soli intellectui offertur, testante Aristotele, qui dicit passiones animae esse signa rerum." Fredborg, Nielsen, and Pinborg, "An Inedited Part," 82.
26. Aristotle, *De Interpretatione*, 16a26. Cf. Boethius, *Commentarii: Editio Prima*, 50: "secundum placitum vero, quoniam naturaliter nominum nihil est, sed quando fit nota."
27. Ockham, *Summa Logicae*, I 1: "terminus conceptus est intentio seu passio animae aliquid naturaliter significans vel consignificans."

to these mental items: "these concept-terms and propositions composed of them are those mental words which exist only in the mind and cannot be revealed externally, whereas sounds as signs subordinate to them can be pronounced publicly."[28] "It is clear that to every true or false spoken utterance there corresponds a mental proposition composed of concepts."[29]

Language is threefold (written, spoken, and mental), but the focus is on mental language. Mental language is common to all, whereas written and spoken languages differ between different peoples, as Aristotle had observed. Mental language provides a "universal semantics,"[30] a natural medium whose properties of signification arise naturally by a causal process. Having a certain concept is not independent of having certain linguistic abilities; it is an ability to exercise those concepts that confers on written and spoken utterances the signification which they have.

The mental language serves to explain many philosophical and semantic phenomena. The presence of the mental proposition distinguishes meaningful utterances from mere parroting—the parrot who recites "Daisy, daisy" is not accompanying the sounds with the appropriate mental commentary. The mental term or concept serves to disambiguate vocal terms, e.g., "*canis*," the much-used example, which can mean "dog," "dogfish," or "dog star." The concept also unites different utterances from different languages, so that, e.g., "*canis*" and "dog" are marks of the same mental item, and so are appropriate translations—the Aristotelian diversity is united in the mental identity. The concept and the mental proposition provide intensionality where the shift to things as what is signified might threaten to remove it. To take a modern example, "renate" and "cordate" will for Ockham signify the same things, those creatures that have a kidney and those that have a heart, since they are, we are told, the very same animals. Signification, now that words signify things, not concepts, is extensional. What distinguishes the spoken words "renate" and "cordate" is that they are marks of different concepts. What distinguishes the concepts? Their makeup. Simple concepts can be distinguished only in what they are concepts of, that is, extensionally. So "renate" and "cordate" must be complex concepts. The one contains reference to the concept *kidney*, where the other contains reference to the concept *heart*.[31]

---

28. Ibid.: "isti termini concepti et propositiones ex eis compositae sunt illa verba mentalia quae . . . tantum in mente manent et exterius proferri non possunt, quamvis voces tamquam signa subordinata eis pronuntientur exterius."

29. G. de Ockham, *Quodlibeta Septem*, ed. J. Wey (St. Bonaventure, N.Y.: Franciscan Institute, 1980), 509 (V quaestio 8): "Patet . . . quod omni orationi vocali verae et falsae correspondet aliqua propositio mentalis composita ex conceptibus."

30. The phrase is Nuchelmans's. See G. Nuchelmans, *Late-Scholastic and Humanistic Theories of the Proposition* (Amsterdam: North-Holland, 1980), 4.

31. Cf. J. Buridan, *Sophismata*, ed. T.K. Scott (Stuttgart: Fromann-Holzboog, 1977), 27–8 (I conclusio 8ª).

Once mental language is extended from concepts to mental propositions, new questions arise. What is the grammar of mental language? Ockham and others were fascinated by this question. Ockham's mental language contains mental nouns, verbs, adverbs, conjunctions, and prepositions.[32] What are omitted are purely stylistic features of spoken and written language. So number and case are preserved in mental language, for they are essential, but gender and differences only of conjugation or declension, differences of verbal form—of synonymous terms, say—are absent. What is essential is whatever is needed to mark distinctions of truth-value.[33] Synonymy and ambiguity are absent from the mental realm, but everything necessary for precise expression is retained.

Concepts are what are apt to be part of the mental proposition,[34] so the mental proposition is, for Ockham, Holcot, Buridan, Marsilius of Inghen, *inter alia*, a complex. But what provides its unity? This is not a problem specific to the medievals.[35] But it arises immediately one recognizes the propositional complexity of the mental. A mental proposition is not just a list of concepts. What gives that set of concepts its unity? This problem struck Gregory of Rimini so forcefully that he was led to deny complexity and parts to mental propositions: "it seems to me more rational to say that such a mental utterance of whatever sort is not composite in any way."[36] Peter of Ailly followed him, at least for the case of categorical propositions. This doctrine raises its own problems, concerning the relation between concepts and mental propositions if the latter do not contain the former as parts.

Buridan is one of the few who did not follow the new non-Aristotelian path (we think of it as Ockhamist, but it was Ockham's conclusion that permeated Paris, not his works[37]), retaining the conception whereby the vocal sign signifies the concept, and only indirectly signifies *res extra*, by means of the concept. Similarly, the vocal proposition signifies the mental proposition. Paul of Gelria and Thomas of Cleves follow this line, perhaps justifying the description of their semiotic as Buridanian, since Buridan is the most famous upholder of the

---

32. See, e.g., Ockham, *Summa Logicae*, I 3.

33. See, e.g., J. Trentman, "Ockham on Mental," *Mind* 79 (1970): 589.

34. Ockham, *Summa Logicae*, I 1: "terminus conceptus est . . . nata esse pars propositionis mentalis."

35. See, e.g., R. Gaskin, "Bradley's Regress, the Copula and the Unity of the Proposition," *The Philosophical Quarterly* 45 (1995): 161–180.

36. Gregory of Rimini, *Super Primum et Secundum Sententiarum* (St. Bonaventure, N.Y.: Franciscan Institute, 1955), f. 4[va]: "videtur mihi rationabilius dici quod talis enuntiatio mentalis cuiuscumque generis mentalium sit non est taliter composita."

37. See W. Courtenay, "The Reception of Ockham's Thought at the University of Paris," in *Logique, Ontologie et Théologie au XIVe siècle: preuves et raisons à l'Université de Paris*, ed. Z. Kaluza and P. Vignaux (Paris: Vrin, 1984), 43–64.

Aristotelian conception in the fourteenth century. But we still need to ask: What provides the propositional unity to that mental proposition? Buridan wrote: "A mental proposition, however, involves a combination of concepts, and so it presupposes in the mind some simple concepts, to which it adds a complexive concept, by means of which the intellect affirms or denies one of those [presupposed simple] concepts of the other. ... That complexive concept is called the copula."[38] Thus the language of concepts also contains a special kind of syncategorematic concept, like "is," whose function is to bind with the categorematic concepts to form a complex thought, a mental proposition.

Returning to the Augustinians, Ockham and others who take the mental term not as the significate of the vocal term, but as sharing a significate with it, *res extra* (the external thing), we are left with one further puzzle. What is the significate of the mental proposition as a whole? Indeed, what is the significate of the vocal proposition? A vocal term, like "man," signifies men, by being subordinate to the concept man which itself naturally signifies men, and "animal" likewise. But what does "A man is an animal" signify? For the true Aristotelians, it signifies the mental proposition, but for Ockham and his followers, both term and proposition signify some thing in the world.

There were at least four answers:

1. It signifies whatever its subject term signifies, i.e., whatever the proposition is about.
2. It signifies what the categorematic terms signify—so "A man is an animal," whether written, vocal, or mental, signifies men and animals. This was Ockham's view.[39]
3. It signifies some state of things in the world, a *propositio in re*—a suggestion of Burleigh's.[40]
4. It signifies some *complexe significabile* (a signifiable complex), as suggested by Wodeham and taken up by Rimini.[41]

---

38. J. Buridan, *Summulae de Dialectica*, trans. G. Klima (New Haven: Yale University Press, 2001), 24. (The final sentence cited is omitted in Klima's translation.) Johannes Buridanus, *Summulae de Propositionibus*, ed. R. van der Lecq (Turnhout: Brépols, 2005), 31: "propositio autem mentalis consistit in complexione conceptuum, ideo praesupponit conceptus simplices in mente et superaddit conceptum simplicem complexivum quo intellectus affirmat vel negat unum illorum conceptuum de reliquo.... Ille autem conceptus complexivus dicitur copula."

39. Nuchelmans, *Late-Scholastic and Humanistic Theories of the Proposition*, 201 (§12.1.4).

40. Ibid., 219 ff. (§13.3).

41. G. Gál, "Adam of Wodeham's Question on the 'complexe significabile' as the Immediate Object of Scientific Knowledge," *Franciscan Studies* 37 (1977): 66–102; Katherine Tachau, *Vision and Certitude* (Leiden: Brill, 1988), chap. 10; Nuchelmans, *Late-Scholastic and Humanistic Theories of the Proposition*, chap. 14.

## CONCEPTS AND SIGNIFICATION

The medievals make the traditional distinction between natural and conventional signification. Natural signs obtain their signification from some dependency or natural relation between sign and significate (thing signified). There are many such relations: natural likeness, identity, contrariety, cause and effect, opposition, relation of part to whole and vice versa, of one part to another, of what contains to what is contained—any real or natural relation of one thing to another. This is a very wide definition, and Thomas of Cleves shows by examples how wide it reaches. For he appeals to natural relations to explain how a term can come to have a secondary signification in addition to its primary signification. Thus "jar" comes to signify wine, "lion" a man's strength, "wolf" cunning, "dove" simplicity, "Job" patience, "to plough the sea-shore" (*arare litus*) laboring uselessly.[42] His first example is intriguing: he says that "mouth" (*os*) comes to signify "face" (*facies*). This happens in the phrase "*os gladii*," the face (i.e., edge) of the sword.[43] These are all metaphorical uses, he says. There are also ironical uses, so that "good" comes to mean "bad," as in "Oh, what a good boy he is!" The point is that, however the primary signification is come by (presumably, conventionally, in all these cases), a natural relation between the things signified transfers that primary meaning onto other things related in various ways—indeed, practically any.

Conventional signification, in contrast, results from arbitrary custom or agreement in use, and this agreement should be regardless of any natural relation of sign and significate. A natural sign is made by nature; a conventional sign is made by free choice. This agreement in use means that no further arrangement or convention is needed for its signification.

Two corollaries follow from these definitions. First, a natural sign always represents the same thing in the same way for everyone, other things being equal; in contrast, a conventional sign will have different signification depending on the practices and customs in place anywhere. Second, error is rare in the case of natural signs but is commonplace with conventional signs. Buridan, Oresme, Marsilius and others all have a question in their *De Anima* commentaries asking whether the senses can be deceived about their proper objects: They support Aristotle's conclusion (*De Anima* II, 6: 418a11) that they cannot be—or at least, rarely in the case of universal judgments. But they can be for "special" judgments and judgments of degree.[44] Conventional signs, writes Paul of Gelria, a follower

---

42. Cf. Ovid, *Tristia* 5 IV 48: "nec sinet ille tuos litus arare boves"; cf. *Heroides* V 116.

43. The phrase occurs several times in the Vulgate, e.g., Luke 21, 24: "and they fell to the edge (face, mouth) of the sword (et cadent in ore gladii)." See also Deuteronomy 13:15, 20:13, 20:17; Jeremiah 21:7; Judith, 2:16, 7:17.

44. Cf. J. Buridan, *Quaestiones in tres libros De anima* II question 11, in P. G. Sobol, "John Buridan on the Soul and Sensation" (PhD diss., Indiana University, 1984), 167–168: "non videmur decipi quantum ad iudicium generale, sed quantum ad specialia. . . . Non enim decip-

of Thomas of Cleves, can so strongly mislead that Jews and Saracens err in what they say and write about sacred matters. It is a nice question to ask how the heathens can err in blindness to the shining truth of Christianity—but to suggest it is because of their heathen tongue adds insult to injury.[45]

Thomas Maulfelt, Albert of Saxony and others in the middle and late fourteenth century distinguish among natural signs those signifying naturally and properly (*proprie*) and those signifying naturally but in a broad sense (*communiter*): "Some concepts signify themselves naturally in a broad sense and also what is similar to them, as this concept 'man' or similar ones. Some concepts signify themselves naturally and properly, like the concepts quality, being and that sort. . . . Hence every concept standing in a mental proposition for what it naturally and broadly signifies supposits materially."[46] Concepts of things signify them naturally; they are significations representing them. Other signs do

---

imur videntes coloratum iudicando quod coloratum est aliquid vel alicubi. Sed in speciali decipimur iudicando quod est lignum vel lapis, quod est in illo loco vel in isto;" and N. Oresme, *Quaestiones in tres libros De anima* II question 10, in P. Marshall, "Nicole Oresme's Questiones super libros Aristotelis De anima" (PhD diss., Cornell University, 1980), 291–292: "quantum ad iudicium universale [vel] nunquam vel raro est decepcio;" 785: "quantum ad iudicium speciale sensus bene decipitur circa proprium eius obiectum. Patet nam visus aliquando album iudicet esse rubeum vel nigrum; vel eciam album iudicat esse remissus vel intensius quam in veritate est"—but such a case is set aside as a matter of a common sensible, not proper, 294: "sensus decipitur circa iudicium magis particulare, scilicet iudicando quantum aliquid est album vel in quo gradu. Et racio est quod hoc est sensibile commune: scilicet iudicare de quantitate sive extensiva sive intensiva."

45. Note that shortly before Paul was writing, the French Parlement had declared (1374): "Certa sententia seu excommunicatio, quam Judaei inter se vocant Niduy. . . . Nostra curia inhibet expresse. . . . Judaeis omnibus . . . ne ipsi de cetero in regno nostro Franciae utantur dictis sententiis seu pronuntiationibus de niduy, samatha et de herem inter eos." Only ten years earlier, King Charles had said: "si aliquis a secta Judaica vellet recedere, spiritu illuminatus divino, ac limitibus erroris derelictus, fidei orthodoxae sacrique baptismatis reciperet sacramenta, quae praehabebat nudaretur omnino . . . unde accidebat, quod tales, qui antea se locupletes cernebant, egeni, et quidam ex eis vitam quasi quaererent mendicantium." See Charles Dufresne (Dominus Du Cange), *Glossarium novum ad scriptores mediae aevi* (Paris, 1766), vol. III, col. 24.

46. The distinction is found in the *Suppositiones* treatise of Thomas Maulfelt (Edinburgh ms. 138, f. 63ʳ): "quidam conceptus significat se communiter naturaliter vel etiam suum simile ut iste conceptus *homo* vel consimilis. Quidam conceptus significat se naturaliter proprie ut isti conceptus *qualitas, ens* et huiusmodi . . . Omnis igitur conceptus stans in propositione mentali pro isto quod significat naturaliter communiter supponit materialiter. Exemplum ut *homo est conceptus anime mee*, posito quod sic intelligam. Sed si conceptus propositionis supponit pro isto quod naturaliter proprie representat dicitur supponere personaliter, ut in exemplo *qualitas concipitur a me*." Cf. anon. ms. BJ 686 f. 22vb: "Thomas de Clivis ponit . . . terminus stat pro isto quod significat naturaliter communiter, et sic dicitur supponere materialiter." See E. P. Bos, *Logica Modernorum in Prague about 1400* (Leiden: Brill, 2004), 438 (Appendix I.1). See also Albert of Saxony, *Perutilis Logica*, tr. 2 ch. 3, in C. Kann, *Die Eigenschaften der Termini* (Leiden: Brill, 1994), 174–175. John of Holland contrasts proper natural signification with "improper or general natural signification": *Suppositiones*, in John of Holland, *Four Tracts on Logic*, ed. E. P. Bos (Nijmegen: Ingenium, 1985), 12–13.

not signify formally by themselves, so they are not significations, but only naturally in the broad sense, or else conventionally. Concepts signify immediately or directly; these signs signifying in the broad sense rely on a further relation of natural and proper signification. An example is the concept whiteness: because of the natural likeness between the *species* (the form) and the concept, whiteness (*albedo*) signifies itself naturally but in the broad sense. For a white thing seen signifies itself principally and consequently other colored things falling under the same concept or intention.

In fact, the same sign can be a natural and a conventional sign for the same things but by different concepts. Take the written sign "substance," for example. Clearly, it conventionally signifies every substance. Since it is a substance itself, it conventionally signifies itself. But "substance" also signifies itself naturally in the broad sense, and every sign similar to it. Another example is the spoken term "utterance" (*vox*): there is a proper concept common to all the spoken sounds "utterance" by which "utterance" signifies those spoken sounds naturally in the broad sense.

So every sign signifies itself—naturally in the broad sense: "every term and indeed anything whatever signifies itself naturally in the broad sense."[47] In addition, some signs signify themselves conventionally. But in each case, the concepts by which the two significations are enabled are different. The concept of substance is different from the concept of (written) "substance"; and the concept of utterance is different from the concept of (spoken) "utterance."

There is a further distinction. Marsilius of Inghen, following Buridan, distinguishes ultimate from non-ultimate signification:

> It should be noted that the non-ultimate significate of a term is the term itself or one similar or equivalent to it, since first, a term always represents itself and those similar to it to the intellect, whence it points out its ultimate significate to the intellect, namely, the external thing for which such a term is said to stand significatively.... Its ultimate significate is the external thing which such a term signifies if it is spoken or written, and is its natural likeness if it is a mental term.[48]

---

47. See, e.g., Johannes Dorp, *Perutile Compendium totius logicae Joannis Buridani cum praeclarissima solertissimi viri Joannis Dorp expositione* (Frankfurt: Minerva, 1965), sig. h4$^{vb}$: "quilibet terminus similiter quelibet res mundi significat se naturaliter communiter;" cf. Peter of Ailly, *Concepts and Insolubles*, trans. P. V. Spade (Dordrecht: Reidel, 1980), 28 (§60).

48. Marsilius of Inghen, *Suppositiones*, in *Treatises on the Properties of Terms*, ed. E. Bos (Dordrecht: Reidel, 1983), 54: "Notandum quod significatum termini non ultimatum vocatur ipse terminusmet aut sibi similis aut equivalens, cum primo semper terminus se ipsum et sibi similem intellectui representet, deinde significatum intellectui ostendit suum ultimatum, scilicet rem extra pro qua talis terminus dicitur stare significative. Exempli gratia: significatum non ultimatum istius termini homo est ipsemet aut sibi similis aut equivalens. Sed significatum ultimatum est ipsa res extra, sicut animal rationale mortale, quia ultimate rem extra significat. Et ideo breviter: significatum ultimatum termini est res extra quam talis terminus

Note that not only mental terms but also spoken and written terms have non-ultimate signification.

The notion of broad natural signification is, however, not found in Marsilius. The two notions are brought together, perhaps for the first time, in Peter of Ailly's treatise on *Concepts*, written only a few years later, in Paris in the early 1370s.[49] But Peter makes an important new observation. "To signify naturally," he observes, "may be taken in two senses: in a proper sense and in a general sense," (§32) as Spade renders "*significat naturaliter communiter*," which I rendered as "broad" natural signification. To signify naturally in this broad or general sense is "to represent not by itself, but by means of something else, something to a cognitive power by vitally changing [that power]. And this pertains to any thing whatever. For any thing is by its nature apt to cause a concept of itself in an intellective power. . . . From this it follows that every thing signifies or is apt to signify itself naturally in a general sense," (§33) that is, broadly. That everything signifies itself naturally in the broad sense is a crucial observation.

Consequently, corresponding to a spoken sign, like "homo," there are two concepts. (§63) There is the concept of man, which it signifies by convention non-ultimately, which properly and naturally signifies men, who are the ultimate significates of the spoken sign. In addition, there is the concept of the sound "homo," which naturally and properly signifies the sound "homo," and by means of which the sound "man" broadly and naturally signifies itself, and by which it is its own non-ultimate significate. Ailly notes that in the latter case, "some people say it has material supposition." Thus, he is aware of Marsilius's view: "when a spoken term . . . supposits or is taken for itself, it is taken for a non-ultimate significate" (§67).

The ultimate significates of "man" are men; the non-ultimate significates of the term are itself and other similar terms. But we have to be careful here in capturing the medievals' manifold use of the term "ultimate." The vocal term "man" signifies non-ultimately (and conventionally) the ultimate concept of man. It signifies ultimately (and conventionally) men. And it signifies itself naturally in the broad sense (*naturaliter communiter*) and is its non-ultimate significate. Indeed, as we saw, anything whatever signifies itself naturally in the broad sense. Moreover, "man" also signifies terms similar to it in this way.

These reflections lead to a surprising consequence, at first glance: Every conventionally significative sign corresponds to at least four significates, namely, two concepts and two (classes of) things conceived by those concepts. For each spoken and written term, as we have seen, corresponds both to a concept embracing its primary (ultimate) signification and to a further concept embracing the

---

ex impositione significat si sit vocalis vel scriptus, et est eius naturalis similitudo si sit terminus mentalis. Significatum non ultimatum dicitur ipsemet terminus vel sibi equivalens."

49. Peter of Ailly, *Concepts and Insolubles*, tr. P. V. Spade (Dordrecht: Reidel, 1980).

class of that term and its natural likenesses. For example, a clock or bell signifies to its hearer the concept of bell, and so itself, and also the concept of time, and so in turn the actual hour of matins, or dinner or singing Compline (*completorium*)[50] or for reading. In the case of the vocal term "man," it is subordinate to the concept naturally embracing the vocal terms "man," thereby signifies itself and other terms like it, further conventionally corresponds to the concept of man (the natural likeness of men), and finally conventionally signifies its ultimate significates, men like Plato and Socrates.

Here matters become delightfully complex: perhaps it is time for a diagram (see Figure 1). Here the concept by which a conventionally signifying term naturally signifies in the broad sense (the concept of terms like it) corresponds to the concept by which that term was imposed to signify conventionally, namely, the concept or cognition of those things that the term ultimately signifies. It follows that many mental terms signify conventionally, but not those

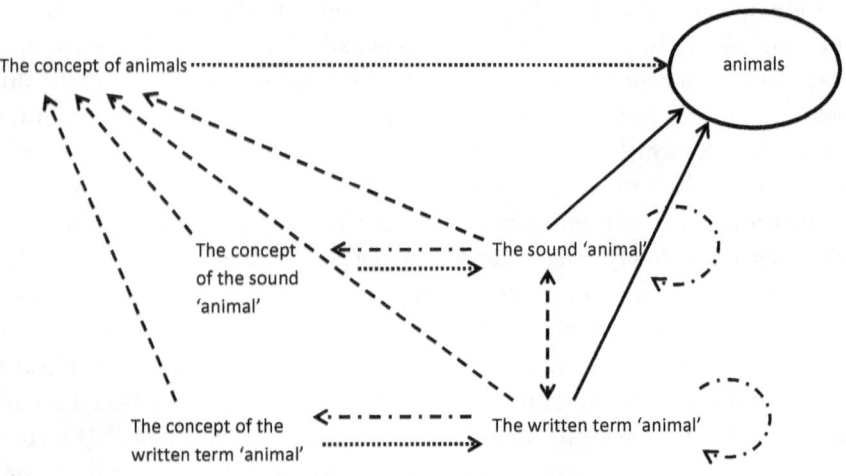

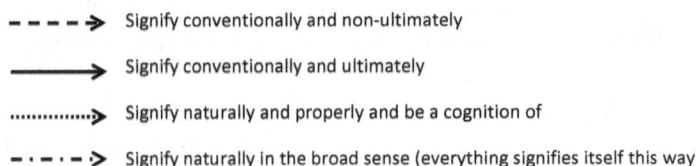

FIGURE 1

50. Cf. Nivard of Ghent, *Reinardus Vulpe* 3, 557, in *Ysengrimus*, ed. and tr. J. Mann (Leiden: Brill, 1987), 392: "Carmina nunc stares ad completoria juxta/Qui tardas demens? hinc eremita sali!"

things of which they are the concept—them they signify naturally and properly, for they are cognitions of them. "Animal," for example, ultimately signifies animals (solid line) by virtue of its relation (dashed line) to the concept of animal, which signifies animals naturally and properly (dotted line). But in virtue of what does "animal" signify itself and its similars? In virtue of a further concept, the concept of the sound "animal." In other words, there are two concepts corresponding to the vocal and written terms "animal," and indeed to every term. Thus to every conventionally signifying term there are four things signified, the two concepts, and the two classes of things conceived by those concepts. In the case of "sound" (*vox*), for example, the classes of things signified overlap (in the sound "sound" itself). See Figure 2.

We find the case of "man" set out explicitly by Paul of Gelria, in his treatise on concepts of around 1380:

> It should be noted that to every sign signifying by convention there correspond at least four significates, namely, two concepts and two things conceived by these concepts. For example, to this term "man" signifying by convention there corresponds first [dot and dash diagonal], the concept which is a natural likeness of this sound "man," and by means of this it signifies itself and anything naturally similar to itself [dot and dash lines], and these

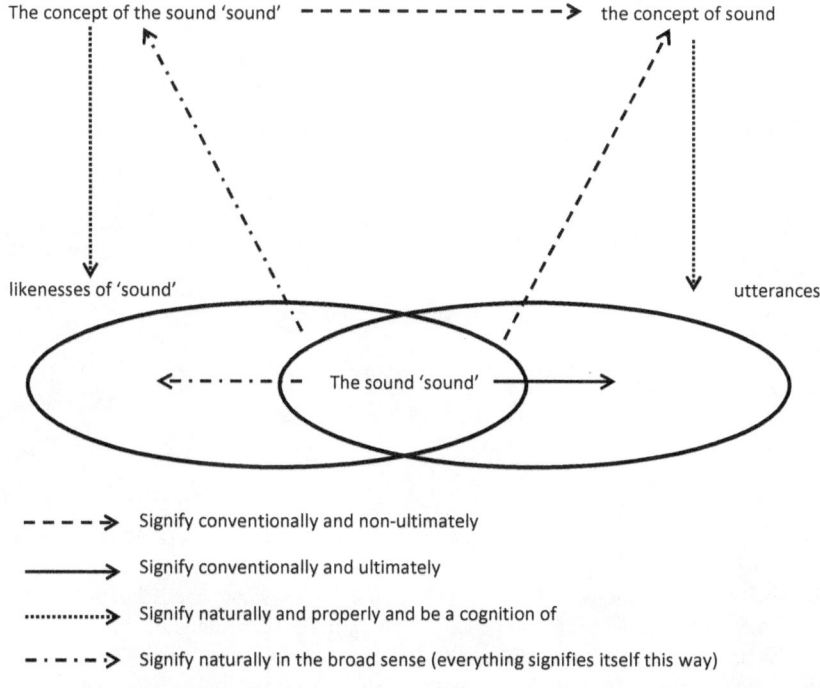

FIGURE 2

are two of its significates which it signifies naturally. Moreover, there corresponds to it [dashed diagonal] the concept which is a natural likeness [dotted line] of men, which it signifies by convention non-ultimately, and by means of this it ultimately signifies by convention [solid line] external things, namely, men, such as Plato and Socrates.[51]

---

51. Paul of Gelria, *De Conceptibus*, in Bos and Read, *Concepts*, 124: "Notandum quod omni signo ad placitum significanti correspondent ad minus quattuor significata, scilicet duo conceptus et res illis conceptibus concepte. Exemplum: huic termino vocali 'homo' significanti ad placitum correspondet primo conceptus qui est naturalis similitudo huius vocis 'homo,' et mediante isto significat se et quodlibet sibi simile naturaliter, et ista sunt duo significata sua que naturaliter significat. Deinde correspondet sibi conceptus qui est naturalis similitudo hominum quam significat ad placitum non ultimate, et mediante isto significat ad placitum ultimate res ad extra, que sunt homines, ut Plato, Sortes."

# Mental Language in Aquinas?

JOSHUA P. HOCHSCHILD

It would be anachronistic, at the very least, to attribute to Aquinas a theory of mental language. As historians of philosophy seem to agree, and I will not question, it is only after Aquinas that thinkers elaborated theories of mental language, or of a "language of thought," with attempts to provide a linguistic (especially semantic and syntactic) analysis of cognition: first within the project of later medieval nominalism, and more recently (and apparently independently) by thinkers in contemporary analytic philosophy (foremost Jerry Fodor).[1]

Nonetheless, allowing that we do not find a recognizable *theory* of mental language to Aquinas, I want to consider the sense in which it is appropriate to attribute to Aquinas some *conception* of "mental language," and then to explore whether, given that conception, a Thomistic theory of mental language would be possible, and, if so, what it might look like and how it would differ from more familiar versions. For, as will become clear, Aquinas did regard cognition as having certain language-like qualities; but as I also hope to show, given his particular understanding of cognition, there are reasons why a syntactic and semantic analysis of the "language" of thought in a Thomistic framework would have only limited similarities to what we recognize in other thinkers as theories of mental language. I will begin, then, with a brief review of some of the features of mental language theory as developed explicitly in medieval nominalism and in contemporary analytic philosophy, in relation to which we can then better appreciate the distinctiveness of Aquinas's own attention to the language-like features of thought.

## MENTAL LANGUAGE: NOMINALIST AND CONTEMPORARY ANALYTIC VERSIONS

Ockham is usually recognized as the first to have developed a theory of mental language. Other thinkers before him had, for various theological and philosophical reasons, treated some aspects of thought as language-like, but, in the

---

1. An exception to this general historical consensus is Peter King, "Abelard on Mental Language," *American Catholic Philosophical Quarterly* 81 (2007): 169–187. Claude Panaccio has responded to this in "Mental Language and Predication: Ockham and Abelard," *Analytica* 14 (2010): 183–194.

words of Claude Panaccio, who has traced this history, "Ockham's originality in the history of the idea of mental language is to have systematically transposed to the analysis of non-linguistic discursive thought the grammatical and semantic categories that the science of his time employed in the study of oral or written language."[2]

Ockham's development of a theory of mental language was, if not determined by, at least fostered within, his nominalist project. Desiring to preserve the universality of scientific knowledge *without* a commitment to universal objects, Ockham found it attractive to take propositions, rather than common natures, as objects of knowledge, for even universal propositions could be verified, on Ockham's nominalist semantics, by reference only to particular individuals in the world. But if they were to transcend the particularity of individual language communities, the universal propositions which are the objects of scientific knowledge could be not just tokens in spoken and written language but items of a "mental language," which is "not in any language," that is, an interior language of the mind not bound by conventional oral or written expression and therefore in principle common to all human beings.[3]

In the mature form of Ockham's theory, the components of mental language, its terms and expressions, are not some *objects* of intellectual acts, but the very intellectual acts themselves. Whether, for Ockham, these intellectual acts or concepts can be said to *represent* or be *similar* to their objects, or whether their direct causal connection to their objects can be described apart from, and even in opposition to, a "representation" or similitude relation, is a controverted point,[4] but what is undeniable is that Ockham's articulation of a theory of mental language, taken up by later nominalists, allowed for the development of a sophisticated semantic analysis of cognition while upholding the characteristic nominalist goal: in this case, to restrict both the *objects* and the *apparatus* of cognition to concrete individuals (and to no more concrete individuals than necessary).

In recent analytic philosophy, Jerry Fodor and other theorists have defended a "language of thought hypothesis," according to which, as for Ockham, thought is language-like in having a compositional structure and bearing semantic prop-

---

2. Claude Panaccio, *Le discours intérieur de Platon à Guillaume d'Ockham* (Paris: Éditions du Seuil, 1999), 278.

3. Ibid., 256.

4. For a variety of positions see, for instance, ibid., chap. 8; Peter King, "Rethinking Representation in the Middle Ages: A Vade-Mecum to Mediaeval Theories of Mental Representation," in *Representation and Objects of Thought*, ed. Henrik Lagerlund (Aldershot: Ashgate, 2005), 83–102; and Gyula Klima, "Ockham's Semantics and Metaphysics of the Categories," in *The Cambridge Companion to Ockham*, ed. P. V. Spade (Cambridge: Cambridge University Press, 1999), 118–142.

erties.[5] Contemporary theorists tend to join this general position to further commitments, identifying mental states with physical states in the brain, and regarding the language of thought as innate, perhaps genetically determined.[6] These physicalist and nativist assumptions indicate something of the underlying motivations of contemporary "language of thought" theories, with their connections to the project of cognitive psychology; but arguably they are not strictly speaking essential to a language of thought hypothesis.[7]

These are brief outlines that do not do justice to the details of the theories, nor to the varieties that they have taken in particular medieval and contemporary authors, but they are sufficient to lead us to expect that Aquinas would not have a theory of mental language. For a simple, not to say simplistic, version of Aquinas's view is that intellectual cognition involves the form or nature of a thing being received immaterially in the mind. This immaterial-reception-of-forms account seems to share very little of (indeed, seems directly at odds with) the theoretical frameworks that have fostered the development of historical mental language theories: materialist functionalism for Fodor, and aversion to extra entities like natures distinct from their individuals for the nominalists.

Nonetheless, this is not enough to help us understand why Aquinas did not develop his own, alternative theory of mental language—after all, we have not presented any reasons why an approach to thought as somewhat language-like (and thus as susceptible to semantic and syntactic analysis) *must* have a particular motive or take place within a framework of particular theoretical assumptions. Furthermore, the immaterial-reception-of-forms account of Aquinas's view that I have given is indeed too simplistic. The real story for Aquinas is more complicated and subtle. Telling it and working out some of its details will allow us to clarify the roles of representation, intentionality, mediation, and other notions central to Aquinas's account of intellectual cognition, and will also prepare us to develop a more nuanced appreciation of how the notion of "mental language" can apply to Aquinas's approach to cognition.

---

5. The founding text is Jerry Fodor, *The Language of Thought* (Cambridge, Mass.: Harvard University Press, 1975). For an overview and other references, see Murat Aydede, "The Language of Thought Hypothesis," *Stanford Encyclopedia of Philosophy* (Fall 2004 Edition), ed. Edward N. Zalta, http://plato.stanford.edu/archives/fall2004/entries/language-thought.

6. Cf. Aydede, sections 1 and 4.

7. Ibid. An assumption apparently more central to contemporary mental language theories is that of "mental representationalism" in the sense typical of modern empiricism: that we know things in the external world only by attending to mental phenomena that somehow represent those things. But there is some question as to how "externalist" or "internalist" the implied representationalism must be. Fodor has apparently developed his view on this point.

## WORKS OF THE MIND

As is well known, Aquinas adopts from Aristotle a view of intellectual cognition that is derived from his hylomorphist conception of nature and the soul. Natural objects are composites of form and matter, and a cognitive being is one whose substantial form or soul endows that being with the power to receive the forms of things, without the matter of those things, in a manner that makes that being aware of those things. Different kinds of cognitive powers—sensation, imagination, intellectual understanding—involve the reception of forms in different manners. What makes sensation different from intellectual understanding is that it is directed to particular physical individuals, while intellectual understanding is universal, common, or general.

While intellectual and sensitive powers can exist independently of each other (in angels and brutes, respectively), in human beings they not only exist together, but one (intellectual cognition) is crucially dependent on the other (sensation). Natural forms, as they exist in things, are sensible, but not immediately intelligible—they have to be made intelligible by being abstracted from all their individuating material conditions. This is the work of the agent intellect, whose role is to operate on the phantasms received in the imagination that are derived from the sensible forms received through the senses. The agent intellect isolates the universal intelligible features of the forms, thus making them available for intellectual cognition. This is the abstraction of the intelligible species.

But the intelligible species is not yet actually understood, and is not the object of intellectual cognition. It is *intelligible*, that is, *able* to be understood, but as intelligible species it is not yet *actually* understood. The agent intellect, having abstracted it from the phantasm, deposits it in the possible intellect, where it serves, in the phrase of David Braine, as a "standing intellectual capacity."[8] Informing the possible intellect, the intelligible species can serve as the formal principle for the action of the intellect that forms a concept by which an object is understood.

This last sentence is carefully phrased. The *intelligible species* can serve as the formal principle for the *action of the intellect* that forms a *concept* by which an *object* is understood. Aquinas carefully insists that we must not confuse the four elements or moments of intellectual cognition suggested by this description: the intelligible species, the act of intellect, the concept, and the object of understanding. As Aquinas puts it in the *De Potentia Dei*:

> Now the one who understands may have a relation to four [things] in understanding: namely to the thing understood, to the intelligible species whereby his intelligence is made actual, to his act of understanding, and to his intel-

---

8. David Braine, "The Active and Potential Intellects: Aquinas as a Philosopher in His Own Right," in *Mind, Metaphysics, and Value in the Thomistic and Analytical Traditions*, ed. John Haldane (Notre Dame: University of Notre Dame Press, 2002), 22.

lectual concept. This concept differs from the three others. It differs from the thing understood, for the latter is sometimes outside the intellect, whereas the intellectual concept is only in the intellect. Moreover the intellectual concept is ordered to the thing understood as its end, inasmuch as the intellect forms its concept thereof that it may know the thing understood. It differs from the intelligible species, because the latter which makes the intellect actual is considered as the principle of the intellect's act, since every agent acts forasmuch as it is actual: and it is made actual by a form, which is necessary as a principle of action. And it differs from the act of the intellect, because it is considered as the term of the action, and as something effected thereby.[9]

The account in this famous and difficult passage has elicited two related objections: First, that it is too complicated, involving too many entities—especially, in addition to the act and object of intellect, the intelligible species and the concept; and second, that these added entities introduce unnecessary steps of "mediation"—some of these entities seem to serve instrumentally as representations of the others. These objections are behind typical nominalist criticisms of the Thomistic picture, charging Thomism with a profligate mental representationalism in comparison with the true, economical "direct realism" of nominalism,[10] and some who would defend Aquinas's treatment of cognition would rather ignore this passage as uncharacteristic. I think that the objections can be handled without dismissing this passage.

In anticipation of the first objection, I have called the four items Aquinas discusses here "moments" or "elements" in cognition, in order to avoid making them sound like *things*. I think it is clear that these are not four *res*; they are distinct, and must not be confused, but we do not have to find here four "entities."

Now it is not controversial to say that the *object*—or what in later medieval philosophy came to be called the *objective concept*[11]—differs from the other three elements, for it is *what is understood*, while the other three are not what is understood but some part of the process of understanding. These other three elements are connected: the concept (or what is sometimes called the *formal concept*), while not identical with the act of intellect, is its terminus, since the act of intellect is the action which forms the quality of mind (the formal concept) by which the objective concept is grasped; and the intelligible species, while identical with neither the formal concept nor the act of intellect, is their formal principle.

If this helps to clear Aquinas of the charge of having too many things involved in cognition, I also think that it helps to clear Aquinas of the charge

9. *Disp. Q. de Potentia Dei*, q. 8, a. 1.
10. Cf. Panaccio, *Le discours intérieur*, ch. 6.
11. See Gyula Klima's contribution to this volume.

of having "mediating representations" that make the thinking subject attend to something internal, rather than to the external object of thought. Aquinas is emphatic that the intelligible species and the (formal) concept are not *what* is understood, not the *object* of intellection. We do not attend to them, and then conclude something about the world by a kind of inferential step. Instead, they are the *principles* by which we can attend to objects. Of course, in describing the "mechanics" of cognition, I may attend to these principles, and make them objects of thought—as when doing logic or philosophical psychology. But in thinking of dogs, I don't think of my (formal) concept of dog; I think about the canine nature.[12]

## INTENTIO INTELLECTUS, REPRESENTATION, MEDIATION

At this point, however, more needs to be said about mediation and representation. For clearly the concept does *mediate* understanding and signification—I understand a thing *by means of* my concept of it, and I can signify that thing because a word can signify the concept immediately, and by its mediation signify the thing of which it is a concept. This does not mean that the signification of things is *indirect*, only that my directly signifying and understanding a thing cannot take place without a concept. An intellectual subject's relationship to an understood object is necessarily *mediated* by his cognitive states—by his intentions or concepts. Even nominalism's alleged "direct realism" cannot avoid *this* kind of mediation. The (formal) concept's mediation of understanding certainly does not entail that the intellectual agent only knows by inferences from introspection, that there is something that stands in the way of direct contact with the world, or that the mind is immediately occupied only with its own concepts. The mind is occupied with the things it conceives, by means of (formal) concepts. This should serve to clear Thomas of the charge of "mental representationalism" in the modern sense we associate with British empiricism.[13]

But it must be further acknowledged that Aquinas says that the concept *represents* its object. The concept "by which our intellect understands a thing distinct from itself originates from another and *represents* another."[14] What can Thomas mean by "represent" in such a claim? What sort of "representation"

---

12. For a recent detailed discussion of the role of the intelligible species, see Yves Floucat, *L'intimé fecondité de l'intelligence: Le verbe mental selon saint Thomas d'Aquin* (Paris: Téqui, 2001), especially chap. 3. On the development of Aquinas's treatment of the concept and intelligible species, see also Lawrence Dewan, "St. Thomas and Pre-Conceptual Intellection," *Études Maritainiennes/Maritain Studies* 11 (1995): 220–233.

13. For an extended treatment differentiating Aquinas on cognition from contemporary mental representationalism, see John O'Callaghan, *Thomist Realism and the Linguistic Turn: Toward a More Perfect Form of Existence* (Notre Dame: University of Notre Dame Press, 2003).

14. "Huiusmodi ergo conceptio, sive verbum, qua intellectus noster intelligit rem aliam a se, ab alio exoritur, et aliud repraesentat." *De Pot.* 8.1. Cf. *In Sent.*, d. 2, q. 1, a. 3, c.; d. 8, q. 2, a. 1d, ad 1.

does he have in mind, and in what sense is it serving to represent? In "mental representationalism" commonly understood, a representation is what is directly attended to, and the representation is somehow a physical likeness or depiction of what it represents. We have already seen that Aquinas does not share the first assumption. He also does not share the second; a concept cannot represent in the way that a picture or a mental image, a phantasm, represents, for as an immaterial quality it cannot *physically* represent, or have a physical similitude to, anything at all.

Even apart from immaterial intellectual intentions, in general for Aquinas a representing thing need not physically resemble the object it represents. The representing thing may encode the represented thing in a different medium, as pits in the surface of a CD that encode but do not physically resemble the sounds that make up a song.[15] On this understanding, any instance of what Aquinas calls an "intentional" reception of a form is a "representation." Such an "intentional" reception, in Aquinas's sense, does not imply a cognitive subject; it implies the reception of a form in a mode other than that appropriate to its natural being.

Presumably, then, every intentional reception of a form is a representation. Something represents to the degree that it has the power to manifest or make known, not necessarily to the extent that it depicts.[16] An intentional reception of a form is an encoding of a form, and it represents to the extent that it could be decoded. The concept's "representation" of its object is due to its formal principle, the intelligible species, which directs the intellect to its object, the nature. We might say that it is an "encoding" of the species, an intentional reception of the form, in such a way as to direct the intellect to its object. Informed by the intelligible species, the intellect is able to produce an intention that directs it toward the nature of which the intelligible species is the formal principle. The concept is thus also called by Thomas the *intentio intellectus*—an *intentio*, in the sense that it is an intentional reception of a form, that is, a reception of the form in something other than the matter proper to that form's natural being; and it is an intentio *intellectus*, because in this case it is received in an intellect, and is that by which the intellect actually understands—in other words, it is the kind of *intentio* that directs an intellect to an object of understanding.[17]

---

15. The example is from the more extended discussion in Klima, "Tradition and Innovation in Medieval Theories of Mental Representation," *Proceedings of the Society for Medieval Logic and Metaphysics* 4 (2004): 4–11.

16. This point is made very clearly in David Braine, "The Active and Potential Intellects."

17. See Max Herrera, "Understanding Similitudes in Aquinas with the Help of Avicenna and Averroes," *Proceedings of the Society for Medieval Logic and Metaphysics* 5 (2005): 4–17, esp. 11: "A species is a type of form that intentionally specifies and determines its subject by communicating a *ratio*, also known as an *intentio*, to its subject. The *ratio* or *intentio* is a formal characteristic that *intentionally* specifies and determines its subject."

So for Aquinas the concept mediates thought and signification because it is a representation of its object, a special kind of representation in an intellectual agent which makes that agent aware of an intellectual object—and we can say this without implicating him in the difficulties of "mental representationalism" with its mediated entities separating the knower from the world.

## VERBUM MENTIS

Further indication that Aquinas considered thought to be language-like is his explicit treatment of concepts as *mental words*. In some of the passages discussed above, and many others in Aquinas, another term for the concept or *intentio intellectus* is *mental word (verbum mentis)*—occasionally *interior word (verbum interius)* or *word of the heart (verbum cordis)*.[18] This "word" terminology is usually presented as synonymous with the other terminology of concept and *intentio intellectus*.[19] Obviously the terms "concept," "intentio," and "verbum mentis" do not have the same connotation, but for Aquinas they all pick out the same element in the analysis of cognition—indeed, all three are used not just of simple concepts, resulting from the first act of intellect, but of complex concepts or judgments, propositions formed by the second intellectual act of combination and division.[20]

In calling the concept a "verbum," the obvious connation, in addition to linguistic, is theological. In the Latin translation of the Gospel of John, "verbum" is the name for the second person of the Trinity, and Christian theologians before Aquinas—especially Augustine—had already attempted to tease out an appropriate analogy between the procession or expression of the Divine *Logos* in God and the formation of a concept or "inner word" in the human intellect. This theological inspiration might suggest that Aquinas's characterization of the concept as a *verbum* is not especially relevant to his philosophical account of cognition. So, for instance, reviewing the context and significance of Aquinas's employment of the term *"verbum mentis,"* John O'Callaghan has concluded that "the *verbum mentis* plays no philosophical role in St. Thomas, but is rather a properly theological discussion. It has the theological purpose of providing

---

18. On Aquinas's use of *verbum*, two classic treatments are Bernard Lonergan, *Verbum: Word and Idea in Aquinas* (Notre Dame: University of Notre Dame Press, 1967) and Henri Paissac, *Théologie du verbe* (Paris: Cerf, 1951). See also Floucat, *L'intimé fecondité de l'intelligence*, and William W. Meissner, "Some Aspects of the *Verbum* in the Texts of St. Thomas," *The Modern Schoolman* 36 (1958): 1–30. Dewan, "St. Thomas and Pre-Conceptual Intellection," mentions some other relevant scholarship.

19. Aquinas occasionally distinguishes between the *verbum cordis* and an interior *verbum* which is an image of the vocal word, apparently out of greater deference to Augustine's use in *De Trinitate*. Cf. *DV* 4.1 and *Sent*. 27.2.1.

20. E.g *Quod. Quest.*, Quod. 5, q. 5, a. 2, c.

nothing more than an image or metaphor for talking about man, made in the image and likeness of God as Trinity."[21]

O'Callaghan is moved to argue for this against several thinkers who have treated the notion of *verbum mentis* as if it were the key to Aquinas's philosophical psychology. O'Callaghan is right that we have no reason to take the notion of *verbum mentis* as the starting point, or central feature, of Aquinas's account of intellectual cognition, especially since, as O'Callaghan notes, the "*verbum mentis*" terminology does not appear in Aquinas's most developed philosophical treatments of cognition: *Disputed Questions on the Soul*, the *De Anima* and *De Interpretatione* commentaries, and questions 75–89 of the *Summa Theologiae* (*prima pars*). Instead, the term "*verbum mentis*" tends to appear in explicitly *theological* contexts and, given its relation to the divine *Verbum*, it is reasonable to infer that the notion of "*verbum mentis*" always retains for Aquinas some of its Christian theological connotations.

Nonetheless, it does not follow that the phrase "*verbum mentis*" is an item of purely theological, *as opposed to* properly philosophical, discourse, and we do not have to conclude with O'Callaghan that the notion of the *verbum* plays *no* properly philosophical role, and serves *only* as a theological metaphor. First of all, a theological metaphor (or analogy) still depends on the natural meanings of terms—or else there is no way to connect revelation to what is known from natural knowledge.[22] Calling God a "Word" does not reveal anything to us unless we can already import something of what we know of the *word* (or *ratio* or *logos*) apart from revelation, as well as import something of what we learn from revelation to enlighten what we naturally know of *words*.

Second, the "theological" connotation of "*verbum mentis*" is not solely a matter of Christian *sacra doctrina* but also of natural theology. In addition to the obvious connection to the Second Person of the Trinity, there is an important connection to the classical philosophical notion of a divine mind that conceives ideas. The extended treatment of the *verbum mentis* in *De Veritate*, q. 4, for instance, seems at least as indebted to the Neoplatonic desire to describe God as a divine mind with ideas as it is to the properly Christian interest in finding an image of the divine Trinity in man.

Furthermore, it seems worthwhile to pay attention to the direction in which the metaphor (or analogy) of human concept and Divine *Verbum* is supposed

---

21. John O'Callaghan, "Verbum Mentis: Philosophical or Theological Doctrine in Aquinas?" *Proceedings of the American Catholic Philosophical Association* 74 (2000): 103–119. O'Callaghan's thesis and arguments are explored further in subsequent exchange: James C. Doig, "O'Callaghan on Verbum Mentis in Aquinas," *American Catholic Philosophical Quarterly* 77 (2003): 233–255, and John O'Callaghan, "More Words on the Verbum: A Response to James Doig," ibid., 257–268.

22. Many articles on analogy could be mentioned here, but I will cite a more subtle and lesser known one: Alasdair MacIntyre, "Which God Ought We to Obey, and Why?" *Faith and Philosophy* 3 (1986): 359–371.

to move. From O'Callaghan's critique, we might assume that we know first that God has/is a "Word" which God conceives and expresses, and it is only by comparing our mind and its concepts with this that we may call our concepts "words." However, Aquinas seems to think that the analogy stretches in the other direction: "Our intellectual word . . . *enables us to speak about* the divine Word by a kind of resemblance."[23]

Why do we call the inner word a "word," according to Aquinas? Not because it is like the Divine Word, since the Divine Word is called a "word" because of its resemblance to the inner word. The inner word, it turns out, is so called because of its relation to the exterior, vocal word:

> We give names to things according to the manner in which we receive our knowledge from things. . . . Consequently, since the exterior word is sensible, it is more known to us than the interior word; hence, according to the application of the term, the vocal word is meant before the interior word, even though the interior word is naturally prior, being the efficient and final cause of the exterior.[24]

In other words, by order of imposition, the term "word" belongs first to the vocal word and is extended then to the interior word or concept, which is more primarily a word in the order of nature (and so from it the term "word" can be extended to the Divine Word—which, presumably, is even more primary in the metaphysical order, but remains last in the order of imposition).[25]

This position in *De Veritate* is consistent with what we learn from the *Summa Theologiae* about the notion of "word," its order of imposition and natural order. First, the notion of *word* is extended from vocal word to concept, insofar as the concept *issues from* a power (the intellect) and directs us *toward* something else (the object of understanding):

> whenever we understand, by the very fact of understanding there proceeds something within us, which is a conception of the thing understood, a conception issuing from our intellectual power and proceeding from our knowledge of that thing. This conception is signified by the spoken word, and it is called the word of the heart signified by the word of the voice.[26]

---

23. *DV* 4.2. Presumably this, and not something heretical, is what John Poinsot (John of St. Thomas) means when he says that the mental word is the principal reason that explains (*praecipuam rationem explicandi*) the Divine Verbum (cited in O'Callaghan, "Verbum Mentis"). That is, the mental word is not a rational principle that makes possible a philosophical demonstration of a mystery, but a rational principle by reference to which the mystery of the Second Person of the Trinity can be expounded.

24. *DV* 4.1.

25. Cf. *DV* 4.1 ad 5.

26. *ST* Ia.27.1, *corpus*.

But the concept, while called a "word" later in the order of imposition, by its nature deserves the name more properly, as being cause of the vocal sound's being a word:

> The vocal sound, which has no signification, cannot be called a word; wherefore the exterior vocal sound is called a word from the fact that it signifies the interior concept of the mind. Therefore it follows that first and chiefly, the interior concept of the mind is called a word.[27]

To be sure, the larger context of both of these quoted passages is Trinitarian theology (q. 27 treats the Procession of the Divine Persons, q. 34 the Person of the Son). But within this larger theological context, the immediate dialectical context of the quoted passages is dedicated to articulating why the different things that we call words, vocal and mental words, are so called; and that is not done by reference to revealed Trinitarian doctrine but, in typical Aristotelian fashion, by reference to the order of natural knowledge.[28]

If we look at another passage, as well, its larger theological context should not blind us to the immediate dialectical trajectory. Treating the notion of Eternal Law, Aquinas responds to an objection that law, which must be promulgated by word, must be related to one Person of the Trinity rather than to the essence of God as a whole. Aquinas's response begins by clearing up why we call different things words:

---

27. *ST* Ia.34.1 *corpus*.
28. Consider Aquinas's reflections in another undeniably theological context, commenting on the Gospel of John (chap. 1, lect. 1, sections 25–29 of *Super Evangelium S. Ioannis lectura*). Aquinas begins by saying that to understand the name "verbum" as it occurs in the first verse, we need to understand its natural sense. Citing Aristotle's account of words as signs of "passions in the soul," Aquinas explains that naturally speaking "word" refers to both the external (vocal) word and to that of which the external word is a sign, namely the internal word (*verbum interius*, also called here *conceptio mentis*, or even simply *ratio*) formed by the act of understanding. Thus, even if the external word is what is called "word" first in the order of imposition, the internal (mental) word is prior in the order of causality, as providing that which gives the external word its signification. The interior word is what is formed by an intellect when it understands, including both the first and second acts of intellect—that is, not only simple concepts but also judgments are a kind of interior speech. Aquinas can thus establish that an interior word is necessarily linked to an intellectual nature, and not as the *activity* of that nature but as *what intellectual activity forms* in the act of understanding—the word is not that *by which* the intellect understands but that *in which* it understands. Interestingly, Aquinas's first illustration of the divine word is not an explicit reference to the second Person of the Trinity as such, but to the creative act of God in Genesis, by speech; and Aquinas only begins to approach what looks like the recognizably Christian notion of the divine Word as the second Person of the Trinity through subsequent reflections on how the divine Word must differ from words uttered by other intellectual natures, given the uniqueness of the divine nature. At no point in this discussion does Aquinas take something that we know by faith about the Son to illuminate what we mean by "mental word"; rather, he reflects on the nature of the mental word to establish the appropriateness of speaking of a divine *Verbum*.

With regard to any sort of word, two points may be considered: viz., the word itself, and that which is expressed by the word. For the spoken word is something uttered by the mouth of man, and expresses that which is signified by the human word. The same applies to the human mental word, which is nothing else than something conceived by the mind, by which man expresses mentally that which he thinks about.[29]

Aquinas does continue by clarifying the sense in which what is conceived by the intellect of God is a Word, but this does not imply that when we speak of mental words we are working with a merely "theological" metaphor that extends to the realm of the human mind a revealed name of the Second Person of the Trinity. Rather, the logic here, as elsewhere, seems to present talk of the Divine Word as (at least in part) a semantic or psychological metaphor (or analogy) relating the Son to intellectual conceptions. In short, these passages suggest that a concept is not called an inner word because it is somehow like the second Person of the Trinity, but because it is like an exterior word, in being expressed by something and in turn expressing something else.[30]

On the basis of these reflections, it is fair to say that in characterizing the concept as a "verbum," Aquinas wants to highlight the following things about human thought: first, concepts behave like words in that they *represent*, and second, that they are a kind of *utterance* or "expression" by the mind that remain within the mind.

Thomas is even willing to say that these representing expressions *signify*, and so they deserve to be called *signs*—as in this passage from *De Veritate*:

> The nature of a sign belongs more properly to an effect than to a cause when the cause brings about the existence of the effect but not its meaning, as is the case in the example given. But when the effect has derived from its cause, not only its existence, but also its meaning, then this cause is prior to the effect both in existence and in meaning. Hence, *signification and manifestation belong more properly to the interior than to the exterior word [verbum interius per prius habet rationem significationis quam verbum exterius]*, for

---

29. *ST* Ia–IIae 93.1 ad 2.

30. Of course, it may still be the case that the notion of the Son of God as the Divine Word gives the Christian a particular reason to make and exploit this comparison of mental and vocal word. Aware that we will try to understand the Divine Word by its comparison with the human mental word, the notion of the *verbum mentis* might always retain, for a Christian theorist, a theological connotation. (In clarifying the distinction between formal and objective concept, Cajetan admits that calling the formal concept a "word" is more a theological than philosophical way of talking: "Conceptus formalis est idolum quoddam quod intellectus possibilis format in seipso repraesentativum objectaliter rei intellectae: quod a philosophis vocatur intentio seu conceptus, a theologis vero verbum." *Commentaria in De Ente et Essentia*, §14.) But that does not make the content of this notion theological as opposed to philosophical.

whatever meaning the exterior word has been adopted to convey is due to the interior word.[31]

Aquinas's point in this passage is that thoughts or concepts have *semantic properties* (they are signs) and are appropriately—even more primarily—called "words" insofar as they *represent* or *signify* objects and are the *foundation* or *cause* of the representation or signification of uttered words. The priority of the signification of the mental word over the spoken word is manifest in a similar passage from the same work, where we learn that even angels (who have no uttered speech) can be said to know by means of signs:

> A thing cannot be called a sign in the *proper* sense unless one can come to know something else as if by reasoning from it. In this sense, signs do not exist among angels, because, as we proved in the previous question, angels' knowledge is not discursive. The signs we use are sensible, because our knowledge, which is discursive, has its origin in sense-objects. But we *commonly* call anything a sign which, being known, leads to the knowledge of something else; and for this reason an intelligible form can be called a sign of the thing which is known by its means. It is in this sense that angels know things through signs; and thus one angel speaks to another by means of signs, that is, through a species which actuates his intellect and puts it perfectly in relation to the other.[32]

We might summarize the further point made in this passage by saying that formal concepts are not just signs but *natural* signs. For Aquinas words of mental language naturally, that is, essentially or by their very intelligible content, signify their objects—for angels, and for human beings. There does not need to be some further account of how the conceptions expressed by the intellect correspond to, signify, or represent their objects, for they bear the same form as their objects.[33]

### COMPOSITIONALITY, SYNTACTIC AND SEMANTIC

It seems clear that Aquinas is not just calling the concept a "word" because of some extraneous theological consideration, but that he regards the concept as having language-like properties—formal concepts are intellectual utterances or expressions that naturally represent or signify their objects. Still, by the standards of Claude Panaccio, who expects a mental language theory to consist

---

31. *DV* 4.1, ad 7.
32. *DV* 9.4, ad 4.
33. The natural or essential connection between thoughts and their object is the crucial point of Thomistic realism, as opposed to nominalism: not whether or not universals or natures are "real," but the role that natures play in guaranteeing a formal identity between knower and known. On this see Gyula Klima, "Ontological Alternatives vs. Alternative Semantics in Medieval Philosophy," *S. European Journal for Semiotic Studies* 3 (1991): 587–618.

in a transposition of grammatical and semantic terminology to the analysis of thought,[34] Aquinas seems not to have developed a mental language theory, as far as formal concepts, the simple qualities of the mind whereby it conceives of its objects, are concerned.

A central element of any mental language theory is the position that mental propositions exhibit compositionality—they are subject to linguistic analysis just insofar as they can be analyzed into their semantic and syntactic components. It is reasonable to ask whether Aquinas's mental language has this feature. Perhaps, given Aquinas's reliance on the notion of a *word*, one might think that what held Aquinas from applying semantic and grammatical analysis to mental language is that the analogy of thought and language did not extend beyond *individual* words and simple concepts. But as we noted earlier, for Aquinas a mental "word" is not just a simple concept; a mental proposition is also a "word."

Indeed, it is at least clear that Aquinas's mental language exhibits *semantic* compositionality: the semantic values of mental propositions (second acts of intellect) are "complex" and can be analyzed in terms of the simpler semantic values of (non-propositional) mental words (first acts of intellect), and similar considerations apply to the operation of reasoning (third act of intellect). Aquinas did not hesitate to offer such analysis—this is, for him, part in the proper business of logic.[35] But note that semantic compositionality concerns the *information content* of mental language—which in this case is the objective concepts, that which is understood by means of the formal concepts that are the mental language. Given that the information content or semantic value of the mental word (or formal concept) just is what that mental word signifies (or the *objective* concept), to say that mental language exhibits semantic compositionality for Aquinas is just to say that the complex objective concept that is a mental proposition, grasped by a second act of intellect, can be analyzed in terms of simpler objective concepts that are grasped by first acts of intellect.

But given the distinction between objective and formal concepts, this *semantic* compositionality does not have to be reflected on the level of the *syntax* of mental language, on the level of formal concepts. If formal concepts exhibited *syntactic* compositionality, it would mean that the structure of a second act of intellect, considered as a quality of mind, could be analyzed in terms of component parts, simpler qualities of mind out of which a complex formal concept is made. Given Aquinas's conception of formal concepts, he is not committed to, and has principled reasons that count against, the idea that formal concepts could exhibit such syntactic compositionality. As immaterial intellectual qualities, formal concepts cannot strictly speaking have structure or sequence or

---

34. Panaccio, "Mental Language and Predication," 184–185.
35. For a thoroughgoing account of Aquinas's conception of logic along these lines, see Robert W. Schmidt, S.J., *The Domain of Logic According to Saint Thomas Aquinas* (The Hague: Martinus Nijhoff, 1966).

parts; and if they could not have any structure or sequence or parts, then it would seem to be a category mistake to subject them to syntactic analysis.[36] Aquinas is clear that the mental act by which a proposition is apprehended is a single act, not a combination or composite of many acts.

It may sound odd to insist that the formal concepts that constitute Aquinas's mental language exhibit semantic, but not syntactic, compositionality. But, as Gyula Klima has explained, it is possible to attribute semantic complexity to ontologically (and so syntactically) simple mental acts, if and insofar as one can analyze the semantic value of the simple mental act as dependent on more simple semantic values, which more simple semantic values could be attributed to other mental acts which are not parts (ontologically, syntactically) of the original mental act.[37] Consider the mental word that is the result of a second act of intellect (judgment, or composition and division), such as "Socrates is white." The formal concept by which it is understood that Socrates is white need not, as a quality of the mind, exhibit a structural (syntactic) compositionality in order to have as its object (semantic content) the relevant judgment.

To be sure, there may be rules that govern how simple formal concepts can be "combined" to create well-formed complex formal concepts; but such rules would not be based on the ontological structure of the formal concepts as qualities of mind, rather they will be based on the *objects* of those formal concepts, the semantic values of the item in mental language. One might apply "syntactic" (structural) analysis to a signified complex *object* (for example, Socrates' being white), but that would in turn lead to an account of the truth conditions of the mental act in familiar metaphysical terms (for example, the inherence of the form of whiteness in Socrates), not to some further linguistic analysis of the formal concepts by means of which Socrates being white is understood. In other words, the mental word (formal concept) is just not subject to syntactic analysis in its own structure, apart from the object that it (naturally) represents. To the extent that the immaterial intellectual quality that is the *formal* concept has an "ontological structure," it would be analyzed in terms of forms inhering in the mind—which would lead to the kind of metaphysical analysis included in Aquinas's philosophical psychology, not to a linguistic analysis that looks like a "theory of mental language" or of a "language of thought."

---

36. To be sure, the objective concepts (the objects of understanding) may exhibit "syntactic" compositionality—after all, the structure of the object of complex propositional understanding may be analyzable into its component parts, such as subject copula, predicate, as the notion of propositional thought as "composing and dividing" implies. But such an analysis of objective concepts is not a syntactic analysis of *mental language*, understanding mental language as the representational system of *formal concepts*.

37. See the introduction to Gyula Klima, *John Buridan, Summulae de Dialectica: An Annotated Translation, with a Philosophical Introduction* (New Haven: Yale University Press, 2001), xxxvii–xxxix.

This clarification should help to account for what Robert Pasnau noticed when he examined Aquinas's treatment of thought's linguistic nature. Pasnau distinguished two theses about the language-like character of thought, one semantic (that is, the content of thought is linguistic), the other syntactic (that is, the structure of thought is linguistic); for Pasnau, it is especially an affirmation of the latter that implies a full-fledged theory of mental language. Pasnau found that Aquinas accepted both the semantic and syntactic theses in only very limited ways,[38] and we are now in a position to see why. Aquinas's (implicit) distinction between formal concept (mental word) and objective concept (the *ratio* of the formal concept, the object of awareness signified by the formal concept, or in other words, the information content of the formal concept)[39] means that for Aquinas there *is* a semantics of mental language (taking mental language to be representational system of *formal* concepts) realized on the level of *objective concepts*, a kind of "concept" not admitted by Ockham (in his mature theory, having abandoned *ficta*) and his followers. On the level of the *formal concepts* themselves—the only kind of concept allowed by nominalist semantics—there is no relevant *syntactic* analysis of mental language, considered just in itself without reference to the *objects* of thought they naturally signify.

## A THOMISTIC THEORY OF MENTAL LANGUAGE

We are now in a better position to characterize the sense in which Aquinas did have a conception of mental language, and at the same time why this conception is not developed in the direction that more recognizable theories of mental language take.

Aquinas undoubtedly considered thought as language-like in relevant ways—he considered thought (formal concepts) as *internally uttered natural signs exhibiting semantic compositionality*.

But if Thomas had found the notion of "mental language" perfectly acceptable, a Thomistic "theory of mental language" would have to be crucially different from the kinds of theories described at the beginning of this chapter. For one thing, unlike certain contemporary versions of mental language, for Aquinas mental language is not innate. Mental words or concepts may signify their objects naturally, but as qualities of the mind they are, like habits, innate only potentially; their actuality is acquired, thanks to the process of abstracting the intelligible species and the further activity of the possible intellect.

Furthermore, as we have seen, while for Ockham a mental proposition can be identical to both an intellectual act and an object of understanding, for Aquinas a word in the mental language is identical with neither. While an actuality in its own right, the mental word is described by Aquinas as the terminus of

---

38. Robert Pasnau, "Aquinas on Thought's Linguistic Nature," *Monist* 80 (1997): 558–575.

39. For this interpretation of Aquinas's notion of *ratio*, see again Gyula Klima's contribution to this volume.

the act of intellect that expresses it. Furthermore, this mental word which is produced or "uttered" by an intellectual act is also not itself the *object* that the intellect understands, but is that by which the intellect understands its object.[40]

Thus, what we in fact find in the way of Aquinas's own conception of mental language is a realist semantics explaining the meaning and truth value of propositions in terms of the forms signified by predicates inhering in the objects supposited for by the subject terms. The formal concepts that make up mental language are *signs*, but to the extent that one would feel a need to provide a semantic analysis of mental language, it is enough for such analysis to occupy itself with an analysis of the objective concepts (and to coincide therefore with the logical semantic analysis of uttered speech).

More commonly recognizable and explicit "theories of mental language," involving the semantic and (some sort of) syntactic analysis of (formal) concepts in their own right, are not only more appropriate but more necessary within an alternative, nominalist approach to language and thought. A Thomistic theory of language of thought, however, would have to be firmly placed within the realm of objective concepts, an ontological realm that Ockham and his fellow nominalists completely abandoned.

---

40. This is thus consistent with O'Callaghan's treatment of Aquinas in *Thomistic Realism and the Linguistic Turn*, which is critical of the mental language hypothesis, esp. in chap. 4.

# Causality and Cognition
## An Interpretation of Henry of Ghent's Quodlibet V, q. 14

MARTIN PICKAVÉ

Among scholars of medieval philosophy Henry of Ghent is well known as a critic of the view (defended, for example, by Thomas Aquinas) according to which intellectual cognition requires so-called intelligible species, that is, cognitive devices that precede the act of the intellective power and that are necessary in order to render the intellect capable of exercising its activity.[1] It is also generally recognized that Henry did not always reject these species. Whereas he admitted their existence in the earlier stages of his career, he is said to have later modified his position.[2] Henry's attitude toward intelligible species is considered as an example of several issues on which he changed his mind.

Recently, however, scholars have come to raise doubts as to whether Henry really rejected intelligible species, and if so, to what extent. Robert Pasnau, for instance, writes:

> Henry of Ghent is often described as having rejected intelligible species. Although this is nominally true, it gives the misleading impression that Henry held a view more radical than the one he actually held. His position, although it has received sustained attention both from his contemporaries and from modern historians, is not nearly as philosophically interesting as that of Olivi and Ockham.

And he concludes his own interpretation of Henry's theory with the following remark:

---

1. In the following I am concerned only with intellectual cognition of *material* objects—that is, the "normal" case of human intellectual cognition. I will not deal with Henry's account of self-knowledge and of cognition of immaterial substances (such as God).

2. See, in particular, T. Nys, *De werking van het menselijke verstand volgens Hendrik van Gent* (Leuven: Nauwelaerts, 1949); E. Bettoni, *Il processo astrattivo nella concezione di Enrico di Gand* (Milan: Vita e Pensiero, 1954); F. Prezioso, *La "species" medievale e i prodomi del fenomenismo moderno* (Padua: CEDAM, 1963), 7–28; J. V. Brown, "Intellect and Knowing in Henry of Ghent," *Tijdschrift voor Filosofie* 37 (1975): 490–512, 692–710; K. H. Tachau, *Vision and Certitude in the Age of Ockham* (Leiden: Brill, 1988), 28–34; J. Spruit, *Species intelligibilis: From Perception to Knowledge* (Leiden: Brill, 1994), 1:205–212; G. Pini, "Il dibattito sulle specie intelligibili alla fine del tredicesimo secolo," *Medioevo* 29 (2004): 267–306.

[I]t's deeply misleading to classify Henry with Olivi and Ockham, as critics of the species theory. It is not species per se that Henry rejects but merely one rather technical aspect of the standard account.[3]

However, Pasnau admits that none of Henry's contemporaries seemed to have had any doubts as to whether or not Henry was critical of the species theory. And indeed many of these contemporaries developed their own defense of intelligible species in reaction to Henry's arguments.[4] Yet, there is some prima facie evidence in favor of Pasnau's reservations with regard to the extent of Henry's criticism. Describing intellectual cognition in his later works, Henry continues to use the term *species* without any hesitation, a move that would be surprising for someone rejecting intelligible species tout court.[5] But if Pasnau is correct, then we might wonder why Henry has constantly been read as a species critic and not just as someone proposing a particular version of the theory of intelligible species. Furthermore, should Pasnau's interpretation move us to conclude that Henry has not changed his mind? Or if there still is a change of mind, what does this change precisely amount to?

The enormous impact Henry's teachings had on later medieval philosophy of mind would justify a reexamination of Henry's cognitive psychology as a whole—an impossible task for a short essay like this. Instead, I would like to focus on one particular text whose importance as a witness for Henry's cogni-

---

3. R. Pasnau, *Theories of Cognition in the Later Middle Ages* (Cambridge: Cambridge University Press, 1997), 306 and 310. I defended a somewhat similar interpretation in W. Goris and M. Pickavé, "Von der Erkenntnis der Engel. Der Streit um die *species intelligibilis* und eine *quaestio* aus dem anonymen Sentenzenkommentar in ms. Brügge, Stadsbibliotheek 491," in *Nach der Verurteilung von 1277: Philosophie und Theologie an der Universität von Paris im letzten Viertel des 13. Jahrhunderts. Studien und Texte*, ed. J. A. Aertsen, K. Emery, and A. Speer (Berlin: W. de Gruyter, 2001), 124–177. For a more recent commentator who thinks that Henry merely reformulates the traditional species theory see M. E. Rombeiro, "Intelligible Species in the Mature Thought of Henry of Ghent," *Journal of the History of Philosophy* 49 (2011): 181–220.

4. For some of the responses to Henry's rejection of species, see the list of authors in Goris and Pickavé, "Von der Erkenntnis der Engel," 150 and n. 92. To this list can be added Roger Marston, *Quaestiones disputatae de anima*, q. 9, ed. Collegium S. Bonaventurae (Quarrachi, 1932), 412–417; Vital du Four, *Quaestiones disputatae de cognitione*, q. 2, ed. F.M. Delorme in ibid.; "Le cardinal Vital du Four. Huit questions disputés sur le problème de la connaissance," *Archives d'histoire doctrinale et litteraire du Moyen Age* 2 (1927): 151–337, at 185–211.

5. See, for instance, *Summa quaestionum ordinariarum*, a. 58, q. 2 ad 3, ed. Badius (Paris, 1520 [repr. St. Bonaventure, 1953]), fol. 130rG: "Hic vero non est aliud re phantasma particulare et species quae est phantasma universale, sicut nec res universalis est alia a re particulari, nec ipsa species quae est phantasma universale abstrahitur a phantasmate particulari per modum separationis realis aut generationis aut multiplicationis in intellectu, ut quem informat ad eliciendum in intellectu actum intellectionis, sed solum per quandam separationem virtualem conditionum materialium et particularium." It is of course peculiar to say, as Henry does, that the species *is* the universal phantasm (and nothing really distinct from the particular phantasm in the imaginative power). But this passage can easily be read as an account of what a species is!

tive psychology in its mature state is generally acknowledged: *Quodlibet* V, q. 14. This choice may seem odd because strictly speaking the text deals with angelic cognition. Yet, many readers, both medieval and modern, regard *Quodlibet* V, q. 14 as equally crucial for Henry's account of human (intellectual) cognition. John Duns Scotus is presumably the best-known example: the arguments by which he describes in his *Sentences* commentaries Henry's rejection of intelligible species in human cognition are all taken from this particular quodlibetal question.[6]

There are, however, two main problems with the traditional readings of *Quodlibet* V, q. 14. No doubt Henry himself constantly alludes to the human case in order to illustrate his reply to what is primarily a theological question. But one might wonder about how much of the actual arguments advanced there can in fact be carried over to the human case. Do (all) the arguments against intelligible species equally apply to the angelic and the human case?[7] Second, if Henry rejects intelligible species, what is his positive account of human cognition and how are we to evaluate his account? Commentators have been surprisingly quiet on these two issues, especially on the more important second issue. I hope this essay will make some progress towards alleviating this deficit.

### THE STRUCTURE OF *QUODLIBET* V, Q. 14

Although I am not interested here in the intricacies of medieval angelology and I am thus not concerned with the argument of the present quodlibetal question as a whole, it might nevertheless be useful to begin by giving a brief outline of the entire question, which asks "whether the intellect of an angel cognizes things that are different from it through its essence or through similitudes of these things or through the presence of their quiddity." According to one widespread opinion (held, for instance, by Thomas Aquinas), angels cognize material objects by means of so-called impressed (intelligible) species. That such species are "impressed" (upon the angelic mind) means primarily that they are not acquired through senses. Angels are purely intellectual beings that do not need (nor possess) sensory faculties to engage in cognitive activities. At the moment of their creation they are endowed by God with something like mental representations of their objects of cognition. For angels do not, like God, understand

---

6. See, for instance, John Duns Scotus, *Ordinatio* I, dist. 3, pars 3, q. 1, *Opera Omnia* III (Vatican City, 1954), 201–244; *Lectura* I, dist. 3, pars 3, q. 1, *Opera Omnia* XVI (Vatican City, 1960), 325–348.

7. Treatments of angelic cognition are common places where medieval authors discuss human cognition. See William Ockham's *Reportatio* II, qq. 12–13, *Opera Theologica* V (St. Bonaventure, N.Y., 1981), 251–310, for another famous example. But we should not infer from this coincidence that in these texts angelic and human cognition are considered in exactly the same way.

everything there is by merely contemplating their own very essences.[8] It is this view, the "familiar" or "common opinion" (*usitata/communis opinio*), to which Henry immediately turns in the present quodlibetal question regarding the cognitive means involved in angelic cognition.[9]

It is important to notice that Henry considers the problem regarding angelic cognition from a specific point of view. Right from the start, Henry wonders whether cognitive means such as species or "similitudes" can explain how cognition is *elicited* in the cognitive powers. He begins his reply to the aforementioned question with the following declaration:

> There is no other difficulty in solving this question than the one touched on in the objection: namely, by means of which agent does an intellect which is potentially understanding become actively understanding? And the doctrine of impressed intelligible species was introduced rather to avoid this difficulty, not because of a grasp of the causality through which the impressed species or the similitude ... works on the intellect.[10]

Thus, one of Henry's main interests is to track down the exact causal mechanisms involved in acts of angelic cognition and part of his strategy in his reply is to show that impressed intelligible species cannot be the moving causes of those acts. But if the occurrence of cognitive acts can be explained without such impressed species then it will equally follow that they do not play any other causal role in cognition.

Henry's proper response in *Quodlibet* V, q. 14 starts with six arguments (A 1–6) against the assumption of impressed intelligible species in angelic cognition. The starting point is the idea that an act of cognition can only be called complete once it has established a union between the cognizer and that which is cognized. Therefore, one can ask either with respect to the cognizer or with respect to that which is cognized whether something like a species is required for the actual occurrence of an act of understanding. Three of the six arguments are advanced to make the case that the angelic intellect does not require

---

8. For this theory see, for instance, Thomas Aquinas, *In II Sententiarum*, dist. 3, q. 3, a. 1; *Summa Theologiae* I, q. 55, a. 2. On Aquinas's theory of angelic cognition, see T. Suarez-Nani, *Connaissance et langage des anges selon Thomas d'Aquin et Gilles de Rome* (Paris: Vrin, 2002). For an overview over the different views medieval authors held concerning angelic cognition see S. Meier-Oeser, "Medieval, Renaissance, and Reformation Angels: A Comparison," in *Angels in Medieval Philosophical Inquiry: Their Function and Their Significance*, ed. I. Iribarren and M. Lenz (Aldershot: Ashgate, 2008), 187–200, esp. 187–192; and the chapters by Harm Goris and Timothy Noone in *A Companion to Angels in Medieval Philosophy*, ed. T. Hoffmann (Leiden: Brill, 2012).

9. *Quodlibet* V, q. 14, ed. Badius (Paris, 1518 [repr. Leuven, 1961]), fols. 175rD and 178rV.

10. Ibid., fol. 174rV.

impressed species *ex parte intellectivi* (A 1–3) for such acts to occur, the remaining three reasons argue *ex parte intelligibilis* for the same point (A 4–6).[11]

The twofold consideration of the cognitive act also provides the setup for Henry's positive account of angelic cognition. Henry stresses that *ex parte intellectivi* no intellect whatsoever requires anything over and above itself:

> Every intellect ... is by itself (*seipso*) a ground of understanding (*ratio intelligendi*) whatever it understands, i.e., its bare essence is the ground of understanding whatever it understands, by means of which the act of understanding actively (*active*) proceeds from the essence itself, so that it does not require anything more *ex parte intellectivi* insofar as the power of understanding is actively understanding.[12]

Yet, if acts of cognition "actively proceed" from the intellect, this simply means that any intellect is itself a cause of its acts.

*Ex parte intelligibilis* only the divine intellect is completely sufficient so that it does not require anything else to actively understand its objects. Created intellects, on the other hand, need in most cases (i.e., in the standard case, in the cognition of material objects) something else by which the object is present to the cognizer. However, in the case of angels this cannot happen via intelligible species, impressed by God on the angelic intellect at the moment of its creation. For (1) if these species are impressed in the angelic mind by God at the moment of the angel's creation, these species are always present and would thus move the angelic intellect to always think all objects simultaneously (A 7), and (2) with regard to such species the angelic intellect would only accidentally be passive, namely insofar as it is a being receiving accidents, but not insofar as the intellect is an intellective power that is passive with respect to its object (A 8).[13]

Now, how can the objects of cognition be present to the angelic intellect if not through impressed species? It is at this point that Henry introduces the idea that angels are endowed with dispositional knowledge or, to use Henry's expression, "scientific habits" (*habitus scientiales*). These habits inhere in the angelic mind, but the objects, which these habits "express" (i.e., represent), do not inhere in the mind themselves. In this sense, the objects of cognition are not merely accidents in the mind.[14] However, such an alternative account of angelic cognition leads to two main questions: (1) In what sense is a scientific habit capable of presenting the intelligible object to the intellective power of the angel? (2) Someone endowed with a scientific habit is normally capable of exercising

---

11. Ibid., fols. 174rV–175rC. The demarcations of the arguments are easy to spot; each of them is introduced by "further" (*praeterea*).
12. Ibid., fol. 175rC.
13. Ibid., fol. 175rD–vF.
14. Ibid., fol. 175vG.

it at will, if nothing external prevents this. Once I have acquired, say, mathematical knowledge I can use it whenever I want. I am not dependent on the appearance of, say, a triangle in front of me. In other words: I am active with respect to the exercise of this knowledge. But doesn't this conflict with the idea that the angelic intellect, like every other created intellect, is essentially a passive power?

Henry's response to the first problem is relatively short.[15] But in order to reply to the second problem he begins a long inquiry into the causal factors involved in cognition in general, starting with the causality involved in human cognition. By comparing it to the human case, Henry intents to shed more light on the angelic case. His final solution consists in downplaying the passivity of the angelic intellect: it is still passive in the sense that it has to be moved by its objects. But its objects are present to it through scientific habits, which enable the angel to exercise acts of understanding whenever the angel desires to do so.[16]

In the last third of the quodlibetal question, Henry returns to the exact wording of the initial question (i.e., "whether the intellect of an angel cognizes things that are different from it through its essence or through similitudes of these things or through the presence of their quiddity") and provides a more direct answer to it. This part repeats many of the points made earlier, and its only really new element is a detailed examination of why the earlier arguments against impressed species do not affect the doctrine of connatural scientific habits impressed upon the angelic mind.[17]

### SENSE PERCEPTION AS CHANGE

It hopefully became clear from the summary above that any serious attempt to read *Quodlibet* V, q. 14 as offering an account of *human* cognition should begin with the remarks about the causal mechanisms involved in human cognition, remarks that Henry offers in his response to the second main question regarding his own account of angelic cognition. For it is in this digression that Henry for the first time clearly and explicitly addresses human cognition as such.

From a general point of view the processes involved in human cognition can simply be described as various sorts of change; after all, when we perceive or think of something, we change from not-perceiving or not-thinking to perceiving and thinking. And these changes can naturally be attributed to the relevant powers, i.e., the senses or the intellect. Yet, not all of the changes involved in cognition are of the same kind and have the same causes. Henry focuses first on sense perception and the sensory powers, and he introduces a distinction

---

15. Ibid., fols. 175vH–176rK.
16. Ibid., fols. 176rL–177vR.
17. Ibid., fols. 177vS–179vG.

between a first and a second change (*immutatio*) by which the senses are affected in sensation.[18] About the first change he writes:

> Therefore, beginning with the change of a sensory power and its reduction from potency to act, it has to be known that, according to the Philosopher in book 2 of the De anima, the first change of the sensory power (by which it proceeds into being from the potency of matter to the actuality of form) is from that which generates it in the form of a sensory power. Such a change does not occur in any intellectual power, for an intellectual power has being only from that by which it is created.[19]

The reference to *De anima* II.5 makes clear what Henry has in mind. There, Aristotle adds to his famous distinction between potentiality and actuality by further distinguishing between two senses of actuality (and potentiality, respectively). A mathematician, for instance, exercising her knowledge can be said to have knowledge in actuality. But it would be ridiculous to deny that she has knowledge in situations where she does not exercise it (for example during sleep). Even in those situations she is definitely in a condition different from that of someone who has not even acquired any mathematical knowledge at all. According to Aristotle's picture, someone who merely has the mental capacities to acquire a certain kind of knowledge is in pure (or first) potentiality, someone who has knowledge yet is momentarily not exercising it is in first actuality (or second potentiality), and someone actively exercising it is in second actuality (417a21–30).[20]

Aristotle advances this distinction because he wants to make his readers aware of the fact that the move from pure potentiality to first actuality is very different from the move from first actuality to second actuality. To make this clear with the help of our example: the mathematician acquired first actuality knowledge by learning, yet she is not said to learn when she moves to exercise her knowledge (417a30–b12). Aristotle calls each of these moves "alteration" (*alloiôsis*), but they are different sorts of alteration. Strictly speaking, alteration is a qualitative change that occurs when a subject receives a new quality through which a previously

---

18. *Quodlibet* XI, q. 5 is another important text in which Henry discusses the different changes involved in sensory and intellectual cognition. For Henry's account of sensation see also J.V. Brown, "Sensation in Henry of Ghent: A Late Mediaeval Aristotelian-Augustinian Synthesis," *Archiv für Geschichte der Philosophie* 53 (1971): 238–266.

19. *Quodlibet* V, q. 14, fol. 176rK: "Inchoando igitur ab immutatione virtutis sensitivae et reductione eius de potentia in actu, sciendum est quod secundum Philosophum 2° De anima, sensitivi prima immutatio qua exit in esse de potentia materiae ad actum formae, est a generante ipsum in forma sensitivi, qualis immutatio non est in aliqua vi intellectiva, quia habet esse a solo creante."

20. For a detailed interpretation of these (and the following) *De anima* passages, see M. Burnyeat, "De anima II.5," *Phronesis* 47 (2002): 28–90.

held quality is destroyed.[21] Now in none of the processes mentioned in the example does, according to Aristotle, real destruction occur. This is most obvious in the case of the move from first to second actuality knowledge: the habitual knowledge of the mathematician is in no way destroyed by being actualized. But for Aristotle this is also true for the move from first potentiality to first actuality: the initial condition of the intellectual power too is not destroyed when someone learns (417b2–16).[22]

Most important for our purpose is Aristotle's claim that actual sensing is a move from first actuality (second potentiality) to second actuality—similar to the move from first actuality (i.e., dispositional) knowledge to the exercise of knowledge, with the difference that in case of knowledge the knowing subject is by itself fully capable of moving from first to second actuality, whereas in sense perception the move is brought about by something outside the cognizer (417b19–28). Yet, if sensing consists in such a transition, there must also be a first transition or change from pure (or first) potentiality to first actuality. It is this first change that Henry alludes to in the quotation above.

But why, someone might rightly ask, is sensing a move from first to second actuality and why is there a preceding first change with regard to sensing? One of Aristotle's—and Henry's—reasons for holding such a view seems to be this: Animals or human beings are subjects that are not right from the beginning of their physical existence capable of every kind of sense perception. Although they are endowed in a certain way with the power of sense perception—namely, insofar as they have everything to develop it—they first have to undergo a development to fully acquire their sensory powers. In the passage quoted above, Henry refers to this process by describing it as a process from the "potency of matter to the actuality of form." We human beings acquire our full sensory powers only when our human form, the human soul, actualizes its formal potential in the matter (i.e., the body) to which it belongs. This first change, caused by that which is responsible for the generation of the subject, is obviously very different from the second change to actual sense perception.

It should be clear from the preceding that a proper account of sense perception has to focus on the second change of the sensory power. But according to Henry, this second change in fact consists of two changes:

> But when the sensory power has been generated, it is in potency with respect to two things: (1) with respect to a species of the sensible object and (2) with respect to actual sensing. And for both of these it needs something existing in actuality, which leads it out and transmits it from potency to act. And this

---

21. Think, for instance, of a surface that was previously white and has now been changed to black (by the process of painting).
22. See also Burnyeat, "De anima II.5," 61–65.

is the sensible object outside without which the sensory power does not actually sense.²³

That the sensory power is in potency with respect to a species of a sensible object obviously means that it is in potency with respect to the *reception* of such a species. Let's concentrate first on this reception before we ask ourselves how the reception relates to the move from sensing in potentiality to sensing in actuality. Henry himself immediately goes on to describe how he wants us to understand the reception involved:

> The sensory power is in potency towards a species of the sensible object, for by receiving an intention of it it does not become the sensible object itself or a thing of that kind according to the truth and perfection of such a form as it exists outside in the sensible object. But the sensory power becomes like the sensible object by receiving an intention through which it is in a certain way it. However, such a form is something real and it happens to occur according to some kind of real change, a change that also occurs in the medium.²⁴

Apparently, species reception in sense perception differs from the normal case of the reception of a form. If, say, the sense of touch senses heat, then it receives a species of that heat without that the sensory power becomes hot itself (at least not insofar as it is sensing). In this respect, the reception is not like the ordinary one that occurs between two material objects one of which heats the other by imparting on it the form of heat. For there the form of heat manifestly exists "according to the truth and perfection of such a form" in the heated object. Similarly, the medium is not (completely) changed by the form it received. Air, for example, the medium of vision, is not colored by a sensible object. However, as Henry tells us in the quote above, the sensory power and the medium nevertheless turn in a way into something "like the sensible object" (*ut sensibile*) and the change underlying this reception is some kind of real change (*realis alteratio*).²⁵

Henry's insistence that such a reception of an intention of a sensible object counts as a material change (and can thus not occur in the intellect)²⁶ seems to

---

23. *Quodlibet* V, q. 14, fol. 176rL.

24. Ibid., fol. 176rM: "Ad speciem sensibilis est in potentia, quia recipiendo eius intentionem fit non ipsum sensibile vel tale aliquid secundum veritatem et perfectionem talis formae qualis est in sensibili extra, sed fit ut sensibile recipiendo intentionem qua quodammodo est illud. Quae tamen forma aliquid rei est et fit secundum realem alterationem quae etiam fit in ipso medio." See also *Quodlibet* IV, q. 21, *Opera Omnia VIII* (Leuven, 2011), 336–337.

25. Although the same kind of reception takes place in the medium and in the sense organ, the medium does of course not sense, for it lacks the *vis formalis sensitiva*; see *Quodlibet* V, q. 14, fol. 176rM.

26. Ibid., fol. 176rM: "Sed talis immutatio per impressionem speciei a nulla re omnino fit in quacumque vi intellectiva, quia non est nisi materialis et per materialem transmutationem et quaelibet vis intellectiva immaterialis est."

blur the distinction between an ordinary reception and an "intentional" reception. Yet, Henry's point simply seems to be this: Every real change of a material object is a material change; for what else could change in such an object if not something related to its material composition? Not every form received in a material object turns the object into that of which it ordinarily is the form. If I am standing on the shore of lake Ontario and I draw a map of the streets of downtown Toronto, the sand in which I make my drawing clearly changes insofar as the arrangement of material parts is now altered so that it represents the different streets.[27] In this sense, the sand receives the form of the downtown street system, but it doesn't turn itself into that very system.

But why in the first place should we accept the distinction between two kinds of real change/reception: ordinary material change/reception and intentional (material) change/reception? And why is the latter involved in sense perception? To the first question Henry would have presumably responded by pointing at the media involved in perception. Take the sense of sight: Visual objects are normally remote and not in direct contact with the eyes. The relevant organ is not directly affected by the object of vision, but since seeing is a kind of being affected by the object of sight the affection of the eyes must be caused by the mediation of some other item. Now the medium, air in this case, does not change in the ordinary sense into something else by being the medium, say, between the tree in front of me and my eyes; there is nothing another person (watching me seeing) could directly observe in the intermediate air. So the affection the medium receives from the object and conveys to the sense organ cannot amount to an ordinary qualitative change. This phenomenon points to the existence of a peculiar kind of (real) change and reception.[28]

However, when we look at Henry's explicit arguments for the involvement of an intentional reception in sense perception, we might be surprised to see him emphasizing the material nature of this reception where we would expect him to draw a sharp distinction between material and intentional reception. For example, Henry presents the detrimental effects of strong sensory impulses as evidence for the occurrence of an intentional reception of a species. An exceedingly loud sound, a very bright light, extreme heat etc., will destroy to a certain extent the relevant sensory powers. They damage the sensory powers by damaging, through the species' impression, the moderate mixture of qualities necessary for being a receiver of sense impressions. The tactile sense, to use Henry's example, is neither too hot nor too cold, that is why it can experience different degrees of heat or cold. By receiving a species of extreme heat or cold

---

27. For this kind of example, see E. Stump, Aquinas (London: Routledge, 2003), 252.
28. In the background is of course the assumption that objects themselves have no causal power over distances, an assumption Henry shares with many other thirteenth-century philosophers. See *Quodlibet* IV, q. 21, 336–337, for a description of the intentional change in the medium of sight and the transmission of an intentionally received form or species to the sense organs.

this mixture gets out of tune and cannot longer serve as the basis for sense perception.[29]

Notice that, according to Henry, there is also more positive evidence for the involvement of an "intentional" species reception in sense perception. Such a reception has to be admitted in order to account for the interaction between the exterior senses and the various inner senses. As described in one of the quotations above, an external sensible object is the active cause of both a species reception and the actualization of one of the exterior senses. But then the species in the sensory power cause the reception of further species in higher sensory powers together with the acts of those powers. In these inner processes, the species play the role of the exterior objects, and since through the species reception the sensory power becomes somewhat like the sensible (*ut sensibile*), we best regard this mechanism as a purely physical process. One of the cases for which Henry describes this process explicitly is memory's interaction with imagination. Like the external sensible object, the species that is present (or revived) in the faculty of memory causes two things to happen: (1) the reception of a species or form through which the power of imagination gets transformed in a certain way and (2) the act of imagining.[30]

It is however a serious problem that none of Henry's two principal reasons for positing an intentional reception of species in sense perception demonstrates that the species reception *cannot* consist in a normal reception involving ordinary material change in the senses. Especially the possible detrimental effects on the sensory powers seem to point to an ordinary material change by which the organs pertaining to a given sensory power are destroyed. This at least is how Aquinas explains the phenomenon.

Finally, before we are able to address the question of how the intentional reception of a species is related to the other change with regard to which a sensory power is in potency, it is opportune to look at what Henry says about this other change itself. Unfortunately, the relevant remarks are rather brief. He grants that this change requires certain material dispositions[31] and then adds:

> Through the sensible object present outside the sensory power is instantly (*statim*) changed so that it is rendered from sensing in potency to sensing in

---

29. *Quodlibet* V, q. 14, fol. 176rM.

30. Ibid., fol. 176vM: "Et est advertendum circa transmutationem sensus quod sicut a sensibili extra per medium generatur species eius in organo sensus particularis extra et ipsum immutat ad actum sentiendi, sic a sensu particulari extra species . . . intra generatur in organo memoriae, in qua conservatur ad absentiam sensibilis extra. Et est species illa in memoria respectu imaginativae virtutis, sicut sensibile respectu sensus particularis. . . . Unde generatur [species] a memoria in imaginativam sicut a re extra in sensum particularem et imaginativam informatam specie. Species existens in memoria immutat ad actum imaginandi, sicut sensibile extra immutat ad actum sentiendi sensum particularem."

31. Ibid., 176rM: "Ad actum autem sentiendi sensus est in potentia, quia dispositus materialiter ad susceptionem immutationis ad actum sentiendi ex parte principii formalis in ipso."

actuality. And in this there is no difference compared with the change through which the intellect is moved by the intelligible object to actual understanding, except that the sensible objects exist as particulars outside the soul and the intellect, but that the intelligible objects are universals and exist in some way in the soul and the intellect itself, as the Philosopher says.[32]

The first lesson we can learn from this characterization (and its juxtaposition to the reception of a species) is that for Henry the act of sensing is different from the reception of a species. But what does Henry mean when he says that the sensible object "instantly" changes the sensory power so that it actually senses? Does this indicate that the actualization of the power and the reception of a form are just two simultaneous events, both caused by one and the same thing, the sensible object? Or do the two events stand in a causal relationship? No doubt, the actualization of a sensory power is *sometimes* caused by a received species. This is clear from Henry's understanding of the way the different sensory powers are functionally related. As we saw, a species received in, say, memory can trigger both an act of the imaginative power and species reception in that power. Here, a form or species received in *one* sensory power causes the actualization of *another* power. But the question is whether with respect to one and the same power the reception involved in an act of sensation is responsible for the actualization of the sensory power itself? The problem is, of course, related to a more important question, namely the question of whether species reception is an essential part of any act of sensation.

In *Quodlibet* IV, q. 21, Henry gives some brief indications regarding the causal role of the species reception. As he explains in this slightly earlier quodlibetal question, the actualization of a sensory power is caused by the impression of a species in it: the received species is that by which the sensory power is moved from potency to act.[33] The language used makes one wonder whether Henry considers the species' impression as the efficient cause of the act of sensation. However this may be, such a role of the species reception seems to exclude that it is part of the act of sensation itself. In *Quodlibet* V, q. 14, Henry is less outspoken about the causal role, but there is no reason to doubt that he still separates between the species reception and the proper act of sensing. In the latter text, Henry remarks that a sense is identical with the sensibles "through species impressed in the sensory power" and he qualifies this by referring to the species as that which is "materially" a ground for sensation

---

32. Ibid.
33. *Quodlibet* IV, q. 21, 337: "... sensus ab obiecto habet speciem receptam impressivam, qua deducitur per transmutationem naturalem sensus de potentia in actum, non solum ut in potentia formatum actu informetur receptione speciei impressivae in subiecto ... sed ut ulterius potentia sentiens fiat actu sentiens ..."

(*ratio sentiendi*).³⁴ There are other passages where he refers to something as being materially the ground for cognizing something else. In his *Summa*, Henry contrasts this way of being a *ratio cognoscendi* with being "formally" a ground for cognition. The latter case applies when that by which something else is cognized provides the formal ground for cognizing that other thing. Something that is only materially a ground of cognition provides merely an occasion for knowing something else.³⁵ We are therefore allowed to conclude that the reception of a species simply leads to what has to be regarded as the act of sensation strictly speaking, without being an essential a part of it. And how such a triggering is possible needs hardly any further explanation, given that our sensory powers are instantiated in sensory organs, which are the precise locations in which the species reception takes place.³⁶

So when Henry says that the external sensible object "instantly" (*statim*) renders the sensitive power actually sensing, he does not hint at a causal immediacy between object and act of sensation.³⁷ All he says is that in normal cases the act of sensing occurs without any delay when the object is present. The sensible object elicits the act of sensation by impressing a species on the sensory power.

### SENSE PERCEPTION: A SPECIES RECEPTION?

To further clarify Henry's analysis of sense perception, it might be useful to compare his account to that of Thomas Aquinas. For Aquinas too, sensation has to do with a reception of a species, a reception that differs from ordinary reception of a form and the change it involves. More precisely, according to Aquinas, sensation involves a "spiritual change" in which a form or species is received with "spiritual being":³⁸

> Change is of two kinds: one is natural, the other is spiritual. Natural change takes place when the form of that causing the change is received according to natural being in that which is changed, as heat is received in the thing heated. But spiritual change takes place when a form of that causing the change is received according to spiritual being in that which is changed, as the form of

---

34. *Quodlibet* V, q. 14, fol. 176rK: "Sensus est sensibilia per species sibi impressas ... ex parte sensus intelligitur solum de specie organo impressa quae non est ratio sentiendi nisi materialiter ..."

35. *Summa quaestionum ordinariarum*, a. 24, q. 7, fol. 144vI. For this distinction, see also my *Heinrich von Gent über Metaphysik als erste Wissenschaft* (Leiden: Brill, 2007), 148–149.

36. In *Quodlibet* XI, q. 5, Henry examines in detail the precise causal role that the species reception has with respect to the act of sensation. In this text, Henry denies that the species reception is an efficient cause of sensation. It merely inclines and "excites" the sensory power. Yet, he still holds (a) that the species reception must precede the act of sensation and (b) that it is not an essential part of sensation itself.

37. This would also be unlikely because, as was already said, we normally perceive objects through media.

38. For more on Aquinas's position, see M. Burnyeat, "Aquinas on 'Spiritual Change' in Perception," in D. Perler, *Ancient and Medieval Theories of Intentionality* (Leiden: Brill, 2001), 129–153; Pasnau, *Theories of Cognition*, 31–47.

color is received in the pupil which does not thereby become colored. But in the operation of the senses the spiritual change is required, through which an intention of the sensible form happens to exist in the sense organ.[39]

And although sense perception is sometimes accompanied by natural changes, sense perception itself does not involve such a change. This is clear, for example, from the following passage in which Aquinas contrasts the natural changes occurring in perception with those connected to the movements of the sensitive appetite:

> The organs of the soul can be changed in two ways. First, by a spiritual change, according to which the organ receives an intention of a thing (*intentio rei*). And this is essential to the act of a sensitive apprehensive power. In this way, the eye is changed by the visible object, not by being colored, but by receiving an intention of color. The other change is the natural change of the organ insofar as the organ is changed with respect to its natural disposition; i.e., when it becomes warm or cold or it is changed in some other similar way. And such a change is accidental to the act of a sensitive apprehensive power; i.e., if the eye is wearied through gazing intently at something or if it is destroyed by the intensity of the visible object. But such a (natural) change essentially belongs to the act of the sensitive appetite. For this reason the material element in the definitions of the movements of the appetitive part, is the natural change of the organ; e.g., anger is said to be a kindling of the blood about the heart.[40]

These passages make clear that Aquinas and Henry disagree with respect to how they treat the "intentional" reception of a form or species. Both agree that such a reception is different from ordinary natural change, but on Henry's account the spiritual or intentional change is somewhat closer to the natural

---

39. *Summa theologiae* I.78.3: "Est autem duplex immutatio: una naturalis, et alia spiritualis. Naturalis quidem, secundum quod forma immutantis recipitur in immutato secundum esse naturale, sicut calor in calefacto. Spiritualis autem, secundum quod forma immutantis recipitur in immutato secundum esse spirituale; ut forma coloris in pupilla, quae non fit per hoc colorata. Ad operationem autem sensus requiritur immutatio spiritualis, per quam intentio formae sensibilis fiat in organo sensus."

40. Ibid., I–II.22.2 ad 3: "Ad tertium dicendum quod, sicut in primo dictum est, dupliciter organum animae potest transmutari. Uno modo, transmutatione spirituali, secundum quod recipit intentionem rei. Et hoc per se invenitur in actu apprehensivae virtutis sensitivae, sicut oculus immutatur a visibili, non ita quod coloretur, sed ita quod recipiat intentionem coloris. Est autem alia naturalis transmutatio organi, prout organum transmutatur quantum ad suam naturalem dispositionem, puta quod calefit aut infrigidatur, vel alio simili modo transmutatur. Et huiusmodi transmutatio per accidens se habet ad actum apprehensivae virtutis sensitivae, puta cum oculus fatigatur ex forti intuitu, vel dissolvitur ex vehementia visibilis. Sed ad actum appetitus sensitivi per se ordinatur huiusmodi transmutatio, unde in definitione motuum appetitivae partis, materialiter ponitur aliqua naturalis transmutatio organi; sicut dicitur quod ira est accensio sanguinis circa cor."

one.⁴¹ As we have seen, Henry insists that "intentional" reception is a real material change and for him it is the "intentionally" received species that can cause the destruction of the sensory organ. It is reasonable to regard Henry's respective views as a criticism of Aquinas. There is some debate in modern Aquinas scholarship concerning whether or not Aquinas holds a materialist account of sensation.⁴² Some commentators deny that he explains sensation in purely material terms. According to them, Aquinas's view of sensation also involves nonmaterial processes. On this background it would not be surprising if Henry too regarded Aquinas as someone proposing a nonmaterial account of sense perception. Henry's insistence on the fact that reception of an intention in a sensory power is a real material change could then well be understood as a reaction to Aquinas.⁴³

If sensory cognition goes along with the reception of a species, why is sensory cognition not simply identical with this reception? Aquinas sometimes speaks as if there were nothing else to sense perception than just the spiritual reception.⁴⁴ However, in distinguishing the species reception from the move from potentially sensing to actually sensing, Henry obviously resists regarding the act of sensing itself as a kind of reception of a form or species. This seems puzzling, for in *Quodlibet* IV, q. 21 (i.e., not long before *Quodlibet* V), he described the two aspects with respect to which the sensory power is in potency as (1) a potency to receive an "impressed species" and (2) as a potency to receive an "expressed species," and he identifies the reception of an expressed species with the move from sensing in potency to sensing in actuality.⁴⁵ But in *Quodlibet* V, q. 14, he is apparently unwilling to apply the expression "expressed species" to the process of sensation. He even goes so far as to say that there are *only* impressed species in the sensitive part of the soul.⁴⁶ So it is hardly an accident that in *Quodlibet* V, q. 14, Henry dissociates the exercise of a sensory power from a species reception.

41. For a somewhat similar conclusion, see Rombeiro, "Intelligible Species," 189.
42. For this debate, see Pasnau, *Theories of Cognition*, 42–47.
43. If this is the case, it might help to explain why Henry is less clear about how the ordinary and the intentional reception actually differ. Presumably, all he wants to say is that they don't differ as radically as Aquinas suggests. A spiritual change/reception is still a material reception!
44. See, e.g., *Summa theologiae* I.17.2 ad 1: "Sensum affici est ipsum eius sentire."
45. *Quodlibet* IV, q. 21, 337: "sensus ab obiecto habet speciem receptam impressivam, qua deducitur per transmutationem naturalem sensus de potentia in actum, non solum ut in potentia formatum actu informetur receptione speciei impressivae in subiecto ... sed ulterius potentia sentiens fiat actu sentiens receptione speciei expressivae." Henry switches between the expressions *species impressa* and *species impressiva* and likewise between *species expressa* and *species expressiva*. I will refer to them as impressed and expressed species.
46. *Quodlibet* V, q. 14, fol. 176rK: "quod dicit [i.e., Aristotle] ad differentiam sensitivae, in qua non est nisi species impressa."

Whether this is an instance of a change of mind or not, it is important to ask what led Henry to deny that the exercise of the sensory power consists in the reception of a species. In *Quodlibet* V, q. 14, Henry offers no explicit argumentative support for this view, but I believe the *De anima* II.5 background provides us with some clues. Remember, one of Aristotle's points there was to argue that in the case of sense perception the move from first to second actuality is not an ordinary change; it is a change that is better described as a transition toward the *perfection* of the underlying subject, the sensory power. However, the interaction between the different sensory powers and the possible damage by extreme sensible objects show, according to Henry, that a real accidental change occurs in sense perception. And such a change is best described as the reception of a species, that is, of an accidental form. This form comes from the object, which acts as an agent and impresses it in the receiving subject. In other words, there is a real transfer of a form from the agent to the patient. Given that this change can lead to the destruction of the sensory organs, it can in no way be that in which the perfection of the sensory power consist. It is for this reason that sense perception cannot be identical with this kind of species reception. One could, of course, employ a loose way of speaking and refer to the act of sensing as the reception of a species. But then, so Henry might respond, the term "reception" is not used in the same way in both cases. In the real accidental change a form is transferred and impressed on the changing subject; the underlying subject really receives something from something else. When the sensory power moves from first to second actuality, it might be said to have received something, i.e., the act of sensing (in the sensory power), but strictly speaking this act is the perfection of that power and is something that intrinsically and exclusively belongs to it. It is only metaphorically received from something else, from the sensible object.

I think there is also another, somewhat related reason, why Henry refrains from calling the act of sensation itself a species reception. This reason has to do with what one might call "cognitive agency." In different places throughout his works, Aristotle distinguishes between two kinds of activities, i.e., changes (*kineseis*) and operations (*energeiai*). To most modern readers this distinction is familiar from *Metaphysics* IX.6 (1048b18–35) where Aristotle seems to develop a so-called tense test for distinguishing between the two kinds of activities. According to this test, those activities are operations for which it is not absurd to say of one and the same instance both that "x is Φing" and "x has Φed." Seeing therefore qualifies as operation (*energeia*) because in every instance of seeing, seeing has already taken place. Building (a house), on the other hand, qualifies as change (*kinesis*) because it is not true in every instance of building a house that a house was built.[47] This notorious passage, however, is missing in the medieval Latin

---

47. On this passage see the influential paper by J. Ackrill: "Aristotle's Distinction between *Energeia* and *Kinesis*," in *New Essays on Plato and Aristotle*, ed. R. Bambrough (London:

translations of the *Metaphysics*, and anyway, as M. Burnyeat has recently shown, does not belong there in the first place.[48] So when medieval authors refer to *motus* as distinct from an *operatio* they have to account for their distinction differently. For Henry, their distinction is simply identical with the distinction between transitive and intransitive activities: a *motus* is an activity terminating in something that is external and different from the agent, whereas an *operatio* terminates in something intrinsic to the agent.[49] The crucial point is now that acts of sense perception as well as intellectual acts are clearly cases of operations.[50] Of course, acts of sensing or thinking are normally about external objects; but both activities do not essentially lead into the creation or production of something extrinsic to sensing and thinking itself. With other words, it does not follow from the intentionality of sense perception and thought, that is, from the fact that they are about something, that intentional acts are transitive acts.

To come back to the issue of sensation and species reception: if sensation were essentially to consist in the reception of a species (in the strict sense), then it would have to be considered a change (*motus*) and not an operation. A species reception is a moment in a transfer of a species from an agent to a patient. The endpoint of this process is distinct from the starting point. Take the example of heating: a hot item conveys a form to another item in proximity whereby this second item becomes hot by receiving the form. Moreover, in the example we attribute the activity of heating to the hot object that initiated and caused the heating of its neighboring object. There is no activity we attribute to the subject of the reception, the heated object. But when we attribute episodes of perception or thought to a cognizer we think of them as the cognizer's activities. And the opposite seems absurd. For then it would not be me who sees, tastes, hears, thinks but all these activities would merely happen in me as a patient.[51] All this is meant to demonstrate that cognition, be it sensory or intellectual, cannot essentially consist in a species reception.[52]

---

Routledge, 1965), 121–141; repr. in Ackrill, *Essays on Plato and Aristotle* (Oxford: Clarendon Press, 1997), 142–162.

48. M. Burnyeat, "*Kinesis* vs. *Energeia*: A Much-Read Passage in (but not of) Aristotle's *Metaphysics*," *Oxford Studies in Ancient Philosophy* 34 (2008): 219–292.

49. See *Quodlibet* XI, q. 5, fol. 451rT, for Henry's most comprehensive explanation of this distinction. The distinction is however also present in *Quodlibet* V, q. 14, fol. 175rD. And of course it is present in Henry's main inspiration, *De anima* II.5. See 417a16–17 and Burnyeat, "De anima II.5," 41–44.

50. See *Quodlibet* XI, q. 5, fols. 451rT and 452rD. See also, e.g., Thomas Aquinas, *Summa Theologiae* I.14.2, and Aristotle, *Metaphysics* IX.6 (1048b22–28).

51. See also *Quodlibet* XI, q. 5, fol. 451vA.

52. By this I mean that cognition cannot strictly speaking be the reception itself of a species or form. But nothing prevents that one refers to cognition as the reception of a species or form in a broader sense. And this is a move later medieval authors are use to make. One example, in my view, is Henry referring to the act of sensing as *species expressa* in *Quodlibet* IV. For another example see the anonymous Thomist who replies to Durandus of Saint-

These worries about cognitive agency also allow us to understand why Aristotle and Henry of Ghent consider sensation, as we have seen earlier, as a move from first to second actuality. For if sensation were merely a move from first potentiality to first actuality, it would be impossible to attribute sensation to that which undergoes this move. For something existing in complete potentiality can hardly be considered as an agent.

However, Henry's account of sensation leaves us with a crucial problem. If sensation is not essentially a species reception and if a species reception is not even an essential part of sense perception (but only something that precedes the act of proper sensation), how can he explain that a particular act of sensation is about this or that object, if the intentionality of the act is not derived from the species received? How does he account for the intentionality of sense perception? To respond to this problem, we will first have to look at his account of intellectual cognition.

### INTELLECTUAL COGNITION

The human intellect and its activities depend on the sensory powers. Or to use a famous phrase: nothing is in the intellect that has not been previously in the senses. The way in which this dependency plays out, according to Henry of Ghent, is that in its most basic act, that is, the act of concept formation, the intellect receives its object through the activity of the inner senses. The activity of the intellect starts where the activity of the inner senses ends: with the act of the imaginative power. More precisely, it starts with the "particular object imagined inside" (*obiectum particulare imaginatum intra*), that is, the object appearing in the act of imagination (as opposed to the external object of sense perception). For Henry, the starting point for intellectual acts is literally the imagined thing in front of the mental eye.[53] For obvious reasons it is not the sensible species in the higher inner senses (or their corresponding organs) from which thinking takes off. Actual sensing, as we saw, does not consist in the reception of these species. If the latter were the starting points for the intellect, the intellect would not be essentially connected to the *activity* of the sensory powers. Note moreover that Henry's analysis implies a distinction between the act of imagination and the imagined inner object, that is, the object appearing

---

Pourçain's view according to which the act of cognition is not a reception of a form. He writes in response to Durandus (ed. J. Koch in *Durandi de S. Porciano O.P Quaestio de natura cognitonis et Disputatio cum anonymo quodam necnon Determinatio Hervei Natalis O.P* [Münster, 1929], 34): "Dicendum quod non est inconveniens quod forme sit forma, accipiendo formam *diversimode*. Actus enim intelligendi cum sit informans intellectum et sibi inherens, sicut accidens et forma quedam, oportet dicere quod sit forma" (my emphasis).

53. *Quodlibet* V, q. 14, fol. 176vO: "Post hoc sequitur operatio intellectus agentis in nobis circa phantasmata, hoc est non circa species impressas in memorativa vel imaginativa, sed circa obiectum particulare imaginatum intra."

in this act.[54] But since it is the latter that expresses the phenomenal character and the specificity of a given act of imagination (and is thus inseparable from it), Henry not surprisingly regards the imagined object rather than the act of imagination itself as the link between sensation and intellection.

Unlike the different senses, the human intellect is not determined to a specific class of objects; its object can be everything. From this medieval authors conclude that the intellect must be immaterial; for the determination of the senses derives from the fact that they are realized in corporeal organs. Moreover, from the immaterial nature of the intellect it follows that the object of the intellect can only be something universal, and not some singular thing. This leads to the central problem medieval accounts of intellectual cognition have to deal with: How can there be a connection between the senses and the intellect if the senses, as is obvious, are involved with matter and singularity?[55] No doubt we have intellectual understanding of sensible objects. So in principle there has to be a transfer from the sensory to the intellectual level. The question is simply how this transfer exactly works.

For Henry, the immateriality of the intellect poses less of a problem. As a sensory act the act of imagination is instantiated in matter, but the imagined object or phantasm (to use Henry's preferred term) is itself immaterial. Sense perception takes place through corporeal organs, but this does not mean that the (external) object of sense perception is received with its matter in the sensory power. In this respect, sense perception already involves abstraction from matter.[56] However, everything that we imagine we imagine as having a certain shape, color, extension etc. Our phantasms provide us with images of objects having individuating features; and as such they are incapable of affecting the intellect.[57] Henry thus assigns the necessary abstraction from individuating features to a special faculty of the human mind, the so-called agent intellect.

---

54. For a stronger version of this distinction (and for a different argument regarding the starting point of intellectual cognition) see *Quodlibet* IV, q. 21, 339–340. On this text see also B. Goehring, "Henry of Ghent's Use of Aristotle's *De anima* in Developing his Theory of Cognition," in *Medieval Perspectives on Aristotle's De anima*, ed. R. L. Friedman and J.-M. Counet (Leuven: Peeters, 2013), 61–99, at 89; and Rombeiro, "Intelligible Species," 207–208.

55. On this important problem and some of the proposed solutions, see P. King, "Scholasticism and the Philosophy of Mind: The Failure of Aristotelian Psychology," in *Scientific Failure*, ed. T. Horowitz and A. I. Janis (Lanham, Md.: Rowman & Littlefield, 1994), 109–138.

56. See *Quodlibet* V, q. 14, fol. 176vO. Aquinas too seems to agree with the idea that sensory perception already involves an abstraction from matter. For Aquinas's spiritual reception of a sensible form is nothing else than a reception of that form without matter. See, for example, *Sentencia libri De anima* II, lect. 24, Opera omnia 45.1 (Rome, 1984), 169.

57. *Quodlibet* V, q. 14, fol. 176vO: "Phantasma autem apprehensa ab imaginatione, ut apprehensa ab illa, sunt immaterialia abstracta a materiae praesentia, non autem abstracta a conditionibus particularibus quae accidunt formae secundum quod est in materia individuata, sicut sunt figura, ubi et huiusmodi. Quae quidem phantasmata sub talibus conditionibus intellectum movere non possunt primo et per se neque ab ipso apprehendi, sed solum secundum quod sunt abstracta non solum a materiae particularis praesentia, sed etiam a dictis

This intellective power does nothing else than rendering what is potentially intelligible and capable of moving the intellect actually intelligible; it is not itself a thinking power. Yet, once the phantasms are made intelligible by the agent intellect they move the so-called possible intellect as its objects and they change the possible intellect so that it arrives at a simple understanding of the essence and the quiddity of the thing understood. After our (possible) intellect is equipped with basic concepts, the products of the simple act of understanding, the intellect has by itself the power to go on to combine these concepts and form judgments and deductions.[58]

In performing higher order intellectual acts, the intellect is more or less active, but with respect to the primary act of understanding, the intellect is passive. Its acts are caused by something other than itself, and for Henry it is clear that its acts are elicited by nothing else than the intelligible (i.e., universalized) phantasms. Because of its name one might be tempted to regard the agent intellect as that what triggers acts of the thinking power, that is, acts of the so-called possible intellect, but this is wrong. As Henry explains, the relationship between the agent intellect, the possible intellect, and the phantasms is similar to that between light, a transparent body, and color. Without light, colors cannot move a transparent body; because neither do colors have any causal power in the darkness nor does the transparent body in this circumstances have the capacity to receive a visual imprint. Yet, it is not the light that moves the transparent object, that is, that makes me see a remote object through the intermediate air; light only provides the conditions in which colors can exercise their causal powers.[59] Similarly, the agent intellect does not move the possible intellect; it enables the phantasms only to exercise causal power on the intellect, so that acts of understanding occur. This picture also explains why, in Henry's view, the activity of the agent intellect does not result in the production of a new item, as various critics object to Henry's account of intellectual cognition.[60] The light of the sun, for instance, does not produce anything by shining on visible objects; it merely allows these objects to now be seen.[61] In the same way, the agent intellect does not cause the existence of a new item.[62] This is why

---

conditionibus individualibus, ita quod phantasmata in imaginativa apprehensa non sunt nisi in potentia universalia et in potentia moventia intellectum."

58. Ibid., fols. 176vO–177rO.

59. Ibid., and, more explicitly, *Quodlibet* IV, q. 21, 338–339. The example is taken from Averroes, *Commentarium magnum in Aristotelis De anima* lib. III, com. 5, ed. F. Stuart Crawford (Cambridge, Mass.: Harvard University Press, 1953), 410–411.

60. For this type of criticism see, for instance, John Duns Scotus, *Ordinatio* I, dist. 3, pars 3, q. 1, n. 359, *Opera Omnia* III, 216ff.

61. This argument fails, of course, once you accept that colors are merely secondary qualities. But Henry does not draw a distinction similar to the early modern distinction between primary and secondary qualities, and neither do his contemporary critics.

62. Moreover, the agent intellect does not produce anything new because, after all, its activity is only negative insofar as it takes all the individualizing features off the phantasms.

Henry insists that the particular phantasm and the universalized phantasm are one and the same thing. It is one and the same content, to which singularity is attached insofar as it is in the imagination, that now under the influence of the agent intellect has the character of universality.[63]

For the sake of completeness it is worth adding that on Henry's picture the will too does not move the intellect to a simple act of understanding. The will does of course move the intellect. It does so by telling it to consider this or that and to reason about this and that. Yet, that does not mean that it directly changes (*immutat*) the intellect so that it moves from understanding in potentiality to understanding in actuality.[64] Only the intelligible object is capable of directly moving the intellect, and such an object exists only as a universalized phantasm.

Here someone might object that universalized phantasms alone will not do. If the phantasms in the imaginative power are by themselves particular and then, under the influence of the agent intellect, universal, then it would follow that the same entities have contrary properties, which is impossible. It seems reasonable to say that due to the activity of the agent intellect some properties emerge that haven't been perceptible before. In the dark, for instance, milk has the property of tasting sweet, but when exposed to light we also see that milk has a white color.[65] These two properties, "white" and "sweet," are not contrary and can thus exist in the same subject. However, in the case of the phantasm only different subjects will do; the universal phantasm must be different from the particular one.

Henry does not discuss this objection in *Quodlibet* V, q. 14.[66] But it is important to notice that he does everything to show the impossibility of what is supposed to follow from it. The phantasm and nothing else elicits our basic acts of intellectual understanding; there is no further item, no intelligible species, involved here. This is so, according to Henry, because there is simply no room

---

63. *Quodlibet* V, q. 14, fol. 176vO. This also means that a given universal phantasm no longer exists when the act of imagination stops. For this account of abstraction, which does not produce a new item, see also *Summa quaestionum ordinariarum*, a. 58, q. 2 ad 3, fol. 130rG.

64. *Quodlibet* V, q. 14, fol. 179rC: "Voluntas movet intellectum imperando ut intelligat et discurrat, non tamen est ponendum quod aliquo modo ipsum ad actum intelligendi immutat. Immo quod immutat non potest esse nisi obiectum."

65. For this example, used by many late thirteenth-century authors, see, e.g., Godfrey of Fontaines, *Quodlibet* V, q. 10, ed. M. De Wulf and J. Hoffmans (Louvain, 1914), 37.

66. It is not difficult, however, to imagine Henry's response to the objection. He would presumably argue that the kind of universality involved here is not contrary to singularity. The particular phantasm in the imagination is some content plus individualizing features. But the content itself is not particular and in so far it is universal, that is, indifferent with respect to this or that particular instantiation. Otherwise, individualizing features could not be added to it. It is important to distinguish this kind of "incomplete" universality from "complete" universality. The latter is indeed incompatible with singularity.

for a species produced by the agent intellect and *impressed* in the intellect. But what exactly does it mean that there is no impressed species (*species impressa*) in the intellect? What does the adjective "impressed" precisely refer to? Species proponents like Aquinas would agree to a certain degree that there is no impressed species in the mind, because the talk of impression leads one naturally to think of a direct causal influence of corporeal entities on the immaterial intellect. This, however, is impossible, for "nothing corporeal can make an impression on something incorporeal."[67] So either Henry expresses a common view or his use of the expression "impressed species" must mean something more specific. Obviously, the latter is the case. What he has in mind becomes clear when we look back at the species reception in sense perception. Despite all the differences between such a species reception and a normal reception, both are receptions of (accidental) forms. In both cases a form is received (from an agent) in a new subject (i.e., the patient). The intentional reception of a species in sense perception is nothing else than the transfer and the reception of a species in the sensory power (or its organ) as in a subject. After a reception has taken place the species exists in that new subject. One of the main features of an impressed species is thus to exist in a subject.[68]

It is hard to overemphasize this last point. According to Aquinas, the presence of species or forms in the cognizing power is absolutely necessary for cognition to occur. He strongly endorses the following principle:

> Every cognition happens according to some form that is the principle of cognition in the cognizer.[69]

As we have already seen, Henry agrees that sensory cognition involves forms or species, namely those that are impressed in the sensory power. Henry also thinks that a representation of the object has to be in the intellect. The human (and the angelic) intellect is simply not the sort of thing that is able to understand everything in the world by merely understanding itself. But to be in the intellect *as in a cognizer* is for Henry not the same as to be in the intellect *as in a subject*. According to him, the phantasms illuminated by the agent intellect *exist* in the cognizer, insofar as they move the intellect to its act and present the intellect with its objects,[70] but such universal phantasms do not exist in the intellect as in a subject. Yet, they would have to if universalized phantasms were

---

67. *Summa Theologiae* I.84.6: "Nihil autem corporeum imprimere potest in rem incorpoream."
68. See, e.g., *Quodlibet* V, q. 14, fol. 176rK.
69. *Quaestiones disputatae de veritate*, q. 10, a. 4, *Opera omnia* 22.2 (Rome, 1970), 306: "Omnis cognitio est secundum aliquam formam quae est in cognoscente principium cognitionis."
70. See *Quodlibet* V, q. 14, fol. 176vO, where Henry says that the agent intellect (1) achieves that the phantasms, which are in themselves only potentially capable of moving the intellect, move the intellect actually ("phantasma quantum est de se solum in potentia mov-

different things than the phantasms themselves. For where else could these separate items exist if not as entities inhering in the intellect as in a subject?

## WHY THERE ARE NO INTELLIGIBLE SPECIES IN THE MIND

We have finally arrived at the main subject of this essay: Henry's rejection of intelligible species, or better, Henry's rejection of species as entities "subjectively" existing (i.e., inhering) in the mind. Not only does Henry *claim* that there are no such impressed species in the human intellect; at the end of his digression on human cognition, he also says that no intellective power whatsoever has impressed intelligible species "as was *shown above.*"[71]

But where exactly has Henry shown that there are no intelligible species inhering in the intellect? Strictly speaking, Henry provides nowhere in *Quodlibet* V, q. 14, an argument that directly establishes that there can be no such species. The most he does is to argue that such species are useless for an account of intellectual cognition. But because nature does nothing in vain, it would be wrong to posit the existence of such needless entities.[72] This is Henry's overall strategy. And as should be clear from the overview given earlier, there are altogether eight arguments Henry advances against the need for species in the *angelic intellect*. Are all of these arguments also establishing that there is no need for species in *any kind of intellect*?[73]

The first three arguments against species (A 1–3) are, as we saw above, all formulated *ex parte intellectivi*. Their aim is to establish that at least *ex parte intellectivi* species are not required for intellective acts to occur. The first one says that for an intellective power to be actually understanding it is enough to be separated from matter, and the angelic intellect is obviously separated from matter. Arguments two and three point out that there are certain kinds of intellectual activities, such as the beatific vision or self-knowledge, which do not require species. Therefore species are never required *ex parte intellectivi*.[74] For when it is sometimes in the power of the intellect to actively produce simple acts of cognition then there seems to be no good reason to deny that this might always be the case. However, it is extremely unlikely that Henry had these three reasons in mind when he later in his quodlibetal question says he has "shown above" that impressed species do not exist in any sort of intellect. Maybe the

---

entia intellectum esse actu moventia") and (2) makes that the phantasms exist in the intellect merely as in a cognizer ("et existentia in eo ut in cognoscente solum").

71. Ibid., fol. 177rR: "Dicimus quod sola vis sensitiva species habet impressas a sensibus et nulla vis intellectiva habet species impressas intelligibilium, ut supra ostensum est."

72. Ibid., fol. 174rV. For the Aristotelian background of this "principle of parsimony" see, e.g., *Physics* I.4 (188a17). See also *Quodlibet* IV, q. 7, 32.

73. I should add that Henry also argues for why there are no intelligible species in the divine intellect; see *Quodlibet* V, q. 14, fol. 175rD. This, however, is not a controversial issue, and I will therefore leave it aside.

74. Ibid., fol. 174r–vV.

arguments are even good ones, but without more details why immateriality entails intelligibility and why there are no species involved in certain specific acts of intellectual cognition they are hardly complete.[75]

Moreover, the third argument *ex parte intelligibilis* (A 6) is hardly an argument intended to show that no intellect *whatsoever* requires species. Here Henry argues that if the species theory were correct, angels must naturally be endowed with an actual infinity of intelligible species, because they are able to understand an infinite number of things. But there can be no actual infinity of intelligible species in the intellect.[76] Later in the text, Henry advances a somewhat related version of the same line of reasoning (A 7): if angels are capable of understanding everything and are naturally endowed with species of all of their objects and if such species are also responsible for eliciting acts of understanding, then an angel would by necessity understand everything at the same time.[77] Obviously, these arguments only deal with the angelic case. If Henry was sincere when he implied that he has given a *general* argument against (impressed) intelligible species—and there is no reason to doubt this—then he cannot have these in mind.

This leaves us with three arguments that merit closer scrutiny. The first one I want to examine (A 4) takes issue with the notions of impression and representation. Intelligible species, we are reminded, were introduced as devices presenting an intelligible object to the intellect. However, this will not do,

> because the intelligible is only an object of the intellect if it is universal and an impressed species can only represent something as singular. For if a species of something is impressed in something else by something other than that of which it is a species, then it is required—if the species is to be a true representation of something—that the species is impressed in the same way by this other thing as it would have been impressed immediately by the thing itself. However, no species can be impressed in the intellect by something universal qua being universal, but only by something universal insofar as it exists as a determinate being in a particular supposit. For a universal does not exist as such in reality, but only as something determinate in a supposit and nothing can cause an impression of its species in something else unless it has real existence in reality. However, in this way it can only impress the species of something particular under the aspect under which it is particular and this is never representative of something universal under the aspect under which it is universal.[78]

---

75. For Henry's rejection of intelligible species in the beatific vision, see *Quodlibet* III, q. 1; for his rejection of species in self-knowledge, *Quodlibet* IV, q. 7.
76. *Quodlibet* V, q. 14, fols. 174vA–175rB. The argument is actually more complex, but the exact details are of no relevance here.
77. Ibid., fol. 175rD–vE.
78. Ibid., fol. 174vY.

Henry does not deny that impressed species represent that by which they have been impressed in something else. He accepts the principle according to which impressed species represent the natural agents causing the impressions.[79] But in order to be able to represent universal objects to the mind an intelligible species would have to be impressed by something universal qua universal, which is impossible. For universals as such do not exist and what does not exist does not have causal efficacy. So if impressed species exist in the mind, they are necessarily species of particular things and could not do the job for which they have been introduced in the first place, namely to represent universal objects. Moreover, if there is no way in which impressed species can represent universal objects, it also follows that the idea of species impressed by God in the angelic mind is a complete nonstarter.[80] For in impressing in the angelic mind species that are truly representing intelligible objects God would have to impress them in the very same way in which they would have been impressed immediately by the universal objects themselves. Yet, the impossibility of the latter includes the impossibility of the former.

It is important to notice that Henry does not reject impressed species as representations of something universal on the ground that species existing in the mind (as in a subject) would be individuated by their subjects and would thus represent only something particular. Such a reasoning would be too open to objections. A species proponent could reply that it confuses the ontological nature of a mental presentation as an accident inhering in a subject (from which stems its singularity) with its representational content. As should be clear, Henry's argument proceeds differently insofar as it addresses directly the very impossibility of providing universal representational content by impression. Because of its general strategy, Henry's argument clearly applies to more than just the angelic case. Nothing in its formulation restricts it to angelic cognition. Although the remark about impression of species by something other than by the normal agent is introduced to apply a general point to the angelic case, this is not a crucial step in the overall argument.

Henry's argument does of course raise further questions, which unfortunately he does not address at all. The most important is probably: Why do impressed species represent the impressing agent at all? But maybe it is inappropriate to ask Henry for a general account of representation. After all, his aim is to argue against opponents who also share the belief that impressed species generally represent, and so he can easily take for granted that they would accept that impressed species or forms represent what brought them into being. Yet, there is no reason to doubt that he himself subscribed to the principle according to which every effect represents its cause. In this sense the footprint

---

79. His account of sense perception depends heavily on this principle.

80. This is the reason why Henry talks in the earlier quote about the case that an impressed species is not impressed by that of which it is the species but is impressed by something else.

in the sand is a natural representation of the foot by which it got imprinted on the sand. What Henry denies, however, is that the particular footprint is a *natural* representation of a "universal foot." But why, so might a species proponent object, can the particular imprint on the sand not represent all possible feet capable of producing such an imprint? And what about a particular triangle drawn on the blackboard? Can it not represent a multitude of particular existing triangles?

This again is an objection Henry himself does not bother replying to. Yet, there can be no doubt concerning his response. The particular footprint and the particular triangle on the board can sometimes be regarded as universal representations if (and only if) the intellect considers them as such. When I draw a triangle to illustrate a geometrical property of triangles, I do of course not take that particular triangle as representing only one single triangle; and there is no reason that Henry would have denied that. But the point is this: the particular representation can only represent universally if the intellect considers it actively as a universal representation, that is, by considering it not with respect to its particular features. In a slightly more scholastic vocabulary: if the intellect is already actively thinking, it can consider particulars as universal representations. But Henry's focus here is on what activates the intellect in the first place, and that can only be something that is by itself a universal. For this important task impressed intelligible species seem useless. And this is all the argument intends to show.

The next argument (A 5) is clearly meant to apply to angelic cognition only. It tries to establish that impressed intelligible species in the angelic mind would not be enough to account for the angelic cognition of an object present to the angel. For one quite reasonably assumes the relationship between the intelligible object and the intelligible species to be the same as the relationship between the sensible object and the sensible species, say, in the visual power: whatever their exact relationship is, the existence of species seems to depend more on the external objects than the other way round, for the latter are usually the causes of the former. The existence of a species in the cognitive power is, on the contrary, not the cause of the presence of the external object. Now think about the angelic case: if angels were to cognize material objects by species impressed on their intellect at the moment of their creation then they would still need something informing them about the actual presence of an external object. In Henry's words:

> A species that is impressed on the intellect by something else than by a universal thing and that is conserved in the intellect cannot cause the presence of the thing so that it is cognized by the intellect under the aspect of an object. Rather for this is required that it is represented by something else, so that the intellect is reduced from potential understanding to actual understanding either by this representing thing or by the represented object itself. But because species impressed in the intellect have been introduced exactly

to explain such a representation of the object it is useless to posit their existence in the intellect.[81]

Obviously this argument does not apply to the human intellect, for human beings are not commonly held to be endowed with impressed species of all possible objects. In our case species are, if they exist at all, ultimately impressed, through a series of mediating instances, by the external objects themselves.

The most important argument against impressed intelligible species is the one Henry mentions last (A 8). Its aim is to establish that even if species existed impressed on the intellect and even if they were able to represent universals, they could play no role in actualizing the intellect and would therefore be useless in explaining the occurrence of a simple act of the intellect. The argument runs as follows:

> Moreover, it would follow that the intellect would not be passive in understanding, except in an accidental way, namely insofar as it receives a species through an impression by God. The intellect receives this species like a subject receives its accident; and this insofar as it [i.e., the species] is something in the genus of being (*in genere entis*), but not insofar as it is something in the genus of intelligibles (*in genere intelligibilium*). And so such a passion would not be caused by an intelligible object insofar as the intelligible is able to move the intellect as belonging to the genus of intellective powers (*in genere intellectivorum*). And so the intellect as belonging to the genus of intellective powers would behave like something active with respect to the act of understanding and would in no way be passive and understanding would not be some sort of passion (*non esset intelligere pati quoddam*). The act of the intellect would not be a movement from the object toward the soul, but the other way round. More correctly, it would not even be a movement from the soul toward the object because such an act is completely unconditioned (*absolutus*) and not terminated with respect to something else, but stays within the agent, like shining is not terminated with respect to something else. And so the thing understood would not be perceived by an act of understanding.[82]

Like the argument discussed earlier, the present one is formulated as an argument against impressed species in the *angelic* mind. If angels had such species impressed by God, then, according to the argument, the angelic mind would

---

81. *Quodlibet* V, q. 14, fol. 174vZ.
82. Ibid., fol. 175vF. For the dictum *intelligere est pati quoddam*, see Aristotle, *De anima* III.4 429a13–15.

have them as accidents in itself as their subject. But insofar as species are accidents, they cannot play the role of representing intelligible objects moving the intellect to act. For what moves the intellect insofar as it is intellect is not an accident but an intelligible object. What the species theory of angelic cognition lacks, so the implicit criticism, is an account of how these accidental qualities are capable of presenting the intellect with intelligible objects.[83] Therefore, to say that objects are presented to the angelic intellect by means of impressed species does hardly explain anything. If there is, however, nothing able to move the angelic intellect in the way of an object, then the intellect would have to be itself the cause of its proper actions, or in other words: the intellect would be essentially an active power of thought. Yet, even if such an impressed species caused, as an accident, the actualization of the intellective power, this would only be coincidental, because the actualization wouldn't occur insofar as the intellect is a passive *cognitive* power.

In the second part of the passage, Henry links the passivity of the intellect to the intentionality of thought. Suppose the intellect is essentially an active power: intellectual understanding could then not longer be conceived of as a movement from the object toward the intellect; thought would not be "affected" by its object. It looks as if the direction of fit between world and mind is then not from the world to the mind, but the opposite. Yet, even that is not possible with a purely active intellect. For if there is nothing that determines it, the intellect will not be directed toward an object. Under these circumstances intellectual understanding is hardly intentional, but resembles a purely diffusive and indeterminate activity like the shining of a light source.

It is easy to see that the key idea with which the argument operates is not restricted to the angelic intellect. Human understanding is fundamentally passive because our cognition is essentially receptive (although there might also be some spontaneity involved). Impressed species are not helpful in explaining the receptivity specific to cognizing powers for the very same reasons that species in the angel mind are irrelevant in explaining angelic cognition. Naturally, a species proponent will try to downplay the ontological features of impressed species. She might grant that species do not contribute to cognition insofar as they are accidents in the intellect but insist that they do insofar as they represent the intelligible object.[84] But even if we grant that species in the human

---

83. Henry's own theory of angelic cognition attempts to explain exactly this point of how some quality of the angelic intellect can present the intellect with intelligible objects. According to his solution, the quality inhering in the angelic mind is an intellectual habit and intellectual habits have natural objects.

84. That this, however, is impossible is shown by A 4. Bringing A 4 into the picture also allows us to answer to the following objection: Maybe the impressed intelligible species activates the intellect by being impressed in it as an accident and the intellect then turns to that what is represented by the impressed species and is moved by the represented object.

intellect can present intelligible objects to the intellect, it is not clear why we would need them in the first place. For the intelligible object is, according to Henry, already present in the universalized phantasm and human intellectual cognition is in any case always accompanied by the operation of the imaginative faculty.[85]

Finding Henry's arguments against impressed intelligible species in *Quodlibet* V, q. 14 turned out to be much more complicated than expected. As we were able to see, only two arguments are developed enough to explain the general rejection of such species in intellectual cognition. The first of these arguments (A 4) doubted that species are principally capable of representing universal intelligible objects, the second (A 8) argued for the irrelevance of species existing in the intellect as in a subject. This result is in sharp contrast to the general anti-species arguments medieval authors ascribe to Henry of Ghent. In John Duns Scotus's discussion of species in the human mind in book I of his *Ordinatio*, we encounter, for instance, a much longer list of arguments against species taken more or less verbatim from Henry's *Quodlibet* V, q. 14.[86] We should not be surprised by this. Duns Scotus and his contemporaries were not interested in interpreting Henry but in defending the species account of intellectual cognition. In their view, Henry's arguments were wrong anyway, so that they might not have felt too much need to distinguish between those of Henry's arguments that were only meant to work for the angelic case and those that carry over to the human case. But it is an unfortunate fact that their reading has seriously distorted our appreciation of Henry's own position.

## HOW EXACTLY DOES INTELLECTUAL COGNITION WORK?

At this point we know more about how, according to Henry of Ghent, human intellectual cognition does not work than about his positive account of cognition. This should not come as too much of a surprise because the text we are interpreting is, allow me to repeat this again, mainly concerned with angelic cognition. But by now we should have enough indications to know better where to look for such a positive account. One expectation we can have with respect to such an account is that it provides us with an explanation for why the intel-

---

Such an account would be somewhat similar to the way sensory cognition works. For there the impression seems to have some sort of causal role. But as Henry argues in A 4, the impressed species would not be able to represent something universal, and for that reason it could not move the intellect even at such a later stage. Yet, the case is different in sensory perception, because there the impression can indeed move the sensory power (the object of which is something particular).

85. See *Quodlibet* V, q. 14, fol. 176vO: "Intellectus noster nihil intelligit nisi coniunctum cum sua imaginatione; ut enim ipse speculetur phantasmata sub ratione universalis, necesse est imaginativam idem simul speculari sub ratione particularis."

86. See *Ordinatio* I, dist. 3, pars 3, q. 1, nn. 333–336 and 340–345, *Opera Omnia* III: 201–203 and 205–208. But Scotus is not the first who comes up with a longer list of Henry's anti-species arguments.

lect can be both a passive power and at the same time a power from which the act of understanding "proceeds actively." Isn't there a contradiction?

To settle these remaining questions it is again helpful to look at Thomas Aquinas and at how he explains understanding as a conjunction of the knower and the known as well as the role species have in all of this. In his *Disputed Questions on Truth*, Aquinas writes:

> But what understands and what is understood (*intelligens et intellectum*), inasmuch as from both one thing results (*prout ex eis est effectum unum quid*), which is the intellect in act, are one principle (*unum principium*) of the act of understanding. And I say that from both one thing results insofar as what is understood is conjoined to what understands either by its essence or by a similitude.[87]

According to Aquinas, the species (or similitude) is one of the things that establish the union between the knower and the known. And it does so by being a feature *intrinsic* to the intellect, causing the intellect to be determined to this or that object.[88] As we know already, Henry considers this model as inadequate, for there is no way impressed species (existing subjectively in the intellect) can do what Aquinas wants them to do. Henry explicitly refers to Aquinas's model:

> The one principle (*unum principium*) of understanding is the intellective power (*intellectivum*) and the intelligible object through its species (*intelligibile per suam speciem*), inasmuch as from both one thing results (*prout ex eis est effectum unum quid*), which is the intellect in act. But the formal part in this union is played by the species by which the intellect is informed. However, it appears immediately that this way of understanding the act of understanding is not adequate.[89]

If this is not the adequate way of understanding the union between the knower and the known, what other model has Henry to offer? In a later passage of his quodlibetal question he explains:

---

87. *Quaestiones disputatae de veritate*, q. 8, a. 6. See also *Summa Theologiae* I.85.2 ad 1. For a thorough account of Aquinas's theory of intellectual cognition, see Pasnau, *Theories of Cognition*; E. Stump, "Aquinas's Account of the Mechanisms of Intellective Cognition," *Revue internationale de philosophie* 52 (1998): 287–307; D. Perler, *Theorien der Intentionalität im Mittelalter* (Frankfurt a.M.: Klostermann, 2002), 31–105.

88. See, e.g., *Quaestiones disputatae de veritate*, q. 10, a. 4, 306: "Omnis cognitio est secundum aliquam formam quae est in cognoscente principium cognitionis. Forma autem huiusmodi dupliciter potest considerari: uno modo secundum esse quod habet in cognoscente, alio modo secundum respectum quem habet ad rem cuius est similitudo. Secundum quidem primum respectum facit cognoscentem actu cognoscere, sed secundum respectum secundum determinat cognitionem ad aliquod cognoscibile determinatum."

89. *Quodlibet* V, q. 14, fol. 175rD. The context of this bit of Henry's text makes it even clearer that Henry here responds directly to Aquinas, *Quaestiones disputatae de veritate*, q. 8, a. 6.

The intellect is identical with what is understood and the sensory power is identical with what is sensed, in this consists the perfect assimilation of the cognizer to that which is cognized, and without this assimilation no cognitive act achieves its end (*perficitur*). And so it is required for the act of understanding that the intelligible object insofar as it is understood according to a disposition (*secundum habitum*) acts on the intellect and changes the intellect, so that it moves from potency to act; and the intellect itself is what is passive here. But in this stage the act of understanding does not exists according to its form and completion, but only insofar as this stage describes its beginning. But the act of understanding exists according to its form and completion in that . . . one thing results out of the intellect insofar as it is an intellective power and out of what is understood insofar as it is the intelligible object. This is one principle (*unum principium*) of the act of understanding which is an operation and the perfection of that which understands insofar as it understands, but the formal part of this is played by the object itself.[90]

Although the primary aim of this passage is, again, to explain angelic cognition, the main ideas also apply to the human case. According to Henry, the objects of the angelic mind are represented by intellectual dispositions (*habitus*) and for this reason he talks above of "the intelligible object insofar as it is understood according to a disposition." In the human case, the intellect is moved directly by the universalized phantasms. But putting this issue aside, the contrast with Aquinas's account of the cognitive union is clear and as the explicit reference to the "one principle of understanding" shows, the contrast is not merely incidental. Note that Henry distinguishes between two stages in intellectual cognition: First, the simple act of human intellectual understanding is triggered by the universalized phantasm but not by something informing the intellect in any way. In this first stage, the intellect is completely passive. In the second stage, when the act of understanding "exists according to its form and completion," i.e., when we arrive at the act of understanding strictly speaking, the intellect and its object are united, but again not by an intelligible species, something intrinsic to the intellect, but insofar as the intellect assimilates itself to the object that is, as presented in the phantasm, something *extrinsic* to the intellect itself. One might picture this in the following way: the object of the intellect "informs" the intellective act only in the way an external boundary shapes what it encloses; this way of how the intellective act receives its specification and determination provides an alternative to the model of intrinsic determination by the inherence of a form.[91]

90. *Quodlibet* V, q. 14, fol. 177vR.
91. It is possible that Henry's solution is connected to a distinction he draws in his account of the beatific vision. For there he distinguishes between a form as something inherent and a form as something merely present. Only in the latter sense can God be the form of the intellect. For this distinction see Pini, "Il dibattito sulle specie," 285.

Notice that this model allows us to understand why for Henry the human intellect is both passive and "actively proceeding" toward the act of understanding. The intellect is passive insofar as it has to be triggered by its object and because in the process of becoming similar to the intelligible object it is "receptive" of the form of that object by becoming in a certain sense like it.[92] Yet, the intellect must also be active. For thought and understanding are attributed to the intellect and not to the intelligible object. But they could hardly be attributed to the cognitive power if it would not play the role of an agent.[93]

A defender of Aquinas would presumably not be too convinced by Henry's understanding of the union between the knower and the known. How, the defender might argue, can the intellect become similar to the intelligible object if it has not received some intrinsic specification that determines it to this specific object and thus makes that it assimilates this object and not some other thing? Aquinas has at least a response to this problem, but Henry's account only talks about the result of the assimilation. It is true that Henry does not explain *how* the intellect assimilates its object; he contents himself with the position that it does so. Yet, his silence may just indicate that there is not much more to say anyway. Cognition is a kind of assimilation and cognitive powers are powers of assimilation. That might be mysterious to some, but Aquinas's reference to species inhering in the intellect is not really a solution either, as Henry's arguments against impressed species were aiming to show.

## CONCLUSION

What are we supposed to think about Henry's account of cognition and his rejection of impressed intelligible species? Is his position really only of minor philosophical interest? A response to the latter question depends on what one considers as philosophically interesting in the first place. To someone committed to direct realism, for instance, Henry's rejection of intelligible species must

---

92. See also *Quodlibet* V, q. 25, fol. 204rI, and *Summa questionum ordinariarum*, a. 58, q. 2 ad 3, fol. 131rL.

93. And for this reason we now see why Henry is justified to emphasize, at the beginning of *Quodlibet* V, q. 14, the active role of the intellect. Some interpreters regard Henry's insistence on the active nature of cognition as an Augustinian influence (see, e.g., Brown, "Sensation in Henry of Ghent"). And although it is true that Henry later, in *Quodlibet* XI, q. 5, develops his views about the activity of cognition into an interpretation of the relevant chapters of Augustine's *On the Trinity*, I am not convinced, *pace* such commentators as Rombeiro, "Intelligible Species," that evoking Augustine helps much to understand the philosophical considerations that lead Henry to his account. The active role of the objects (as they are represented in the phantasms) has led commentators to talk of them as efficient causes of the first act of the intellect (see, e.g., Pasnau, *Theories of Cognition*, 307). But we can now see why this is a misunderstanding. For obvious reasons, Henry frequently talks about the active role of phantasms and objects, but there is not a single passage in which he calls them efficient causes of cognitive acts.

definitely seem lukewarm. For although Henry rejects species in the intellect, he seems not to reject intermediate representational devices such as universalized phantasms. But why should Henry's philosophical success be measured with respect to how successful he argues for direct realism? There is no evidence that he had any problems with intermediate representations as such. On the contrary: in one of his treatments of the beatific vision, Henry is explicitly confronted with the problem of whether a species or some other medium would prevent us from having an immediate cognition of God. He is very outspoken against any theory that explains the beatific vision by means of species in the mind, but his opposition to such a view is not at all related to worries about indirect realism. As he says himself, he has no problems with cognitive theories as long as the species or the medium in cognition is not meant to serve as an intermediate *object*.[94] Henry does obviously not believe as his contemporary Peter John Olivi that entities in between the extramental object and the cognitive powers constitute a sort of veil between us and the world.[95] And this is just what we expect from a philosopher who holds that sensation requires species and who holds that the object of intellectual cognition is the object as actively imagined by the faculty of imagination.

It looks as if for Henry the only way to make sense of our intellect's dependence on sensation is exactly endorse a more indirect realist account of cognition. For that reason he seems to have no quarrels talking about species as such. Henry might also have in mind Aristotle's dictum according to which in cognition the stone is not in our soul by the species of the stone[96] when he writes that "it belongs to the nature of our intellect to understand the abstracted *species* in the phantasms" or that our intellect understands through *species* existing in the phantasms.[97] In short, Henry agrees that in order to have intellectual cognition our intellect must be moved by an object and that the object must be *in* the intel-

---

94. *Quodlibet* III, q. 1, fol. 47vR: "Nec est haec opinio repellenda ut quidam credunt, quia privat omnino divinae essentiae visionem immediatam.... Videre autem per medium ut per speciem informantem visum, quae solum est ratio videndi et non obiectum visum, non privat immediatam visionem divinae essentiae."

95. See his *Quaestiones in secundum librum Sententiarum*, q. 58, ed. B. Janssen (Quaracchi, 1924), 2:469: "Si aliquid aliud interponeretur inter aspectum potentiae et ipsum obiectum, illud potius velaret rem et impediret eam praesentialiter aspici in se ipsa quam ad hoc adiuvaret." Henry actually addresses this sort of veil-of-perception argument against species in *Summa quaestionum ordinariarum*, a. 1, q. 1, *Opera Omnia XXI* (Leuven, 2005), 27–28. For a discussion of medieval accounts of cognition in terms of the distinction between indirect and direct realism, see D. Perler, "Essentialism and Direct Realism: Some Late Medieval Perspectives," *Topoi* 19 (2000): 111–122.

96. *De anima* III.8 431b29f. Aristotle talks about the *eidos* of the stone, but the Latin translators render this as *species*. In this way the passage becomes one of the key inspirations for the medieval species theory.

97. *Quodlibet* V, q. 14, fol. 177rR: "Natura nostri intellectus est quod species intelligat in phantasmatibus abstractas"; ibid., fol. 179rC. Henry sometimes uses the expression *species expressa* or *expressiva* when he talks about these species in the phantasms on which our intellect is dependent. See *Quodlibet* IV, q. 21, 337–347.

lect. Moreover, the object is in the intellect through a species of the object. However, according to Henry, Aquinas and others were misled in adopting a too literal reading of this principle, for they took existing *in the intellect* to mean existing in the intellect as *in a subject* (*ut in subiecto*). Yet, on Henry's understanding, the object has merely to exist in the intellect as in a cognizer (*ut in cognoscente*). This does not mean that there is some new kind of being that objects enjoy in the intellect. There is no reason to doubt that for Henry being as an object in a cognizer just means to be related to a cognizer. If someone were to ask where exactly these objects exist in the strict sense, Henry would point to the imaginative faculty as the place where they exist qua species in a subject.[98]

From this perspective it looks indeed as if Henry were merely concerned with a "technical aspect" (Pasnau) of the species doctrine, namely the problem of how exactly species can be said to move the intellect and to exist in the intellect.[99] Yet, the impression is absolutely misleading. For the core difference between Henry's account of cognition (in *Quodlibet* V, q. 14) and that of the species proponents he is arguing against is a difference regarding the very nature of intentionality. On Henry's account, our intellect is not determined toward a certain object because it receives a form of that object through which the intellect is intrinsically determined. The intellect is naturally directed toward whatever object will move it to act. In other words, the intentionality of thought is not derivative on auxiliary items inhering in the intellect; the intellect has its intentionality through itself and through the object moving it. Henry does not reject the traditional view that cognition occurs by means of mediating representation. It is the representation of the object that gets our cognitive powers going and the states of the powers represent their objects at every stage of the cognitive process insofar as cognition is nothing else than assimilation. Yet, intellectual cognition does not require a representation intrinsic to the intellect.[100]

And there is reason to suspect that the same account also applies to sensory perception. Although Henry's account of sense perception in *Quodlibet* V, q. 14 does not rule out that he considers sensation as a different case, i.e., that he thinks the sensible species determine the sensory power intrinsically with regard to this or that object, a text from *Quodlibet* XI, q. 5 is more explicit. In the later quodlibetal question, Henry emphasizes the distinction between the sensory power as a power of the soul and the sensory organ; the species is said to inhere in the sensory organ (*organum*), but not in the power of the soul (*vis animae*) itself. The species inclines and determines the power thus as something that is

---

98. See also *Quodlibet* IV, q. 21, 337–339.
99. I have myself defended such an interpretation in Goris and Pickavé, "Von der Erkenntnis der Engel."
100. For this reason I disagree with Rombeiro ("Intelligible Species," 219), for whom Henry is committed throughout his career "to the doctrine that the intellect passively *receives* the intelligible form by which it operates" (my emphasis).

somewhat external to the power, and the power uses the species informed organ as an instrument of sense perception.[101]

As I said at the outset of my contribution, my aim was to provide a partial interpretation of *Quodlibet* V, q. 14, and not a comprehensive interpretation of Henry of Ghent's cognitive psychology. Yet, if the presented interpretation of *Quodlibet* V, q. 14 is correct, then a new overall study might be a great desideratum. For Henry's theory of cognition may turn out to be much more interesting than expected.

---

101. See, e.g., *Quodlibet* XI, q. 5, fol. 451vZ: "Agens principale est vis animae inclinata, agens autem instrumentale est organum informatum specie."

# Two Models of Thinking

*Thomas Aquinas and John Duns Scotus on Occurrent Thoughts*

GIORGIO PINI

Suppose I am thinking about what it is to be a cat. What sort of activity am I engaging in? What is it to think about something? Thomas Aquinas and John Duns Scotus answered this question in two remarkably different ways. Even though Scotus did not develop his theory of thinking in direct opposition to Aquinas, a comparison between their treatments can shed some light on what is distinctive of their respective views on what they called "acts of thinking."[1]

It will be convenient to break down the question "What is it to think about something?" into the following three subquestions:

1. What sort of thing is an act of thinking?
2. How and when does an act of thinking occur?
3. What accounts for an act of thinking's being about something?

The first question concerns the ontological status of an act of thinking. The second question concerns the mechanisms of cognition. The third question concerns the intentionality of an act of thinking. It is a typical trait of later medieval theories of intellectual cognition to regard these three questions as interconnected. Specifically, the answer given to the first question was supposed to have a bearing on the answers given to the other two questions.

Interpreters of later medieval philosophy have recently devoted much attention to the second and especially the third question, that is, to the mechanisms of intellectual cognition and thought's intentionality. In particular, much effort has been recently spent to investigate medieval theories of mental represen-

---

I worked on his essay while I was in Leuven in 2008–2009 thanks to a Fordham University Faculty Fellowship and a Katholieke Universiteit Leuven Research Grant. I am grateful to both institutions for giving me that opportunity. I wish to express special thanks to Russell Friedman for making my stay in Leuven so enjoyable and to Gyula Klima for commenting on a previous version of this essay.

1. By "act of thinking," I translate the following Latin expressions: *actus intelligendi, actus cognoscendi, actualis cognitio, intellectio, notitia, notitia actualis, notitia actualis genita in intellectu*. Both acts of thinking and their contents were referred to as "concepts" (*conceptus*).

tation.² By contrast, the question regarding the ontological status of an act of thinking has attracted less attention. In this essay, I hope to show that the contrast between Aquinas's view that acts of thinking are actions and Scotus's alternative view that acts of thinking are mental qualities is more than a negligible disagreement concerning a technical issue in cognitive psychology and has a deep influence on their respective accounts of what to think about something is.³

Before starting with Aquinas and then moving to Scotus, some clarifications are needed. When dealing with Aquinas's and Scotus's accounts of what it is to think, I will focus on human rather than angelic or divine thinking. I will also consider simple acts of thinking, such as my thought about what it is to be a cat, as opposed to complex acts of composition and division, such as my thought that cats are graceful animals or that they do not fly, and to acts of reasoning, such as my thought that, since cats are animals and animals need to eat, cats need to eat.⁴ When dealing specifically with Scotus's account, my focus will be on what were called "abstractive" as opposed to "intuitive" acts of thinking, that is, thoughts whose identity is independent of whether their object exists or not, such as my thought about what it is to be a cat, which remains the same whether cats actually exist or not.⁵ Finally, my focus will be on general

---

2. See R. Pasnau, *Theories of Cognition in the Later Middle Ages* (Cambridge: Cambridge University Press, 1997), 31–124; D. Perler, *Theorien der Intentionalität im Mittelalter* (Frankfurt: Kostermann, 2002); D. Perler, *Théories de l'intentionnalité au moyen âge* (Paris: Vrin, 2003); J. P. O'Callaghan, *Thomist Realism and the Linguistic Turn. Toward a More Perfect Form of Existence* (Notre Dame, Ind.: University of Notre Dame Press, 2003); P. King, "Rethinking Representation in the Middle Ages: A Vade-Mecum to Medieval Theories of Mental Representation," in *Representation and Objects of Thoughts in Medieval Philosophy*, ed. H. Lagerlund (Aldershot: Ashgate, 2007), 81–100; J. E. Brower and S. Brower-Toland, "Aquinas on Mental Representation: Concept and Intentionality," *The Philosophical Review* 117 (2008): 193–243.

3. My claim is not that Thomas Aquinas was the only supporter of the view that thoughts are actions or that Duns Scotus was the only supporter of the view that thoughts are qualities. But they are arguably the most articulate proponents of their respective positions.

4. In the later Middle Ages, it was common to distinguish among three kinds of intellectual acts: simple apprehension (which will be the focus of my essay), composition and division, and reasoning. See for example Aquinas, *In Peryerm.*, I, 1, 1,5; *In An. Post.* I, 1, 2, 4–5; *In IV Meta.*, lect. 4, n. 574; *In IV Meta.*, lect. 17, n. 736. See R. W. Schmidt, *The Domain of Logic according to Saint Thomas Aquinas* (The Hague: Nijhoff, 1966), 53–57; R. Pasnau, *Thomas Aquinas on Human Nature: A Philosophical Study of* Summa theologiae Ia 75–89 (Cambridge: Cambridge University Press, 2002), 273; E. Stump, *Aquinas* (New York: Routledge, 2003), 265–266. Aristotle distinguished two acts of the intellect in *De anima* III, 6, 430a26–b6.

5. On the distinction between abstractive and intuitive cognition in Scotus, see S. J. Day, *Intuitive Cognition. A Key to the Significance of the Later Scholastics* (St. Bonaventure, N.Y.: Franciscan Institute Publications, 1947), 39–139; K. H. Tachau, *Vision and Certitude in the Age of Ockham. Optics, Epistemology and the Foundations of Semantics 1250–1345* (Leiden: Brill, 1988), 68–75; S. D. Dumont, "The Scientific Character of Theology and the Origin of

acts of thinking, such as thoughts about what it is to be a cat, as opposed to singular thoughts, such as thoughts about this or that individual cat.[6]

### AQUINAS'S MODEL OF THINKING: THINKING AS ACTING

Aquinas adopted Aristotle's insight that to think is akin to change as both thought and change can be explained at a general level as the reception of a form in a patient.[7] Just as something is heated when it receives the form heat, so I think about what it is to be a cat when the form felinity is received in my intellect.

Within this general framework, Aquinas faced five separate questions. First, what is the relationship between the form in my intellect and the form of the thing I am thinking about, for example, between the form felinity in my intellect and the form felinity as instantiated in extramental cats? Second, what sort of thing is an act of thinking—a passion or an action? In other words, when I think about what it is to be a cat, does my intellect receive a form or does it produce a form? Third, if it is granted that an act of thinking is an action, what sort of action is it? Fourth, is the presence of a certain form in my intellect both necessary and sufficient for an act of thinking to occur? Fifth and finally, what accounts for an act of thinking's intentionality, that is, for its being about what it is about?

I will address each of these questions in turn.

### *The Form in the Intellect: The Intelligible Species as Likeness*

So, first, what is the relationship between the form felinity present in my intellect when I think about what it is to be a cat and the form felinity as it is instantiated in cats?

Aquinas rejected the view that the form present in my intellect is numerically the same as the form that is the organizing principle of the thing I am thinking about.[8] Rather, the form in my intellect and the form of the thing I am thinking about are two numerically distinct items. Following the standard usage of his time, Aquinas called the form in the intellect "intelligible species." He claimed that the relationship holding between the intelligible species and

---

Duns Scotus' Distinction between Intuitive and Abstractive Cognition," *Speculum* 64 (1989): 579–599; R. Pasnau, "Cognition," in *The Cambridge Companion to Duns Scotus*, ed. T. Williams (Cambridge: Cambridge University Press, 2003), 296–300.

6. On singular thoughts in Scotus, see Peter King's essay in this volume.

7. On Aristotle's account of thinking as implying a "hylomorphic model" in which the form of the thing cognized is received in the cognizer, see C. Shields, "Intentionality and Isomorphism in Aristotle," *Proceeding of the Boston Area Colloquium in Ancient Philosophy* 11 (1995): 308–310; C. Shields, *Aristotle* (New York: Routledge, 2007), 293–305; and C. Shields, "The Peculiar Motion of Aristotelian Souls," *Proceedings of the Aristotelian Society. Supplementary Volume* 81 (2007): 140, 145–150.

8. In this respect, Aquinas is indebted to Avicenna. See Avicenna, *Liber de anima*, pars V, c. 6, 134–135. See D. L. Black, "Conjunction and the Identity of Knower and Known in Averroes," *American Catholic Philosophical Quarterly* 73 (1999): 162–163; M. Sebti, *Avicenne. L'âme humaine* (Paris: Presses Universitaires de France, 2000), 97–99.

the thing thought about is not numerical identity but a specific kind of asymmetrical likeness (*similitudo*). Specifically, the intelligible species is a likeness of the thing thought about (but not the other way around). Thus, to think about something is to have a likeness of that thing in the intellect:

> That which is understood is within that which understands through its likeness. And the saying that "what is actually understood is the actualized intellect" holds in this way: insofar as a likeness of the thing understood is the intellect's form. (Similarly, a likeness of a sensible thing is the form of the actualized sense.)[9]

### Acts of Thinking as Actions

Second, what kind of event is that by which the intelligible species comes to be present in the intellect?

At times, Aquinas seemed to suggest that there is nothing more to thinking than the reception of a form. Thus, acts of thinking should be regarded as instances of passions as opposed to actions.[10] This, however, should only be taken as a very general description of what happens when I think about something. Any time Aquinas provided a more detailed account of how thought occurs, he claimed that, when I think about something, I am genuinely doing something. Specifically, he defended three points. First, he argued that, even though the material object does not act on the intellect, the intellect nevertheless receives its form. Second, he granted that the object plays some causal role in the act of thinking. Third, he distinguished between the intellect's reception

---

9. *ST* I, q. 85, a. 2, ad 1: "intellectum est in intelligente per suam similitudinem. Et per hunc modum dicitur quod intellectum in actu est intellectus in actu, inquantum similitudo rei intellectae est forma intellectus; sicut similitudo rei sensibilis est forma sensus in actu." The English translation is taken from Thomas Aquinas, *The Treatise on Human Nature. Summa theologiae 1a 75–89*, trans. Robert Pasnau (Indianapolis: Hackett, 2002), 164. Contemporary interpreters disagree about the way the claim that the intelligible species is a likeness should be spelled out. Some argue that the notion of likeness is to be taken as primitive. See, for example, C. Panaccio, "Aquinas on Intellectual Representation," in *Ancient and Medieval Theories of Intentionality*, 185–200; Brower and Brower-Toland, "Aquinas on Mental Representation." By contrast, other interpreters argue that the notion of likeness between a species and what it is a likeness of should be interpreted as a relation of "co-formality" or "formal identity" or "sharing of form." See for example G. Klima, "Tradition and Innovation in Medieval Theories of Mental Representation," *Proceedings of the Society for Medieval Logic and Metaphysics* 4 (2004): 4–11; Stump, *Aquinas*, 273–275; King, "Rethinking Representation." What I say in this essay is independent of which of the two positions is adopted on this issue.

10. See *De Ver.*, q. 10, a. 4: "Hoc autem differenter contingit in mente humana quae formas accipit a rebus, et in divina vel angelica quae a rebus non accipiunt. In mente enim accipiente scientiam a rebus, formae existunt per quandam actionem rerum in animam; omnis autem actio est per formam; unde formae quae sunt in mente nostra primo et principaliter respiciunt res extra animam existentes quantum ad formas earum."

of the object's form on one hand and, on the other hand, the intellect's act of thinking proper.

Concerning the first point, Aquinas held that the form of an object is impressed on the intellect not by that object but by the intellect itself. Specifically, he distinguished between the active and the passive role the intellect plays in cognition. Both roles are played by numerically the same intellect. In its active role, the intellect performs an operation called "abstraction," which results in the production of a mental quality that has the same form as the sensory impressions and images caused by the object. That mental quality is called "intelligible species."[11] The intellect also plays the passive role in the impression of the intelligible species. In that passive capacity it is called "possible intellect."[12]

Concerning the second point, Aquinas held that the object, through the intermediary of a sensory image (the phantasm), plays some causal role in intellectual cognition. Admittedly, the image of an object is not the sole or even the principal agent in the process of reception of that object's form in the possible intellect. Rather, the agent intellect is the main agent in that production. The image of the object, however, plays the role of "instrumental or secondary agent." Even though the details of this view may not be completely clear, Aquinas intended to reject the claim that the object, through the intermediary of its sensory image, plays merely a noncausal role in the process of intellectual cognition.[13] Subsequently, Aquinas preferred to refer to sensory images as something like (*quodammodo*) the matter on which the agent intellect performs its action.[14]

---

11. On the history of the notion of intelligible species, see L. Spruit, *Species Intelligibilis: From Perception to Knowledge* (Leiden: Brill, 1994); G. Pini, "Il dibattito sulle specie intelligibili nel tredicesimo secolo," *Medioevo* 29 (2004): 267–306.

12. *ST* I, q. 79, a. 2–4; q. 85, a. 1. See Pasnau, *Thomas Aquinas on Human Nature*, 310–318; Stump, *Aquinas*, 263–264. On the role of the agent intellect in Aristotle and the controversial interpretation of *De anima* III, 5, see M. Frede, "La théorie aristotélicienne de l'intellect agent," in *Corps et âme. Sur le* De anima *d'Aristote*, ed. G. Romeyer Dherbey and C. Viano (Paris: Vrin, 1996), 377–390; M. F. Burnyeat, *Aristotle's Divine Intellect* (Milwaukee: Marquette University Press, 2008).

13. *De Ver.*, q. 10, a. 6, ad 7: "Ad septimum dicendum quod in receptione qua intellectus possibilis species rerum accipit a phantasmatibus, se habent phantasmata ut agens instrumentale vel secundarium, intellectus vero agens ut agens principale et primum; et ideo effectus actionis relinquitur in intellectu possibili secundum condicionem utriusque et non secundum condicionem alterius tantum; et ideo intellectus possibilis recipit formas ut intelligibiles actu ex virtute intellectus agentis, sed ut similitudines determinatarum rerum ex cognitione phantasmatum. . . ."

14. *ST* I, q. 84, a. 6: "ex parte phantasmatum intellectualis operatio a sensu causatur. Sed quia phantasmata non sufficiunt immutare intellectum possibilem, sed oportet quod fiant intelligibilia actu per intellectum agentem; non potest dici quod sensibilis cognitio sit totalis et perfecta causa intellectualis cognitionis, sed magis quodammodo est materia causae." Aquinas rejected the view that senses and sensory images merely provide the intellect with an opportunity for producing the intelligible species or obtaining them from something else (such as a separate intelligence). Rather, senses and sensory images play a genuinely causal role in the production of an intelligible species. See *ST* I, q. 84, a. 4.

But it is the third point in Aquinas's strategy that is particularly worth noticing. Aquinas held that the possible intellect, once it receives the form of a certain object from the agent intellect, becomes itself an agent. Because the human intellect is potential with respect to its operation of actually thinking about something, it must be made actual by the reception of a form (i.e., an intelligible species). For example, before learning what a cat is, I only have the capacity to think about cats. Thus, in order to actually think about what a cat is, I must receive the form felinity in my possible intellect. But even though the possible intellect's reception of a species is necessary for an act of thinking to occur, to think about something is not to receive a species. Rather, it is a distinct event.[15]

Accordingly, it is necessary to distinguish between two different actions carried out by the intellect in the process of thinking. First, there is the agent intellect's act of abstracting an intelligible species and of impressing it on the possible intellect. In this first event, the possible intellect plays the role of a patient. Second, there is the act of thinking proper. In this second event, the possible intellect plays the role of an agent. These two distinct events can be compared to a sense's being changed by a sensory object and the imagination's forming a sensory image. In sensory cognition, these two events are carried out by two distinct powers, namely, sense and imagination, respectively. By contrast, in intellectual cognition both events are carried out by the intellect. But they are still two distinct events, not just numerically but also categorically different. The possible intellect's act of reception is a passion. By contrast, the possible intellect's act of thinking is an action.[16]

It may be useful to illustrate this distinction with a comparison. Consider a light bulb. When the light is on, it is possible to distinguish two separate events. On one hand, the light bulb receives electricity in its circuits. On the other hand, that light bulb, once it has received electricity in its circuit, gives out light. Even though these two events occur simultaneously, they should be considered as distinct. Each event can be considered as an action resulting in a distinct effect.

---

15. *ST* I, q. 14, a. 2: "Ex hoc enim aliquid in actu sentimus vel intelligimus, quod intellectus noster vel sensus informatur in actu per speciem sensibilis vel intelligibilis. Et secundum hoc tantum sensus vel intellectus aliud est a sensibili vel intelligibili, quia utrumque est in potentia." See also *ST* I, q. 56, a. 2.

16. *ST* I, q. 85, a. 2, ad 3: "In parte sensitiva invenitur duplex operatio. Una secundum solam immutationem: et sic perficitur operatio sensus per hoc quod immutatur a sensibili. Alia operatio est formatio, secundum quod vis imaginativa format sibi aliquod idolum rei absentis, vel etiam nunquam visae. Et utraque haec operatio [scil. immutatio et formatio] coniungitur in intellectu. Nam primo quidem consideratur passio intellectus possibilis secundum quod informatur specie intelligibili. Qua quidem formatus, format secundo vel definitionem vel divisionem vel compositionem, quae per vocem significatur."

The first action's effect is the illumination of the bulb. The second action's effect is the bulb's illuminating its environment.[17]

### Acts of Thinking as Self-Contained Actions: Aquinas's Two Accounts

So Aquinas held that occurrent thoughts are actions. Following Aristotle, he also distinguished between two kinds of actions. Some actions produce a result distinct from the exercise of the action itself. They are accordingly called "transitive actions." For example, fire's action of heating produce the form heat, which is distinct from the action of heating and is received in a patient such as a kettle. Other actions, however, do not produce any result distinct from their exercise. They are accordingly called "immanent" or "self-contained actions."[18] Aquinas held that cognitive and appetitive acts, such as sensing, imagining, thinking and willing, are self-contained actions, which he also called "activities" (*operationes*).[19] He actually held that only cognitive and appetitive acts are self-contained actions. All natural actions are transitive.[20]

There is, however, a complication. For Aquinas gave two different analyses of self-contained actions. In his first account, a self-contained action is an action that consists merely in the exercise of an activity that produces no result distinct from the activity itself. In his second account, a self-contained action is the exercise of an activity that does produce an effect distinct from the activity itself. Contrary to what happens in transitive actions, however, the effect of a self-contained action remains within the agent and is received in no patient distinct from the agent itself.

---

17. The distinction between these two events may be made apparent if we leave the first event untouched but we tamper with the second, for example by putting a sheet of opaque paper around a bulb. The bulb is still illuminated but does not illuminate anymore.

18. Aristotle *Meta.* IX, 8, 1050a23–b6. See Aquinas, *CG* III, 2: "Actio vero quandoque quidem terminatur ad aliquod factum, sicut aedificatio ad domum, sanatio ad sanitatem: quandoque autem non, sicut intelligere et sentire. Et si quidem actio terminatur ad aliquod factum, impetus agentis tendit per actionem in illud factum: si autem non terminatur ad aliquod factum, impetus agentis tendit in ipsam actionem." Aquinas drew this distinction between two kinds of actions in many passages of his works. See for example *Super I Sent.*, d. 40, q. 1, a. 1, ad 1; *De Ver.*, q. 8, a. 6; q. 14, a. 3; *De Pot.*, q. 3, a. 15; q. 8, a. 1; *CG* II, 23, n. 993; *ST* I, q. 18, a. 3, ad 1; q. 23, a. 2, ad 1; q. 27, a. 1; q. 27, a. 3; q. 27, a. 5; q. 28, a. 4; q. 54, a. 1, ad 3; q. 54, a. 2; q. 56, a. 1; q. 85, a. 2; *ST* I-II, q. 3, a. 2, ad 3; *De unitate intellectus*, 3; *In Meta.* IX, lect. 8, nn. 1862–1865; *In Meta.* VI, lect. 1, n. 1152; IX, lect. 2, n. 1788; XI, lect. 7, n. 2253.

19. Aristotle himself had considered perception and thought as activities and had contrasted them to changes in a strict sense, because in activities there is no progress and no new form is acquired. See Aristotle, *Meta.* IX, 6, 1048b18–35 (a passage that was unknown to medieval interpreters) and *Nicomachean Ethics* X, 3–5. See J. L. Ackrill, "Aristotle's Distinction between *Energeia* and *Kinesis*," in *New Essays on Plato and Aristotle*, ed. R. Bambrough (London and New York: Routledge, 1965), 121–141; M. F. Burnyeat, "*Kinesis* vs. *Energeia*: A Much-Read Passage in (but not of) Aristotle's *Metaphysics*," *Oxford Studies in Ancient Philosophy* 34 (2008): 219–292.

20. *CG* II, 23, n. 993.

Accordingly, Aquinas gave two different analyses of acts of thinking as actions. In his first analysis, an act of thinking is an action that has no end product distinct from the act of thinking itself. Thus, the term of that action is not distinct from its principle; what makes an intellect actual is also the term of the intellect's act.[21] In his second analysis, an act of thinking is an action that results in the production of an internal term. Specifically, the intellect produces a concept, which must be distinguished both from the intellect's act of thinking and from the intelligible species received in the intellect. The species is the formal principle of an act of thinking. This means that the species is the form that makes the possible intellect actually think about something. By contrast, the concept (which Aquinas called "conception" and "inner word") is the term of an act of thinking, that is, what the intellect produces when it performs the action triggered by the reception of the species.[22]

## Dispositional versus Occurrent Knowledge

So far, I have presented Aquinas's position as if the abstraction/reception of a species were both necessary and sufficient for an act of thinking to occur. Granting that the act of abstraction and the act of thinking triggered by the reception of a species are two distinct acts, Aquinas seems indeed at times to suggest that an act of thinking occurs if an only if a species is abstracted and received in the intellect.[23] But this view clashes with some of Aquinas's explicit claims on this topic. For Aquinas was aware that, if the presence of a form in the intellect were

---

21. *CG* I 53, first draft, printed as *Appendix* II, A in *Liber de Veritate Catholicae Fidei contra errores Infidelium seu Summa contra Gentiles*, vol. 1, ed. C. Pera, P. Marc, and P. Caramello (Turin: Marietti, 1961). I quote the relevant passage in note 29. See also *ST* I, q. 56, a. 2: "Sed in actione quae manet in agente, oportet ad hoc quod procedat actio, quod obiectum uniatur agenti: sicut oportet quod sensibile uniatur sensui, ad hoc quod sentiat actu. Et ita se habet obiectum unitum potentiae ad huiusmodi actionem, sicut forma quae est principium actionis in aliis agentibus: sicut enim calor est principium formale calefactionis in igne, ita species rei visae est principium formale visionis in oculo." The same point is made in *ST* I, q. 85, a. 2. On the three successive drafts of *CG* I, 53, see L.-B. Geiger, "Les rédactions successives de *Contra Gentiles* I, 53, d'après l'autographe," in *Saint Thomas d'Aquin aujourd'hui* (Paris: Desclée de Brouwer, 1963), 221–240.

22. *CG* I, 53 (third and definitive draft); *CG* IV, 11; *ST* I, q. 27, a. 1; q. 28, a. 4, ad 1; q. 34, a. 1; q. 85, a. 2, ad 3; *De Pot.*, q. 8, a. 1; q. 9, a. 5; *Quodl.* V, a. 2; *Super Evang. Ioan.*, I, 1; *De spirit. creat.*, 9. Some elements of this account were already present in *De Ver.*, q. 4, a. 2. On Aquinas's evolution in this respect, see H. Paissac, *Théologie du verbe. Saint Augustin et Saint Thomas* (Paris: Les Éditions du Cerf, 1951); R. Gauthier, *Saint Thomas d'Aquin. Somme contre les gentils. Introduction par René-Antoine Gauthier* (Paris: Éditions Universitaires, 1993), 105–108; A. F. van Gunten, "In principio erat Verbum. Une evolution de saint Thomas en théologie trinitaire," in *Ordo Sapientiae et Amoris. Hommage au Professeur Jean-Pierre Torrell OP à l'occasion de son 65ᵉ anniversaire*, ed. C.-J. Pinto de Oliveira (Fribourg: Éditions Universitaires, 1993), 119–141.

23. See, for example, *ST* I, q. 14, a. 2.

sufficient for an act of thinking to occur, one of the following two undesirable scenarios would obtain: either any time I think about something I carry out a new act of abstraction and I acquire a new intelligible species or I always think about all the things of which I have a species in my intellect. And both situations were unacceptable for Aquinas.[24]

Accordingly, Aquinas introduced the view that an intelligible species can be related to the intellect in three ways. First, a species can be in the intellect only potentially. In that case, I am ignorant of what something is but I am able to learn what it is. Second, a species can be in the intellect in complete actuality, that is, when I actually think about something. Third and crucially, a species can be present in the intellect in an intermediate way, which is neither entirely potential nor entirely actual. In that case, I know what something is but I do not think about it. Because a species can be present in this intermediate way, I keep some knowledge of the things I have learned even though I do not always think about all the things I know:

> An intelligible species is sometimes present only potentially in the intellect, and then the intellect is said to be in potentiality. Sometimes it is there inasmuch as the act is entirely complete, and then the intellect is actually thinking. Sometimes it stands midway between potentiality and actuality, and then the intellect is said to have a disposition. It is in this way that the intellect preserves species, even when it is not actually thinking.[25]

Aquinas never gave a detailed description of how the passage from dispositional to occurrent knowledge takes place. It is very likely that the intelligible species is brought to the state of complete actuality by what Aquinas called the intellect's "turning back toward the sensory images" (*conversio ad phantasmata*). By turning back to the sensory image from which a certain intelligible species has been abstracted, the intellect fully actualizes that species, which until

---

24. On Aquinas's rejection of the first option, see his criticism of Avicenna at *De Ver.*, q. 10, a. 2; *ST* I, q. 79, a. 6; *CG*, II, 74; *Quodl.* III, q. 9, a. 1; *Quodl.* XII, q. 9, a. 1. On Aquinas's rejection of the second option, see for example the distinction between dispositional and occurrent knowledge in *De malo*, q. 1, a. 5: "Actus autem est duplex, scilicet primus, qui est habitus uel forma, et secundus, qui est operatio, sicut scientia et considerare. Actu autem primo inherente adhuc est potentia ad actum secundum, sicut sciens nondum actu considerat set considerare potest."

25. *ST* I, q. 79, a. 6, ad 3: "Ad tertium dicendum quod species intelligibilis aliquando est in intellectu in potentia tantum: et tunc dicitur intellectus esse in potentia. Aliquando autem secundum ultimam completionem actus: et tunc intelligit actu. Aliquando medio modo se habet inter potentiam et actum: et tunc dicitur esse intellectus in habitu. Et secundum hunc modum intellectus conservat species, etiam quando actu non intelligit." The English Translation is from Thomas Aquinas, *The Treatise on Human Nature*, trans. Pasnau, 92. See also *De Ver.*, q. 10, a. 2, ad 4; *De Ver.*, q. 19, a. 1; *CG* II, 74, n. 16; *Quodl.* III, q. 9, a. 1; *Sent. libri de anima*, III, cap. II, p. 208.

then was lying dormant in the intellect itself, as it were.[26] Thus, thinking is cognate to the process of learning something. When the intellect learns something, it acquires a certain form for the first time. By contrast, when the intellect thinks about something, it reacquires in full actuality a form that had been partially forgotten and that was in a state of incomplete actuality. This act of reacquisition is effected through the intellect's turning back toward the sensory image, and in turn that act of turning back is triggered by an act of the will, which Aquinas calls by the Augustinian term of "attention" (*intentio*).[27] Thus, I actually think about what a cat is if and only if I decide to focus on the sensory image of a cat and in that way I bring back to my mind what I already know about cats.

The claim that an intelligible species can be possessed in complete or incomplete actuality sounds like an *ad hoc* move to account for the passage from dispositional to occurrent knowledge. In itself, the view that a form can be possessed in incomplete actuality is obscure. A form is just what makes something actual. In this specific case, an intelligible species is what brings the possible intellect to a state of actuality. How can what makes something actual be possessed in incomplete actuality? Aquinas never clarified this issue.

## Aquinas on the Intentionality of Acts of Thinking

A curious consequence of Aquinas's view that intentional acts in general and acts of thinking in particular are actions is that those acts are not related to the things they are about. Let it be reminded that, according to Aquinas's first account of what a self-contained action is, self-contained actions are actions whose term coincide with the form that triggers them. Thus, an act of thinking is related only to an intelligible species, not to an extramental thing. According to Aquinas's second account of self-contained actions, self-contained actions are actions that produce their own inner term. Thus, an act of thinking is related to the concept it produces, not to the extramental thing it is supposed to be

---

26. *De Ver.*, q. 10, a. 2, ad 7: "Nulla potentia potest aliquid cognoscere nisi convertendo se ad obiectum suum ... unde ... quantumcumque aliquam speciem intelligibilem apud se intellectus habeat, numquam tamen actu aliquid considerat secundum illam speciem nisi convertendo se ad phantasmata." See also *Quodl.* XII, q. 9, a. 1: "et non solum propter hoc [scil. corpus] phantasmata indigemus, sed ad utendum huiusmodi species." And more in general *ST* I, q. 84, a. 7. See Pasnau, *Theories of,* 135–136; Pasnau, *Thomas Aquinas on Human Nature,* 284–295.

27. *De Ver.*, q. 13, a. 3: "ad actum alicuius cognitivae potentiae requiritur intentio;" *CG* I, 55: "Vis cognoscitiva non cognoscit aliquid actu nisi adsit intentio: unde et phantasmata in organo conservata interdum non actu imaginamur, quia intentio non fertur ad ea." See also *In 1 Sent.*, d. 3, q. 5, a. 5: "Ad talem enim cognitionem non sufficiet praesentia rei quolibet modo; sed oportet ut sit ibi in ratione obiecti, et exigitur intentio cognoscentis." See Pasnau, *Theories of Cognition,* 134–135. For Augustine's notion of attention, see Augustine, *De Trin.*, XI, 2.2–3.

about. In neither account is there room for a relation between an act of thinking and the extramental thing it is about.[28]

But then, why is a certain act of thinking about a certain object?

According to Aquinas's first account of acts of thinking as self-contained actions, the intentionality of an act of thinking is due to that act's occurring after the likeness of a certain thing (i.e., the intelligible species of a certain thing) has been received in the intellect. That intelligible species, and not the act of thinking, is related to the extramental thing that is thought about by virtue of that act of thinking. Thus, it is in some way not accurate to say that a certain occurrent thought is about something. Rather, it would be more precise to say that the intellect becomes assimilated to a certain thing because it receives the form of that thing (i.e., an intelligible species) and the form of that thing is what activates the intellect, that is, what makes us actually think.[29]

According to Aquinas's second account of thinking as a self-contained action, the intentionality of an act of thinking is explained in an even more complicated way. A certain act of thinking is about a certain thing because the concept produced by that act is a likeness of its agent, that is, of the intellect. Now any effect is a likeness of its cause insofar as that cause produces that effect. A cause produces an effect insofar as that cause is actual. And what makes a cause actual is its form, whether essential or, as in this case, accidental. Since the intellect is made actual

---

28. *In Meta.* V, lect. 17, n. 1027: "Unde [scil., relativum tertii modi ut visibile et scibile] non dicitur relative propter aliquid quod sit ex eorum parte . . . ; sed solum propter actiones aliorum, quae tamen in ipsa non terminantur. Si enim videre esset actio videntis perveniens ad rem visam, sicut calefactio pervenit ad calefactibile; sicut calefactibile refertur ad calefaciens, ita visibile referretur ad videntem. Sed videre et intelligere et huiusmodi actiones, ut in nono huius dicetur, manent in agentibus, et non transeunt in res passas; unde visibile et scibile non patitur aliquid, ex hoc quod intelligitur vel videtur. Et propter hoc non ipsamet referuntur ad alia, sed alia ad ipsa." The view that is presupposed here is that an action is a relative item, and that, like any relative item, it has a foundation (the form present in the agent) and a term at which it is directed (the form received in a patient or, more properly, the patient informed by that form). For example, the action of heating is founded on the form *heat* present in fire and directed at the form *heat* present in the kettle heated by fire or, more properly, the hot kettle. Similarly, an act of thinking is founded on the intelligible species that actualizes the intellect and either has no term distinct from that species (according to Aquinas's first account) or is directed at the concept it produces (according to Aquinas's second account). On subjects and terms of relations, see M. G. Henninger, *Relations: Medieval Theories 1250–1325* (Oxford: Clarendon Press, 1989), 4–6.

29. *CG* I, 53, first draft: "Harum igitur potentiarum operatio non terminatur ad res exteriores neque sicut ad principium agendi neque sicut ad subiectum patiens, sed ad eas terminatur sola relatio potentiae operantis, quae quidem relatio consequitur formam operantis per quam operatur: sicut imaginatio per formam relictam a sensu habet operationem propriam in imaginatione consistentem, ad rem vero exteriorem quam imaginatur habet relationem per formam qua informatur, et ex hac relatione contingit quod imaginando cognoscit rem imaginatam. Et similiter intellectus per formam intelligibilem qua intelligit, refertur quadam similitudinis relatione ad rem extra quam intelligendo cognoscit. Unde et dicitur quod scientia est assimilatio scientis ad rem scitam."

by an intelligible species and since that species is a likeness of an extramental object, the concept produced by the intellect, which is a direct likeness of the intellect, is an indirect likeness of the intelligible species, which in turn is a direct likeness of the extramental object. Accordingly, a concept is removed from the extramental object of which it is an indirect likeness by two degrees. For example, my act of thinking about what a cat is is about the essence of cats because the concept produced by my act of thinking is a likeness of my intellect made actual by the intelligible species of cats, which in turn is a likeness of cats:

> And this [i.e., that a concept is a likeness of the thing thought about] happens because the effect is like its cause in respect of its form, and the form of the intellect is the thing understood. Wherefore the word that originates from the intellect is the likeness of the thing understood.[30]

The relation between the concept produced by my intellect and the extramental thing it represents is a relation of final causality—the thing is the end at which my concept is directed—not a relation of aboutness, no matter how aboutness is going to be spelled out.[31] Aquinas also described the relation between the concept and the extramental thing it represents as a containment relation—the concept is that "in which" (*in quo*) I understand the extramental thing. For example, my concept of what a cat is is that "in which" I think about what a cat is. What Aquinas seems to mean is that I think about what a cat is by thinking about the definitional account I form in my intellect of what a cat is.[32] As Aquinas also stated, the concept my intellect forms of what a cat is is the tool by which I think about what a cat is.[33]

Based on what I have presented, Aquinas answered the three questions I have mentioned at the beginning of this essay in this way:

1. An act of thinking is an item in the category of action. More specifically, an act of thinking is a self-contained action. Aquinas, however, had two accounts of self-contained actions. According to his first account, thinking

---

30. *De Pot.*, q. 8, a. 1: "Et hoc ideo contingit, quia effectus similatur causae secundum suam formam: forma autem intellectus est res intellecta. Et ideo verbum quod oritur ab intellectu, est similitudo rei intellectae." The English translation is from Thomas Aquinas, *On the Power of God*, trans. English Dominican Fathers (London: Burn Oates & Washbourne, 1932), 3:71.

31. *De Pot.* q. 8, a. 1: "et iterum conceptio intellectus ordinatur ad rem intellectam sicut ad finem: propter hoc enim intellectus conceptionem rei in se format ut rem intellectam cognoscat."

32. *Super Evang. Ioan.*, I, 1: "Istud ergo sic expressum, scilicet formatum in anima, dicitur verbum interius; et ideo comparatur ad intellectum, non sicut quo intellectus intelligit, sed sicut in quo intelligit; quia in ipso expresso et formato videt naturam rei intellectae."

33. *Quodl.* V, a. 2, ad 1: "Ad primum ergo dicendum quod intellectus intelligit aliquid dupliciter: uno modo formaliter, et sic intelligit specie intelligibili qua fit in actu; alio modo sicut instrumento quo utitur ad aliud intelligendum, et hoc modo intellectus uerbo intelligit, quia format verbum ad hoc quod intelligat rem."

is an action that does not produce anything. According to his second account, thinking does produce something: a term. That term, however, is not received in a patient distinct from the agent.
2. The mere presence of a form in the possible intellect (the so-called intelligible species) is a necessary but not a sufficient condition for an act of thinking to occur. The additional requirement is that that form should be present in complete actuality. This passage to complete actuality is effected by the intellect's turning back to a sensory image.
3. An act of thinking is about a certain thing because its starting point is the reception of a certain form present in complete actuality in the possible intellect. By itself, however, an act of thinking is not related to its object. Rather, a certain act is about a certain object only because the intellect has been activated by a certain form.

As I have mentioned, there are two problematic aspects in Aquinas's account of thinking as I have presented it. First, Aquinas posited that an intelligible species is present in different degrees of actuality in the intellect in order to account for the difference between dispositional and occurrent knowledge. But this view is obscure. Second, Aquinas's explanation of the intentionality of acts of thinking is quite convoluted. The very idea that an act of thinking is not directly related to its object is at first sight implausible. Both problems are consequences of Aquinas's assumption that acts of thinking are actions. Accordingly, it does not come as a surprise that some thinkers after Aquinas rejected that assumption. Scotus was among those who approached the whole issue from a different perspective.

### SCOTUS'S MODEL OF THINKING: THINKING AS A QUALITY

Scotus laid the foundations of his account of thinking some forty years after Aquinas had developed his mature views on that issue. In the eventful period between Aquinas and Scotus, several thinkers subjected Aquinas's treatment to careful scrutiny and occasionally harsh criticism. Among the elements that were most often criticized were Aquinas's account of abstraction and his analysis of the act of thinking as an act of concept formation. Concerning the agent intellect's act of abstraction, thinkers as diverse as Henry of Ghent,[34] Godfrey of Fontaines,[35]

---

34. Henry of Ghent, *Quodl.* V, q. 14, ff, 174Y, 176O–177R. See Martin Pickavé's essay in this volume. See T. V. Nys, *De psychologia cognitionis humanae secundum Henricum Gandavensem* (Rome: Gregorian University, 1947); M. Rombeiro, "Intelligible Species in the Mature Thought of Henry of Ghent," *Journal of the History of Philosophy* 49, no. 2 (2011): 181–220.

35. Godfrey of Fontaines, *Quodl.* IX, q. 19 (PhB IV, 271–275). In general, on Godfrey's views on abstraction, see *Quodl.* V, q. 10 (PhB III, 3540). See Wippel, "The Role of the Phantasm in Godfrey of Fontaines' Theory of Intellection," 573–582.

and Peter John Olivi[36] argued that the agent intellect's act of abstraction does not result in the production of an intelligible species in the possible intellect. Concerning Aquinas's view that an act of thinking results in the production of a concept, Henry of Ghent[37] and William of Ware[38] conceded that a concept is actually produced when an act of thinking occurs but disagreed with Aquinas's specific analysis of how a concept is produced. None of these authors, however, seems to have questioned the fundamental assumption that acts of thinking are actions.

If we have to judge from some casual references to the mechanisms of intellectual cognition in Scotus's early writings, Scotus himself initially held that any cognitive act is an action.[39]

In just a few years, however, Scotus developed a sophisticated position on intellectual cognition. The main elements of this position can be gathered from his writings dating from the years 1301–1305: *Ordinatio*, *Reportatio* I-A, and *Quodlibet*. In those writings, he made three characteristic moves. First, he distinguished between two actions, both of which are ordinarily necessary for an act of thinking to occur. The first action is the agent intellect's act of abstraction and production of an intelligible species. The second action is the production of an act of thinking. Second, Scotus distinguished the act of thinking from the *production* of an act of thinking and consequently argued that an act of thinking is a quality rather than an action. Third, he accounted for the intentionality of acts of thinking by introducing a special relation holding between acts of thinking and their objects.

I will consider each of these three aspects in turn.

## Two Actions: Abstraction and the Production of an Act of Thinking

Scotus distinguished between two actions that must ordinarily occur in order for an act of thinking to occur.[40] The first action is the agent intellect's abstraction of a form—the intelligible species—from a sensory image present in the imagination. This action is identical with the possible intellect's reception of

---

36. Peter John Olivi, *Quaestiones in secundum librum Sententiarum*, q. 74, 106–135. See Pasnau, *Theories of Cognition*, 236–247.

37. Henry of Ghent, *Summa quaestionum ordinariarum*, art. 58, q. 1, vol. 2, 124H–L. See S. P. Marrone, *The Light of Thy Countenance: Science and Knowledge of God in the Thirteenth Century* (Leiden: Brill, 2001), 270–298; G. Pini, "Henry of Ghent's Doctrine of *Verbum* in Its Theological Context," in *Henry of Ghent and the Transformation of Scholastic Thought: Studies in Memory of Jos Decorte* (Leuven: Leuven University Press, 2003), 307–326.

38. William of Ware, *Sent.* I, d. 27, q. 3, 258*–263*. It should be noticed that William of Ware is often thought to have been one of Scotus's teachers.

39. Scotus, *Quaest. super Meta.*, V, q. 12–13, n. 98, OPh III, 638: "cognitio est in genere actionis [...];"

40. I say "ordinarily" because God can bypass both actions and produce an act of thinking immediately in my intellect, as I indicate below. Also, notice that here I am considering acts of *abstractive* cognition.

the intelligible species, as the agent intellect's production of a species and the possible intellect's reception of a species are just two descriptions of one and the same process. Against Henry of Ghent and Godfrey of Fontaines, Scotus argued that the agent intellect's act of abstraction is an act of producing a form in the possible intellect, because such a form must be present in the intellect prior to the occurrence of an act of thinking.[41] Scotus's argument for this claim was based on the assumption (which Scotus took to be self-evident) that the object of an act of thinking must be present to the intellect prior to the occurrence of that act of thinking as well as on the further assumption that the object of an act of thinking (as far as abstractive cognition is concerned) is known in a universal way, that is, like "what it is to be a cat" as opposed to "what it is to be this particular cat." Given these two assumptions, Scotus argued that only a form present in the intellect prior to the occurrence of an act of thinking could account for the presence of a universal object prior to the occurrence of an act of thinking.[42] Since the form present in the intellect prior to the occurrence of an act of thinking is the intelligible species produced by the agent intellect, it follows that the agent intellect's abstraction of a species is a prerequisite for the occurrence of an act of thinking and must be distinguished from it.[43]

Scotus regarded the agent intellect's act of abstraction as a real action, that is, an event that ends up in the production of a real quality, the intelligible species.[44] That real quality, however, also represents an extramental thing. It is by virtue of its being a representation that the intelligible species contributes to the production of an act of thinking.[45] The details of this view, which are complicated and controversial, should not retain us here.[46] Suffice it to say that the agent intellect produces a form, and by that production it also makes some specific content potentially present in the possible intellect.

---

41. *Ord.* I, d. 3, p. 3, q. 1, Vat. III, 201–244; *Lect.* I, d. 3, p. 3, q. 1, Vat. XVI, 325–348; *Rep.* I-A, d. 3, q. 4 and q. 5, ed. Wolter and Bychkov, 207–220 and 221–232.

42. *Ord.* I, d. 3, p. 3, q. 1, nn. 349–350, Vat III, 210–211. For Scotus's argument that only a form present in the intellect can account for the presence of the object as a universal prior to the act of thinking, see *Ord.* I, d. 3, p. 3, q. 1, nn. 352–358, Vat. III, 211–216; *Lect.* I, d. 3, p. 3, q. 1, nn. 266–273, Vat. XVI, 331–334; *Rep.* I-A, d. 3, q. 4, nn. 95–97, 210–211. See King, "Rethinking Representation."

43. Scotus contrasted the agent intellect's act of abstraction to the act of thinking proper in *Ord.* I, d. 3, p. 3, q. 1, n. 359–360, Vat. III, 216–218; *Rep.* I-A, d. 3, q. 4, n. 103, 212–213; *Quodl.*, q. 15, n. 14, Vivès XXVI, 145. See also *Lect.* I, d. 3, p. 3, q. 1, n. 275, Vat. XVI, 335.

44. *Ord.* I, d. 3, p. 3, q. 1, n. 359, Vat. III, 216: "intellectus agens est mere potentia activa ... ergo potest habere actionem realem. Omnis actio realis habet aliquem terminus realem." See also *Rep.* I-A, d. 3, q. 4, n. 103, 212–213.

45. *Ord.* I, d. 3, p. 3, q. 1, n. 386, Vat. III, 235: "Ad quartum dico quod intellectus non tantum patitur realiter ab obiecto reali, imprimente talem speciem realem, sed etiam ab illo obiecto ut relucet in specie patitur passione intentionali: et illa secunda passio est 'receptio intellectionis'—quae est ab intelligibili in quantum intelligibile, relucens in specie intelligibili—et illud 'pati' est 'intelligere' ..."

46. See King, "Scotus on Mental Content," 84–85.

The agent intellect's production of a form representing a certain object, however, is not sufficient for an act of thinking about that object to occur. I may have as much information about cats as I can gather, but this is not sufficient for me to perform an act of thinking about what it is to be a cat. In addition to the presence of the form felinity in my intellect, Scotus argued that a separate intervention of the intellect is necessary in order for an act of thinking about what it is to be a cat to occur.[47]

So two causal events must be distinguished. First, there is the act of abstraction caused by the agent intellect and the sensory image (the "phantasm"). Its term is a mental quality, i.e. the intelligible species. Second, there is the production of an act of thinking, which is caused by the intelligible species and the intellect after the abstraction of the species.[48] The product of that second event is the act of thinking proper. As I will show, Scotus argued that the act of thinking is also a mental quality.

By clearly distinguishing between two actions involved in the act of thinking and by claiming that the intellect must play the role of an efficient cause not just in the act of abstraction but also in the production of an act of thinking, Scotus managed to lay the foundation for the distinction between dispositional and occurrent knowledge. Only when the second event occurs does an act of occurrent knowledge occur, that is, do I actually think about something. When only the act of abstraction and reception of a form occurs, some information is memorized and stored in the intellect, but no actual thought follows. This is the situation I experience when I know what it is to be a cat but I do not think about it.

### Acts of Thinking as Qualities

Scotus's most characteristic insight, however, is not his distinction between the two actions involved in the production of an act of thinking. Rather, his most typical claim is that both the act of abstraction and the posterior act carried out by the intellect and the species together must be distinguished from the act of thinking proper.[49]

The distinction between an act of thinking on one hand and, on the other hand, the joint action of the intellect and an intelligible species is a consequence

---

47. *Ord.* I, d. 3, p. 3, q. 2, Vat. III, 245–330; *Lect.* I, d. 3, p. 3, q. 2–3, Vat. XVI, 349–395; *Quodl.*, q. 15, nn. 7–9, Vivès XXVI, 137–141. It is clear that the act of thinking is distinct from the act of abstraction carried out by the agent intellect. It is an open question, however, whether the act of thinking itself is performed by the agent intellect, the possible intellect or both the agent and the possible intellect. Scotus considered each of these possibilities in *Quodl.*, q. 15, nn. 13–20, Vivès XXVI, 141–153.

48. See *Ord.* I, d. 3, p. 3, q. 2, Vat. III, 245–330; *Lect.* I, d. 3, p. 3, q. 2–3, Vat. XVI, 349–395; *Quodl.*, q. 15, nn. 7–10, Vivès XXVI, 137–143.

49. More precisely, an act of thinking is what Scotus calls the "formal term" of the process carried out by the intellect and the species together. The proper term of that process is the whole constituted by the intellect thinking about something or an individual person thinking about something. See *Rep.* I-A, d. 3, q. 6, nn. 183–184, 239.

of Scotus's general claim that acts of thinking are neither actions nor passions. Scotus's argument for that claim was that actions and passions are necessarily related to the term they bring about. For example, fire's action of heating is necessarily related to what it produces—for example, a hot kettle. Similarly, a kettle's passion of being heated is necessarily related to its term, that is, that kettle's being hot. By definition, an action produces something and a passion entails the production of something. There can be no action or passion if a term is not produced by that very action or passion. Scotus, however, remarked that an act of thinking produces nothing apart from itself. It is true that sometimes acts of thinking produce a habit. For example, if I repeatedly think about what it is to be a cat, it becomes easy for me to entertain that act because I get used to performing it. This, however, is an accidental result of my act of thinking. A certain act of thinking is essentially the same act even though it does not produce any habit (as with acts of thinking that are performed only occasionally.) In any case, it is clear that an act of thinking does not produce its object, because what I think about is presupposed, not produced, by my act of thinking about it.[50]

So what sort of thing is an act of thinking, if it is neither an action nor a passion? Assuming that all things belong to one of the ten Aristotelian categories, Scotus proceeded by elimination.[51] Apart from actions and passions, he held that there are only two plausible candidates. First, an act of thinking may be a relation. Second, an act of thinking may be a quality.

Scotus had three arguments to demonstrate that acts of thinking are not relations. I will leave aside his first argument, which concerns the theological notion of beatific vision,[52] and consider the other two.

Scotus's first philosophical argument that in any act of thinking there is an irreducible nonrelative feature is based on the view that two things become newly related to each other if and only if a new nonrelative item is acquired by either or both of them. For example, a chair becomes similar in color to a wall only if the chair has been colored like the wall or the wall has been colored like the chair

---

50. *Rep.* I-A, d. 3, q. 6, n. 171, 235–236: "Item, de actione et passione probatur idem [scil., quod intellectio non est actio vel passio]: nam actio et passio necessario sunt alicuius termini accipientis esse per actionem et passionem; quia non est intelligibile quod sit calefactio et quod nullius ulterioris termini, scilicet quod nihil accipiat calorem per eam; sed operationes sunt termini ultimi quibus nihil ulterius accipit esse, quia sunt fines, I *Ethicorum* et IX *Metaphysicae*. Obiectum vero operationis ad quod terminatur operatio non accipit esse per eam, sed praesupponitur operationi, quia sunt fines operantis, ut dictum est; ergo etc." See also *Ord.*, d. 27, q. 1–3, n. 55, Vat. VI, 86: "intellectio non est actio productiva alicuius termini: tunc enim incompossibile esset intelligere eam esse, et non esse termini, sicut incompossibile est intelligere calefactionem esse et non esse calorem ad quem sit calefaction. Non est autem impossibile intelligere intellectionem in se, non intelligendo quod sit alicuius termini ut producti per ipsam."

51. *Quodl.* q. 13, n. 25, Vivès XXV, 570–571; *Rep.* I-A, q. 6, nn. 169–237, 234–237.

52. Scotus, *Quodl.*, q. 13, nn. 3–4, Vivès XXV, 508–509; *Rep.* I-A, d. 3, q. 6, n. 169, 234–235.

or both the chair and the wall have been colored in the same way. But an act of thinking can occur without the reception of a new form either in the intellect or in the thing thought about. For example, suppose that I already know what it is to be a cat; then, I do not have to acquire any new information in order to actually think about what it is to be a cat. My intellect must acquire a new form only when it is in essential potency with respect to the knowledge of what it is to be a cat, that is, when I am ignorant of what it is to be a cat. By contrast, when I know what it is to be a cat but I do not think about cats, my intellect is in a state of accidental potency, that is, it can perform an act of thinking about what it is to be a cat without acquiring any new form. Similarly, cats do not acquire a new form when I think about what it is to be a cat. Since a new act of thinking can be brought about without the acquisition of a new form in the intellect, it follows that acts of thinking are not relations.[53]

Scotus's second philosophical argument in support of his claim that thinking is not a relation is based on the fact that an act of thinking is itself related to its object. For example, my act of thinking about what it is to be a cat is related to what it is to be a cat, that is, (according to Scotus) the essence of cats. Now it was a common assumption that only a nonrelative item can be related to something else, because only a nonrelative item can play the role of the foundation of a relation. For example, the relation of paternity holding between a father and his child is grounded in a nonrelative feature pertaining to the father, namely, presumably, his power to procreate. The father's power to procreate must be interpreted as a nonrelative item in order to exclude the possibility of an infinite regress. Acts of thinking, however, are related to their objects. It follows that they are not relations.[54]

Behind the technicality of Scotus's arguments, it is easy to detect his general strategy. Aquinas's commitment to the view that acts of thinking are actions forced him to embrace some implausible conclusions, that is, that acts of thinking are not related to their objects or that they produce their own terms. Scotus

---

53. Scotus, *Quodl.*, q. 13, n. 4, Vivès XXV, 509: "Secundo probatur conclusio principalis [scil., quod in omni intellectione et generaliter operatione quacumque de qua loquimur, est aliqua entitas absoluta] sic. Relatio proprie dicta non est nova sine novitate alicuius absoluti prioris, et hoc in subiecto vel in termino. Operatio autem potest esse nova sine novitate cuiuscumque alterius prioris absoluti in ipso operante, sine etiam cuiuscumque alterius absoluti novitate in termino. Igitur operatio non est praecise relatio proprie accipiendo relationem. Igitur etc.... Minor probatur quantum ad primam partem, quia illud quod exit de potentia accidentali ad actum non recipit aliquam formam novam priorem ipsa operatione, quia tunc non fuisset prius in potentia accidentali sed essentiali. Secunda pars minoris est manifesta. Patet enim quod nihil asbolutum advenit visibili quando videtur actu nec intelligibili quando intelligitur actu, et consimiliter de aliis." For an English translation, see John Duns Scotus, *God and Creatures. The Quodlibetal Questions*, trans. F. Alluntis and A. B. Wolter (Princeton: Princeton University Press, 1975), 286–287.

54. *Quodl.*, q. 13, n. 5, Vivès XXV, 509; *Rep.* I-A, d. 3, q. 6, n. 170, 235.

managed to avoid these implausible conclusions by rejecting the view that acts of thinking are relative items and more specifically that they are actions.

Since acts of thinking are neither relations nor actions or passions, Scotus concluded that they are qualities. Specifically, he argued that they are in the first of the four species of qualities Aristotle had distinguished in the eighth chapter of the *Categories*. Since Aristotle sorted out the qualities belonging to the first species into habits such as virtues and more fleeting conditions such as heat, cold, disease and health, it seems likely that Scotus regarded acts of thinking as those fleeting dispositions (*diatheseis, affectiones*), which can be easily acquired or lost.[55]

Scotus seems to have been aware of the novelty of the claim that acts of thinking are qualities. According to Aquinas and to the standard Aristotelian theory, acts of thinking are, in some crucial respects, akin to fire's action of heating. By contrast, Scotus proposed to consider them akin to the form heat. Scotus's position clashed with the intuition that to think is something I do. By contrast, Scotus held that I do perform an action that results in an act of thinking, but the act of thinking itself is not something I do but something I have, just as I have the form heat or the form coldness.

Scotus admitted that acts of thinking belong to a special sort of qualities called 'activities' (*operationes*). In calling acts of thinking 'activities', Scotus was just following Aristotle and was in agreement with Aquinas. There is, however, a fundamental difference between Scotus and Aquinas. As I have indicated, Aquinas regarded activities as genuine actions, albeit self-contained and not transitive. By contrast, Scotus held that activities are not actions but qualities, even though he conceded that it is easy to mistake activities for a certain class of actions. Specifically, both a certain class of actions and activities share two properties. First, both a certain class of actions and activities are nonpermanent or *in fieri*, that is, they exist only as long as their causes produce them. For example, the action of heating exists only as long as fire heats and an act of thinking exists only as long as its causes (ordinarily, an intellect and an intelligible species) produce that act. Second, both a certain class of actions and activities are about (*circa*) a certain term.[56] For example, fire's act of heating is about a certain object, such as a kettle, and my act of thinking is about a certain

---

55. *Rep.* I-A, d. 3, q. 6, nn. 175–176, 237: "Restat ergo necessario concedere quod istae operationes sint qualitates, cum non sint nihil nec in aliquo genere, sicut superius est probatum. Sed non sunt de secunda specie qualitatis, quia non sunt naturalis potentia vel impotentia; nec de tertia vel quarta specie, quia istae tantum conveniunt corporalibus. . . . Relinquitur ergo quod operationes sunt in prima specie qualitatis, et universaliter omnis perfectio naturae spiritualis, si non sit substantia eius—sive sit in fieri, sive sit permanens et in facto esse—est in prima specie qualitatis." See also *Quodl.*, q. 13, n. 15, Vivès XXV, 570–571. For Aristotle's text, see *Cat.* 8, 8b26–9a4.

56. In the light of what I say in the next section, however, it seems that actions and activities are about their term in two different senses of "about."

object, for example what it is to be a cat. Only actions, however, and not activities produce something, or, as Scotus said, are turned toward (*ad*) a certain term. For example, fire's act of heating produces a hot kettle. My act of thinking about what it is to be a cat, however, produces nothing (unless it accidentally produces a habit).[57]

## Scotus on the Intentionality of Acts of Thinking

What consequences does Scotus's view that thoughts are qualities have on his explanation of their intentionality?

Since acts of thinking are in themselves nonrelative items, Scotus, unlike Aquinas, could contend that they are directly related to their objects. And this is what he did.[58]

But Scotus not only held that the intentionality of acts of thinking is accounted for by a feature pertaining to those acts themselves, that is, by their being related to their objects; at least in a couple of passages, he also argued that the intentionality of acts of thinking is explained *only* by the relation holding between those acts and their objects. Specifically, the presence of a certain form in the intellect prior to an act of thinking does not play any essential role in explaining intentionality. The presence of a certain species in my intellect is neither a necessary nor a sufficient condition for a certain act's being about a certain thing. For example, my act of thinking about what it is to be a cat is about the essence of cats because it is related to the essence of cats, not because my intellect has previously received the form felinity. Scotus admitted that in most cases my intellect must have received such a form prior to the actual occurrence of a thought. The prior reception of a form, however, is necessary only in order to account for the universality of a thought (e.g., for the fact that I think about what it is to be a cat rather than about what it is to be this or that individual cat). The presence of that form, however, does not play an essential role in explaining why my act is about what it is about. Scotus demonstrated this point by an appeal to divine omnipotence. Since acts of thinking are nonrelative items, they can be created directly by God. Thus, God can create my act of thinking about what it is to be a cat even though I have no form felinity in my intellect. Nevertheless, my act of thinking would still be

---

57. *Quodl.* q. 13, n. 27, Vivès XXV, 575; *Rep.* I-A, d. 3, q. 6, n. 191, 241–242. For a previous attempt to distinguish activities from actions and nonpermanent qualities, see *Ord.* I, d. 3, p. 3, q. 4, nn. 601–603, Vat. III, 354–356.

58. *Rep.* I-A, d. 3, q. 6, n. 170, 235: "Minor [scil., quod intellectio et omnis operatio est ad aliquid] patet per Philosophum, V *Metaphysicae*, dicentem operationem [*pro*: scientiam?] dici relative ad obiectum, ut mensuratum ad mensuram, quia obiectum est mensura operationis; unde si scientia dicatur ad aliquid, multo magis operatio et actus scientiae quae immediatius respiciunt obiectum quam habitus; immo habitus non respicit obiectum nisi mediante actu." Scotus analyzed the act of thinking's role as the foundation of a relation directed at its object in *Quodl.*, q. 13, nn. 6–7 and nn. 11–14, Vivès XXV, 525–541.

about cats, not about God, even if God and not cats were the cause of my act of thinking about cats.[59]

So what sort of relation is intentionality, according to Scotus? Here it is necessary to distinguish two separate issues. First, one must consider the nature of the relation linking an act of thinking to its object. Second, one must consider the relationship between the intentional relation itself and an act of thinking.

Concerning the first issue, Scotus was willing to consider the intentional relation holding between an act of thinking and its object as a relation of likeness (*similitudo*). He stressed, however, that such a likeness cannot be accounted for as the sharing of a common form. An act of thinking is a likeness of its object not because it has the same form of its object but because it is an "imitation" (*imitatio*) of its object, just as something modeled against a certain idea is an imitation of that idea.[60] Admittedly, this amounts to little more than saying that the intentional relation holding between an act of thinking and its object is a *sui generis* relation. Acts of thinking are about their objects just because of the kind of things they are. Scotus also stressed that such a relation cannot be reduced to any of the four Aristotelian causes. An object is not the formal, material, efficient or final cause of the act of thinking that is about that object.[61]

But Scotus also attempted to give a more positive description of the intentional relation holding between an act of thinking and its object. Aristotle had already mentioned a class of relations involving "the measure and the measured." He had illustrated that class of relations by making reference to the relation holding between something known (playing the role of the measure) and knowledge (playing the role of the measured).[62] The idea was that, if an object $o$ acquires a relation $R$ to a knower $k$, no real change occurs in $o$. This implies that the relation $R$ holding between $o$ and $k$ is not real. The explanation for this is that the relation $R$ is not founded on any real feature of $o$ that $o$ lacked when it was not related to $k$ by $R$ and that $o$ acquired when it became related to $k$ by $R$. Thus, when I know a certain thing, that thing does not acquire any real feature and does not undergo any real change. By contrast, if a knower $k$ acquires a relation $R_i$ to an object $o$, some real change occurs in $k$. This implies that the relation $R_i$ holding between $k$ and $o$ is real. The explanation for this is

---

59. *Ord.* I, d. 3, p. 3, q. 2, nn. 477–479, Vat. III, 285–286. See also *Lect.* I, d. 3, p. 3, n. 392, Vat. XVI, 377. See G. Pini, "Can God Create My Thoughts? Scotus's Case against the Causal Account of Intentionality," *Journal of the History of Philosophy* 49 (2011): 39–63.

60. *Quodl.*, q. 13, n. 12, Vivès XXV, 526.

61. By contrast, Aquinas maintained that the object is the final cause of the act of thinking. See note 3.

62. *Meta.* V, 15, 1021a26–b3; *Meta.* X, 1, 1053a31–b3; *Cat.* 7, 6b1–6. See Henninger, *Relations*, 6–8. See Scotus, *Quodl.*, q. 13, nn. 11–12 (Vivès XXV, 525–526). In that passage, Scotus distinguished the measure/measured relation from another kind of relation, which he called "*relatio attingentiae.*" He clarified, however, that the *relatio attingentiae* is a real relation only in acts of intuitive cognition. See ibid., n. 14 (Vivès XXV, 540). Since I focus on abstractive cognition, I do not take the *relatio attingentiae* into account.

that the relation $R_i$ is founded on a real feature of $k$, which $k$ lacked when it was not related to $o$ by $R_i$ and acquired when it became related to $o$ by $R_i$.

These relations were called "nonmutual," because one of them is real and the other one is not. By contrast, mutual relations are either both real or both nonreal. For example, the relation holding between a father and a son is mutual, because there is a corresponding real relation holding between the son and the father.

Aristotle had developed this framework to account for the relation holding between dispositional knowledge and its objects. Scotus applied Aristotle's insight to the relation holding between occurrent knowledge and its objects, that is, between acts of thinking and what they are about. When I think about something, the object of my thought acquires no new feature. By contrast, I do acquire a real feature: a thought. Even though a thought is a *mental* quality because it exists in my mind, it is *real* because it exists no matter whether I think about it or not.

Concerning the second issue, as I have already mentioned, Scotus held that the intentional relation holding between an act of thinking and its object is a relation founded in an act of thinking and directed at its object. Since acts of thinking are nonrelative items, the intentional relation holding between an act and its object cannot be part of the essence of an act of thinking. Thus, the link between an act of thinking and its object is not an essential property of an act of thinking. As a consequence, if an act of thinking is an item belonging to just one category (as it is likely to be), it follows that an act of thinking and its relation to its object are two distinct items belonging to two distinct categories.[63]

With regard to the relation holding between an act of thinking and its object, Scotus held that, even though that relation is not part of the essence of that act of thinking, nevertheless it pertains to that act of thinking necessarily. Thus, it is impossible for a certain act of thinking to exist and not to be about the object is it about. For example, my act of thinking about what it is to be a cat is necessarily about the essence of cats, even though at least in principle it could be defined without ever mentioning the essence of cats.[64] In this respect, the relation between an act of thinking and its object is akin to the relation between a creature and God. Even though the relation between a creature and God is not

---

63. *Quodl.*, q. 13, n. 24, Vivès XXV, 569: "Ex his sequitur quod actus cognoscendi vel non est aliquid per se aliquid per se unum unius generis vel non per se includit illa duo, quae probata sunt concurrere [scil., aliquid absolutum et relatio]. Videtur autem probatum in primo articulo quod essentialiter includat absolutum. . . . Igitur videtur quod actus talis non sit essentialiter relativus, sicut per se includens relationem." For an English translation see John Duns Scotus, *God and Creatures*, 303–304.

64. *Quodl.*, q. 13, n. 13, Vivès XXV, 539–540. A further complication is that the object of an act of abstractive cognition does not have to exist. For example, I may be thinking about what it is to be a cat even though cats may be extinct. For that reason, Scotus described the relation between an act of thinking and its object as a real *potential* relation.

part of the essence of a creature, no creature could exist if it did not depend on God. Therefore, that relation of dependence pertains to a creature necessarily but not essentially. Similarly, the relation to an object is not part of the essence of an act of thinking, but no thought could exist without that relation.[65]

Scotus's answer to the three questions I have mentioned at the beginning of this essay should now be clear.

1. An act of thinking is a quality. Admittedly, it is a special kind of quality: a nonpermanent quality that requires the constant action of its causes to be kept in existence. Also, it is a quality that is about something, namely, its object. Nevertheless, a quality it is, not an action. Thus, an act of thinking is not something I do but something I have. In the current order of things, my intellect and a form present in my intellect perform the action that produce an act of thinking. God, however, could bypass both my intellect and the form present in my intellect and create an act of thinking directly in my intellect.
2. In the current order of things, the presence of a form in the intellect and the intellect's own action as an efficient cause are separately necessary and jointly sufficient for an act of thinking to occur. God, however, could bypass both intellect and form, and act as the sole cause of an act of thinking.
3. An act of thinking's intentionality is accounted for by a special relation founded on the act of thinking itself and linking it directly to its object. Such a relation between an act of thinking and its object cannot be reduced to any of the Aristotelian causes.

Scotus's key move in his account of thinking was the insight that to think is neither to do something nor to be related to an object. Rather, it is a mental quality, that is, a nonpermanent state of the intellect. By taking that step, Scotus gave up both the view that the occurrence of thoughts can be explained as akin to natural changes such as the production and reception of forms and the cognate view that the intentionality of an act of thinking can be explained by virtue of the reception of a form in the intellect.

---

65. On Scotus's position on the relation between creatures and God, see Scotus, *Ord*. II, d. 1, q. 4–5, nn. 260–75, Vat. VII, 128–36; *Lect*. II, d. I, q. 4–5, nn. 238–58, Vat. XVIII, 80–88. See Henninger, *Relations*, 78–85.

# Thinking About Things
## Singular Thought in the Middle Ages

PETER KING

In one corner, Socrates. In the other, on the mat, his cat, Felix. Socrates, of course, thinks (correctly) that Felix the Cat is on the mat. But there's the rub. For Socrates to think that Felix is on the mat, he has to be able to think about Felix, that is, he has to have some sort of cognitive grasp of an individual—and not just any individual, but Felix himself. How is that possible? What is going on when we think about things?

These questions have a contemporary flavor. First, whether an act of thinking is able to grasp an individual is the problem of "singular thought." Second, whether an act of thinking is able to single out some particular individual, that is, to latch onto a given object in the world, is roughly the issue of *de re* thought (so-called from its relation to issues of *de re* belief). Third, whether a thinker can know what thing a thought is about touches on the debate between internalism and externalism, narrow content and wide content.

My agenda is mediaeval rather than contemporary, however. These selfsame questions are the key to understanding the evolution of cognitive psychology under High Scholasticism (1250–1350). For difficulties in explaining how it is we can think about things posed a challenge to the working paradigm of cognitive psychology, prompting a variety of responses and spurring innovative theories, fragmenting the initial consensus on an Aristotelian approach to the philosophy of mind. In what follows, I will sketch the main lines of the mediaeval debates: Aquinas presenting the dominant paradigm for cognitive psychology (§1), the initial challenges to the paradigm over the question of singular thought (§2), Scotus devising a "hybrid" account in response (§3), and Ockham proposing a radically different approach to psychological explanation altogether (§4).

---

A version of this essay was presented at Claude Panaccio's workshop on singular terms and singular concepts in late mediaeval nominalism held at the Université du Québec à Montréal, 12–13 May 2006. Anna Greco commented on the penultimate version and improved it greatly. All translations are mine.

## OUR STORY THUS FAR

Aquinas offers a sophisticated and elegant theory to explain psychological phenomena, a theory based on Aristotle as interpreted by the late Greek commentators and the Arabic commentators, especially Avicenna and Averroes, with an eye to particular points of Christian doctrine, most notably the prospect of personal immortality. The additions and accretions have made it a "neo-Aristotelian" account; the tensions and conflicts among its various parts have been ironed out, and the whole is an admirable blend of disparate elements into a unified theory. Similar attempts at synthesis were underway in other branches of philosophy, with greater and lesser success; the critical assimilation of Aristotelian philosophy was the new intellectual project of the Latin Christian West. In psychology, at least, it seemed to triumph.

The fundamental principle of the neo-Aristotelian synthesis in psychology is that *psychological phenomena are to be explained in terms of the internal mental mechanisms that bring them about*. In the case of cognition, these mechanisms are subpersonal and semiautonomous, causally connected to one another and analyzed in terms of potency and act; their existence and nature is deduced from the functions they discharge. Typically, these mechanical modules—usually called "faculties"—transfer or "transduce" information—a process the Scholastics described as the "transmission of form" and, when information-preserving, as "having the same form." The vehicle[1] for the form is a kind of mental representation, called a *species*, that mediates among the several faculties of the mind. Therefore, the best explanation of psychological phenomena, or at least of cognition, is given by functionally defined subpersonal mechanisms operating on representations. At this level of generality, the neo-Aristotelian synthesis closely resembles the project of contemporary cognitive science.

Details make the picture concrete without altering this fundamental similarity. When Socrates encounters Felix the Cat on the mat, the following train of events is set in motion.[2] Felix, through the intervening medium,[3] has a causal impact on Socrates's various sense organs: each of the affected sense organs is put into one of its possible determinate states $d_i$ by the way in which Felix

---

1. The term "vehicle" deliberately straddles the difficult question whether it *is* the form of the object or merely *contains* it somehow. See Peter King, "Rethinking Representation in the Middle Ages," in *Representation and Objects of Thought in Medieval Philosophy*, ed. Henrik Lagerlund (London: Ashgate Press, 2005), 83–102.

2. The following account of sensitive cognition is ultimately derived from Aristotle, *De anima* 2.12 424ª17–24, who likens the process to the impression of a seal in wax by a signet ring.

3. How an external object exercises its causality through the medium is dealt with by the appropriate science: in the case of vision, the science of optics (*scientia perspectiua*). I shall ignore the details here in the interests of the larger picture. See Katharine Tachau, *Vision and Certitude in the Age of Ockham: Optics, Epistemology, and the Foundations of Semantics 1250–1345* (Leiden: Brill, 1988).

causally acts on it. Each particular sense organ corresponds to a particular sense faculty in the expected way—the eye is the sense organ of the faculty of vision, the ear the sense organ of the faculty of hearing, and so on. In general, a sense faculty is the *form* of its associated sense organ, which is a particular instance of the form-matter relation between soul and body. When a sense organ is part of a living whole, animated by a sense faculty, it is receptive to a range of causal influences and responds differentially to differential causal input. In the case of vision, for example, rods and cones in the eye fire in patterns that are correlated with distinct external causes (and undergo complex integration for binocular vision). The receptivity of the sense faculty just is its associated sense organ's differential responsiveness to stimuli, such that the sense organ is able to be in a range of determinate states $d_1, \ldots, d_n$; each state $d_i$ corresponds to an act of "seeing" $s_i$ of a given sort of visual appearance.[4]

When Socrates encounters Felix, then, an event transpires that may be described in three theoretically rich ways:

Felix causes Socrates's eye to be in state $d_i$
Socrates's faculty of vision, which is in potency to $s_i$, becomes actually $s_i$
Socrates sees Felix

So, too, *mutatis mutandis* for the other senses. The particular states of each sense organ then causally affect the sense organ associated with the "common" sense (the heart), which unites the diverse external sense modalities, coordinating their deliverances through the common sensibles, such as shape and number, which are able to be sensed by more than one faculty, in contradistinction to the proper sensibles. This results in a composite determinate configuration of the heart as a sense organ, reducing the commonsense faculty from potency to act in the sensing of the object. In the case at hand, it is the combined sight and sound (perhaps smell) of Felix, on the mat. The sensing of Felix is known as the *sensible species*, which is stored for later reference in memory whence the imagination can draw it forth (in which case it is known as the *phantasm*). The systematic correlation of objects with such species is part of the information-preserving aspect of perception: a given object regularly causes sensitive cognition of a given kind, and the sensible species is a concrete particular preserving the relevant information about the external object. In short, the object and the sensible species are isomorphic—they have literally the same form, the mediaeval way of saying that the representation of an object encodes information about that object uniquely.

To summarize: the neo-Aristotelian analysis of sensitive cognition turns first on an exact understanding of the form-matter relation of the sense faculty and

---

4. The given determinate state of the sense organ $d_i$ is known as the *species impressa*, and the corresponding determinate actualizing of the sense faculty's potencies $s_i$ is known as the *species expressa*.

its associated sense organ, treating this relation as a variety of the act-potency relation. The object and the sensing are "formally identical." Initially the sense faculty is merely passive with respect to sensing.[5] In general, something is reduced from potency to act only by an agent cause, that is, whenever there is some actualizing process going on there is an agent that causes the occurrence of that process.[6] In sensitive cognition, the sensed object is therefore the agent cause of the determinate actualization of the potencies of the sense faculty. External objects are actually sensible; in standard circumstances, they causally bring it about that they are actually sensed. The distinction of external and internal senses seems required by the evident facts of experience, but each faculty is given the same kind of potency-act-cause analysis.

The analysis of sensitive cognition is common to humans and other animals. In the case of humans, the same conceptual apparatus is deployed to explain intellective cognition, on analogy with sensitive cognition. There are three main points of difference. First, the intellective soul is immaterial and therefore has no associated "organs"; although the close connections between the brain and thought were recognized, the brain is not the organ of thought the way the eye is the organ of vision or the ear the organ of hearing. Second, an agent cause must be postulated for intellective cognition, the operation of which is analogous to the causal activity of the external object in sensitive cognition; this is the agent intellect, in contradistinction to the possible intellect (less commonly "material intellect"). Third, whereas sense deals with particulars, the intellect deals with universals, and so the information passed along from the senses has to be appropriately altered.

Bearing in mind these points of difference, Aquinas works through the analogy as follows. There are two faculties involved in intellective cognition, the agent intellect and the possible intellect. The possible intellect is the faculty that is potentially able to think—that is, the faculty whose actualization is an occurrent act of thinking, just as the sense faculty associated with a given sense organ is potentially able to sense an object. No intermediate step of affecting matter is needed, since intellective cognition does not depend on an organ, or indeed on the body at all. By the same token the processes of sensitive cognition do not of themselves set in train the events constitutive of intellective cognition.

---

5. The sense faculty is not totally passive; it is the potency of a living sense organ, quite a different thing from an inanimate receptacle such as a mirror or a lump of wax. The point is that sensing must involve an actualization of the sense organ, which is passive in respect of its cause.

6. Unless there were an agent cause for the actualization of the potency, there would be no more reason for the potency to be actualized at one time rather than another; hence the process would either always be actualized or never be actualized, each of which is evidently false.

Hence there are two distinct functions discharged by the agent intellect in bringing about thought:[7]

1. The agent intellect *abstracts* from the sensible species (or the phantasm) its universal features, thereby creating an item in intellective soul with the requisite generality. This item is the intelligible species; in the case at hand, felinity is abstracted from the sensible species of Felix.
2. The agent intellect *impresses* the intelligible species on the possible intellect, reducing it from potency to act in a determinate act, namely a thinking-of-felinity.

The transduction of information from the sensitive soul is performed in the first. The sensible species is appropriately "dematerialized" and thereby rendered less concrete, since it is freed from its individualizing conditions. No change in form takes place, though. The structural features of the information carried by the intelligible species are the same as that carried by the sensitive species. This general representation is then the vehicle for bringing about an occurrent act of thinking, as spelled out in the second. The content of this act of thinking is provided by the only information available: the common nature abstracted from the sensible species and present in the intelligible species. Hence, it is an act of thinking about felinity, about cats in general. The intelligible species is then stored in memory, able to be used at will in future acts of thinking.

It is but a short step from occurrent acts of general thought to the rest of intellectual cognition. Once general concepts are available in the intellective soul, stringing them together into propositions is a matter of mental acts of "combination" or "division" (corresponding respectively to affirmation and denial); sequences of propositions constitute chains of reasoning. So it is that all cognitive psychology is explained by the mental mechanisms postulated by the neo-Aristotelian synthesis.

There is much to admire in the theory. An economical set of principles yields a theoretically rich and articulated structure, one that can plausibly lay claim to being a complete theory of cognitive psychological phenomena.

### CORRECTIONS AND CHALLENGES

The attack on the neo-Aristotelian synthesis was not long in coming. Shortly after Aquinas's death, the English Franciscan William de la Mare published a short treatise entitled *Correctorium fratris Thomae*. In it he listed a series of claims attributed to Aquinas (usually directly quoted from his works), reasons not to adopt or endorse the claim, and arguments for an alternative to Aquinas's

---

7. These functions are usually taken to be sequential. However, some philosophers hold that there is only a single process that effectively discharges these distinct functions: abstracting universal features is the same as impressing the species on the possible intellect. See the discussion of this point in Giorgio Pini's essay in this volume.

view—the "corrections" of the title. William's treatise provoked a flurry of responses; its adoption in 1282 as the official Franciscan position with regard to Aquinas vis-à-vis his Dominican defenders lent a further sectarian air to an already bitter quarrel.

The second of the ninety-odd articles William de la Mare wrote to correct Aquinas raises the problem of singular thought. He puts the problem as follows:[8]

> [Aquinas] says in *Summa theologiae* 1ª q.14 art.11 *ad* 1 that our intellect has no cognition of singulars. For our intellect abstracts the intelligible species from individuating principles, and, accordingly, the intelligible species in our intellect cannot be a likeness of the individuating principles.

Note the exact form of William's complaint. He tries to explain Aquinas's denial of singular thought by referring to how the faculties of the intellective soul function. In particular, William charges Aquinas with not being able to provide a mechanism that allows singular thought to take place. That is the substance of his point about abstraction "from individuating principles," for everyone agrees that we are capable of singular thought; we can tell Peter from Paul, however this may occur. The trick is to provide an explanation that grounds this everyday ability, and that is what William claims Aquinas cannot do.

The many vehement replies indicate that William had indeed touched a raw nerve. Richard Knapwell, likely the author of the *Correctorium corruptorii "Quare"* (perhaps the first reply), is typical. He presents William's claims and arguments in careful detail, and then offers a blizzard of citations to refute them, pointing, as do contemporary defenders of Aquinas, to *Sum. theol.* 1ª q.86 art.1. The question at stake there is whether our intellect cognizes singulars. Aquinas declares that it does not and cannot, at least, in a straightforward or direct way. He explains this qualification by stating that the intellect can have cognition of singulars "indirectly" (*indirecte*), "as if by some kind of reflection" (*quasi per quandam reflexionem*). Reflection on what? Ever since Knapwell, defenders of Aquinas have linked this cryptic and hesitant remark to Aquinas's earlier declaration in *Sum. theol.* 1ª q.84 art.7 that the intellect must "turn to phantasms" (*conuersio ad phantasmata*) in order to think. Yet it is unclear how these texts are supposed to go together. Does the intellect turn to the phantasm by "reflecting" on it? If so, what does this mean? How does it work? Even with the best will in the world, the partisans of Aquinas's "indirect" knowledge cannot say that his vague references to mental functions count as specifying a mechanism

---

8. As reported by Richard Knapwell in *Les premières polémiques thomists*, ed. Palamon Glorieux (Le Saulchoir: Kain, 1927), 12–13: "Item, quaestione 14 articulo 11, in responsione primi argumenti dicit quod intellectus noster non cognoscit singularia; quia intellectus noster abstrahit speciam intelligibilem a principiis indiuiduantibus; unde species intelligibilis nostri intellectus non potest esse similitudo principiorum indiuiduantium."

by which singular thought takes place—at best it is no more than a suggestion about where an answer might be found, not an answer itself.[9]

There are reasons to be skeptical that an account of singular cognition is available to Aquinas—at least, singular thought of material composite substances. Roughly, if the content of an act of thinking is given by the intelligible species, namely when the agent intellect impresses it on the possible intellect to cause an occurrent act of thought, then in order to think of Felix at all Socrates would have to have an individual intelligible species. Yet as we have seen, it is not possible in this life to have an individual intelligible species naturally, given Aquinas's account of human psychology. (If mental content is provided in some other way Aquinas owes us an account of it.) There is no psychological means for Aquinas to distinguish:

a thought *occasioned* by the phantasm
a thought *directed* to the phantasm

Yet distinguish these he must, since the one is naturally universal and the other purportedly not.

Without a detailed response to William de la Mare's criticism, the neo-Aristotelian synthesis in psychology founders on the problem of singular thought, despite the best efforts of Knapwell and others. This is not to deny its genuine virtues; Aquinas's thought was powerful and systematic enough to command defenders even beyond partisanship, and continues to do so. But the wall had been breached and the battering ram was the intellectual cognition of singulars.

Even if we grant William his criticism, it is not as though he is in a better position; to point out that we need to have an account of singular cognition is not to provide one, and the Franciscans as well as the Dominicans had no theory to hand. Broadly speaking, the Dominicans tried to patch up the neo-Aristotelian synthesis by elaborating theories of how "indirect" knowledge was possible. Others—seculars and Franciscans alike—were less tempted by this route than by the prospect of redesigning some or all of Aristotelian psychology. Bonaventure, Matthew of Aquasparta, and later Peter John Olivi tried to revive an "Augustinian" account of cognition. Durand of St.-Pourçain argued that no mechanism was necessary. Most noteworthy of all such attempts was the "illuminationist" approach of Henry of Ghent, who argued that in intellective cognition the phantasm is not transformed but viewed "in a new light" (and hence

---

9. Bérubé charges Aquinas's opponents with conflating "only indirect knowledge of the singular" with "no knowledge of the singular at all." But surely this misrepresents William's objection, which is that Aquinas has no way to explain even indirect cognition of the singular. Camille Bérubé, *La connaissance de l'individuel au Moyen Âge* (Montréal: Presses Universitaires de France, 1964).

not necessarily universalized). But none of these approaches commanded wide assent, and there was no consensus.

## JUST WHAT THE (SUBTLE) DOCTOR ORDERED

John Duns Scotus not only recognized and addressed the problem of singular thought, he correctly distinguished it from *de re* thought—roughly, admitting the former but denying the latter. In so doing he set the terms of the debate in psychology for the centuries to come.[10] For over the course of several works, Scotus invented and pioneered the distinction between *intuitive cognition* and *abstractive cognition*, which rapidly became a staple.[11] In his late and mature quodlibetal questions, Scotus introduces intuitive cognition as follows (*Quodl.* 6.19):[12]

> There is an act of understanding ... that is cognition precisely of a present object *qua* present and of an existing object *qua* existing ... This sort of intellective act can properly be called "intuitive" since it is an intuition of a thing as existing and present.

He offers a more concise description slightly later (*Quodl.* 13.27):[13]

> There is some cognition of the existent *per se*, which attains the object in its proper actual existence.

Taking each characterization into account, we can say that an intuitive cognition is a cognition of a present existing individual as present and existing. By contrast, Scotus describes abstractive cognition as follows (*Quodl.* 6.18):[14]

---

10. "The history of medieval theories of knowledge from *ca.* 1310 can be traced as a development of this dichotomy." Tachau, *Vision and Certitude*, 81.
11. There were intimations before Scotus, most notably in Vital du Four; see John Lynch, *The Theory of Knowledge of Vital du Four* (St. Bonaventure, N.Y.: Franciscan Institute Press, 1972) 463 n. 13, though Lynch's claim that Vital has a theory to rival that of Scotus is, as John Boler remarks, "unduly enthusiastic." Boler, "Intuitive and Abstractive Cognition," in *The Cambridge History of Later Medieval Philosophy*, ed. Norman Kretzmann (Cambridge: Cambridge University Press, 1982), 460–478. Scotus's texts are collected in Sebastian Day, *Intuitive Cognition: A Key to the Significance of the Later Scholastics* (St. Bonaventure, N.Y.: Franciscan Institute Press, 1947), and discussed in Robert Pasnau, "Cognition," in *The Cambridge Companion to Duns Scotus*, ed. Thomas Williams (Cambridge: Cambridge University Press, 2003), 285–311.
12. "Alius autem actus intelligendi est ... qui scilicet praecise sit obiecti praesentis ut praesentis et exsistentis ut exsistentis ... Ista, inquam, intellectio potest proprie dici intuitiua, quia ipsa est intuitio rei ut exsistentis et praesentis."
13. "Aliqua ergo cognitio est per se exsistentis, sicut quae attingit obiectum in sua propria exsistentia actuali."
14. "Unus indifferenter etiam respectu obiecti exsistentis et non-exsistentis, et indifferenter etiam respectu obiecti non realiter praesentis sicut et realiter praesentis.... Iste actus intelligendi potest satis proprie dici abstractiuus, quia abstrahit obiectum ab exsistentia et non-exsistentia, praesentia et absentia."

> One [kind of cognition] is indifferent whether the object exists or not, and also whether it is present in reality or not ... This act of understanding can quite properly be called "abstractive" since it abstracts the object from existence or nonexistence, from presence or absence.

He again offers a more concise description later (*Quodl.* 13.27):[15]

> There is also a cognition of the object, but not as existing as such—either because the object does not exist at all, or at least because the cognition is not of it as actually existing.

Hence, an abstractive cognition is a cognition of an object without regard to either its presence or existence. It does not exclude the existence or the presence of the object in its content; those features are merely not included, which is not the same as being positively excluded from the conception of the object.

Scotus's distinction between intuitive and abstractive cognition therefore rests on whether "existence" and "presence" are part of the mental content of the cognition, or "abstracted" away. Hence abstractive cognition may, and intuitive cognition must, be directed at individuals. This is reflected in Scotus's technical account of each kind of cognition. According to Scotus, Socrates has an intuitive cognition of Felix when two real relations obtain: a third-mode real relation of the measureable to the measure, and a relation of "getting hold of the thing as its terminus" (*relatio attingentiae alterius ut termini*).[16] The first condition says in essence that the cognition is accurate to the extent that it lives up to the object at which it is directed, capturing the object as it is; the second, that it latches onto the object. Socrates has a merely abstractive cognition of Felix when the first condition is relaxed to be merely potential or aptitudinal rather than real and actual, and the second is replaced by an actual relation of reason to a nonexistent possible object.[17] In either case, Socrates is cognitively related to Felix as an individual, not to felinity or something else. For this to be possible, of course, Scotus has to reject Aquinas's contention that the intellect is capable only of universal cognition. He explicitly does so. In *Quodl.* 6.19 he offers the following argument:[18]

---

15. "Aliqua etiam est cognitio obiecti, non ut exsistentis in se, sed uel obiectum non exsistit uel saltem illa cognitio non est eius ut actualiter exsistentis."

16. See *Quodl.* 13.35. The scholastic theory of third-mode relations is derived from Aristotle, *Met.* 5.15 1020$^b$26–32; see Scotus, *In Met.* 5.11. There is no critical discussion of the extremely difficult paragraphs 13.37–39 in the literature; Day simply skips them (*Intuitive Cognition*, 64).

17. Scotus allows for another possibility, namely that the abstractive cognition can be the object of a reflexive act that is then related to its object by a relation of reason (*Quodl.* 13.44). Since abstractive cognition need not be of singulars whereas intuitive cognition must be, I will not pursue the details of abstractive cognition further here.

18. "Quia omnis perfectio cognitionis absolute, quae potest competere potentiae cognitiuae sensitiuae, potest eminenter competere potentiae cognitiuae intellectiuae; nunc autem per-

Every perfection which is a perfection of cognition absolutely and which can be present in a faculty of sense knowledge can pertain eminently to an intellective cognitive faculty. But it is a matter of perfection in the act of knowing *qua* knowing that what is in fact known be attained perfectly, and this is so when it is attained in itself and not just in some diminished or derivative likeness of itself. On the other hand, a sense power has such perfection in its knowledge, because it can attain an object in itself as existing and present in its real existence, and not just diminutively in a kind of imperfect likeness of itself. Therefore this perfection pertains to an intellective power in the act of knowing. It could not pertain to it, however, unless it could know an existing thing and know it as present either in itself or in some intelligible object which contains the thing in question in an eminent way.

The key idea here is that if sense can do it, then the intellect must be able to as well; we sense individuals, and therefore must equally be able to conceive them—that is, singular thought must also be possible.

Scotus clearly intended intellective intuitive cognition to be addressed to the issue of singular thought, and to the shortcomings in the neo-Aristotelian synthesis.[19] The doctrine is meant to explain how singular thought takes place; it does so in standard mediaeval fashion by describing how singular concepts are acquired: in the case of intellective intuitive cognition, through direct contact with individuals in the world—exactly what was missing in Aquinas. There is some indirect textual evidence that Scotus had William de la Mare's specific criticisms of Aquinas in mind. For Scotus usually introduces his distinction between intuitive and abstractive cognition in connection with worries about the Beatific Vision, which, after all, is meant to be the direct intellective experience of an individual,

---

fectionis est in actu cognoscendi, ut cognitio est, perfecte attingere primum cognitum; non autem perfect attingitur quando non in se attingitur sed tantummodo in aliqua deminuta uel deriuata similitudine ab ipso; sensitiua autem habet hanc perfectionem in cognitione sua, quia potest obiectum attingere in se, ut exsistens et ut praesens est in exsistentia reali, et non tantum deminute attendendo ipsum in quadam perfectione deminuta; ergo ista perfectio competit intellectiuae in cognoscendo; sed non posset sibi competere nisi cogosceret exsistens et ut in exsistentia propria praesens est, uel in aliquo obiecto intelligibili eminenter ipsum continente." Scotus gives a similar argument in *Quodl.* 13.29.

19. It used to be thought—presumably in the wake of the criticism offered by Ockham and Aureol—that the motive for the doctrine of intuitive and abstractive cognition was epistemological, namely to avoid skepticism by providing a secure ground for contingent truths. On the reading offered here, the motive is not epistemological (concerned with explaining and grounding claims to knowledge) but psychological (concerned with explaining and grounding singular thought). Once singular thought is possible, we can sensibly raise questions about contingent knowledge, that is, knowledge involving singulars. But the initial impetus for the doctrine is psychological.

namely God (or more exactly Christ as Savior);[20] it is no coincidence that the first objection given by William de la Mare to Aquinas's claim that we do not have cognition of singulars is that it makes it impossible for the blessed in Heaven to have the Beatific Vision:[21]

> [Aquinas's view] gives an occasion for going astray, since according to it neither separated souls nor angels can cognize Christ in Heaven by an intellectual cognition.

The doctrine of intuitive and abstractive cognition was designed to remedy this defect. The resulting psychological theory is no longer a "neo-Aristotelian" account, since it includes foreign elements; the doctrine is just bolted onto the side of the existing theory, which is now a hybrid. So much for the traditional view of mediaeval philosophers as slavish followers of Aristotle.

When Socrates encounters Felix, he can have an intellective act that stands in a dual real relation to Felix. On one hand, it "represents" Felix, at least to the extent of having its accuracy assessed with respect to Felix rather than anything else. On the other hand, it "gets hold" or "latches on" to Felix as an external object in the world. These are indeed the key features of singular thought. But we need to draw another distinction. For Scotus wants to distinguish sharply between two different cases: singular thought, in which Felix as an individual is conceived, and *de re* thought, in which Felix is grasped as Felix, that is, as the very individual he is. Put another way, Scotus holds that there is a difference between conceiving of an individual *qua* individual and conceiving of it *qua* the very individual it is, roughly the distinction between individuality and identity.[22]

Scotus's reasons for insisting on the distinction between singular thought and *de re* thought are metaphysical at bottom. For Scotus maintains that there are singular essences, so that Felix has an essence beyond his specific feline nature, an essence proper to Felix alone that cannot be had by anyone else.[23] Although Felix does have singular (individualized) forms, his singular essence is not a form—there is no form *Felixity* for the singular essence paralleling

---

20. Stephen Dumont proves, beyond the shadow of a textual doubt, that Scotus's doctrine of intuitive and abstractive cognition is deeply linked with his attempt to find a philosophically and theologically adequate account of the Beatific Vision: Dumont, "The Scientific Character of Theology and the Origin of Duns Scotus's Distinction Between Intuitive and Abstractive Cognition," *Speculum* 64 (1989): 579–599.

21. Glorieux, *Les premières polémiques thomists*, 13: "Hoc praebet occasionem errandi, quia secundum hoc animae separatae et Angeli Christum in patria intellectuali cognitione non cognoscerent."

22. This seems to be the distinction Boler has in mind when he writes: "It was with Scotus, however, that a distinction between the knowledge of individuality and the knowledge of existent individuals was systematically developed." Boler, "Intuitive and Abstractive Cognition," 463. See also Giorgio Pini's essay in this volume.

23. For Scotus's theory of singular essences, see Peter King, "Duns Scotus on Singular Essences," *Medioevo* 30 (2005): 111–137.

the form *felinity* for the specific essence. Instead, Felix has his singular essence in consequence of being an individual, that is, in consequence of having an "individual differentia,"[24] which is what makes Felix the very thing he is, namely Felix. Of course, Felix is an individual cat. But each and every cat is an individual cat, whereas only one cat is, or for Scotus could be, Felix. Yet the singular essence is not known by us in this life (*In Met.* 7.13.158 and 7.15.20–30). His argument is simple and direct. Take two individuals $a_1$ and $a_2$ belonging to the same species; if they are sufficiently similar we cannot tell whether the one before us is $a_1$ or whether it is $a_2$, something we could easily do if we were to grasp the individual differentia, for then we would know of any individual which one it is (*In Met.* 7.13.158):[25]

> The individual differentia is generally not known by anyone in this life. Proof: The difference between it and anything else would then be known, and so one could not be in error about anything else shown to oneself intellectually;[26] one would judge it to be something else. But this is false for something else wholly similar [to the original].

The individual differentia, a component of the singular essence, includes the identity of the individual it partially constitutes. If it cannot be grasped—and evidently it cannot, for if it could we should be infallible regarding the identity of things, and we manifestly are not—then the singular essence cannot be known: Scotus concludes "thus *we* cannot define the individual due to our incapacities, not due to anything on its side." We do have a cognitive grasp of individuals, of course; that is the point of the doctrine of intellective intuitive cognition. But we do not grasp an individual *as* the very individual it is: Socrates has a cognitive grasp of Felix, but not of Felix *qua* Felix. Our powers of intellectual discrimination can reach to individuals, but not to which individuals they are—that is, not to identifying them.

---

24. The individual differentia is often called the "haecceity." But this is mistaken and misleading. It is mistaken because Scotus uses the term *haeceitas* to pick out the individuality of the individual rather than the individual differentia (roughly the identity) of the individual—though the term is uncommon in Scotus's writings. It is misleading because it suggests that the individual differentia is a form, and further that there is a generic kind to which all individual differentiae belong, each of which is incorrect. See King, ibid.

25. "Differentia indiuidualis a nullo nota est in hac uita communiter. Cuius probatio est: quia tunc nota esset differentia eius ad quodcumque aliud, et ita non posset errare de quocumque alio sibi intellectualiter ostenso quin iudicaret illud esse aliud. Sed hoc est falsum de alio omnino simili." See also *In Met.* 7.15.20, where Scotus further argues that we could not tell if two sufficiently similar patches of white were superimposed whether there were one or two.

26. The phrase "shown to oneself intellectually" is meant to rule out incapacities or limitations stemming from the senses or the process of sense-cognition; it is an oblique reference to intellective intuitive cognition.

Therefore, when Socrates has an intellective intuitive cognition of Felix, the content of his (singular) thought is *an individual cat*. To be sure, the cat occasioning Socrates's thought may be Felix. But even in that case Socrates's thought is only contingently a thought of Felix, not a *de re* thought of him, which would necessarily be about Felix no matter the identity of the cat (or the apparent cat-façade) before Socrates. Scotus endorses a clear and sharp distinction between singular thought and *de re* thought, admitting the possibility of the former and rejecting that of the latter.[27] Hence, the content of Socrates's cognition depends on purely internal features, whereas its character depends on the world's being a certain way. External factors determine what a singular thought is indeed directed at, as a contingent matter. With Scotus, then, we have an explicit account of singular thought and *de re* thought, carefully distinguished. It is no wonder that the doctrine became a touchstone for subsequent discussion.

### AND NOW FOR SOMETHING COMPLETELY DIFFERENT

William of Ockham identified what he took to be a fatal flaw in Scotus's account. According to Ockham, Scotus has made the same mistake as Aquinas: he hasn't specified any mechanism to explain how intellective intuitive cognition is possible. Rather than explaining *how* singular thought happens, Scotus just asserts *that* it happens.

There is some justice in Ockham's charge, just as there is in William de la Mare's charge against Aquinas, though loyal partisans of each have rallied to defend their respective views. There is no consensus among Scotists about how to respond to Ockham's criticism, however. Put the challenge like this: For Scotus, does intellective intuitive cognition require an intelligible species? No answer seems satisfactory. Suppose that it does require an intelligible species, in keeping with the way other intellective activities are explained. The doctrine of intuitive cognition then seems less like a mere addition to the rest of psychology, conforming, at least in broad outlines, to the rest of the philosophy of mind. But then Scotus owes us a story about the mechanism at work—how it is we can somehow acquire an individual concept from an individual without being able to grasp the individual differentia. Suppose, instead, that intellective intuitive cognition does not require an intelligible species. Then Ockham's criticism that there is no mechanism seems well founded. Worse yet, Scotus seems to have mixed together psychological phenomena explicable by describing a quasi-causal mechanism that bring them about with psychological events that just happen. In contemporary terms, Scotus has proposed an uneasy

---

27. Scotus may have thought that *de re* mental acts are possible but that they essentially involve the operation of the will rather than the intellect. It is the will, for example, that stretches forth and latches on to a designated individual, such as Christ (for we love Christ rather than an indistinguishable duplicate even if we cannot tell them apart).

hybrid of representationalism with direct realism, an account that is neither fish nor fowl.

Ockham draws a surprising moral. From Scotus's omission of a psychological mechanism underpinning the doctrine of intuitive and abstractive cognition, Ockham concludes that none is really needed—that the project of explaining psychological phenomena by the causal interaction of subpersonal mechanisms is misguided. Hence he rejects such appeals. Rather than endorse a hybrid, Ockham dispenses with the remnants of the neo-Aristotelian synthesis, adopting in its stead a radical externalism with as little "mentalistic" psychology as possible. In its place he puts forward direct realism and an account of acquired competencies, as follows.[28]

On one reading of Scotus's doctrine of intuitive and abstractive cognition, as noted, these kinds of cognitive acts "just happen." They are produced by causal interaction with the world, to be sure, but this fact does not require a reductive explanation; Ockham elevates this into a general principle (*Rep.* 2 qq.12–13):[29]

> Given a sufficient agent and patient in proximity to each other, the effect can be postulated without anything further.

Applied to ordinary cases of cognition, this means that we can dispense with the complex details of subpersonal agents. Now Ockham holds that acts of singular intuitive cognition are the building blocks of mental life. On his view, a sensory intuitive cognition occurs when in the presence of an object, and, together with the object, cause an intellective intuitive cognition of that same object; after repeated exposure, the mind is caused to have an abstractive general concept of that kind of object.[30] Along the way, habits are created, which account for overt acts of memory as well the dispositional abilities that make up the concept of the object. Thus in the presence of Felix, Socrates has an intuitive cognition of Felix, which in its turn causes an abstractive cognition of Felix. Nothing more needs to be said about how this happens, other than to point to

---

28. For a more complete discussion of Ockham's radical revolution in philosophy of psychology, see Peter King, "Two Conceptions of Experience," *Medieval Philosophy and Theology* 11 (2004): 1–24; "Rethinking Representation"; and "Le rôle des concepts selon Ockham," *Philosophiques* 32 (2005): 435–447. Here I only sketch the details necessary for the account of singular thought and *de re* thought.

29. "Posito activo sufficienti et passivo in ipsis approximatis, potest poni effectus sine omni alio" (OTh 5 268).

30. See *Ord.* Prologue q.1 art.1 and q.12 (OTh 1 16–47 and 355–356 respectively); *Rep.* 2 qq.12–13 (OTh 5 261–263); *Exp. Phys.* 1.1.2 (OPh 4 25–26); *Summa logicae* 3-2.10 and 3-2.29. Ockham further sketches the foundational role of intuitive cognition in his *Exp. Isag.* 2.11 (OPh 2 45). In *Quaest. uar.* q.5, Ockham suggests that even a single sensory intuitive cognition might be enough to cause the associated abstractive general concept, though he denies this in *Quodl.* 1.13. The "mentalism" of Mental Language seems to be no more than a way of talking about the mind in terms of linguistic competence, despite Ockham's occasional nods in the direction of compositionality.

the "proximity" of Socrates and Felix. To the objection that this requires a material agent (Felix) to cause an effect in an immaterial patient (Socrates's intellect)—a suggestion other philosophers rejected; Durand of St.-Pourçain calls it "absurd"—Ockham simply asserts that it is indeed possible, and leaves it at that. What is more, since there is no need to postulate subpersonal psychological mechanisms, there is equally no need to postulate any intermediary representations; Ockham therefore rejects both sensible and intelligible species, on the grounds that any job they might have performed can be accounted for adequately by postulating complexes of competencies (*habitus*).[31] Nor, for that matter, are there large-scale distinctions among the "parts" of the soul (*Ord.* 1 d.3 q.6):[32]

> The agent intellect isn't distinct from the possible intellect at all; instead, one and the same intellect is denominated in different ways.

The packages of interrelated abilities with which Ockham replaces the neo-Aristotelian synthesis are capable of being articulated in a logical structure: one ability may presuppose another, or require further abilities for its exercise. Yet, there isn't anything "in the head" about such sets of skills. They should be thought of as skills possessed by the whole person rather than inner mental episodes.

So, too, for intuitive cognition. For Ockham, the content of these mental acts is not an "internal" feature of the mind. Instead, it is determined by the external world, in particular by the very item that *caused* the intuitive cognition. In contemporary terms: Ockham is a (strong) externalist with regard to singular thought.[33] Socrates's thought of Felix is of Felix precisely because it was caused by Felix rather than anything else.

Like Scotus, Ockham is impressed by the fact that we cannot tell the difference between two extremely similar objects, be they patches of white, amounts of

---

31. Ockham's classic statement of this thesis is in the first conclusion of *Rep.* 2 qq.12–13 (OTh 5 268). Similar arguments are found in *Ord.* 1 d.2 q.8 and d.27 q.2, as well as in his *Exp. Isag.* 2 and *Exp. De int.* preface. In *Rep.* 2 qq.12–13, Ockham lists the functions typically played by the intelligible species: to inform the intellect, to unite the object with the potency, to determine the potency to the kind of act, to cause the act of understanding, to represent the object, and to account for the unity of mover and moved. In each case Ockham argues that the function is either unnecessary or can be accomplished by an acquired skill (*habitus*). See Leen Spruit, *Species intelligibilis: From Perception to Knowledge*, vol. 1, *Classical Roots and Medieval Discussions* (Leiden: Brill, 1994). He holds the same thesis in the case of the sensible species; see Tachau, *Vision and Certitude*, 130–148.

32. "Intellectus agens nullo modo distinguitur ab intellectu possibili sed idem intellectus habet diversas denominationes" (OTh 2 520).

33. See also Claude Panaccio, *Ockham on Concepts* (London: Ashgate, 2005), 12–14. Susan Brower-Toland challenged the thesis that Ockham is a radical externalist, particularly with respect to the counterfactual criterion given here, in her "Intuition, Externalism, and Direct Reference in Ockham," *History of Philosophy Quarterly* 24 (2007):317–335.

heat, human beings, or anything else.³⁴ Scotus drew the conclusion that singular thought only extends to the individual, not to its identity; *de re* thought is beyond our powers in this life. Ockham, by contrast, concludes from such examples that "likeness is not the precise reason why we think of one thing rather than another."³⁵ Instead, he has recourse to a feature of causality, namely that "it is part of the very notion of an impression that it be caused by that of which it is the impression" (*Ord.* 1 d.3 q.9 OTh 2 547). A likeness need not be fashioned from the original, whereas an impression must be. More exactly, Ockham holds that it is the nature of an impression to be producible by a given individual rather than another, that is, that it is apt to be so produced even were God to supplant the causal chain. He states his view succinctly in *Quodl.* 1.13 (OTh 9 76):³⁶

> Intuitive cognition is a proper cognition of a singular not because of its greater likeness to one than to another, but because it is naturally caused by the one and not by the other; nor can it be caused by the other. If you object that it can be caused by God alone, I reply that the following is true: Such a sight is always apt to be caused by one created object and not by another; and if it were caused naturally, it is caused by the one and not by the other, and it is not able to be caused by the other.

He reiterates the point, alluding to the same case, in *Rep.* 2 qq.12–13 (OTh 5 289):³⁷

> Suppose you were to object that a given concept can be immediately and totally caused by God, and so through that given concept the intellect would no more understand one singular than another extremely similar one, since it would be as much similar to one as to the other; nor does causality make it be of one and not of the other, since it is caused by neither but rather immediately by God. I reply that any given concept of a creature that is caused by God can be partially³⁸ caused by the creature,

---

34. *Rep.* 2 qq.12–13: patches of white, OTh 5 281–282; amounts of heat, 287; humans, 304.
35. "Similitudo non est causa praecisa quare intelligit unum et non aliud," *ibid.* (OTh 5 287).
36. "Dico quod intuitiua est propria cognitio singularis, non propter maiorem assimilationem uni quam alteri, sed quia naturaliter ab uno et non ab altero causatur, nec potest ab altero causari. Si dicis, potest causari a solo Deo: uerum est, sed semper nata est talis uisio causari ab uno obiecto creato et non ab alio; et si causetur naturaliter, causatur ab uno et non ab alio, nec potest ab altero causari."
37. "Si dicas quod illa intentio potest immediate causari totaliter a Deo; et tunc per illam intentionem non plus intelligeret intellectus unum singulare simillimum quam aliud, quia tantum assimilatur uni sicut alteri. Nec causalitas facit ad intentionem unius et non alterius, quia a nullo causatur sed a solo Deo immediate. —Respondeo: quaelibet intentio creaturae causata a Deo potest a creatura causari partialiter [perhaps emend to *naturaliter*] licet non causetur de facto. Et ideo per illam intentionem cognoscitur illud singulare a quo determinate causaretur si causaretur a creatura; huiusmodi autem est unum singulare et non aliud, igitur *etc.*"
38. Ockham says 'partially' because he holds that God is a necessary co-cause of any effect.

even if it weren't actually so caused. Hence a given singular is cognized through that cognition by which it would be determinately caused were it caused by a creature; this is a feature of one thing and not of another; therefore, *etc.*

A mental act that occurs as the result of an object's causal activity counts as an "impression" in Ockham's sense, so that Socrates's intuitive cognition of Felix, as an impression, is a (singular) thought *of* Felix—at least, so long as it "co-varies" with Felix: present in Felix's presence and absent in his absence. Ockham's view, then, is that the intuitive cognition of Felix is a thought of Felix for the precise reason that it is the thought that Felix naturally causes us to have.[39] This is externalism: what a given act of thinking is about depends solely on its cause, which is a matter of the external world rather than any "internal" mental feature.

Ockham's externalism led him to reject Scotus's sharp distinction between singular thought and *de re* thought. For Ockham, singular thought is necessarily *de re*. That is because what an act of thinking is about is a matter of what causes it, and, as we have just seen, the intuitive cognition of Felix is necessarily caused by Felix and not by anything else (barring divine interference). Put another way, the singular term "Felix" is a rigid designator in Mental Language.[40] Socrates cannot have an intuitive cognition of Felix that fails to latch on to Felix, by definition. Scotus's notion of singular thought, that grasps an individual without its identity, is for Ockham an abstractive rather than an intuitive cognition. The upshot is that Ockham gives pride of place to *de re* singular thought as the foundation of his new psychology of "habits," designed as the successor to the preceding psychological theories.

## CONCLUSION

With Ockham, we have come full circle from Aquinas: an ideal of psychological explanation by the interaction of subpersonal internal mental mechanisms, fundamentally a representationalist account of the mind, has given way to a radical externalist account that eschews mental processes as far as possible, fundamentally a direct realist account. The central issue in the evolution of the positions is singular thought—the apparently simple process of thinking about

---

39. The proviso "naturally" is important. As Ockham notes, God could supplant the ordinary causal chain. But what matters is what happens in the ordinary course of events, not what might occur due to miraculous intervention. Technically, then, Ockham endorses a counterfactual causal account of singular thought. But for most purposes we can put its counterfactual nature aside.

40. Hence, it permits quantification across opaque contexts: "Socrates thinks that Felix is on the mat" and "Socrates thinks of Felix that he is on the mat" are equivalent if "Felix" is a rigid designator, despite the fact that the former is *de dicto* and the latter *de re*. It is straightforward to apply this to belief contexts, though Ockham, unlike Buridan, seems not to have done so.

things. Not that the evolution was uniform and unidirectional, any more here than in the case of natural history: defenders of the neo-Aristotelian synthesis continued to push their agenda cheek-by-jowl with Scotists defending a hybrid account and Ockhamists trying to change the basic terms of the debate, each group playing up the advantages of its position while downplaying the others. Yet, the issue of singular thought is the key to understanding the conceptual heart of the debates in mediaeval philosophy of psychology, and by concentrating on it the main lines of the debates stand out clearly from what otherwise appears to be a disorderly welter of texts.

# Singular Terms and Vague Concepts in Late Medieval Mental Language Theory
## Or, the Decline and Fall of Mental Language

HENRIK LAGERLUND

William Ockham and John Buridan belong to the same late medieval philosophical tradition. What primarily unites this tradition is a shared metaphysical stance, which can be traced at least up to Thomas Hobbes, and which through Hobbes had a profound influence on British philosophy and also on Leibniz. The most salient feature of this tradition's metaphysics is, of course, the rejection of universals in extramental reality. According to both Ockham and Buridan, universals exist only in language. All things existing in extramental reality are singular.

By saying that they think universals exist only in language, I mean that they think universals are primarily mental concepts in a mental language. Universal or common terms in a written or spoken language, in turn, derive their signification from these mental concepts. Even though they agree about this, Ockham and Buridan fundamentally disagree about how to treat singular concepts in the mental language. Since they agree that everything existing is individual or singular, it is quite surprising that they disagree about singular concepts. The reason for this is that they have different views about how the basic significative constituents of the mental language are acquired.

Ockham argues that the first concepts acquired are simple and singular, primarily since they are caused through the simple act of cognition of a singular object. Buridan, on the other hand, argues that the first concepts acquired are singular, but complex, since they are caused by a species or similitude in the soul. Buridan calls these concepts vague singulars, since they might signify different things in different circumstances.

As will hopefully become clear in the course of this article, this difference between Ockham and Buridan has a profound effect on the theory of mental language as it is further developed by their followers in the fourteenth and fifteenth centuries. In struggling to hold on to some of Ockham's basic ideas and to incorporate Buridan's view on singular concepts, these followers radically change the theory into one that no longer takes a mental language hypothesis as its basis, but that it seems to me instead bears many similarities to the theory of thought defended by René Descartes in his *Meditations on First Philosophy*.

In this essay, I start by outlining the difference between Ockham and Buridan on singular concepts, and I then discuss the development of Buridan's ideas in Nicholas Oresme (d. 1382), Marsilius of Inghen (d. 1396), Peter of Ailly (d. 1420) and Gabriel Biel (d. 1495). I conclude by spelling out the consequences of this discussion as I see them.

### OCKHAM AND BURIDAN ON SINGULAR TERMS

Ockham's most extensive discussion of cognition is in the Prologue to the *Ordinatio*,[1] but he also deals with it in several other places of his works. He begins the section on cognition in the *Ordinatio* by drawing a distinction between acts of apprehension and acts of judgment. Acts of apprehension are divided into simple and complex, while acts of judgment are always complex. Acts of apprehension can be either sensitive or intellective, while acts of judgment are also always intellective. The acts of apprehension are further divided into intuitive and abstractive acts.[2]

According to Ockham, there are two souls in each human, and hence there are two distinct levels of apprehension, namely the sensitive and the intellective.[3] As a consequence, there are two kinds of intuitive and two kinds of abstractive acts of cognition. The object of perception acts by efficient causation on the senses to produce an intuitive cognition in the sensitive soul,[4] and then that intuitive cognition in turn acts by efficient causation on the intellective soul and causes an intuitive cognition in the intellect.[5] These two intuitive cognitions are of the very same thing, namely, the individual object acting on the senses.

---

1. See William Ockham, *Ord.*, ed. P. Boehner et al. (St. Bonaventure, N.Y.: Franciscan Institute, 1967–1988), prol. 1.1, OTh I, 16–47.

2. Ockham's account of intuitive and abstractive cognition is very much in dispute. See Elenore Stump, "The Mechanisms of Cognition: Ockham on Mediating Species" (168–203), and Elizabeth Karger, "Ockham's Misunderstood Theory of Intuitive and Abstractive Cognition" (204–226), both in *The Cambridge Companion to Ockham*, ed. P. V. Spade (Cambridge: Cambridge University Press, 1999), for two other different accounts of Ockham's theory. See also Kathrine Tachau, *Vision and Certitude in the Age of Ockham* (Leiden: Brill, 1988), 123–129, and Claude Panaccio, *Ockham on Concepts* (Aldershot: Ashgate, 2004), 5–8. I have presented my own view of it in Henrik Lagerlund, "What Is Singular Thought? Ockham and Buridan on Singular Terms in the Language of Thought," in *Mind and Modality: Studies in the History of Philosophy in Honor of Simo Knuuttila*, ed. V. Hirvonen, T. Holopainen, and M. Touminen (Leiden: Brill, 2006), 217–237.

3. See Henrik Lagerlund, "John Buridan and the Problem of Dualism in the Early Fourteenth Century," *Journal of the History of Philosophy* 42 (2004): 369–387, for a discussion of Ockham's theory of the nature of the soul.

4. See William Ockham, *Rep.*, ed. P. Boehner et al. (St. Bonaventure, NY: The Franciscan Institute, 1967–1988), II, q. 13, OTh V, 276.

5. See ibid., III, q. 2, OTh VI, 65.

There is no need for any intermediary here, argues Ockham. The object itself is sufficient to cause at a distance the act of apprehension. "I say that a thing itself is seen or apprehended immediately, without any intermediary between itself and the act."[6] It need not be the case that a mover and what is moved are in contact with each other, but "something can act at a great distance, with nothing acting in between."[7]

The end products of both intuitive and abstractive cognitions are concepts, or mental terms. Concepts caused by an intuitive cognition will be singular concepts and concepts caused by an abstractive cognition will be general or common concepts, argues the later Ockham.[8] Any concept caused by an intuitive cognition will be proper to the object causing it, that is to say, no other object can cause it (leaving God aside).[9] Thus, this means that my thinking about the book on the table is having the concept in mind that was caused by the book on the table. The concept is then a sign of the book. These two singular things, that is, the book on my table in the external world and the concept or sign of the book in my mind, stand in a unique causal relation to each other.

There has been considerable disagreement in the secondary literature about whether Ockham on his later view of cognition uses the notion of similarity to account for or explain the relationship between the object and the cognition of the object.[10] Ockham seems to want to eliminate similitude or at least appeal to a minimal notion of similitude. One reason for this is that a similitude or likeness is a general property that will not uniquely link a cognition to a specific object. Ockham himself brings up this problem in relation to the species theory. In the passages in the *Reportatio* that include his rejection of the species theory, he lists some arguments for the species theory and against his own theory. For example, he writes that:

---

6. See William Ockham, *Ord.*, ed. P. Boehner et al. (St. Bonaventure, N.Y.: Franciscan Institute, 1967–1988), I. d. 27, q. 3, OTh IV, 241, and *Rep.*, III, q. 3 OTh VI, 121.

7. "aliquid potest agere in extremum distans, nihil agendo in medio." (ibid., III, q. 2, OTh VI, 60).

8. See William Ockham, *Quodlibet*, ed. P. Boehner et al. (St. Bonaventure, N.Y.: Franciscan Institute, 1967–1988), I, q. 13, OTh IX, 74. For a discussion of the views of the earlier Ockham see Claude Panaccio, *Ockham on Concepts* (Aldershot: Ashgate, 2004), chap. 2.

9. See Lagerlund, "What Is Singular Thought?" for a detailed argument.

10. Claude Panaccio has argued that one must take very seriously the passages where Ockham uses the terminology of concepts as similitudes. He gives a detailed account of how he thinks this should be spelled out in *Ockham on Concepts*, chap. 7. The example Panaccio uses is that of a hand gripping a ball. When the ball is taken away, the hand still has the outer shape of a ball. This is the kind of similitude Panaccio thinks Ockham appeals to in order to account for how a concept is about an object. I have contributed my own view in "What Is Singular Thought?" It is very close to the accounts given in Peter King, "Rethinking Representation in the Middle Ages: A Vade-Mecum to Medieval Theories of Mental Representation," in *Representation and Objects of Thought in Medieval Philosophy*, ed. Henrik Lagerlund (Aldershot: Ashgate, 2007), 81–100, and Calvin G. Normore, "The Invention of Singular Thought," in *Forming the Mind*, ed. Henrik Lagerlund (Dordrecht: Springer, 2007), 109–128.

it is proved that a singular is not understood by an intuitive or an abstractive [cognition], because when some [of the things understood] are similar, then whatever is similar to one is [similar to] the other; for example, if many whitenesses of the same degree are received, then whatever is a similitude of one is [a similitude of] another. But the intellect is a similitude of the object, and by this it understands through that assimilation with the object.[11]

Later on in the same question he answers that:

to this I say that it concludes as much against positing species either in the intellect or in the *phantasia* as it does against me ... because by this [similitude] the intellect is not assimilated more to one of the similar singulars than to another. ... And therefore a similitude is not the precise cause whereby one thing is understood and not another.[12]

The argument against Ockham's view given above is that he cannot properly account for how we grasp singulars since there is nothing on his view to explain why an act of cognition is similar to some particular whiteness. On the species view of cognition, there is something that explains this, namely, the species itself, which is a likeness of the object. In his reply, Ockham does not directly address the problem at hand, but instead notes that the objection can also be seen as an objection against the species theory of cognition, since a similarity gives us no account of the singularity of the cognition of the whitenesses cognized. It might give us an account of the similarity between the whitenesses, but it only does this by not distinguishing between the different whitenesses.

Turning now to Buridan, he seems, on the contrary, to accept the very theory of cognition that Ockham rejects and hence must face the problem Ockham points to, which he also explicitly does. Despite its problems, the theory of species in the medium at least gives Buridan a scientific account of how an object can cause a representation of itself in us without involving the mysterious notion of action at a distance. On this theory, sense information from the external senses is compiled in the soul into a representation or likeness of the external world. In question 15 of Book III of the third redaction of the *De anima* commentary, he explains:

11. "Item, quod singulare non intelligitur intuitive nec abstractive probatur, quia quando aliqua sunt similia, quidquid est similitudo unius et alterius. Exemplum: si accipiantur multae albedines in eodem gradu, quidquid est simile uni et alteri. Sed intellectio est similitudo obiecti, et per hoc intellectus intelligit per quod assimilatur obiecto." Ockham, *Rep.*, II, q. 13, OTh V, 281–282.

12. "Ad aliud dico quod illud concludit aequaliter contra ponentes speciem sive in intellectu sive in phantasia sicut contra me ... quia per illam non magis assimilatur intellectus uni singulari simillimo quam alteri. ... Et ideo similitudo non est causa praecisa quare intelligit unum et aliud." Ibid., OTh V, 287.

It was stated in Book II that actual sensations are received subjectively in the soul as well as in the body, and derived from the potentiality of both. It seems to me that the intellect is sufficiently actual by the actual cognition or apprehension, so that with it, it can form an actual intellection in itself that is not already received in the body (as derived from its potentiality), but in the intellect alone. It is, therefore, apparent that the phantasm, that is, the actual apprehension, is related to the intellection in the same way that the species caused by an object in the organ of sense was said to be related to the sensation.[13]

As is obvious from this quotation, there is a double aspect of the phantasm, according to Buridan, and hence one side of sensation corresponds to changes in the internal bodily organ while another side corresponds to the subjective reception of sensation in the intellective soul.[14] The representation in the soul can be said to be both confused and confusing. It is confused because it is put together from so much diverse information. He says that substance is confused with accidents, that is to say, the information about substance and its accidents is put together or fused into one phantasm or image representing the thing(s) perceived. This was a rather common idea already before Buridan, particularly among thinkers relying on a species-theory of perception. Scotus expresses it in his *Metaphysics* (VII, q. 15) in the following way:

In the fantasy the substance is confused with accidents, or there are simply many accidents that are interconnected with one another. The intellect in understanding the universal abstracts each of them [one at a time], so that it might eventually understand the singular, namely the nature which is [in fact] "this" but not *qua* "this."[15]

This confused representation is also confusing, since it is difficult to tell exactly what is perceived; in order to tell what we are perceiving, according to Buridan, we need to focus in on or attend to the specific things represented. Attending to some individual thing represented is called putting the thing in prospect (*in*

---

13. "Cum enim dictum fuit in secundo libro quod actuales sensationes recipiuntur subiective tam in anima quam in corpore, et de utriusque potentia educuntur, videtur mihi quod per illam actualem cognitionem seu apprehensionem, intellectus sit sufficienter in actu, ut ipse cum illa posset actualem intellectionem formare in se quae iam non recipiatur in corpore (tanquam educta de eius potentia), sed in intellectu solum. Unde sic apparet quod illud phantasma, id est illa actualis apprehensio, se habet proportionaliter ad intellectionem sicut species causata ab obiecto in organo sensus dicebatur se habere ad sensationem." John Buridan, *Questions on Aristotle's De anima, III*, in Jack Zupko, "John Buridan's Philosophy of Mind" (Ph.D. diss., Cornell University, 1989), q. 15, 168–169.

14. Buridan assumes a strong dualism between body and soul. See Lagerlund, "John Buridan and the Problem of Dualism" and "What Is Singular Thought?" for an explication of this dualism. See also Jack Zupko, *John Buridan: Portrait of a Fourteenth-Century Arts Master* (Notre Dame, Ind.: Notre Dame University Press, 2003), chap. 11.

15. John Duns Scotus, *Questions on the Metaphysics of Aristotle*, 2 vols., trans. G. Etzkorn and A. Wolter (St. Bonaventure, N.Y.: Franciscan Institute, 1997–8), VII, q. 15.

*prospectu*) or in view. In his commentary on Aristotle's *Metaphysics*, Buridan notes that the same thing is called intuitive cognition by others.[16]

It is important to note that, in the preceding quote from Scotus, it is taken for granted that what is first understood or grasped by the intellect is a universal, and that a singular can be grasped only after the confused representation is sorted out. Since the representation in the soul is a likeness or similitude, it is natural to think that we first grasp the universal or general aspects presented to us, but Buridan wants to have it the other way around. The question facing him is this: How come the generality of a likeness pointed out by Ockham does not exclude singular cognition? Buridan is well aware of this difficulty.[17] To explain this he writes in his *De anima* that:

> To resolve these doubts, we need to see from *Metaphysics* VII in what way a thing is perceived singularly, namely, because it is necessary to perceive it in the way something exists in the prospect (*in prospectu*) of the cognizer.... Therefore, because exterior [sense] cognizes a sensible in the way something exists in its prospect in accordance with a certain location, even if sometimes it judges falsely about the place due to the reflection of the species, it cognizes it singularly or as something designated [*consignate*], namely, as this or that. Therefore, even though exterior sense cognizes Socrates, or whiteness, or white, nevertheless this is not done without the species representing it confusedly together with the substance, the whiteness, the magnitude, and the location, in accordance with what appears in the prospect of the cognizer. And this sense cannot sort out this confusion, namely, it cannot abstract the species of the substance, the whiteness, the magnitude, and the location from each other; therefore, it cannot perceive the whiteness, or the substance, or the white unless in the way something exists in its prospect. Therefore, it can only cognize the aforesaid things singularly.[18]

---

16. "Et sic finaliter videtur mihi esse dicendum quod nullus est conceptus singularis nisi sit conceptus rei per modum existentis in praesentia et in prospectu cognoscentis, tanquam illa res appareat cognoscenti sicut demonstratione signata. Et istum modum cognoscendi vocant aliqui intuitivum." John Buridan, *Quaestiones in Metaphysicen Aristotelis* (Paris, 1518), VII.20, f. 54va.

17. Buridan actually formulates the question himself. He writes: "Secunda dubitatio est cum sensus etiam cognoscat res per suas similitudines, quare non cognoscit eas universaliter?" Buridan in Zupko, "John Buridan's Philosophy of Mind," q. 8, 75.

18. "Ad solvendum illas dubitationes, debemus ex septimo Metaphysicae videre modum percipiendi rem singulariter: scilicet quia oportet eam percipere per modum existentis in prospectu cognoscentis.... Sensus ergo exterior quia cognoscit sensibile per modum existentis in prospectu suo secundum certum situm, licet aliquando false iudicat de situ propter reflexiones speciorum, ideo cognoscit ipsum singulariter vel consignate, scilicet quod hoc vel illud. Quamvis ergo sensus exterior cognoscat Sortem vel albedinem vel album, tamen hoc non est nisi secundum speciem confuse repraesentatem cum substantia et albedine et magnitudine et situ secundum quem apparet in prospectu cognoscentis. Et ille sensus non potest distinguere illam confusionem: scilicet non potest abstrahere species substantiae et albedinis

By putting things perceived in prospect or in view, we cognize them as this or that. This is a singular cognition, but it is one quite different from the singular cognition Ockham argues for, since for him all singular (intuitive) cognitions are simple.[19] To explain this further, Buridan expands on what these singulars first cognized are like. He writes,

> there are two kinds of sensible singular [terms], as has been noted: one, which is usually called vague, as "this man" and "this man approaching," which must be called singular absolutely and strictly (nevertheless, it is only called vague conventionally, because a similar utterance fits several things depending upon the different ways of picking it out), and another, which is usually called determinate, such as "Socrates" or "Plato," in accordance with which [something is] described by a collection of properties determined to one referent in such a way that, as a matter of fact, such a collection is not received in another determinate referent, as Porphyry correctly states.[20]

In this passage, Buridan distinguishes between vague and determinate singular terms and the corresponding concepts.[21] A concept is first of all acquired by putting something in prospect (*in prospectu*),[22] and such a concept is called a vague concept because it fits several things depending on what is perceived at that particular time or what is in our view or prospect; thus, "that human" may signify both Socrates and Plato—though at different times. A determinate con-

---

et magnitudinis et situs ab invicem, ideo non potest percipere albedinem vel substantiam vel album nisi per modum existentis in prospectu eius. Ideo non potest cognoscere praedicta nisi singulariter." Ibid., 76.

19. In *Summa logicae* I, 19, Ockham distinguishes three kinds of singular terms, namely, proper names, demonstrative pronouns, and a common noun taken together with a demonstrative pronoun like "this human." This last category looks like Buridan's vague singular, but this is not the case since, as Pannacio explains (*Ockham on Concepts*, 14–15) this kind of singular is for Ockham a mixed cognition, that is, a cognition combined by an intuitive cognition and an abstractive cognition. For Buridan a vague singular corresponds to one singular cognition.

20. "Et hoc provenit ex parte sensus, quoniam duplex ponitur singulare sensibile, ut tactum fuit: unum quod solet vocari vagum, ut 'hic homo' vel 'hic veniens', quod vocari debet singulare simpliciter et propria (solum tamen, vocatur ad placitum vagum, quia similis vox convenit pluribus secundum diversas demonstrationes), aliud quod solet vocari determinatum, ut 'Sortes' vel 'Plato', secundum quod describitur per collectionem proprietatum determinatum sic ad unum suppositum, quod defacto non recipitur talis in alio supposito determinato, ut bene dicit Porphyrius." Buridan in Zupko, "John Buridan's Philosophy of Mind," 76.

21. See Jenny Ashworth, "Singular Terms and Singular Concepts: From Buridan to the Early Sixteenth Century," in *John Buridan and Beyond*, ed. R. Friedman and S. Ebbesen (Viborg: Royal Danish Academy of Science and Letters, 2004), 121–152, for a discussion of Buridan's theory of singular terms, and see Jenny Ashworth, "Medieval Theories of Singular Terms," in *The Stanford Encyclopedia of Philosophy* (Winter Edition), ed. Edward N. Zalta, http://plato.stanford.edu/archives/win2003/entries/singular-terms-medieval, for a general overview of medieval theories of singular terms including Buridan's theory.

22. For the arguments, see Lagerlund, "What Is Singular Thought?"

cept, on the other hand, is uniquely determining; thus, the concept from which the term "Socrates" is taken signifies Socrates and nothing else, and it does this because a collection of properties uniquely picks him out—these properties do not fit anything else.[23]

In the *Physics* commentary, Book I, q. 4, Buridan writes:

> [I] have initially a confused concept that represents substance and accident together, because when I perceive something white I do not simply see whiteness, but a white thing and later I perceive the same thing moving and changing from white to black. I judge this to be something else than whiteness and the understanding then has the power to sort out this confusion.[24]

Again, in the *De anima* commentary, he writes:

> It must be said that we understand singularly before we understand universally, because a representation confused with size, place and other things is produced in the intellect before the intellect can sort out, and abstract from, this confusion.[25]

In the *Physics* commentary, by confused concept he seems to mean what is expressed in the quote from the *De anima* commentary, namely, some concept representing many properties together. Further, he says, the concept must also be singular, since these properties pick out unique individuals. Abstraction, that is, the process of moving from universal to singular concepts, is a matter of getting rid of these properties—sorting out the confusion and then arriving at universal concepts.

To explain how the process he is here advocating works, he uses an example that, after him, became a standard example used to explain singular cognition. In the example, which originated with Avicenna, Socrates approaches me from afar. At first I cannot tell exactly what I see approaching; something (a substance) is coming closer and closer to me. After a while, I see that it is an animal of some sort, but I cannot tell exactly what kind of animal it is. As it comes closer, I realize that it is a human being, and, finally, when he is close enough, I recognize

---

23. For an explication of what this means, see ibid.
24. "Tertio modo abstractive ut quia habeo primo conceptum confuse et simul representantem substantiam et accidens, ut cum percipio album non enim solam albedinem video, sed album et tamen postea percipio idem moveri et mutari de albo in nigtum. Iudico hoc esse aliud ab albedine et tunc intellectus naturaliter habet virtutem dividendi illam confusionem et intelligendi substantiam abstractive ab accidentem et accidens abstractive a substantia, et potest utriusque formare simplicem conceptum et sic etiam abstrahendo fit conceptus universalis ex conceptu singulari sicut debet videri tertio de anima et septimo metaphisice." John Buridan, *Subtilissimae Quaestiones super octo Physicorum libros Aristotelis* (Paris 1509), I, q. 4, Vrb-va.
25. "Ex illis dictis, apparet manifeste quod sit respondendum ad quaestionem, dicendum est enim quod prius intelligimus singulariter quam universaliter, quia prius fit in intellectu representatio confusa cum magnitudine et situ et aliis, quam intellectus posset distinguere et abstrahere illam confusionem." Buridan in Zupko, "John Buridan's Philosophy of Mind," q. 8.

Socrates. Although this example seems to have had a long tradition, nowhere else did it play as important a role as it does for Buridan and some of his followers. Cognition, it shows, is always in the first instance about "that thing," "that animal," "that human being," and finally about "Socrates." Hence, it is always about a singular thing in the first instance. The example can be found in John Buridan, Nicholas Oresme, Marsilius of Inghen, Peter of Ailly, Gabriel Biel, and later authors, and all these authors used it in virtually the same way. The example can thus be said to reform the theory of thought developed by Ockham.

### NICHOLAS ORESME ON CONFUSED CONCEPTS

In q. 14 of Book III of his *De anima* commentary, Oresme discusses the question of whether we cognize universals before singulars. In his answer to the question, he writes:

> We make the following distinction. Some concept is universal with which some singular circumstance is not conceived, such as when the intellect conceives humans absolutely, not imagining quantity, figure, color, place or time, and so forth. Such a concept is said to be absolute, quidditative, [and] not connotative. And certain such [concepts] are more general than others, such as substance [is more general] than animal, animal than human, etc. Secondly, there is another concept that someone conceives with some singular circumstance, such as here and now. And sometimes it is in this way that a body seen from afar is conceived, by conceiving that it is this body situated here, while it is not yet known which color or figure it has, or if it is a human or a horse. In conformity with this such a concept is said to be singular, but it is in some ways also universal, since by the same concept one would conceive also another thing, if it were place there, and one would not perceive the difference at such a distance. And some such concepts are more common, when they are conceived with fewer circumstances, and others are more specific, when they are conceived with more circumstances, as when the thing is getting closer and it is seen moving, it is conceived that it is an animal, then that it is a human being, and at last, when nearly all circumstances are apprehended, it is perceived that it is Socrates. And then such a concept is, thirdly, said to be singular, since it is perceived that it is white, and of such a figure, and so on.[26]

26. "Quantum ad primum est distinctio quod quidam est conceptus universalis quo non concipitur aliqua singularis circumstantia, sicut quando intellectus concipit hominem absolute, non imaginando quantitatem nec figuram nec colorem nec tempus, et sic de aliis: et talis conceptus dicitur absolutus quidditativus non connotativus. Et quidam talium sunt communiores aliis, sicut substantia quam animal, animal quam homo, etc.
Secundo est alius conceptus quo aliquid concipitur cum aliqua circumstantia singulari, sicut hic aut nunc. Et isto modo quandoque concipitur corpus visum a longe, concipiendo quod hoc est hoc corpus hic positum; et nescitur adhuc cuius coloris sit aut figurae, vel si est homo aut equus. Et secundum hoc talis conceptus dicitur singularis, et cum hoc etiam est quodam-

Before commenting on this, let us have a look at another passage from the same question, in which Oresme discusses the second type of concepts mentioned above, those which pertain to the example of something approaching from afar. There he writes,

> The second conclusion is that a concept in the second sense is . . . not simple, but connotative, as was said. And this is evident in the example: if a body is seen from afar, then it is conceived to be a body, and together with this that it is here and now. It can be said that the concept in a sense is confused. . . . The fourth conclusion is that every concept in the second sense is said to be universal in one sense and singular in another. It is singular in that it is conceived with some singular circumstance. It is universal in that such a concept would represent another thing, if it were entirely similar in all its sensible accidental qualities, as is the case with two eggs. Furthermore, if there is but a slight difference [between the two things], then the senses would not always notice it.[27]

On Oresme's view, there are, thus, three types of basic concepts. These concepts are:

1. Universal absolute/quidditative concepts
2. Singular "confused" concepts
3. Singular concepts

Concepts of the second type are, as he says, confused, since they involve different properties or circumstances. Such concepts are also complex or, as he says, using Ockhamistic terminology, connotative. (Note that Buridan's example of something approaching from afar also figures prominently in Oresme's discussion.) The concepts of the second type are also vague in the same sense as Buridan's

---

modo universalis, quia isto eodem conceptu conciperetur unum aliud, si poneretur, nec a tali distantia perciperetur differentia. Et talium conceptuum quidam sunt communiores, quando concipiuntur paucae circumstantiae, et alii specialiores, quando concipiuntur plures circumstantiae, sicut approximando et videndo motum concipitur quod est animal, deinde quod est homo, et tandem, apprehensis quasi omnibus circumstantiis, percipitur, quod est Socrates. Et tunc talis conceptus tertius dicitur singularis, quia iam percipitur quod est album et taliter figuratum, et sic de aliis." Nicholas Oresme, *Quaestiones in Aristotelis De anima*, ed. B. Patar (Louvain: Édition Peeters, 1995), III, q. 14.

27. "Secunda conclusio est quod conceptus secundo modo dictus est in intellectu et in sensu: patet, quia simul componitur ex specie quae est in intellectu et speciebus quae sunt in sensu. Nec est simplex, sed connotativus, ut dictum est. Et hoc patet in exemplo: si quis videat corpus de longe, concipit quod est corpus; et cum hoc quod est hic et nunc. Et licet iste conceptus sit aliqualiter confusus. . . . Quarta conclusio [est] quod omnis conceptus secundo modo dictus est aliqualiter universalis et aliqualiter singularis. Est singularis in eo quod concipitur aliqua circumstantia singularis. Est universalis in eo quod per talem conceptum repraesentaretur unum aliud, si esset omnino simile in omnibus accidentibus sensibilibus, sicut de duobus ovis. Et adhuc, si est parva dissimilitudo non sepmer sensus sciret eam cognoscere." Ibid., q. 14.

vague concepts are vague, namely, in that they are each about one particular thing although, in a sense, they apply to several things. It seems safe to assume that these concepts are the same type of concepts that Buridan calls vague. Consequently, Oresme's third type of concepts corresponds to those that Buridan calls determinative concepts.

An interesting aspect of Oresme's view is that as a concept becomes more determinate, or less vague, that is, as more circumstances are added to it, the concept gets more complex. It seems to me that a determinate concept, for example, "Socrates," must be something very complex, since it includes all the properties and all the circumstances together with which he was perceived as Socrates. It is this complexity that makes it a proper name picking out no one else but Socrates.[28]

### MARSILIUS OF INGHEN ON VAGUE CONCEPTS

The view developed by Buridan and expanded on by Oresme seems to become somewhat of a standard doctrine defended by many nominalists after them. I will here note some examples, beginning with Marsilius of Inghen in the late fourteenth century. In question 2 of the first book of his *Sentence* commentary, he writes:

> Among incomplex [acts of knowing (*notitia*)] some are singular and others are common. The singular ones are of two kinds, namely, vague, which follow upon a sensitive act of knowing, and determinate, which are the most difficult of the acts of knowing, since they are the most distinct. The latter are those to which individual [names] in the category of substance correspond, such as the concept to which the terms "Socrates" and "Plato" correspond. A common [act of knowing] is a simple apprehension of a thing that is common to several *supposita* in accordance with its mode of signification.[29]

Further down in the same passage, he writes, "among intellective acts of knowing, a vague singular is first, because this is how sense first represents [its object]."[30]

Marsilius is here talking about intellective acts of knowing or cognitions (*notitiae intellectivae*), that is to say, concepts. Singular simple concepts are

---

28. See Lagerlund, "What Is Singular Thought?" for a discussion of Buridan's view on the complexity of a singular concept.

29. "Incomplexarum aliqua est singularis et aliqua communis. Singularis est duplex, scilicet vaga, quae sequitur notitiam sensus, et determinata, quae difficillima est inter notitias incomplexas, quia distinctissima. Et est illa, cui correspondent individa praedicamenti substantiae sicut conceptus quibus correspondent hi termini 'Socrates' et 'Plato'. Communis est simplex apprehensio rei ex modo suae significationis communis multis suppositis." Marsilius of Inghen, *Quaestiones super quattuor libros sententiarum I–II*, ed. M. Santos Noya (Leiden: Brill, 2000), I, q. 2.

30. "Tertio, inter intellectivas vaga singularis est prima, quia ita primo repraesentat sensus." Ibid.

either vague or determinate, and the vague ones are primary in acquisition. Let us stop here for a moment, since there now emerges a very interesting problem. Buridan and Oresme never claimed that vague and determinate concepts were simple—on the contrary, Oresme explicitly claimed that they were complex. For someone like Ockham, on the other hand, it was obvious that the first concepts acquired through intuitive cognitions were simple, but this was not Buridan's view, as I have claimed.[31] How can Marsilius claim that his vague concepts are simple? Let us attempt to answer this by looking at how Peter of Ailly treats this topic.

### PETER OF AILLY ON VAGUE CONCEPTS

In his *De anima*, Peter of Ailly writes:

> There are two kinds of singular concepts. For some such concept is called a vague singular, such as "that human," "that animal" . . . another such concept is one that is called a determinate singular, such as "Socrates" and "Plato". . . . If Socrates is approaching from afar, I first cognize him to be an animal before [cognizing him to be] a human; and finally I cognize him to be Socrates, but I cognize him to be *this* animal singularly before [I cognize him to be] an animal universally.[32]

Further down he writes:

> Therefore, every universal has its [corresponding] vague singular, such as "body"/"this body," "animal"/"this animal," "human"/"this human." Now, when a sense cognizes singularly, by means of a vague singular and not a determinate singular, it has first a vague singular of a major universal than of a minor universal, namely, this body before this animal and this animal before this human; therefore, correspondingly, the intellect in its abstractive activity cognizes more universally at first.[33]

---

31. See Lagerlund, "What Is Singular Thought?"
32. "Circa quod tamen est advertendum, quod duplex est conceptus singularis; nam quidam est, qui vocatur singulare vagum, ut 'hic homo,' 'hoc animal,' et tale est proprie singulare, licet ad placitum vocetur vagum, quia vox ei correspondens convenit pluribus secundum diversas demonstrationes. Alius est conceptus singularis, qui vocatur singulare determinatum, ut 'Socrates,' 'Plato' et huiusmodi, et quantum ad tale singulare videtur, quod non oportet prius intelligere singulariter quam universaliter, sed bene quantum ad singulare vagum. Nam, si Socrates a longe veniat, prius cognosco ipsum esse animal quam hominem et ultimo cognosco ipsum esse Socratem, sed prius cognosco ipsum esse hoc animal singulariter quam animal universaliter." Peter of Ailly, *Tractatus de anima*, in *Die philosophische Psychologie des Peters von Ailly*, ed. Olaf Puta (Amsterdam: Verlag B. R. Grüner, 1987), c. 12, secunda pars.
33. "Unde quodlibet universale habet suum singulare vagum, ut 'corpus' 'hoc corpus,' 'animal' 'hoc animal,' homo' 'hic homo'; modo sensus cognoscens singulariter singulari vago et non singulari determinato prius habet singulare vagum magis universalis quam minus universalis, scilicet huius corporis quam huius animalis et huius animalis quam huius hominis; ideo intellectus abstrahendo correspondenter prius cognoscit magis universaliter." Ibid.

As is obvious from these quotes, Peter is working with the same distinctions and the same theory that seems to be common among Buridan and his followers. Peter's psychology is generally a mix or unification of Ockham's and Buridan's theories, and according to him vague concepts are first acquired through an intuitive cognition, or by putting something in prospect, which for him are the same things. In the *De anima*, he also notes that "an intuitive act of knowing (*notitia*) is a simple act of knowing."[34] The idea seems to be the same as the one Marsilius expressed, namely, that since concepts are acquired through simple acts of cognition, they must themselves be simple. But Peter does not stop at this; in the *Insolubilia* he famously claims that "No categorical mental sentence is essentially put together out of several partial acts of knowing, one of which is the subject, another the predicate and another the copula."[35] Not even mental sentences seem hence to be complex, according to him.[36]

This, I think, suggests that when Marsilius and Peter talk about these concepts as simple, they mean that they are simple metaphysically and not semantically. They are obviously not simple semantically, since under this theory neither vague concepts ("that cup") nor Peter's mental sentences ("that cup is on the table") are simple. However, they might still be simple metaphysical entities or simple qualities of the intellective soul; hence, a simple act, an intuitive cognition, may produce a simple concept, even though the content of such a concept is not simple. The richness of the content of an act of cognition derives from the richness of the representation in the soul causing the concept, which in turn is derived from the richness of the world of which the representation is a likeness. In other words, something metaphysically simple in the soul might have a semantically complex content. It is only in light of such a distinction that Marsilius's and Peter's discussions make any sense.[37]

The distinction I just drew may also be used to answer the question: What individuates mental terms in the mental language? There are two likely candidates, I think: they are individuated either by their syntax or by their content,

---

34. See Henrik Lagerlund, "Representations, Concepts and Words: Peter of Ailly on Semantics and Psychology," *Proceedings of the Society for Medieval Logic and Metaphysics* 3 (2003) for a discussion of Peter's theory of cognition.

35. "Secunda conclusio: nulla propositio mentalis cathegorica est essentialiter composita ex pluribus partialibus noticiis, quarum una sit subiectum et alia predicatum et alia copula." Peter of Ailly, *Conceptus et insolubilia* (Paris, 1500), fol. Biv$^b$.

36. See Lagerlund, "Representations, Concepts and Words," for a detailed discussion about this.

37. Many commentators have noted that some kind of distinction must be drawn between metaphysical and semantical simplicity. See, for example, Klima's introduction to John Buridan, *Summulae de Dialectica*, trans. G. Klima (New Haven: Yale University Press, 2002), xxxvii–xli, and Lagerlund, "Representations, Concepts and Words." See also Panaccio, *Ockham on Concepts*, 32, as well as the detailed discussion about connotative concepts in later chapters for Ockham's use of a somewhat similar distinction.

that is, by their semantics. It seems immediately clear that Peter and Marsilius rule out the first candidate. This is exactly the view they seem to be opposing. Mental sentences are simple unstructured acts that do not have syntax, and hence they can only be individuated by their content. This means that the picture Peter and Marsilius are painting for us is a picture where there are metaphysically simple mental terms with different contents, and where it is their content that makes mental terms either simple or complex.

I think an interesting analogy arises here between Peter's use of concepts and Descartes' use of ideas. In the Third Meditation, Descartes writes:

> In so far as ideas are considered simply as modes of thought, there is no recognizable inequality among them: they all appear to come from within me in the same fashion. But in so far as different ideas are considered as images which represent different things, it is clear that they differ widely.[38]

As this quote shows, an idea has two sides to it, which correspond to what I have called the metaphysical and the semantical in Peter's case—the act and the content or, to use Descartes's terminology, the mode and the image—and the mode is said to have formal being while the image has objective being (*esse obiectivum*).

However, the view that Peter flirts with and that Descartes defends leaves room for some serious doubts concerning the mental language itself, since on this view it becomes unclear in what sense the mental language is really a language at all. Before returning to this problem in the conclusion, I will outline Gabriel Biel's view on these issues.

### GABRIEL BIEL ON VAGUE CONCEPTS

In his *Sentence* commentary, Book I, dist. 3, q. 5–7, Biel discusses whether universal or singular cognition is primary. The most important question in this distinction for my purpose here is the sixth, in which he asks whether the first intellective cognition is an intuitive cognition of something singular, but before answering that question he explains the context of this discussion of universals in question five. He begins by saying that one must make a sharp distinction between universals in the world and universals in the mind. The question he is here discussing is not whether there are universals in the external world, since he takes it for granted that all things existing in reality (*in re*) are singular. Thus, the question at issue here concerns only universals in the mind (*in mente*). These universals have only objective being (*esse obiectivum*), and are only universal in representation (*in repraesentando*), not in essence (*in essendo*). Every genuine *thing* that we cognize is a singular; even the mental acts in the

---

38. René Descartes, *The Philosophical Writings of Descartes*, ed. J. Cottingham, R. Stoothoff, and D. Murdoch (Cambridge: Cambridge University Press, 1984), 2:27–28.

mind that we cognize in a reflexive act are singular.[39] The distinction between the metaphysical and semantical aspects of an act of thought mentioned earlier is thus taken for granted by Biel as something in light of which the question of universal cognition must be discussed.

Having covered this issue, Biel goes on in question six to explain how singular cognition works. His discussion in this question is divided into a discussion of the operations of the senses and the intellect. I will here only briefly note the division of sensory cognition he outlines. The reason one must start with an explanation of sensory cognition, he says, is that all cognition begins in the senses.[40] The first kind of cognition outlined is a cognition that is immediately caused by an external object. It is an intuitive cognition because it cognizes a thing to be or to exist. It is also a singular cognition.[41] The second cognition is of the same object; it represents the object in the same way as the first cognition, but it also includes a cognition that something is cognized or seen. This cognition includes a judgment about the first cognition. Biel remarks: "by the first, exterior vision, I do not cognize that I see, because sometimes one sees something without realizing that one sees it." The second cognition is also an intuitive cognition, since I evidently cognize myself as seeing something.[42]

39. "Quod etiam quaestio investigat, an primum cognitum sit singulare, dumtaxat locum habet secundum opinionem tenentem universalem conceptum esse obiectum cognitionis universalis et habere in mente tantum esse obiectivum, quia secundum oppositam opinionem tenentem quod talia ficta non sunt ponenda quodque universale nihil sit nisi cognitio universalis aut signum sibi subordinatum, quod est res quaedam singularis, licet universaliter repraesentet, et ideo dicatur universalis non in essendo, sed repraesentando, nulla est quaestio. Cum enim omne cognoscibile sit singulare, certum est quod primum cognitum et medium et ultimum est singulare, eo quod quidquid cognoscitur, est singulare. Nec habet quaestio dubium, si fieret comparatio obiecti cogniti ad cognitionem, quia, cum cognitio quae est actus cognoscentis, non cognoscitur nisi per actum reflexum, certum est quod prius actu recto cognoscitur obiectum singulare quam ipse actus rectus actu reflexo, ad minus prius natura." Gabriel Biel, *Collectorium circa quattuor libros sententiarum*, ed. W. Werbeck and U. Hofmann (Tübingen: J. C. B. Mohr/Paul Siebeck, 1973–84), I, dist. 3, q. 5, 226.

40. "Pro articulo primo et pro clariori intellectu dicendorum est hic notandum breviter de ordinata cognitionum generatione, et primo de operatione sensitive cognitive, quod pro statu viae huius nostra cognitio incipit a sensu." Ibid., I, dist. 3, q. 6, art. 1, 231.

41. "Est ergo prima cognitio primitate generationis sensatio exterior, quae causatur immediate ab obiecto. Immediate dico, id est sine cognitione media, sive ponatur species media sive non. De quo in II q. 2 dist. 3. Haec notitia est intuitiva, quia ea cognosco rem sensatam esse, et dependet ab obiecto non solum in fieri, sed etiam in esse. Unde remoto obiecto, statim corrumpitur haec cognitio. Haec singulariter repraesentat obiectum, id est qualitates sensibiles tam proprias quam communes." Ibid.

42. "Secunda cognitio est cognitio eiusdem obiecti, quam elicit sensus communis, eodem modo repraesentans obiectum sicut cognitio prima et cum hoc ut sensatum vel visum etc. Nam sensus interior est qui iudicat de actibus sensuum exteriorum. Prima enim visione, scilicet exteriori, non cognosco me videre, quia nonnumquam aliquis videt nesciens se videre. Illa cognitio similiter est intuitiva, quoniam ea evidenter cognosco me sentire. Quae similiter cedente prima sensatione corrumpitur. Huius obiectum est res sensata et cum hoc sensatio exterior." Ibid.

The third and fourth kinds of cognitions outlined by Biel are both abstractive cognitions. The third kind of cognition is similar to the second, but it can occur without the exterior sensation; it distinctly cognizes a thing even when the thing is removed from the external senses.[43] The fourth kind of cognition is the cognition of memory (*cognitio memorativa*), cognizing the same thing as something perceived in the past.[44] Biel further notes that all these sensitive cognitions are simple, singular, and material, that is, they are cognitions in the body and in the sensitive soul.[45]

The intellect, he goes on to claim, is immaterial and is a superior power, yet its operations have their beginning in the senses. The first intellectual cognition is a cognition of a thing sensed. This cognition is caused or generated by an interior sensation. He calls this interior sensation a phantasm.[46] After considering how an inferior power can act on a superior one, Biel explains the nature of this first intellective cognition and what follows from it in the following way:

> Therefore from the first intuitive intellective notion [the intellect] abstracts a singular abstractive vague intellective notion in the same way as the senses. Thereafter it abstracts two notions, one singular and one common. For by having a vague singular signifying many circumstances of sensible perceptions and considering some of these to be variable and some others to remain the same, the intellect abstracts two concepts: one of that which changes, and another that represents precisely that which remains unchanged. All of these are singular. Abstraction does not end here, however, since it continues until it arrives at simple concepts that signify only one quality absolutely.

---

43. "Tertia notitia est synonyma secundae, manens remoto obiecto, etiam cessante sensatione exteriore, per quam cogito de re etiam absente. Si quidem experimur, quod videntes rem aliquam, ipsa amota ab oculis, adhuc manet in nobis notitia quaedam, quae repraesentat rem distincte et eodem modo, quo novi praesentem. Et haec non est aliqua duarum praecedentium, quia per illam non possumus evidenter scire aliquam veritatem contingentem de re cognita sicut per praecedentes; ergo distinguitur ab eis. Et ita non est intuitiva, sed abstractiva, quia abstrahit ab existentia rei hic et nunc, id est per eam non possumus evidenter scire de re, quam repraesentat, an sit vel non, an sit hic vel ibi. Est tamen notitia rei distincta." Ibid., 231–232.

44. "Quarta est cognitio memorativa, quae formatur per species vel habitus a prioribus cognitionibus decisas vel decisos in organo memoriae reservatos. Et illa cognitio memorativa cum obiecto importat tempus praeteritum, id est importat obiectum ut prius etiam cognitum. Haec notitia etiam abstractiva est sicut tertia et distincta vel rei in se, sed non intuitiva." Ibid., 232.

45. "Hae quattuor notitiae sensitivae sunt simplices. Quae regulariter producuntur de quolibet obiecto sensato, praesertim tres primae, quae sunt rei in se distinctae, singulares et materiales, inhaerentes organo sensus, quod est compositum ex corpore et anima sensitiva." Ibid., 232. Biel's use of the terms "intuitive" and "abstractive" cognition is very similar to Peter of Ailly's usage; compare Lagerlund, "Representations, Concepts and Words."

46. "Prima ergo cognitio intellectiva est cognitio singularis rei sensatae, synonyma sensationi interiori, quae interior vocatur phantasma. Dicitur autem intellectio prima a sensatione interiori, quia illa est penitus immaterialis, inhaerens tantum intellectui et non organo." Biel, *Collectorium circa quattuor libros sententiarum*, I, dist. 3, q. 6, art. 1, 232.

Considering several singulars that are more similar to one another than they are to others, [the intellect] abstracts a common concept that adequately represents these similar things. If their agreement is essential, then it can form absolute concepts, and if it is accidental, it forms connotative [concepts]. And, depending on whether these agreements are of more or fewer [individuals], it forms more or less common concepts.[47]

Biel's way of describing the intellective cognition of a singular is slightly different than what we have seen so far, but it is obvious that all the elements I have identified are present in his description. In the same way as in sense cognition, there is first an intuitive cognition in the intellect (which is here left undescribed), followed by what he calls a vague abstractive cognition. From this vague cognition the intellect arrives at determinate singular concepts and common concepts through a process of repeated abstractive cognitions. As with Oresme, it is clear that having a singular intellective cognition is something very complex (at least in semantic content).

Common concepts are formed through a process of comparison between the similar and dissimilar aspects of singular concepts. As Biel explains this process, the common concept thus formed will be absolute or connotative depending on whether the agreement between these singular concepts is essential or accidental. He does not give examples, but it is not difficult to see what he has in mind. "Human being" is at least for Ockham an absolute concept and to form such a concept we have to compare the singular concepts of humans we have and notice the essential agreement between these concepts, as, in this case, the rationality represented in the concepts. An example of a connotative concept is "father." Such a concept has according to Ockham a primary signification, which is the male animal that is a father, and a secondary signification, which is the child or children of the male animal. In Biel's terminology, we have to explain the psychological acquisition of such a concept with reference to animals that are male and have children. By comparing the singular concepts we have of such male animals, we notice of course that having children is an accidental trait of such creatures.

Biel develops a very interesting empiricist theory of concept acquisition, but it is important to note that the process I just described of the acquisition of

47. "A notitia ergo prima intellectiva intuitiva abstrahit intellectivam abstractivam singularem vagam sicut sensus. Deinde abstrahit duplicem notitiam, singularem et communem. Singularem, nam habita singulari vaga significante multas circumstantias sensu perceptibiles, considerans aliquas variari aliis manentibus, abstrahit duos conceptus: unum eius quod mutatur, alium repraesentantem praecise illud quod manet immutatum. Et omnes hi sunt singulares. Nec ab illa abstractione cessat, donec perveniat ad conceptus simplices significantes tantum unam qualitatem absolute. Item: Considerans plura singularia convenientia sibi similiora inter se in aliquibus quam cum aliis, abstrahit conceptum communem adequate repraesentantem huiusmodi convenientia. Et si fuerit convenientia essentialis, potest formare conceptum absolutum. Si accidentalis, format conceptum connotativum. Et secundum quod convenientiae sunt plurium vel paucorum, format conceptus magis vel minus communes." Ibid.

common concepts is not a process suitable for a theory of thought involving a mental language hypothesis. The description is much more suitable if concepts are taken to be images of some kind. But if one combines two images, one does not get a mental sentence, just another image. It seems clear that to allow for the kind of comparison needed for abstraction of common concepts, the singular concepts compared must have a very complex content similar to that of an image, or else they must contain a very large number of descriptions of the objects they are concepts of.[48]

It seems to me that what we are witnessing in Biel's outline of the acquisition of singular and common concepts is the complete breakdown of the mental language theory. Concepts are simple individual qualities or acts of the intellectual soul and as such they are all the same, but they can have very different representational contents, which in turn have only objective being. This content seems also, on Biel's account, to have the characteristics of an image and hence it represents its object as a likeness.

## CONCLUSION

In this essay, I have argued that Buridan can be viewed as developing his view of singular concepts in the mental language as a reply to a challenge posed by Ockham to any theory of cognition based on the reception of species. Buridan's view is quite distinctive and involves a distinction between vague and determinate singular concepts. His vague concepts are always primary in acquisition, but they are also complex in content and are best described by complex expressions like "this animal" or "this book." Although Buridan manages to save the idea central in Ockham's own theory of cognition, namely, that what is first cognized is always a singular, he introduces a very complicated notion into his theory of thought. The notion of vague singular concepts is both defended and developed by the thinkers following Buridan. I have presented excerpts from Nicholas Oresme, Marsilius of Inghen, Peter of Ailly, and Gabriel Biel.

An absolutely central part of Ockham's theory of mental language is that the basic constituents of the language are simple and that complex signs are generally constructed or composed out of simple ones. In order to defend Buridan's view of the acquisition of singular concepts while still trying to remain faithful to an atomistic view of concept formation, the followers of Buridan needed to introduce, either implicitly or explicitly, a distinction between concepts as metaphysical entities and the semantic content of these concepts. They can then talk about simple and singular concepts in two ways.

This distinction, however it seems to me, spells the end of the theory of mental language. Given these authors' acceptance of nominalism and the view that all things existing are singular, the thought they put forward that all concepts

---

48. See my presentation of Buridan's view of singular concepts in "What Is Singular Thought?" 233–236.

first acquired are also metaphysically simple acts or qualities of the mind implies that such concepts are indistinguishable. If mental acts all "look" the same, that is, if they are all simple metaphysical entities or qualities of the mind, while at the same time they have different complex contents, then the language of thought seems not to have a syntax, which destroys the notion of compositionality. The mental language is simply not a language anymore! A further problem introduced by the distinction is that thinkers who accept it must also draw a distinction between the priority of acquisition and the priority of signification, and this pulls apart the mental acts and their linguistic roles. This is another blow to the mental language.

As I argue here, the theory of thought that results from the theory introduced by Buridan can be found in Gabriel Biel. It is no longer a mental language theory. Instead, it is a theory, which bears striking similarities to the one defended by Descartes in the *Meditations on First Philosophy*. On this theory, concepts or ideas are simple acts or modes of the mind and the content of these acts or ideas are images or representations with objective being.

# Act, Species, and Appearance
*Peter Auriol on Intellectual Cognition and Consciousness*

RUSSELL L. FRIEDMAN

The study of consciousness is without question one of the hottest topics in contemporary philosophy of mind, cognitive psychology, and neuroscience. Among other issues currently being debated are: whether consciousness even exists; if it does exist, then can we explain it or characterize it; and if we can do that, then can we explain or characterize the relation between consciousness, on one hand, and, for example, cognition or intentionality, on the other, and further can we say which of these is a more primitive feature of human mental life. All of this contemporary activity in the study of consciousness has been to some extent reflected in historical studies looking for how the notion of consciousness—if not the actual term "consciousness," then at least the characteristics that today we tend to associate with that term—evolved in two and a half millennia of philosophical debate.[1] The present essay fits into that historical project. Here, in my attempt to find a historical figure who isolated something approaching what we denote by the word "consciousness," I am going to focus on aspects of the theory of cognition elaborated in the late 1310s by the French Franciscan Peter Auriol (d. 1322). In order to see why Auriol might be of special interest in the search for a medieval description of consciousness, one need only consider the process that Auriol claims is involved in our coming to understand something or in having intellectual cognition of something. Auriol says that you begin with a mental representation, which has some kind of real existence in the soul of, say, a human being; you add this mental

---

An earlier version of this paper was read at a conference on Intentionality in Medieval Thought held at the University of Parma. I want to thank the conference organizer, Fabrizio Amerini, as well as the following conference participants for their comments and questions: Richard Cross, Bernd Goehring, Peter King, Gyula Klima, Calvin Normore, Claude Panaccio, and Martin Pickavé. In what follows, all references to the "Electronic Scriptum" are to electronic texts found at www.peterauriol.net; references like "X 725b" are to pages in the Rome 1596 printing of Auriol's *Scriptum*. On the Rome 1605 edition of Auriol's II *Sent.*, see note 38.

1. For a nice sketch of some of the issues involved in the historical study of consciousness, see especially the introduction to Sara Heinämaa, Vili Lähteenmäki, and Pauliina Remes, eds., *Consciousness: From Perception to Reflection in the History of Philosophy* (Dordrecht: Springer, 2007).

representation to a cognitive power, in this case, an intellect; this intellect has an ability or characteristic that we would today call "consciousness" or "awareness," but that Auriol calls the ability to be *appeared* to. As soon as you add the mental representation to the intellect, an intentional production is initiated, and what is produced is the concept, the word of the mind (*verbum mentis*), and this is the real world object of intellection put into intentional being; Auriol characterizes this intentional being as "in itself nothing" (*nihil in se*). This is not the end of the process, however, since for Auriol what is significant about understanding (or sensing, or cognizing in general) is that it involves something *appearing* to a conscious knower, and so the last and all important step on the way to intellectual cognition is the intentional object, the extramental object of cognition in intentional being, *appearing* to the intellect of the conceiver through the very same intellectual act through which the intentional object was formed in the first place. That is the big picture. In what follows, by examining in some detail the mechanics of intellectual cognition according to Peter Auriol, I want to show that as much as anyone in the medieval period, and more than most, Auriol recognized and brought into his philosophy of mind the fact that cognitive states involve phenomenal experience, or, as Auriol himself puts it, the distinctive feature of the cognitive is the fact that something appears to whatever is said to be cognitive; all cognition involves the appearing of something to someone or something. To this extent, Auriol was developing, I want to suggest, a theory of cognition in which what we today would call "consciousness" played the central role, so much so that one can say that consciousness is a more primitive feature in Auriol's philosophy of mind than is either cognition or intentionality, the latter being explained by the former. Along the way, I will explore some of Auriol's views on mental representation, mental acts, and intelligible species.

First, let me clarify what I intend to argue by specifying what I am *not* intending to argue. I am not going to try to claim that Peter Auriol has a compelling or even a coherent theory of consciousness. Although, as I mention below, Auriol does make statements that can be considered attempts at minimal criteria for classifying something as conscious, he does not have or attempt to develop an elaborate theory of consciousness along the lines of contemporary philosophers, cognitive psychologists, and brain researchers. Nor am I going to try to claim that Auriol "invented" consciousness or that he was the first to think of it; in fact, I am inclined to believe that many of Auriol's contemporaries—for example, Aquinas, Scotus, and Ockham—would have agreed with Auriol concerning the fact that something's appearing to the cognizer is a necessary element in any cognition. Nevertheless, I also believe that Auriol's contemporaries would have thought that appearing and awareness weren't the really interesting part of the cognitive process, and I take as evidence for this claim the lack in their writings of detailed explicit statements concerning this aspect of the cognitive process. On the basis of what they *do* write about at great length, I would argue further that what did interest Auriol's contemporaries was the actual mechanics of cognition, that is to say, what has to take place in order for reality to appear to us (the nature of the sensory and intellectual faculties and their relations to each other; whether there are cognitive mediators, and if so what sorts; the ontology of concepts, and so on), but not the appearance itself. So, I imagine his contemporaries saying to Auriol: "Yes, yes, awareness and being appeared to, that's all well and good; now let's move on to the important stuff." And this leads me to my final preliminary point: as we will see, like his contemporaries, Auriol was also highly interested in the mechanics of cognition, but, in contrast to those contemporaries, he shifted the emphasis in his theory of cognition away from the mechanics aspect (how we come to have cognition) to the awareness or consciousness aspect. For Auriol, the most important part of cognition—indeed, its defining feature—is precisely the fact that $x$ appears to $y$, or, conversely, that $y$ is conscious or aware of $x$. It is this change of emphasis that I want to maintain is important and innovative about Peter Auriol's theory of cognition, not least because what Auriol emphasizes became in the early modern period a central aspect of cognitive theory, and it remains so to this day.[2]

With those preliminary remarks, I would like first to give a short description of Auriol's ideas on the ontology of concepts. Auriol's claim, today quite well known, is that "in every intellection there emanates and proceeds nothing other than the cognized thing itself in a certain objective existence insofar as (*secundum quod*) it serves to terminate the intellect's gaze (*intuitum*)."[3] Thus, for Auriol concepts *are* extramental particulars, but having a different type of existence—a different *modus essendi*—than the real existence they have extramentally. Auriol calls this special type of existence "intentional" or "objective"

---

2. The centrality of Auriol's theory of cognition to the medieval development of a theory of what we would call "consciousness" has already been suggested by Robert Pasnau in *The Cambridge Translations of Medieval Philosophical Texts*, vol. 3: *Mind and Knowledge* (Cambridge: Cambridge University Press, 2002), 219, and more extensively explored in Joël Biard, "Intention and Presence: The Notion of *Presentialitas* in the Fourteenth Century," in Heinämaa, Lähteenmäki, and Remes, *Consciousness*, esp. 129–136.

3. Auriol, *Scriptum*, d. 27, q. 2, a. 2: "in omni intellectione emanat et procedit, non aliquid aliud, sed ipsamet res cognita in quodam esse obiectivo, secundum quod habet terminare intuitum intellectus." Electronic Scriptum, ll. 365–66; X 622a. For a discussion of Auriol's ideas on concepts and their formation, along with references to further literature, see Russell L. Friedman, "Peter Auriol," *Stanford Encyclopedia of Philosophy* (Fall 2009 Edition), ed. Edward N. Zalta, http://plato.stanford.edu/archives/fall2009/entries/auriol, esp. §§3–4. On Auriol's theory of intentionality per se, see most recently Fabrizio Amerini, "Realism and Intentionality: Hervaeus Natalis, Peter Aureoli, and William Ockham in Discussion," in *Philosophical Debates at Paris in the Early Fourteenth Century*, ed. S. Brown, T. Dewender, and T. Kobusch (Leiden: Brill, 2009), 239–260.

existence, or, most famously, *esse apparens*, apparent being.[4] What characterizes this type of existence is that it is a particular extramental object, for example, Socrates, but indistinguishably mixed together with (*indistinguibiliter immiscetur*) passive conception, that is, the formation of a concept of Socrates. A concept of Socrates, then, *is* Socrates as conceived; it is Socrates as an object of the intellect.[5] Upon intellectual acquaintance, Socrates as really existing is converted through the act of conception, that is, by being conceived, into Socrates as intentionally existing. Thus, for Auriol, Socrates and a concept grasping Socrates are the same thing with differing modes of existence. Now, when Auriol claims that Socrates and a concept of Socrates are "the same," he means it in a very strict sense, even saying that "a thing and its intention do not differ numerically with respect to anything absolute"; they are numerically the same thing. What thing and concept differ by, says Auriol, is a respect or a relation; and this is no ordinary respect "fixed to or superimposed upon that thing, as are other relations, rather it is utterly intrinsic and indistinguishably joined to it." This intrinsic relation, Auriol tells us, is the appearing of the thing (*apparere*) as an object of cognition to a cognizer.[6] Hence, for Auriol, it is intrinsic to each and every thing to have two different modes of being: real or extramental being on the one hand, and intentional or objective being on the other. In contrast to its real being, the thing's intentional being needs a cognizer in order to actualize it, since in intentional being the thing is appearing to the conceiver. Through the act of conceiving, then, a thing is put into intentional being and appears to the conceiver. It should be noted that Auriol describes the *esse apparens* or the thing in intentional being as "nothing in itself" (*nihil in se*) and as diminished being (*esse deminutum*). Making more precise what he means by this, Auriol, basing himself upon Aristotle and Averroes, draws a distinction between, on

---

4. See, e.g., Auriol, *Scriptum*, d. 27, q. 2, a. 2: "Relinquitur ergo ut detur septimum, scilicet quod [conceptus] sint verae rosae particulares et flores, non quidem ut existunt exterius, sed ut intentionaliter et obiective, et secundum esse formatum concurrunt in unum quid simpliciter, quod est praesens in intellectu per speciem intelligibilem vel per actum." Electronic Scriptum, ll. 520–523; X 624b.

5. Auriol, *Scriptum*, d. 23: "obiectiva conceptio passive dicta non respicit rem per modum substrati, immo res quae concipitur est aliquid sui et immiscetur indistinguibiliter sibi. Unde conceptio rosae idem est quod rosa, et conceptus animalis idem quod animal. Iste nimirum conceptus claudit indistinguibiliter realitates omnium particularium animalium et quendam modum essendi, qui est intentionalis, qui non est aliud quam passiva conceptio." In Dominik Perler, "Peter Aureol vs. Hervaeus Natalis on Intentionality: A Text Edition with Introductory Remarks," *Archives d'histoire doctrinale et littéraire du Moyen Age* 61 (1994): 227–262, at 248, §22.

6. Auriol, *Scriptum*, d. 27, q. 2, a. 2: "considerandum est quod res in esse formato posita non claudit in se aliquid absolutum nisi ipsam realitatem. Unde non ponit in numerum res et sua intentio quantum ad aliquid absolutum, claudit tamen aliquid respectivum, videlicet apparere. Quod non debet intelligi ut affixum aut superpositum illi rei, sicut ceterae relationes, sed omnino intrinsicum et indistinguibiliter adunatum." Electronic Scriptum, ll. 584–588; X 625a–b.

the one hand, pure nothings, existing neither in themselves nor in the soul, and, on the other, the type of mental being that intentional being is, that is, a being that is nothing in itself but exists in the soul as the object of the intellect or of another cognitive power.[7]

With Auriol's view of the cognitive process in mind, we can focus our attention on the central feature for Auriol in all cognition: the fact that something *appears*. This feature is the source of the most famous name that he gives to intentional existence: *esse apparens*, apparent being. As mentioned earlier, I think that in the medieval discussion over mental representation and intentionality, Auriol perhaps laid the most stress of anyone on what we would today probably call "phenomenal consciousness." In what follows, I want to show just *how* Auriol draws consciousness or awareness into the heart of his explanations for cognition, intentionality, and mental representation. Indeed, as I will argue, consciousness seems to be the most primitive feature of mind and the mental for Auriol. Thus, what makes a mental representation *mental* in the relevant way is the fact that it is involved in some $x$ appearing to some $y$. For Auriol, if a representation existing in the mind is not involved in the occurrent appearance of something to a cognitive faculty, then it is *mental* only inasmuch as it exists in the mind, and in no more meaningful sense. The fact that appearing is going on is basic to Auriol's description of the cognitive.[8]

What does it mean for something to "understand" some thing, according to Peter Auriol? Or, more generally, what does it mean for something to cognize some thing? In d. 35, q. 1, of Auriol's *Scriptum*, the large commentary on I *Sentences* that he wrote mostly before he started lecturing at Paris in 1316–1318, Auriol discusses whether and how we can say that God understands (*intelligere*). Here, Auriol deals at length with the nature of intellectual cognition and of cognition in general. Much of this discussion is directed against Godfrey of Fontaines, Thomas Aquinas, John Duns Scotus, and Durand of St. Pourçain, but I want to leave Auriol's specific criticisms of his contemporaries' theories basically to the side. The general problem that Auriol finds with all of the other solutions to the issue of what understanding (*intelligere*) is, is that

---

7. Auriol, *Scriptum*, d. 27, q. 2, a. 2: "nullus dubitare debet qui noverit mentem Philosophi et Commentatoris sui quin aliqua sint nihil et non-entia simpliciter, quae tamen sunt entia secundum quid in anima cognitiva entitate quadem intentionali et deminuta. Hoc enim expresse dicit Philosophus, IX *Metaphysicae*, et Commentator exponit, com. 7, dicens quod entia quae non sunt extra animam non dicuntur esse simpliciter, sed dicuntur esse in anima cognitiva. Sic igitur nullum est inconveniens, si eo modo quo sunt, producantur; sunt autem in esse apparenti tantummodo, quod quidem stat cum nihilitate simpliciter, et relinquit entitatem in anima deminutam. Illa vero sunt nihil utroque modo quae nec sunt in se nec in anima obiective." Electronic Scriptum, ll. 603–611; X 625b.

8. See Robert Pasnau, *Theories of Cognition in the Later Middle Ages* (Cambridge: Cambridge University Press, 1997), 74: "Aureol in fact claims that being in the proper relationship to this *esse apparens* is both necessary and sufficient for being cognitive." (As evidence for this claim, Pasnau refers to the text in note 9.) On Auriol, see ibid., 69–76.

they all postulate that it involves some specific type of thing, whether that is a passion (Godfrey) or an action (Aquinas), a quality (Scotus) or a relation (Durand). Auriol cannot see that any of these solutions can account for what we know happens in cognition, and he proposes a solution that is in many ways typical of his strategy in philosophical problem solving. For Auriol, the term "understanding" cannot signify a certain, determinate thing (taking "thing" broadly to include actions, passions, qualities, and relations), rather it is a *connotative* term for him. What this means is that directly (*in recto*) the term *intelligere* indicates no particular item (it indicates the univocal concept of being, which, for Auriol, is all things and all *rationes* (i.e., all basic units of conceptual acquaintance and content) wrapped up in one totally unexplicitated conceptual mass), but *intelligere* connotes or indicates indirectly (*in obliquo*) that the following situation obtains: something *appears* to whatever is said to understand.[9] Thus, for Auriol, you can find understanding anywhere that one particular condition is met, that is, the condition that something appears to the person or thing who is said to understand. To illustrate this, Auriol claims that

> if nothing were to appear objectively to someone's mind, no one will say that that person understands something, rather he or she will be in a state similar to those who sleep . . . and similarly, if through a picture on a wall, Caesar depicted [in the picture] would appear to the wall, then the wall would be said to cognize Caesar depicted. Thus, it manifestly appears that the formal meaning of understanding, or of cognizing in general, is nothing more than "having something present through the mode of appearing."[10]

Wherever there is *appearing* going on, even if that were (very much counterfactually) in a wall, there we would say that cognition is going on. Appearing is the hallmark of the cognitive and of cognition. Wall example aside, Auriol in fact basically sets up an equivalency between the possession of life and life forces, on the one hand, and appearing and cognition, on the other: since cognition only happens when there is appearing going on, and appearing only happens

---

9. Auriol, *Scriptum*, d. 35, q. 1, a. 1: "Prima siquidem est quod intelligere formaliter non includit determinate aliquid in recto, sed solum connotat aliquid ut apparens illi quod dicitur intelligere. . . . Sed manifestum est quod a quacumque re tollitur ne sit quoddam habere aliquid praesens per modum apparentis, ab illa tollitur ne sit formaliter intelligere; cuicumque vero hoc competit, illud dicitur quoddam comprehendere. *Si enim menti nostrae nihil appareat obiective, nullus dicet se aliquid intelligere, immo erit in dispositione simili dormienti, ut Philosophus dicit XII Metaphysicae. Similiter etiam si per picturam in pariete existentem, Caesar pictus appareret parieti, paries diceretur cognoscere Caesarem pictum. Ergo manifeste apparet quod non est plus de formali ratione ipsius intelligere, aut cognoscere in universali, nisi habere aliquid praesens per modum apparentis.*" Electronic Scriptum ll. 320–321, 326–336; X 751b–752a. On Auriol's views concerning the concept of being, see, e.g., Friedman "Peter Aureol," §2.2, and especially the literature referred to there.

10. See the italicized text in note 9.

where there is life or a vital force, only living things can be cognitive and all cognition requires a life force of some kind. Auriol says,

> we have to consider that the likeness alone of the thing is not sufficient in order to put a thing into apparent being ... otherwise species in the air would put color into apparent and intentional being, and similarly [species] existing in the sensory memory would make the thing appear, and this is false. Thus, since appearing is a type of vital being (*quoddam esse vitale*), no thing can hold such being except when a vital force acts along with it.[11]

Ignoring the fact that Auriol here (and elsewhere) appears to have forgotten plants, his intuition seems to be one that most people would share: we have a difficult time thinking about air or outer space cognizing things just because there are sensible species or radio waves in them. It is not entirely clear whether anyone in the Middle Ages did in fact hold the view that the medium is cognitive simply because it has sensible species in it, nor, if someone did hold the view, how it was to have been understood.[12] But for Auriol, the view is nonsense: cognition happens when something appears to someone, and that involves a

---

11. Auriol, *Scriptum*, d. 35, q. 1, a. 1: "considerandum quod sola rei similitudo non sufficit ad ponendum res in esse apparenti ... alioquin species in aere poneret colorem in esse apparenti et intentionali, et similiter existens in memoria sensitiva faceret res apparere, quod falsum est. Unde cum apparere sit quoddam esse vitale, nulla res potest capere tale esse, nisi concurrente virtute vitali. *Unde necesse est quod intellectus informatus rei similitudine sit unum sufficiens principium et una causa totalis apparentiae obiectivae.*" Electronic Scriptum ll. 683–689; X 757a. For discussion of the view presented in the italicized text, see notes 17–26.

12. There is some disagreement in the modern literature concerning whether Thomas Aquinas held, or at least is implicitly committed to, the view that the medium is in some sense cognitive because of the existence in it of sensible species. Thus, Robert Pasnau, *Theories of Cognition*, 12–13, 31–60, esp. 47–60, and Peter King, "Rethinking Representation in the Middle Ages: A Vade-Mecum to Medieval Theories of Mental Representation," in *Representation and Objects of Thought in Medieval Philosophy*, ed. Henrik Lagerlund (Aldershot: Ashgate, 2007), 81–100, esp. 84–85, have both argued that Aquinas was committed to the view, and this because, for Aquinas, (1) the medium receives a form according to spiritual alteration (receiving the form of something without becoming that thing), and (2) the mark of the cognizant is the ability to have more than one form; ergo (3) the medium in some way or another is cognizant (and Aquinas even calls air "perceptive"). On the other hand, Gyula Klima has argued against assigning the view to Aquinas, drawing a distinction between a carrier of information (e.g., air) and a cognizer of information (e.g., a human being); see Klima, "Tradition and Innovation in Medieval Theories of Mental Representation," in *Mental Representation*, ed. G. Klima and A. Hall (Newcastle upon Tyne: Cambridge Scholars Publishing, 2011), 7–16. For my present purposes, whether Aquinas held this view or not is immaterial, I merely want to stress that Auriol decisively rejects it (for another rejection of particularly Pasnau's view, see John P. O'Callaghan, "Aquinas, Cognitive Theory, and Analogy: A Propos of Robert Pasnau's Theories of Cognition in the Later Middle Ages," *American Catholic Philosophical Quarterly* 76 (2002): 451–482, esp. 469–473, with a reply by Pasnau in "What Is Cognition? A Reply to Some Critics," *American Catholic Philosophical Quarterly* 76 (2002): 483–490. Auriol may have picked up this line of thought from John Duns Scotus; see for Scotus's use of it, Giorgio Pini's essay in the present volume.

living, vital force—in the case of intellectual cognition, an intellect. Moreover, even with a representation existing in the mind, some type of *mental* representation, like a species existing in the sensory memory, that representation on its own cannot serve to make something appear to us: there has to be something more than simply the representation, and Auriol will insist that the "something more" is some activity of a cognitive power. Thus, moving to the case of the intellect, Auriol tells us that the intellect can be informed by a mental representation (a likeness, *similitudo*) and yet the thing represented by the likeness might well not appear to the intellect so informed. The thinker's gaze (*acies cogitantis, intuitus, conspectus*), what we would today call *attention*, is in some way distinct from the intellect informed by the mental representation, and both are necessary for the represented thing to appear to the thinker. Indeed, Auriol claims that the gaze of the mind is the very intentional action that constitutes the putting of a thing into *esse apparens*, and this is a step added onto the mind's being in possession of a representation of the object. Thus, according to Auriol, when the thinker's gaze rests on the intellect informed by a particular mental representation, that represented thing then appears to the thinker; when, under the command of our will, our attention shifts to another mental representation in the intellect, whatever is represented by that then appears: "the intentional action that comes about from the intellect informed by the species is subject to the power of the will, not with respect to its total suspension, but with respect to its alternation." To bring this point home, Auriol brings up a fact that can be expressed in the following example: we can be walking around in a crowded street, but thinking so intensely of something else—say, a mathematical proof—that we do not even register the many sensory images that are impinging upon us; this is because our attention is not alighting on those sensed objects—the cart rolling by, the children screaming—and hence they are not *appearing* to us. Even with our eyes wide open, it is possible for us to remain uncognizant of our environment because our mind's gaze is elsewhere.[13]

13. Auriol, *Scriptum*, d. 35, q. 1, a. 1: "Illa namque similitudo cum intellectu sufficit ad faciendum rem praesentem et apparentem, cum similitudinis sit praesentare et absens praesentialiter exhibere. Quod ergo dicitur non esse possibile apparentiam de novo fieri sine acquisitione alicuius realis, dicendum quod intellectus informatus similitudine potest ab huiusmodi apparentia separari, quamvis sit intentionalis. Quod patet multipliciter. Tum quia in visu separantur, recipit enim quandoque videns ab obiecto qualitatem illam, quae non est aliud quam visio, et tamen obiectum non apparet nec iudicatur, sicut quilibet experitur dum oculos habens apertos, de alio considerat; quod enim tunc recipiat visionem patet ex hoc quod sensibile agit in visum; actio autem sensibilis et qualitas visibilis idem sunt. . . . Tum quia species vel similitudo habet repraesentare obiectum et exhibere praesens praesentia intentionali tantum; nullus autem negat quin absolutum speciei possit separari ab actu repraesentandi, qui est pure intentionalis. . . . *Ex quibus patet quod res in esse apparenti et formato posita habet modum intentionalem ex natura ipsius animae. Actio igitur intentionalis, quae provenit ab intellectu specie informato, redigitur sub potestate voluntatis, non quidem quantum ad sus-*

I want to make two points about this theory. The first is that the example that Auriol introduces here seems to allow for a rudimentary criterion for recognizing that something is conscious: it is able *not* to register its environment. Take a thermometer: most everyone would agree that a thermometer is not conscious, and yet it has the ability to register one certain fact about its environment. Auriol can at least be read to suggest here that a rock bottom reason why a thermometer cannot be said to be conscious is that, unless it is broken, it cannot help but register its environment in precisely the same way it always has. This in contrast to the much more complex system that a human being represents, where examples abound of our ability to not register our environment. It is a crude criterion, and by no means sufficient (although perhaps necessary); but an attempt at a criterion it does seem to be.[14] A second point is that the only thing that likenesses or representations, mental or otherwise, do, according to Auriol, is *present* something to you.[15] They cannot in and of themselves make anything appear. Thus, when we have a cognitive power informed by a representation, the offer is there, but actual cognition requires still more: it requires that something *appear* to you, that is, that you are conscious of it. And this is where the thinker's gaze and the will as directive of our intentional awareness comes into the picture; they are the final element in our coming to conscious awareness of this or of that.

To sum up: Putting something into intentional being, and hence making it appear to yourself, has to do with the nature of the soul and it involves the will. We can look at Auriol's cognitive theory as presented thus far as answering two different questions, a general and a specific one. The general question is why do we (in this case) understand or have intellectual cognition; the specific

---

*pensionem totalem, sed quantum ad alternationem....* Secundum hoc ergo formatio obiecti atque positio in esse apparenti, quae non est aliud quam acies cogitantis vel intuitus seu conspectus, potest separari ab intellectu informato similitudine rei. Non est enim impossibile quod actus intentionalis sive repraesentare vel facere apparere obiectum sit quodam modo voluntarium, et ideo Augustinus dicit frequenter quod voluntas copulat aciem cogitantis cum forma sive cum obiecto formato. Quod ergo dicitur non posse de novo fieri talem formationem intentionalem nisi realis qualitas aliqua acquiratur, non est verum, sicut patet." Electronic Scriptum ll. 696–727; X 757a–b. The last sentence of the passage shows that Auriol is here dealing with intellectual memory, how we can have repeated intellectual cognitions of something without the necessity of acquiring a new real representation of that thing each and every time. Auriol played an important role in disambiguating the term *intentio*, so that it was confined only to mental appearances; see on this esp. Katherine H. Tachau, *Vision and Certitude in the Age of Ockham: Optics, Epistemology and the Foundation of Semantics, 1250–1345* (Leiden: Brill, 1988), 93–98.

14. For the thermometer example and discussion of it, I thank Peter King. Of course, even this point about a thermometer not being conscious might meet with disagreement: for instance, David Chalmers (*The Conscious Mind: In Search of a Fundamental Theory* [Oxford: Oxford University Press, 1996], 293–297) considers the possibility that a thermostat has experiences in virtue of its being an information-processing system.

15. See, e.g., the texts in notes 13 and 39–40.

question is why do we understand this as opposed to that. With regard to the general question, Auriol would claim that it is precisely because our intellects have the ability to be appeared to (to be conscious of certain phenomena) that we are able to have intellectual cognition in the first place; consciousness, for Auriol, is a more primitive feature of mind than is cognition (or intentionality), since the former explains the latter. In answer to the specific question, Auriol would say that it is because our will guides our attention to one thing or another (what we should be conscious of) that we understand either this or that.[16]

In another context, in d. 9, q. 1 of his *Scriptum*, Auriol looks at the issue of "saying" or the formation of the divine word, and, in true medieval fashion, he models his description of divine saying on the way he thinks that concepts are formed in human beings. Hence he deals here with the necessary and sufficient condition for our forming a concept or putting a thing in intentional being (these are equivalent for him). According to Auriol, this is what happens:

> In us "to say" names the intellective power informed by a real likeness of the object, insofar as through the likeness the thing cognized holds formed and apparent being. Thus, the active formation is called "diction" or "locution." But [the term] "intellection" names the same power with the same likeness, as it is that to which [something else] is an object, or that to which [something else] is formed and posited, so that it shines and makes apparent. Thus, it is clear how, in understanding, the mind speaks to itself, for it expresses to itself the thing that it forms.[17]

This is Auriol's first stab at the intellectual process that is the immediate source of the mental word or concept: the cognitive power, informed by some real likeness of the object of cognition, says the word, which is the object of cognition in intentional or apparent being, and this saying of the word is called *dictio* or *locutio*. The same cognitive power, informed by the same real likeness, is also that to which the intentional object *appears*, and when this happens we have *intellectio*, and we are said to understand. The mind, as Auriol tells us in the preceding

---

16. See, e.g., the text in note 13. Of course, Auriol's answer to the specific question immediately raises at least one question of its own: how does the will direct us to become conscious of something of which we are *not* presently conscious. This (and the nature of attention more generally) is a major issue in recent discussions of consciousness, but only more research will uncover whether Auriol has a position on it.

17. Auriol, *Scriptum*, d. 9, q. 1, a. 1: "Ex praemissis ergo colligitur quid sit dicere et intelligere in nobis et quid etiam in divinis. In nobis quidem 'dicere' nominat intellectivam potentiam informatam reali similitudine obiecti, in quantum per eam capit res cognita esse formatum et apparens; unde illa activa formatio, 'dictio' seu 'locutio' appellatur. 'Intellectio' vero nominat eandem potentiam cum eadem similitudine, prout est id cui obiicitur, seu formatur et ponitur, ut luceat et apparescat. Unde patet quomodo intelligendo mens loquitur sibi ipsi: exprimit enim sibi rem quam format." Electronic Scriptum, ll. 580–585; X 323b. The Augustinian turn of phrase (that I have been unable to locate in Augustine) "mens loquitur sibi ipsi," is one of Auriol's typical sayings; see, e.g., also note 31.

quotation, speaks to itself. Now, Auriol describes in several ways the cognitive power informed by the real likeness of the object: at times he calls it the "absolute of intellection" (*absolutum intellectionis*), but he also calls it the intellectual act,[18] and it is through this intellectual act that the intentional object, the object of cognition in apparent being, is both formed (*dictio*) and appears to us (*intellectio*). Thus, there are two moments in every intellectual act for Auriol: there is *dictio*, the production of the thing in apparent being, and there is *intellectio*, the "reading" of that same intentional object by the same intellectual act that produced it.[19] I want now to discuss some of Auriol's ideas on the intellectual act, why it is the "absolute of intellection," and how it relates to the intentional object.

Why must the intellectual act be something absolute, and what does that mean anyway? Auriol is clearly using "absolute" here to mean something with subjective being in the soul, that is, something that in and of itself has some being. His major reason for claiming this is clearly that the absolute of intellection is what grounds the diminished being that it causes: since *esse apparens* or intentional being is, as we have seen, nothing in itself (*nihil in se*), it has to have a basic causal dependency on some real being or it wouldn't exist at all, "neither in itself nor in anything else," as Auriol puts it.[20] The mental being that it depends on, in Auriol's view, is the mental act, which hence has to have some real subjective being of its own. Moreover, just as Caesar couldn't have "depicted being"—that is, Caesar couldn't be understood from a picture of Caesar—unless there were in fact some *real* picture of Caesar, so it works in the intellect: There cannot be apparent being without its depending upon some real likeness of the object with its own subjective being existing in the intellect.[21]

Of course, one might reply to this that respects, that is to say, relational entities, can also have real being. So, why couldn't the source of the intentional

---

18. E.g. in the texts in notes 29 and 30, and more diffusely, 31 and 32.

19. The term "reading" here is mine, but is based on the common medieval etymology (a variation of which is offered by Auriol at, e.g., *Scriptum*, d. 9, q. 1, a. 1, Electronic Scriptum, ll. 546–547, X 323a) that understanding is an internal reading (*intelligere* as *intus legere* or *intellectio* as *intus lectio*).

20. Auriol, *Scriptum*, d. 9, q. 1, a. 1: "res non potest habere tale esse apparens nisi ratione alicuius absoluti realis existentis in intellectu: omne namque deminutum reducitur ad aliquid reale, alioquin nihil esset et in se et in alio. Sed res in esse apparenti sive rei apparitio est omnino quid deminutum; unde nihil est in se. Ergo necesse est quod sit aliquod reale in intellectu, ratione cuius dicatur esse." Electronic Scriptum, ll. 364–369; X 320b. On the diminished ontological status of the *esse apparens*, see also the text in note 7.

21. Auriol, *Scriptum*, d. 9, q. 1, a. 1: "Praeterea, sicut se habet realis pictura ad esse pictum, sic se videtur habere realis apparitio ad dare esse apparens. Sed numquam Caesar caperet esse pictum nisi quatenus est aliqua realis pictura. Ergo nec res erunt apparentes intellectui nisi quatenus est aliqua formalis apparitio et realis in intellectu." Electronic Scriptum, ll. 370–373; X 320b. Interestingly, Auriol seems to use the term *apparitio* here in a different sense than he does in, e.g., notes 20, 29, 30, and 31. There the *apparitio* refers to the appearing of an object of cognition to a cognizer, here it is a likeness with real being, which is a necessary condition for a cognitive appearing to take place.

object's diminished being be a respect and not an absolute at all? Auriol's arguments against the intellectual act being relational in nature boil down to the claim that likeness, and relations in general, are not the kinds of items that can bring about cognition. In particular, no similarity relationship makes one thing appear to another: for instance, by the very fact that they are similar to one another, one white thing does not appear to another.[22] Auriol seems to be assuming here that the only relevant kind of relation is a likeness or similarity relation, and that this type of relation in and of itself is insufficient to get cognition off the ground. It requires more than just similarity or likeness to make something *appear* to someone, and for Auriol, as we have seen, appearing, conscious experience, is what cognition is all about.

Thus, we need to have some absolute in the intellect that serves as the necessary foundation of the diminished being of the *esse apparens* that is itself necessary for actual intellectual cognition. What is that absolute?

> What makes cognized things appear is something absolute. But it cannot be maintained that it is a quality alone or a species or an operation from the genus of quality. For if it were a species, then the medium in which species are received would be able to comprehend, and things would appear to it, and that's false. But if it were an operation from the genus of quality, like "to light" or "to be white," then to light would put the thing in apparent being, and there would be just as good a construction when you said "I light you" or "I white you" as when you say "I understand you." Therefore it is not a quality alone through which things hold apparent being objectively. Further, it cannot be said that it is a quality [along] with a respect to an object. Both because the species has both [of these], even as it exists in the medium; and because it's been explained that the respect of likeness does not make things appear, otherwise Caesar would appear to a wall through a picture [of Caesar on that wall], which is false. What we are left with, then, is that the absolute from which objective knowledge arises is a conjunction of the intellective potency and the likeness. For the potency on its own account does not put things into formed being, and neither does the likeness, or any quality whatsoever, but both at once give birth to objective knowledge or put the thing into apparent being.[23]

---

22. Auriol, *Scriptum*, d. 9, q. 1, a. 1: "Hoc autem impossibile est, quod [intellectio actus] sit purus respectus.... Tum quia nulla similitudo quae sit respectus vel relatio facit res apparere, est enim similitudo inter duo alba, et inter iustitiam existentem in voluntate unius iusti et alterius, et similiter inter grammaticam unius grammatici et alterius, nec tamen ista similitudo facit grammaticam aut iustitiam alterius apparere. Tum quia similitudo-relatio maior est inter duas animas vel inter duas albedines, cum sint eiusdem speciei, quam inter ipsam albedinem et speciem illius in oculo existentem, istae nempe non sunt eiusdem speciei; claret autem quod anima non facit apparere animam, nec albedo albedinem; unde relinquitur quod relatio similitudinis non facit res intellectui apparere." Electronic Scriptum, ll. 374–384; X 320b.

23. Auriol, *Scriptum*, d. 9, q. 1, a. 1: "Restat ergo ut illud quod facit res cognitas apparere sit aliquid absolutum: istud autem poni non potest quod sit qualitas sola, sive species, sive

The first thing worth noticing about this rich passage is that toward the end of it, Auriol tells us explicitly that the absolute of intellection is, as we also saw above,[24] the intellectual power together with a likeness of the object of intellection; these make up one conjoined or composite absolute of intellection that puts the object of intellection into apparent being, making it appear as an intentional object to the absolute of intellection itself. Indeed, here Auriol seems to tell us specifically that the likeness of the thing is a quality (*similitudo, aut qualitates quaecumque*).[25] But no quality, whether a species or something else, could ever on its own make things appear. As we have seen, that requires life and the capacity to be appeared to, and Auriol appeals in this passage to some of his favorite examples of why a species on its own account could not bring about cognition; if that were the case, then the medium would be cognizant, and a wall could understand Caesar in virtue of the fact that he is painted on it. All of this pushes Auriol to say that, in order to bring about intellectual cognition, in order to make something appear to our intellect, the likeness of the thing found in the intellect must be conjoined with the intellectual power. For a positive reason that an *intellectual power* must be involved in intellectual cognition, Auriol resorts basically to his view that only living things can have comprehension of any type, and hence in order to have intellectual cognition, or in order for things to appear to the intellect, there has to be a living being with an intellect: no nonvital nature can constitute something in apparent being.[26] On the other hand, the reason that he gives for a *likeness* of the thing being involved in cognition is based on what looks to be a standard notion of assimilation: the only way that an extramental thing can be united to the mind is through the existence of the thing's

---

operatio de genere qualitatis. Si enim esset species, tunc medium in quo recipiuntur species esset comprehensivum, et sibi res apparent, quod falsum est. Si vero esset operatio de genere qualitatis ut lucere et albere, tunc lucere poneret res in esse apparenti, et esset bona constructio dicendo 'luceo te' vel 'albeo te,' sicut dicendo 'intelligo te'; non est igitur sola qualitas illud quo res capiunt esse apparens obiective. Ulterius non potest dici quod sit qualitas cum respectu ad obiectum: tum quia species habet utrumque, etiam prout existit in medio; tum quia declaratum est quod respectus similitudinis non facit res apparere, alias per picturam appareret Caesar parieti, quod est falsum. Relinquitur ergo quod sit illud absolutum a quo oritur notitia obiectiva coniunctum quoddam ex potentia intellectiva et ex similitudine ipsa. Nec enim potentia per se ipsam ponit res in esse formato, nec similitudo, aut qualitas quaecumque, sed utrumque simul parit notitiam obiectivam sive ponit res in esse apparenti." Electronic Scriptum, ll. 385–397; X 320b–321a.

24. See notes 11, 13, 17, and 26.
25. Compare the final sentence of the quotation in note 13.
26. Auriol, *Scriptum*, d. 9, q. 1, a. 1: "Secundo vero idem patet quia esse apparens, quod capit res per intellectionem et visionem, est proprium rei comprehensivae et vitam habentis, nulli enim naturae res apparent nisi sit comprehensiva; unde illud est proprie susceptio formae sine materia. Nulla ergo natura non-vitalis potest constituere res in esse apparenti. Oritur ergo apparitio obiectiva simul ab utroque, videlicet a potentia et impressa similitudine." Electronic Scriptum, ll. 406–410; X 321a. See also note 11.

likeness there.[27] Of course, it goes nearly without saying that the intellectual potency completely on its own cannot bring about intellectual cognition, because if it could, then it could understand all things without any input from the extramental world, and this is tantamount to a theory of innate ideas (Auriol uses this argument against Durand of St. Pourçain on several occasions).[28]

Thus, Auriol's position on the absolute of intellection is that:

> The act of intellection does not name the likeness alone nor one simple form, but a composite of the power and the likeness of the thing, for both constitute the intellection, because neither the likeness alone nor the power alone is the intellection, but both at once, and from both is born the appearing (*apparitio*) of the object or its intentional presence and objective shining out.[29]

How does this work in detail? Auriol argues that the absolute of intellection, the intellectual act, which is the intellect informed by the real likeness of the object, and is in fact a composite of the intellectual power and that likeness, has a twofold relation to the intentional object. Auriol says:

> the actual knowledge that indicates the composite of the thing's likeness and the intellective power has two separate respects to the thing put objectively into intentional being. And the first respect belongs to the genus of action,

---

27. Auriol, *Scriptum*, d. 9, q. 1, a. 1: "Tertio quoque patet idem, quia partus debet assimilari ei a quo nascitur: notitia vero obiectiva est res in quodam esse intentionali posita, et in esse prospecto, quapropter oritur a re ipsa, et a prospiciente anima. Res autem non facit idem cum anima nisi per similitudinem suam. Quare relinquitur ut conceptus seu partus mentis oriatur ab utroque." Electronic Scriptum, ll. 411–414; X 321a.

This seems to be Auriol's general reason for positing the real existence of likenesses in cognition, since a similar notion of assimilation is to be found in Auriol's II *Sent.*, d. 11, pars 3, q. 1: "Anima per unam potentiam est assimilabilis obiecto mediante unica tantum similitudine; sed per nullam aliam potentiam quam per intellectum anima assimilatur rei intellectae; igitur mediante unica tantum similitudine; sed illa est ipse actus; igitur intellectus non est alia similitudo obiecti quam actus ipse." Florence, Biblioteca Nazionale Centrale, conv. soppr. A.3.120, f. 47va; ed. Rome 1605, p. 128a. For discussion of the issues addressed in this text from Auriol's II *Sent.*, see at notes 36–49.

28. For an example of Auriol's use of this argument against Durand, see R. L. Friedman, "Peter Auriol versus Durand of St. Pourçain on Intellectual Cognition." *Recherches de Théologie et Philosophie Médiévales/Studies in Medieval Theology and Philosophy/Forschungen zur Theologie und Philosophie des Mittelalters*, 2014.

29. Auriol, *Scriptum*, d. 9, q. 1, a. 1: "*Ex quo patet quod intellectio actus non nominat solam similitudinem nec unam formam simplicem, sed compositum ex potentia et ex similitudine rei, ambo enim constituunt intellectionem, quia sola similitudo non est intellectio, nec sola potentia, sed simul utrumque et ab utroque paritur obiecti apparitio sive praesentia intentionalis et relucentia obiectiva*. . . . Unde decipiuntur, qui quaerunt intellectionem tamquam unam formam simplicem, cum sit quoddam compositum ex duobus, quorum unum est potentia, reliquum complementum. Utrum autem ista similitudo sit species, aut oporteat speciem ponere praeter similitudinem quae est pars actus, locum habebit in secundo libro. Unde ad praesens haec inquis[it]io relinquatur." Electronic Scriptum, ll. 415–425; X 321a–b. For a consideration of the view expressed in the untranslated part of this text, see at note 36.

the second to the genus of relation. For such an appearing as an object (*obiectalis apparitio*) [1] arises efficiently from the power and the likeness informing it, i.e. the two items that constitute the act of intellection, and [2] arises inside the power so informed.[30]

The intellectual act relates directly in two very different ways to one and the same intentional object, that is, the thing in apparent being: the intellection has a respect (*habitudo*) of (as we will see, *metaphorical*) efficient causality because it produces the intentional object through an intentional production; it also has a relational respect to that same intentional object as that *to which* the intentional object appears. Thus, one and the same intellectual act has, as we saw, two moments: *dictio*, the production of the intentional object (putting the thing into *esse apparens*), and *intellectio*, the appearing of the intentional object to the very same intellectual act that produced it. Each of these moments involves a separate respect of the intellectual act to the intentional object.

Auriol offers several arguments as to why the intellectual act needs this twofold respect to the intentional object. For example, since the concept, as all would agree, remains within the conceiver, it depends on the act of the intellect in two ways: efficiently as a product of that act, and "contentwise" (*contentive*) as what is contained within the act. The intentional object is both produced by the act and serves as its content, and the latter in virtue of the fact that it is literally contained in the act of the mind producing it. A second argument is simply in keeping with Auriol's often used phrase that the mind speaks to itself (*mens loquitur sibi ipsi*): for this reason, the same act of intellection through which the intentional object, the thing in apparent being, is formed, is also the act to which the intentional object appears. Finally, because everything that appears, appears to someone or something (otherwise it wouldn't be appearing in the first place), the act of the intellect is both that in virtue of which the object understood appears (or takes on apparent being) and that to which the object appears. Basically, what produces the object in intentional being must also read or be appeared to by that object; because the object is contained within the act, there is nothing else to which the object could so appear. In this way, Auriol deduces the intellectual act's twofold respect to the intentional object, that is, the object of cognition in *esse apparens*.[31]

---

30. Auriol, *Scriptum*, d. 9, q. 1, a. 1: "Quod intellectio actus duplicem habitudinem habet ad rem positam in esse apparenti. Tertia quoque propositio est quod notitia actualis quae dicit compositum ex similitudine rei et ex intellectiva potentia, istud inquam sub duplici habitudine respicit rem positam obiective in esse intentionali. Et est prima habitudo de genere actionis, secunda vero de genere relationis. Talis namque apparitio obiectalis et oritur effective a potentia et a similitudine informante, quae duo constituunt actum intellectionis, et oritur intra potentiam sic informatam." Electronic Scriptum, ll. 427–432; X 321b.

31. Auriol, *Scriptum*, d. 9, q. 1, a. 1: "Primo quidem, quoniam res posita in esse apparenti dicitur concipi per actum intellectus, immo est conceptus intellectualis. Conceptus autem

In elaborating this view, quite interesting are Auriol's attempts to defend the difference in two ontological levels that he maintains exist in one and the same intellect: the intellection itself being an absolute, something with *real* existence, while the concept produced through it and necessarily dependent upon it having merely *intentional* or *diminished* existence. Thus some unnamed opponent objects to Auriol's theory that, since any absolute can be conceived without a respect, and since the intellect's act is something absolute (i.e., the composite of power and the object's real likeness), therefore the intellect's act can be conceived without its own relational activity, that is to say, without the production of the object in *esse apparens* and the reading or appearance of that object to the same act. In answer, Auriol flatly denies that this can be the case: "The act of the intellect can only be conceived as making the thing appear objectively."[32] The intellectual act and its activity, then, are so intimately linked that the one cannot even be thought to exist without the other. Indeed, although Auriol seems to consistently maintain that the act of the intellect always produces an intentional object, that is, the thing in *esse apparens*, nevertheless he also insists that the intentional production does not necessarily result in the thing appearing to us, because the intellect might not have conscious access to its own intentional production and "reading." We have already seen this suggested when Auriol maintained that "attention" or the thinker's gaze was something separate from the intellectual act (the intellect informed by the mental representation) and could be guided by our will to alternate between one object and the next.[33] Thus, although Auriol thinks that a distinction can indeed be drawn in the various moments in the process of intellectual cognition, nevertheless the distinction he draws is very different from the one suggested by his anonymous opponent: the opponent claims that an act of the intellect can be conceived (and hence can exist) without its activity, while Auriol claims that act

---

remanet intra concipientem, et est a concipiente. Ergo res ut apparens dependet ab actu intellectus effective et per modum producti, et contentive et per modum contenti.

Secundo vero, quia formando huiusmodi conceptum mens dicitur sibi loqui, et per consequens ille conceptus habet habitudinem ad mentem loquentem, et ad eandem mentem, tamquam ad id cui locutio fit.

Tertio autem, quia omne quod apparet, alicui apparet, et omne quod lucet, alicui dicitur lucere; talis autem conceptus dicitur apparitio et relucentia quaedam; habet ergo habitudinem ad intellectum in actu tamquam ad id cui lucet et cui apparet. Constat autem quod habet habitudinem tamquam ad id cuius virtute est, ut declaratum est supra quod relucentia obiectiva non est nisi propter realem relucentiam, quae est actus. Ergo patet quod res posita in esse intentionali, dupliciter se habet ad actum intellectus, videlicet quia virtute eius lucet, et quia sibi lucet." Electronic Scriptum, ll. 434–447; X 321b. For *mens loquitur sibi ipsi*, see note 17.

32. Auriol, *Scriptum*, d. 9, q. 1, a. 1: "Omne enim absolutum potest concipi absque respectu. Sed actus intellectus, qui resultat ex potentia et ex reali similitudine obiecti, est aliquid absolutum. Ergo poterit intelligi sine respectu activitatis ... actus intellectus concipi non potest nisi ut faciens res obiective apparere." Electronic Scriptum, ll. 456–458, 495; X 321b–322a.

33. On the thinker's gaze, see note 13.

and both aspects of its activity (production and "reading") are inseparable, although we may indeed not be conscious of the results of the act's activity. There can be situations, Auriol seems to want to say, in which we are blocked conscious access to the act's activity, but the intellectual act and both its moments are, for Auriol, a package deal: if there is an intellectual act, it involves both an intentional production and "reading." We will return to this below where I suggest a way of making sense of Auriol's hints. In response to another objection to his view, an objection stating that since the thing in apparent being is nothing, and since pure nothing can be the object of no production, the thing in apparent being cannot be produced, Auriol maintains that the production of something in diminished, intentional being is a "metaphorical" production. Thus, just as a real product is produced by a real action, a merely intentional product is produced by a "metaphorical" intentional action.[34]

Thus far, then, we have seen that Auriol claims that the intellectual act, the absolute act of intellection, is the intellectual power informed by some representation or likeness. The intellectual act cannot exist without its activity, and this activity comprises two respects: both a production of the intentional object and a reading of that same intentional object. When the thinker's gaze or attention is fixed on a particular object of intellection, that object becomes available to conscious thought because it appears to the thinker. And Auriol strictly links the thinker's gaze with the appearing of the object to the thinker. Consciousness, for Auriol, is thus the mark of the cognitive, and is a more primitive explanatory feature than either cognition or intentionality.

This account, however, might lead us to ask Auriol just what *is* the representation in the intellect? Is it, for instance, an intelligible species?[35] Auriol had in fact anticipated this question, and at several junctures in his discussion of this material in the *Scriptum* version of his commentary on the first book of the

---

34. Auriol, *Scriptum*, d. 9, q. 1, a. 1: "omnia verba ista videntur phantasiae, quod enim nihil est, produci non potest. Res in esse apparenti nihil sunt, ut supra dictum est. Ergo produci non possunt, nec intellectio habet annexam aliquam activitatem.... Tertia quoque deficit, quia res in esse apparenti nihil est in se nisi deminute et metaphorice, eo modo quo entia rationis dicuntur esse; et ea quae non sunt simpliciter, sunt in anima.... Sicut ergo res in esse apparenti est tantum metaphorice, sic actio [qua] formatur est metaphorica." Electronic Scriptum, ll. 461–463, 513–514, 517–518; X 321b–322b.

35. Tachau, *Vision and Certitude*, 95 n. 30, considers erroneous the claim made by Faustino Prezioso and Gedeon Gál that Auriol rejected intelligible species; Dominik Perler, "Peter Aureol vs. Hervaeus Natalis," 239 n. 37, supports her. As will be clear, I agree that Auriol creates some space in his theory for using the term "intelligible species," but I also think that, at least in his II *Sent.*, he has effectively emptied the term of most of the significance it had for his contemporaries. For Auriol, all there are in the intellect are acts, some of which are not consciously registered. If you want to use the term "intelligible species" to describe those acts that are not consciously registered, this will not upset Auriol. But this is very far from a normal understanding of intelligible species. Auriol deals with similar issues in a somewhat different way in his magisterial *Quodl.*, q. 8, a. 3 (ed. 1605, 81–88, esp. 85–88); see note 50 for some remarks on the quodlibetal text.

*Sentences*, he promises that in the second book of the *Sentences* he will return to the issue of whether for his theory of intellectual cognition to work there has to be an intelligible species in addition to the intellectual act.[36] Clearly there has to be a likeness or representation, but are *both* the species and the act necessary? And one could ask further: what is the relation between the act and the intellectual power? True to his word, Auriol takes up this issue in his II *Sentences*, d. 11, part 3, q. 1, in a text that can be accurately described as Auriol's parallel text to Ockham's *Reportatio* II, qq. 12–13. Here Auriol rejects, in rather explicit opposition to Scotus, that intelligible species are either (1) a necessary prerequisite or necessary corequisite for the intellectual act or (2) an endpoint of the intellectual act. Auriol's conclusion is that "species and intellection, both in angels and us, are really (*realiter*) the same as the act of understanding."[37] In order to understand the view that Auriol is endorsing here, something needs to be clarified about his use of the term "intellection" or *intellectio*. In normal scholastic parlance, *intellectio* is a synonym for *actus intellectus* or *actus intelligendi*, and Auriol uses the term in this way as well, although when he does so, he often uses the phrase *intellectio realis* (e.g., note 46): this is an *intellectio* with real being, that is, the intellect's act. But as we have seen from *Scriptum*, d. 9, q. 1, Auriol also uses the term *intellectio* to denote the second respect that the act of understanding has to the intentional object, that is, the reading of the intentional object or the appearing of the intentional object to the intellectual act; we can call this the "intentional *intellectio*." With that terminology in mind, Auriol's view is that the species, the real *intellectio*, and the intellectual act are the same in their reality (*realiter*), they are the same real item; but he thereby holds open the possibility that they differ in some other, less-than-real way.

Auriol's main argument for the view that species and intellectual act are really the same—one he uses specifically against Scotus's theory of intellectual cognition—is that there are never two likenesses of the same type in the same power at the same time: if these two likenesses were completely the same, then one would clearly be redundant, but if one of the two likenesses were more perfect than the other, then the less perfect one would certainly be superfluous, roughly like both tepidness and extreme heat being in the same glass of water.[38]

36. See, e.g., the text in note 29, and compare what Auriol says at the end of the text in note 4.

37. See note 38.

38. Auriol, II *Sent.*, d. 11, pars 3, q. 1 ("Utrum in intellectu angeli species et intellectio realiter distinguantur"): "Quoad primum pono propositionem istam, quod *species et intellectio tam in nobis quam in angelis est realiter idem quod actus intelligendi*. Hanc propositionem probo rationibus quibusdam. Prima haec: impossibile est respectu eiusdem ponere duas similitudines realiter differentes, et hoc respectu eiusdem et in eodem; sed species est quaedam similitudo perfecta rei, et intellectio similiter; igitur impossibile est quod species et intellectio differant realiter. Maior patet, quia illae duae similitudines [1] vel essent distinctae solum numeraliter, et si sic, tunc duo accidentia eiusdem speciei essent in eodem, [2] aut erunt alterius rationis, et si sic unum erit perfectius altero, et [in] virtute continebit ipsum sicut

This is precisely what Auriol thinks obtains with regard to the species and the act: the purpose of a species is "to represent the object and make the object present to the intellect,"[39] and that's also the purpose of the act.[40] Indeed, Auriol claims that it is "not so clear" that the species has this property, while the property especially (*maxime*) applies to the act.[41] Thus, Auriol's line of reasoning seems to be: since we *know* that the intellect has an act, and since the act is better at making the object present to the intellect than any intelligible species would be, a separate intelligible species is redundant, and Ockham's razor dictates eliminating it. Auriol goes on to suggest that the agent intellect together with the phantasm are perfectly suited to moving the possible intellect to its act with no intelligible species involved, asking why the phantasm and agent intellect should be able to cause a species in the possible intellect, but not an intellectual act directly?[42]

That is not entirely the end of the story, however. One of the reasons that Scotus had postulated the intelligible species was to account for dispositional knowledge: the intelligible species in the possible intellect was the intellectual memory awaiting actualization. Auriol brings this up: Isn't *this* a reason to claim that we need intelligible species, that is, to reduce the intellect from

---

perfectum continet imperfectum in virtute; sed impossibile videtur quod duo accidentia, quorum unum continet aliud in virtute, sint distincte in eodem subiecto, sicut tepiditas et calor in summo; igitur species, quae est similitudo rei imperfecta et remissa, non poterit esse in eodem intellectu distincta ab intellectione, quae est in eodem perfecta et expressa similitudo eiusdem obiecti." Florence, Biblioteca Nazionale Centrale, conv. soppr. A.3.120, f. 47va; ed. 1605, pp. 127bF–128aB. All quotations from Auriol's II *Sent.* are taken from the Florence manuscript with minor modifications clearly indicated; the early printed edition of 1605 is rife with errors, making the text nearly impossible to understand. I am preparing a working edition of the text for publication.

39. Auriol, II *Sent.*, d. 11, pars 3, q. 1: "species ponitur in intellectu ad repraesentandum obiectum et facere obiectum praesens intellectui, et ad exhibendum ipsum in esse praesentiali; sed hoc maxime competit intellectioni; igitur non videtur quod sit ponenda species alia ab intellectione." Florence, BNC, conv. soppr. A.3.120, f. 47vb; ed. 1605, p. 128aE.

40. Auriol, II *Sent.*, d. 11, pars 3, q. 1: "ubi est eadem ratio, ibi est idem illud quod sequitur ex ratione illa; sed actus intelligendi habet quod exhibeat rem praesentem in prospectu mentis, quia est vera similitudo rei. Hoc autem convenit speciei, ipsa enim est rei similitudo, licet non ita clara. Igitur ipsa species vere exhibet rem praesentem, ac per consequens est vera rei intellectio." Florence, BNC, conv. soppr. A.3.120, f. 47vb; ed. 1605, p. 128bD-E. Cp. also the beginning of the text in note 13 for the same claim about the function of mental likenesses.

41. See notes 39 and 40.

42. Auriol, II *Sent.*, d. 11, pars 3, q. 1: "Praeterea: non videtur ratio quare intellectus agens cum phantasmate non possit reducere intellectum possibilem ad actum respectu intellectionis, sicut respectu speciei quam ponis in intellectu; non videtur enim quod phantasma et intellectus agens simul habeant maiorem repugnantiam ad causalitatem intellectionis quam speciei. Et confirmo hoc per Aristotelem, III *De anima*, qui dicit quod sicut se habent sensibilia ad sensum, sic phantasmata ad intellectum; sed secundum eum ibidem actio sensibilis est passio ipsius, sonatio enim est auditio, coloratio est visio; quare in intellectu prima impressio formae a phantasmate in intellectu erit ipsa intellectio." Florence, BNC, conv. soppr. A.3.120, f. 48ra; ed. 1605, p. 129aF–bA.

essential potency to a merely accidental potency (i.e., the readiness to issue into act that is associated with being able to remember as opposed to learning something for the first time)? Auriol's answer looks to be a firm *no*: with regard to simple intellection, that is, first-order knowledge of things and their natures, Auriol claims approvingly that "Aristotle doesn't think that the intellect is brought from essential potency to accidental potency with respect to the act that is simple intellection or consideration through anything inhering in the intellect"—Aristotle only thought that about complex acts of composing and dividing.[43]

Now, as far as I can see, the most promising way of interpreting Auriol's claim that, with regard to simple acts of intellection, the intellect is not brought from essential to accidental potency through anything inhering in the intellect, that is, anything with its own subjective being, is that the intellect goes directly from essential potency—the bare intellectual capacity completely unactualized as a *tabula rasa*—to full actuality as soon as a representation with its own subjective being is in the intellect. At least two reasons can be given that appear to argue for this interpretation. First, it is well known that Auriol is committed to the fundamental activity of cognitive powers in general, and the intellect in particular;[44] this view of the intellect as fundamentally active would militate against having anything simply "lying around" in the intellect, and this is probably precisely how Auriol saw the type of accidental potency that some of Auriol's contemporaries thought species to be. So Auriol probably thought that holding species to be nonoccurrent knowledge, priming the intellect for actual knowledge, compromised the intellect's fundamental activity. And this leads us to a second reason to take this interpretation seriously: once Auriol had rejected species, he had also rejected the common way of explaining intellectual memory (i.e., dispositional or habitual knowledge), and so, in order to say how we can have memory of things we have thought in the past, he was pushed to say that all those thoughts remain in act. If past mental events are not dispositionally available for recall (as an intelligible species account of memory would have it), then they have to be *actually* available for recall—unless you are willing to

---

43. Auriol, II *Sent.*, d. 11, pars 3, q. 1: "Dices quod immo, ipse [scil., Aristoteles] enim dicit quod anima ante actum fit de potentia essentiali in potentia accidentali, hoc autem non est nisi per speciem. Dico quod Aristoteles non intelligit ibi quod intellectus fiat de potentiali essentiali in potentia accidentali respectu actus qui est simplex intellectio et consideratio per aliquid inhaerens intellectui, sed intelligit hoc respectu actus complexi, qui est considerare. Considerare enim proprie est unum cum alio per intellectum componere et dividere, et tunc ipse vult quod respectu talis actus complexi intellectus primo fiat de potentia essentiali in potentia accidentali per aliquid inhaerens intellectui. Illud autem est habitus scientiae secundum mentem suam." Florence, BNC, conv. soppr. A.3.120, f. 48ra; ed. 1605, p. 129bB–C. In discussion, Richard Cross pointed out that claiming that we have habitual knowledge of complexes but not of the components of complexes, seems at the very least ad hoc if not nonsensical. I do not know what Auriol has to say about this (if anything).

44. See, e.g., Tachau, *Vision and Certitude*, 90, 93.

deny the existence of intellectual memory (which Auriol is not). And this is what Auriol appears to be proposing.

As mentioned, however, what is entailed by this interpretation is that, for Auriol, for there to be a mental representation in the intellect just *is* for the intellect to be in act or have an act. To put it in another way, if there is a real likeness of a thing in the intellect, then it exists in the intellect as an intellectual act, and this is what Auriol called "the absolute of intellection." As we have seen, Auriol rejects the distinction between essential and accidental potency in simple intellectual cognition, at least as it was normally understood in his day, and that means that the intellect is either bare (essential) potency or fully in act—there is no dispositional, accidental potency in between. But, as mentioned before, from Aristotle and on, the whole point of some type of essential/accidental potency distinction in cognition, was to explain the *fact* of dispositional knowledge, namely, that we can store away experiences and knowledge, recalling them later without having to acquire them from scratch. In short, not all of the knowledge in our possession is occurrent, and the device of accidental potency was an elegant way to explain how this could be the case. However, by doing away with the essential/accidental potency distinction in cognition, by making all of our simple intellectual knowledge actual, Auriol seems to be committed to the view that we think occurrently everything that we ever have thought, and that is manifestly false.

He has a way out, of course, and it works off of the intellect's constant need in this life to work with the senses and especially the imagination.[45] Thus, Auriol tells us that something's existing in *esse apparens*, and hence that thing's appearing to us, depends on (1) that thing's being in the intellect as the object of the intellectual act (i.e., the absolute of intellection), and (2) that thing's being in the imagination as the phantasm, that is, the occurrent object of the imagination. This appeal to the phantasm is how Auriol answers precisely the charge that, on his view, according to which all simple knowledge is actual, we should right now know occurrently everything that we have ever known:

> There is a doubt concerning whether a human being actually understands all the things of which she has a species. I say she doesn't, because in order for a thing to be understood there is required, besides the reality of the intellection [i.e. the intellectual act], that the thing be put in judged and apparent being founded in that same thing's phantasized cogitated being, and since many things at once cannot actually (*actu*) have that phantasized being, thus even though there are many intellections actually in the intellect, nevertheless there will not be many things understood through

---

45. Thus, here we could consider Auriol to be filling in gaps in Thomas Aquinas's famous device of "turning to the phantasm."

these intellections, but only the one that holds phantasized being in the phantasm.[46]

Auriol claims that the reason that we do not know everything at once is because there is a logjam at the imagination, and the logjam arises because the imagination is an organic power, capable of sending on merely one phantasm at a time to the agent intellect.[47] On his theory, all of us have lots of acts of the intellect at once—everything that we have ever learned or experienced or known is actually in the intellect right now. Each one of those acts, moreover, is, as we saw, a "package deal" involving the production of the intentional object (*dictio*) and the reading of the same object (intentional *intellectio*). All of our simple intellectual knowledge is *actual* in this way. Nevertheless, it isn't all *occurrent*, because in order for the object of intellectual cognition to appear to us, that is, in order for us to have conscious awareness of it and thereby intellectual cognition, there has to be a coincidence between the thing I am thinking in the intellect and the thing I am phantasizing (imagining) in the imagination. For us human beings in this life, only one thing can appear to us at once—that is, we can be conscious of only one thing at a time—and that is because of the necessity for our conjoined intellect to work with the imagination.[48]

---

46. Auriol, II *Sent.*, d. 11, pars 3, q. 1: "Sic igitur ex his colligitur quod res secundum esse quod habet in prospectu mentis quod est esse intentionale et apparens dependet realiter a duobus, et ab illa intellectione reali, a qua habet quod sit esse distinctum de non-ente, et ab esse rei phantasiato, in quo habet necessario fundari in quantum suum esse est esse iudicatum. Deficiente igitur altero istorum, puta intellectione reali vel esse rei in phantasmate in actu, deficit necessario res habere esse obiectivum et praesentiale in intellectu; et ideo res ut sic non potest habere esse intellectivum quocumque illorum deficiente, propter colligantiam necessariam harum intentionum, scilicet intentionis intellectae et imaginatae. . . . Tunc ad propositum, *cum dubiatur si actu homo intelligit omnia quorum habet species, dico quod non, quia ad hoc quod res intelligatur, requiritur ultra realitatem intellectionis quod res ponatur in esse iudicato et apparenti fundato in esse eiusdem rei phantasiato cogitato, et quia plures res simul non possunt habere esse actu phantasiatum, ideo licet actu sint plures intellectiones in intellectu, non tamen erunt plura intellecta per illas intellectiones, sed unum tantum quod capiet in phantasmate esse phantasiatum.*" Florence, BNC, conv. soppr. A.3.120, f. 48va; ed. 1605, p. 130bB–E.

47. Auriol makes a very clear statement of this at II *Sent.*, d. 11, pars 4, q. 3 (ed. 1605, p. 139bD), quoted and discussed briefly in Friedman, "On the Trail of a Philosophical Debate: Durandus of St. Pourçain vs. Thomas Wylton on Simultaneous Acts in the Intellect," in *Philosophical Debates at Paris in the Early Fourteenth Century*, ed. S. Brown, T. Dewender, and T. Kobusch (Leiden: Brill, 2009), 442.

48. One wonders how Auriol will deal with the cases of disembodied souls or angels, neither of which have the organic power of the imagination, and hence would appear, on Auriol's view, to have necessary occurrent conscious experience of all their past intellectual acts. An answer to that will require another venue, but perhaps he could use "attention" or the gaze of the mind to explain this, the will directs the gaze of the mind to focus on some of the intentional objects being produced by the many actual intellectual acts in the intellect. Thus, attention, just as much as the imagination, could be a device to explain why we have only a limited number of thoughts at once, and one that could be used also with separated souls.

Interestingly, Auriol does in fact give a way of positing a difference between the species in the intellect, on the one hand, and the intellectual act (*intellectio*), on the other; in addition, he claims that there is a way to talk about the intellect's being in first and second actuality with regard to its cognition. Both of these return us to the material we dealt with in the first part of this paper. Recall that for Auriol intellection—true understanding—is only said to occur when the object of understanding *appears* to the one who is said to understand. For Auriol, cognition is based upon consciousness, and in order to be said to understand $x$, you have to be conscious of $x$ because $x$ appears to you. With that in mind, Auriol's suggestion is that we can use the term "species" to denote all of those intellectual acts of which we are in possession, but of which we have no awareness because the object of those acts are not *appearing* to us: this is the intellect in first act (not, however, in accidental potentiality, since the intellect is fully actualized, just not accessible to conscious experience). On the other hand, we can call "intellection" that one intellectual act at a time whose object does appear to us, and this is the intellect in second act.[49] When we go from the intellect in first act to the intellect in second act, we possess the same reality— the same absolute of intellection is inhering in the intellect—there is a merely "intentional" difference, inasmuch as the object of intellection now appears to the conscious cognizer. This fits well with the claims of Auriol that we saw earlier: that species and *intellectio* are really (*realiter*) the same as the intellectual act. So, Auriol can save in his cognitive theory the use of the term "species," and the distinction between first and second act, through a type of semantic distinction. But that should not obscure the fact that he has rejected the intelligible species on any normal understanding of it, claiming that in the intellect we have only intellectual acts, and that these intellectual acts are all in full act—we have no dispositional or habitual knowledge as such, what we have is actual knowledge that is non-occurrent on account of the fact that we can entertain in the imagination only one image at a time, and in order to be con-

---

49. Auriol, II *Sent.*, d. 11, pars 3, q. 1: "*Ex hoc patet quomodo in intellectu distinguitur actus primus, qui est species, ab actu secundo, quae est intellectio. Non enim sunt duae realitates in intellectu, sed eadem realitas dicitur species quoad realitatem praecisam et absolutum intellectionis, et ex hoc habet praecise quod sit actus primus. Eadem autem realitas ut connotat rem secundum esse obiectivum apparens, dicitur intellectio. Et quia potest realitas illa esse in intellectu absque hoc quod res per illam capiat esse obiectivum et praesens, puta si phantasia non sit in actu circa rem illam, hinc est quod species potest esse in intellectu absque intellectione.* . . . *Ideo facta intellectione rosae in intellectu, quae idem est quod species eius, et facta phantasia in actu respectu eiusdem, statim sequitur per modum sequelae necessariae esse intellectivum et obiectivum ipsius rosae in intellectu. Sic ergo mutatio non est ad esse intentionale in intellectu per se; sed sequitur ad ipsam intellectionem et actum phantasiae simul vel ad alterum si alterum praefuit.*" Florence, BNC, conv. soppr. A.3.120, f. 48va; ed. 1605, pp. 130bF–131aC. See also ibid., p. 131bB–D.

scious of something there has to be a coincidence between the object of the intellect and the object of the imagination.[50]

Summing up: For Peter Auriol, concept formation comes about in the following way: a true mental representation, a likeness of the thing, informs the intellectual power, and the intellect so informed simply is in act. The intellectual act issues into a metaphorical production of the thing understood in intentional being, the thing itself in another mode of existence, *esse apparens*; the same intellectual act also "reads" the intentional object that it produces and contains. The intellectual act is inseparable from both of these respects towards the intentional object; it cannot even be thought to exist without them. When the object considered in the imagination coincides with the object of one of these acts of the intellect, then the intellect and the person understanding truly cognize that object, because the intentional object—the object of cognition in apparent being—appears to the conceiver. At that point we are having conscious experience, precisely because we are being appeared to. This is the hallmark of the cognitive for Auriol. According to him, all the other mental representations might as well be shone to a wall or a floor; only when a thing *appears* to a cognitive power is there cognition. In this way one can say that consciousness, or the ability to be appeared to, is the most primitive category in Auriol's theory of cognition, that which is explanatorily basic.

There are a great number of problems or at least puzzles about Auriol's view: It is very "spooky" in its use of intentional being, and Auriol owes us an explanation for how a real intramental representation can help us put the extramental object itself into a different type of being. And to return to the caveats with which I began this chapter, I think neither that Auriol has a compelling theory of consciousness nor that he would have been alone among medievals in thinking the appearance of the thing to be an important part of cognition. But for him the fact that something appears to a cognizer, the fact that the cognizer is

---

50. In his *Quodl.*, q. 8, a. 3, Auriol claims (ed. 1605, p. 85bC) that "licet species et actus cognitivus idem sint secundum suum absolutum, tamen differunt ratione in hoc quod ubicumque in potentia non-apprehensiva, aut vitali dispositione existente in qua non est apprehensiva, similitudo illa ponatur, habet rationem tantummodo speciei et non actus, et ideo species in memoria sensitiva aut in medio non est comprehensio; in potentia vero cognitiva est comprehensio, non additur autem, dum est comprehensio, nisi sola praesentialitas et apparentia obiect<iv>i, quod est purum ens rationis," and he appeals (ed. 1605, p. 86aE–F) to the coincidence of the object of the imagination and intellect as the reason that there can be "species" (which seem also here to be intellectual acts we are not currently conscious of) in the possible intellect. All of this is based on what we can call "Auriol's cognitive rule" (ed. 1605, p. 84aA): "omnis similitudo existens in potentia cognitiva ultimate disposita est actus cognitivus." Thus, in his magisterial *Quodlibet*, Auriol has nuanced his view: a species and an act differ only rationally; when a species is in a fully (*ultimate*) disposed apprehensive power, then it is a cognitive act; otherwise it is merely a species; a part of the intellect's being fully disposed is the coincidence of the object of imagination and intellect.

aware or conscious, is the all-important point in his cognitive theory; it is what cognition is all about. This overwhelming emphasis on cognition as the thing's appearing does seem to be something significant and interesting about Peter Auriol, especially inasmuch as it is an emphasis that will only gain in importance as we enter the modern world.

# Ockham's Externalism

CLAUDE PANACCIO

Externalism in recent philosophy is the idea that the internal states of an agent do not suffice in general to determine the content of what she thinks, or knows or does not know, or the meaning of what she says. Under one guise or another, externalism has been defended by some of the most prominent analytic philosophers of the last three or four decades, including Hilary Putnam, Saul Kripke, Tyler Burge, Jerry Fodor, Donald Davidson, Ruth Millikan, David Armstrong, and Alvin Goldman. What I would like to show here is that there was already an important externalist drive in William of Ockham's theory of language and mind in the early fourteenth century.[1]

Of course, there are different varieties of externalism to be distinguished:

*Linguistic externalism* is the thesis that the meaning of the words a speaker utters does not solely depend on the internal state of the speaker at the moment of their utterance, but on certain external factors as well.

*Mental content externalism* is the thesis that the very content of what an agent thinks does not solely depend on the internal states of the agent, but on certain external factors as well.

*Epistemic externalism* is the thesis that what an agent believes or knows does not solely depend on the internal states of the agent, but on certain specific external factors as well.

---

I would like to express my deepest gratitude to the Canada Research Chair Program, the Social Sciences and Humanities Research Council of Canada, and the University of Quebec at Montreal, for having generously supported the work that led to the present paper. I have also greatly benefited from the discussions that followed preliminary presentations of it in St. Louis (Missouri), Pisa, and Montreal, and thank, consequently, all those who participated in these stimulating exchanges.

1. All references to Ockham's works will be to the standard critical edition in two series: *Opera Theologica* (*OTh*), 10 vols., ed. by G. Gál et al. (St. Bonaventure, N.Y.: Franciscan Institute, 1967–1986); and *Opera Philosophica* (*OPh*), 7 vols., ed. by G. Gál et al. (St. Bonaventure, N.Y.: Franciscan Institute, 1974–1988). The source of the English translation will be given for each particular quotation.

All three varieties have often been presented as radical innovations with respect to traditional philosophy of mind, language and knowledge. And the explosion of externalism in recent decades is indeed a phenomenon of major importance. Yet it is not something entirely new in the history of philosophy. What I would like to show here about Ockham is:

> First, that there is a full-fledged form of *linguistic externalism* to be found in his philosophy.
> Second, that there is a robust form of *mental content externalism* as well.
> Third, that Ockham is committed to a large extent to *epistemic externalism*, especially with respect to knowledge.

## LINGUISTIC EXTERNALISM

It would be interesting to scrutinize how linguistic externalism gradually developed in the late thirteenth and early fourteenth centuries. Henry of Ghent seems to have opened the way for this, but the real pioneer was John Duns Scotus. Scotus clearly broke with a principle that was largely accepted before him concerning the relation between language and thought, namely, the principle that something can be signified—or named—only as it is understood: *sicut intelligitur, sic et significatur*, sometimes called the modistic principle. The meaning of uttered words, according to this principle, was supposed to be entirely determined by the intellections of their speaker. Scotus explicitly rejected this internalist principle:

> this proposition which is common to many doctrines—namely that "something is named only as it is understood"—is false if it is understood precisely, since something can be signified more distinctly than it is understood.[2]

Scotus's point in this passage is theological: we can use spoken names that precisely and distinctly signify God, he wants to hold, even though we do not have a precise and distinct understanding of God. For him, the meanings of words are still connected with concepts somehow, but there need not be a one-to-one correspondence between what is in the mind of a particular speaker when she refers to God and the meanings of the words she uses. Scotus's rejection of the modistic principle, then, does amount in the end to a rejection of linguistic internalism, and it would be fascinating, no doubt, to look at this more closely. My focus here, however, will be on Ockham, who follows Scotus on this, but

---

2. John Duns Scotus, *Ordinatio* I, 22, q. unica, Editio Vaticana V:343 (my translation). See on this E. Jennifer Ashworth, "'Can I Speak More Clearly than I Understand?' A Problem of Religious Language in Henry of Ghent, Duns Scotus, and Ockham," *Historiographia Linguistica* 7 (1980): 29–38, e.g. p. 36: "Henry of Ghent, Duns Scotus and Ockham ... agreed ... that the Thomistic connection between spoken language and understanding had to be loosened."

goes much further in that he places this rejection in the context of a full-fledged semantic theory.

The main Ockhamistic idea to which I want to draw attention in this context is the idea of *subordination* (*subordinatio*). Spoken words, for Ockham, do not signify concepts (as they do in Thomas Aquinas, for example), but rather things. The English spoken word "horse" signifies not the concept of horse, but horses themselves, real singular horses.[3] In itself, however, this particular semantic thesis is not sufficient to warrant the attribution of linguistic externalism to Ockham. For even though spoken words do not *signify* concepts according to his manner of speaking, their signification, nevertheless, is not independent from concepts. The semantic dependence of words on concepts is what Ockham calls "subordination":

> I say that spoken words are signs subordinated to concepts or intentions of the soul not because in the strict sense of "signify" they always signify the concepts of the soul primarily and properly. The point is rather that spoken words are imposed to signify the very things that are signified by concepts of the mind, so that a concept primarily and naturally signifies something and a spoken word signifies the same thing secondarily. . . . The same sort of relation I have claimed to hold between spoken words and impressions or intentions or concepts holds between written words and spoken sounds.[4]

Concepts signify things naturally—they are "natural signs" of things (*signa naturalia*). Then, certain spoken sounds are conventionally subordinated to certain concepts, thus inheriting the signification of these concepts. Written marks in turn can be conventionally subordinated to spoken words, thus inheriting the signification of these spoken words. This last point is to be especially noted: Ockhamistic subordination is not always a relation between a spoken word and a concept. There is a more general idea here, and a very useful one too as far as I can see, the gist of which is: when a new sign is subordinated to a previously existing one, the result of this conventional operation is that the newly instituted sign inherits the signification—or more generally, the semantic features—of the previously existing sign, *whatever that signification was*.

A salient aspect of Ockham's idea of subordination, which has often been missed by commentators, is that the conventional subordination of a new sign is something that takes place at the moment of the *imposition* of the new sign. What the medievals called the "*impositio*" of a sign was its *original* institution as a conventionally significant unit (whether by an explicit decision or by tacit

---

3. For an overall presentation of Ockham's theory of concepts, see Claude Panaccio, *Ockham on Concepts* (Aldershot: Ashgate, 2004).

4. Ockham, *Summa logicae* I, 1, *OPh* I, 7–8. In Michael J. Loux, *Ockham's Theory of Terms. Part I of the Summa Logicae* (Notre Dame, Ind.: University of Notre Dame Press, 1974), 50. There is one amendment: I translate "*imponuntur*" by "are imposed" rather than by "are used," as Loux does; as we are about to see, the point is of some significance.

agreement based on common use). When Ockham says (in the passage quoted before) that subordination occurs when "spoken words are imposed [*imponuntur*]," he is explicitly referring, with the right technical term, to the original introduction of the conventional sign (however this introduction may have taken place). The point deserves to be stressed, because many commentators suggest that subordination in Ockham is the relation that holds between the spoken utterance of a given speaker and the concept that *that* speaker has in mind at the moment of utterance. That is not case.

Subordination, for Ockham, relates the spoken word with the concept chosen by the person (or group of persons) who originally instituted the word, the "impositor" (*imponens*) in Ockham's vocabulary. Here is another passage drawn from the *Ordinatio*, where the point is made even more explicitly:

> a certain spoken word primarily signifies several things equally because *it has been imposed by a single imposition* to everything which a determinate concept *of the impositor* is common to, so that the word and the concept are to each other like ordered signs.... Such is the spoken word "man," and this is why it is simply univocal: *the person who imposed this word "man"* intended [*intendebat*] that it should signify every thing which a determinate concept of the mind is true of.[5]

"Man" is a univocal word in spoken language insofar as it has been subordinated to one single concept *when it was originally instituted*.

An equivocal word, by contrast, is characterized by Ockham as a word which, in the course of its history, was subordinated to several different concepts: "A spoken word is equivocal if, in signifying different things, it is a sign subordinated to several concepts rather than one concept or intention of the soul."[6] This definition of equivocation confirms that subordination is not the relation that holds between a word and the concept that the speaker has in mind in uttering the word. If that were the case, a word such as "bank" would *not* be equivocal if the speaker happened to have a single determinate concept in mind when using it. This is not what we want, and it is not what Ockham wanted either. If I say "the bank is far," my utterance of "bank" is equivocal even though in uttering it I may very well have in my mind one particular meaning. The precise reason why this is so, according to Ockham's semantics, is that equivocation depends on subordination, and subordination in turn depends on imposition (or *impositions* in the plural, if there happen to have been several such impositions for the same spoken word).

In contrast, a term is univocal when it depends on a single imposition even if it should signify many things at once. The word "man," for example, signifies

---

5. Ockham, *Ordinatio* I, 2, q. 4, *OTh* II, 139–140 (my translation and italics).
6. Ockham, *Summa logicae* I, 13, *OPh* I, 45 (trans. Loux [1974], 75; with minor emendations).

several things at once, namely, all the men there are, but it is nevertheless univocal since this meaning has been instituted by a single imposition:

> Whoever it was that *first instituted* the use of the term "man" saw some particular man and coined the term to signify that man and every substance like him.... But even though it signifies indifferently many men, "man" is not equivocal, for in signifying indifferently many men it is a sign subordinated to just one concept and not many.[7]

The mention of "whoever it was that first instituted the use of the term" leaves no doubt here that Ockham is self-consciously referring to the original imposition rather than to what happens in the mind of the speaker at the moment of utterance.

I propose, therefore, to reconstruct Ockham's idea of subordination in the following formula:

> A sign $S_2$ is subordinated to a sign $S_1$ if and only if $S_2$ has been imposed to signify whatever it is that $S_1$ signifies (and to signify it under the same modes, if any).

The consequence I want to draw attention to is that a *gap* now becomes possible between the meaning of the words a certain speaker uses and the concepts that this speaker has in mind at the moment of utterance. Consider the following passage from Ockham's *Summa Logicae*: "since words are conventional, merely absolute spoken words [roughly: natural kind terms] can be imposed on those things of which we have, *or others have*, such concepts."[8]

What this implies is that some of the words we use may be subordinated to concepts that we do not have, but that *others* have. Ockham gives the example of the concept of lion, informing us in the process (in a rare personal note!) that he himself had never seen a lion.[9] Given his own view that simple absolute concepts are normally acquired on the basis of singular intuitive encounters, it follows that Ockham himself, having never seen a lion, could not have in his own mind the simple absolute concept of lion. So whenever a speaker such as himself uses a sentence with the word "lion" in it (or *"leo"* in Latin), what he has in mind on the occasion is not the simple absolute concept that the word is supposed to have been originally subordinated to, but a certain complex description. Yet, this does not prevent the word "lion" from being subordinated to the simple absolute concept of lion, even in the mouth of somebody (like Ockham himself) who does not have this concept.

This is precisely the reason why Ockham thinks that a particular speaker can fail to notice that some of the words he uses are synonymous with one another:

7. Ibid. I, 43, *OPh* I, 124 (trans. Loux [1974], 136; my italics).
8. Ibid. III–2, 29, *OPh* I, 558 (my translation and italics).
9. Ibid. III–2, 25, *OPh* I, 550; see also III–2, 29, *OPh* I, 559.

> More broadly, expressions are synonymous which simply signify the same thing.... In this sense terms are called synonymous even when those using the terms do not believe that they signify the same thing, but rather wrongly think that something is signified by one which is not signified by the other. Some people could think, for example, that the name "God" signifies a certain whole while "Divinity" signifies a part of that whole [although those two terms are in fact synonymous (in the broad sense)].[10]

The point here is that two different spoken words could have been subordinated to the same concept by their original impositors without some of their users being clearly aware of that fact, even though they are able to use those words correctly in most cases.[11]

It is then both possible and legitimate that we should sometimes use words—and use them correctly—without having in mind the concepts from which these words draw their signification. Ockham goes so far as to consider, in the *Ordinatio*, a case where even the impositor does not himself have the relevant concept in mind at the moment of imposition:

> Moreover, it is possible for somebody to impose this name *a* to signify whatever animal will appear to him tomorrow. This being done, the word *a* distinctly signifies this animal, and it will signify it for all those who are willing to use the word as it was imposed, even though the impositor does not have a distinct intellection of this animal, and maybe will not have one when it appears to him.[12]

A sufficient condition for the success of imposition, here, is that the concept to which the newly instituted word is subordinated should be, somehow, uniquely determined. Some individuating condition for this concept must be made clear by the impositor, but she does not need to have the concept actually in mind at the moment of imposition.

A wide variety of similar cases could be imagined. I could ask someone, for example, to have a particular concept in mind without telling me which, and I

---

10. *Ibid.* I, 6, *OPh* I, 19 (trans. Loux, 58, with minor amendments).

11. David Chalmers thinks that there is a contradiction in Ockham between the admission that a particular speaker could fail to notice that some of the spoken words she uses are synonymous with each other, and his (well-known) thesis that there should be no synonymy among the concepts of a given person. Chalmers, "Is There Synonymy in Ockham's Mental Language?" in *The Cambridge Companion to Ockham*, edited by Paul V. Spade (Cambridge: Cambridge University Press, 1999), 88. Chalmers reasons that since the signification of a spoken word is supposed to come from its being subordinated to a given concept, any normal speaker should be in a position to know which concept it is that the words she uses are subordinated to. The mistake here, as we can now clearly see, is precisely that Chalmers wrongly thinks of Ockhamist subordination as being the relation that holds between a spoken word and the concept that the speaker has in mind when uttering it.

12. Ockham, *Ordinatio* I, 22, q. unica, *OTh* IV, 56 (my translation).

could then choose a word—"*b*," for example—and subordinate it to that precise concept that the person in question has in mind, even though I do not have the slightest idea which concept it is. Ockham's general approach to subordination opens up many such possibilities.

Another interesting point to be noted about the particular passage I just quoted is its reference to "all those who are willing to use the word as it was imposed." This suggests that the condition which must be fulfilled for a word to have a certain determinate meaning when it is used by a given speaker is not that the speaker should have that meaning in mind, but that she should be willing to use the word in conformity with a certain determinate imposition. Suppose, for example, that you have baptized your dog "Fred." I can be willing to use the name "Fred" as you have imposed it, even though I have never seen the dog in question. I might not even know that Fred is a dog. I could try to guess, for example, who Fred is, by asking questions such as "Is Fred a human being?" In my asking of the question, the word "Fred" designates your dog, even if I do not know it, because it is clear, in this context, that I am accepting your imposition for the name. This yields a proto-Kripkean conception not only of proper names, but of every other category of words as well.

What we arrive at in the end is a clear form of linguistic externalism, quite similar to that proposed by Hilary Putnam in the 1970s. Ockham's position on such matters strikingly contrasts with, for example, John Locke's paradigmatically internalist position:

> words, in their primary or immediate signification stand for nothing but the ideas *in the mind of him that uses them*. . . . That then which words are the marks of are the ideas of the speaker: nor can any one apply them as marks, immediately, to anything else but the ideas that he himself hath.[13]

Against this form of internalism, Ockham is on Putnam's side: the signification of words does not essentially depend on what the speaker happens to have in mind when uttering the words.

Ockham's specific contribution to linguistic externalism lies in his idea of *subordination*, which strikes me as a fruitful and illuminating idea. It makes clear, in particular, how a certain word can be conventionally introduced into a language without a definition being given, and even without the word being in any way semantically located with respect to other words of the same language. Suppose, for example, that there is no word in French corresponding to "mutton" in English. I can introduce one, "*muton*," let us say, simply by subordinating this newly coined French word "*muton*" to the English word "mutton." From then on, for all the speakers (if any) who are willing to accept *my* imposition, the French word "*muton*" will have the same meaning as the English word

---

13. John Locke, *An Essay Concerning Human Understanding* III, 2, 2, ed. Alexander C. Fraser (New York: Dover, 1959), 2:9.

"mutton," even if I myself am in no way familiar with this meaning. Ockham's notion of subordination turns out to be a well-defined idea, opening appealing perspectives for linguistic externalism.

## MENTAL CONTENT EXTERNALISM

Now, what about mental content? Can Ockham be credited with mental content externalism, in addition to linguistic externalism? The situation here, as we will see, is a bit more complicated, but the answer is still affirmative.

For Ockham, mental concepts are natural signs. Our present question, then, primarily has to do with how the natural signification of concepts is determined. But distinctions have to be made. Here I will discuss, first, the case of singular intuitive acts; second, the case of general natural concepts; and third, the special case of what I will call "conventional concepts."

### Intuitive Acts

Ockham distinguishes between sensitive intuition, which is perception proper, and intellectual intuition, which is the actual singular grasping of an object by the intellect.[14] However, this does not concern the present inquiry. Our question is: How, in general, is the content of an intuitive grasping determined, whether it be perceptual or intellectual?

To this question, Ockham's answer is strictly externalistic, as can be seen by the ingenious thought experiment he devises in his *Reportatio*.[15] Suppose, he says, that an angel could see what is in my mind when I have an intuitive grasping of something. Could the angel tell exactly which object it is that I am intuiting? His answer is: if there are two singular objects equally close to me (which the angel could see), then the angel would not know which one I am intuiting simply by scrutinizing my internal intuitive act, especially, Ockham adds, if the two objects are similar to each other. What the angel would have to know in addition is which one is the *cause* of my present intuitive grasping. The internal aspect of my intuitive grasping, in other words, is not in itself sufficient to uniquely determine the object of my particular intuition. *Causality* is required.

Consider the following passage, also from the *Reportatio*:

> I say then that an intellection is a similitude of the object . . . and no more a similitude of one object than another [supposing those two objects to be similar to each other]. And therefore *similitude is not the precise cause why the mind intelligizes one object rather than another one* . . . for although the intellect assimilates equally to all these individuals in the case under consid-

---

14. See, for example, Ockham, *Quodlibeta* I, 15, *OTh* IX, 83–86: "Does our intellect know sensible things intuitively in this life?" William of Ockham, *Quodlibetal Questions*, trans. Alfred J. Freddoso and Francis E. Kelley (New Haven: Yale University Press, 1991), 72–74.
15. Ockham, *Reportatio* II, 16, *OTh* V, 378–379.

eration, nevertheless, it can cognize one of them determinately, and not the other one. But this is not in virtue of assimilation, but in virtue of the fact that every naturally producible effect by its very nature is such that it is produced by one efficient cause and not by another.[16]

Like all mental representations, singular intuitive graspings are likenesses of their objects for Ockham. But if so, they are likenesses as well of whatever it is that sufficiently resembles their singular object. A singular grasping of a given object, then, might be a likeness of several objects at once. What makes it the grasping of one of these, and not of the others, is that it is caused by only *one* thing, which *is* its object (just as in the case of a photograph).

It follows from this that two cognizers could be in maximally similar internal states, while one of them is intuiting something and the other one is intuiting something else. The observing angel would not notice any internal differences between the states of mind of these two persons. Their objects, nevertheless, would be different, because the states of these two cognizers would have been caused by two different objects. Ockham, consequently, is a full-fledged externalist with respect to the content of singular intuitive graspings.

## Natural General Concepts

There are *prima facie* reasons to think that the same holds for general concepts. Let us return to a passage from the *Summa Logicae* which I quoted earlier. "Whoever it was that first instituted the term 'man,'" Ockham writes, "saw some particular man and coined the term *to signify that man and every substance like him*."[17] This passage, admittedly, has to do with the institution of a spoken word, the spoken word "man" or "*homo.*" But, we have good reasons to think that the process described here closely corresponds to what happens when a general concept is naturally acquired.

The reason is this: Ockham holds that one encounter suffices for the acquisition of basic species concepts such as "man" or "horse" (although it does not suffice for more general genus concepts like "mammal" or "animal").[18] Suppose I see a horse for the first time under good conditions of observation. I auto-

---

16. *Ibid.* II, 12–13, *OTh* V, 287–288 (my translation and italics). The last sentence of this quotation expresses a principle about causality in general to which Ockham firmly adheres: in the natural order, every singular thing has one and only one (possibly complex) efficient cause. For every natural effect, then, the actual cause of this particular effect is always uniquely determined. This, however, does not yield any special internalistic consequences for our present discussion, since, as the angelic thought experiment makes clear, nothing in the internal structure of the effect is such for Ockham as to reveal the identity of the cause to an ideal observer who would not already know it from some other source. In other (non-naturally) possible worlds, the same effect could be caused by a different cause.

17. Ockham, *Summa logicae* I, 43, *OPh* I, 124 (trans. Loux, 136; my italics).

18. See Ockham, *Quodlibeta* IV, 17, *OTh* IX, 385: "the concept of the species can be abstracted from a single individual" (trans. Freddoso and Kelley, 317). But also: *Quodlibeta*

matically acquire, then, Ockham thinks, the concept of "horse." This is an *absolute* concept, in Ockham's vocabulary, that is to say, a natural kind concept, by and large. And it is a *simple* concept, which is not represented in the mind by a complex definition. What is it, then, that determines its content? Since we are speaking of a simple absolute concept, what *we* call its "content" is nothing but its extension. My concept of "horse" is a natural sign in my mind for all horses indifferently, and it refers, directly or indirectly, to nothing but horses. So when we ask, "What is it that determines the content of a concept of this sort?" what we are asking in effect is, "What is it that determines its extension?" And the answer, I gather, must lie in the process alluded to in the passage from the *Sum of Logic* I, 43, quoted earlier. What must happen is this: I see some particular horse, and I automatically form a concept signifying both *that* horse (the one that caused the formation of the concept) *and* every substance like it.

The extension of such "absolute" concepts, in other words, is determined by two relations, *both external*. There is a causal connection on the one hand, just like in the case of intuitive graspings: which singular thing was it that caused the original formation of my concept? And there is, in addition, the relevant similarity *among substances*, what Ockham expresses by "every substance *like him.*" This is a wholly externalistic process. It is a Putnamian process, actually, except that it applies to concepts and not merely to words. Ockham's account of general absolute concepts is fundamentally externalistic.

Yet more must be said. Calvin Normore, in a recent paper within a collection of essays on Tyler Burge's externalism, has credited Ockham with a doctrine of what he, Normore, calls *"bare concepts."*[19] Bare concepts, in Normore's vocabulary, are signs of whatever they are the concepts of, but they do not connect these objects with anything else in the world, and they do not represent them *as* anything. In particular, these bare concepts do not convey any information whatsoever as to what their objects look like. "If my concepts are bare," Normore says, "nothing in them gives us a hook out to perception."[20] And Normore thinks this is what we have in Ockham. Tyler Burge, in his lengthy reply, responds very severely to this doctrine:

> It would be absurd to think that finite beings can perceive or think about ordinary objects and properties *neat*—incorporate them into perception and thought without doing so by representing them in some way.[21]

---

I, 13, *OTh* IX, 77: "the concept of a genus is never abstracted from [just] one individual" (trans. Freddoso and Kelley, 67).

19. See Calvin Normore, "Burge, Descartes, and Us," in *Reflections and Replies: Essays on the Philosophy of Tyler Burge*, ed. M. Hahn and B. Ramberg, 1–14 (Cambridge, Mass.: MIT Press, 2003).

20. Ibid., 4.

21. Tyler Burge, "Reply to Normore," in ibid., 305.

All mental representations, for Burge, convey in some way or other a representation *as* (something).

But did Ockham really deny that? I do not think so. Ockham, as I read him, was *not* a proponent of the "bare concept" account that Normore credits him with. As I see it, from his very first philosophical writings up to his last, Ockham always stuck to the idea that concepts are likenesses—or similitudes—of whatever they represent. And, I supposed this to hold for simple absolute concepts as well. I have documented the point in detail in chapter 7 of my *Ockham on Concepts*, where I quote several relevant passages—some of them from Ockham's later philosophical writings.[22] Consider the following, for example, from the *Quodlibeta*, which was obviously written in Ockham's mature period when he subscribed to the identification of concepts with intellectual *acts* rather than with purely ideal objects (called *"ficta"*):

> For like a *fictum, an act of understanding is a similitude of an object*, and is able to signify and supposit for things outside the soul, and is able to be the subject or the predicate in a proposition, and is able to be a genus or a species, etc.[23]

This is not a slip on Ockham's part. The idea that concepts are schematic representations, or *likenesses*, is indispensable if concepts are to fulfill one of the roles he expects them to play, namely, that of allowing the *recognition* of new objects as falling within their extension. Back when he still embraced the *fictum*-theory of concepts, Ockham had written, "we can have a cognition of a certain *fictum* which is equally related to all men, and *according to which we can judge about anything whether it is a man or not.*"[24] The point must hold as well within Ockham's later theory of concepts as mental acts. Even "absolute" concepts, then, do not simply have an extension. Whether they are thought of as *ficta* or as mental acts, one thing concepts are expected to do, for Ockham, is to help *in some way* in recognizing which individuals fall within their extension and which do not. In today's terminology, we would say that concepts should help somehow in the *categorizing* of new objects. This is why they have to represent

---

22. See Panaccio, *Ockham on Concepts*, 119–122. In discussing this part of my book, Peter King has expressed doubts about the significance of Ockham's appeal to cognitive similitude in his latest works. King, "Le rôle des concepts selon Ockham," *Philosophiques* 32, no. 2 (2005): 435–447; see also King, "Two Conceptions of Experience," *Medieval Philosophy and Theology* 11 (2004): 203–226, and "William of Ockham: Summa Logicae," in *Central Works of Philosophy*, ed. J. Shand (Chesham, UK: Acumen, 2005), 2:242–269. The passages I quoted from the *Quodlibeta*, however, still seem decisive to me. For my reply to King, see Claude Panaccio, "Réponses à mes critiques," *Philosophiques* 32, no. 2 (2005): 449–457.

23. Ockham, *Quodlibeta* IV, 35, *OTh* IX, 474 (trans. Freddoso and Kelley, 390; with minor amendments; my italics).

24. Ockham, *Ordinatio* I, 2, q. 8, *OTh* II, 278 (my translation and italics).

their objects *in some way*, just as Burge says. Ockham's absolute concepts, consequently, are not "bare concepts."

But how is this consistent with Ockham's externalism with respect to general concepts, as I described it a few paragraphs back? Ockham himself is not explicit on the point. Yet there is, I think, a straightforward way of reconciling his idea that concepts are likenesses with his strong endorsement of mental content externalism. The key to it is that the similarity of the concept to what it represents should not be thought of as what determines the *extension* of the concept. *How* the concept represents whatever it is that it represents should not, in this view, determine uniquely *what* the concept represents. What fixes the extension of an absolute concept, for Ockham—as I stressed earlier—is what object caused it, plus what other objects are essentially similar to that one. The extension of the concept is determined externalistically. But that in no way prevents the concept from representing its objects *in some way*. If the concept is to be helpful for categorizing objects, it must incorporate some perceptual schema. This is what conceptual likeness is all about. Ockham's concepts thus do offer, after all, "a hook out to perception" (to use Normore's phrase). They do provide perceptual schemata, which, however, do not determine their extension.

That the perceptual schemata enclosed in concepts should not determine their extension also has the advantage of smoothly accounting for the fact that these perceptual schemata can sometimes be misleading. My concept of "horse" could very well be a likeness of horses, in the sense that it could incorporate a perceptual schema for categorizing something as a horse. Still, there could be cases where the perceptual schema fails: it might happen, after all, that something which looks like a horse is not a horse, or that a certain horse, in some circumstances, does not look like a horse.[25]

Ockham's theory of concepts, then, is committed to integrating *within* absolute concepts some sort of recognitional schemata. But those are not what determine the extensions of the concepts. As it turns out, this is something Tyler Burge entirely agrees with: all thoughts and perception, according to him, provide a certain perspective on their objects; but such a perspective, he adds, could be "erroneous."[26] This is to say that concepts represent their objects in some way: they are not "bare concepts." But, how they represent their objects is not what fixes their extensions. For both Burge and Ockham, the extensions of simple concepts are externalistically determined.

Ockham, therefore, is committed to a robust form of mental content externalism, as well as to a robust form of linguistic externalism, even though he does not subscribe to the doctrine of "bare concepts."

25. See on this Panaccio, *Ockham on Concepts*, esp. 126–129.
26. Burge, "Reply to Normore," 304.

## Conventional Concepts

There is, in addition, another intriguing suggestion to be found in the *Venerabilis Inceptor* that goes even further in the direction of mental content externalism: the signification of some of our concepts is allowed by him, in at least one passage, to be determined by social linguistic conventions. What I have in mind is a development in the *Ordinatio* where Ockham discusses the acquisition of various kinds of *nonabsolute* concepts, namely: syncategorematic concepts, connotative concepts, and negative concepts. The doctrine he proposes there holds that such concepts are not naturally acquired, but are implemented in the mind on the basis of the representation *of words*:

> I say that there are no syncategorematic, or connotative, or negative concepts, except by mere institution. . . . Such concepts, however, can be imposed or they can be abstracted from words, and this is what happens in fact either always or generally. . . . From words which thus signify, then, the intellect abstracts common concepts which can be predicated of them, and *it imposes these concepts to signify the same thing that these external spoken words signify*. And in the same way, it forms with such concepts propositions which are similar to the spoken propositions and have similar properties.[27]

The process Ockham postulates here has two steps. First, the mind naturally forms mental representations of spoken or written words, just as it does for any other objects in the world, such as horses, men, and so on. I can naturally form, for example, a concept representing the spoken word "carburetor," or rather its tokens. This concept will *naturally* signify all the tokens of the spoken word "carburetor," just as my concept of horse naturally signifies all horses. From words, Ockham says in the passage just quoted, "the intellect abstracts common concepts *which can be predicated of them*"; concepts, that is, that apply to words: my *concept of* the word "carburetor," for example, is naturally apt to be truly predicated of certain linguistic tokens, each one of which, then, naturally belongs to its extension. That is the first step.

But there is also a second one: "and it [the intellect] imposes these concepts to signify the same thing that these external words signify." In the vocabulary I introduced earlier, this is to say that the intellect *subordinates* the concept it has just formed to the very word that this concept naturally signifies. The

---

27. Ockham, *Ordinatio* I, 2, q. 8, OTh II, 285–286 (my translation and italics). For a detailed analysis of this passage, see Panaccio, *Ockham on Concepts*, 146–151. For other references by Ockham to voluntarily instituted concepts or mental signs, see, e.g., *Ordinatio* I, 3, q. 2, OTh II, 403: "Thirdly, I say that [God] can be cognized by us in a concept which is simple in a certain way and voluntarily instituted [*ad placitum instituto*] to signify" (my translation); and *Quodlibeta* IV, 35, OTh IX, 471, where Ockham says that a second intention is sometimes "able to signify mental signs that signify voluntarily [*ad placitum*]" (trans. Freddoso and Kelley [1991], 388; with a minor amendment: I prefer to translate *"ad placitum"* as "voluntarily" rather than as "conventionally").

concept, then, inherits the signification of the spoken word, just as in every other case of subordination the newly instituted sign inherits the signification of the previously existing sign to which it is subordinated. My concept, which naturally signified the tokens of the word "carburetor," now acquires *by imposition*—Ockham does use the technical term *"imponere"* here—a *new signification*, that of the word "carburetor." It now signifies not the tokens of the word "carburetor" as it naturally did, but the carburetors themselves as the word does; and it can, from then on, stand for carburetors in my mental propositions. Whereas before it could be truly predicated of linguistic occurrences, it can now, in its new meaning, be truly predicated of the *significates* of these linguistic units.

A striking consequence of it all, of course, is that I will now be stuck with an *ambiguous* concept with two different significations: a *natural signification*, on the one hand, which it does not lose (how could it?) and according to which it signifies the tokens of a certain spoken word, namely, the tokens of the word "carburetor"; and an *instituted signification*, on the other hand, according to which it signifies the carburetors themselves. Yet this is presumably the sort of ambiguity that the mind can live with in Ockham's view, an ambiguity it can successfully cope with in most cases. Ockham is not explicit on this in this particular case, but he does admit elsewhere that there are ambiguities of a closely related sort in mental language: "the third mode of equivocation," he holds, "can be found in a purely mental proposition."[28] This is the kind of ambiguity that occurs when a given term is allowed to have different suppositions depending on the propositional context in which it occurs. Use/mention ambiguities are the paradigmatic cases here: they occur when the propositional context is such as to allow for both personal and material supposition, for example (or personal and simple supposition; or even all three of them, as it may happen). And this is a situation that does obtain sometimes in mental language, according to Ockham. Now, it is true that the ambiguity between the natural signification of a concept representing words and its instituted signification is not exactly a use/mention ambiguity. But it is very similar to it. And if, according to Ockham, we are able to live with certain use/mention ambiguities in our mental language, we should be able to live with these ones as well without being confused all the time. Certain extrapropositional disambiguating factors might be available sometimes in both sorts of cases.[29]

The process Ockham postulates, in short, is a *reverse subordination*. Instead of subordinating a spoken word to a concept, we now subordinate a concept to

---

28. Ockham, *Summa logicae* III-4, 4, *OPh* I, 763 (my translation).
29. How suppositional ambiguities can (sometimes) be disambiguated in Ockham's mental language by the intervention of certain extrapropositional factors is briefly discussed in Claude Panaccio and Ernesto Perini-Santos, "Guillaume d'Ockham et la suppositio materialis," *Vivarium* 42 (2004): 202–224, esp. 220–223.

a spoken word. And as a result, we can use this concept in our mental propositions with this new signification, just as with any other mental term. This strikes me as a great idea. Admittedly, Ockham eventually renounced using it as a general account for the acquisition of all syncategorematic and connotative concepts. Yet the suggestion is independently intriguing that in certain cases—never mind which—such a reverse subordination process might occur, through which some of our natural representations—namely, our representations of words—could come to be used in our mental computations with the meanings of the very words that they naturally represent.

The suggestion, moreover, brings us a step further into externalism. What we are led to, if we follow the hint, is that the signification of *some* of our concepts can depend upon the conventional imposition of certain words by *other speakers*. This is why I speak of "conventional concepts" here. The interesting thing is that it could happen, according to this picture, that a thinking agent has but a very vague idea of the original signification of the word in question. I, for one, do in fact have but a very vague idea of the signification of the word "carburetor." Yet the Ockhamistic process of reverse subordination allows me to have a very precise concept of carburetor with all and only carburetors in its extension. The contribution of this concept to the truth-conditions of the mental propositions in which it occurs will be very definite indeed, even though I do not have myself a good grasp of these truth-conditions. In other words, the possibility that is opened by Ockham's hypothesis concerning reverse subordination is that some of my own concepts might be opaque to me to some extent—and, in some cases, even opaque to a very large extent—and still the concepts in question would not be vague or fuzzy; their signification would be entirely "determinate." What would be deficient in such situations would not be the signification of the concept, but my mastery of it. That the two can thus be distinguished points toward a very radical form of mental content externalism, much more radical, probably, than the *Venerabilis inceptor* ever consciously envisioned.

### EPISTEMIC EXTERNALISM

How Ockham is committed to epistemic externalism, finally, can be gathered from a close examination of his development of the very idea of *knowledge* in the Prologue of his *Ordinatio*, where he discusses the status of theology as a science, and in the Prologue of his commentary on Aristotle's *Physics*, where he discusses the epistemological status of natural sciences.[30] In the latter text, in particular, he distinguishes four senses of the term "*scientia*" (best translated as "knowledge" rather than "science").[31] According to all four senses, knowledge

---

30. See Ockham, *Ordinatio* I, Prologue, q. 1–8, OTh I, 3–225; and *Expositio in libros Physicorum Aristotelis*, Prologue, OPh IV, 3–14.
31. See Ockham, *Expositio in libros Physicorum Aristotelis*, Prologue, 2, OPh IV, 5–6.

is a mental state of the person who knows something: it is the assent the person gives—or is inclined to give—to certain mental propositions. Not any mental proposition will do, of course. At a minimum, a known proposition, according to all four senses, must be *true*: if I assent to a false proposition, my assent in that case, no matter how strong it may be, cannot correctly be assessed as knowledge.

Strictly speaking, that the known proposition must be true already constitutes an externalistic condition for knowledge: the truth of a proposition, most of the time, depends on the external world rather than on the internal states of the agent. But this is a rather trivial externalistic condition. No serious philosopher, after all, ever doubted that a known proposition must be true. The real disagreement between externalism and internalism in epistemic matters is about whether there is a subjectively recognizable feature of our states of knowledge which would allow the knower to distinguish them by mere introspection from other sorts of beliefs, whether, in other words, a person who knows something should normally be able to know by introspection that she knows it. This seems to be what Descartes, for one, would have liked, at least for the most basic cases of knowledge, when he proposed as a general rule that any thought is true which turns out upon inspection to be clear and distinct for the thinker himself.[32] Yet this is not something Ockham could have agreed with.

To see this, let us turn to the various senses of "knowledge" that he distinguishes. According to the first sense, a person $A$ knows that $p$ if and only if $A$ believes "$p$" with certainty *and* "$p$" is true.[33] What "certainty" means here is left unexplained, unfortunately, and it is not clear, in particular, whether it should correspond to a subjective condition such as the absence of doubt (as suggested by Ockham's own comments on the examples he gives) or to the fact that the belief in question is well-justified (as would seem more reasonable).[34] Whichever it is, the important thing to notice is that the certainty condition is not treated here by Ockham as sufficient by itself: *in addition to* being certain, the belief in question must be true in order to be a piece of knowledge. This strongly suggests that some beliefs could be both certain and false, and that certainty, therefore, whether it be purely internal and subjective or not, is not in Ockham's eyes a sufficient condition for the truth of what is believed. Since

---

32. See René Descartes, *Discours de la méthode IV*, ed. André Bridoux (Paris: Pléiade, 1953), 148: "je jugeai que je pouvais prendre pour règle générale, que les choses que nous concevons fort clairement et fort distinctement sont toutes vraies."

33. Ockham, *Expositio in libros Physicorum Aristotelis*, Prologue, 2, *OPh* IV, 5.

34. Ibid.: "For example, we say that we know that Rome is a big city, although we haven't seen it; and similarly, I say that I know that this is my father and that this is my mother, and so on, although these are not evidently known; but since we assent to these things without any doubt, and they are true, we say we know them" (my translation and italics). Note that although Ockham explicates his point by mentioning the absence of doubt in such cases, the examples themselves are all well-justified beliefs.

no other internal feature is mentioned, it is to be gathered that no internally recognizable mark of knowledge (in this first sense) is to be found within the knower himself according to Ockham.

The point indeed comes out more clearly with the second sense of "*scientia.*"[35] Knowledge, in this sense, is succinctly defined as "evident cognition" (*evidens notitia*), this latter phrase being taken, as the context makes clear, in the very same sense Ockham had defined in the Prologue of his *Ordinatio*:

> as to which cognition is evident, I say that an evident cognition is a cognition of some true propositional compound, which is such as to be sufficiently caused, either immediately or mediately, by the incomplex cognition of the terms.[36]

The first point to be noticed about this passage is that no cognition can be evident, in Ockham's sense, unless the cognized proposition is true. Even God could not give me an evident cognition of a falsehood since this would "involve a contradiction":[37] the very idea of an evident cognition, Ockham says, "implies that things are in reality as they are asserted to be by the proposition to which the assent is given."[38] Second, aside from its having a true proposition as its object, for Ockham, a certain belief is evident on account of *how it is caused*, namely, by the "incomplex cognition of the terms." By this, Ockham does not mean that the only evident propositions are those that are known to be true in virtue of our understanding of the meanings of their terms. It is clear from Ockham's own explanations that the "incomplex cognition of the terms," in this context, can be taken to be the incomplex cognition of the *referents* of the terms:

> For instance, even if nobody told me that the wall is white, from the very fact that I see the whiteness in the wall, I would know that the wall is white, and so on for other cases. In this sense, then [i.e. the second one], knowledge is not only of necessary propositions, but of contingent ones as well.[39]

When my incomplex apprehension of a wall plus my incomplex apprehension of the whiteness of this wall jointly cause in me an assent to the (true) proposition that the wall is white, the proposition in question can properly be said to be *known* (in the second sense).

Knowledge in this sense, then, is a matter of how the relevant belief is apt to be caused, and not a matter of how it is subjectively entertained by the agent. God, for example, could deceive me into believing that the wall is white when

---

35. Ibid., 6.
36. Ockham, *Ordinatio* I, Prologue, *OTh* I, 5 (my translation).
37. Ockham, *Quodlibeta* V, 5, *OTh* IX, 498 (trans. Freddoso and Kelley [1991], 415).
38. Ibid. (trans. Freddoso and Kelley [1991], 416).
39. Ockham, *Expositio in libros Physicorum Aristotelis*, Prologue, 2, *OPh* IV, 6 (my translation).

it is not. In such a case, my internal experience could be subjectively indiscernible from what it would be if I were really perceiving the white wall. In only one of these two situations, however, would I correctly be said to *know* that the wall is white, not only because the believed proposition happens to be true in one case and false in the other, but also because it is caused by the wall and its whiteness in one case and cannot have been so caused in the other. Since the actual causal process involved in a particular situation of this type is not something that I am normally aware of, it follows that even when I do in fact know that the wall is white, I do not automatically know that I know it.[40] Ockham's idea of knowledge in the second sense, consequently, is fully externalistic.

The same holds for the third and fourth senses of *"scientia"* as well, both being but specifications of the second. "In the third way," Ockham says, "we call 'knowledge' the evident cognition of something necessary"[41]; and in the fourth way, we call it "the evident cognition of some necessary truth, capable of being caused by the evident cognition of true premises through syllogistic reasoning."[42] The point of introducing these two restricted definitions is to accommodate the Aristotelian conception of science as the knowledge of what is necessary, the difference between them being that the former applies to the knowledge of principles as well as of conclusions while the latter holds only for conclusions insofar as they are reached by syllogistic means (the knowledge of principles in this last case being called by a name other than *"scientia,"* namely, *"intellectus,"* Ockham says, or maybe *"sapientia"*).[43] What is important for us, however, is that both definitions are built upon the idea of "evident cognition" introduced earlier. The externalistic implications of the second sense are thus carried over to the third and fourth as well.

The only special thing to mention in this regard is that the connection between the knowledge of principles and the knowledge of conclusions is also characterized by Ockham in this context as being *causal*. Syllogistic reasoning, for him, is a computational mechanism naturally implemented in the human mind in such a way that, in favorable cases at least, the assent to certain premises causally brings about the assent to the conclusion. Since the whole process is supposed to occur within the mind, it does not, strictly speaking, add to the

---

40. It cannot be the case, then, that Ockham's doctrine of intuitive cognition and evident knowledge is designed to allow the perceiving agent to rule out the possibility that she is presently being deceived by God, as suggested by Elizabeth Karger in "Ockham and Wodeham on Divine Deception as a Skeptical Hypothesis," *Vivarium* 42 (2004): 225–236. If a contingent belief is naturally caused in the right way, it cannot be false, admittedly, but since the agent cannot in principle *subjectively* distinguish this sort of situation from a case of divine deception, she cannot in principle rule out the latter on the basis of her subjective experience.

41. Ockham, *Expositio in libros Physicorum Aristotelis*, Prologue, 2, OPh IV, 6 (my translation).

42. Ibid.

43. Ibid.

externalistic import of Ockham's epistemology. But it clearly goes in the same direction insofar as no special awareness of the causal mechanism itself is postulated within the agent: an inclination to assent to certain conclusions, in such a case, occurs in the agent as a natural result of the assent she previously gave to some necessary premises, and the agent, then, can correctly be said to *know* the conclusions (in the strongest sense of "to know"), even though it cannot be inferred in such a situation that the agent has any introspectively accessible guarantee that she has the knowledge in question.

## CONCLUSION

On all three counts, in the end, Ockham clearly comes out as holding strongly externalistic theses: the meaning of our words does not directly depend on what we happen to have in mind when we utter them; the content of what we think generally depends on the causal history of our relevant mental states; and our knowledge has no introspectively accessible subjective mark that would internally distinguish it from mere belief. Ockham never brought all of this together, of course, nor did he fully explore its implications, some of which, one gathers, would probably have startled him. Ockham, admittedly, cannot be said to have self-consciously promoted a well-organized externalistic system. But the basic elements are there, and they jointly point to a radical renunciation of what Ruth Millikan calls "meaning rationalism," the idea, roughly, that what we mean, think, believe, or know is normally transparent to our own mind.[44]

The various elements of Ockham's externalism, moreover, are not merely scattered in his works and independent from each other. Two central driving ideas hold them together: Ockham's resolutely causal approach to intentionality on the one hand, and his articulate conception of the imposition and subordination of conventional signs on the other hand.

That the intentionality of the mental should basically be accounted for by causal connections with external things was, as we have seen, already strongly hinted at in Ockham's first writings, the *Ordinatio* and the *Reportatio*, yet the idea is even more consonant with his mature theory of concepts as mental acts. All mental intentional units, whether intuitive or abstractive, conceptual or propositional, are identified in this theory with real qualities of the mind.[45] None of them, then, is more intrinsically relational than, for example, a whiteness is, and none can have by itself anything like an intrinsic content. Whatever representational import they have—their extension, in particular, in the case of concepts, and their immediate object in the case of intuitive acts—always depends in the end upon their external causes. Even their intentional similarity with external objects—which is never renounced—comes out in this view as

---

44. See in particular Ruth G. Millikan Millikan, *White Queen Psychology and Other Essays for Alice* (Cambridge, Mass.: MIT Press, 1993), chap. 14.

45. See on this Panaccio, *Ockham on Concepts*, chap. 2: "Intellectual Acts."

secondary and instrumental with respect to what is causally determined. And knowledge itself occurs as such in human minds only insofar as certain assents are caused in them in some particular way. Since the causal processes that relevantly bear upon these conceptual and epistemic qualities of the mind are not immediately conspicuous to the agents themselves, in Ockham's view, both mental content and epistemic externalism directly follow.

The intentionality of the mental thus being implemented by natural causes, that of external linguistic signs is derived from it, according to Ockham, through the imposition/subordination process. The nature of this process, admittedly, is entirely different from the former one; there is nothing causal about it. What is effective in this case are the *decisions* or *volitions* of agents: the impositor, typically, attributes a meaning to a newly coined sign by *deciding* to subordinate it to a preexisting sign, and the other speakers, then, use the new sign with this instituted meaning insofar as they *voluntarily* accept this imposition. Linguistic institution for Ockham is a matter, not of natural causes, but of human decisions. And the scope of such institutive decisions can extend to whatever can serve as a sign, whether spoken, written, or even in some cases merely mental (as when certain naturally implemented signs are subjected to what I called "reverse subordination" earlier). The important point, nevertheless, is that these voluntary impositions are no more necessarily conspicuous to the users of the instituted signs than the relevant causal processes are to the possessors of natural mental signs. A strong version of linguistic externalism thus follows, and is even extended to the "conventional" meanings of some of our internal concepts.

The dynamics of our human world, for Ockham, simultaneously depend on natural causal processes and on autonomous acts of will, the two aspects being taken to work in completely different ways. As to intentionality, however, whether mental, linguistic, or epistemic, both converge toward a radically externalistic account.

# Was Adam Wodeham an Internalist or an Externalist?

ELIZABETH KARGER

Conceiving of the mind as a substance, Adam Wodeham regarded thoughts as accidents within the mind and their contents as fixed independently of things existing outside of it. He also recognized, however, that, in the normal course of nature, our simplest and most basic mental acts, by which we conceive of the nonmental things we form complex thoughts about, are ultimately caused by things existing outside our mind and within our environment. This doctrine is the subject of the present writing, the issue being whether it should be regarded as internalist, as the former feature suggests, or as externalist, as does the latter.[1]

In order to settle the issue, I provide first an account of the most general features of Wodeham's theory of mind. I next consider more especially those thoughts—presupposed by all others—that are acts by which things or states of affairs[2] are simply conceived of, not also feared or loved, for example, thoughts I call "intellections." I then focus more specifically on those intellections by which things, in particular nonmental things, rather than states of affairs, are conceived of, called "intuitive" and "abstractive" cognitions. They are the simplest and most basic mental acts referred to in the preceding paragraph. I shall explore first how the content of these cognitions is fixed, according to Wodeham, and second how, according to him, they are or could be caused. On the basis of this exploration of Wodeham's theory of mind, especially his theory of intuitive and abstractive cognitions, I propose to settle the issue at stake.

---

1. Evidence for the views I ascribe to Wodeham is given in these footnotes, where I quote mainly from Adam Wodeham's *Lectura secunda in librum primum Sententiarum* (ed. R. Wood and G. Gál, 3 volumes), hereafter referred to as *LS*. Occasionally, I quote from the so-called *Abbreviatio*, made by Henry Totting de Oyta from Wodeham's *Lectura oxoniensis*, edited by John Major, entitled *Adam Goddam super quatuor libros Sententiarum*.

2. Wodeham's ontology includes individual things, "natures" as he calls them, in particular substances and qualities, but not universals. It also includes, however, states of affairs. See footnote 14.

## WODEHAM'S SUBSTANTIALIST THEORY OF MIND

### Minds as Substances, Thoughts as Qualities

With the exception of the divine mind, all minds—or, as Wodeham often calls them, intellects—are, according to him, souls. Some souls, the angelic ones, do not inhabit bodies, but others, such as human souls, do. Not all souls are minds, however, for animal souls are not. Only angelic and human souls are minds or intellects.[3]

Being a soul, a mind is a substance, though a spiritual one. Spiritual and material substances, however, have some properties in common. A substance, material or spiritual, does not depend for its continuing existence on the existence of any other contingently existing thing. In this respect, substances differ from qualities. Qualities are things that depend for their continuing natural existence on the substance in which they inhere.[4] Another feature common to substances is that qualities inhere in them. Many of these qualities are short-lived, and when they go out of existence others replace them. This flow of qualities within a substance accounts for the qualitative changes a substance undergoes. For example, a leaf's change in color from green to yellow is accounted for by the going out of existence of one quality, a greenness, which was first produced in the leaf and its replacement by another quality, a yellowness.[5] In the case of a mind, there are qualities that inhere there as well, and many of them are also short-lived. The resulting flow of qualities in the mind is its flow of thoughts, and each of these short-lived qualities is an occurrent thought. Conversely, every occurrent thought is a short-lived quality inhering in the thinking mind.[6]

### Thoughts from a Third-Person Perspective

Material substances and the qualities that inhere in them are, in principle, publicly observable. Wodeham was bold enough to infer that, if minds are substances, the same must hold for them. Minds, then, and the qualities that inhere in them are observable by other minds. Wodeham recognizes, of course, that we do not, as a matter of fact, ever observe what is going on in another mind.

---

3. Wodeham held that human beings have but one soul, an intellective soul: "anima intellectiva . . . nulla alia anima est in homine," *LS*, d. 2, q. 4 (vol. II, 101).

4. By God's power, a quality could enjoy independent existence, but its existence would then not be "natural."

5. These qualities are individual things, not universals. See note 2.

6. Concurring here with Ockham, whom he quotes, Wodeham writes: "Intellectio enim (et universaliter omne accidens informans animam) est vera qualitas, sicut est calor vel albedo," *LS*, d. 8, q. 2 (vol. III, 42). "Intellectio" and "intentio" share the same manuscript abbreviation, and the editors of the *Lectura Secunda* have used both transcriptions. Preferring a uniform use of "intellectio" in all contexts where both terms are acceptable, I have substituted here and in other quotations "intellectio" for "intentio."

But he has an explanation for this fact. In punishment for our original sin, God has prevented the exercise of this particular capacity, which our mind nonetheless has by nature.[7]

Wodeham makes another bold move. He describes what we would see if, still in a state of innocence, we could look into another mind. We would, he claims, see the various mental acts, or as he calls them, "vital acts," present in the mind at the time of our looking. We would see them as the short-lived qualities they are. We would realize that some of these qualities cause others to appear, whereas some appear spontaneously. We would also see in the mind, as qualities, various dispositions to call to mind certain contents, dispositions which Wodeham calls "habits." These latter qualities, however, being more durable than the former, are not of the same sort. If we were dedicated enough in our observation, we would surely find that a quality of the latter sort tends to cause repeatedly, though not necessarily, a quality of the former sort. We might also note that there are qualities in both categories that are too dissimilar to be of the same kind. In fact, on the basis of systematic observations, we might set out to study other minds scientifically, thus initiating a new branch of natural science.[8]

There is, however, one thing we would not know of those short-lived qualities, which are all occurrent thoughts. We would not know what it is they are thoughts of, or, in other words, what their content is.[9] In fact, we would not even know *that they have a content at all*. A thought without content, however, would not be a thought. We would have to acknowledge, therefore, that we were seeing thoughts in the mind of another *as qualities*, not *as thoughts*. A branch of natural science could, then, be developed, having as its object the spiritual substances that minds are and the thoughts that inhere in them. It

---

7. "Intellectus enim humanus, si non impediretur ex condicione status poenalis, et etiam intellectus angelicus, posset per actus rectos, circumscriptis quibuscumque actibus reflexis, habere notitiam perfectam intellectionum, et quarumcumque cognitionum et actuum vitalium in aliena potentia...." *LS*, d. 23, q. un. (vol. III, 317–8).

8. "Intellectus enim humanus ... posset ... habere notitiam perfectam intellectionum, et quarumcumque cognitionum et actuum vitalium in aliena potentia, et multarum proprietatum naturalium earum. Puta quod quidam actus vitales [necessario] eliciuntur et causantur, et quidam contingenter, quod quidam nati sunt relinquere habitus inclinativos in similes actus, et quidam non; et multa similia [sicut] distinctionem specificam talium [actuum] et majorem vel minorem similium convenientiam vel disconvenientiam [eorum]. Potest enim perpendere de quibusdam actibus in alieno intellectu quod semper ponuntur ad praesentiam talium causarum, et de aliis quod non semper sed quandoque et quandoque non, et quod ad positionem talis qualitatis vel entitatis quae est intellectio, aliquando sequitur talis entitas quae est habitus." *LS*, d. 23, q. un. (vol. III, 317–8).

9. "Sed ... per hoc quod videt tales qualitates in alieno intellectu non potest sibi constare quod illae qualitates sunt cognitiones vel signa talium objectorum." *LS*, d. 23, q. un. (vol. III, 318). Nor would angels be more perceptive: "licet unus angelus videat intellectiones alterius, non per hoc novit quarum rerum iste intellectiones sunt signa." *Abbreviatio*, lib. I, d. 1, q. 2 (fol. 11ra). As we shall see in the next section, those thoughts which are intellections (or cognitions) are regarded by Wodeham as signs of their objects.

would be developed, as all natural sciences are, from a third person perspective. This branch of natural science would not, however, deal with thoughts *as thoughts*. Dealing with thoughts as thoughts does not, and cannot, therefore, pertain to natural science.[10]

### Thoughts from a First-Person Perspective

It is nevertheless possible to see the mind-inherent quality that a thought is insofar as it is a thought and to know what its content is. This is possible, however, only for the mind in which the quality exists, in other words, from a first-person perspective, or so Wodeham claims. Let us, then, follow his lead and describe what, according to him, we might see by looking into our own mind.

One way to proceed, he recommends, is to first look at something outside your mind, say, a stone. Now, while you are seeing that stone, look into your own mind. You are bound to "see" there the vision or, as Wodeham calls it, the "intellection" you are having of the stone. You are now having two intellections, by each of which you are apprehending just one thing. One is an intellection of a stone, the other an intellection of that intellection, that is, of the quality within your mind that the first intellection is. Moreover, having both intellections, you can form the complex thought that the intellection you are seeing is an intellection of a stone, a thought that immediately strikes you as true.[11] You are, therefore, now seeing a certain quality within your mind, which is an intellection of a stone, *as such*. This result could be generalized: provided the mind-inherent quality you are seeing is one existing in your own mind, you can see it as a thought and realize what its content is.

There are many kinds of occurrent thoughts and, therefore, many kinds of short-lived qualities that may exist in a person's mind.[12] Basic to all other kinds of thoughts, however, are those that Wodeham calls "intellections," of which we just considered two examples. Intellections are acts of apprehending some given object. The object apprehended may be just one thing, as when one sees a thing, or many things, as when one thinks of roses, though of none in particular,[13] or a state of affairs, possible or impossible, as when, preferring to

---

10. According to Wodeham, dealing with thoughts as thoughts pertains to logic. For more on this view, see E. Karger, "Adam Wodeham on the Intentionality of Cognitions" in *Ancient and Medieval Theories of Intentionality*, ed. D. Perler (Leiden: Brill, 2001), 295–296.

11. "scio me intelligere lapidem virtute notitiae intuitivae habentis intellectionem lapidis pro objecto. Non quia illa intuitiva cadit super intellectionem quae est lapidis et simul etiam super lapidem. Sed [quia] cadit super intellectionem tantum et illa intellectio super lapidem, ita quod anima assentit se intelligere lapidem non virtute alicuius unius actus simplicis, sed duorum, quorum unus habet pro objecto intellectionem quae est lapidis et alius lapidem...." *LS*, d. 1, q. 2 (vol. I, 217). See also *LS*, prol. q. 2 (vol. 1, 61–2).

12. Acts of willing, for example, are qualities of a certain kind: "ponendo volitionem qualitatem receptam in anima." *LS*, d. 1, q. 5 (vol. I, 282). See also the text quoted in note 27.

13. Acts of apprehending many things indiscriminately are called by Wodeham "abstractive cognitions." We shall consider these later.

remain silent rather than to speak, one conceives of both possibilities.[14] Intellections are basic to all other thoughts, for you cannot, for example, hate or love a person unless you have the person "in mind" whom you are loving or hating, unless, in other words, you are "apprehending" her.[15] Nor could you hope to win a race if your winning the race were something that never crossed your mind, that is, if you had never apprehended that state of affairs. Intellections thus provide all other thoughts with their content. Rather than take into account all thoughts or mental acts, it suffices, then, for our present purpose, that we examine Wodeham's theory of intellections.

## A THEORY OF INTELLECTIONS AS MIND-INHERENT QUALITIES

### Mind-Inherent Qualities as Mental Mediators

Every intellection by which a person apprehends a given object is, according to Wodeham, a quality inhering in the mind of that person.[16] As we have just seen, if you look into your own mind and see there a quality that is an intellection of a certain object, you see it as being the intellection it is and as having the object it has. This implies, however, that when a person apprehends a given object, her apprehending is a relation involving *three relata*: her mind (subject of the apprehending), the object apprehended, and a particular quality existing in her mind, which is the thing her intellection is. Why, however, is this quality needed? Why are not two entities, the mind and an object, provided it is present to the mind, sufficient to account for the mind's apprehension of the object? Among Wodeham's contemporaries, some apparently thought that this parsimonious mental ontology was indeed sufficient.[17] Nor did Wodeham himself believe that God needed any quality within his mind to think a thought, whatever its content. He did believe, however, that such qualities are needed for human thought, and in particular for those thoughts that are intellections.

---

14. In the *Abbreviatio*, lib. I, d. I, q.10 (fol. 35ra), in a passage Oyta copied from Wodeham's Oxford Commentary (the same passage is contained in codex Maz915, Bibliothèque Mazarine, Paris, fol. 46ra–b), it reads: "data mihi opportunitate silendi vel loquendi, si eligam silere non eligo aliquid, sumendo ly aliquid pro aliqua natura, nec etiam si eligo loqui, et tamen utroquemodo eligo aliquid eo modo quo dicimus eum aliquid cogitare qui ... cogitat antechristi animam non esse et dicitur secundo modo sumendo aliquid; et non esse sic loquendo est aliquid et omne significabile complexe sive negative sive affirmative [est aliquid]."

15. "omnis amor causabilis a voluntate, ad hoc quod sit ab ea, necessario requirit cognitionem realiter distinctam ab amore," *LS*, d. 1, q. 5 (vol. I, 277).

16. The quality can be simple or complex, as explained in note 21.

17. "illi qui ponerent quod intellectio et volitio non essent accidentia distincta ab anima ... ponerent animam esse intellectionem respective, et ideo non esse intellectionem nisi ad positionem vel approximationem etiam alicuius extrinseci, sicut albedo, secundum eos, non est similitudo nisi ad positionem alterius albedinis." *LS*, d. 3, q. 5 (vol. II, 224).

Mind-inherent qualities are needed, Wodeham believed, as *that by which* the mind apprehends an object.[18] Only the divine mind can directly apprehend an object because all objects are immediately present to it. This is not the case, however, with created minds. A created mind can apprehend an object only if the object is presented to it by a mental quality, which mediates between the mind and the object.[19] From the subject's point of view, however, it is as if the mental quality by which he apprehends an object were not there, for he is aware only of the object, not of the mental quality that presents the object to him. As we have seen, he can, by introspection, become aware of the mental quality itself, but that is by a new intellection, itself a new mental quality, of which, in turn, he is not aware except by yet another intellection.[20] In other words, whatever the object a mind apprehends, there is always a quality inherent in the mind—namely the quality that intellection is—which presents the object to the mind but of which the mind is not aware. It follows that direct realism is not compromised by Wodeham's doctrine. It would have been compromised only if the doctrine had required, for an object to be apprehended, that the mental mediator presenting the object to the mind be itself apprehended.

Wodeham describes the role a mind-inherent quality plays in the mind's apprehension of an object by saying that it *signifies* that object to the mind and is therefore a *sign* of that object.[21] The notion of signifying that Wodeham uses here is not, however, a new notion. It is rather the notion of apprehending under a new guise. For it holds by definition that a mind-inherent quality *signifies* to the mind in which it exists whatever it is that the mind *apprehends* by it.[22] Signifying in this sense differs therefore from apprehending only insofar as the items related are taken in a different order.

---

18. As Crathorn writes, in the counterfactual mode, because he does not share the view described: "si cognitio vel actus cognoscendi *quo* cognoscens cognoscit formaliter esset una qualitas superaddita potentiae cognitivae. . . ." *In primum librum Sententiarum*, q. 1, ed. F. Hoffmann (Munster: Aschendorff, 1988), 74; emphasis mine.

19. "illud, quo offeruntur menti res extra formaliter, maxime videtur ponendum esse cognitio; sed per istam qualitatem offeruntur potissime res menti . . ." *LS*, d. 8, q. 1 (vol. III, 10).

20. "concedo quod scilicet visio intellectionis lapidis videtur per aliam visionem quando judico certitudinaliter me videre visionem primae intellectionis, et sic de tertia et quarta." *LS*, prol., q. 2 (vol. I, 57).

21. "qualitas est signum repraesentativum et expressivum talis objecti." *LS*, d. 23, q. un. (vol. III, 318). Note, however, that if the object signified is a state of affairs, it is primarily signified not by a simple quality, but by a mental proposition, itself a complex quality that the mind composes out of simple ones: "sciendum quod quando intellectus format propositionem, componit aliquid cum aliquo, non aliquid unum per se constituendo," *LS*, prol., q. 6 (vol. I, 147). A state of affairs is accordingly called by Wodeham a "*complexe significabile*." See the text quoted in note 14.

22. "esse signum contingit . . . expressive per modum quo omnis apprehensio offert et exprimit potentiae, in qua est, illud quod apprehenditur." *LS*, d. 23, q. un., (vol. III, 316).

## Mind-Inherent Qualities as Things and as Signs

However, the mind-inherent quality any given intellection is has the paradoxical property that it is not necessarily an intellection. As with any quality, it could, by God's power, enjoy independent existence and exist outside any mind. But, if it existed in that way, it would not be that by which a mind apprehends something and would not, therefore, be an intellection.[23] Nor would the quality signify anything, there being no mind to whom it could signify.

Accordingly, Wodeham distinguishes two uses of the term "intellection" and its cognates. The term can be used to designate the mind-inherent quality that a given intellection is just as the quality it is. Used in that way, the term "intellection" is taken as an "absolute" term.[24] But the term can also be used to designate the quality insofar as it exists in a mind and the mind apprehends a certain object by it. In that case, Wodeham says, the term is then taken as a "relative" term.[25] Provided its subject-term is taken as an absolute term and its predicate-term as a relative term, the following sentence, which appears paradoxical, is perfectly legitimate and true: "This intellection is possibly not an intellection."

For an intellection in the absolute sense to be an intellection in the relative sense, it is both *necessary and sufficient* that it exist in a mind. This is a *necessary* condition, for no one could apprehend anything by an intellection existing elsewhere than in her mind or by an intellection which once existed in her mind but no longer does.[26] It is also a *sufficient* condition. As Wodeham writes, it

---

23. "licet non sit idem rem istam que est visio esse rem talem et esse visionem, eo quod si talis res per divinam potentiam fieret sine subjecto posset non esse visio." *Abbreviatio*, lib. IV, q.12 (fol. 152ra).

24. "hoc nomen 'intellectio' potest accipi, vel apud diversos de facto accipitur, pro signo subordinato conceptui absoluto illius qualitatis quae est intellectio." *LS*, d. 23, q. un., (vol. III, 318). Terms for other kinds of mental acts, as for example, 'volition,' can also be used as absolute terms, designating the mind-inherent quality that the mental act is: "illud quod est volitio vel nolitio vel cognitio absolute est volitio et cognitio." The same holds of terms such as "love" and "hate": "illud quod est amor vel odium vel cognitio absolute est amor vel odium vel cognition." *LS*, d. I, q. 5 (vol. I, 280).

25. "Vel [potest accipi] pro signo [subordinato] conceptui relativo illius qualitatis, pro quanto ipsa est cognitio et signum expressivum objecti cuius est intellectio <corr. ex: intellectus> menti in qua est." *LS*, d. 23, q. un., (vol. III, 318).

26. Immediately following the text quoted in footnote 11, Wodeham writes: "... in tantum ... quod si per potentiam Dei tolleretur prima intellectio et servaretur visio illius intellectionis et suspensa activitate memoriae et omnium talium, anima non assentiret se intelligere lapidem sed tantum se intelligere et quid, nesciret." *LS*, d. 1, q. 2 (vol. I, 217). The supernatural possibility Wodeham is considering here is one where the intellection of a stone (i.e., the quality that that intellection is), which existed in the mind of a person, is destroyed by God, while the vision of that intellection (i.e., the quality that vision is), which also existed in her mind, is preserved by God. It is further assumed that the person cannot—again by God's power—remember having seen a stone. If all this were the case, what would the person know in virtue of her vision of a now nonexistent intellection that was once an intellection of a stone? She would not, as in the normal case, where her intellection of the stone coexists in her mind with her vision of that intellection, know that the intellection she is seeing is of a

would be contradictory that an intellection should exist in a mind and that the mind not apprehend anything by it.²⁷ It follows that the quality a given intellection is necessarily signifies something to the mind in which it exists and only to that mind.²⁸

## The Object a Mind-Inherent Quality Can Signify

The identity of the object a given quality signifies to the mind in which it exists does not, however, depend on whose mind it is in which the quality exists. Rather, there is, according to Wodeham, one and only one determinate object (consisting in just one thing, or in many things or in a state of affairs) that the quality a given intellection is *can* signify to a mind in which it exists, no matter whose mind this may be, and whenever that may be.²⁹

This is made vivid by a thought experiment Wodeham considers. Suppose, he writes, that you are seeing a particular whiteness, and that God, while you are looking at it, replaces in an instant that whiteness by another exactly similar, while maintaining in existence in your mind the vision, that is, the quality that the vision is, by which you were seeing the original whiteness. Which whiteness would you now be seeing by that vision? Wodeham answers that the new whiteness is not capable of being seen by the vision by which the original one was.³⁰ You would be seeing, therefore, the original whiteness.

---

stone. The reason she could not know this is precisely that that intellection no longer exists in her mind (in fact it no longer exists at all) and that, therefore, she is no longer apprehending anything by it. Not realizing that the intellection she is seeing no longer exists, since she is seeing it, she would believe it to be—absolutely—an intellection, but she would have no idea what its object might be.

27. "Contradictio est intellectionem quamcumque esse subjective in mente . . . quin mens per eam formaliter aliquid concipiat." *LS*, d. 8, q. 1 (vol. III, 7). The same can be said of the qualities that other mental acts are, as for example volitions: "actus volendi ita (est) volitio quod ipsa posita in anima contradictio est quin ipsa anima velit, sicut contradictio [est] quod albedo informet aliquid quin illud sit album." *LS*, d. 1, q. 5 (vol. I, 280). Note that "habits" are not intellections, although they tend to cause some. They exist in a mind, therefore, without the mind apprehending anything by them. Nor are intellections and "habits" mind-inherent qualities of the same sort, as a mind that were to see them in another mind would recognize.

28. As we saw earlier, Wodeham further holds that the quality a given intellection is can be *seen as signifying something* only by the mind in which it exists. By any other mind, it would be seen only as being a quality. In other words, it would be seen by that other mind as being an intellection only in the absolute sense of the term "intellection"; it would not be seen as being an intellection in the relative sense of the term.

29. "iste actus qui semel representat potentie quam informavit objectum aliquod vel aliqua, semper, dum informat talem potentiam, precise eadem objecta sibi representabit per modum cognitionis." *Abbreviatio*, prol., q. 2 (fol. 7ra).

30. "sit albedo *a* visa visione *b* et post hoc instans annihilata *a* ponitur in eodem loco albedo *c* similis *a*, conservata priore visione scilicet *b*. Tunc quero: aut per *b* videbit *c* vel non . . . dicendum est quod *c* albedo non est nata videri visione *b* qua videtur *a*." *Abbreviatio*, lib. I, d. 3, q. un. (fol. 52rb–vb).

Another thought experiment where the object apprehended is a state of affairs brings home the same point. Suppose that by a certain (complex) intellection (a mental proposition), that is, by the (composite) quality a certain complex intellection is, Socrates thinks that he is seeing an angel.[31] Suppose that God, as he might, transfers that intellection from the mind of Socrates into that of Plato. What would Plato be thinking by that intellection? The very same state of affairs, namely, that Socrates is seeing an angel.[32]

Wodeham held, then, the rather startling view that the object of any given intellection is entirely fixed by the nature of the mind-inherent quality that intellection is. For that quality is *by nature* such that there is one and only one determinate object that *can* be apprehended by it. Accordingly, if that quality exists in a mind, that mind *necessarily* apprehends by it that object and no other.[33] The quality, moreover, has or would have that property even if, by God's power, it were not to exist in a mind at all. In that case, one would have to say that, *were* the quality to exist in a mind, that mind *would necessarily* apprehend by it the one and only object that *can* be apprehended by it.[34]

Was Wodeham entitled to this view, however? In other words, did he provide a theory of intellections within which this view can be consistently upheld? He did, at least with respect to simple intellections. The theory in point is his theory of intuitive and abstractive cognitions. Because intuitive and abstractive cognitions are all simple intellections and conversely every simple intellection is either an intuitive or an abstractive cognition, the theory is a theory of simple intellections. I therefore now turn to this theory with the purpose of showing that, with respect to simple intellections, Wodeham was indeed entitled to the view I have described here.

Complex intellections, the object of which is a state of affairs, will not be further considered. To my knowledge, there is, in Wodeham's writings, no sufficiently elaborate theory of these intellections as there is one of simple intellections. Besides, simple intellections are the more basic ones, being contained in the complex intellections whose object is a state of affairs.[35]

My first topic in the next section will therefore be intuitive and abstractive cognitions, as Wodeham conceived of them. Particularly noteworthy is the fact

---

31. Because its object is a state of affairs, the intellection in this case must be a mental proposition. Therefore, the quality that intellection is must be complex. See note 21.

32. "(arguitur per eos quod) per intellectionem qua Sortes experitur se intelligere angelum, si eadem ponatur in Platone, Plato experiretur se intelligere angelum. . . . Ad (istud) dicendum est quod . . . si intellectio qua Sortes experitur se intelligere [angelum] poneretur in Platone, ille judicaret Sortem intelligere [angelum]." *Abbreviatio*, lib. I, d. 3, q. un. (fol. 52ra–va).

33. "contradictio est quod sit (intellectio) et tamen quod non sit intellectio istius cuius nata est esse intellectio." *LS*, d. 8, q. 1 (vol. III, 16).

34. "si intellectio vel visio Sortis poneretur in lapide, adhuc esset intellectio vel visio, licet actu nullus per eam intelligeret vel videret, sed quia de natura sua est, si esset in subjecto, . . . per eam aliquid videretur vel intelligeretur." *Abbreviatio*, lib. I, d. 3, q. un. (fol. 53ra).

35. See note 21.

that, according to Wodeham, these cognitions do not require any actually existing things as their object but only possibly existing ones. On this basis, as I will proceed to show, it is perfectly consistent to hold that the object of any such cognition is entirely fixed by a property the cognition has by nature.

## THE NATURE OF INTUITIVE AND ABSTRACTIVE COGNITIONS

### Things Apprehended Need Only Possibly Exist

Both an intuitive and a singular abstractive cognition, if it exists in a mind, are cognitions by which just one individual thing is apprehended.[36] Although an intuitive cognition and a singular abstractive cognition can be of the very same thing, these cognitions differ in kind.[37] When a person has an intuitive cognition of a thing, as she does when she is seeing it, it appears to her evident that the thing exists; however, this is not so if her cognition of the thing is abstractive, as it is when she is imagining the thing.[38]

General abstractive cognitions come in various degrees of generality. The least general are occurrences of some specific concept and the most general are occurrences of the transcendental concept of being. Abstractive cognitions that are occurrences of a specific concept are cognitions by which the mind apprehends indiscriminately all the infinitely many actual and possible things of a certain specific sort. For example, any cognition by which the mind apprehends all actual and possible human beings, but only human beings, and neither asses nor oxen nor individuals of any other species, is an occurrence of the specific concept of man.[39] As such, it signifies all actual and possible human beings to the mind in which it exists. In the same way, any cognition by which all actual and possible animals are apprehended indiscriminately, but only animals, is an occurrence of the generic concept of animal. It signifies to the mind in which it exists all actual and possible animals.[40] Abstractive

---

36. "omnis notitia simplex et propria alicuius objecti est intuitiva vel abstractiva." *LS*, prol., q. 5 (vol. I, 112).

37. "anima respectu eiusdem cognoscibilis singularis potest habere duos actus absolutos proprios, realiter et specifice distinctos." *LS*, prol., q. 2 (vol. I, 35).

38. "omnis actus ... se habens ad suum objectum ... sicut se habet sensatio exterior ad suum, congrue vocatur notitia intuitiva.... Sed talis est notitia incomplexa virtute cuius judico rem exsistere quae tamen potest non exsistere.... Omnis autem imaginatio sensitiva et actus conformiter se habens ad objectum suum sicut actus imaginandi ad suum est abstractiva cognitio, quia scilicet omnis talis abstrahit ab exsistentia et praesentia cogniti quod eius virtute non potest cognosci exsistere vel non exsistere." *LS*, prol., q. 2 (vol. I, 37).

39. "habere intellectionem communem hominis non est aliud quam habere unam intellectionem qua non magis intelligatur unus homo quam alius, sed indifferenter offertur quilibet homo menti per eam, non tamen asinus vel bos vel individuum aliquod alterius speciei." *LS*, d. 8, q. 2 (vol. III, 39). See the continuation of this text in note 45.

40. " 'notitia animalis' ... potest ... accipi ... pro notitia quae repraesentat omne animal et solum animal sicut completum significatum." *LS*, d. 8, q. 4 (vol. III, 106).

cognitions that are occurrences of the transcendental concept of being, on the other hand, have as their object all the infinitely many actual and possible things, substances or qualities, that there are or could be, including even God. This collection of things is the most inclusive there is.

In the case of both intuitive and abstractive cognitions, the thing or things of which their object consists must possibly exist, but need not actually exist. Neither the object of an intuitive cognition nor that of a singular abstractive cognition need be an actually existing thing. Although an intuitive cognition of a given thing tends to cause the belief that that thing exists, the belief may be mistaken and the thing may fail to exist.[41] What is impossible, however, is that the object of an intuitive or of a simple abstractive cognition be something that cannot exist. The object of an intuitive cognition need, then, only be a *possibly existing thing*.[42] The same holds of the object of a singular abstractive cognition.[43]

Nor do the infinitely many things that are the objects of general abstractive cognitions, specific or generic, need actually exist. For example, by a cognition that is an occurrence of the specific concept of roses, the mind in which it exists apprehends all possible roses, and would apprehend them even if actually there were no roses.[44] Similarly, by a cognition that is an occurrence of the specific concept of man, the mind in which it exists apprehends all possible human beings and would apprehend them even if actually there were no human beings. Indeed, even if there were now no human beings, and even if it were now no longer possible that there be any human beings, still all human beings who existed in the past or were in the past possible would be apprehended.[45] Accordingly, when we say that the human beings apprehended need only possibly exist, we are taking "possible" in the sense in which whatever was, is or will be possible (in one sense) is possible, a sense of "possible," therefore, in which whatever is possible is always possible. All abstractive cognitions, specific or generic, are similar in this respect. In other words, the collection of things

---

41. "notitia intuitiva . . . est notitia incomplexa virtute cuius iudico rem exsistere quae tamen potest non exsistere." *LS*, prol., q. 2 (vol. I, 37).

42. "fiat igitur argumentum sic: video *a*, igitur aut videtur aliquid a me aut nihil. Si aliquid, et nonnisi hoc, igitur hoc est aliquid, et ultra: igitur est ens et exsistens. —Responsio: istam deductionem concedo, et ideo do secundam partem quod nihil videtur a me, tamen hoc *a* quod videtur a me non sit aliquid, verumtamen potest esse aliquid." *LS*, prol., q. 2 (vol. I, 49).

43. "omne imaginabile (id est omne simplici conceptu conceptibile vel imaginabile) saltem de Dei omnipotentia est possibile." *Tractatus de indivisibilibus*, q. 2 a. 3 (ed. R. Wood, p. 158).

44. "ista intellectio est indifferens conceptio omnium rosarum tam exsistentium quam non exsistentium. Immo, si nulla exsisteret in rerum natura, nihilominus offerretur menti quod nunc sibi offertur posita intellectione communi rosae." *LS*, d. 8, q. 1 (vol. III, 19).

45. "concedo quod confuse, indistincte et imperfecte concipiuntur infiniti homines per talem intellectionem et indifferenter illi qui possunt esse sicut illi qui sunt. Immo si nullus esset nec esset possibilis, dummodo remaneret intellectio, offerret menti omnes qui fuerunt vel qui fuerunt possibiles." *LS*, d. 8, q. 2 (vol. III, 39).

apprehended by any such cognition need only include *possible things*, each of these possible things being, however, always possible. This ensures that the collection of things apprehended by any such cognition is invariant, as Wodeham's doctrine requires.[46]

The exception here is the transcendental concept of being. Because by that concept, the things the mind in which it exists apprehends include everything possible or actual, they include God as well as both the cognition itself and the mind in which it exists. But God necessarily exists and both the cognition and the mind by hypothesis exist. The object of a cognition that is an occurrence of this concept must, then, include three actually existing things, although all the other things it includes need only possibly exist.

No intuitive or abstractive cognition requires, then, if it is singular, that its object be an actually existing thing, and, if it is general, and either specific or generic, that its object include any actually existing things. It requires only, if it is singular, that its object be a possible thing and, if it is general, and either specific or generic, that its object consist of possible things.[47]

### An Intrinsic Object-Fixing Property of These Cognitions

Because intuitive and abstractive (specific or generic) cognitions are so conceived that their object need include only possibly existing things, it is consistent to hold, as Wodeham did, that the object of any such cognition is entirely fixed by a property the quality which that cognition is has by nature.

Consider intuitive cognitions first. Consider, for example, a vision by which a person apprehends a particular whiteness. The person apprehends that whiteness rather than any other thing, not because that whiteness happens to be present, for it need not be, it may even fail to exist, but because of the nature of the mind-inherent quality that vision is. For that quality is by nature such that the only thing that can be apprehended by it is that actual or possible whiteness. Accordingly, when it exists in the mind of a person, that person will necessarily apprehend that whiteness, whether the latter actually exists or not.[48] Even if, by God's power, it were to exist outside all minds, the quality would

---

46. "conceptio universalis offert menti indifferenter quae non sunt actu individua sicut quae sunt actu, sed fuerunt, vel erunt vel esse possunt, quia qualitercumque singularia varientur in re quoad esse, fore vel fuisse, nulla tamen penitus contingit varietas aut disconformitas ex parte actus in offerendo et praesentando menti talia." *LS*, d. 8, q. 2 (vol. III, 41).

47. "Contradictio est intellectionem quamcumque esse subjective in mente, sive propriam sive communem in significando, quin mens per eam formaliter aliquid concipiat, ut ita loquar. Non [dico] quod illud quod concipitur sit aliquid, quia hoc non oportet . . . sed ad istum sensum loquendo quo ante rerum creationem Deus intellexit res omnes, et ad istum sensum quo dicimus istum aliquid intelligere qui praecise intelligeret chimeram, *si tamen hoc non esset impossibile*." *LS*, d. 8, q. 1 (vol. III, 7–8), emphasis mine.

48. "contradictio est ponere—per te—visionem qua albedo nata sit videri quin ipsa videatur. Igitur sive albedo circumscribatur sive non, videbitur." *LS*, d. 8, q. 1 (vol. III, 16). Here, by "per te," Wodeham is referring to himself.

not lose its nature and would, therefore, still have the property of being such that, were it to exist in a mind, that mind would necessarily apprehend by it that whiteness and nothing else.[49] In other words, it has by nature the property of being such that the only thing that can be apprehended by it is that actual or possible whiteness and nothing else.

We can now go one step further. We can argue that this property the quality has by nature can be regarded as *intrinsic* to it. Suppose that, by God's power, the quality that that vision is were the sole contingent thing in existence. It would not thereby lose its nature. It would, then, still have the property of being such that the only thing that *can* be apprehended by it is that possible individual whiteness and nothing else. A property may be regarded as *intrinsic*, however, if the thing that has it would have it even if it were the sole contingent thing in existence.[50] Nor is there any inconsistency involved in the notion that a thing is related by an intrinsic property to another thing, if that other thing need only possibly exist.[51] This property, then, which the quality that vision is has by nature, is a property intrinsic to it. Generalizing from this result, we may say that, according to Wodeham, the object of any intuitive cognition is entirely fixed by an intrinsic property of the mind-inherent quality that the given cognition is.

This result can be further generalized to all abstractive cognitions, singular or general, including those which are occurrences of a specific concept, of a generic concept, or of the transcendental concept of being. Consider, for example, a cognition that is an occurrence of the specific concept of roses. The quality that cognition is is *by nature* such that the only things that *can* be apprehended by it are all the roses there are (if any) or could be. Accordingly, when that quality exists in the mind of a person, that person necessarily apprehends all possible roses, whether or not any roses actually exist. That quality could, however, by God's power, be the sole contingent thing in existence. It would not thereby lose its nature and would therefore still have the property of being such that the only things that *can* be apprehended by it are all the roses there are (if any) or could be. This property is therefore intrinsic.

As a second example, consider a cognition that is an occurrence of the transcendental concept of being. The quality that cognition is is by nature such that

---

49. See the text quoted in note 34.

50. This presupposes that "intrinsic" is defined as follows: "an intrinsic property is . . . a property that could belong to something that did not coexist with any contingent object wholly distinct from itself." David Lewis and Rae Langton regard this definition as requiring further refinement. It is, however, adequate for our present purpose. See "Defining 'Intrinsic,'" *Philosophy and Phenomenological Research* 58 (1998): 333.

51. A property can be intrinsic though it relates the thing which has it to another thing, provided the other thing need not be a contingently existing thing. Thus, as Lewis/Langton point out (ibid.), if it is assumed that God necessarily exists, the property of being divinely created turns out to be intrinsic (if "intrinsic" is defined as it is in the preceding note).

nothing less than all things, actual (if any, besides God and that quality) or possible *can* be apprehended by it. Clearly, this is a property that quality would have even if it were the sole contingent thing in existence. The property is therefore intrinsic.

In general, then, the object of an intuitive or abstractive cognition is, on Wodeham's theory, entirely fixed by an *intrinsic* property of the mind-inherent quality that cognition is.[52] This also holds, in particular, when the cognition is of a nonmental thing or of nonmental things of a certain sort.

Nevertheless, intuitive and abstractive cognitions of nonmental things naturally require the existence of certain things within the subject's environment. They require this, according to Wodeham, not for being the acts they are, but for being caused the way they are caused, when they are caused naturally.[53] Let this feature of Wodeham's doctrine be our final topic.

## THE DEPENDENCE OF INTUITIVE AND ABSTRACTIVE COGNITIONS ON THE SUBJECT'S ENVIRONMENT

### *A Causal Dependence within the Normal Course of Nature*

Abstractive cognitions, both singular and general, have a causal history that, if entirely natural, originates in an intuitive cognition. Let us therefore consider first how, according to Wodeham, intuitive cognitions are caused when they are caused naturally.

Intuitive cognitions, when caused naturally, are not all caused in exactly the same way. Introspective intuitive cognitions, when caused naturally, are simply caused by their object. Intuitive cognitions of external things,[54] in contrast, are caused naturally by two partial causes. One cause is the object of the cognition;

---

52. Although Wodeham himself does not, as far as I know, call the property "intrinsic," later authors did. Thus, Gervasius Waim, in the early sixteenth century, writes: "Qualitas ex *intrinseca sua natura* habet quod sit noticia huius objecti potius quam alterius sic quod a priori nulla potest dari ratio nisi natura rei. Adverte tamen quod quando dico quod qualitas ex *intrinseca sua natura* habet quod sit noticia huius objecti, nolo dicere quod aliqua qualitas accidens sit intrinsece noticia, immo nulla talis est intrinsece noticia, cum possibile sit qualibet talem esse et non esse noticiam. Sed volo dicere quod qualitas que est noticia huius objecti ex natura sua habet quod non stat ipsam esse noticiam et non esse noticiam huius objecti. Nec habet istud ex efficientia illius vel illius objecti." *Tractatus noticiarum*, pars I, fol. b4vb, emphasis mine.

53. An effect is naturally caused when it is caused by a secondary cause, i.e., by a finite agent, God's indispensable contribution (as primary cause) consisting in his collaborating with the finite agent.

54. The only intuitive cognitions of external things that we are allowed in this life are of material things, not of other minds or of qualities existing in them. See the first section of this essay.

the other is a quality existing in a sense organ (called by Wodeham a "sensible species"), which in turn is itself caused naturally by the same object.[55]

An intuitive cognition, then, when caused naturally, is caused, at least in part, by the thing that is its object. But nothing can be a cause unless it exists. It follows that the object of an intuitive cognition, if the cognition is caused naturally, can only be an existing thing.[56] If the intuitive cognition is of a nonmental thing, it is, moreover, required that the thing exist in the environment of the person in whose mind the intuitive cognition is caused. Otherwise, if it were too distant, the thing could not act on the mind of the person (or on her sense organ) to cause an intuitive cognition of itself. Each of our naturally caused nonintrospective intuitive cognitions requires, then, that a certain thing, namely the thing that is its object, exist within our environment.

The way an abstractive cognition is caused, when caused naturally, is more complex. For the sake of brevity, I will consider here only the case of abstractive cognitions that are occurrences of some specific concept. According to Wodeham, one cannot naturally have an abstractive cognition of this kind unless one has had an intuitive cognition of at least one thing of the relevant sort.[57] Several intuitive cognitions of things of that sort are not required. He infers that, when a certain sort of thing is apprehended in one of its instances intuitively for the first time, that intuitive cognition naturally causes a first general abstractive cognition of all things, actual and possible, of the same sort as it is,[58] although we are not conscious of this abstractive act.[59] This act of general abstractive cognition in turn causes a "habit," which is, as we have seen, a mind-inherent quality of a durable kind. This "habit" has by nature the capacity to elicit, at will, an abstractive cognition similar to the first abstractive cognition that caused it and therefore a cognition of the very same things.[60] If the cognition is an

---

55. "licet res extra requiratur ad causandum speciem istam (scilicet speciem sensibilem in organo sensus exterioris) et visionem consequentem . . ." *Abbreviatio*, lib. I, d. 3, q. un. (fol. 54rb). A naturally caused intuitive cognition of a material thing *can*, however, be caused just by its object. In a pure intellect (that of an angel), it would have to be.

56. "omnis notitia simplex et propria ad quam naturaliter causandum necessario coexigitur exsistentia objecti sui, ita quod aliter causari nullo modo potest praeterquam a Deo solo, est intuitiva." *LS*, prol., q. 5 (vol. I, 115).

57. "licet (communi intellectioni) praesupponatur secundum cursum naturae cognitio propria alicuius singularis." *LS*, d. 8, q. 2 (vol. III, 38–39).

58. "pono tres conceptus simul causari ad minus in prima conceptione singularis talis vel talis speciei, id est intuitivam, abstractivam propriam et abstractivam specificam." *LS*, d. 8, q. 4 (vol. III, 91).

59. Because our mind is occupied by the thing we are seeing, we are unaware of any abstractive act caused by and simultaneous with the intuitive cognition we are having: "quia potentia occupatur circa objectum quod intuetur, in tantum quod anima naturaliter non perpendit se habere aliquem actum abstractivum circa illud, nec etiam perpendere potest nisi ductu rationis et discursive, pro statu isto saltem." *LS*, d. 3, q. 5 (vol. II, 221).

60. "Quia statim, cessante sensatione intuitiva, experior quod possum in duplicem abstractivam: communem et propriam . . . oportet quod eliciam illos mediante habitibus." *LS*, d. 8, q. 4 (vol. III, 91). This text follows immediately the one quoted in note 58.

occurrence of a specific concept of nonmental things, its object will, then, include a thing that has existed in the environment of the subject, namely that thing in which the causal history of the cognition originates. Every abstractive cognition that is an occurrence of a specific concept of nonmental things requires, then, if its causal history is entirely natural, that at least one thing of the relevant sort has existed within the environment of the subject.

It can be shown that, if the causal history of a singular abstractive cognition is entirely natural and if its object is a nonmental thing, then that thing must have existed in the environment of the subject. It can also be shown that, if the causal history of an abstractive cognition that is an occurrence of a generic concept is entirely natural and if it is a concept of nonmental things, then at least two things, each of a different specific sort, but both of the same relevant genus, must have existed in the environment of the subject.[61]

## A Contingent Dependence

Intuitive or abstractive cognitions of nonmental things require, then, when naturally caused, the existence of certain things or of things of certain kinds within the environment of the subject. It is, however, by no means *necessary* that a thing, which, as a matter of fact, is naturally caused, should have been naturally caused. For when a thing is naturally caused, it is partially caused by God and partially by finite agents. Yet God could always have chosen to be himself the sole cause of the thing, dispensing with other agents altogether. This is, at any rate, a principle Wodeham assumed, as did most of his contemporaries.[62]

It follows that one's having a given intuitive or abstractive cognition of a nonmental thing or of nonmental things only *naturally* requires that some item exist in the environment of the subject, not *necessarily*. Consider, for example, the intuitive cognition you are having of a lemon. If the intuitive cognition is naturally caused, it requires the existence of the lemon in your environment. It could have been caused by God alone, however, were the lemon not to exist in your environment and perhaps not at all.[63] Your having that cognition does not, then, necessarily require the existence of the lemon, nor of anything else, in your environment.

---

61. "omne universale communius specie specialissima ad hoc ut habeatur, praehaberi supponit—saltem natura—cognitionem individuorum alterius rationis aliquo modo, ita quod generalis notitia colorum requirit cognosci individua diversarum specierum colorum, non sic de cognitione specifica." *LS*, d. 8, q. 4 (vol. III, 100).

62. "quidquid potest Deus facere per causam efficientem mediam, potest per se immediate." *LS*, prol., q. 2 (vol. I, 46).

63. "supernaturaliter posset esse notitia intuitiva sine exsistentia objecti sui. . . . Quia quidquid potest Deus facere per causam efficientem mediam, potest per se immediate, igitur et visionem quam [facit] mediante objecto." *LS*, prol., q. 2 (vol. I, 46). For an example of an introspective intuitive cognition supernaturally caused (or preserved) while its object does not exist, see the text quoted in note 26.

The same holds of abstractive cognitions. Suppose that, hearing someone mention roses, you elicit an abstractive cognition by which you apprehend all actual and possible roses. If the causal history of your cognition is entirely natural, your having that cognition requires that there should have existed at least one rose in your environment. But it is by no means necessary that the causal history of your cognition should have been entirely natural. At any of its stages, God alone could have caused the relevant entity in your mind, even though no roses exist or ever have existed in your environment. Thus, God alone could have caused your "habitual concept" of roses,[64] without which you could not have naturally elicited your present abstractive cognition.[65] He could have done this, although no roses exist or ever have existed in your environment. Alternatively, that habitual concept might have been naturally caused, but God could have caused the initial abstractive cognition of roses that caused it, even though there were no roses in your environment. Or that abstractive cognition might have been naturally caused, but God could have caused the intuitive cognition of a rose that caused it, even though there were no roses in your environment. Finally, God alone could have caused your present cognition itself, although no roses exist in your environment. In each of these cases, you would apprehend all actual and possible roses by your abstractive cognition, although perhaps no roses exist or ever have existed in your environment. Your having that cognition does not, then, *necessarily* require the existence of anything in particular in your environment.

We may conclude that, on Wodeham's theory, we could not *naturally* have any intuitive or abstractive cognitions of nonmental things if our environment did not contain or had not contained the appropriate things or kinds of things. Yet, we *could* have them nonetheless. Admittedly, this possibility could not be realized unless God were to intervene in the normal course of nature. But God *can* intervene in this way *because* neither intuitive nor abstractive cognitions of nonmental things require, in order to be the mental acts they are with the objects they have, that anything in particular exist in the environment of the subject. In other words, the nature of these acts does not hinge on the way they are caused, when they are caused naturally.

CONCLUSION

Colin McGinn has sought to explain why externalist views of the mind appear counterintuitive, at least at first glance. This may be, he suggests, because we

---

64. Wodeham calls a disposition (habitus) to elicit an abstractive cognition by which, for example, all actual and possible whitenesses are apprehended, a "conceptus habitualis albedinis" or a "notitia habitualis albedinis" (cf. *LS*, d. 3, q. 4 (vol. II, 183–4)).

65. "si Deus ante primum actum causaret talem habitum qualis esset naturaliter causabilis per actus, tunc posset anima sine intuitiva etiam in primum actum." *LS*, prol., q. 6 (vol. I, 171).

unreflectively take minds to be substances.⁶⁶ But if minds were substances, he argues, an externalist theory of mind would seem inconsistent.⁶⁷ Now Wodeham's theory of mind is substantialist. Is it therefore internalist? The answer, it seems to me, is definitely affirmative.

Considering Wodeham's theory of our simplest and most basic mental acts, namely his theory of intuitive and abstractive cognitions, I have argued that the content of any such cognition is entirely fixed by an intrinsic property of the cognition itself, a mind-inherent item. Although, in the normal course of nature, every such cognition of an external thing (or of external things of a certain kind) is caused (proximately or remotely) by that very thing (or by a thing of that kind), the cognition is not *of* that thing (or *of* things of that kind) in virtue of being so caused. Rather, the reverse is true. It is in virtue of the cognition being by nature *of* that thing (or *of* things of that kind), that it can be naturally caused (proximately or remotely) only by that thing (or by a thing of that kind). In holding this theory of intuitive and abstractive cognitions of nonmental things, Wodeham was undoubtedly an internalist. Yet, despite his internalism, he was able to account for the fact that, in the normal course of nature, most of our thoughts latch onto the external world.⁶⁸

---

66. "Internalism feels pretheoretically attractive—there is a strong gut undertow towards it—precisely because (I am suggesting) it respects the implicit substantialist presumption." C. McGinn, *Mental Content* (Oxford: Blackwell, 1989), 18.

67. "Suppose the mind were metaphysically akin to the body or brain, autonomous and exclusive like them; then externalism could not be true of it—for it would have its own world-independent intrinsic nature determined by its (quasi-) primary qualities." Ibid., 17. This is, however, quite precisely how Wodeham conceived of the mind.

68. There is good reason, however, for not considering Wodeham's theory of intuitive and abstractive cognitions as *purely* internalist. Every such cognition requires, for being the cognition it is, with the content it is internally determined to have, that the set of all possible things be the set it is. Suppose that, *per impossibile*, this set were other than it is, that it includes, say, possible chimeras but no possible horses. If this were the case, there could be no general abstractive cognition by which all possible horses would be apprehended, whereas there could be a general abstractive cognition by which all possible chimeras would be apprehended, impossible as this may be (see the text quoted in note 47). These suppositions are themselves impossible because the set of possible things is necessarily the set it is, given, as it were, to God himself, who knew each and every possible thing even "before" he created anything (see again the same note). His knowledge of possible things does not, however, make them possible. Rather, a possible thing is possible of itself and is therefore necessarily possible. So the dependence of our general abstractive cognitions (and of our intuitive and singular abstractive cognitions as well) on the set of possible things being the set it is is a dependence on something that cannot fail to hold. The dependence is nonetheless real and, unless our cognition is introspective, on something definitely nonmental, external therefore to the mind. This suggests that we should, then, consider Wodeham's theory of intuitive and abstractive cognitions of nonmental things as *both* internalist and "weakly externalist," to use a term coined by Colin McGinn (see *Mental Content*, 7), provided "weak externalism" is understood in a sense (not contemplated by McGinn himself), in which a given cognition requires only the *possible existence* of items "belonging to the nonmental world," a form of weak externalism I propose to call "modal externalism."

# How Chatton Changed Ockham's Mind
## William Ockham and Walter Chatton on Objects and Acts of Judgment

SUSAN BROWER-TOLAND

Recent scholarship has begun to uncover the nature and extent of the reciprocal—and typically adversarial—relationship between William Ockham (d. 1347) and Walter Chatton (d. 1343). We now know, for example, that Chatton, a slightly younger contemporary of Ockham, is both enormously influenced by and, at the same time, highly critical of his older colleague. Chatton often takes up precisely those questions Ockham treats (and likewise the terminology and conceptual framework in which he expresses them) only to reject Ockham's conclusions.[1] We also know that Chatton's criticisms leave their mark on Ockham. Ockham frequently rehearses and responds to Chatton's objections, occasionally refining or even altogether revising his views in light of them. Perhaps the best-documented case of such influence concerns Ockham's developing views of concepts, where, in direct response to Chatton's criticisms, Ockham famously abandons his early "fictum" theory of concepts in favor of Chatton's own "men-

---

I am grateful to Jeff Brower for helpful comments and criticism on earlier drafts of this essay. I would also like to thank Rondo Keele for helpful discussion of a number of aspects of this paper (especially, issues surrounding the dating of Ockham and Chatton's texts) and for his willingness to share several of his unpublished papers with me.

1. For a general introduction to Chatton's philosophy, see Rondo Keele, "The So-Called *Res* Theory of Walter Chatton," *Franciscan Studies* 61 (2003): 37–53. A number of studies have been made of Chatton's reaction to (and, typically, criticism of) Ockham's views. See, for example, Luciano Cova, "L'unità della scienza teologica nella polemica di Walter Chatton con Guglielmo D'Ockham," *Franciscan Studies* 45 (1985): 189–230; Armand Maurer, "Ockham's Razor and Chatton's Anti-Razor," *Mediaeval Studies* 46 (1984): 463–475; Noel A. Fitzpatrick, "Walter Chatton on the Univocity of Being: A Reaction to Peter Aureoli and William Ockham," *Franciscan Studies* 31(1971): 88–177; Gedeon Gál, "Gualteri de Chatton et Guillelmi de Ockham controversia de natura conceptus universalis," *Franciscan Studies* 27 (1967): 191–212; and Jeremiah O'Callaghan, "The Second Question of the Prologue to Walter Catton's Commentary on the Sentences on Intuitive and Abstractive Knowledge," in *Nine Mediaeval Thinkers*, ed. J. R. O'Donnell (Toronto: Pontifical Institute of Mediaeval Studies), 1955.

tal act" account.[2] Although this may be the best-documented case, it is by no means the only example of such influence—a handful of others have been discussed in the literature.[3] In this essay, I hope to extend our current understanding of the relationship between these two Franciscan thinkers by looking in some detail at a debate between them over the objects of judgment.

The broad outlines of Ockham's place in the development of late medieval debates about judgment are fairly well drawn. Scholars have traced the discussion and controversy generated by Ockham's account among a host of fourteenth-century thinkers at both Oxford and Paris.[4] It is well established, moreover, that Chatton is among the earliest and most vehement critics of Ockham's account of objects of judgment.[5] What has gone overlooked in the

---

2. For a fuller discussion of Chatton's criticisms of Ockham and his role in Ockham's eventual change of mind, see Gál, "Gualteri de Chatton et Guillelmi de Ockham"; Francis E. Kelley, "Walter Chatton vs. Aureoli and Ockham Regarding the Universal Concept," *Franciscan Studies* 41 (1981): 222–249; and Katherine Tachau, *Vision and Certitude in the Age of Ockham: Optics, Epistemology and the Foundations of Semantics 1250–1345* (Leiden: Brill, 1988), chap. 7.

3. Joseph Wey provides a list of places in Ockham's *Quodlibetal Questions* in which Ockham explicitly rehearses arguments or objections offered by Chatton. In addition to these, Wey also finds some 68 other textual parallels between Ockham's *Quodlibeta* and Chatton's writings. Wey, introduction to *Reportatio et Lectura super Sententias: Collatio ad Librum Primum et Prologus*, ed. J. C. Wey (Toronto: Pontifical Institute of Medieval Studies, 1989); see also Wey, introduction to *Quodlibeta Septem* (*Opera Theologica* IX), ed. J. C. Wey (St. Bonaventure, N.Y.: St. Bonaventure University Press, 1980). In "Walter Chatton's Lectura and William of Ockham's Quaestiones in libros Physicorum Aristotelis," in *Essays Honoring Allan B. Wolter*, ed. W. A. Frank and G. J. Etzkorn (St. Bonaventure, N.Y.: Franciscan Institute, 1985), Stephen Brown (1985) presents evidence that Ockham draws on Chatton's *Lectura* in the course of his discussion of Aristotle's physics. See also Keele, "The So-Called *Res* Theory," and Brower-Toland, "Medieval Approaches to Consciousness: Ockham and Chatton," *Philosophers Imprint* 12 (2012).

4. For example, see Gabriel Nuchelmans, *Theories of the Proposition: Ancient and Medieval Conceptions of the Bearers of Truth and Falsity* (Amsterdam: North Holland, 1973); Tachau, *Vision and Certitude*; Onorato Grassi, "The Object of Scientific Knowledge in Some Authors of the Fourteenth Century," in *Knowledge and the Sciences in Medieval Philosophy: Proceedings of the Eighth International Congress of Medieval Philosophy*, ed. S. Knuuttila, R. Tyorinoja, and S. Ebbesen (Helsinki: Luther-Agricola Society, 1990), 180–189; Elizabeth Karger, "William of Ockham, Walter Chatton, and Adam Wodeham on the Objects of Knowledge and Belief," *Vivarium* 33 (1995): 171–186; Susan Brower-Toland, "Later Medieval Theories of Propositions: Ockham and the 14th Century Debate at Oxford over Objects of Judgment" (PhD diss., Cornell University, 2002); Laurent Cesalli, "Some Fourteenth Century Realist Theories of the Proposition: A Historical and Speculative Study," in *Signification in Language and Culture*, ed. H. S. Gill (Shimla: Indian Institute of Advanced Study, 2002), 83–118.

5. Maria Elena Reina, "La prima questione del Prologo del 'Commento alla Sentenze di Walter Catton,'" *Rivista critica di storia della filosofia* 25(1970): 48–74, 290–314; Keele, "The So-Called *Res* Theory." Brower-Toland, "Can God Know More? A Case Study in the Late Medieval Debate about Propositions," in *Later Medieval Metaphysics: Ontology, Language & Logic*, ed. R. Keele and C. Bolyard, 161–187 (New York: Fordham University Press, 2013).

literature, however, is the fact that Chatton's criticisms of Ockham have an important influence on Ockham himself. Not only has this gone unnoticed, but scholars have at times also thought that Chatton so misunderstood Ockham's position that, in the end, his objections to it fail even to apply. In what follows, I argue that Chatton's criticisms not only find their target in Ockham, but that they were felt by Ockham himself to be sufficiently forceful as to lead him to radically modify his views. Indeed, Ockham's most mature treatment of judgment contains revisions that not only resolve the problems Chatton identifies, but that also bring his final account of objects of judgment fairly close to Chatton's own.

My discussion in what follows divides into three parts. In the first, I provide the background necessary for understanding Chatton's criticisms—namely, a description of Ockham's early theory of judgment. I then turn in the second part to sketch Chatton's central objections to that theory and the role these objections play in shaping Ockham's mature views. Here, I argue, first, that Ockham initially does defend a view susceptible of Chatton's criticisms and, second, that he is eventually persuaded by these criticisms to abandon it. Although the changes Ockham introduces into his final theory of judgment significantly reduce the distance between him and Chatton, important differences remain. In the third and final section, I consider these differences, arguing that they are important both to our understanding of Ockham and Chatton's respective theories of judgment, and to our understanding of the subsequent development of the debate about judgment.[6]

## BACKGROUND: OCKHAM'S EARLY THEORY OF JUDGMENT

In order to appreciate Chatton's objections and the developments in Ockham's account to which they give rise, it is necessary to begin with a brief overview of Ockham's early theory of judgment and certain features of Chatton's interpretation of it.[7]

Ockham's views about judgment are framed in terms of a much broader theory about the nature of human cognition—a theory that Chatton himself largely shares. According to this theory, all thought (that is, intellective cogni-

---

6. In what follows, citations of Ockham's Latin texts are to *Opera Philosophica et Theologica* (St. Bonaventure, N.Y.: St. Bonaventure University Press, 1967–88). I use the following abbreviations in referring to particular volumes: Ord. (= *Ordinatio. Scriptum in Librum Primum Sententiarum*); Expos.Praedic. (= *Expositio in Liburm Praedicamentorum Aristotelis*); Expos.Perih. (= *Expositio in Librum Perihermenias Aristotelis*); Quodl. (= *Quodlibeta Septem*); SL (= *Summa Logicae*). Translations are my own.

7. Ockham's earliest account of judgment is developed in his *Ordinatio* commentary—primarily in q.1 of the prologue to it. It is this text that Chatton relies on for his interpretation of Ockham. In setting out Ockham's initial theory of judgment, therefore, I will be drawing primarily from his account in this work. I have discussed Ockham's early theory of judgment in more detail elsewhere. See Susan Brower-Toland, "Ockham on Judgment, Concepts, and the Problem of Intentionality," *Canadian Journal of Philosophy* 37 (2007): 67–110.

tion) forms a kind of mental language—one structured in much the way natural language is. Thus, like spoken and written language, the language of thought is compositional: it is comprised of simple or atomic units (namely, "concepts"), which, via the mental operation of "composition," can be combined in various ways to form complex, propositional expressions.[8] Accordingly, Ockham divides mental expressions into two broad categories: sentential or propositional expressions, and the nonsentential terms or units—subject, predicate, and copula expressions—that comprise them.[9] Ockham thinks this division maps Aristotle's distinction in the *Categories* between expressions that are "said in combination" (*dicuntur cum complexione*), and those "said without combination" (*dicuntur sine complexione*). Propositional expressions (*complexa, propositiones*) are those produced by the operation of composition and so are appropriately characterized as expressions only "said in combination"; by contrast, "simple terms" (*simplex termini, incomplexa*) are semantic units that precede and are used in the operation of composition.

On Ockham's view, the intellect's formation of a judgment involves not only its formulating or "composing" a propositional thought (that is, a mental sentence), but also its adopting some stance or attitude with regard to it. In order to accommodate this aspect of judgment, Ockham distinguishes between two different psychological modes, or types of mental act associated with the intellect's formation of a mental sentence, namely, apprehension and judgment. Acts of apprehension are, on his view, acts or states in which the intellect merely considers or entertains a given content—whether nonpropositional (as when the intellect forms or possesses an individual concept) or propositional (as when it entertains a mental sentence). Acts of judgment, by contrast, arise only in connection with the intellect's formation of a mental sentence; these are acts or states in which the intellect not merely entertains a given content, but also takes some positive stance with respect to its truth. As Ockham puts it, judgment is an act "by which the intellect not only apprehends its object, but also gives its assent or dissent."[10] Thus, in keeping with the interpretation of thought as an inner, mental language, we can perhaps think of judicative acts as mental *assertions*—that is, acts involving a kind of assertoric force.

Broadly speaking, acts of judgment fall into one of two categories: assent or dissent. Acts of assent and dissent, however, can be further subdivided into particular propositional—or, we might say, "judicative"—attitudes, namely,

---

8. According to Ockham: "whatever the intellect can apprehend in a simple act of thinking, it can combine (*componere*) with another thing by saying 'this is that.'" *Ord.* Prol., q. 1 (*OTh* II, 49).

9. *Expos. Praedic.* Cap. 4, § 1 (*OPh* II, 148). Ockham argues that while Aristotle was speaking primarily about spoken language in the passage from which this distinction is taken, he, nevertheless, intended it to apply to mental language as well.

10. *Ord.* Prol., q. 1 (*OTh* I, 16).

belief, knowledge, doubt, opinion, faith, and so on. Thus, when one takes something as true (say, by believing, knowing, or opining) she is said to *assent*; when she takes it to be false (say, by disbelieving, or doubting) she is said to *dissent*. Accordingly, a given judicative act may be an act of knowledge, belief, doubt and so on depending on the grounds for and causes of that act or state. For this reason, Ockham (and Chatton, who adopts his terminology and conceptual framework) will often move freely between terms like "judgment," "act of assent," "act of knowledge/belief."

In addition to distinguishing between apprehension and judgment, Ockham also develops a certain picture of the logical and causal ordering among such acts. In particular, he holds that acts of judgment presuppose the occurrence of several (logically) prior acts of apprehension.[11] For our purposes, we need only focus on one part of this account, namely, Ockham's claim that every act of judging presupposes a (logically) prior act of apprehending the object judged. As he explains, "an act of judgment with respect to a mental sentence presupposes an act of apprehension relating to the same thing."[12] The motivation for this claim is just the intuition that one does not form a judgment with respect to some content without first having apprehended or considered that same content. Indeed, on Ockham's view, the prior act of apprehension is itself partly causally responsible for the occurrence of the subsequent judicative act. For, as he sees it, part of what explains one's coming to assent (or dissent) to something is one's prior consideration or "apprehension" of it. Since, as we shall see, Chatton draws heavily on this particular feature of Ockham's account, it will be useful to set it out explicitly as follows:

> *Ordering Principle:* Every act of judgment is always preceded and caused by an act of apprehension relating to the same object (at least in the natural order, apart from supernatural intervention).

Now, with this much of Ockham's theory of judgment Chatton is in perfect agreement. He shares Ockham's conception of thought as occurring in a type of mental language, and he accepts Ockham's account of the distinction between and ordering among acts of apprehension and judgment. What he objects to, and what he wants to reject, is Ockham's account of the *objects* of judgment. Ockham claims that all acts of judgment—that is, all acts of believing, knowing, opining, etc.—relate to mental sentences as their object. In fact, this claim about objects of judgment is central to Ockham's understanding of the nature of judgment itself—so much so, that Ockham's first argument for it comes in the very passage in which he introduces acts of judgment as distinct from acts of apprehension.

---

11. See, Ockham's *Ord*. Prol., q. 1 (*OTh* I, 17–21).
12. *Ord*. Prol., q. 1 (*OTh* I, 17).

The second type of act may be called an act of *judgment*. It is that act by which the intellect not only apprehends its object, but also gives its assent or dissent to it. This act is only in relation to a mental sentence (*complexi*). For our intellect does not assent to anything unless we consider it to be true and it does not dissent from anything unless we judge it to be false.[13]

Because this claim about objects of judgment is at the heart both of Ockham's early theory of judgment and Chatton's criticisms of it, it will be useful to consider briefly the motivation behind it.

Ockham's commitment to the view that mental sentences are objects of judgment has a twofold source: one rooted in his nominalism, the other in his understanding of Aristotelian demonstrative science. As the foregoing passage makes clear, Ockham thinks that judicative acts or attitudes pertain only to what is truth-evaluable, that is, only to what is capable of being true or false. But since Ockham's ontology has no place for abstract propositional entities such as sentence types, propositions, or states of affair, he holds that only sentence tokens—and, in the first place, mental sentence tokens—are the bearers of truth or falsity.[14] Indeed, he is committed to what we would nowadays think of as a nominalist account of truth bearers. As he says, "nothing is true except a sentence [token]."[15] This, together with his understanding of acts of assent as relating to what is true (and dissent to what is false), entails that judicative attitudes such as belief and knowledge must take mental sentences as object.

The other motivation for Ockham's views about the nature of objects of judgment comes from his understanding of the nature of demonstrative science (what he refers to as "knowledge properly so called," *scientia propria dicta*). Following Aristotle's account of demonstrative knowledge in the *Posterior Analytics*, Ockham holds that what is known or assented to in demonstration is not only something that is *true*, but also something that is necessary and universal. For this same reason, he concludes that the immediate objects for all demonstrative knowledge (that is, of all sciences) must be mental entities since, on his view, there is nothing in extramental reality that is universal and, likewise,

---

13. *Ord.* Prol., q. 1 (*OTh* I, 16).

14. Ockham is, of course, well known for his nominalism. In general, he appears willing to allow only concrete, particular things (*res*) falling in the category of substance and quality. Thus, he denies the reality not only of universals, but also of *abstracta* including propositions (as they are nowadays conceived) and states of affairs. For an overview of Ockham's ontology, see Marilyn M. Adams, *William Ockham* (Notre Dame, Ind.: Notre Dame University Press, 1987), chaps. 1–9. See also C. Normore, "Some Aspects of Ockham's Logic," and Paul Spade, "Ockham's Nominalist Metaphysics: Some Main Themes," both in *The Cambridge Companion to Ockham*, ed. P. Spade (Cambridge: Cambridge University Press, 1999).

15. *Quodl.* III.8 (*OPh* IX, 236). Sentences in natural language are also truth bearers, but their truth-value (and, truth conditions) is wholly derivative on that of the corresponding sentence in the language of thought.

nothing there (besides God) that is a necessary being.[16] Mental sentences, however, can possess universal concepts (that is, concepts which can be predicated of numerically distinct things) as constituent terms, and can be true necessarily (which, on his view, is just to be true whenever formed); thus, they alone are the only sorts of entity suitable to function as objects for demonstrative *scientia*.[17] Accordingly, Ockham's entire theory of demonstration is predicated on the assumption that the terms, the premises, and the objects of Aristotelian *scientia* are mental entities—namely, concepts and mental sentences. As he insists: "every science (*scientia*) whatsoever—whether it is real or rational—concerns only mental sentences. For it concerns those things which are known (*scita*) and only mental sentences are known (*scitur*)."[18] For convenience, in what follows, I refer to Ockham's position on objects of judgment simply as "Ockham's conclusion," where this is shorthand for his view that every act of judgment—every act of believing, opining, knowing, demonstrating, and so forth—relates to a mental sentence as its immediate object.

Now, it is precisely this conclusion that Chatton wants to reject. Chatton denies not only that the objects of demonstrative science are mental sentences, but also, and more generally, he denies the conclusion that objects of *all* propositional attitudes are mental entities. Although Chatton is, as we shall see, willing to grant that in some special cases mental entities can be said to serve as objects of judgment, he insists that, in the normal course of things, the objects for judicative attitudes are extramental things (*res*). In order to appreciate the details of Chatton's criticisms, however, it is important to see that, throughout his discussion, he is presupposing a commitment on Ockham's part to a very specific conception of the metaphysical structure of mental language—and, so, to a very specific conception of the nature of the entities that serve as objects of belief and knowledge. To see what this assumption amounts to, I need to say just a word or two about the developments in Ockham's account of concepts.

When Ockham originally formulates his theory of judgment, he is operating with what we might think of as a kind of act-object analysis of mental language. According to this analysis, mental sentences (and the concepts from which they are composed) are taken to be mind-dependent entities—what Ockham refers to as "*ficta*," where these are taken to be inner thought-objects distinct from and

---

16. Eileen Serene, "Demonstrative Science," in *The Cambridge History of Later Medieval Philosophy*, ed. N. Kretzmann, A. Kenny, and J. Pinborg (Cambridge: Cambridge University Press, 1982), 513.

17. As Ockham explains: "In one way something is called 'necessary' . . . because it can begin and cease to exist by no power; in such a way God alone is necessary. . . . In another way, a sentence called 'necessary' . . . which is such that it cannot be false—namely, which is true in such a way that, if it is formed it is not false but only true. And in this sense demonstration is of necessities . . . that is, of sentences which cannot be false but only true." SL III–2, 5 (*OPh* I, 512).

18. *Ord.* d.2, q.4 (*OTh* II, 135).

dependent on mental *acts* of apprehension or awareness directed at them.[19] As is well known, however, Ockham eventually rejects the act-object account of mental language—in no small part because of Chatton's criticisms of it. Indeed, in its place, he adopts Chatton's own, adverbial (or "mental act"), analysis of mental language. On this view, concepts and mental sentences are not understood as intentional *objects* of acts of thinking, but are rather identified with *acts* of awareness themselves.[20] Thus, on Ockham's mature view, mental sentences are no longer understood as complex or structured thought-objects, but rather as complex or structured mental acts—what both Ockham and Chatton refer to as "*complexa apprehensiones,*" and which we might call "propositional apprehensions."[21]

Obviously, such a shift in Ockham's conception of mental language required *some* amendment to his account of objects of judgment, since it entails, at the very least, a change in his views about the nature of the mental sentences that serve as objects of judgment.[22] Chatton simply assumes that Ockham means to hold fixed all the central elements of his early theory of judgment—and, in particular, the conclusion regarding mental sentences serving as objects of judgment—while merely replacing his early account of mental sentences with an adverbial, or "mental act," analysis of them. Thus, on Chatton's interpretation, Ockham's considered view is that objects of judgment are mental acts, namely, complex or propositional acts of apprehension. And it is *this* account of objects of judgment that is the target for his criticisms. Indeed, we can think of Chatton's objections as an attempt to demonstrate why Ockham's early conclusion regarding objects of judgment cannot be conjoined with an adverbial analysis of mental language.

## CHATTON'S CRITICISMS AND CHATTON'S INFLUENCE

Chatton takes up the question of objects of judgment in the first article of the first question of his *Sentences* Prologue (hereafter, q.1, a.1).[23] Although he is

---

19. Ockham frequently refers to the mental entities that serve as objects of thought as "*ficta.*" On his early theory of concepts and mental language, concepts or *ficta* are construed as entities that have a special (mind-dependent) mode of existence—they are, as Ockham describes them, "objectively existing" beings. Because, on his early view, concepts are characterized as "ficta" and as "objectively existing" his early theory of mental language is sometimes referred to in the literature as the "fictum-theory" or as "objective-existence theory."

20. Hence, Ockham's later theory of concepts is sometimes referred to as the "mental-act" theory.

21. As Chatton explicitly says at one point in his discussion: "I am supposing that a mental sentence is a propositional apprehension." *Rep.* I, Prol. q.1, a.1, 41.

22. Although commentators have generally recognized that Ockham is forced to modify his early theory of judgment in light of his changing theory of concepts, there is disagreement as to what these modifications involve. See Brower-Toland, "Ockham on Judgment, Concepts, and the Problem of Intentionality."

23. References to q. 1, a.1 are to Chatton, *Reportatio et Lectura Super Sententias: Collatio ad librum Primum et Prologus*, ed. J. C. Wey (Toronto: Pontifical Institute of Mediaeval

clearly interested in the objects of judgment generally, the focus of his discussion in this context is a question about the objects of belief (or, more precisely, faith). This is not surprising given the broader context: not only does his discussion occur in a commentary on a theological textbook, but the specific issue Chatton is concerned with in this part of the commentary has to do with the evidentness (*evidentia*) of the articles of faith. The bulk of his discussion in q.1, a.1 consists in a detailed consideration and critique of Ockham's account of the objects of judgment. Indeed, he begins, at the outset of his discussion with a lengthy quotation from Ockham's early discussion of apprehension and judgment, followed by a long list of places in the same work in which Ockham claims that mental sentences are objects for all acts of judgment—whether the act in question is belief, knowledge, opinion, or any other kind of judgment.[24] Then, in response, Chatton proceeds to develop a series of arguments, all of which are designed to establish the falsity of Ockham's conclusion and the truth of Chatton's own, namely, that "the act of believing (and the act of knowing and opining...) has an external thing and *not* a mental sentence for its object."[25]

In what follows, I want to focus on just three general lines of criticism that emerge over the course of Chatton's discussion as a whole. In each of these three lines of criticism, Chatton attempts to establish the falsity of Ockham's conclusion on *objects* of judgment by drawing on various features of Ockham's *own* account of judgment and apprehension.

### Chatton's Criticisms

The first two lines of criticism take their start from Ockham's ordering principle. As I noted earlier, Chatton wholly accepts this principle, and so accepts Ockham's account of the logical and causal ordering among judgment and apprehension—as he says: "I concede that every act of assent naturally presupposes an apprehension of its object."[26] But, as we shall see, he also thinks that acceptance of Ockham's ordering principle provides an important first step toward establishing both the falsity of Ockham's account of judicative objects and the truth of his own.

To see why this should be the case, let us turn to Chatton's first line of criticism. Here, Chatton concedes Ockham's ordering principle only to argue that its conjunction with Ockham's conclusion regarding objects of judgment entails something obviously false: namely, that every act of judgment involves some sort of second-order awareness (what Chatton himself refers to as "reflex-

---

Studies, 1989). Wey provides a brief introduction to the prologue of Chatton's *Sentence* commentary.

24. Prol. q.1, a.1, 18–20. Chatton draws exclusively from Ockham's *Ordinatio* discussion of judgment.

25. Prol. q.1, a.1, 20.

26. Prol. q.1, a.1, 42.

ive" apprehension) of one's own mental states. Since Chatton accepts the ordering principle, he thinks the result tells against Ockham's conclusion.

That the conjunction of the ordering principle and Ockham's conclusion about judicative objects has this untoward consequence is clear, Chatton thinks, since, on Ockham's view, the mental sentences that serve as objects of judgment are themselves acts of apprehension. But, given Ockham's ordering principle, it follows that

> one does not assent to some mental sentence unless he first apprehends it.... This is because, as he [namely, Ockham] proves, the *apprehension* of a mental sentence is the cause of the [*judgment*] by which the intellect assents to the sentence.[27]

Clearly, if the sentences that serve as the objects for judgment are propositional apprehensions, and if every judgment presupposes an apprehension of the object judged, it follows that every act of judgment—that is, any act of believing, knowing, opining, etc.—involves some kind of second-order awareness or apprehension of one's own (first-order) mental acts or mental sentences. But this, as Chatton goes on to argue, is implausible insofar as it conflicts with our experience of the phenomenology of judging. As Chatton repeatedly points out, we seem to form judgments all the time without any second-order awareness or apprehension of our own mental states. Indeed, he thinks that mere reflection on the process by which we form a judgment (whether assent or dissent, belief or knowledge, and so on) makes perfectly clear that we can and do form judgments without any "reflexive" apprehension of our own states and, so, likewise clear that mental sentences cannot serve as objects for every judgment.

To illustrate the point, Chatton takes as a case in point the belief that God is three and one. The process by which one comes to form such a belief begins, he explains, with an act of propositional apprehension—that is, with the intellect's formulation of the thought or mental sentence "God is three and one." This is then immediately followed by an act of judgment, in this case, an assent—an act in which the intellect affirms or accepts the sentence as true. Now, as Chatton points out,

> when the intellect, in forming this mental sentence "God is three and one," assents with an act of belief, that act [of believing] does not presuppose an apprehension of the mental sentence "God is three and one" ... This is because the assent requires on the part of the intellect only that the mental sentence be formed in the intellect. It does not require that any mental sentence be apprehended.[28]

---

27. Prol. q.1, a.1, 17.
28. Prol. q.1, a.1, 39.

Of course, if it were true that a mental sentence was the object for this judgment, it would follow (given Ockham's ordering principle) that the formation of this belief would involve some kind of second-order apprehension of the mental sentence "God is three and one." Yet, as Chatton here points out, there is no reason to think this is the case. In forming such a belief, one typically does not—and need not—have any reflexive awareness of sentences in one's own language of thought. If this is right, however, it follows that Ockham's conclusion is mistaken: not every judgment has a mental sentence as its object.[29] Indeed, on Chatton's view, in *most* cases they do not.

So much for Chatton's first line of criticism. If we turn now to the second, we can see that, like the first, it takes Ockham's ordering principle as its point of departure. This time, however, he argues not merely against Ockham's conclusion, but for a positive claim of his own, namely, that "assent has for its object an extramental thing or things (*res*)"—where by "things" Chatton has in mind individual substances and/or some attribute of them. To see how Chatton arrives at this conclusion using Ockham's ordering principle, consider, once again, the formation of the belief that God is three and one. As we have seen, to believe or judge *that God is three and one* is just a matter of the intellect's forming the mental sentence "God is three and one" followed by a subsequent act of assent. What Ockham's ordering principle tell us, however, is that the object of the assent is the object of the act of apprehension that precedes and causes it. It follows, therefore, that whatever serves as the object of the propositional apprehension "God is three and one" is the object of the assent in question. Chatton then proceeds to argue that since "the mental sentence is an apprehension of God," we should be led by the ordering principle to conclude that God (and not some mental sentence) is the object of the belief that God is three and one.

In general, Chatton holds that what is cognized in a given act of propositional cognition is some external thing (or things)—specifically, substances and, perhaps, some property of them. This is because, as he sees it, the object (or, as he often characterizes it, the "significate") of sentences in the language of thought is just the entity (or entities) cognized by its constituent terms. And, in most cases what is cognized by each of the terms of a mental sentence is some extramental object. As he explains:

> a mental sentence is a certain propositional cognition. Thus, it is a cognition of just that which is cognized through the subject, or the predicate or the

---

29. As Chatton puts it elsewhere: "Supposing that a mental sentence [is present] in the intellect, and ruling out any apprehension of the mental sentence (*omni apprehesione complexi circumscripta*), the intellect is inclined to assent. But, having ruled out any apprehension of the metal sentence, [it is clear that] the intellect does not assent *to the sentence*.... [This is clear] since according to [Ockham] (and according to the truth of the matter) the intellect does not assent without a cognition or apprehension [of that to which it assents]. Therefore, if the mental sentence is not apprehended, the intellect does not assent to it." Prol. q.1, a.1, 21.

copula [of that mental sentence]. For its being a cognition accrues to it through its parts—but its parts are cognitions of an extra-mental thing.[30]

What is more, Chatton can see no reason why Ockham would disagree with this claim about the objects of propositional cognitions given his acceptance of Chatton's own adverbial analysis of mental sentences and of the concepts that comprise them.

Of course, if this is right and the object of the complex or propositional apprehension that precedes and causes a given act of assent (or dissent) is an extramental entity it follows that the object of the judgment is likewise something extramental. As Chatton insists,

> if we suppose that the intellect forms a sentence that signifies an external thing, and suppose further that it does not apprehend that sentence (which assumption is plausible since the parts of that sentence are not apprehensions of the whole sentence), then (assuming all of this), I claim that this mental sentence is suited to cause an assent, but that it does not cause an assent that relates to that sentence [as its object]. For, by assumption, the sentence is not what is apprehended. Therefore, the assent has for its object the external thing (or things) that are signified by that sentence.[31]

In the end, therefore, Chatton contends that Ockham's account of the relations which obtain between apprehension and judgment tell not only *against* his own conclusion about the objects of judgment but also *in favor* of Chatton's alternative account. "On the basis of [Ockham's] own claims," he says, "I have my principal point in this question—namely, that the assent that the intellect has when it forms a mental sentence signifying an extramental thing has that thing (and not the mental sentence) for its immediate object."[32]

All of this leaves open the possibility that there are nevertheless *some* cases in which we do direct attention toward our own mental states and even go on to form second-order thoughts or judgments about them. Chatton is perfectly

---

30. As Chatton proceeds to explain: "An external thing (*res*) is cognized through the subject, and the predicate and the copula since those terms are cognitions of an external thing. Throughout the whole time in which the sentence signifying an external thing is formed in the mind, the external thing is cognized—sometimes by the subject of the sentence, sometimes by the copula, sometimes by the predicate." Prol. q.1, a.1, 24. That Chatton does indeed think that what is apprehended by a mental sentence is a *thing* (i.e., an individual substance or attribute) one has only to consider his own examples. For instance when considering what is signified by the mental sentence 'God is three and one,' he claims that it is just God. "This is because that assent [viz. to the mental sentence *God is three and one*] requires on the part of the intellect only that that mental sentence be formed in the intellect. It does not require that any mental sentence is apprehended, because each part of that sentence is an apprehension of God and not of any accident in the mind." Prol. q.1, a.1, 39. God is the object for a number of other theological articles: "God is incarnate," "God is God," and so on.
31. Prol. q.1, a.1, 26.
32. Ibid., 38.

willing to acknowledge this possibility. Indeed, he explicitly allows that sometimes judgments do have mental sentences as their object. Cases in which an act of judgment relates to a mental sentence as its object are, on Chatton's view, cases in which one apprehends a given mental sentence and then goes on to make some judgment regarding its truth. Thus, for example, an act of *assent* that is directed at a mental sentence as its object will be an act in which one judges (believes, knows, etc.) that *that sentence* is true. Such judgments are, thus, not about or principally directed at some *thing* in extramental reality, but are rather directed at one's own mental acts.

In order to accommodate this possibility, Chatton thinks it is necessary to draw a distinction, already anticipated above, between two kinds of judgment or assent: those that are about extramental things (*res*) and so require no awareness or apprehension of one's own mental states, and those which are about one's own states (i.e., about sentences in one's language of thought) and so do require some sort of second-order or reflexive awareness of them. Accordingly, Chatton explicitly distinguishes between

> [1] the assent which the intellect has when it forms a mental sentence that immediately signifies an external thing—such as when one forms the sentence "God is three and one"—and [2] the assent the intellect has when it forms a mental sentence that immediately signifies another mental sentence—such as when one forms this mental sentence "the article of faith [e.g., "God is three and one"] is true."[33]

As Chatton points out, one sort of assent (call it a "nonreflexive" assent) is caused by the intellect's formation of a first-order mental sentence regarding some extramental thing (e.g., "God is three and one"), and, so, has that thing (e.g., God) as object. The other sort of assent, which Chatton labels "reflexive" assent, is caused by the intellect's formation of a second-order or metalinguistic mental sentence (e.g., "'God is three and one' is true"), and has (the first-order) mental sentence (e.g., "God is three and one") as object.

Obviously, the introduction of this distinction involves conceding to Ockham that *some* judgments do have mental sentences as objects. Chatton draws on this concession, however, to bolster his own position regarding objects of judgment. This brings us to the third line of criticism he pursues against Ockham. Here, after conceding that in some cases mental sentences do serve as objects of judgment, Chatton goes on to insist that the very possibility of such reflexive judgments presupposes the truth of his own view about the objects of nonreflexive judgments. This is because, Chatton maintains, every occurrence of a reflexive judgment directed at a mental sentence as object, requires the (logically) prior occurrence of a nonreflexive act of judgment that has an extramental thing as its object. As he explains:

33. Ibid.

Assent to a mental sentence necessarily presupposes [a prior act of] assent to the *thing* (*res*) signified by that sentence. This is the case because assenting that it is the case in reality (as the sentence signifies it to be) is prior to assenting that the sentence itself is true.[34]

On Chatton's view one cannot judge that a thought or mental sentence is true unless one has first formed a belief or judgment about how things stand in reality. To judge a sentence (mental or otherwise) to be true is to judge that it corresponds to reality. Hence, if one assents to a mental sentence—that is, if one believes or judges that one's thoughts (or apprehensions) are true, this must be because one has already formed a belief or judgment about *things* in the extramental world. Thus, the formation of a judgment directed at a mental sentence presupposes a prior judgment that is not directed at a mental sentence—indeed, it presupposes a prior judgment about *things* in extramental reality. Hence, the concession that acts of judgment sometimes have a mental sentence as object by itself entails the falsity of Ockham's position since it entails that not *every* act of judgment has a mental sentence as object.[35]

Although Chatton raises a number of other objections for Ockham's account, what we have seen already will be sufficient for establishing his influence on the subsequent development of Ockham's views.

## Chatton's Influence

Chatton's criticisms, as we have seen, are predicated on the assumption that Ockham continues to defend his early conclusion about mental sentences serving as objects of judgment even when his views about the nature of mental language itself began to evolve. Some commentators have questioned the accuracy of this assumption, however.[36] There is evidence to suggest that once Ockham comes to accept the adverbial analysis of concepts and mental sentences, he also abandons his early claim that mental sentences serve as objects for every

---

34. Ibid., 27.
35. Thus, as Chatton explains, at one point, even if one apprehends and assents that the article "God is three and one is true," this "does not entail that he first assents that the article is true. Rather it is the reverse. Assenting that an article is true requires that one [first] assent that something is the case in reality. And then, with the assent that relates to the external thing remaining in place, by virtue of that assent it then appears evident [to the person] that the article is true." Ibid., 42.
36. This was, in fact, my own view for a time. See also Karger, "William of Ockham, Walter Chatton, and Adam Wodeham," 183, who contends that Chatton's arguments against Ockham are "misleadingly presented" and, in general characterizes Chatton's criticisms of Ockham in terms of their "unfairness" to Ockham. Apparently, Adam Wodeham—a contemporary of both Ockham and Chatton—seems to have shared much the same view. He too denounces Chatton as being unfair to Ockham on this score. See ibid., n. 46.

act of judgment.[37] In the *Quodlibetal Questions*—a work which contains Ockham's most mature treatment of judgment and which also reflects his full acceptance of the adverbial analysis of mental language—Ockham explicitly claims that "an act of assent by which something is known to be such-and-such or known not to be such-and-such . . . does not have a mental sentence (*complexum*) as its object."[38] In fact, Ockham's treatment of judgment throughout his *Quodlibetal Questions* reflects a consistent and wholesale rejection of his early contention that mental sentences are the objects for all acts of judgment. But, if this is right—and Ockham never attempted to combine an adverbial analysis of mental language with his early theory of judgment—it follows that Chatton either misrepresents the views of his colleague (and, so, unfairly criticizes them) or is simply mistaken about the way they develop.

In point of fact, however, Chatton's criticisms clearly do find a target in Ockham's developing views about judgment. To see this, we need only consider some of Ockham's remarks in his commentary on Aristotle's *De Interpretatione*—a work written just a few years before his *Quodlibetal Questions* were completed. In this work, Ockham defends precisely the view that Chatton criticizes.[39] What is more, it looks as if Ockham comes to abandon this theory

---

37. Ockham's transition from the act/object or "fictum" theory of concepts to the adverbial or "mental act" theory proceeds in three stages: in the earliest stage he advances the *fictum* theory, in the middle stage he defends both the *fictum* and the mental act theory as equally plausible views, and in the final stage he wholly endorses the mental-act theory. The earliest drafts of his *Sentences* commentary—that is, his *Reportatio* commentary and the early draft of his *Ordinatio*—belong to the early period. To the middle period belong his later additions to the *Ordinatio* commentary and his commentary on the *Perihermenias*. The *Quodlibetal Questions*, the *Questions on the Physics*, and the *Summa Logicae* all belong to the last period. For relative dating of these texts, see Boehner 1946 and 1951 and Leff 1975, chap. 2. I argue at length in "Ockham on Judgment, Concepts, and the Problem of Intentionality" that Ockham's views about judgment also undergo a three-stage development—one corresponding to each of the three phases in the development of his theory of concepts. The view Chatton is attacking corresponds to the view that Ockham endorses during the second phase of his thinking about judgment. Thus, on my analysis, Chatton plays a role in Ockham's move from the second to the third and final theory of judgment.

38. *Quodl*. III, q. 8 (*OTh* IX, 233–234).

39. Although Chatton does not actually cite this work when criticizing Ockham's account of judgment, it dates to roughly the same period as the redaction of the *Ordinatio* commentary (on which Chatton does rely). What is more, there is good reason to think that Chatton knew of—perhaps was even present at—Ockham's lectures on *De Interpretatione*. This is because Ockham delivered his lectures on the "old logic" in 1321–22 while staying at the Franciscan studium in London, and it is widely supposed that Chatton was at the London studium during this same time. For discussion of the issue of Chatton's presence in London, see Gadeon Gál and S. Brown, "Introduction to *Summa Logicae* (*Opera Philosophica* I)," ed. P. Boehner, G. Gál, and S. Brown (St. Bonaventure, N.Y.: St. Bonaventure University Press, 1967), 53–56; and William Courtenay, "Ockham, Chatton, and the London Studium: Observation on Recent Changes to Ockham's Biography," in *Gegenwart Ockhams*, ed. W. Vossenkuhl and R. Schönberger (Weinheim: VCH-Verlagsgesellschaft, Acta Humaniora, 1990), 327–337.

precisely in response to Chatton's criticisms. Thus, if Ockham does eventually develop a view immune to Chatton's criticisms, this does not owe to any misunderstanding or unfairness on Chatton's part; rather, it owes to the fact that Ockham came to appreciate the force of Chatton's objections and revised his view in response to them.

The nature and extent of Chatton's influence can best be seen if we begin by looking briefly at Ockham's remarks about judgment in the prologue to his *De Interpretatione* commentary. Ockham's discussion in this context represents his earliest attempt to modify his initial account of the objects of judgment in order to accommodate the adverbial model of mental language.[40] In the prologue of the commentary, Ockham surveys a variety of views about the nature of concepts and of mental language, turning specifically in section 6 to a discussion, and a limited defense, of the adverbial model of mental language. Over the course of his discussion, Ockham specifically addresses a question about what, on this way of thinking about mental language, serves as object for judgment. His response is clear: objects of judgment are mental sentences—where these are understood as *acts* of propositional apprehension. As he explains:

> To apprehend a mental sentence is nothing other than to form a mental sentence. [ . . . ] But, if we speak of an act of *knowing* some mental sentence, then it can be said that this act is an act that is distinct from the act [of apprehension] that *is* the mental sentence. And, therefore, when some mental sentence is known, there are two acts of the intellect occurring simultaneously, namely, the act that is the sentence and the other act by means of which the mental sentence is known. Nor does one ever find Aristotle denying that two acts of the intellect can exist at the same time in the intellect, especially when it comes to acts ordered in the way these are: mental sentence and act of knowing it.[41]

What this passage shows is that, when Ockham first begins to entertain the adverbial model of mental language, he clearly does continue to hold fixed his earlier views about mental sentences serving as objects of judgment. He is, at least at this stage in his thinking, willing to accept both that mental sentences can be taken as acts or modes of propositional apprehension, and that mental sentences, so understood, function as objects of judgment. Indeed, as the foregoing passage makes clear, Ockham initially sees nothing untoward in conjunction

---

40. As noted earlier, at this stage in his thinking, Ockham has not wholly abandoned his early "fictum" theory of concepts, he is simply now willing to entertain the mental-act account alongside it. In this particular section of the prologue to the *De Interpretatione*, he is attempting to develop an account of judgment that would accommodate the mental act account of concepts, but does so without wholly endorsing the mental-act account of concepts.

41. *Expos. Perih.* Prol., sec. 6 (*OPh* II, 358). Cf. section 12 (*OPh* II, 375), where Ockham says much the same thing.

of the adverbial analysis of mental language and his earlier claim about objects of judgment.

When we turn to his most mature treatment of judgment in the *Quodlibetal Questions*, however, it becomes evident that the objections Chatton raises against this account have had their impact. In fact, the revisions Ockham makes in his account of objects of judgment appear to be a direct response to Chatton's discussion in q.1, a.1, and to take a great deal from Chatton's discussion in that context.[42]

Consider, for example, what Ockham says when, in his *Quodlibetal Questions*, he returns once again to the question about the objects of judgment. As noted earlier, he responds here by rejecting the claim that judicative acts always take mental sentences as their object. Significantly, however, he gives precisely Chatton's reasons for doing so: he claims that acceptance of such a view would entail something implausible, namely, that judgments would involve some kind of second-order, reflexive awareness of one's own mental states. Thus, in Quodlibet III.8, Ockham says that, in the ordinary case, an act of judgment

> does not have a mental sentence (*complexum*) as its object because such an act is able to exist through the mere formulation of a mental sentence and without any apprehension of a mental sentence. For this reason, it cannot be an act of assenting to a mental sentence. Furthermore, when an ordinary person knows *that a rock is not a donkey*, he is not thinking about a mental sentence at all, and as a result he is not assenting to a mental sentence.[43]

---

42. The dates assigned to Ockham's Quodlibetal disputations are 1322–1324. Although Ockham's discussion of judgment in the *Quodlibetal Questions* makes perfectly clear that he is not only aware of Chatton's objections, but even drawing material directly from Chatton's discussion in q.1, a.1, the precise means by which he had access to this material is a bit difficult to pin down. This is because the only extant version of Chatton's q.1, a.1 comes from the *Lectura* version of his *Sentences* prologue, and the dates for the completion of the *Lectura* range from 1324 to 1330. It is not unreasonable, however, to suppose that Chatton was already revising the prologue for the *Lectura* even as he was still giving his *Reportatio* lectures—namely during the years of 1321–23. And since Ockham and Chatton were likely together at the London studium during these years, it may be that Chatton was composing the *Lectura* version of the prologue at roughly the same time Ockham was engaged in his Quodlibetal disputations and, therefore, that Ockham had access to the material during the period he was presiding over these disputations. Or, it may be that Ockham incorporated material from Chatton's prologue into his Quodlibets some time after the disputations themselves were completed. After all, Ockham is thought to have revised and completed his *Quodlibetal Questions* some years after the disputations were held—perhaps during 1324–26 while he was in Avignon. Or, finally, it is even possible that Ockham had access only to the earlier *Reportatio* version of Chatton's Q.1, a. 1, but that the *Lectura* version is a simply a close parallel of the *Reportatio* discussion. For a discussion of the respective dating of Ockham's *Quodlibeta Septem* and Chatton's *Reportatio* and *Lectura*, see Wey's introductions to *Reportatio et Lectura super Sententias: Collatio ad Librum Primum et Prologus* (53–56) and *Quodlibeta Septem* (36–38), as well as Keele, "The So-Called *Res* Theory."

43. *Quodl.* III.8 (*OTh* IX, 233–234).

These remarks make perfectly clear that Ockham is both aware of and accepts as decisive Chatton's argument against his earlier theory. For he explicitly acknowledges that to claim that a judgment relates to a mental sentence as object requires that such a judgment involves reflexive awareness of one's own mental states and, likewise, acknowledges that in the normal course of things we form judgments without any consciousness of our own thoughts or mental acts. He concludes with Chatton, therefore, that mental sentences cannot, in general, serve as objects of judgment.

What is more, Ockham is now even willing to allow that there is a sense (albeit, a qualified or restricted one) in which we can say that things (*res*)—namely, substances and accidents—in extramental reality are objects of judgment. After all, in many cases, when we form a judgment we are aware of and judging about external things and, in this sense, the things themselves can be said to be the objects of judgment. Consider, for example, what Ockham says in connection with the previous example of judging *that a rock is not a donkey*:

> Although it is by means of a mental sentence formulated in the intellect that one affirms and knows that things are such and such in reality or that things are not such and such in reality, one nonetheless does not perceive this [mental sentence]. Instead, the act of assenting has as its object things outside the mind, namely, a rock and a donkey.[44]

Here Ockham concedes not only that this judgment involves no apprehension of the mental sentence that precedes and causes it, but also that since the judgment does clearly involve some awareness or apprehension of extramental things—namely, rocks and donkeys—these things can be said to be its objects. As he proceeds to explain: "by means of an assent of this sort I apprehend things (*res*) outside the mind, since every assent is an apprehension but not vice versa."[45] Thus, to the extent that objects of judgment are those entities that are apprehended in the judgment—or in one or more of the acts leading up to the formation of the judgment—Ockham is willing to grant Chatton's view that extramental entities—that is, *things* such as rocks and donkeys—can serve as objects of judgment. Thus, a bit later in this same discussion, when considering the question of objects of faith or belief, Ockham explicitly concedes Chatton's own conclusion about the object of the belief that God is three and one. As Ockham puts it: "by such an act it is believed that God is three persons; and the object of that act (in the sense in which it has an object) is God."[46]

Although Ockham holds that substances or accidents can be called objects of judgment only in a restricted or qualified sense, the extent of Chatton's influence is evident, nonetheless. Not only does Ockham now reject his earlier conclusion

---

44. Ibid. (*OTh* IX, 234).
45. Ibid.
46. Ibid. (*OTh* IX, 236).

about mental sentences serving as objects for all acts of judgment while also granting the view that *things* can serve (in some sense at least) as objects, but he also appropriates Chatton's distinction between the two different types of judgment, that is the distinction between nonreflexive and reflexive assent.[47]

Indeed, one of the most distinctive features of Ockham's treatment judgment in the *Quodlibetal Questions* is the appearance of this distinction—it shows up only in his most mature treatment of judgment and it matches exactly the distinction Chatton draws between acts of assent that require no awareness or apprehension of one's own mental acts (and so do not have mental sentences as objects) and those which do. In fact, at every point in the *Quodlibetal Questions* at which Ockham treats questions about judgment he begins his discussion by marking this very distinction. Consider, for example, his remarks at the outset of Quodlibet IV.16:

> I claim, as was explained in another Quodlibet, that acts of assenting are of two sorts. One sort is an act by which I assent that some thing is or is not such-and-such in the way that I assent to its being the case that God exists, and to its being the case that God is three and one, and to its being the case that God is not the devil. . . . The second sort of assent is an act by which I assent to something, with the result that the act of assenting does bear a relation to something, in the way that I assent to or dissent from a mental sentence (*complexum*) For example, I assent to the mental sentence "a human being is an animal," since I consider it to be true.[48]

Although there is a great deal going on in this passage, one thing that emerges perfectly clearly is that Ockham has adopted Chatton's distinction between nonreflexive and reflexive assent, and does so in order to make just the same point Chatton did—namely, that mental sentences can be the objects only of reflexive acts of assent. Indeed, like Chatton, Ockham now wants to distinguish between cases in which one apprehends and forms thoughts and judgments about *things* in extramental reality—for instance, about God and the devil, *that the one is not the other*, say—and cases in which one apprehends and forms (second-order)

---

47. The distinction that Ockham, following Chatton, draws here between two acts of judgment is one that he comes to apply to other mental acts as well. Indeed, in a number of places throughout his *Quodlibetal Questions* Ockham marks a distinction between what he calls "direct" and "reflexive" mental acts, claiming that "an act by which we understand an object outside the mind is called a *direct act*, and an act by which a direct act itself is understood is called a *reflexive act*" (*Quodl*. II.12 [OTh IX, 165]). What Ockham here refers to as "direct" mental acts are just *first-order* acts involving an awareness only of items in the extramental world; reflexive acts, by contrast, are *second-order* as they involve awareness of other, first-order mental acts. Although Ockham does not restrict this distinction to acts of judgment, and while he never uses the terms "direct" and "reflexive" in the context of his treatments of judgment, it is clear, nevertheless, that the distinction between two types of assent corresponds to his distinction between direct and reflexive mental acts.

48. OTh IX, 376–377.

thoughts and judgments about one's own (first-order) thoughts—for example, about the mental sentence "a human being is an animal," *that that sentence is true*, say. Since cases of the former sort are about *things* in extramental reality and not about sentences in one's head, they clearly require no reflexive awareness of such sentences. As Ockham goes on to explain:

> without exception it is never the case that the first sort of assent necessarily presupposes an apprehension of a mental sentence, since this sort of assent is not an assent relating to a mental sentence as object. Rather this assent presupposes apprehension of singular *thing*, though the intellect does not assent to singular things. By contrast, the second sort of assent, speaking naturally, does necessarily presuppose apprehension of a mental sentence . . . and the reason is that this sort of assent has a mental sentence for its object.[49]

Thus, insofar as it is only reflexive judgments that are about mental sentences, it is also only reflexive judgments that have mental sentences as object. Here again, Chatton's influence on Ockham is unmistakable.[50]

## CHATTON AND OCKHAM ON THE OBJECTS AND STRUCTURE OF JUDGMENT

To this point, I have been emphasizing the similarities between Ockham's final treatment of judgment and Chatton's discussion in q.1, a.1 in order to call attention to Chatton's influence on Ockham. What we have seen is, I think, sufficient to establish not only that Ockham does, at one point, advance precisely the view Chatton criticizes, but also that he is moved by these criticisms to revise this view—taking much from Chatton's own account in the course of doing so. Yet, while the revisions Ockham makes do bring his account much closer to Chatton's, the remaining disagreements between them should not be overlooked. Indeed, as I now want to show, there are still a number of important differences between Chatton and Ockham's views about both *objects* and *acts* of judgment.

---

49. Ibid.
50. Not only can Chatton's influence be seen in the changes Ockham introduces to his final theory of judgment, but it can also be seen in the structure the discussion itself. For example, in *Quodlibet* III.8, the three points Ockham considers in connection with the first of the objection he discusses turn out to be precisely the first, second, and seventh principle objections raised by Chatton in q.1, a.1 (21–22, 27, 29–30). Likewise, all three objections Ockham treats in *Quodlibet* IV.16 are points raised by Chatton. In *Quodlibet* V.6, a number of arguments Ockham adduces in favor of each of his two theses have a close parallel in Chatton's discussion. For instance, the argument Ockham offers in favor of the conclusion that reflexive acts of judgment must be distinct from reflexive acts of apprehension is roughly the same argument Chatton offers in response to the first objection brought against his position (Prol. q.1, a.1, 33ff.). There, however, he is using the argument to argue for a distinction among nonreflexive apprehensions and judgments.

## Objects of Judgment

As we have seen, Ockham concedes Chatton's point that in cases of first-order, nonreflexive acts of judging what is apprehended is not a mental sentence, but rather one or more extramental things. And insofar as extramental entities are what is cognized or apprehended in such judgments Ockham allows that such things can be said to be the "objects" of judgment. Where he diverges from Chatton, however, is in his insistence that extramental things are not objects of judgment in the more strict sense of being "that which known" (or believed) or, more generally, that to which assent or dissent is given. Consider his remarks in a passage cited just above from Quodlibet IV.16 where he discussing the objects of first-order acts of faith:

> by [this sort of act] I assent that some thing is or is not such-and-such—in the way that I assent to its being the case that God exists, and to its being the case that God is three and one, and to its being the case that God is not the devil. *I do not, however, assent to God or to the devil; rather I assent to its being the case that God is not the devil. Hence, strictly speaking, I assent to nothing through this act even though I apprehend God and the devil through this act.* (Italics added.)

Drawing on Chatton's own example of the belief that *God is three and one*, Ockham argues that although what is apprehended is God (and not a mental sentence about God), nevertheless, one does not "assent to God." Indeed, Ockham thinks that, strictly speaking, in cases of first-order judgments there is "nothing"—that is, no entity or object—to which the act of judging relates as *what is assented to*. Although this may seem an odd claim, it is, nevertheless, one Ockham returns to a number of times. In fact, he makes much the same point in Quodlibet III.8 when talking about the first-order judgment "A rock is not a donkey." As we have seen, Ockham grants that "this act of assent has as its object things outside the mind, namely, a rock and a donkey," yet, he also insists that "it is not, nevertheless, the case that a rock is known or that a donkey is known. . . . Indeed, if you ask whether there is something known by this act, I reply that, properly speaking, it should *not* be said that something is known by this act."[51] Ockham's point here is not that the act in question is empty or devoid of content; rather his point is simply that the relation in which it stands to extramental things (in this case, rocks and donkeys) is not the relation of "being known" (or believed) or "being assented to."

Thus, while Ockham is willing to grant Chatton's point that *things* such as rocks and donkeys (or God and the devil) can be called objects of judgments in the sense that they are the objects toward which one's attention is directed in judgment (or, in Chatton's terms, what is "apprehended"), he also wants to resist

---

51. *OTh* IX, 234.

saying that such entities are objects that can be judged or to which assent (or dissent) can be given. Indeed, as he says at one point, "there is no such thing as assent with respect to a thing (*res*), since it makes no sense to say that I assent to a rock or to a cow."⁵² The emphasis Ockham's puts on this point is clearly an attempt to distance himself from Chatton's own account of objects of judgment. For not only is Chatton perfectly comfortable with the claim that, in cases of first order judgments, the intellect "assents to a thing," but he holds that this is what one *must* say. After all, he argues, if "the intellect does not [in such cases] assent to a mental sentence, it therefore assents to a thing (or to things) signified by the sentence."⁵³ And, to his mind, there is nothing particularly worrisome about this. For, as he explains, it is "no more absurd [to say] that assent has for its immediate object one thing (or many things) than [to say] that the thing (or things) are signified simultaneously by the sentence that the intellect forms in assenting."⁵⁴

This difference between what Chatton and Ockham are each willing to count as "objects" of judgment owes, ultimately, to the fact that each thinker approaches the question about objects of judgment with a different set of interests and aims in mind. For Chatton, the question about objects of judgment is, ultimately, a question about the broadly intentional or semantic features of mental language. On his view, therefore, the objects of judgment are whatever is apprehended or "signified" by the mental sentence that precedes and causes it. Thus, for him, the question about objects of judgment is, fundamentally, a question about the nature of the entities that serve as the referent or "significate" for sentential expressions (namely, mental sentences). And, as we have seen, he thinks that mental sentences refer just to the thing (or things) to which their subject and predicate expressions refer—where these include substances and/or their attributes. Hence, these are objects of judgment.⁵⁵

52. *Quodl.*, IV.16 (*OTh* IX, 380).
53. Prol. q.1, a.1, 21.
54. Prol. q.1, a.1, 30.
55. To some extent, therefore, my reading of Chatton diverges from that offered by Rondo Keele in "The So-Called *Res* Theory," where he claims that while "Chatton does sometimes drift over to talking about the signification of [mental] propositions ... it would be wrong to view Chatton's goal in q.1, a.1 as establishing or defending a *res*-theory as an answer to [this] question" (48). Indeed, according to Keele, Chatton "has a small theoretical contribution on [the] question [about the significates of mental sentences] primarily because his interest in [that] question ... was quite low" (40). Although, I would concur with Keele's contention that (a) we must look beyond q.1, a.1 for a *complete* understanding of Chatton's account and (b) the complete account will ultimately show that Chatton takes "res"—namely, individual substances and attributes—to function as *truth-makers* for sentences, nevertheless, none of this undermines the fact that for Chatton the question about the "significates" of mental sentences was of central importance. As I read him, Chatton holds that the significate of a mental sentence (and of the corresponding act of assent) is precisely that which serves its truth maker. Indeed, it is precisely this claim that his younger colleague Adam Wodeham attacks. See Susan Brower-Toland, "Facts vs. Things: Adam Wodeham and the Later Medieval Debate about Objects of Judgment," *Review of Metaphysics* 60 (2006): 597–642.

Ockham approaches the question about objects of judgment from a rather different set of concerns. From the start, he is thinking of objects of judgment in terms of truth and, in particular, in terms of truth-bearers.[56] Thus, on his view, properly or "strictly" speaking, only *what is true* can be an object of assent—since only what is true is said to be "known" (*scitum*), "believed" (*creditum*), or, in general, an object for assent (or dissent). And since, mental sentences are, even on his mature view, the primary bearers of truth and falsity he is resistant to the notion that ordinary things (*res*) are objects of assent in any strict sense. Indeed, Ockham goes so far as to insist that it is only second-order judgments that can be said to have objects properly speaking; for only these sorts of act relate to something in such a way that that it is appropriate to say of the *relatum* that it is *known* or believed or assented to. After all, only second-order judgments relate to something true (i.e., truth-bearing). As he explains, "the second [namely, reflexive] sort of [judgment] is an act of assenting by which I assent to something in such a way that the act of assenting does bear a relation to something—as it does when I assent to or dissent from a mental sentence."[57] Thus, for Ockham the question about objects of judgment is closely tied to questions about the nature of truth-bearers; only what is true can, strictly or properly speaking, be said to be an object of judgment.

Because Ockham and Chatton approach the question about objects of judgment with different interests and aims they arrive at different conclusions about what sorts of thing count as "objects" of judgment. This same divergence in starting points also lies behind a second, and much more substantial disagreement between them—one having to do with the nature of objects of demonstration. As we have already noted, Ockham's general approach to the issue of objects of judgment is tied to particular concerns he has about objects of *scientia*—that is, demonstrative knowledge or science. As we have seen, in order to accommodate the standard definition of demonstrative knowledge (namely, as knowledge of what is not only true, but also necessary and universal) Ockham argues that all acts (and habits) of assent produced by a demonstrative syllogism relate to mental sentences as object. Despite all the other changes he makes to his early theory of judgment, this is a claim he retains. Thus, even in his most mature writings, Ockham insists that "the science (*scientia*) of nature is not about corruptible and generable things or about natural substances . . . rather, properly speaking, natural science is about intentions in the mind which are common to [external] things and which stand precisely for such things."[58] What

---

56. As we noted earlier, his initial definition of judgment and assent is in terms of truth: "our intellect does not assent to anything unless we consider it to be true and does not dissent from anything unless we judge it to be false."

57. *Quodl.* III.8 (*OTh* IX, 233).

58. *Expos.Phys.*, Prol. (*OPh* IV, 11). Cf. *SL* III-2, qq. 1–12 (*OPh* I, 505–526).

this means for his mature theory of judgment is that demonstrative knowledge turns out to be a type of reflexive judgment—as Ockham himself explicitly points out:

> speaking about the second [namely, a reflexive] sort of knowing or assenting, I claim that such an act is a propositional act that properly speaking has a mental sentence as its object.... And it is this sort of act that philosophers are commonly speaking of. For they claim that the effect of a demonstration is a habit that relates to a conclusion. Consequently, the act corresponding to that habit is an act that relates to a conclusion as its object. Philosophers also claim that nothing is known except what is true, and they are speaking of a mental sentence. They also claim that a demonstrative science is based on first and true principles. Therefore, only what is true is an object of a science.[59]

Here Ockham draws on his new distinction between reflexive and non-reflexive judgments (which, as we have seen, he takes from Chatton) in order to defend his early view about objects of demonstration. For, by restricting demonstration to reflexive acts of judgment, he is able to retain his original claim that demonstrative knowledge relates to mental sentences as object and in this way accommodate the strictures of demonstrative science within his nominalist ontology.

Ockham's final position on objects of demonstration stands in stark contrast to Chatton's. For, throughout his discussion in q.1, a.1 Chatton makes clear that acts of demonstration can be nonreflexive in nature. For, as he sees it,

> it suffices for an act of knowing that the intellect demonstrates. And, as a result, even if neither the demonstration nor any of its parts is apprehended through a reflexive act, still that demonstration would exist, and would no less cause an act of assenting.[60]

Although demonstrative knowledge is the result of the formation in the intellect of a demonstrative syllogism, Chatton does not think demonstrative knowledge requires any second-order awareness of the syllogism—its premises or its conclusions. Indeed, on his view, it is perfectly possible for us to syllogize nonreflexively and so perfectly possible for us to have acts of scientific knowledge that relates to things in extramental reality. As he explains, "when someone demonstrates, that is, forms a demonstration that does not signify things in the mind, but rather things outside the mind ... the external thing (whether one or many) which is signified by the conclusion is the object of the assent." As opposed to Ockham, therefore, Chatton holds that demonstrative knowledge can be a first order act and, therefore, like any other act of judgment, can have some extramental *thing* as its object.

---

59. *Quodl.* III. 8 (*OTh* IX, 234).
60. Prol., q.1, a.1, 21.

These various points of disagreement between Ockham and Chatton regarding objects of judgment are significant not only because they mark the differences in their own positions, but also because they serve as starting point for subsequent debates about objects of judgment. Indeed, the differences that remain between Ockham and Chatton provide a good deal of fodder for later discussions. This is perhaps nowhere more evident than in the writings of Ockham and Chatton's immediate contemporaries and successors at Oxford. For thinkers such as Adam Wodeham, William Crathorn, Robert Holcot the positions marked out by Ockham and Chatton provide the main dialectical alternatives in terms of which the debate as a whole is framed—such authors either explicitly side with one or the other or else present themselves as attempting to develop some middle ground between the two.[61] And even beyond this immediate sphere of influence, the debate between Ockham and Chatton has a role in shaping the direction of the debate. As the debate about objects of judicative attitudes unfolds in the mid and latter half of the fourteenth century, the two issues which come to occupy the center of the discussion are precisely those which come to the fore in the debate between Ockham and Chatton: namely, the question of the nature of the objects of Aristotelian demonstrative knowledge, and the question about the nature of the entities "signified" by propositional expressions.[62]

---

61. Thus, for example, Wodeham, who commences his *Lectura Secunda* (D.1, q.1, a.1) with a question about the nature of objects of *scientia*, opens his discussion with the following question: "I ask first whether the act of knowledge (*scientia*) has as its immediate object things (*res*) or signs (*signum*)—that is, whether it has a sentence in the mind [as object] or the things signified by the sentence." Adam Wodeham, *Lectura Secunda in Librum Primum Sententiarum*, ed. R. Wood and G. Gál (St. Bonaventure, N.Y.: St. Bonaventure University Press, 1990), 180. Although he does not name Chatton and Ockham explicitly here, he does mention them later on in the discussion. Similarly, Robert Holcot (d. 1349) opens his *Quodlibet* I.6, which focuses on a question about objects of God's knowledge, by rehearsing Ockham and Chatton's views on the question of objects of knowledge generally. "There is," he says, "uncertainty regarding what should be said to be known as object. One view, namely, Ockham's, is that only a mental sentence is known. Another view, namely, Chatton's, is that the object of an act of knowing or believing is not a sentence but the thing signified by the sentence." See Robert Holcot, *Quaestiones quodlibetales*, in W. J. Courtenay, "A Revised Text of Robert Holcot's Quodlibetal Dispute on Whether God Is Able to Know More Than He Knows," *Archiv für Geschichte der Philosophie* 53 (1971): 3. Crathorn, too, frames his discussion on objects of *scientia* as a question about whether such objects are sentences (*complexa*) or things (*res*). See William Crathorn, *Quaestiones super librum sententiarum. In Questionen Zum ersten Sentenzenbuch*, Ed. F. Hoffmann (Munster: Aschendorff, 1988), 269–306. For further discussion of these figures see Tachau, *Vision and Certitude*; Nuchelmans, *Theories of the Proposition*, chaps. 12–13; Grassi, "The Object of Scientific Knowledge"; Jack Zupko, "How It Played in the rue de Fouarre: Reception of Adam Wodeham's Theory of the Complexe Significabile in the Arts Faculty at Paris in the Mid–Fourteenth Century," *Franciscan Studies* 54 (1994): 211–225; Karger, "William of Ockham, Walter Chatton, and Adam Wodeham"; Brower-Toland, "Later Medieval Theories of Propositions," chaps. 4–5; Brower-Toland, "Facts versus Things."

62. Wodeham, for example, considers both issues in a single question—he argues that the object of demonstrative *scientia* is something that is only *"complexe significabile"* (that is,

Although Ockham and Chatton are not the first to consider these issues, their treatment of them seems to lend new momentum to the discussion.

## Acts of Judgment

I want to call attention to one further difference between Ockham and Chatton's respective accounts of judgment. Here, the difference has to do not with their views about *objects* of judgment, but rather with they way in which each conceives of the *act* of judging itself. As will become clear, the disagreement between them on this issue is far less conspicuous; neither Ockham nor Chatton ever explicitly remark on it, and perhaps did not even clearly recognize it. Nonetheless, I think we can detect a difference in way in which each conceives of, and so characterizes, the intentionality associated with acts of judgment.

Recall that both Ockham and Chatton assume that every judgment is caused by a (logically) prior apprehension. Despite their shared commitment to this assumption, Ockham allows that it would be possible for God to act directly on the intellect to produce an act of judgment—without any prior act of apprehension. For, as he explains,

> one should not deny of any absolute thing that it can exist by divine power apart from another absolute thing, which is really distinct from it unless some evident contradiction arises. But there appears to be no evident contradiction in thinking that the judgment that follows an apprehension could exist even though the apprehension does not.[63]

Interestingly, however, Ockham goes on immediately after this to argue that while an act of judgment can occur in the absence of a *distinct* act of apprehension, it is, nevertheless, impossible for a judgment to occur without any apprehension whatsoever. As he says: "it is not a contradiction for an intellect to assent to a

---

something that can only be signified by a complex, sentential expression). A number of thinkers after Wodeham take an interest specifically in questions about the nature of the entities that are *complexe significabile* (i.e., signified by sentences). This debate clearly has its roots in the debate between Ockham and Chatton—in particular, in Chatton's focus on questions about the significate of mental sentences. For discussion of the development of the later fourteenth-century discussion of objects of *scientia* and of *complexe significabilia*, see Kretzmann, "Medieval Logicians on the Meaning of the Propositio," Journal of Philosophy 67 (1970): 767–787; Nuchelmans, *Theories of the Proposition*, chaps. 14–16; Nuchelmans, *Late Scholastic and Humanist Theories of the Proposition* (Amsterdam: North Holland, 1980), chap. 4; Jack Zupko, "How It Played in the rue de Fouarre"; Cesalli, "Some Fourteenth Century Realist Theories of the Proposition"; R. Gaskin, "Complexe Significabilia and Aristotle's Categories," in *La tradition médiévale des categories (XIIe–XVe siècles)*, ed. J. Biard and I. Rosier-Catach (Louvain: Éditions Peeters, 2003), 187–205; and Alessandro Conti, "Complexe Significabile and Truth in Gregori of Rimini and Paul of Venice," in *Medieval Theories on Assertive and Non-Assertive Language*, ed. A. Maierù and L. Valente (Florence: Olschki, 2004), 473–494.

63. *Ord*. Prol. Q.1 (*OTh* I, 59).

mental sentence without apprehending it by an act of apprehension really distinct from that assent; nevertheless, it can be conceded that assenting without apprehension of any sort does involve a contradiction."[64] This is because, as he immediately goes on to add, "assent is itself a certain sort of apprehension."[65] His point, I take it, is that acts of judging, just like acts of apprehending, are fully representational states. That is to say, they are intellective acts or states that are of or about something—states in which something is thought or "apprehended." Thus, it is impossible for there to be an act of assent without apprehension at all since, on his view, this would be tantamount to saying that an act of judgment can be devoid of intentionality.

For Ockham, therefore, judgment is a type of apprehension insofar as it is itself a fully representational state. An act of judgment is propositional in content in just the way propositional apprehensions (i.e., mental sentences) are. In fact, at one point, Ockham explicitly refers to acts of assent as "propositional" (*complex*) acts—much in the way he characterizes the propositional apprehensions with which he identifies mental sentences.[66] It would appear, therefore, that the only difference between apprehension and judgment, on his view, has to do with the force associated with each: acts of judgment carry a kind of assertoric force not present in acts that are *merely* apprehensive. As Ockham expresses it, in judgment "the intellect *not only apprehends* its object, but *also* gives its assent or dissent with respect to it." On his view, therefore, acts of apprehension and judgment are acts belonging to the same genus—for they are each cognitive or intentional states. Indeed, as he says, if "one asks how these acts [namely, apprehension and judgment] differ, I say they are distinct in species; nor is it unfitting for there to be acts of distinct species in the same power with respect to the same object."[67]

---

64. Ibid.
65. Ibid. Although the texts on which I am relying here are early, there is no indication that Ockham changes his mind about this. Indeed, in his discussion of judgment in the *Quodlibetal Questions*, Ockham explicitly reiterates his early claim that "every act of assenting is an act of apprehension" at a couple of points (see *OTh* IX, 234, 311). In his mature account of the ordering among acts of judgment vis-à-vis apprehension (namely, in Quodlibet IV.16), Ockham continues to emphasize that acts of judging presuppose the prior occurrence only "naturally speaking"—that is, only in cases where God's influence is not under consideration.
66. See Quodlibet III. 8 (*OTh* IX, 234). There is some complication here, however, for in Quodlibet V.6 he characterizes acts of knowing and believing as "simple." It is not clear what to make of this claim, however. In any case, it is not at all clear that his calling such acts "simple" counts against the interpretation I am offering. For according to Ockham, a simple or "incomplex" mental act is just an act that is such that no part of it is itself an intellectual act. I take this definition from Claude Panaccio, *Ockham on Concepts* (Haddon: Ashgate, 2004), 32. According to it, however, even mental sentences can be simple acts. Indeed, Ockham himself explicitly acknowledges this possibility. See, *Expos. Perih.* Prol., sec. 6 (*OPh* II, 355–357) and I.4 (*OPh* II, 395).
67. *Ord.* Prol. Q.1 (*OTh* I, 60).

Chatton, by contrast, seems to presuppose a different view about the nature of judgment. Not only does he nowhere indicate that acts of judging are a type of apprehension, capable of existing apart from the apprehensions that cause them, his remarks imply a rather different view of the nature of the relation between apprehension and judgment. It appears that, for Chatton, acts of judgment are not merely *causally* dependent on prior acts of apprehension, but are also dependent on them for their *representationality*—that is, for their representational content. In fact, some of his remarks in other contexts suggest that he takes acts of assent (and dissent) to be more akin to noncognitive acts such as willing (and refusing) than to acts of apprehension. Indeed, at one point, he explicitly characterizes acts of will as a type of assent or dissent and, later on in the same discussion, describes intellective assent and dissent as analogous to acts of appetite insofar as "what is affirmation and negation in the intellect is attraction and repulsion in the appetite."[68]

In the context of his discussion in q.1, a.1, Chatton's most explicit remarks about the difference between acts of apprehension and judgment come in a passage in which he is explaining how, in the case in which one comes to believe an article of the faith, the act in which assent is given differs from that in which one merely entertains (i.e., "apprehends") the article in question. His account here suggests that he takes the act of apprehending the article and the act of assenting to it to be not merely distinct numerically, but also distinct in kind. For, he says,

> the act of believing is a simple act, whereas the act of forming the article [i.e., forming a mental sentence stating an article of faith] occurs successively over time. Therefore, these acts are distinct. . . . The first premise is clear since if it were not a simple act (one that does not include many acts) there would be no single instant at which it could be posited. After all, a mental sentence (which does include many acts) is usually formed by a wayfarer in succession—in that order in which it is formed in spoken words (or at least it can be so formed). And so [if the two acts were not distinct] there would be no one instant at which the faithful person believes.[69]

As Chatton emphasizes here, on his view, a propositional apprehension—that is, a mental sentence—is an aggregate of mental acts: one act serving as the subject term, another as the predicate term, and a third as the copula. By contrast, the act of believing or assenting is "simple." Thus, unlike the propositional

---

68. Earlier in the same discussion, Chatton compares acts of willing and judging in this way: "Every act of the will is willing or resisting since it is no less the case here than in other respects that any act of the intellect following deliberation is assenting or dissenting. For it is clear from the Philosopher that in the intellect there is affirmation and negation and here there is attraction and repulsion" (*Rep.* I, D. 1, q.2, a.2, 40).

69. Prol. q.1, a.1, 34.

act of apprehension that precedes and causes it, assent does not "include many acts" but, rather, in some sense attaches to or accompanies the existing aggregate that is the already formed mental sentence. As Chatton goes on to explain, however, "although an act of knowing or believing is a simple act of the intellect" and, so, not a "complex" or propositional act, he wants to insist that "it remains the case that it is a truth-evaluable (*veridicus*) act—insofar as it is caused by means of composition [and division] and is such that it is not had prior to composition and division." Indeed, on his view, the act of assent is "simple" inasmuch as it "does not include a plurality of acts *intrinsically*." Yet, unlike other simple or nonpropositional acts, an act assent is such that it can exist only in connection with a complex or propositional apprehension and so will relate to that which is represented (or apprehended) by that apprehension. As Chatton seems to be thinking of it, therefore, the act by which the intellect assents or judges is not, as it is for Ockham, a species of apprehension; it is, rather, an act that in some sense attaches to or follows on apprehension and adds a kind of judicative force to it.

In light of the foregoing, we might summarize the difference between Ockham and Chatton in terms of their respective ways of accounting for the force and content associated with any given judgment. For Ockham, judgment is a single act—one that possesses both propositional content as well as assertoric force. Chatton, by contrast, seems to analyze the force and content involved in judgment into distinct types of act, one of which is a content bearing act, with the other functioning as the mental equivalent of a judgment stroke. Thus, for Chatton, a single judgment is comprised of two distinct *types* of act: a complex or propositional *apprehension* and a separate act of assent "by virtue of which the intellect takes (*asserit*) the complex apprehension (*complexum*) to be true."[70]

Here again, the difference between Ockham and Chatton is significant for understanding later medieval developments. Indeed, we can find in thinkers such as Adam Wodeham—an immediate successor and student of both Ockham and Chatton—evidence of this disagreement and some indication of how it came to shape later discussions. Since Wodeham's treatment of this issue not only appears to corroborate my reading of the difference between Ockham and Chatton, but also illustrates how such different conceptions of judgment made their way into subsequent discussions, it is worth considering briefly.

Wodeham's discussion of this issue occurs in the context of a discussion about God's ability to directly cause an "evident" act of judgment. At one point in this discussion, he pauses briefly to summarize what he takes to be two different ways of thinking about the nature of judicative acts themselves. The first of these bears a remarkable resemblance to the view I have attributed to Chatton, whereas the second looks to be Ockham's. Thus, on the first model, as Wodeham describes it, "no judgment ... is an apprehension" but

70. Prol., q.1, a.1, 43.

> rather, judgment is only a certain nod by which the mind grants that it is the case as the mental sentence (or sentences) signifies. But for the fact that there is this nodding there would be [just] some apprehension concerning its being such and such. Thus, [judgment] is a certain mental concession or refusal that, according to nature, always presupposes and also co-occurs with a propositional apprehension, which when posited, one can grant or not grant as if mentally saying "yes" or "no" or by hesitating. And according to this, such an act might be a certain act of the soul that conforms more to acts of the appetite than to acts of apprehension. . . . Thus, if God were to cause such an act in us without apprehension, we would, inwardly, assess nothing by it since it is not a perceptive act. Rather we would remain totally blind.[71]

On this analysis, judgment is not an intentional or representational state, but is rather more like a mental "nod" that, as Wodeham explains, "always co-occurs" with a propositional apprehension. Indeed, if it were to somehow occur without being accompanied by an act of apprehension it would be, as he puts it a "blind" mental nod for the intellect would be assenting or dissenting (giving a mental nod, or shake) but not to anything. Thus, as Wodeham nicely puts it, on this view "no single mental act would be knowing [or believing or judging], rather it would be as much as an aggregate of multiple acts."

On the second of Wodeham's two models, however, an act of judgment "is itself a certain . . . apprehension." Indeed, as Wodeham goes on to explain, on this analysis

> it may be said that this sort of judgment is a single act that is simple in being, but in representing [it represents] just as much as the propositional and the nonpropositional acts that are necessary (naturally speaking) for causing and conserving it—although perhaps it represents and signifies in a less perfectly manner than these. . . . For the two representative natures are of a different species—that is, the two acts belong to representations of their own species.[72]

Here, judgment is conceived as a type or species of apprehension; it is, as Wodeham says, an act that "represents and signifies" things in much the way as acts of apprehension do. On this view, therefore, judging is not a composite mental state, but rather a single act in which one both represents or entertains a certain content and intellectively assents (or dissents) to it.

Although Wodeham does not mention Ockham or Chatton by name in connection with either of these views, the resemblance to each seems clear.[73] What

---

71. *Lectura Secunda*, Prol., q.6 (I, 173).
72. Ibid. (I, 174).
73. What is more, this issue arises in the context of a broader question in which he is addressing and adjudicating the differences between Ockham and Chatton's views on cognition—in particular, what sort of acts are required in order for the intellect to form an evident judgment. It is, therefore, not unlikely that in rehearsing (and ultimately deciding between)

is more, Wodeham's discussion not only provides a nice way of summarizing the differences between them, but also shows how the dispute between Ockham and Chatton on judgment may well have been responsible for initiating a wide-ranging debate about both the nature of *objects* of judgment and the nature and intentional structure of acts of judgment. Indeed, in the latter part of the fourteenth century, questions and debate about the nature of judicative acts comes to the fore alongside questions about objects of judgment.[74]

CONCLUSION

In this essay, I have argued that Chatton's criticisms of Ockham find a target in Ockham's developing views about judgment and that they play an important role in shaping the outcome of that development. I have also attempted to show that while Ockham's final theory of judgment is clearly influenced by Chatton, significant differences between them remain—differences in the sorts of philosophical interests that motivate their respective accounts, differences in the conclusions they draw about the nature of objects of judgment, and, finally, differences in the way each conceives of the nature and structure of judicative states themselves. These points of disagreement serve to highlight the nature of the formative relationship between the two. For here, as in so many other cases, the exchange between them provides an occasion for each to refine and sharpen his views—and, by so doing, to further the philosophical debate itself. Indeed, as we have seen, understanding the differences between Chatton and Ockham sheds new light not only on what is distinctive in each, but also on the development of the later medieval debate about judgment as a whole.

---

these two ways of thinking about judgment Wodeham means to be addressing yet one more difference between Ockham and Chatton.

74. See Nuchelmans, *Late Scholastic and Humanist Theories of the Proposition*, 90–102.

# The Nature of Intentional Objects in Nicholas of Autrecourt's Theory of Knowledge

CHRISTOPHE GRELLARD

If we admit that all mental states share a common feature, namely, the feature of being about something, or being directed toward something, then we can describe "intentionality" as this property of aboutness or directedness. But what is this thing that a mental state is about? More precisely, two questions should be answered: What makes a mental state intentional? Why is this mental state about *this* object (rather than *that*)? The first question is supposed to explain the ontological status of a mental state, the second, to describe how a mental state can be related to an object. Of course, answering the second question presupposes answering the first one. It is well known that Brentano (whose aim is to preserve the autonomy of the science of mental phenomena against physical science) provided an answer that still determines all contemporary reflections on intentionality. Brentano holds that mental phenomena are characterized by their intentional or mental inexistence, that is, that all mental states are related to an inner object, different from the external one, and irreducible to it. Indeed, a mental event is directed toward an object that is not the concrete reality as such, but an "immanent objectivity."[1] Thus, this intentional object is included in a triadic relation, with the mind of the knower on one side, and the reality outside the mind on the other. But this triadic relation leads to a rather puzzling ontological commitment. Indeed, we may wonder what kind of reality these intentional objects have. In the first version of his theory, Brentano is a phenomenalist, since he seems to claim that we have direct access only to these intentional, immanent objects and not directly to material objects. But, in the second version of his theory (in the 1911 edition of his *Psychology*), he explicitly rejects these "ghostly" mental objects and defends a kind of direct realism, in which the objects of the mind are real things. Such an evolution is quite common in contemporary epistemology, since the failure of theories of sense data and phenomenalism is generally recognized.

1. F. Brentano, *Psychologie von empirischen Standpunkt*, ed. O. Kraus (Hamburg, 1973), 1:124–125: "Jedes psychische Phänomen ist durch das charakterisiert, was die Scholastiker des Mittelalters die intentionale (wohl auch mentale) Inexistenz eines Gegenstandes gennant haben, und was wir, obwohl mit nicht ganz unzweideutigen Ausdrücken, die Beziehung auf einen Inhalt, die Richtung auf ein Objekt (worunter hier nichteine Realität zu verstehen ist), oder die immanente Gegenständlichkeit nennen wollen."

I have mentioned Brentano's evolution not in order to pay tribute to a classical reference of contemporary philosophy of mind, but rather because Nicholas of Autrecourt's evolution is, in fact, strictly the reverse of Brentano's. Indeed, in the first part of his work,[2] Autrecourt (ca. 1300–1369) defends a kind of direct realism. The *apparentia* is the mental act, which is isomorphic to the external object. But in his later work, toward the end of his academic teaching, Autrecourt espouses a theory close to phenomenalism: the object of knowledge, on this conception, is not the *esse subjectivum* of the external thing, which is unknowable *in se*, but the *esse objectivum* of the object in the mind. Thus, we find here the same triadic relation as in Brentano's first theory. Hence, we may wonder why Nicholas follows such a path, rejecting direct realism for phenomenalism.[3] To answer this question, we may propose two main reasons: First, the principal interest of the phenomenalist theory (as it appears in the theory of sense data or Brentano's first thesis) is to explain how a mental state can be about something even when there is nothing corresponding to it outside the mind. Indeed, Nicholas wants to give a uniform account of all mental states. Hence, even if in his first theory intentional objects are used only in the case of illusions, while in veridical cases the mental state is directly about a real object, in his second theory, intentional objects are utilized to account for all kinds of perception (whether sensory or intellectual). The second reason for his shift is not episte-

---

2. This main treatise of Nicholas has a special status. Only the prologues and the first chapter were "published," that is, copied and known by Nicholas's contemporaries. The other chapters always remained in draft form. Thus, the *Exigit ordo* is really a work in progress wherein we can discover Nicholas's inquiries, doubts, and sudden changes. On this question, see Z. Kaluza, *Nicolas d'Autrécourt, ami de la vérité* (Paris: Histoire littéraire de la France, 1995), esp.170. I assume that chapters 1–6, which deal mostly with natural philosophy and epistemology, are contemporary to Nicholas's teaching in the Arts Faculty. They were probably written before his lecture on *Sentences*, that is, between 1330 and 1335. From the seventh chapter on, Nicholas's interests are more ontological, and we may assume that these chapters were written after 1335. As to the disputed question on vision, see C. Grellard, "L'usage des nouveaux langages d'analyse dans *la Quaestio* de Nicolas d'Autrécourt. Contribution à la théorie autrécurienne de la connaissance," in *Quia inter doctores est magna dissensio. Les débats de philosophie naturelle à Paris au XIV<sup>e</sup> siècle*, ed. S. Caroti and J. Celeyrette (Florence: L. Olschki, 2004), 69–95.

3. In *Croire et savoir. Les principes de la connaissance selon Nicolas d'Autrécourt* (Paris: Vrin, 2005), I was not fully aware of this evolution and tried to give a unitary and systematic account of Nicholas's entire philosophy. I give some arguments for the evolution thesis in both "L'usage des nouveaux langages d'analyse" and "*Sicut specula sine macula*. La perception et son objet chez Nicolas d'Autrécourt," in *Chôra. Revue d'études anciennes et médiévales* 3–4 (2005–2006): 229–250. Dallas Denery challenges this thesis in *Seeing and Being Seen in the Later Medieval World* (Cambridge: Cambridge University Press, 2005), and "Nicholas of Autrecourt on Saving the Appearances," in *Nicolas d'Autrécourt philosophe*, ed. S. Caroti and C. Grellard (Cesena: Stilgraf editrice, 2006), 65–84. In my opinion, Denery's thesis is weakened by the fact that he never explains why Nicholas stops using the notion of *apparentia* in the last part of the *Exigit ordo*, and by the fact that he does not take a clear position on the opposition of direct realism and phenomenism.

mological but ontological; by the end of his career, Nicholas seems to assent more firmly to a Platonic conception of reality in which only separate principles can be called "real." By examining the case of Nicholas, which is certainly not an isolated one,[4] I would like to investigate the reasons *why* anyone would need intentional objects, and to determine *who* needs such objects. My claim is that phenomenalism is firmly connected to a certain kind of ontology.

## THE FAILURE OF DIRECT REALISM

Since I claim that Nicholas changed his position from direct realism to phenomenalism, I shall explain why he may have done so. My aim will be first to show what could be the failure of direct realism according to Autrecourt. My thesis is that Nicholas changed his mind because of some ontological considerations.

The sixth chapter of the *Exigit ordo* is entitled "Whether all that appears is true?" There Nicholas examines the problem of the truth of our perception. In this perspective, he has to confront the skeptical challenge and to explain how our experiences could be wrong. His answer relies on a strict separation between the veridical perception directed toward a real thing outside the mind, and the false perception directed toward an image of the thing, that is, something unreal that exists only in the mind. Thus, the intentionality of the perception does not require an intentional object-theory, except in the exceptional cases of illusions.

### *What Is Apparentia?*

The key notion in Nicholas's first epistemology, as expounded in the sixth chapter of the *Exigit ordo*, is the concept of *apparentia*. As is well known, *apparentia* is above all a normative concept and the foundation of Autrecourt's general trust in sensory cognition: all that appears to our external senses under good conditions is true. Nevertheless, this principle cannot be proved, but can only be assumed as true if we want to have any certitude about the external world. Hence, appearance is immediately connected with the problem of certitude and with the claim that we usually do have such certitude. But how can appearance lay claim to this kind of certitude? Nicholas's answer is clear on this point: all sensory appearance "in the full light" (that is, under optimal conditions) has a necessary relation with its object. Such a relation warrants us to hold that the object of our knowledge actually exists and that we are not deceived. In brief, a true and evident appearance is a mental state which occurs if and only if (1) the external senses are affected by an object, (2) this object actually exists and is present, (3) the external and internal conditions of the apprehension are optimal, and (4) a necessary relation is produced between the

---

4. See, for example, D. Perler, "What Are Intentional Objects? A Controversy among Early Scotists," in *Ancient and Medieval Theories of Intentionality*, ed. D. Perler (Leiden: Brill, 2001), 203–226.

mental state and the object. Of course, the question is: how can we know that we are under the optimal conditions of perception? Nicholas answers that we *just do* know it. An evident appearance is strong enough to lead to assent and impose its own evidentness. If there is any doubt, we should say that the perception is not "in the full light."

Admittedly, this general theory of perception is indifferent to direct realism or phenomenalism, since it gives us only the internal conditions of certitude.[5] Now, how can we connect the notion of appearance with direct realism? To answer this question, we have to consider the nature of appearance and determine why a given appearance is about a given object. At one point, Nicholas defines appearance as "the configuration of the object" (*configuratio objecti*). He also clearly holds that any object can be grasped by means of different configurations, depending on the way in which we perceive the object. Unfortunately, Nicholas does not tell us precisely what such a configuration is. But we may assume that this is a kind of likeness, even though, as we will see below, our mental state is not properly an image of the thing. It seems that the best way to understand such a likeness depends on the atomistic theory of perception that Nicholas develops.

Indeed, Nicholas claims that, just as material atoms move and come together to form a body, spiritual atoms gather to form a mental act suitable to an external thing that is grasped:

> Yet one must know that the combination of such spiritual atomic beings sometimes turns out inharmonious, sometimes harmonious. Just as external material things because of disharmony or harmony in their combination are sometimes said to be monstrosities, sometimes to be composed well, so in the case of the soul an inharmonious combination is called a false composition, a harmonious one (i.e. when it is properly related to what is in reality outside) a true composition.[6]

Hence, the mental act is built from spiritual atoms that are perceived not by themselves but only as a whole. And this construction corresponds to another external one. Two questions remain to be solved: How is this atomic construc-

---

5. I assume that Nicholas defends an internalist and foundationalist theory of knowledge. See Grellard, *Croire et savoir*, especially chaps. 2, 3, and 9.

6. N. Autrecourt, *The Universal Treatise of Nicholas of Autrecourt*, trans. L. A. Kennedy, R. E. Arnold, and A. E. Millward (Milwaukee: Marquette University Press, 1971), 70 (slightly modified); Autrecourt, "Exigit ordo" in J. R. O'Donnell, "Nicholas of Autrecourt," *Medieval Studies* 1(1939): 268–280: "Sciendum tamen quod aliquando fit congregatio talium entium atomalium spiritualium disconveniens, aliquando conveniens, et sicut in rebus materialibus extra, propter disconvenientiam [et convenientiam] in congregatione dicuntur interdum monstra interdum bene composita, sic et in anima propter congregationem disconvenientem dicitur . . . compositio falsa; propter convenientiam vera cum est modo convenienti ei quod est extra in re."

tion possible and how can such a spiritual compound correspond to external reality? To answer these questions, Nicholas relies on his reductionist conception of natural events, according to which all phenomena depend on the local motion of atoms.[7] There is no exception when we turn toward psychological events. Hence, perception is explained by the diffusion of some sort of atoms from the thing to the senses, in the same way as a *species sensibilis*:

> In connection with the act of seeing one must reckon with a twofold power. One is more corporeal, which unites the spirits and the visual rays. In or by their union the species is conveyed right to the organ of sight. Whether it be for receiving the species or for whatever other purpose, it is certain that such a union of spirits is prerequisite to the act of seeing. Only after this should we consider the power of the soul which elicits the act of seeing.[8]

Nicholas assumes that the human body contains two main spiritual atoms, one called "sense" and the other "intellect." These two atoms, respectively, receive material and spiritual (that is, less material) exemplars, so that the sense-atom produces an atomic image from these exemplars, and then the intellect-atom builds a universal exemplar. Therefore, the atomic construction is the result of the local motion of atoms to the senses and from them to the intellect. And the same atoms, in a spiritual form, are the constituents of our image of the thing. Hence, the relation between the atomic image and the external compound is founded on a structural likeness. Now, what is the object of such knowledge? Is it the atomic compound outside the mind, or the atomic image inside the mind? We may assume that, for Autrecourt, spiritual exemplars have no representational properties, but only sensational ones.[9] Indeed, an atom by itself cannot be perceived. It is known only when it acts in a compound. It should be the same for exemplars: they affect the senses but are not perceived. Hence, the image is not the object of perception, but what allows us to have a perception. To prove this last point, Nicholas carefully examines the case when we perceive the image and not the thing, that is, the case of illusions. Direct realism is established at this level.

---

7. See C. Grellard "La causalité chez Nicolas d'Autrécourt," *Quaestio* 2 (2002): 267–289, and "Nicholas of Autrecourt's Atomistic Physics," in *Atomism and Its Place in Late Medieval Philosophy*, ed. C. Grellard and A. Robert (Leiden: Brill, 2009), 107–126.

8. Autrecourt, *Universal Treatise*, 162; Autrecourt, "Exigit ordo," 265, 7–12: "Circa actum videndi est considerare duplicem virtutem, unam magis corporalem unitivam spirituum et radiorum visualium in quibus unitis vel quibus unitis fit delatio speciei usque ad organum visus, sive sit propter receptionem speciei, sive propter quodcumque aliud, certum est quod ad actum videndi prerequiritur talis unio spirituum, postea consideranda est quaedam virtus animae eliciens actum videndi."

9. On this distinction, see C. Peacocke, *Sense and Content* (Oxford: Oxford University Press, 1983), 5.

## The Problem of Illusions

As we have seen, according to Nicholas, veridical perception depends on the conformity between a mental state and a thing outside the mind. This relation requires that the thing actually exists, and that it is perceived by the senses. Nevertheless, we have all experienced cases when we are convinced we perceive something real when in fact nothing of that sort exists in front of us. The problem here is to determine when our appearance is "in the full light," and to explain how it can be not "in the full light."

Nicholas carefully examines the arguments frequently discussed in the Middle Ages concerning the reliability of the senses. There are two kinds of arguments: first, relativist arguments arguing from variation in taste or sight; and, second, skeptical arguments based on illusion and hallucination (like the broken stick, the size of the sun, and the moving tree seen from a boat), the dream argument, and the argument from disagreement. All these arguments are discussed by Peter Aureole, on whom Nicholas clearly depends.[10] On the first approach, Nicholas tries to evade these arguments by means of the classical distinction between perception and judgment. Relativist arguments demand an *a posteriori* answer, namely, the correction of some judgment by reference to other correct appearances. In other words, different cognitive faculties have to be consistent with each other.[11] But for our purposes, Nicholas's second approach is much more interesting since it relies on the atomist theory of perception. Nicholas's aim is to carefully distinguish between the image of the thing and the thing itself as the term of an intentional act. Hence, he claims that under normal conditions, the perceptual act is about the thing itself, while in situations of illusion, perception is about the image of the thing. Indeed, our perception of the external world is made of a multitude of spiritual motions, that is, atomic emanations from things to our senses. But, as soon as we perceive several things simultaneously, the multiplication of the motions weakens our faculties and disturbs them. Therefore, spiritual atoms will be imperfectly grasped and the images made of them will also be imperfect, that is, partial:

> These spirits, some of which carry the image of one thing, and others the image of another thing, can impede one another in their movement. Then the image of neither thing is carried without mutilation. It is men in this condition who judge of things defectively and imperfectly.[12]

---

10. See Denery, *Seeing and Believing*; H. Thijssen, "The Quest for Certain Knowledge in the Fourteenth Century: Nicholas of Autrecourt against the Academics," *Acta Philosophica Fennica* 66 (2000): 199–223. In some of my previous studies, I have unduly underestimated Aureole's influence on Autrecourt's thought.

11. On this point, see C. Grellard, "Nicholas of Autrecourt's Skepticism: The Ambivalence of Medieval Epistemology." In *Rethinking the History of Skepticism: The Missing Medieval Background*, ed. H. Lagerlund (Leiden: Brill, 2010), 119–144.

12. Autrecourt, *Universal Treatise*, 146; "Exigit ordo," 254, 44–47: "Spiritus isti quorum aliqui deferunt imaginem istius rei, alii imaginem alterius rei in suo motu ad invicem possunt

Mutual distraction among the spiritual movements is the main physiological cause of misperception. Since the atomic image of the thing is truncated, it cannot have any relation of conformity with the thing, and any judgment founded on this appearance will be defective. In this case, there is a gap between the appearance and the thing, and the appearance does not have the thing itself as an object but only the image of the thing.

In this way, Nicholas can give an atomistic account of sensible illusions or delusions. In the case of the broken stick or the moving tree, the appearance we have is not of the real thing, called the *res fixa*, but of a changing image. When we say that the stick is broken or the tree is moving, we do not speak about the thing, but about the environment or the context in which we perceive it, and the way in which we are affected. All these perceptions need to be corrected by other perceptions, such as the tactile sensation of the stick, or the perception of the tree from a fixed point of view, or even by a mathematical concept as in the case of the sun's size. The case of ill taste is slightly different, but also depends on this atomist theory. Exemplars in the organ usually have a relation of conformity with the corresponding atoms in the thing that move them—for example, with atoms of sweetness in honey.[13] But if the organ is modified by illness, the nature of the exemplars will change, and we will no longer have any kind of conformity.

Finally, it appears that when some atoms are lacking, the atomic image or configuration of the object will not be complete. In this case, the appearance is of the image of the thing, not the thing itself.[14] Nicholas compares this situation to that of a man looking at himself in a mirror.[15] This man will have indirect access to the thing. Conversely, when the appearance is complete, that is, "in the full light," there is no difference between the image of the thing and the thing, and we have direct access to the thing. The appearance, that is, the mental state, directly refers to the thing outside the mind without any intermediate entity. Hence, Nicholas is able to answer the two questions raised at the beginning. First, what makes the mental state intentional is the movement of spiritual atoms. So, we need no special ontological items to explain intentionality, but only spiritual and material atoms in movement. Second, a mental state is about *this* object rather than *that*, because its configuration is isomorphic to the object's and shares the same atomistic structure.

---

se impedire, et tunc neutrius affertur imago rei nisi truncate; et isti sunt qui truncate et imperfecte judicant de rebus."

13. Significantly, Autrecourt supports qualitative atoms in his theory. See Grellard, *Croire et savoir*, 214–218, and "Nicholas of Autrecourt's Atomistic Physics," 113–117.

14. Autrecourt, "Exigit ordo," 232, 2–3: "illa apparentia terminatur ad imaginem rei et non ad aliquid existens subjective in re extra." On this point, the influence of Peter Aureole's distinction between the thing and the *esse apparens* is manifest.

15. Ibid., 231, 24–26: "sed sciendum propter quaedam alia quod aliquando dicitur videri res in suo proprio lumine, aliquando in lumine sui imaginis ut cum homo videtur in speculo."

## Ontological Models for Perception

It seems clear enough that Autrecourt's version of direct realism is connected to his atomism. The key to understanding Nicholas's thought is a text at the beginning of the *Exigit ordo*, in the first chapter, "On the Eternity of Things." Here, Nicholas examines how things can be said to be eternal, and tries to determine the existential import of appearance. Can we make an inference such as "the thing has ceased to appear, therefore the thing no longer exists"? In order to reject this inference, Nicholas introduces three ontological models for explaining what is perceived. The first one is the atomistic model:

> The first way seems to me to be more probable than the others, even though I do not have an evidently demonstrative conclusion. Here it is: As regards the major premise,[16] let it be said that it does not contain truth. For natural forms are divisible into their smallest units in such a way that these, when divided off from the whole, could not perform their proper action. And so, though they are visible when existing in the whole, they are not visible when dispersed and divided or separated. For this is true even according to the mind of Aristotle when he says that natural beings have a maximum and a minimum limit.[17]

Atoms are the real things (*vera entia*) and are only perceptible when they are acting together in a whole. When they are separated from a compound, they cannot act and do not appear to us. This atomistic explanation is labeled the most probable. There are also two other ways. The second could also be understood as a form of atomism, or at least is not inconsistent with atomism; it states that in each thing there is a power of movement (*potentia* or *virtus*). When this power is at rest, the thing does not appear. Later on, Nicholas interprets this power as a particular kind of atom that is an essential part moved by celestial bodies.[18] Hence the two first models are both atomistic, but with a greater or lesser mechanistic emphasis, since the notion of power is not really mechanistic:

---

16. Nicholas is criticizing the following argument: "Everything which previously appeared to a sense but now does not appear, no matter what the sense fixes its attention on, no longer exists. But this is the case with the whiteness that previously appeared but now does not appear. Therefore, etc." Autrecourt, *Universal Treatise*, 61.

17. Ibid., 61 (slightly modified); Autrecourt, "Exigit ordo," 199, 40–46: "primus modus inter alios mihi probabilior esse videtur, licet non habeam conclusionem evidenter demonstrantem, et est hic: dicatur ad majorem quod veritatem non continet; nam formae naturales sunt ita divisibiles in minima quod seorsum divisa a toto non possent habere actionem suam et ita licet ipsa existentia in toto videantur, dispersa tamen et divisa seu segregata non videntur. Hoc enim veritatem habet etiam secundum intellectum Aristotelis dicentis: entia naturalia esse terminata ad maximum et minimum."

18. See Grellard, "La causalité chez Nicolas d'Autrécourt," 283–289, and "Nicholas of Autrecourt's Atomistic Physics," 120–123.

The second way would be to say that the case is analogous with the power of movement, which sometimes performs its act and sometimes is at rest. When it functions, it appears. When it is at rest, it does not appear, but it is not therefore said to be destroyed.[19]

The last possible explanation places atoms in the realm of Platonic ideas. This theory assumes that when two people see some whiteness, they see exactly the same one Whiteness. Indeed, we may imagine that, if several mirrors were put around the same person, that very same person would appear in each mirror. For Nicholas, the situation is the same in the case of perception: what we directly perceive is the reflection of the real whiteness, which is the separate Whiteness. Material things only reflect the action of separated principles. When the latter cease to act, material things stop reflecting them and do not appear. This radically Platonic claim would lead us to assume that the material world is only a world of images or phenomena and that reality is on the side of separated ideas:

> The third way would be to say that no reason [*ratio*] for a thing's appearance is lost. . . . For place in front of or around you several mirrors in diverse places. According to the common doctrine, if you fix your gaze in one direction, you will see yourself and nothing else formally inhering in the mirror. Similarly, if you look in another direction, you will see yourself. Thus in looking in diverse directions you will see something which will not be in numerically diverse places. So in the case under discussion the position might be stated that there are only material things in this physical reality [*hic inferius*], and that separated principles are responsible for the actions of things, as Plato claimed, as for example, a separated whiteness for the action of this whiteness. . . . And then the material thing that is looked at is only a sort of mirror in which Whiteness can be seen when the gaze is fixed in that direction. This is how Plato understands it.[20]

---

19. Autrecourt, *Universal Treatise*, 61; "Exigit ordo," 200, 47–200, 1: "Secundus modus esset ut diceretur quod sicut potentia motiva aliquando habet actum suum, hoc est quando movet est in apparentia, et aliquando quiescit, et tunc non est in apparentia, et tamen propter hoc non dicitur quod sit corrupta."

20. Autrecourt, *Universal Treatise* (modified), 61–62; "Exigit ordo," 200, 7–40: "Tertius modus ut diceretur quod a nulla re substrahitur ratio apparentiae . . . pone ante vel circa te plura specula ad diversa ubi, secundum doctrinam communem si defingas aspectum tuum ad unum ubi, videbis te et nihil aliud formaliter inhaerens speculo. Similiter si aspicias ad aliud ubi, videbis te et sic aspiciendo ad diversa ubi videbis aliquid quod non erit in diversis locis numero; et sic in proposito diceretur ponendo quod hic inferius non est nisi materiale et quod actiones rerum reducuntur in principia separata quemadmodum ponebat Plato; puta actio albedinis hujus in albedinem separatam . . . tunc non est illud materiale ad quod aspicitur nisi ut speculum, ita quod ad illud ubi defingendo aspectus nata est albedo videri; et iste est intellectus Platonis. Uterque istorum modorum trium possibilis est, nec video quod ab Aristotele sufficienter fuerit aliquis eorum reprobatus; primum tamen pro nunc eligo."

At this stage of the argument, Nicholas merely asserts that such a claim is possible, but he prefers to adopt the first, strictly atomistic, hypothesis. Indeed, the subsequent chapters of *Exigit ordo* clearly rely on a materialist, atomistic mechanism. However, from Chapter 7 on, the Platonic hypothesis comes back and progressively becomes more and more prominent. Therefore, my hypothesis is that the failure of direct realism in the Ultricurian epistemology is linked to the failure of atomism as a convenient explanation of nature. In the course of this discussion, Autrecourt keeps hesitating between Democritus and Plato, but in the end he chooses the latter.[21] Eventually, Nicholas recognizes the failure of atomism.[22] This failure leads Nicholas to adhere firmly to Platonism and to modify his conception of reality and of the perception of reality.

### WHAT IS REALITY? A PHENOMENALIST ANSWER

Beyond the partial failure of atomism, Nicholas seems to have changed his stance on our apprehension of reality because of a change of paradigm: a new reflection on clarity. Indeed, there is a change of paradigm in the last part of the *Exigit ordo*, when the notions of *apparentia* and *evidentia* disappear simultaneously and are replaced by *esse objectivum* and *claritas*. I will first show the steps that lead to the introduction of *esse objectivum*, and, second, I will examine the relationship between *esse objectivum* and *esse subjectivum*, that is, between reality and the apprehension of reality.

### From Evidentness to Clarity

In the sixth chapter of the *Exigit ordo*, Nicholas still uses the terms *clarum* and *evidens* together as synonyms. But, while evidentness cannot admit any degrees, later in the chapter he introduces degrees of clarity. This distinction between

---

21. On this hesitation, see S. Caroti "'Or i est or n'i est une', Nicolas d'Autrécourt et le 'ludus baterellorum' ou de la génération et de la corruption," in *Chemins de la pensée médiévale. Etudes offertes à Zénon Kaluza*, ed. P. Bakker et al. (Turnhout: Brepols, 2003), 135–168; Grellard, *Croire et savoir*, esp. chap. 6. On Nicholas's ontological realism, see Z. Kaluza, "Les catégories dans l'*Exigit ordo*. Etude de l'ontologie formelle de Nicolas d'Autrécourt," *Studia Mediewistyczne* 33 (1998): 97–124.

22. Autrecourt, "Quaestio de qua respondit," 257, 15–28: "Supra in tractatu de aeternitate rerum dixi quod quando ignis dicitur produci quantum ad veritatem non est nisi adventus aliquorum corporum calidorum, et frigidditas per recessum illorum et adventum corporum frigidorum ut in aqua calida quae sibi derelicta revertitur ad naturam priorem, scilicet frigiditatem, per recessum calidorum corporum et accessum frigidorum. Et in hoc ultimo non videtur improbabilitas magna nisi quod, cum ignis apparet ubi prius non apparebat, non videtur quomodo motus localis corporum calidorum potuerit ita cito fieri. De sole etiam dicimus quod non calefacit, sed quaedam corpora calida in regione ignis sunt nata assequi motum solis. Similiter est in frigiditate cum dicitur: iste planeta frigefacit, et sic in aliis suo modo de motu corporum calidorum imaginaretur quod sunt satis propinqua, sed prohibita sunt a sua actione propter admixtionem multam contrarii; nunc concurrunt ad locum ubi est ignis quem consequitur virtus expulsiva frigidorum, et tunc ibi facit suam actionem."

clarity and evidentness is probably the first reason why Nicholas embraces phenomenalism. The second reason is the thesis that a difference of clarity implies a difference of object.

Indeed, in the seventh chapter of his book, Nicholas claims that each cognitive power has a different object (that is, that the whiteness grasped by imagination is different from the one grasped by the intellect and the one perceived by sight), and that, conversely, two different objects cannot be grasped by the same power. The problem Nicholas has to face, then, is the following: what can be perceived by two people whose sight or intellect is unequal? In his answer, he provides some interesting observations about the object of vision:

> The ninth conclusion is that every lower degree of whiteness is present where the brightest whiteness exists. For, looking at a white spot, as the light gradually recedes, every whiteness below that whiteness becomes visible in its turn. Indeed, where there is the greatest whiteness even blackness will be more capable of being seen as the light leaves; and so contraries coexist.[23]

One and the same thing is the source of different, even contrary, visions, since the most perfect quality includes the less perfect ones. Once again, it seems clear that Nicholas is trying to claim that all that appears is true. But while in the sixth chapter he makes a distinction between complete and incomplete appearances, only the first being veridical, here he accepts a more problematic relativism. Degrees of perfection in vision depend on the way the thing appears to us. But this claim becomes more significant in the following chapter, when Nicholas introduces the problem of *esse objectivum*. The notion is clearly introduced in order to give an account of the degrees of clarity in vision or intellection. While subjective being remains the same, objective being is multiplied, as different people perceive different things on account of the different degrees of clarity of their perception:

> Likewise, the objective being is multiplied, while the subjective being remains one, because if there are two persons, one of whom understands an object more clearly than the other, what each understands is not the same thing, as was proven above, even when it seems more probable that the thing is one in its subjective being. For when a bright and a dull intellect attend to the same thing, regardless of its unity, what the bright intellect

---

23. Autrecourt, *Universal Treatise*, 122 (modified); "Exigit ordo," 239, 32–36: "Nona conclusio est quod ubi est albedo clarissime ibi est omnis albedo inferioris gradus; nam inspiciendo ad illud ubi, paulatim recedente lumine, paulatim potest videri omnis albedo infra illam albedinem, immo etiam nigredo magis poterit videri recedente lumine ubi est maxima albedo, et sic contraria simul."

conceives is different from what the dull one conceives, as has been shown sufficiently above.[24]

Of course, we could ask: Which one knows the real thing? If by "real thing" we mean the *esse subjectivum*, Nicholas will be led progressively to a rather radical answer: neither of them. Indeed, the object of perception is not the thing in itself as a subjective being, but one of the objective beings that appear to us according to such or such external conditions. We may identify two reasons leading Nicholas to such a thesis: first, a new interest in the divine paradigm, and second, the development of a theory of the intension and remission of forms. Indeed, it must be underscored that Nicholas does seem to hesitate before accepting the phenomenalist account of perception. At the beginning of the eighth chapter, he is still asserting that there is a clear objective being, and that it corresponds to subjective being. Hence, any difference of objective being depends on a process of clarification the terminus of which is the subjective being. Since things are finite in number, this process of clarification can be finite, and we will always have the possibility of access to the subjective being.[25] But the two aforesaid reasons challenge this assertion.

Ultricurian speculation on divine knowledge is probably the more fundamental with respect to this point. Indeed, the divine intellect is superior to the human intellect since God knows all things by knowing his own essence. Therefore, we absolutely cannot know what God knows, and conversely, God does not know what we know.[26] This divine paradigm allows Nicholas to claim that we do not know the reality of *esse subjectivum*. In a strict sense, the clearest form of knowledge is intuitive knowledge, and only God, as the most perfect

---

24. Autrecourt, *Universal Treatise*, 128 (slightly modified); "Exigit ordo," 243, 16–22: "Item esse objectivum multiplicatur esse subjectivo remanente uno, quia si sunt duo quorum unus intelligit objectum clarius alio, non est idem quod uterque intelligit, ut probatum est supra. Et cum videtur probabilius quod res secundum esse subjectivum sit una; nam ad quamcumque rem quantumcumque unam aspicerent intellectus clarus et obscurus, aliud esset quod conciperet intellectus clarus quam quod obscurus ut satis ostensum est supra"; 262, 4–11: "Juxta dicta supra circa principium tractatus hujus dicebatur quod, si duo videntes eandem rem vel intelligentes quorum unus habet visum clariorem vel intellectum, non idem vident de re, sed unus videt albedinem claram magis ubi alius videt albedinem obscuram, et tamen illae albedines in esse subjectivo sunt una albedo, et illud quod quaerit quilibet videre, quando aspiciunt, idem est in numero subjective, licet veniat ad eos secundum diversum esse objectivum. Et secundum istum modum dicendi posset sustineri probabiliter quod albedo et nigredo sunt unum in esse subjectivo."

25. Autrecourt, "Exigit ordo," 242, 30–36: "Et si res sit finita, tunc non videtur, cum unum objectum sit perfectius et clarius alio, licet sint ejusdem rei, quod in talibus circa eandem rem finitam sit procedere in infinitum. Quodlibet enim esse objectivum videtur deficere a perfectione quam habet res in se secundum esse subjectivum quod habet. Tunc secundum hoc est dare aliquod esse objectivum finitum supra quod, si procederetur clarius cognoscendo rem, res cognosceretur secundum esse subjectivum."

26. Nevertheless, in the seventh chapter, Nicholas still hesitates to commit to such a radical claim. Cf. ibid., 239, 5–48. This hesitation is overcome in the subsequent discussion.

and clearest intellect, has such knowledge. Hence, only God has knowledge of subjective being, that is, of a thing as it is in itself. Correspondingly, the subjective being remains unknowable to us, since our cognitive power is not refined enough. In sum, there is a difference in nature, not only in degree, between *subjective being* and the *objective being* that we perceive of it. This point is established by a consideration of the intensification of vision. In the *Exigit ordo*, Nicholas quickly denies that our apprehension of a thing could be clarified to the point of reaching its subjective being.

The explanation is found in the "theological question." In this text, Nicholas deals with the possibility of a vision being intensified, that is, becoming clearer and clearer. Such intensification is made possible by the addition of qualitative degrees (e.g., as whiteness becomes whiter and whiter by the addition of degrees of whiteness).[27] This question of intension and remission of a quality is clearly linked to the problem of the clarity of vision or cognition. And Nicholas asserts that there is no limit, neither minimal nor maximal, to the perfection of cognition. There is no absolutely perfect creaturely cognition, nor an absolutely imperfect one. Nicholas argues that an act of cognition is indefinitely perfectible, either by natural means (a better disposition of the object, the medium or the organ), or by supernatural means (by God's absolute power). The conclusion we should infer is that it is impossible to have comprehensive knowledge of a thing, that is, complete knowledge that is one, evident and "in the full light." It will always remain possible that some aspect of the thing remains unknown to us, since we cannot know whether the sum of all objective being we have in our cognition is equal to the subjective being.

### What Do We Know When We Perceive Socrates?

Nicholas clearly introduces a new type of entity into his ontology, which seems to have an intentional status. Indeed, objective being is something related both to subjective being outside the mind and to a mental state inside the mind:

> But, concerning what has been said about objective being it should be noted that by objective being I understand that being of an object which has such a conjunction with and inseparability from an act that, wherever the act is posited, that objective being will be posited also. For example, when someone is in a boat on a river and it seems to him that the bank is moving, in whomever such an act of seeing was posited, the object would come with that kind of being.[28]

---

27. Actually, Nicholas seems to sustain the theory of addition in the *Question*, and the theory of succession in the *Exigit ordo*. See Grellard, "L'usage des nouveaux langages d'analyse." This problem is not relevant to the present discussion.

28. Autrecourt, *Universal Treatise*, 128; Autrecourt "Exigit ordo," 243, 11–16: "Notandum autem circa illud quod dictum est de esse objectivo quod per esse objectivum intelligo illud esse objecti quod habet quamdam copulationem et indivisionem cum actu, ita quod ubicumque

Hence, on the knower's part, we have an intentional act, that is, an act that is about something. But the object of this act is not *subjective being*, but *objective being*. The latter is *the mode of appearing of the thing* (i.e., of the thing in subjective being). Clearly, Nicholas is generalizing the theory of image he developed in the sixth chapter; since he emphasizes that objective being allows us to give an account of the case of illusions. Objective being is the way the knower is affected by the thing, but it remains something different from the act. Now, what is the relation between objective being and subjective being? Subjective being is the unifying principle of the objective beings we have, that is, their foundation. Nicholas maintains that the last step in the process of clarification results in a unique subjective being. But this last step is unattainable for us and is proper only to God's knowledge. It is the target of any process of clarification or approximation of the truth. Nevertheless, it remains beyond our capacities. We may only suppose that there is something beyond the objective beings presented to our cognitive powers. In the end, we *can* assign a temporary terminus to the multiplication of objective beings by identifying what Nicholas calls a *quasi-subjective being*:

> For example, when someone, not having had the experience, first sees Socrates, he grasps one confused objective being, which confuses in itself many objective beings. Later on, however, he compares him with Plato and grasps one objective being, namely, man. Later, comparing him with a donkey, he grasps another objective being, namely, animal, and so on. By collecting many such ideas he establishes a definition which explicates what was implicitly contained in the confused being. Those objective beings were distinguished above from the subjective being because they are multiplied while the thing's subjective being remains one in itself.[29]

Since all knowledge is an approximation of truth, the quasi-subjective being will be the temporary goal of the inquiry. It is the closer entity to the real thing since it is the sum of our experiences clarified by abstraction and comparison. But, the quasi-subjective being is still an objective being.

---

ponitur actus, ponetur et illud objectivum esse, ut cum quis in riparia existit in navi et videtur sibi quod ripa movetur; in quocumque poneretur talis actus videndi, veniret objectum secundum tale esse."

29. Autrecourt, *Universal Treatise*, 161 (modified); Autrecourt, "Exigit ordo," 264, 35–45: "cum aliquis non habituatus vidit primo Socratem, habuit unum esse objectivum confusum quia multa esse objectiva confundit in se; nam postea comparet eum ad Platonem et habet unum esse objectivum, videlicet homo, post comparans ad asinum habuit aliud esse objectivum, scilicet animal et sic de aliis. Et ex collectione multorum talium constituit definitionem quae explicat illud quod implicite continebatur in illo esse confuso, et illa esse objectiva distincta sunt superius ab esse subjectivo [objectivo, ms.] quia ipsa multiplicantur esse subjectivo rei in se remanente uno."

Let us briefly reconsider Nicholas's example: If I see Socrates for the first time, I will receive from this perception a confused objective being, that is, an objective being containing several other objective beings. By abstracting and comparing, I will be able to clarify the confused objective being and extract the other, latent objective beings. For example, by comparing Socrates and Plato, I recognize the objective being of man, and by comparing Socrates and a donkey, the objective being of animal, and so on. If I can order these different objective beings, I will obtain a definition of Socrates that makes explicit what was implicit. And this definition will be a close approximation of Socrates' subjective being. Thus, abstractive knowledge in Autrecourt's epistemology consists in multiplying the various aspects of a thing in order to combine perceptions and concepts and elaborate a special objective being that can be used as a focal point of the knowledge of the thing. Admittedly, each objective being is relative to the context of its perception and to the other objective beings one has of a thing. Thus, black and white are identical in a subjective being, and differ only at the level of objective being, in the appearance of the thing. Indeed, if we consider several acts of vision ordered from the more perfect to the less perfect, what appears "white" to the perfect one will appear "black" to the less perfect, while the subjective being concerned remains the same.

Now, what is this subjective being? Even if Nicholas never clearly states what subjective beings are, we can make an educated guess. Two theses seem important in this respect. First Nicholas claims that God knows all things by knowing his own essence. Second, he asserts on one occasion that the unique subjective being is God Himself:

> Therefore, what each objective thing seeks, and what it moves [us] toward, is the one subjective being which is God. And this being understands Himself by a knowledge which is the same as Himself in subjective being, and He attains Himself in the subjective being according to which He exists.[30]

From this, we can conclude that subjective beings are the divine ideas. And, while this is only an assumption, since Nicholas does not clearly state his position, it is certainly consistent with the Platonic model of perception presented at the beginning of the *Exigit ordo*.

### CONCLUSION

There are clearly two theories of intentionality and intentional objects in Autrecourt's epistemology. The first one, linked to his atomism, relies on direct realism and holds that an intentional state of knowing or perceiving is about

---

30. Autrecourt, *Universal Treatise*, 158 (modified); Autrecourt, "Exigit ordo," 262, 20–24: "Illud igitur quod quaerit quaelibet res objectiva, et in quod movet, est unum esse subjectivum quod est Deus; et illud ens intelligit se cognitione eadem sibi in esse subjectivo et attingit in esse subjectivo secundum quod est."

a real thing compounded of atoms. Hence, there is a correspondence between the atomic structure of our mental act and the atomic compound outside the mind. The second one does not use the atomistic vocabulary, but relies on the common notions of objective and subjective being. The gap between the two theories consists in the fact that subjective being (whether an atomic compound or not) is no longer the object of knowledge. Indeed, intentional acts have their own intentional objects, that is, objective beings. Therefore, we can say that Nicholas of Autrecourt follows a path opposite to Brentano's, since Nicholas leaves direct realism for a kind of phenomenalism, founded on the special status of intentional objects. How can we explain such an evolution?

The first point worth noting is the link between Ultricurian phenomenalism and his theological turn. In the first part of the *Exigit ordo*, probably written while he was teaching at the Arts Faculty, Nicholas is not at all interested in theological problems and focuses on a strict mechanistic atomism. On the other hand, in the last part of the treatise, which is probably coming from a later period, the divine paradigm is markedly present.

The second point concerns the place of images in his thought. Indeed, the image theory, used in the sixth chapter of *Exigit ordo* to give an account of sensible illusions, later seems to be generalized to account for all perceptive events. This generalization leads Nicholas to introduce an intentional object linking the act of appearance (a mental state) and subjective being. Thus, whereas in the first theory the image was merely negatively considered as something "abnormal," in the second theory, it becomes regular to all perception. A sign of this evolution is the disappearance of a consideration of tactile perception (which was described as the best access to fixed things, that is, subjective being), and the importance given to visual events. Therefore, the second reason of the Ultricurian evolution is perhaps Nicholas's desire to give a unitary account of all intentional acts, which covers both illusions and normal perception. Indeed, in the second theory, illusions are only obscure objective beings, and this obscurity is always relative to an "ideal" but unknowable subjective being. Nicholas defends a strong phenomenalism wherein (1) the object of knowledge is a mode of the appearance of a thing, (2) this mode is distinct from the mental state, and (3) the thing in itself is unknowable.

The last point to be noted is the consistency between this phenomenalism and Nicholas's Platonism. Phenomenalism appears to be the best epistemological alternative for him once he adopts a Platonic ontology. In this ontology, material things are not real, but are only images of what is real, the ideas. The closer an image is to the idea, the more the thing is known. In other words, objective beings do have degrees of participation in the ideas, and these degrees determine their clarity. Hence, Nicholas's evolution from direct realism to phenomenalism is strongly linked to his shift from a Democritean vision of the world to a Platonic one. Who needs intentional objects? The Platonist, undoubtedly.

# On the Several Senses of "*Intentio*" in Buridan

JACK ZUPKO

What is intentionality? It is a useful concept, but its essence is hard to define, especially if we look at how it has actually been used by philosophers since Greek and Roman antiquity. It behaves like a quality, though it is not always clear what kind of quality it is or what it is a quality of. Sometimes it is specified as a quality of qualities, a concept of concepts, though we also see it ascribed to things outside the mind, as when Thomas Aquinas uses it to characterize the sensory species transmitted through the medium between object and perceiver.[1] In terms of its mode of existence, it is usually glossed quantitatively in terms of a degree of being somewhere between "full" existence and nothingness.[2] But it also seems to defy placement in any metaphysical category, like the transcendental notions of being, truth, and goodness, though it is never treated as a Platonic form, or that toward which all things strive, or anything quite so sublime. Indeed, if we consider its history, it might be better to think of it as a Swiss Army knife: it is a knife, to be sure, but also so much more.

The concept became more stable in the last century, thanks to the work of Franz Brentano (1838–1917), who thought he had found in one of its historical moments, specifically the medieval concept of *intentio*, that elusive "positive criterion" capable of distinguishing the mental from the physical. Writing as if he has made a major discovery, Brentano explicitly connects his doctrine of intentional inexistence (*intentionale Inexistenz*) with certain medieval authors (he mentions Augustine, Anselm, and Thomas Aquinas) whose works he had read as a seminary student. The oft-quoted paragraph where he introduces the notion of intentional inexistence in *Psychology from an Empirical Standpoint* (1874) is prefaced by the remark that "psychologists in earlier [i.e., medieval] times [had] already pointed out that there is a special affinity and analogy which exists among all mental phenomena, and which physical phenomena do not share." The paragraph continues:

---

1. Thomas Aquinas, *Summa Theologiae* Ia, q.56, a.2.
2. Hence Roderick Chisholm: intentionality is "short of actuality, but more than nothingness" (*Encyclopedia of Philosophy* 1967, IV, 201).

Every mental phenomenon is characterized by what the Scholastics of the Middle Ages called the intentional (or mental) inexistence of an object, and what we might call, though not wholly unambiguously, reference to a content, direction toward an object (which is not to be understood here as meaning a thing), or immanent objectivity. Every mental phenomenon includes something as object within itself, although they do not all do so in the same way. In presentation something is presented, in judgment something is affirmed or denied, in love loved, in hate hated, in desire desired and so on.[3]

By "inexistence," Brentano means the inherence of mental phenomena in the mind—*Inexistenz* is just his rendering of the Scholastic term for metaphysical inherence, *inesse*,[4] which of course adds to the appearance of medieval pedigree. Even so, Brentano does not examine the historical origins of the concept. If he had, he probably would have been more careful about what he attributed to the "Scholastics of the Middle Ages,"[5] because his concerns are transparently those of a modern thinker: he is interested in intentionality because he takes it to be "characteristic exclusively [*ausschließlich*] of mental phenomena" and because intentional phenomena are always (for him) *conscious* phenomena. Physical phenomena lack intentionality. This made intentional phenomena directly relevant to his aim of developing a modern science of psychology based on phenomenological, or proto-phenomenological, methods. Brentano's psychology was to be an autonomous science, distinct from physical science and immune from its reductionist pull.

Like Brentano, philosophers today have also shown interest in the history of intentionality, though they rarely look farther back than Brentano's own suggestive remarks. Typically, Brentano is mentioned as having "revived" the

---

3. Franz Brentano, *Psychology from an Empirical Standpoint*, ed. Linda McAlister (London: Routledge & Kegan Paul/Humanities Press, 1973). The German original reads as follows: "Jedes psychische Phänomen ist durch das charakterisiert, was die Scholastiker des Mittelalters die intentionale (auch wohl mentale) Inexistenz eines Gegenstandes genannt haben, und das wir, obwohl mit nicht ganz unzweideutigen Ausdrücken, die Beziehung auf einen Inhalt, die Richtung auf ein Objekt (worunter hier nicht eine Realität zu verstehen ist), oder die immanente Gegenständlichkeit nennen würden. Jedes enthält etwas als Objekt in sich, obwohl nicht jedes in gleicher Weise. In der Vorstellung etwas vorgestellt, in dem Urteile ist etwas anerkannt oder verworfen, in der Liebe geliebt, in dem Hasse gehaßt, in dem Begehren begehrt usw." *Psychologie vom Empirischen Standpunkt*, ed. Oskar Kraus (Leipzig: Felix Meiner, 1924), 2:124–125.

4. See Victor Caston, "Towards a History of the Problem of Intentionality among the Greeks," in *Proceedings of the Boston Area Colloquium in Ancient Philosophy IX*, ed. John J. Cleary and William Wians (Lanham, Md.: University Press of America, 1993), 229 n. 42.

5. One is reminded here of the kind of "exegetical thinking" Walter Kaufmann finds in Heidegger's treatment of Nietzsche and the pre-Socratics. Thus, the exegetical thinker "endows his text with authority, reads his ideas into it, and then gets them back endowed with authority." Walter Kaufmann, *Discovering the Mind* (New Brunswick, N.J.: Transaction, 1980).

scholastic concept,[6] which simply accepts Brentano's account of what he was doing. Like Brentano, contemporary authors focus on the question of whether intentionality is really the "mark of the mental." More recently, however, historians of philosophy have been looking at possible precursors of Brentano's idea in the work of medieval and ancient philosophers,[7] producing interesting studies of the way thinking was understood in premodern philosophy. But do these investigations shed any light on our notion of intentionality, which comes from Brentano? This seems a valid question, since premodern thinkers did not write treatises on intentionality, or treat it as "the mark of the mental," or employ it in any systematic way to explain human cognition. There are medieval discussions that *look* relevant to our modern concept, but appearances can be deceptive, and differences in context and genre surely demand that we examine such texts on a case-by-case basis, being wary of false positives as we go.[8]

---

6. For examples, see John Searle, *Intentionality: An Essay in the Philosophy of Mind* (Cambridge: Cambridge University Press, 1983), 14; Simon Blackburn, *The Oxford Dictionary of Philosophy* (New York: Oxford University Press, 1994), 186; Tim Crane, "Intentionality," in ibid., 438–439; Peter Simons, "Brentano," in *A Companion to the Philosophers*, ed. Robert L. Arrington (Malden, Mass.: Blackwell, 1999), 179–178; William G. Lycan, "Philosophy of Mind," in *The Blackwell Companion to Philosophy*, 2nd ed., ed. Nicholas Bunnin and E. P. Tsui-James (Malden, Mass.: Blackwell, 2003), 184–188.

7. See especially Richard Sorabji, "From Aristotle to Brentano: The Development of the Concept of Intentionality," in *Aristotle and the Later Tradition*, ed. Henry Blumenthal and Howard Robinson, 227–259 (Oxford: Clarendon Press, 1991); Caston, "Towards a History of the Problem of Intentionality among the Greeks"; Daag Nikolaus Haase, *Avicenna's De Anima in the Latin West: The Formation of a Peripatetic Philosophy of the Soul, 1160–1300* (London/Turin: Warburg Institute/Nino Aragno Editore, 2000), 127–153; Dominik Perler, ed., *Ancient and Medieval Theories of Intentionality* (Leiden: Brill, 2001); Perler, *Théories de l'intentionnalité au moyen âge* (Paris: Vrin, 2003); and Anthony Lisska, "Medieval Theories of Intentionality: From Aquinas to Brentano and Beyond," in *Analytical Thomism: Traditions in Dialogue*, ed. Craig Patterson and Matthew S. Pugh, 147–169 (Burlington, Vt.: Ashgate, 2006). Sorabji and Caston focus on the concept of intentionality in late antiquity, Haase on Islamic sources. Perler's edited volume collects sixteen papers on intentionality in Greco-Roman antiquity and the Middle Ages; his monograph focuses three later medieval authors: Peter John Olivi, Dietrich of Freiburg, and John Duns Scotus. The German edition, *Theorien der Intentionalität im Mittelalter* (Frankfurt: Klostermann, 2004), expands his account to include Thomas Aquinas, Peter Aureol, Hervaeus Natalis, William of Ockham, and Adam Wodeham. Lisska relates Thomas Aquinas to contemporary philosophy of mind. Interestingly enough, Ryan Hickerson's *History of Intentionality: Theories of Consciousness from Brentano to Husserl* (New York: Continuum, 2007) omits discussion of Brentano's ancient and medieval precursors entirely on grounds of dissimilarity, finding it better to treat Brentano as a "Comtean positivist" (39).

8. Victor Caston, "Connecting Traditions: Augustine and the Greeks on Intentionality," in Perler, *Ancient and Medieval Theories of Intentionality*, is more sensitive than most to the dangers of Whig history, that is, to our seeing "everything as progressing towards our own enlightened state, while falling short in various measures" (29). But then he seems to move in that direction anyway with his alternative of looking for "contributions that form

That we should turn to the history of philosophy for clarification is certainly understandable. Even today, the use of "intentionality" to mean the directedness or "aboutness" of mental states runs together two very different aspects of its meaning: (1) an ethical-volitional sense, in which we speak of the action a person *intended*, or meant to perform; and (2) a logico-epistemic sense (sometimes known as "intensionality" or "intentionality-with-an-s"), which concerns the special conditions that obtain when we analyze certain mental acts and their corresponding propositional forms, such as the referential opacity induced by belief-states. It is partly for this reason that one recent author describes the topic of intentionality as "a well-known quagmire."[9]

Now, one might think that the best way out of the quagmire would be to finish what Brentano started and return to the Middle Ages, where we might find the pristine, original sense of the term, before it became part of the explanatory program of modern philosophical psychology. Well, not exactly. Anyone familiar with the sources knows that precisely the opposite is true: the conceptual history of intentionality becomes *more* complicated as we go back in time, not less. If we look at scholastic usage of the Latin term *intentio* or "intention"—medieval philosophers did not name the phenomenon with an abstract noun as we do—it turns out that Brentano recovered only small part of what *intentio* meant for medieval philosophers and theologians, and missed the part they would have regarded as the most important. When we look for medieval insights on Brentano's idea, what we find instead are dissonances, beginning with a huge difference in outlook: the distinction between the psychical and the physical, between mind and body, was simply not as problematic for pre-Cartesian thinkers as it was for Brentano, and still is for us. No one seems to have thought that the mind is special or that its operations are unique in the sense that they are found nowhere else in creation. Indeed, what is most striking about medieval intentionality is the very *ordinariness* of the phenomenon, in contrast to the special psychic significance Brentano wished it to have.

But the ordinary has no single prooftext. To that end, I will survey some medieval texts that use the term *intentio*, asking whether it is really the same concept we are interested in today. Though my survey will cover only one author, the influential Parisian arts master John Buridan (c. 1295–1361), I hope it will be sufficient to show, in an exemplary way, how the concept was used in ordinary philosophical discourse. The texts I will be discussing are mostly in

---

part of a single discussion, in an effort to respond to a single problem or, more exactly, a single *worry*—that is, what is perceived to constitute a problem" (ibid.). What constitutes a problem is partly a normative question, of course, and it is an open—and frequently very interesting—question whether philosophers writing in different historical periods are operating from the same norms. Thus, whether there are single problems or single worries is something that must be shown, I think, rather than assumed.

9. Joseph Margolis, "Reflections on Intentionality," in *The Cambridge Companion to Brentano*, ed. Dale Jacquette (Cambridge: Cambridge University Press, 2004), 131.

the form of question commentaries on the works of Aristotle, all of which began life in the classroom, as lectures on books students were required to read for the bachelor's degree: *Categories, De Interpretatione, Posterior Analytics, Physics, De Anima, Metaphysics*, and *Nicomachean Ethics*. Like other arts masters, Buridan's classroom practice was to explain the literal sense of Aristotle's text along with any philosophical questions he took to be raised by it.[10] The latter gave him plenty of room to expound his own views, as well as to respond to student queries and arguments made by his predecessors.

What follows may be thought of as part of a natural history of intentionality, insofar as it attempts to recover what Buridan himself understood by the term *intentio*. I have identified five different senses, documented from the most commonly used to the least. The result will constitute, at most, only a small panel in a much larger storyboard. But my suggestion will be that what Brentano handed down to us as *the* scholastic notion of intentionality is just one aspect of a very complex idea.

### INTENTIONES AS MEANINGS

The commonest use of the Latin term *intentio* and its verbal form *intendere* in Buridan is "intend" in the sense of "to mean." There are literally hundreds of examples in his writings. Here the sense is almost always that of authorial intention, whether the author in question is Buridan himself, Plato, Aristotle ("the Philosopher"), Porphyry, Boethius, Averroes ("the Commentator"), Robert Grosseteste ("*Lincolniensis*"), Thomas Aquinas ("*Beatus Thomas*"),[11] or any of the numerous other figures whose views he discusses, including authors unknown (*anonymi*):

> It should be noted that it was not my intention, nor was it Aristotle's [*non est intentio mea, nec fuit intentio Aristotelis*], to maintain that it is only with regard to these four circumstances that a refutation or contradiction [of the fallacy of *ignoratio elenchi*] can be impeded.[12]

> [I]t was my intention to treat of moral questions in this book [i.e., the *Questions* on Aristotle's *Nicomachean Ethics*).[13]

---

10. Contemporary testimony suggests that the practice was common, going back (at least) to Albert the Great (c. 1193/1206–1280), whom Buridan seems to have regarded as a model for commenting on Aristotle. See Jean Dunbabin, "The Two Commentaries of Albertus Magnus on the Nicomachean Ethics," *Recherches de Théologie Ancienne et Médiévale* 30 (1963): 232–250.

11. Pope John XXII had canonized Thomas in 1323.

12. *Summulae* 7.4.3 (trans. Klima: 570). All Buridan translations are my own with the exception of the *Summulae*, for which I use Gyula Klima's *John Buridan: Summulae de Dialectica* (New Haven: Yale University Press, 2001).

13. *Quaestiones super libros Aristotelis Ethicorum Aristotelis ad Nicomachum* X.5; revised Latin text in R. J. Kilcullen, ed., "Buridan, On Aristotle's Ethics, Book X" (1996), www.humanities.mq.edu.au/Ockham/wburlat.html: "fuit intentio mea tractare de moralibus in hoc libro"

By "singulars," Plato intended the things signified singularly by singular terms such as "Socrates" and "Plato," and by "universals" he understood the things signified by universal terms such as "man" and "animal"; and he held that universals are distinct from singulars.[14]

And so it seems to me to be the intention of Aristotle, and also the truth, that however much it is disposed to particular arts and sciences, the human intellect cannot in this life naturally form an act of understanding without the existence of interior sense, viz., without the imagination, or the cogitative power in its second actuality, viz., in cognizing. That is why, when both interior and exterior senses are ensconced in a deep sleep, viz., a sleep without dreams, or a sleep caused by illness, no one understands.[15]

This was not Porphyry's intention in asking those difficult and sublime questions [at the beginning of the *Isagoge*], which he deliberately avoided answering.[16]

But those wishing to harmonize the aforementioned opinion [i.e., that practical reasoning is located in the sensory part of the soul] say that it was not the intention of St. Thomas that prudence be ascribed to the cogitative power subjectively, but to the intellect—and not in any way at all, but as conjoined to sense, or by reflection on the sense itself.[17]

Authorial intention is what an author intended his words to signify as he wrote them. This idea has a long history in medieval hermeneutics, going all the way back to Augustine, who announces in his *Literal Commentary on Genesis* that his audience should expect him "to defend the literal meaning of the narrative

---

14. *In Metaphysicen Aristotelis Questiones* VII.15 (Paris 1518: 50va–vb): "per singularia intendebat Plato res significatas per terminos singulares singulariter, ut per istos 'Socrates,' 'Plato,' et per uniuersalia intelligebat res significatas per terminos uniuersales, ut per istos terminos 'homo,' 'animal' et tunc ille dicebat uniuersalia separata a singularibus."

15. *Quaestiones in libros Aristotelis De anima* III.15 (ed. Zupko, §15): "Ideo videtur mihi esse intentio Aristotelis, et veritas, quod intellectus humanus, quantocumque singulis artibus et scientiis habituatus, non potest in hac vita naturaliter formare actum intelligendi non existente sensu interiori, scilicet phantasia vel cogitativa in actu suo secundo, scilicet cognoscendi, propter quod sensibus tam interioribus quam exterioribus ligatis per somnum perfectum scilicet sine somnio aut per aegritudinem, nullus intelligit."

16. *Quaestiones in Isagogen Porphyrii* I.4 (ed. Tatarzynski in "Jan Buridan, Kommentarz do Isagogi Porfiriusza," *Przegląd Tomistyczny* 2 (1986) 139, ll. 616–618): "Ideo hoc non intendebat Porphyrius per illas quaestiones difficiles et altissimas, a quibus se volebat abstinere."

17. *Quaestiones super decem libros Ethicorum Aristotelis ad Nicomachum* VI.4 (Paris 1513: 120ra): "Quid autem opinionem praedictam ad sensum congruentem volentes reducere dicunt quod intentio beati Thomae non erat quod prudentia poneretur in potentia cognitiva subiective, sed in intellectu—non tamen quocumque modo sed ut copulatio sensui seu ut habente reflectionem ad ipsam sensum."

as it is set forth by the author."[18] "Intention" here reflects an act of the will, as indicated by Augustine's use of the verb *volere* for the "mind" or "will" of the writer: "if the tenor of the words of Scripture does not militate against our taking this teaching as the mind of the writer [*hoc voluisse intellegi scriptorem*], we shall still have to inquire whether he could not have meant something else besides."[19]

In an extended sense, Buridan also ascribes *intentio* impersonally, to a significant term or phrase in a proposition, and sometimes to the proposition as a whole:

> Similarly, in the mind, I believe that I can have the concept of the term "double" without the concept of the term "half" [*ego possum habere intentionem huius termini 'duplum' sine intentione huius termini 'dimidium'*].[20]

> Grosseteste says that if the conclusion, "the earth is round," is demonstrated in both natural science and astrology, these conclusions are the same in name only and not in intention.[21]

> The intention of the question [i.e., whether there are four main kinds of causes—material, formal, efficient, and final—and not more] is . . .[22]

The use of *intentio* to refer to the concept of a term or proposition with which the term or proposition is conventionally associated (hence the translation of *intentio* as "concept"), is related to a second, somewhat less common, sense of intention, that is, as a mental quality distinguishable from the particular volition that expresses it in a speech act. Here we might imagine intentions in an "unwilled" state, naturally signifying certain things outside the mind, which an author or speaker then chooses to "invest" in a piece of conventional discourse. When we analyze such discourse, Buridanian semantics posits that meaningful terms and propositions signify concepts in the minds of those who use them (the "capital" in this analogy), and ultimately signify the things conceived of or

---

18. Augustine, *De Genesi ad litteram* 11.1.2: "ut ad proprietatem litterae defendatur quod gestum narrat ipse qui scripsit." St. Augustine, *The Literal Meaning of Genesis*, trans. J. H. Taylor (Mahwah, N.J.: Paulist Press, 1982), 41–42.

19. Augustine, *De Genesi ad litteram* 1.19.38: "Si autem contextio Scripturae hoc voluisse intellegi scriptorem non repugnaverit, adhuc restabit quaerere utrum et aliud non potuit." The sense of *volere* here is the same as *vouloir* in the French expression, "Ça veut dire?" Ibid.

20. *Summulae* 3.4.6 (trans. Klima, 180).

21. *Quaestiones in duos libros Aristotelis Posteriorum Analyticorum* I.26 (ed. Hubien): "Dicit enim Lincolniensis quod si ista conclusio 'terra est rotunda' probetur in scientia naturali et in astrologia, tamen illa non est eadem conclusio nisi secundum uocem, et non secundum intentionem."

22. *In Metaphysicen Aristotelis Questiones* V.1 (Paris 1518: 26vb): "Intentio quaestionis est . . ."

represented by those concepts (the "collateral").²³ Thus, when Buridan speaks about the *"intentio"* or meaning of a piece of discourse, he is thinking primarily of the concept(s) corresponding to it, for example, the idea Plato or Aristotle or Thomas had when they wrote the words we attribute to them, or the idea(s) we have when we read or hear those words—which may, of course, be different.

> For names are significative by convention [*ad placitum*]; therefore, diverse authors and philosophers often use the same names equivocally, according to diverse intentions [*secundum diuersas intentiones*], and any author who uses those names can legitimately expound those names in accordance with the intentions according to which he uses that name [*secundum quas intentiones ipsi utuntur illi nominibus*], and his audience and readers should take his words in accordance with the intention which the author had or would appear to have had [*secundum intentionem quam auctor habebat aut uidebatur habere*].²⁴

Where the meaning is unclear, determining the intention immediately signified by an expression has the effect of disambiguating it, which for Buridan is the essential first step in determining its logical structure: "in our expressions, where truth and falsity, consequences and oppositions are concerned, we should pay attention more to the intentions than to the utterances, although we should pay attention to both [*magis intendere debemus ad intentiones quam ad voces, licet ad utramque debeamus attendere*]."²⁵

A brief example will suffice. I might argue that the sophism "Nobody can contradict my proposition" is true if my proposition is "Socrates runs" and Socrates is in fact running when I utter it. You would not know what to say to contradict me until I utter my proposition, but by then it would be too late: "if, wanting to contradict, you say that Socrates does not run, it may be the case that I said something true and you also say something true, for when I spoke, he was running, and when you speak, he is not running; but a true proposition never contradicts a true proposition."²⁶ But Buridan argues that the sophism is false because:

> Contradictory propositions have to have the same subject and predicate in utterance and also in intention [*secundum vocem et etiam secundum inten-*

---

23. So the ultimate signification occurs via the concept or intention: "significative utterances signify affections, i.e., concepts of the soul, and signify other things only by the mediation of the signification of the concepts [*voces significativae significant passiones, id est conceptus, animae, et non alias res nisi mediante significatione conceptuum*]" (*Summulae* 9.1, 2nd conclusion, 832). Thus, as Gyula Klima notes, "according to Buridan, what a meaningful utterance signifies is neither simply 'an extramental thing' nor simply something 'in the head'" (*Summulae*, xxxv).
24. *Summulae* 6.2.3 (trans. Klima, 404–405).
25. *Summulae* 7.4.3 (trans. Klima, 566).
26. *Summulae* 9.7, 2nd sophism (trans. Klima, 942–943).

*tionem*]. Therefore, in intention [*secundum intentionem*] I have to refer the verb of my proposition to the same time as that to which you referred the verb of your proposition, so that the intention [*intentio*] should be to deny what you affirmed, or conversely [to affirm what you denied], for the same time, even if that time coexisted with your proposition and not with mine. For I speak with this intention [*secundum intentionem*], as if I were speaking at that time, and this is allowed so that we can relate to the same intention [*ad eandem intentionem*]. This is often the case in the Holy Scripture; for we say that Christ is born today, or will be born tomorrow, speaking with the intention [*loquentes secundum intentionem*] as if we were in the time when he was born.[27]

Intentions are relevant to the truth conditions of propositions because they represent, in conceptual form, the tacit assumptions of those who use them. Accordingly, the logician is interested not just in the conventional form of an utterance, but also in the "mental syntax" of its corresponding concept.[28] In practical terms, this means that when testing a proposition for contradictoriness, "it is [sometimes] necessary to add other utterances when contradicting it . . . For one should primarily attend to the intention, since we use words only to express the intention [*Oportet enim principaliter inspicere ad intentionem, cum non utamur voce nisi ad intentionem exprimendam*]."[29] It is important to note that we are not talking here about meanings as eternal, disembodied forms. For Buridan, abstract intentions are always traceable to their more natural and concrete mode of existence as speaker's intentions. For example, we can easily resist an opponent who tries to persuade us to deny "All men are risible" by pointing to a man on his deathbed who is unable to laugh: such an opponent is "absolutely refuted" as long as the proposition is taken "in the sense in which everyone commonly intends it," that is, as a *proprium* or property following from the essence of man, which is present as long as the man exists even if it is not actually being exercised.[30]

---

27. *Summulae* 9.7, 2nd Sophism (trans. Klima, 943).
28. Indeed, Buridan likens mental intentions to spoken utterances and written letters, placing all three in a structural hierarchy: "letters are related subordinately to utterances, and analogously, even as utterances are related to the intentions of the soul [*subordinate et proportionaliter se habent litterae ad voces sicut voces ad intentiones animae*]" (*Summulae* 9.1, 2nd conclusion; trans. Klima, 832). Lying involves a breakdown in the conventional subordination relation between an utterance and the intention with which it is uttered; thus, "someone knowingly and intentionally asserting something false lies [*dicens falsum scienter et ex intentione mentitur*]" (*Summulae* 1.7.1; trans. Klima, 58).
29. *Summulae* 9.8, 11th sophism (trans. Klima, 979).
30. *Questiones longe super librum Perihermenias* I.3 (ed. van der Lecq, 17, ll. 36–38): "dico quod iste primo concedebat illam 'omnis homo est risibilis' secundum sensum quem omnes communiter intendunt, ipse est simpliciter redargutus in ista excusatione sua."

## *INTENTIONES* AS MENTAL QUALITIES

In its next most frequent sense, Buridanian intentionality covers what we might call mental or psychological phenomena, that is, anything that has its primary mode of existence in the mind. As we saw above, this sense may be more primary in that it seems to be assumed by *intentio* in its authorial meaning. Here, the term *intentio* is synonymous with the terms "concept" and "reason":

> If a single utterance is imposed to signify several things according to a single concept, or according to a single nature, or according to a single intention (for I am taking all of these to mean the same in the present context), then that utterance signifies those things univocally, and is said to be univocal.[31]

The context is the opening section of Aristotle's *Categories*, where univocity and equivocity are defined in terms of the reason or definition of the utterance in question (*Cat.* 1.1a1–11). Buridan's Latin text of the *Categories* had the word *ratio* for "definition," which translates Aristotle's term *logos*. That alone should convey something of the scope of the term *ratio* and its synonyms *conceptus* and *intentio*. We are talking here about something as wide-ranging as the Greek concept of *logos*.

"Intentional" in this sense seems to come to nothing more than "conceptual" signifying that something is a concept or idea in the mind. But this raises a further question about the ontological status of concepts. How does the existence of things that are conceptual differ from things that are physical? Buridan argues that concepts are singular mental qualities or "dispositions" (*habitus*) of the intellectual part of the soul, and he explicitly differentiates mental from physical qualities using the criterion of bodily extension: "our concepts exist in our intellect as singularly and distinctly from one another and from other things as colors and flavors do in bodies: although such concepts do not have extension or corporeal location in it, they certainly all exist singularly."[32] Buridan the nominalist prefers to speak of singularity adverbially, as an act of existence, rather than as a static property or attribute that might be reified: "the intellect understands universally, even though it exists singularly, as do the things under-

---

31. *Quaestiones in Praedicamenta* I.1 (ed. Schneider: 4, ll. 46–49): "si una vox imponitur ad significandum plures res secundum unum conceptum vel secundum unam rationem vel secundum unam intentionem (haec omnia capio pro eisdem in proposito), tunc illa univoce significant illas res, et dicitur univocum."

32. *Quaestiones in libros Aristotelis De anima* III.8 (ed. Zupko, §23): "conceptus nostri in intellectu nostro ita singulariter et distincte ab invicem et ab aliis existunt sicut colores et sapores in corporibus, quamvis conceptus tales in eo non habeant extensionem nec sitem corporeum, immo omnia existunt singulariter." Buridan specifies that concepts lack both extension and corporeal location in order to distinguish them from points, which lack extension but do have corporeal location.

stood, and also the intention [by which it understands]."³³ Likewise, the extramental things and the concepts or intentions by which they are understood are related all by themselves by a kind of natural similarity, which in turn grounds the meaning of conventional signs: "passions, i.e., concepts in the mind, naturally resemble those extramental things, and spoken utterances only signify them by voluntary conventional imposition and by the mediation of those intentions of the soul."³⁴ Other than the fact that they inhere "in" the mind, the only thing separating mental from real qualities is their lack of extension and corporeal location, or as later medieval authors put it, their "having parts outside one another."

In another work that, until recently, was thought to be an earlier version of Buridan's Question commentary on Aristotle's *De Anima*, the anonymous author (whom I shall call Ps.-Buridan) diversifies these intentions or mental qualities into a triadic discourse of act, species, and habit, which he uses to mark the different stages of conceptual thinking:

> To sum up, then, it is clear that it is the same quality which is called (1) the act of understanding while it is being acquired; (2) the intelligible species when the intellect is no longer cognizing it or understanding through it; and (3) the intellectual habit, once it has been sufficiently established in the intellect to incline it [to act]. It is obvious, then, in reply to the question that the intelligible species, that the act of understanding, and the intellectual habit are not distinct things, but the terms, "intelligible species," "act of understanding," and "intellectual habit" signify the same thing, disposed in different ways.³⁵

These intentional moments are distinct phases in the thought process, differentiated via their affective relation to the cognizing subject. Thus, "the intellectual habit is that same likeness which is called the species, connoting a greater

---

33. *Quaestiones super octo Physicorum libros Aristotelis* I.7 (Paris 1509: 8vb): "intellectus intelligit uniuersaliter, licet existat singulariter, et res intellecta singulariter, et intentio etiam singulariter."

34. *Questiones longe super librum Perihermenias* II.11 (ed. van der Lecq: 100, ll. 31–33): "passiones idest conceptus anime sunt naturales similitudines harum rerum. Et voces non sunt significative earum, nisi secundum impositionem voluntariam ad placitum et mediantibus intentionibus anime."

35. Ps.-Buridan, *Quaestiones in tres libros De Anima Aristotelis* III.10 (ed. Patar: 459, ll. 26–34): "Patet igitur recapitulando quod eadem qualitas quae, dum acquiritur, vocatur actus intelligendi, et quando acquisita est et intellectus non cognoscit nec intelligit per eam, vocatur species intelligibilis; sed quando est bene firmata in intellectu et est inclinativa intellectus, vocatur habitus. Patet igitur ad quaestionem quod species intelligibilis, actus intelligendi, habitus intellectualis non sunt res distinctae, sed isti termini 'species intelligibilis,' 'actus intelligendi,' 'habitus intellectualis' significant eandem rem, alio tamen et alio modo se habentem."

firmness, and also the fact that it inclines the intellect [to act by cognizing it]."[36] The name we use for it changes depending on whether the intention stands to the intellect as a pure potentiality (in which case it is a species), or exists in the first (an act) or second (a habit) degrees of actuality. Here, intention has been assimilated to Aristotelian motion, like the kinetic difference between a ball suspended above the ground, then dropping through the air, and finally resting on the ground. Although movement cannot belong to the human soul in any literal sense, we can still conceptualize the process of thought in terms of motion.[37] Ps.-Buridan does not multiply intentions to account for these different states, preferring instead to speak of a single mental quality that gets called different things as it passes through the different stages of the thought process. For him, these mental qualities have multiple guises: statically, they exist as reasons, definitions, and concepts; dynamically, as intelligible acts, species, and habits. By contrast, the actual Buridan prefers to restrict the reference of "species" or "intention" to what acts of cognition leave behind in the imagination or memory, since he thinks we cannot explain the different operations of our cognitive powers unless there is some real distinction in the qualities they produce.[38]

### INTENTIONES AS CLASSIFICATIONS

Buridan also uses *intentio* as a term of classification, by means of which we distinguish between two basic kinds of names and their corresponding concepts:

> from what has been said it is clear that the names "universal whole" and "subjective part," or even "superior" or "inferior in predication," are names of second intention, or imposition [*sunt nomina secundae intentionis, seu impositionis*]; for they appropriately suppost for predicable and subjectible significative terms. But the terms "integral whole" and "integral part" are terms of first intention or imposition [*sunt termini primae intentionis, seu impositionis*], for they aptly suppost for external things, existing apart from

---

36. Ps.-Buridan, *Quaestiones in tres libros De Anima Aristotelis* III.10 (ed. Patar: 459, ll. 24–26): "habitus intellectualis est illa eadem similitudo quae vocatur species, connotando maiorem firmitatem et etiam quod inclinat intellectum." Note that firmness here has to do with the *intellect's* confidence in the concept, that is, in its readiness to assent to it, rather than any quality in the concept itself.

37. See Arist. *De an.* I.3, 406a1; 407a20. The association of thinking with a kind of moving is also present in the Augustinian tradition. See Augustine, *De ordine* II.xi.30: "Reason is a movement of the mind, the ability to distinguish and connect the things that are learned [*ratio est mentis motio, ea quae discuntur distinguendi et connectendi potens*]."

38. See *Quaestiones in libros Aristotelis De anima* II.23 (ed. Sobol, trans. Klima, §16) and III.15 (ed. Zupko, §23). Thus, the third mode of the fallacy of *ignoratio elenchi* occurs when "identity with respect to the utterance is maintained, but not with respect to the thing and its concept [*si observetur identitas secundum uocem et non secundum rem et intentionem*]" (*Summulae* 7.4.3; trans. Klima, 568).

the operations of the soul; for a house is an integral whole, as well as a man, or a stone, for any of these consists of many parts, and is those parts.[39]

This is, of course, the commonplace medieval distinction between terms that refer to things and terms that refer to other terms, or between concepts that stand for things outside the mind and those that stand for other concepts.[40] The ordinal words "first" and "second" express causal and logical priority: the intellect first forms concepts of what is outside the mind and then, by reflecting on those concepts, forms a second tier of concepts about those primary concepts. Therefore, as terms of second intention, "universal whole" and "subjective part" are similar in function to the terms "genus" and "species," so that, Buridan says, "we call a common term taken absolutely a whole with respect to itself taken with some determination, as when we call the term 'animal' a universal whole with regard to the terms 'rational animal' and 'irrational animal,' and consequently also with regard to the species 'man' and 'brute.'"[41] There is not supposed to be anything mysterious about how the intellect does this. Buridan notes elsewhere that specific universal wholes are composed of proper names, not individuals: if we impose the proper name "A" on water and "B" on half of it, "the name 'water' would be a universal whole with respect to the names 'A' and 'B,' as is a species to its individuals."[42]

Second, intentions are concepts or terms that express a kind of attitude or way of construing (*acceptum*) other concepts or terms that do refer to things outside the mind. Thus, they incorporate the features of both of the aforementioned uses of "*intentio*": they are mental qualities or terms that express the will or intention of their author as regards some object. The intention here may not be deliberate on the part of the intellect forming the intention, but only an indication of how it is being understood or cognized:

> Qualitative names pertaining to the second intention, however, are those which are predicated of the aforementioned qualitative terms strictly qualitatively, as passions of them, rather than of substantial terms, e.g., that one whiteness is clear, another obscure; that in sounds of the same species—e.g., in the same baritone—one is strong, another weak, one is rough, another

---

39. *Summulae* 6.4.4; trans. Klima, 428.

40. A "commonplace," that is to say, from the latter part of the thirteenth century on. Its origins can be traced to Alfarabi and Avicenna, but its pre-Buridanian history need not detain us here. Christian Knudsen's 1982 article "Intentions and Impositions," in the *Cambridge History of Later Medieval Philosophy*, remains an excellent source on the question.

41. *Quaestiones in libros Aristotelis De anima* II.7 (ed. Sobol, trans. Klima, §17): "terminum communem simpliciter acceptum, vocemus totum respectu sui ipsius accepti cum determinatione, sicut istum terminum *animal* vocamus totum universale ad istos terminos *animal rationale* et *animal irrationale*, et per consequens etiam ad istas species *homo* et *brutum*." Buridan is here interpreting what he takes to be Aristotle's view in *De Anima* II.2 on how the parts of the soul can be distinguished in definition.

42. *Summulae* 6.4.4; trans. Klima, 434.

plain; that a certain heat is intense, another diminished; that one illness is acute, another less so; that a certain health or knowledge is firm, another unsteady or infirm, and so on.[43]

It is important to notice that these are modes of cognition rather than qualities of things; that is what Buridan means when he says that second intentions are predicated *as passions* of qualitative rather than substantial terms. In more modern parlance, we might put the distinction adverbially: whiteness may be cognized more or less clearly; a baritone voice more or less loudly, or smoothly; heat more or less intensely; illness more or less acutely; and health or knowledge more or less firmly.

Though it slips by almost unnoticed, the distinction between first and second intentions is also where Buridan provides his nominalist solution to the problem of universals. We find it first in an early work, the *Tractatus de differentia universalis ad individuum* (also called *Quaestiones de universali*),[44] but the basic position is one he maintained throughout his long career:

> it is commonly held that universals or genus or species or things of this kind are second-intentional names that denominate things belonging to diverse genera, for we say that man is a species and whiteness is a species, etc., and that man is a universal, and also whiteness and quantity. And it seems necessary to concede this as regards individuals as well, for Socrates is an individual, and also this whiteness and this quantity.[45]

---

43. *Quaestiones in Praedicamenta* I.15 (ed. Schneider: 116, ll. 253–259): "Illa autem nomina pertinerent secunda intentione ad qualitatem, quae de prius dictis terminis qualitatis praedicarentur proprie in quale tamquam passiones eorum, potius quam de terminis substantialibus, ut quod albedo quaedam est clara, quaedam obscura, et vox eiusdem speciei, scilicet in eodem tono gravitatis quaedam fortis, quaedam debilis, quaedam rauca, quaedam plana, et caliditas quaedam intensa, alia remissa, et aegritudo quaedam acuta, quaedam hebes, et sanitas vel scientia quaedam firma, quaedam labilis vel infirma, et sic de aliis."

44. The treatise is one of five polemical works dating from 1332–35, perhaps the earliest of Buridan's surviving writings. Of four known manuscripts, one (Uppsala C.615) indicates in the explicit that the question was determined in 1334. Another (München SB Clm 18 789) interestingly mentions that Buridan wrote the treatise "against certain Englishmen who assume that universals are entities existing outside the soul, just like the heresiarch Wyclif and his followers [*contra quosdam Anglicos ponentes universalia esse encia extra animam, sicut posuit Vickleff heresiarcha cum suis sequacibus*]," though of course Wyclif himself could not have been Buridan's target, as he would have only been a child when the *Treatise* was composed. See Bernd Michael, "Johannes Buridan: Studien zu seinem Leben, seinen Werken und zu Rezeption seiner Theorien im Europa des späten Mittelalters" (PhD diss., University of Berlin, 1985), 434. The treatise is directed against two unidentified realist opponents, possibly Walter Burley, who is named as the author of one of the opposing arguments.

45. *Tractatus de differentia universalis ad individuum* (ed. Szyller: 145, 35–146, 5): "universale vel genus vel species et huiusmodi sunt nomina secundarum intentionum prout communiter conceditur. Et certum est, quod denominant res diversorum generum. Dicimus enim, quod homo est species et albedo est species et cetera, similiter homo est universale et

What is striking about Buridan's position is not the fact that he regards universals as second intentions; that much was "commonly held," as he says. Rather, it is his identification of universality with the dynamic activity of thinking of concepts in a certain way. His reply to the realists is that universals are not things,[46] but events, or more precisely, *cognitive acts* of relating particular concepts or things to other particular concepts or things:

> Some things are taken to be universal with respect to signifying or representing because they do not signify one thing or another determinately, but all things alike in genus or species indifferently (in the way that the term "man" signifies all men, [and] the term "color" all colors). And so universals are significative terms, be they vocal, mental, or written. And those mental or vocal terms exist as singularly as the color does in a wall, although they are called universals with respect to signifying. And in this way, it must be conceded that universals are certainly as generable and corruptible in the mind or in speech as color is in a wall.[47]

Universals are second intentions in the sense that they are concepts of concepts, distinguished not by their objective content but by their mode of conception. Such modes also serve to differentiate concepts: "sometimes concepts are distinct not because of diversity in the things conceived, but because the modes of conceiving them are different, just as the concepts of *rational animal* and *man* are different, though it is the same thing [that is both]."[48] Buridan argues that

---

albedo et quantitas etc.; et sic de individuo etiam concedendum esse videtur, nam Socrates est individuum et haec albedo et haec quantitas."

46. Indeed, Buridan is concerned to block reifying moves even at the level of individuals. See *Summulae* 2.3.5: "To the first I reply that the term 'individual' is not an individual, just as the term 'man' is not a man; indeed, the name 'individual' is a name of second intention, suppositing for many terms, and it is one species among the species and names of second intentions [*Ad primam dicitur quod hoc nomen 'indiuiduum' non est indiuiduum, sicut nec iste terminus 'homo' est homo, immo hoc nomen 'indiuiduum' est nomen secundae intentionis supponens pro multis terminis. Et est una species inter species et nomina secundarum intentionum*].

47. *In Metaphysicen Aristotelis Questiones* I.7 (Paris 1518: 6vb–7ra) (the Latin text of this passage, based on two manuscripts and the 1518 edition, can also be found in de Rijk 1993, whom I follow in correcting the edition's reading of *ignorantia* for *incorruptibilia* in the third sentence): "Alia ponuntur esse universalia in significando vel representando, quia non significant determinate hoc vel illud, sed indifferenter omnia similis generis vel speciei; ut iste terminus 'homo' omnes homines, iste terminus 'color' omnes colores. Et sic universalia sunt termini significativi sive in voce sive in mente sive in scriptura. Et isti termini ita singulariter existunt vel in mente vel in voce, sicut iste color in pariete, quamvis dicantur universales in significando. Et isto modo concedendum est quod universalia sunt ita bene generabilia et corruptibilia in mente vel in voce sicut color in pariete."

48. *Tractatus de differentia universalis ad individuum* (ed. Szyller: 156, 34–37): "aliquando conceptus sunt diversi non propter diversitatem rerum conceptarum, sed propter diversitatem modi concipiendi, sicut alius est conceptus animalis rationalis et alius hominis, licet sit eadem res."

universals are complex concepts whose elements—first-intentional concept, thing, and the relation between them—are all particular. In this way, we might think of universals as dynamic aggregates consisting of a mental component and an extramental component standing in a certain active relation to each other.[49] His use of the term "intention" here suggests the part contributed by the mind, the "directionality" of its act, toward extramental objects (first intentions) or other mental acts (second intentions).

### NONHUMAN ANIMAL *INTENTIONES*

Buridan also attributes intentionality to certain perceptual judgments made by nonhuman or brute animals, though this usage is less frequent and almost always in reference to Avicenna's use of intention to account for animal behavior. Thus, when enumerating the ways in which one concept may give rise to another concept noninferentially, or "without the consequence of one proposition to another [*sine consequentia alicuius propositionis ad aliam propositionem*]," Buridan says that this happens "evocatively [*elicitative*]" as

> Avicenna says that the estimative power elicits an unsensed intention of friendliness or hostility from the sensed intention of color or figure or motion; this is how a sheep fears and flees from the wolf and follows the shepherd.[50]

---

49. The mental component is in this case connected with the activity of representing something in some way to itself. See *Quaestiones super octo Physicorum libros Aristotelis* I.7 (Paris 1509: 8vb): "Therefore, if all asses are in essential agreement and resemble each other, it must be that if an intelligible species will represent some ass to the intellect through the mode of likeness, it will at the same time indifferently represent any ass at all, unless something prevents it (as we will consider later). This is how a universal intention is produced [*Ideo si omnes asini ex natura rei habent adinuicem conuenientiam et similitudinem, oportet quod quando species intelligibilis in intellectu repraesentabit per modum similitudinis aliquem asinum, ipsa simul indifferenter repraesentabit quemlibet asinum, nisi aliud obstet (de quo postea dicetur). Ideo sic fit uniuersalis intentio*]." As for the relations themselves, these too are second intentional, or concepts of concepts (*In Metaphysicen Aristotelis Questiones* V.9 (Paris 1518: 32ra): "I say that a relation is strictly speaking a certain concept of the soul by which the soul understands one thing compared with another (lit. 'this in comparison with that'), and the name imposed from such a concept is called a relative or respective term [*dico quod proprie loquendo relatio est quidam conceptus animae quo anima intelligit hoc in comparatione ad illud, et nomen impositum secundum talem conceptum vocatur terminus relativus sive respectivus*]."

50. *Quaestiones super octo Physicorum libros Aristotelis* I.4 (Paris 1509: 5rb) (cf. *Quaestiones in libros Aristotelis De anima* I.6 (ed. Hartman, §9)): "sicut dicit Avicenna quod virtus estimativa ex intentione sensata scilicet coloris aut figurae aut motus elicit intentionem non sensata puta amicitiae vel inimicitiae; ideo ovis timet et fugit a lupo et sequitur pastorem." Buridan uses the same example in his *De anima* commentary to argue that the human intellect should likewise be able to generate the concept of an underlying substance from its accidents. For discussion, see Jack Zupko, *John Buridan: Portrait of a Fourteenth-Century Arts Master* (Notre Dame, Ind.: University of Notre Dame Press, 2003), 106–108 and 214–216. The sheep example was a later medieval commonplace. As Haase puts it in *Avicenna's De*

Buridan contends that we should not find this at all surprising since brute animals have souls and souls outrank inanimate agents such as fire; therefore, if fire is capable of generating heat and thereby causing other things in its proximity to become lighter and more rarified, then surely the soul can generate one intention from another. What is generated is the will's primary, receptive act of agreement (*complacentia*) or disagreement (*displicentia*), which in the case of humans—though not in brute animals—freely gives rise to a secondary act of acceptance (*acceptatio*), rejection (*refutatio*), or deferment (*differre*).[51] In brute animals, the generated intention is naturally ordained to a certain type of action, so that the sheep's awareness of the wolf's hostility disposes it to flee, which it will do as long as there are no obstacles in its path. The intentionality of willing is thus not proper to the human intellect, but common to all creatures with cognitive appetites.

## NONPSYCHOLOGICAL INTENTIONALITY

The last sense of intentionality found in Buridan does not fit at all with the sense outlined by Brentano. This is the *intentio* of inanimate bodies. Thus,

> the natural intention or appetite of fire for heating is not disposed in a singular way to this or that heatable thing, but indifferently to anything it could make hot; therefore, it would heat whatever is present to it.[52]

Buridan makes the same point in his *Physics* commentary, where the term "intention" or "appetite" indicates that fire is disposed to heat things "in a universal way [*in modo universale*]," that is, not to heat this or that particular stick of wood, but indifferently to heat whatever is capable of being heated. Of course, the act of heating something is concrete and determinate because it is directed to a certain particular. Buridan likens this to the power of vision, which he says is disposed "in a universal way" to see whatever is visible, even though it actually sees only one thing at a time. The intentionality of a particular body, whether animate or inanimate, is a function of its elemental constituents—earth (cool and dry), air (warm and moist), fire (warm and dry), and water (cool and moist)—so a fiery body is naturally disposed to heat whatever is placed next to it.

---

*Anima in the Latin West*, "Almost every [Latin] writer after 1200 who wrote on the soul—and there are few scholastic writers in the thirteenth century who did not write on the soul—mentioned at least the basic ingredients of Avicenna's doctrine: the name of the faculty, the connotational attributes, and the example of the sheep and the wolf" (141).

51. For discussion, see Zupko, *John Buridan*, 252–53.

52. *Quaestiones in libros Aristotelis De anima* III.8 (ed. Zupko, §23) (cf. *Quaestiones super octo Physicorum libros Aristotelis* I.7 (Paris 1509: 8vb): "intentio naturalis vel appetitus ignis ad califaciendum non se habet modo singulari ad hoc calefactibile vel illud, sed ad quodlibet indifferenter quod ipse posset calefacere. Ideo quodcumque sibi praesentetur, calefaceret ipsum."

This kind of intentionality was a favorite of Buridan's realist opponents, since it suggests that inanimate bodies might be oriented to real universals—after all, how could something that lacks a mind have a merely conceptual object? In his *Tractatus de differentia universalis ad individuum*, Buridan remarks that "Walter [Burley], in his *Expositio* on Book I of the *Physics*, argues that universals actually exist outside the mind" by appealing to Avicenna's remark in his commentary on the *Physics* that "nature does not intend the genus or the individual, but the species."[53] Thus, if a particular fire A intends to produce at most one other particular fire B, then, once B is produced, A's natural intention must either disappear or continue to exist pointlessly (*frustra*), since it has done what it intended to do; but this is absurd, since A can ignite other fires and nothing exists pointlessly in nature. The specter is thus raised not only that inanimate bodies have intentional objects, but also that their intentionality forces us to posit real universals.

Buridan handles this realist objection by carefully distinguishing between an agent's causal and productive powers. An inanimate agent like fire does not intend anything by cognizing it, of course, though its active power naturally "moves toward what is outside it [*transiens in rem extra ipsam*]."[54] Conceived as causes, inanimate agents have specific being, and so we can speak of fire as having the specific power of heating, and of this power as being directed toward whatever happens to be placed next to it; nevertheless, this same intention can also be understood in terms of the act it produces, in which case it is particular since these acts are individuated by their effects on particular bodies, which are numerically distinct.[55] Buridan illustrates this with a quaint example:

> It's like the communal ass in some villages back in Picardy: the ass is indifferently related to all men in the village as far as carrying their grain to the mill is concerned, and yet these men do not say that the ass is useless, even though he has not carried all grain in the village to the mill, or even all of their grain at the same time. On the contrary, they believe that the ass is

---

53. *Tractatus de differentia universalis ad individuum* (ed. Szyller: 138, 17–22) (cf. *In Metaphysicen Aristotelis Questiones* VII.16 (Paris 1518: 51vb)): "Tertio autem Gualterus in sua *Expositione super primum Physicorum* arguit sic probando, quod aliquid est extra animam quod non est singulare; illud, quod natura primo intendit, est res extra animam, sed illud, quod natura primo intendit , non est singulare; illa patet per Avicennam primo suae *Physicae* capitulo primo, ubi dicit, quod natura non intendit genus nec individuum, sed speciem."

54. In a parallel discussion elsewhere, Buridan suggests that even so, we should speak of noncognitive agents *as if* they were cognitive, since we ascribe names to them on the basis of their similarity to us (*In Metaphysicen Aristotelis Questiones* VII.16 (Paris 1518: 51vb–52ra): "quia ista nomina attribuuntur illis naturalibus secundum similitudinem ad nos, ideo oportet dici in illis agentibus non cognoscentibus sicut diceretur si cognosceret."

55. *Tractatus de differentia universalis ad individuum* (ed. Szyller: 163, 18–30).

very useful because no matter which one of them comes to him, he will carry their grain.[56]

The communal ass is a universal in the sense that he is understood by everyone in the village to be their carrier of grain to the mill, even though this intention is always realized in particular acts of carrying grain to the mill.

But is the intention to carry grain to the mill any more "in" the communal ass than the intention to heat is "in" the fire? That is, should an intentional state be ascribed to the donkey or fire as such? Even if we can speak of the donkey as a beast of burden, or fire as a specific kind of heating agent, we must remember that we are the ones who are doing the speaking and classifying. If we are thinking of it *qua* cause, then as far as Buridan is concerned we are still in the realm of the psychological because "cause," like "relation,"[57] is a second-intentional term, a concept of concepts having no real existence outside the mind. As a concept, "cause" signifies other concepts that are causes, which connote concepts of their effects, which stand for their relata, which are particular things outside the mind—particular donkeys and sacks of grain, or particular fires and sticks of wood. Buridan is careful not to reify intentions or any other kind of relational notion. His remarks about the heating power of fire are instructive. He says that the proposition, 'Every fire is hot,' compels our assent as a natural principle, but not before we have experience of particular fires. We cannot intuit a priori that every fire is hot, nor do we have any means of demonstrating this "as the formal conclusion of an argument." We concede the truth of such propositions, he says, "just because we have seen many singulars like this, and have been unable to find a counter-instance in any of them."[58] Thus, even though we cannot claim that cause and effect are related by essential or virtual containment, Buridan thinks we can adequately demonstrate their relation a posteriori by the natural resemblance of particular cases. He famously attacks those who demand a much stricter standard of proof, who contend that philosophical demonstrations must always be reducible to the principle of non-

---

56. *Tractatus de differentia universalis ad individuum* (ed. Szyller: 165, 10–16: "Et est simile de asino communi in aliquibus villis de partibus nostris; ille asinus est indifferenter omnium hominum unius villae ad portandum blada sua ad molendinum, et illi homines non dicunt istum esse frustrum, licet non portaverit totum bladum istius villae ad molendinum, vel etiam licet non simul portaverit blada omnium istorum hominum; sed ipsi multum utilem reputant eum, quia quicumque illorum hominum indifferenter venerit ad asinum, ipse portabit bladum suum."

57. See note 49.

58. *In Metaphysicen Aristotelis Questiones* II.2 (Paris 1518: 9vb) (cf. *Quaestiones super decem libros Ethicorum Aristotelis ad Nicomachum* VI.11 (Paris 1513: 127ra): "Sed ideo dicuntur principia quia sunt indemonstrativa et omnino non possunt demonstrari nec etiam probari per rationem formaliter concludendum. Immo solum conceduntur quia sicut vidimus in pluribus singularibus et in nullis potuimus invenire instantiam." For discussion, see Zupko, *John Buridan*, 190–192.

contradiction, as "wicked men" who threaten "to destroy the natural and moral sciences" by making genuine empirical knowledge impossible.[59] On Buridan's view, intentions would be ascribed to inanimate bodies as a kind of shorthand for the causal dispositions we observe them to have, and the utter dependency of such ascriptions on our fallible, human modes of cognition would render the question of their extramental inherence moot.

## CONCLUSION

What light does Buridan's account shed on our current understanding of intentionality? Let me try to answer this first based on the evidence I have sketched here, and then somewhat more speculatively.

If by "our current understanding of intentionality" we mean the axial doctrine of Brentano, the two accounts seem only distantly related. Brentano has the criteriological concerns of the modernist; he believes he has found in intentional inexistence "the mark of the mental," the distinctive property that will justify treating mental phenomena separately from physical phenomena and thereby underwrite a new science of psychology irreducible to physical science. By contrast, intentionality for Buridan seems to be no more than a family-resemblance term: though it begins as a way of expressing what belongs to the conceptual and semantic realms, it is soon pressed into service in other contexts to designate nonintellectual dispositions and other unrealized potentialities. Brentano, needless to say, would have rejected the idea that the potentialities of purely physical things like fire could be intentions or that there could be intentionality if there were no minds. But even if we limit Buridanian intentionality to the conceptual and semantic realms, Buridan's notion is still too general to add any precision to Brentano's idea that intentionality is the mark of the mental. For it looks to be saying no more than that the mark of the mental is the conceptual, or that the intentional is in some sense proper to the mind, which is like saying that opium makes us sleepy because it possesses the dormitive virtue. Now it may be that Brentano's intentionality is a sui generis phenomenon, so that it would be a mistake to try to specify it in terms of some other physical or psychological property that it is not. But this is Brentano's problem, not Buridan's. Buridanian intentionality is not predicated on the existence of a sharp boundary between the mental and the physical.

That said, there is greater richness in the several senses of Buridanian intentionality, although the location of these riches may not be immediately evident.

---

59. The stricter standard is supposed to insulate human knowledge from divine deception, which it can do only at the cost of radically limiting what counts as human knowledge. See *In Metaphysicen Aristotelis Questiones* II.1 (Paris 1518: 9ra): "aliqui valde mali dicunt volentes interimere scientias naturales et morales eo quod in pluribus earum principiis et conclusionibus non est evidentia simplex sed possunt falsificari per casus supernaturaliter possibiles."

Here we must remember that Buridan's account, like virtually all discussions of intentionality in the medieval Latin tradition, was powerfully influenced by Augustine, an authority he hardly ever mentions because Buridan was a master of arts and the interpretation of Augustine was seen as proper to the Faculty of Theology. For Augustine, *intentio* is first and foremost ascribed to the will, which in cognition "is acknowledged to be the more spiritual element [*magis spiritalis agnoscitur*]," such as when it combines the body seen and the power of vision in a single act of perception.[60] Likewise, "the will . . . directs the sense informed [by vision] to the thing it sees and keeps the act of vision focused on it [*voluntas . . . et sensum formandum admoveat ei rei quae cernitur, et in ea formatum teneat*]."[61] Augustine conceives of *intentio* as something contributed by the mind to cognition, rather than as an objective feature or property we might "find" in mental phenomena. Whether he was conscious of it or not, Buridan shares the assumption that the human intellect contributes massively and comprehensively to its own picture of the world. This much is clear in the second-intentional status of common natures and sortal concepts as mental acts by which we organize our experience of what is outside the mind—an experience consisting at the most basic level of singular concepts that refer to particular things.

But does it follow that Buridan is committed to a kind of constructivism in the philosophy of mind, where there is nothing to ensure that our mental picture of the world corresponds to the way it really is? How, for example, is our second-intentional notion of fire as a cause of heating related to particular hot fires outside the mind? Here is Augustine's answer to this question:

> The human mind, therefore, knows all these things which it has acquired through itself, through the senses of its body, and through the testimonies of others, and keeps them in the treasure-house of its memory; and from them a true word is begotten when we say what we know, but a word that is anterior to every sound and to every thought of sound. For then the word is most like the thing that is known, from which its image is also begotten, since the sight of thought arises from the sight of knowledge. This is the word that belongs to no language, the true word about a true thing, having nothing from itself, but everything from that knowledge from which it is born. Nor does it make any difference when he who says what he knows has learned this, for sometimes he speaks as soon as he learns, provided only that it is a true word, that is, born from things that are known.[62]

60. Augustine, *De Trinitate* XI.4.7–5.9.
61. Augustine, *De Trinitate* XI.2.5.
62. Augustine, *De Trinitate* XV.12.22: "Haec igitur omnia, et quae per se ipsum, et quae per sensus sui corporis, et quae testimoniis aliorum percepta scit animus humanus, thesauro memoriae condita tenet, ex quibus gignitur verbum verum, quando quod scimus loquimur, sed verbum ante omnem sonum, ante omnem cogitationem soni. Tunc enim est verbum

Understood in this broader sense, intentionality is the mark not just of the mental but also of the "true word": the intelligible structure of a world created by a provident God. On this view, fires and donkeys and men are all suffused with meaning, and what they signify is the rational hand of their creator. Thus, understanding things in the natural order comes down to our ability to grasp, however derivatively in thought and speech, God's intention in creating them. I suspect that some such assumption underlies Buridan's rather sanguine belief in the veridicality of sense perception and the mind's ability to grasp the truth when confronted with the conclusions of natural science.

Is the intellect ever in a position to understand the nature of its own mental states, beyond their intentional content or meaning? Here the answer must be "no," because such knowledge would assume a God's-eye perspective on the world that is simply not available in this life. If he were around today, Buridan would probably sympathize with Colin McGinn's view that the mind/body problem is unsolvable because "we are cut off by our very cognitive constitution from achieving a conception of that natural property of the brain (or of consciousness) that accounts for the psychophysical link."[63] The difference would be that for Buridan, the mind/body problem was not a problem.

---

simillimum rei notae, de qua gignitur et imago eius, quoniam de visione scientiae visio cogitationis exoritur, quod est verbum linguae nullius; verbum verum de re vera, nihil de suo habens, sed totum de illa scientia de qua nascitur. Nec interest quando id didicerit; qui quod scit loquitur; aliquando enim statim ut discit, hoc dicit; dum tamen verbum sit verum, id est, de notis rebus exortum."

63. Colin McGinn, "Can We Solve the Mind-Body Problem?" *Mind* 98 (1989): 349–366.

# Mental Representation in Animals and Humans
## Some Late Medieval Discussions

OLAF PLUTA

In his *Philosophical Investigations* (*Philosophische Untersuchungen*), Ludwig Wittgenstein makes the following remark about animal thinking:

> It is sometimes said that animals do not talk because they lack the mental capacity. And this means: "they do not think, and that is why they do not talk." But—they simply do not talk. Or to put it better: they do not use language—if we except the most primitive forms of language.[1]

We should thus be careful not to assume a necessary connection between the use of language and a capacity for thought. In fact, thinking may be an ability not connected to language at all, even though for humans it is natural to express thoughts with words.

As far as language is concerned, some animals *are* capable of understanding what Wittgenstein calls "a complete primitive language"[2] where words are linked to actions. Wittgenstein gives the example of a builder and his assistant. The builder calls out words such as "block," "pillar," "slab," "beam," and the trained assistant brings the particular stone that he has learnt to bring in response to a given command.

As reported in an article published in *Science*, a nine-year-old border collie named Rico knew more than two hundred words.[3] Rico had been trained to fetch items, and he usually retrieved the correct item when asked by his owner. Even more impressive, however, was the dog's ability to learn in just a single trial, akin to the "fast mapping" abilities of children. That is to say, Rico inferred the names of novel items by exclusion learning and correctly retrieved those items right away. In general, Rico's retrieval rate was comparable to that of

---

1. Ludwig Wittgenstein, *Philosophische Untersuchungen/Philosophical Investigations*, trans. G. E. M. Anscombe (Oxford: Blackwell, 1953), 12; 3rd ed., trans. G. E. M. Anscombe (Oxford: Blackwell, 2001), 11.

2. Ibid., 3.

3. See Juliane Kaminski, Joseph Call, and Julia Fischer, "Word Learning in a Domestic Dog: Evidence for 'Fast Mapping,'" *Science* 304 (June 11, 2004): 1682–1683; and Paul Bloom, "Can a Dog Learn a Word?" ibid., 1605–1606, a commentary accompanying the original article.

three-year-old toddlers. The authors of the article conclude that word learning "appears to be mediated by general learning and memory mechanisms also found in other animals and not by a language acquisition device that is special to humans."[4] The limitations of animals would thus reflect differences in degree, not in kind.

While Rico's vocabulary of around two hundred words is comparable to that of language-trained apes, dolphins, and parrots, his word-learning abilities surpass those of nonhuman primates such as chimpanzees, who have so far never demonstrated this sort of fast mapping. Rico's word-learning abilities will, however, appear less amazing if one considers that humans and dogs have coevolved for a very long time—the fossil record offers evidence that domestic dogs originated about fifteen thousand years ago.[5] Ever since dogs and humans started to live together, dogs have been close to children and have thus been constantly exposed to word learning. And border collies are known for their intelligence and their eagerness to learn.

In what way Rico interprets or mentally represents a command such as "Rico, where is the sock?" does, however, remain an open question. When Rico is requested by his owner to fetch a sock, he may or may not understand that the word "sock" refers to a group of objects, and that the rest of the command means that he should act in a particular way (fetching) toward a member of this group.[6]

This brings me to the topic of my essay. I would like to introduce you to some late medieval discussions concerning mental representation in animals and humans, and dogs will play a major part in these discussions. Given the ubiquity of dogs during the Middle Ages, it is no surprise that their abilities were studied and that dogs were used as examples for animal thinking. For this paper, my focus will be on the works of John Buridan, a fourteenth-century arts master in Paris.

We come across dogs in almost all of John Buridan's works. In his writings on logic, dogs appear in logical fallacies such as: "Every dog runs; a star (*sidus caeleste*) is (called) dog;[7] therefore, a star runs."[8] Or, "This dog is a father; this dog

---

4. Kaminski, Call, and Fischer, "Word Learning in a Domestic Dog," 1682.

5. See Elisabeth Pennisi, "A Shaggy Dog History: Biologists Chase down Pooches' Genetic and Social Past," *Science* 298 (November 22, 2002): 1540–1542.

6. Bloom, "Can a Dog Learn a Word?" 1605.

7. Sirius, a star of the constellation *Canis Major*, is the brightest star in the heavens—also called the Dog Star. Alternatively, "*sidus caeleste*" also refers to the constellation dog, that is to say, either to *Canis Major*, the Great Dog (Sirius marks the dog's nose), or *Canis Minor*, the Small Dog, which comprises just a few stars dominated by bright Procyon.

8. "Secundo, nam hic est bonus syllogismus simpliciter: 'omnis canis currit; celeste sydus est canis; igitur celeste sydus currit.' Et tamen est syllogismus sophisticus; committitur tamen in eo fallacia equivocationis." (Buridan, *Quaestiones Elenchorum*, ed. R. van der Lecq and H. A. G. Braakhuis [Nijmegen: Ingenium, 1994], 2.2.2, see also 20.3.2.3) "Notandum quod, licet iste terminus 'canis' praedicetur de latrabile, de pisce marino et de caelesti sidere, tamen non est genus ad illa, nec iste terminus 'ens' ad decem praedicamenta, quia non praedicantur de

is yours; therefore, this dog is your father."[9] In Buridan's works on natural philosophy, dogs appear in examples of animal intelligence—sometimes alongside horses, donkeys, cows, or apes. We do not know if Buridan himself owned a dog, but he certainly had plenty of opportunities to study dogs. Buridan was an astute observer, and the astounding abilities of dogs clearly amazed him.

As far as the question of mental representation in animals and humans is concerned, we need to distinguish between particular knowledge and universal knowledge, and between conceptual knowledge and propositional knowledge.[10] It is obvious that animals do not use language—if we exclude language in its most primitive forms—and hence do not possess propositional knowledge in the sense that they could utter propositions such as "Every fire is hot." However, it remains to be seen if animals are able to represent mentally all these forms of knowledge in a way that is similar or maybe even equal to the corresponding ability in humans.

## PARTICULAR AND UNIVERSAL KNOWLEDGE

In a passage from his *Questions on Aristotle's Prior Analytics*, which has so far escaped the attention of scholars,[11] Buridan distinguishes four different forms of knowledge[12] that also differ with regard to their mental representation.

---

eis univoce, sed aequivoce" (Buridan, *Summulae de praedicabilibus*, ed. L. M. de Rijk [Nijmegen: Ingenium, 1995] 16, 29–31).

9. "Sicut iste paralogismus 'ille canis est pater; et ille canis est tuus; ergo ille canis est pater tuus'" (ibid., 14.4.4, see also 14.3.3.3) "Ad septimum sophisma, dicitur quod non valet consequentia 'iste canis est pater, et est tuus; ergo est pater tuus': quia mutatur appellatio huius termini 'tuus,' sicut dictum est." (John Buridan, *Sophismata*, ed. T. K. Scott [Stuttgart/Bad Cannstatt: Frommann-Holzboog, 1977], Pars II, Sophisma 7).

10. For the distinction between conceptual knowledge and propositional knowledge in medieval philosophy see, for example, Duns Scotus, *Ordinatio*, Prol. q. 1: "Whether man in his present state needs to be supernaturally inspired with some special knowledge he could not attain by the natural light of the intellect." Scotus answers that (a) all conceptual knowledge that is required for our perfection, can in fact be obtained naturally, that is to say, we can obtain the concepts "God," "perfect happiness," "highest possible perfection," "specific end," "face-to-face vision," etc. in a natural manner; (b) all propositional knowledge, however, that is required for our perfection, such as "the face-to-face vision and enjoyment of God are the end of man," cannot be obtained naturally.

11. Jack Zupko, *John Buridan: Portrait of a Fourteenth-Century Arts Master* (Notre Dame, Ind.: University of Notre Dame Press, 2003), makes use of Hubien's unpublished edition of Buridan's *Questions on Aristotle's Prior Analytics* but fails to discuss this particular question (see the Index of Quotations at 429).

12. "Alia autem sunt principia quorum termini non manifeste et evidenter se includunt vel excludunt, tamen dicuntur 'principia' quia sunt indemonstrabilia, et quia sine demonstratione et sine necessaria consequentia possunt nobis fieri evidentia. Et hujus modi principia fiunt evidentia aliquo quattuor modorum." (Buridan, *Quaestiones in Analytica Priora*, ed. H. Hubien [unpublished typescript, 1987], lib. II, q. 20a: Utrum per inductionem probabur propositio immediata) Buridan refers to *synthetic knowledge* here. In the case of *analytic knowledge*, by contrast, the propositions are manifest and evident (propositiones verae et immediatae) due to their inclusion ('albedo est color') or exclusion ('nulla albedo est nigredo') in the nominal definition.

The first kind of knowledge is based on actual sensation (*per actualem sensum*). For example, in the proximity of a fire you sense: "This fire is hot."[13] The second form of knowledge, which requires prior sensation, is based on memory (*per memoriam*). You may, for example, later recall, "This fire was hot." In memory, the sensation of fire is associated with the sensation of heat.[14] The third form of knowledge is based on experience (*per experientiam*) and presupposes sensation and memory. For example, if you were to sense that fire A is hot, and later sense the same of fire B and so on, you would, upon seeing a subsequent fire C, be able to judge—by referring to your past sensations in memory and on the grounds of the similarity between fire C and the previous fires—that this fire C is hot—without having to get physically close to it. According to Buridan, this judgment is neither based on sense alone—because you have not actually come close to the fire and have thus not experienced its heat—nor on memory alone—because you have not actually seen this particular fire before. Such a judgment Buridan calls "experimental" (*experimentale*), and he continues to say that "not only humans, but also animals in the very same way (*aequaliter*) make use of such a judgment." A single sense experience may actually be enough to form such kind of experimental knowledge: a dog fears a stone, even if it has only hurt him once. All this "experimental knowledge" is, however, particular in the sense that it refers to a particular sensation and memory or associates a series of particular sensations and memories.[15]

The fourth and final form of knowledge, which Buridan calls universal and scientific in the strict sense, is based on induction and presupposes sensation, memory, and experience (*per inductionem supponentem sensum, memoriam*

---

13. "Unus modus est per actualem sensum, sicut quod iste ignis est calidus: hoc enim est tibi evidens quando sentis ipsum; ita similiter quod Jacobus scribit, quando Jacobum vides scribere; et sic de pluribus aliis. Et non obstante quod tales propositiones sunt contingentes et singulares, et, per consequens, quod non sunt principia in demonstratione, nec intrant scientias demonstrativas, tamen habent locum in artibus et in prudentia, ut manifestatur sexto Ethicorum. Et ideo hujus modi propositiones singulares, ad sensum evidentes, sunt bene principia ratiocinationum artis et prudentiae" (ibid.).

14. "Secundo modo hujus modi principia sunt nobis evidentes per memoriam, ut quod ille ignis erat calidus, et quod Jacobus tunc scribebat. Et adhuc illa principia habent locum in artibus et in prudentia. Saepe enim in moralibus, ad corrigendum, et ad praemiandum vel ad puniendum, oportet ratiocinari ex singularibus de praeterito nobis notis per memoriam" (ibid.).

15. "Alia principia sunt nobis manifesta per experientiam, quae quidem experientia supponit sensum et memoriam. Verbi gratia, si tu ad sensum cognovisti quod ignis A erat calidus, et postea idem de igne B, et sic de multis aliis, tu postea videns ignem C, et non tangens ipsum, judicabis per memoriam de aliis et propter similitudinem quod ille ignis C est calidus; et hoc non est, proprie loquendo, judicium per sensum, quia non tangis ipsum, nec solum per memoriam, quia memoria proprie non est nisi prius cognitorum et tamen ipsum ignem C numquam alias vidisti nec cognovisti; sed hoc judicium vocatur 'experimentale.' Et non solum homines, immo aequaliter brutae hujus modi judicio utuntur; unde propter hoc canis timet lapidem si aliquis laesit ipsum. Et omnia praedicta principia sunt singularia, et sunt principia in arte vel in prudentia, et non in scientia speculativa vel demonstrativa" (ibid.).

*and experientiam*). To arrive at a universal knowledge such as "every fire is hot," "every magnet attracts iron," or "all rhubarb purges bile," the following steps are required: (1) In the past, you will have had many a *sensation* that "fire is hot" and (2) all these sensations have been stored in *memory*. (3) You will have considered this phenomenon in many diverse circumstances—that is to say, you will have compared your current sensation with similar sensations you have had in the past and which you have stored in memory—and your *experience* (i.e. experimental judgment) has never revealed any factual counterinstance in any of your past sensations, nor any reason why there should be a counterinstance in another. When these three conditions are met, your intellect is bound to assert the universal knowledge "every fire is hot" and will consider it to be evident—not because of a necessary conclusion, but simply on the basis of your intellect's natural inclination toward truth. The induction over all of your past experiences works as follows: "This fire is hot, and this," and so on with many others. Finally, the intellect completes this sequence by adding the clause "and so in all other instances," thus considering it to be universally true that "fire is hot."[16]

Buridan is clearly aware of what today is called the "problem of induction": no experiment, however extensive, can render more than a finite number of observations; therefore, the statement of a natural law always transcends experience. In the twentieth century, this problem was most prominently discussed by Karl Popper in his *The Logic of Scientific Discovery* (*Logik der Forschung*).[17]

Buridan describes the problem of induction in the following terms: a universal proposition such as "every fire is hot" is not valid due to a necessary consequence. Even the sum of all past experiences is not sufficient to allow us to infer a universal conclusion, for there are potentially many other experiences that have not been taken into consideration. Therefore, such a universal proposition

---

16. "Alia principia indigent inductione ad hoc quod fiant evidentia, et illa principia sunt universalia, ut quod omnis ignis est calidus, et quod omne rheubarbarum est purgativum cholerae. Illa enim principia sunt nobis nota per inductionem supponentem sensum, memoriam et experientiam. Cum enim saepe tu vidisti rheubarbarum purgare choleram et de hoc memoriam habuisti, et quia in multis circumstantiis diversis [hoc] considerasti, numquam tamen invenisti instantiam, tunc intellectus, non propter necessariam consequentiam, sed solum ex naturali ejus inclinatione ad verum, assentit universali principio et capit ipsum tamquam evidens principium per talem inductionem 'hoc rheubarbarum purgabat choleram, et illud,' et sic de multis aliis, quae sensata fuerunt et de quibus memoria habetur; tunc intellectus supplet istam clausulam 'et sic de singulis,' eo quod numquam vidit instantiam, licet consideravit in multis circumstantiis, nec apparet sibi ratio nec dissimilitudo quare debeat esse instantia, et tunc concludit universale principium" (ibid.). See also the corresponding passage in Buridan's *Summulae de dialectica*, 6.1.4, trans. G. Klima (New Haven: Yale University Press, 2001), 396. To bring it into line with the previous examples, I replaced "all rhubarb purges bile" with "every fire is hot."

17. Originally published in German in 1934. First published in English in 1959. See also Karl Popper, "Conjectural Knowledge: My Solution of the Problem of Induction," in *Objective Knowledge: An Evolutionary Approach* (Oxford: Clarendon Press, 1972), 1–31.

is not called a "conclusion," but a "principle" in the demonstrative sciences; and it is called an "immediate proposition" because it cannot be proved by a necessary conclusion. Nevertheless, such a universal proposition is accepted by the intellect due to the latter's natural inclination toward truth if the sum of past experiences is sufficient to infer the clause "and so in all other instances."[18]

Buridan does not explicitly mention higher animals here, and so the question remains as to what extent higher animals can perform such inductions. Obviously, they cannot utter the proposition "Every fire is hot," but this does not exclude the possibility that animals can mentally represent this kind of knowledge in a similar or even in the same way as humans do. The question as to how animals mentally represent such knowledge is particularly difficult to answer since we cannot easily judge from their behavior whether they possess particular knowledge ("this fire is hot") or universal knowledge ("every fire is hot"). Animals will hesitate to approach a particular fire in both cases.

To find a solution, I will first show that Buridan maintains that animals are capable of universal reference in the realm of conceptual knowledge. In our context, we may define conceptual knowledge as the ability to represent mentally an individual object of sensation as a member of a class or universal category or, conversely, to signify a plurality of individual objects by a single mental entity.

## CONCEPTUAL AND PROPOSITIONAL KNOWLEDGE

During the Middle Ages, it was generally assumed that the capacity to form universal concepts is characteristic of and unique to human thinking. While animal souls were considered to be material forms, that is to say, educed from the potency of matter, the human intellective soul was taken to be immaterial and immortal. Thomas Aquinas, for example, used the ability to form universal concepts as the key argument in his demonstration that the human intellect is immaterial and hence immortal.[19]

---

18. "Et vos bene videtis quod illa non est perfecta probatio virtute consequentiae necessariae. Quia omnia quae sensata fuerunt non sufficiunt ad inferendum conclusionem universalem, quoniam praeter illa sunt multa alia; et si sufficiunt cum ista clausula 'et sic de aliis,' tamen illa est accepta per intellectum sine probatione quae sit necessaria consequentia. Et ideo talis universalis propositio vocatur in scientiis demonstrativis non 'conclusio' sed 'principium'; et vocatur 'propositio immediata' quia caret medio per quod posset probari illatione necessaria. Et sic habetis declaratum quo modo per inductionem, propter naturalem inclinationem intellectus ad verum, probatur propositio immediata" (Buridan, *Quaestiones in Analytica Priora*).

19. See Thomas Aquinas, *Disputed Questions on the Soul*, q. 14: "It is also evident that an intellective principle of this kind is not composed of matter and form, because species are received in it in a wholly immaterial way. This is made clear from the fact that the intellect is concerned with universals, which are considered in abstraction from matter and from material conditions" (Thomas Aquinas, *Questions on the Soul* [*Quaestiones de Anima*], trans. James H. Robb [Milwaukee: Marquette University Press, 1984], 177):

Buridan, however, argues against this common opinion, which, as he says, is held by many contemporaries and nearly all ancient commentators (*multi et quasi omnes expositores antiqui*), against the opinion, that is, that the human intellect apprehends universally because it is immaterial and unextended. In two parallel and complementary texts from his *Questions on Aristotle's Physics* and *Questions on Aristotle's De anima* respectively, Buridan shows that the human intellect is capable of universal cognition even if we assume that it is a material form.[20]

What Buridan outlines here is a theory of representative likeness or similarity. According to Buridan, universal cognition is not constituted by directly referring to something universal but by a process of abstraction that finally results in a common concept (*conceptus communis*), which, while existing singularly in the intellect, becomes universal by indifferently representing or signifying all members of the same species. Thus, for Buridan the universality of concepts does not consist in their mode of existence, but in their capacity to signify a plurality of individuals.

Summarizing his theory of universal cognition, Buridan finally credits Alexander of Aphrodisias as the most famous ancient commentator who upheld a materialistic theory of universal cognition, emphasizing that Alexander actually permitted that this faculty in humans be called "intellect" on account of its excellence and nobility over the cognitive powers of brutes.

In a series of four questions contained in his *Questions on Aristotle's De anima*, Buridan defends Alexander of Aphrodisias, who held that the human intellect is a generated and corruptible material form, educed from the potency of matter (*educta de potentia materiae*), extended like matter, just like the soul

---

"Manifestum est etiam quod huiusmodi intellectiuum principium non est aliquid ex materia et forma compositum, quia species omnino recipiuntur in ipso immaterialiter. Quod declaratur ex hoc quod intellectus est uniuersalium, que considerantur in abstractione a materia et a materialibus conditionibus." (*Opera Omnia* [editio Leonina] XXIV, 1: *Quaestiones disputatae de anima*, ed. B.-C. Bazán [Rome: Commissio Leonina/Paris: CERF, 1996], 126, 210–216)

20. Buridan's question is formulated in the following way: Can something extended and material (*extensus et materialis*) have universal knowledge? Buridan did not devote an entire question to this problem. Instead, his considerations form a digression within his question as to "Whether universals are more known to us than singulars" (*Utrum universalia sunt nobis notiora singularibus*), which is discussed in the first book of his *Questions on Aristotle's Physics* (*Quaestiones in octo libros Physicorum* [ultima lectura], I, q. 7). A similar question (*Utrum intellectus prius intelligat universale quam singulare vel e converso*) and a similar digression can be found in his *Questions on Aristotle's De anima* (*Quaestiones in tres libros De anima* [ultima lectura], III, q. 8). Surprisingly, the question is more elaborate in Buridan's commentary on Aristotle's *Physics*, and he expressly refers to this fact in his commentary on Aristotle's *De anima*. For an edition and analysis of these texts, see Olaf Pluta, "John Buridan on Universal Knowledge," *Bochumer Philosophisches Jahrbuch für Antike und Mittelalter* 7 (2002): 25–46.

of animals—"like the soul of a cow or a dog" (*sicut anima bovis aut anima canis*)—and hence mortal.[21]

Aristotle and Averroes had claimed that if the intellect were educed from the potency of matter and extended, it would be unable to apprehend anything except singularly and individually, just as the senses, and it would cognize nothing universally. Thomas Aquinas had used this argument in his *Disputed Questions on the Soul* to demonstrate that the human soul is immaterial and hence immortal.[22]

To this argument, Buridan replies on behalf of Alexander that an extended power (*virtus extensa*) is indeed carried to its object in a universal way (*modo universali*), just as a thirsty horse or dog does not desire this water or that water, but indifferently any water whatsoever. If an extended power such as the appetite (*appetitus sensitivus*) desires in a universal way, we may readily assume that the human intellect, if taken to be a material and extended form, can cognize universally.[23]

Buridan clearly affirms that animals, and dogs in particular, can refer to things universally. This also means that they can mentally represent a particular bowl of water as a member of the class or universal category "water." We do not know if the mental representation of dogs is identical to human thought in this respect, but we can readily assume that dogs can form a simile of a universal concept.[24]

After having dealt with conceptual knowledge in animals, we now come to the most intriguing question, namely whether or not animals can possess universal knowledge in the strict sense, that is universal propositional knowledge such as "Every fire is hot." As we have seen above, such knowledge is based on induction and presupposes sensation, memory, and experience.

Once again I would like to emphasize that animals obviously do not possess propositional knowledge in the sense that they could utter propositions such

---

21. For a detailed analysis of these four questions, see Olaf Pluta, "Persecution and the Art of Writing. The Parisian Statute of April 1, 1272, and Its Philosophical Consequences," in *Chemins de la pensée médiévale. Études offertes à Zénon Kaluza*, ed. Paul J. J. M. Bakker (Turnhout: Brepols, 2002), 563–585.

22. See note 19.

23. John Buridan, *Questions on Aristotle's De anima*, book III, q.3: "Ad quartam rationem dixisset Alexander quod virtus extensa bene fertur in obiectum suum modo universali, sicut appetitus ipsius equi. Equus enim sitiens appetit aquam, et non determinate hanc vel illam, sed quamlibet indifferenter appetit. Ideo quamcumque invenit, eam bibit." See also the following parallel passage from his *Questions on Aristotle's Physics*, book I, q.7: "appetitus sensitivus ita est extensus et materialis sicut sensus, et tamen equus et canis per famem et sitim appetunt modo universali, non enim hanc aquam vel hanc avenam magis quam illam, sed quamlibet indifferenter; ideo quaecumque eis praesentetur, bibunt eam vel comedunt."

24. Buridan would not claim that a dog (or any other animal) is capable of developing a geometry by precisely defining a circle or by deriving a theorem such as "The center of a circle lies on the perpendicular bisector of any chord." However, Buridan would affirm that dogs can refer to circles or circular objects in a universal way.

as 'Every fire is hot.' Nevertheless, they may be able to represent such universal knowledge mentally.

We already know that animals are capable of having sensation, memory, and experience (in the sense of experimental judgment). Higher animals such as dogs may be able to mentally perform the induction that is required for universal knowledge in the strict sense.

The answer to this problem can be found in another redaction of Buridan's *Questions on Aristotle's De anima*.[25] This redaction has not yet been studied thoroughly, even though, if the sheer number of surviving manuscripts is any indication, it was widely read.[26]

Here, Buridan first talks about the mental abilities of humans and apes; please note that humans and apes are grouped together here and thus stand apart from other higher species of animals. Buridan then continues to say that "dogs and other animals are similarly capable of thinking in a logical way, albeit not in as sophisticated and complete a way as man or ape. This is obvious, for if a dog sees his home and wishes to go there and encounters a large pit on the direct route, it does not enter the pit, but searches for another way, even if it is longer. The dog would not do this unless he reasoned logically (*nisi ratiocinaretur et syllogizaret*) that it would not be good to fall into the pit."[27]

Buridan here refers to a well-known example, namely a dog's use of logical reasoning—Buridan speaks of *ratiocinari* and *syllogizare*—in determining which way to go. This ability of dogs had been known since antiquity.[28] The Stoic philosopher Chrysippus,[29] for example, describes a hunting dog's behavior as

---

25. See Bernd Michael, "Johannes Buridan: Studien zu seinem Leben, seinen Werken und zur Rezeption seiner Theorien im Europa des späten Mittelalters," PhD diss., Berlin, 1985, 684–689.

26. Michael lists fifteen manuscripts for this redaction (B) and nineteen manuscripts for the final redaction (*tertia sive ultima lectura*) (C).

27. "canes et alia animalia ratiocinantur et syllogizant, quamvis non ita subtiliter ac complete sicut homo vel simia. Quod apparet, quia, si canis videt dominum suum et vult ire ad ipsum et in directa linea inveniat magnam foveam, non intrabit in illam, sed quaerit aliam viam, licet longiorem, quod non faceret, nisi ratiocinaretur et syllogizaret, quod non est bonum cadere in foveam et cetera." (Paris, Bibliothèque Nationale, Cod. lat. 15888, f. 70ra) See Olaf Pluta, "Der Alexandrismus an den Universitäten im späten Mittelalter," *Bochumer Philosophisches Jahrbuch für Antike und Mittelalter* 1 (1996): 81–109, at 95. For a description of this manuscript, see Michael, "Johannes Buridan," 586–587.

28. The most important ancient text relating to animals is Porphyry's *On Abstinence from Animal Food*, which contains a wealth of arguments from other authors. See Porphyry, *On Abstinence from Killing Animals*, trans. Gillian Clark (Ithaca, N.Y.: Cornell University Press, 2000). For a general defense of animals, see Plutarch's treatise *Animals Use Reason* (*Bruta Animalia Ratione Uti*) 985d–992e.

29. Chrysippus was the head of the Stoic school from 232 to 207 BC. For a comprehensive account of his philosophy, see Josiah B. Gould, *The Philosophy of Chrysippus* (Leiden: Brill, 1971).

follows. When the dog comes to a three-way crossroads, he is said "virtually" (*dunamei*) to go through a syllogism (*logizesthai*) about his prey. "The animal went either this way, or that way, or the other way. But not this way, or that way. So that way."[30] To come to a decision, the dog may, for example, refer to the absence of footprints or scent; and he may make use of previous hunting experiences stored in memory.[31]

This example appears, with slight variations, in many places. In Philo and Aelian, the hunting dog comes to a pit (closely resembling Buridan's example) and has to decide if the prey turned left or right or went straight ahead and crossed the pit. Sextus Empiricus, who ascribes the example to Chrysippus, even specifies the syllogism: "the dog makes use of the fifth complex indemonstrable syllogism."[32] According to Stoic logic, this syllogism was of the form "Either A or B or C; but neither A nor B; therefore C."[33]

The dog cannot, of course, verbalize his decision or do so in propositional form, but he may mentally represent the three possibilities in a manner that may be akin to the way humans would try to figure out which way to go. We do not in fact know if dogs possess propositional knowledge, but we should not

---

30. Sextus Empiricus, *Outlines of Pyrrhonism* 1.69; Plutarch, *On Animal Cleverness* (*De Sollertia Animalium*) 969a–b; Philo *De Animalibus* 45; Porphyry *On Abstinence from Animal Food* 3.6; Aelian *On the Nature of Animals* 6.59; Basil *Hexaemeron* 9.4. See Richard Sorabji, *Animal Minds and Human Morals: The Origins of the Western Debate* (Ithaca, N.Y.: Cornell University Press, 1993), 26. See also Urs Dierauer, *Tier und Mensch im Denken der Antike. Studien zur Tierpsychologie, Anthropologie und Ethik* (Amsterdam: B. R. Grüner, 1977), 253–273. Thomas Aquinas refers to Chrysippus's dog in *Summa Theologiae* Ia IIae, q. 13, a. 2, objection 3: "We see this plainly, in wonderful cases of sagacity manifested in the works of various animals, such as bees, spiders, and dogs. For a hound in following a stag, on coming to a crossroad, tries by scent whether the stag has passed by the first or the second road: and if he find that the stag has not passed there, being thus assured, takes to the third road without trying the scent; as though he were reasoning by way of exclusion, arguing that the stag must have passed by this way, since he did not pass by the others, and there is no other road. Therefore it seems that irrational animals are able to choose."

31. The logical reasoning of Buridan's dog on his way home or Chrysippus's hunting dog—"not this way, or that way. So that way"—is very similar to the "fast mapping" ability of Rico mentioned above. When Rico hears a new word, he maps it—by excluding a number of familiar objects—to the single new object within sight, apparently appreciating, as young children do, that new words tend to refer to objects that do not already have names (see Bloom, "Can a Dog Learn a Word?" 1605).

32. Sextus Empiricus, *Outlines of Pyrrhonism*, 1.69, trans. R. G. Bury (Cambridge, Mass.: Harvard University Press, 1955), 43.

33. The Stoics had five syllogisms that they termed "indemonstrable," since they required no proof themselves but served to prove others. The syllogism was called "complex" because of its multiple disjunctions. This special form of the fifth indemonstrable syllogism of Stoic logic is discussed by Michael Frede, *Die stoische Logik* (Göttingen: Vandenhoeck & Ruprecht, 1974), 153–157; Chrysippus's dog is mentioned at 155. See also Benson Mates, *Stoic Logic* (Berkeley: University of California Press, 1953/1973), 80.

simply dismiss the possibility of propositional attitudes in animals, provided their behavior can be analyzed by us in intentional terms.[34]

Even according to Aristotle, we would have to grant animals the capacity to engage in practical syllogism or reasoning (*sullogizesthai*). In the case of the thirsty horse or dog, appetite says "I must drink," and perception says "This is a drink." The linking of the premises with the conclusion is a causal process as appears from Aristotle's discussion of human practical syllogisms in the *Nicomachean Ethics*.[35] And there is no apparent reason why animals should not be capable of such causal processes. Thus, even if animals do not "explicitly" go through a practical syllogism, this fact does not suffice to justify the conclusion that they do not think logically.[36]

How can the blind man's guide dog learn to refuse the command to cross the road in certain circumstances in which it would be unsafe to proceed, something termed "intelligent disobedience"? How do sheepdog and shepherd communicate in order to protect the sheep day and night and keep the flock together—a particularly interesting example of interspecific communication? Dogs certainly do have amazing abilities.

But the question still remains: Do dogs possess universal propositional knowledge? According to Buridan, this would require that dogs can perform an induction over all past experiences such as "this fire was hot, and this," and so on, and finally arrive at the universal propositional knowledge that "every fire is hot." We already know that dogs can perform logical reasoning, or to be more precise, that they can make use of syllogistic reasoning.

In another passage from his *Questions on Aristotle's Prior Analytics*, Buridan does indeed show that syllogistic reasoning is, in fact, sufficient for performing an induction. Buridan claims that every induction can be reduced to a syllogism if a supplement is added. If an induction is thus reduced to a syllogism, it is, in fact, a valid consequence. Buridan starts his argument with a distinction between different kinds of consequence. Consequences are divided into formal consequences and material consequences; material consequences are further subdivided into simple conclusions and conclusions "*ut nunc*."[37]

---

34. See Daniel Dennett, "Conditions of Personhood," in *The Identities of Persons*, ed. A. Oksenberg Rorty (Berkeley: University of California Press, 1976), esp. 181–187.

35. Aristotle, *Nichomachean Ethics* 7.3, 1147a24–28.

36. See Sorabji, *Animal Minds*, 88. According to Buridan, there is no inconsistency in attributing semantic complexity to ontologically simple mental acts (see Buridan's *Summulae de dialectica*, xxxviii). For Buridan, a syllogism is a simple mental act within the soul, even though it is a complex semantical structure. Such a simple mental act may easily be possible for animals, even though they cannot express it by means of language.

37. "Notandum est primo quod consequentia dividitur in materialem et formalem. Et vocatur 'formalis' quae in omnibus terminis valet, vel cui omnis consequentia valet sibi consimilis in forma. Sed consequentia materialis est quae valet gratia terminorum, ita quod in multis aliis terminis non valet, quamvis consimilis forma observetur.

According to Buridan, no induction is a formal consequence—unless it is reduced to a syllogism by adding a supplemental proposition. For example, if a common term A has only two referents, namely B and C, then a valid induction would be "B runs and C runs; therefore, all A's run." Now, if we replace the common term A with "homo" and the two referents B and C with "Socrates" and "Plato," then it is obvious that the consequence does not hold "Socrates runs and Plato runs; therefore, all humans run." Thus, the consequence is not formal, that is to say, valid independently of the terms used.[38]

An induction that is reduced to a syllogism is a formal consequence in the same sense as a universal syllogism of the first figure (*syllogismus in primo modo primae figurae*). For example, let us assume the following induction: "Socrates runs, Plato runs, and John runs; therefore, all humans run." If you were to add the proposition that "all humans are Socrates, Plato, and John," then you would arrive at the following valid consequence: "Socrates runs, Plato runs, and John runs; all humans are Socrates, Plato, and John; therefore, all humans run," because "all humans" would be equivalent to "all that is Socrates, Plato, and John"—provided that there is no equivocation and more than one person is called by this name.[39]

---

Et cum hoc vos debetis supponere quid in proposito debeat dici pertinere ad formam consequentiae. Dicendum est quod numerus terminorum et numerus propositionum, et omnia syncategoremata, et ordo terminorum, propositionum et syncategorematum, omnia haec pertinent ad formam consequentiae; consequentiae enim non erunt consimiles in forma si in aliquo praedictorum est discrepantia. Sed ad materiam consequentiae, prout in proposito loquimur, pertinent solum termini categoremextici, scilicet subjecta et praedicata propositionum categoricarum. Si ergo aliqua consequentia sit formalis, numquam mutabitur nec falsificabitur propter mutationem dictae materiae, scilicet dictorum terminorum, retentis praedictis quae ad formam dicebantur pertinere.

Deinde materialis consequentia dividitur in consequentiam simplicem et in consequentiam ut nunc. Et vocatur consequentia 'simplex' quae, quocumque casu possibili posito, numquam possibile est antecedens esse verum sine consequente. Sed consequentia 'ut nunc' vocatur quando rebus stantibus ut nunc stant non est possibile antecedens esse verum sine consequente, licet simpliciter hoc sit possibile" (Buridan, *Quaestiones in Analytica Priora*, lib. II, q. 29a).

38. "Et tunc breviter pono conclusiones. Prima conclusio est quod nulla inductio est consequentia formalis nisi per supplementum sit reducta ad syllogismum. Et causa est quia retenta forma consequentiae, tamen possent sic mutari termini quod consequentia non valeret, immo antecedens esset verum sine consequente. Verbi gratia, si iste terminus communis 'A' habeat solum duo singularia, scilicet 'B' et 'C,' tunc erit inductio sic 'B currit et C currit; igitur omne A currit'; et tunc mutes terminos, et ponas pro 'A' 'hominem,' et pro 'B' et 'C' 'Socratem' et 'Platonem,' tunc manifestum est quod consequentia non valebit; manifestum est enim quod non sequitur 'Socrates currit et Plato currit; ergo omnis homo currit,' et tamen manent omnia consimilia quae ad formam consequentiae pertinere dicebantur" (ibid.).

39. "Secunda conclusio est quod inductio per supplementum reducta ad syllogismum est consequentia bona et formalis, eo modo quo syllogismus in primo modo primae figurae est formalis. Quia sic inductio fit syllogismus in primo modo primae figurae, supponendo unam propositionem in qua de subjecto conclusionis praedicentur omnia singularia sub disjunctione in quibus fit inductio. Verbi gratia, fiat inductio sic 'Socrates currit, Plato currit et Johannes currit,' tunc addatur ista propositio quod omnis homo est Socrates, Plato vel Johannes, et

No induction, however, can be a valid simple material consequence, that is to say, a conclusion where the antecedent can never be true without the consequent being true as well, if the singular premises refer to the realm of generation and corruption. For example, let us assume that there are only three horses, namely Brunellus, Morellus, and Favellus. Then the following induction would be valid: "Brunellus runs, Morellus runs, and Favellus runs; therefore, all horses run." But it would be possible that another horse will be generated that does not run. In this case, if the three other horses still run, the antecedent would still be true, but the consequent would be false.[40]

In the given case, that is, in the case of the singular premises referring to the realm of generation or corruption, an induction can, nevertheless, be a valid material consequence "*ut nunc,*" that is to say, a consequence where the antecedent—as things now stand (*rebus stantibus ut nunc stant*)—can be true without the consequent being true as well. A simple material consequence can be reduced to a formal consequence by adding a necessary proposition; a material consequence "*ut nunc,*" however, can be reduced to a formal consequence by simply adding a contingent proposition that is true.[41]

---

sequitur, in prima figura, quod omnis homo currit. Et est in syllogismo major extremitas 'currit,' minor extremitas 'homo,' et medium est haec tria singularia 'Socrates,' 'Plato' et 'Johannes'; et in majori propositione hoc medium sumebatur universaliter, quia copulatio habet modum distributionis (sicut enim ad terminum distributum sequitur quodlibet singulare, ita ad copulationem plurium sequitur quodlibet illorum), et etiam quia ad istam 'Socrates currit, Plato currit et Johannes currit' sequitur haec universalis 'omne quod est Socrates, Plato vel Johannes currit,' nisi sit aequivocatio quod plures vocentur eodem nomine singulari; et tunc, facta illa resolutione, manifesta est forma syllogistica" (ibid.).

40. "Tertia conclusio est quod in individuis corruptibilibus si non sunt praemissae nisi singulares, numquam inductio est bona consequentia simpliciter. Et hoc probabat prima ratio quae in principio quaestionis fuit adducta."

"1. Arguitur quod non: quia consequentia non est bona cujus antecedens potest esse verum consequente exsistente falso; sed sic est de inductione; igitur . . . et cetera. Major est nota de se. Et minor probatur, ponendo quod modo sint solum tres equi, Brunellus, Morellus et Favellus; et erit inductio sufficiens sic dicendo 'Brunellus currit, Favellus currit et Morellus currit; ergo omnis equus currit'; modo constat quod antecedens compositum ex illis tribus praemissis potest esse verum consequente exsistente falso; probatur, ponendo quod generetur quartus equus, qui non currat et tamen illi tres adhuc currant; in hoc enim casu, qui est possibilis, remanebit illud antecedens verum, et tamen consequens erit falsum, quia non omnis equus curret" (ibid.).

41. "Quarta conclusio ponenda est, quod in dictis individuis potest esse consequentia bona ut nunc. Unde in casu posito prius erat bona consequentia ut nunc 'Brunellus currit, Favellus currit, Morellus currit; ergo omnis equus currit,' quia rebus stantibus ut nunc stant, scilicet quando non sunt plures equi, non potest antecedens esse verum sine consequente. Et hoc etiam probatur. Quia consequentia materialis simpliciter et consequentia materialis ut nunc in hoc conveniunt quod utraque per additionem potest reduci ad formalem; sed differunt quia consequentia simpliciter potest reduci ad formalem per additionem propositionis necessariae vel propositionum necessariarum, sed consequentia ut nunc est bona si possit reduci ad formalem per additionem propositionis verae, licet contingentis. Modo sic erat in proposito, quoniam haec consequentia est formalis, ut dicebatur 'Brunellus currit, Morellus currit, Favel-

The interesting point here is that any kind of induction can be reduced to a syllogism. When the intellect performs an induction such as "this fire is hot, and this," and so on, and when it then completes this sequence by adding the clause "and so in all other instances," the intellect is in fact adding the required supplement, which reduces the induction to a valid syllogism and thus comes to the valid conclusion that "every fire is hot."[42]

According to Buridan, dogs can perform logical syllogistic reasoning, and every induction can be reduced to a syllogism. We may thus conclude that dogs can perform such an induction and mentally represent universal propositional knowledge such as "every fire is hot." We do not know if dogs do in fact represent universal propositional knowledge in the same way as humans do—this would require a window into their consciousness—but we should not easily dismiss the possibility that they can.[43]

Mental representation in animals might in fact be quite different from ours. As Wittgenstein put it later in his *Philosophical Investigations*: "If a lion could talk, we could not understand him."[44]

---

lus currit, et omnis equus est Brunellus, Morellus vel Favellus; igitur omnis equus currit,' et minor quae apponitur est vera secundum casum positum, licet sit contingens; igitur erat bona consequentia ut nunc" (ibid.).

42. In his *Summulae de dialectica*, Buridan expresses some doubt if every induction can be reduced to a syllogism. Sometimes, it may be impossible to induce "based on all the singulars because of their infinity or exceedingly large number" (*Summulae de dialectica*, 6.1.5, 398). Buridan continues: "Now if we were to say that the clause 'and so on for the others' should not be added in the reduction, then the situation is such that the induction is performed over all the singulars or such that this is at least not impossible." In fact, one may argue that adding the clause "and so on for the others" constitutes a *petitio principii* if the number of singulars is infinite or exceedingly large.

Buridan replies that the validity of the statement "every fire is hot" is not based on the possibility of reducing such an induction to a syllogism—for practical reasons, it may be impossible to perform the induction over all the singulars—"but because of the intellect's natural inclination toward truth" (ibid., 399). Formally speaking, an induction (and its reduction to a syllogism) requires that the antecedent consists of all the singulars, but because of the intellect's natural inclination toward truth it is sufficient to enumerate "as many as would suffice to generate belief in the universal conclusion that is inferred" (ibid., 400). Consequently, any kind of induction can be reduced to a syllogism.

43. Buridan concedes that (1) animals have *propositional* knowledge, such as "This fire is hot" (particular knowledge), and that (2) animals have *universal* knowledge in the case of "water" or "fire" (conceptual knowledge). There is no reason why animals should not have *universal propositional* knowledge as well.

44. Wittgenstein, *Philosophische Untersuchungen/Philosophical Investigations*, 223/190.

# The Intersubjective Sameness of Mental Concepts in Late Scholastic Thought

STEPHAN MEIER-OESER

The short introductory remarks of Aristotle's *De interpretatione*, as unimposing as they may appear, have provided the starting point of some of the most intense and long-lasting debates in the history of semantics and epistemology.[1] Quite a number of these discussions are more or less closely related to the Stagirite's well-known statement that "mental concepts are the same for all" (*eaedem omnibus passiones animae sunt*). What at a first glance might appear to be but an arcane issue in the scholastic exegesis of Aristotle, i.e. the attempt to provide a reasonable interpretation and account of his thesis of the intersubjective sameness of concepts (henceforth referred to as ISC), on a closer look, turns out to be historically connected with topics that, from different points of view and different perspectives, have been identified as crucial for the foundation of modern semantics as well as for the origin of modern analytical philosophy.

Many late nineteenth- and early twentieth-century authors, disapproving of what they called the "magical theory of names"[2] or, hardly more adequately, the "nominalistic view of language," considered it as "one of the glories of Locke's philosophy that he established the fact that names are not the signs of things, but in their origins always the signs of concepts."[3] While it had been "familiar to the naive thinking to see the word meaning as nothing but the thing designated by the word," as Meinong's disciple Eduard Martinak held, this "naive correlation of a thing and a word" was vanquished by Locke, who in his *Essay Concerning Human Understanding* "unremittingly pointed to the fact that . . . there is always and with strict necessity an idea (representation/*Vorstellung*)

---

1. I am referring especially to *De interpretatione* I, 16a2–8: "Now spoken sounds are symbols of affections in the soul, and written marks symbols of spoken sounds. And just as written marks are not the same for all men, neither are spoken sounds. But what these are in the first place signs of—affections of the soul—are the same for all; and what these affections are likenesses of—actual things—are also the same." *The Complete Works of Aristotle*, ed. Jonathan Barnes, vol. 1 (Princeton: Princeton University Press, 1984).

2. Cf. C. K. Ogden and I. A. Richards, *The Meaning of Meaning* (New York: Harcourt, Brace and Co., 1956), 9.

3. F. M. Müller, *The Science of Thought* (Oxford: Longmans, Green and Co., 1888), 77; cf. L. Noiré, *Logos. Ursprung und Wesen der Begriffe* (Leipzig: Engelmann, 1885), 21.

inserted between the thing and the word.... And in this sense the word-meaning, up to the present day, is tantamount to the representation we have of the pertaining thing."[4] Although it is not at all clear precisely which authors were alleged to have advocated the "magical theory of names," it is true that, in the succession of Hobbes, Descartes, and Locke, postscholastic semantics was dominated by the view that "the meanings of words ... are always conceptions of the mind,"[5] so that words, as "conventional signs of thoughts" (*signes d'institution des pensées*),[6] "in their primary or immediate Signification, stand for nothing, but the Ideas in the Mind of him who uses them."[7]

While this position was extolled by its promoters as overcoming the "magical theory of names," it has itself become, especially since the late nineteenth century, increasingly condemned by those who consider it a form of "psychologism" and a disastrous implementation of some insurmountable semantic and epistemological "subjectivism." This change of appraisal was based on a fundamental alteration in the notions of idea, concept, and thought that came about together with the advancement of empiricist epistemology. For whereas mental concepts or simple apprehensions, that is, the bare conceptions of things, were considered by the scholastics to be basic mental units (acts or qualities) simply representing or signifying the *quod quid est* of the object apprehended, they were seen as structurally complex by empiricist epistemology, which restricted the notion of "simple idea" to elementary sensory perceptions. The *conceptus simplex* of the Aristotelian tradition (as, e.g., the concept of man) was thus transformed into a (very) "complex idea."[8] In this sense, for instance, David Hartley in the mid–eighteenth century spoke of "clusters of ideas"[9] and regarded

---

4. E. Martinak, *Psychologische und pädagogische Abhandlungen*, ed. E. Mally and O. Tumlirz (Graz: Leykam, 1929), 129.

5. T. Hobbes, *On Human Nature*, ed. G. Molesworth (London: J. Bohn, 1839–45), 4, 28.

6. A. Arnauld and P. Nicole, *L'Art de penser*, I, 4, ed. P. Clair and F. Girbal (Paris: Presses Universitaires de France, 1965) 54; cf. G. de Cordemoy: *Discours physique de la parole* (1666), ed. P. Clair and F. Girbal (Paris: Presses Universitaires de France, 1968), 209.

7. J. Locke, *An Essay Concerning Human Understanding* (Oxford: Oxford University Press, 1975) II, 2, 2, 405sq; cf. II, 11, 9, 159; II, 31, 6, 378; III, 1, 2, 402; III, 4, 1, 420; III, 4, 6, 422. For further references, see S. Meier-Oeser, "Signifikation," in *Historisches Wörterbuch der Philosophie 9*, ed. J. Ritter and K. Gründer (Basel: Schwabe, 1995), 759–795, esp. 785 ff.

8. Cf. John Locke, *An Essay Concerning Human Understanding*, II, 23, 14: "our specifick Ideas of Substances are nothing else but a Collection of a certain number of simple Ideas, considered as united in one thing. These Ideas of Substances, though they are commonly called simple Apprehensions, and the Names of them simple Terms; yet in effect, are complex and compounded"; II, 12, 3: "Ideas thus made up of several simple ones put together, I call complex; such as are beauty, gratitude, a man, an army, the universe; which though complicated of various simple ideas, or complex ideas made up of simple ones, yet are, when the mind pleases, considered each by itself, as one entire thing, and signified by one name."

9. D. Hartley, *Observations on Man* (1749; Gainesville, Fla.: Scholars' Facsimiles and Reprints, 1966), I, 74: "the simple Ideas of Sensation must run into Clusters and Combina-

it as the "very Essence" of intellectual ideas "to be *complex.*"[10] According to Destutt de Tracy, one of the leading figures of the influential French school of *idéologues*, this complexity is such that all our ideas, except elementary sensory perceptions, are "extremely composed assemblages" made up not only of many simple ideas but also of judgments.[11]

It is understandable that under such conditions the intersubjective sameness of mental concepts (ISC) must lose a good deal of its plausibility. Already Locke, affirming something like the ISC with regard to simple sensible ideas,[12] considered it a mere supposition that any idea one man has is "conformable to that in other men's minds, called by the same common name; e.g., when the mind intends or judges its ideas of justice, temperance, religion, to be the same with what other men give those names to."[13] Later on the ISC became more and more subject to doubt. "No one is thinking on a certain word," Wilhelm von Humboldt claimed, "precisely what another does. . . . Any understanding, therefore, is always a not-understanding, and any accordance in thoughts and feelings is a divergence."[14] Where emphasis is placed on the claim that "it is impossible that one and the same sign should have the same value for all those who are using it and even for each of them at different moments of time,"[15] a view that even found its way into some late nineteenth-century neo-Thomist textbooks on logic,[16] the foundations of logic as well as a publicly accessible notion of meaning become problematic.

---

tions, by Association; and . . . each of these will, at last, coalesce into one complex Idea, by the Approach and Commixture of the several compounding Parts."

10. Ibid., I, 56.

11. A. L. C. Destutt de Tracy, *Éléments d'idéologie*, vol. 1 (Paris: Courcier, 1804), 375 ff.: "toutes nos idées sont extrêmement composées . . . toutes sont [376] des assemblages d'une foule de souvenirs et de jugemens."

12. Cf. Locke, *Essay Concerning Human Understanding* II, 32, 15: "I am . . . very apt to think, that the sensible Ideas, produced by any Object in different Men's Minds, are most commonly very near and undiscernibly alike."

13. Ibid., II, 32, 5, 385.

14. W. von Humboldt, *Ueber die Verschiedenheit des menschlichen Sprachbaues und ihren Einfluss auf die geistige Entwicklung des Menschengeschlechts* (1830), in *Gesammelte Schriften*, ed. A. Leitzmann (Berlin: B. Behr Verlag, 1903–1936), VII:64 ff.: "Keiner denkt bei dem Wort gerade, was der andere. . . . Alles Verstehen ist daher immer zugleich ein Nicht-Verstehen, alle Übereinstimmung in Gedanken und Gefühlen zugleich ein Auseinandergehen."

15. Destutt de Tracy, *Éléments d'idéologie*, 2:405: "il est impossible que le même signe ait exactement la même valeur pour tous ceux qui l'emploient, et même pour chacun d'eux, dans les différens momens où il l'emploie."

16. Cf. Tilmann Pesch, *Institutiones logicae*, § 110 (Freiburg: Herder, 1888), 72: "Vocabula per se significant conceptus non audientium, sed loquentium. Cum experientia teste diversi sint in diversis hominibus pro diversa cognitione de una eademque re conceptus . . . necesse est, ut eadem vox ab aliis pronuntiata aliam etiam vim habeat et significationem. . . . Ex quo evidens est in cuiuslibet ore eodem vocabulo alium tegi conceptum et exprimi multum discrepantem."

As a reaction against this semantic and epistemological "psychologism," authors such as Bolzano, Brentano, Frege, and the early Husserl attempted to reestablish semantic and epistemological objectivity by expelling, in a sort of exorcism, the concepts and thoughts from the mind, and placing them into a realm of "objective concepts." With them, the double nature of the scholastic concepts, being both particular mental qualities or acts and intersubjectively the same for all, has been split up into an internal sphere of mere subjective representations (*Vorstellungen*) and a sphere of objective concepts, in which, as a "third realm" (Frege) "representations as such" (*Vorstellungen an sich*), namely, concepts or thoughts (*Gedanken*) only have an "ideal being" (Husserl).[17]

The imaginative representation (*Vorstellung*), always being subjective, such that the representation of *x* of anyone is not equal to that of anyone else, differs from the sense of a sign (*Sinn eines Zeichens*), which, as Frege stated, can be the common property of many and is therefore no part or mode of a single soul.[18] Correspondingly, "the thought (*Gedanke*) does not belong particularly to those who think, as the imaginative representation does to those who imagine, but rather is the same object for all those who are grasping it."[19]

According to Michael Dummett's reconstruction of the origins of analytical philosophy, this antipsychologist approach to the "philosophy of thought," as problematic as it may be regarding some of its ontological implications, "pre-

---

17. In his *Wissenschaftslehre*, Bolzano undertakes the curious venture of introducing the notion of "representations as such" ("Vorstellungen an sich," cf. § 48) into logic while at the same time demonstrating that it has already been frequently used there—though under different names (cf. § 51). Regarding this point his lack of acquaintance with scholastic philosophy is regrettable the more as he believed to have found a perfect equivalent to his notion of "representations as such" in the *conceptus objectivus*, which, however, he knows only from the eighteenth-century author of the Wolffian school, Johann Gottlieb Baumgarten. After quoting a short passage of his *Acroasis logica* (Halle, 1761), § 51 ("Unum quod percipitur, est objectum conceptus, et conceptus objectivus; perceptio ipsa conceptus formalis est"), he remarks: "what Baumgarten designates with this name is obviously the same with that which I call thus." This, however, is not quite correct in all respects. For Baumgarten as well as the scholastic authors held that objective concepts owe their existence to the formal concepts (*conceptus formales*) inhering in individual minds, rather than being, as Bolzano takes it, independent of any subject representing them.

18. Gottlob Frege, *Über Sinn und Bedeutung* (1892), in *Funktion, Begriff, Bedeutung. Fünf logische Studien*, ed. G. Patzig (Göttingen: Vandenhoeck & Ruprecht, 1994), 44: "Die Vorstellung ist subjektiv: die Vorstellung des einen ist nicht die des anderen. Damit sind von selbst mannigfache Unterschiede der mit demselben Sinne verknüpften Vorstellungen gegeben.... Die Vorstellung unterscheidet sich dadurch wesentlich von dem Sinne eines Zeichens, welcher gemeinsames Eigentum von vielen sein kann und also nicht Teil oder Modus der Einzelseele ist; denn man wird wohl nicht leugnen können, daß die Menschheit einen gemeinsamen Schatz von Gedanken hat."

19. G. Frege, *Logik* (1897), in *Schriften zur Logik und Sprachphilosophie. Aus dem Nachlass*, ed. G. Gabriel (Hamburg: F. Meiner, 1990), 46: "Der Gedanke ist den Denkenden nicht so besonders zu eigen, wie die Vorstellung den Vorstellenden, sondern steht allen, die ihn auffassen, in derselben Weise und als derselbe gegenüber."

pared the ground" for the "crucial step" toward a full-fledged philosophy of language, taken by Wittgenstein in his *Tractatus Logico-philosophicus*:

> Before the philosophy of language could be seen, not as a minor specialised branch of the subject, but as the stem from which all other branches grow, it was first necessary that the fundamental place should be accorded to the philosophy of thought. That could not happen until the philosophy of thought had been disentangled from philosophical psychology; and that in turn depended upon ... the extrusion of thoughts from the mind and the consequent rejection of psychologism.[20]

However, what none of the representatives of "philosophy of thought" had in view while attacking "psychologism" is the fact that, already in the scholastic tradition, at least according to its own pretension, semantic and epistemological subjectivism was ruled out by the doctrine of the ISC without resorting to "ideal entities" situated outside the realm of reality. Was, therefore, as Putnam has stated, "the whole psychologism/Platonism issue somewhat a tempest in a teapot, as far as meaning-theory is concerned?"[21] For, as he argues, "even if meanings are 'Platonic' entities rather than 'mental' states ... 'grasping' those entities is presumably a psychological state (in the narrow sense)." The strict correlation between the "Platonic entities" and the mental states "grasping" them lets it "appear to be somewhat a matter of convention" whether "one takes the 'Platonic' entity or the psychological state as the 'meaning.'" In addition to this point, which, looking farther back, can be seen as the revival of Ammonius's polemic against the Stoic semantics of the *lekton*,[22] "taking the psychological state to be the meaning would hardly have the consequences that Frege feared, that meaning would cease to be public. For psychological states are 'public' in the sense that different people ... can be in the same psychological state." Frege's argument against psychologism is, in Putnam's view, "only an argument against identifying concepts with mental particulars, not with mental entities in general."[23]

Putnam's accentuation of the possibility that "different people can be in the same mental state" structurally corresponds to, and therefore leads us back to, our main issue: the ISC as it was put forward, analyzed, and substantiated in scholastic logic. For while, according to Putnam, "to be in the same mental state" means "to grasp or to have the same concept," this "having the same concept" is precisely what the scholastic authors felt to be in need of further explication.

---

20. M. Dummett, *Origins of Analytical Philosophy* (London: Duckworth, 1993), 127.
21. H. Putnam, *Mind, Language and Reality* (Cambridge: Cambridge University Press, 1975), 222.
22. Cf. Ammonius, *In Aristotelis De interpretatione* 17,24–28; cf. A. A. Long and D. N. Sedley, eds., *The Hellenistic Philosophers* (Cambridge: Cambridge University Press, 1987), 33 n.
23. H. Putnam, *Mind, Language and Reality*, 222.

## THE MEANING OF THE ISC

The scholastic authors were especially concerned with two aspects of Aristotle's ISC-thesis: First, what precisely is meant by it, and second, how it is to be justified. Let us begin with the first. What, then, could reasonably be meant by the statement that mental concepts, being in any case particular mental qualities or acts of individual intellects, are the same for all? Obviously, as all medieval thinkers agreed, this statement does not suggest a numerical identity of concepts[24] which, as John Dullaert (ca. 1480–1513) opined, would be impossible even under the conditions of an Averroistic theory of intellect (positing numerically one separate intellect for all humans).[25] Rather, as the scholastics saw it, the thesis claims a specific sameness.[26] This way of spelling out the statement, however, makes the ISC only slightly more intelligible. For it still remains unclear what it means that mental concepts are specifically the same for all—because appar-

---

24. Different is the case with Bolzano's, Brentano's, and Husserl's "representations as such" or Frege's "thought" (*Gedanke*), the numerical identity of which appeared to these authors as the only way of guaranteeing the possibility that two or more persons may have the same concept. As the "objective representation" or "representation as such," according to Bolzano, does not presuppose any subject representing it, but persists—though not as something existing but rather as a certain something—even if no thinking being should conceive it, "it is not multiplied by one, two, three or many beings thinking it." ("Diese objective Vorstellung bedarf keines Subjectes, von dem sie vorgestellt werde, sondern bestehet—zwar nicht als etwas Seyendes, aber doch als ein gewisses Etwas, auch wenn kein einziges denkendes Wesen sie auffassen sollte, und sie wird dadurch, daß ein, zwei, drei oder mehrere Wesen sie denken, nicht vervielfacht"; Bolzano, *Wissenschaftslehre*, 29.) Therefore, "the objective representation is only one while there are innumerably many subjective representations.... We are, however, used to call all those subjective representations the same to each other which have the identical objective representation as their subject matter" ("Die objective Vorstellung . . . ist deshalb nur eine einzige: der subjectiven Vorstellungen aber, gibt es unzählige... Wie pflegen aber alle diejenigen subjectiven Vorstellungen, die einerlei objective Vorstellung zu ihrem Stoffe haben, einander gleich zu nennen"; ibid.)

25. Johannes Dullaert, *Quaestiones super duos libros Peri Hermeneias Aristotelis* (Paris, 1515) fol. 4va: "Unus sensus illius propositionis potest esse quod eedem passiones sunt apud omnes per realem inhaerentiam: ita quod eedem notiones omnibus insint et hoc est falsum: immo licet teneretur opinio commentatoris quod idem est intellectus in omnibus hominibus adhuc non esset illud concedendum."

26. Cf. Martinus Dacus, *Quaestiones super librum perihermeneias*, in: Opera, ed. H. Roos, Corpus philosophorum danicorum medii aevi, 2 (Copenhagen: G. E. C. Gad, 1961), 244: "dicendum, quod passiones animae sunt eaedem in specie apud omnes, et non numero"; Richard Brinkley, "*Summa logicae*, ed. G. Gál and R. Wood, Richard Brinkley and his 'Summa logicae,'" *Franciscan Studies* 40 (1980), 81: "Intelligendum est . . . quod Aristoteles non loquitur de identitate in numero, . . . sed tantum loquitur de identitate in specie. . ."; Johannes Raulinus, *In logicam Aristotelis commentarium* (Paris, 1500) fol. g4ra; Petrus Rauledius, *Commentaria in Librum Aristotelis de Interpretatione* (Paris, 1519) fol. 33ᵛa; Lovanienses, *Commentaria in Isagogen Porphyrii, et in omnes libros Aristotelis de Dialectica* (Louvain, 1553) 229; Conimbricenses, *Commentarii in universam Aristotelis dialecticam* (Cologne, 1607) 2.6; Franciscus Toletus, *Introductio in universam Aristotelis logicam* (Cologne, 1615) 1:207a.

ently it does not simply mean that all men have concepts of the same kind—or what it is for different intellects to have specifically same concepts.

An important conceptual feature used to shed more light on the ISC-thesis was provided when, in the mid–thirteenth century, mental concepts—without at first losing their status of being likenesses of things—began to be considered primarily as "signs of things" (*signa rerum*). Against this background it was now possible to render the Aristotelian dictum more intelligible and, as some felt, more correct, by interpreting the claim of concepts "*being* the same for all" in terms of concepts "*signifying* the same for all." For, as Scotus noted, while it is false that mental concepts (*passiones*) are in themselves (*in se*) the same for all, it is true that they are the same for all insofar as they are signs, such that any concept, remaining the very same in itself, would represent the same thing to the mind of whomsoever.[27] In this way, Walter Burley stated:

> We should say that the proposition "the concepts of the soul are the same for everyone" is to be understood so that a concept of the soul, a similitude of the thing, signifies the same for everyone, for it signifies for everyone the thing of which it is a similitude.[28]

Most late scholastic authors agreed on this *semantic* interpretation of the ISC.[29] As soon as concepts were regarded as signs, the phrase "*idem apud omnes*," which already for Aristotle was a reliable indicator of naturalness, was plausibly interpreted as expressing one of the basic criteria of natural signification. The understanding of concepts as signs, nevertheless, does not exclude interpreting the ISC with reference to concepts as likenesses or mental images of things,[30]

---

27. Duns Scotus, *Super librum I. perihermenias*, q. 4, *Opera omnia* (Lyons, 1639), 1:190a: "passiones non sunt eaedem apud omnes in se, sed inquantum sunt signa rerum, omnis enim passio eadem in se, apud cuiuscumque mentem fuerit, eandem rem se repraesentat."

28. "dicendum quod ista propositio 'eaedem sunt passiones animae apud omnes' debet intelligi quod passio animae, scilicet similitudo rei, significat idem apud omnes, quoniam apud omnes significat rem cuius est similitudo." "Walter Burley, *Commentarius medius*, ed. S. F. Brown, W. Burleigh's Middle Commentary on Aristotle's Perihermeneias," *Franciscan Studies* 33 (1973): 56 ff.

29. Cf. Pierre d'Ailly [?], *Destructiones modorum significandi*, ed. L. Kaczmarek, Die modi significandi und ihre Destruktion (Amsterdam: Brill, 1994), 50: "signa mentalia, scilicet conceptus et passiones animae, sunt eadem apud omnes, id est naturaliter apud omnes idem significant"; George of Brussels, *Quaestiones Georgii in logicam aristotelis*, in: *Logica magistri Georgii inserto textu Bricoti* (Paris, 1493) fol. 40rb: "potest intelligi quod aliquid sit idem apud omnes quoad significationem: hoc est quod omne illud quod uni significat cuilibet alteri ex significatione sive impositione quam actu habet natum est significare, et hoc modo intelligit philosophus dictum suum et verum est quod passiones sunt eaedem apud omnes"; Antonius Rubius, *Logica Mexicana sive commentaria in universam Aristotelis logicam* (Alcalá, 1603), 11.

30. Cf. Thomas Aquinas, *In Libros Perihermeneias*, lib. 1, lect. 2, n. 9: "in passionibus autem animae oportet attendi rationem similitudinis ad exprimendas res, quia naturaliter eas designant, non ex institutione."

for images (*imagines, picturae, similitudines*) were generally seen as one of the major classes of natural signs.³¹ And so it is not surprising that Burley continued his aforementioned exposition of the ISC by taking up the example of pictorial representation:

> Thus, if there were a faithful image of Hercules, wherever this image were presented, it would always signify Hercules; and it would not be the image of Hercules at one place and the image of someone else at another, whence this image would signify the same thing for everyone. And it is in the same way that the concept of the soul signifies the same for everyone.³²

This way of illustrating the ISC by referring to the contextual invariance of pictorial representation has been taken up frequently in later accounts. The reformulation of Aristotle's claim in terms of concepts being signs opened new ways not only for explaining the meaning of the ISC but, as we shall see, also for justifying it. This interpretation, however, is not sufficiently transparent in itself to answer all questions. For what does it mean, after all, to say that concepts signify the same for all?

Taking into account that concepts are particular qualities or acts of individual intellects, it is clear that the meaning of this statement could not be explained, nor its correctness tested, in the same way as the complementary claim about spoken words not signifying the same for all. While the latter claim can be explained in terms of the same word or vocal sound not being connected with or subordinated to the same mental concepts among people of different languages,³³ an analogous explication is obviously not viable regarding concepts themselves—unless one is willing to take recourse to Bolzano's "objective representations" and to call "all those subjective representations the same to each other which have the identical objective representation as their subject matter."³⁴

Without such a *tertium comparationis*, however, it is not possible to substantiate the ISC by describing the concepts in different intellects as tokens of the same type. While the sameness of word meaning for different people is easily tested by confronting each of them with the same word, or with word tokens of the same type, and letting them respond to it in a certain prescribed way, for example, by pointing to its *significatum*, the difficulty with mental concepts is that within the normal course of nature it is impossible to confront

---

31. Roger Bacon, *De signis* I, 5; K. M. Fredborg, L. Nielsen, and J. Pinborg, "An Inedited Part of Roger Bacon's Opus Maius: 'De signis,'" *Traditio* 34 (1978): 75–136, at 83.

32. "Unde si esset aliqua vera imago Herculis, ubicumque foret ista imago semper significaret Herculem, nec esset in uno loco imago Herculis et in alio loco imago alterius, unde ista imago significaret idem apud omnes. Et eodem modo passio animae quae est similitudo rei in anima significat idem apud omnes." See note 28.

33. It has to be noted, however, that this explanation is problematic in itself because it ultimately inherits the difficulties involved in the notion of the ISC.

34. See note 24.

different intellects with the very same concept. An analogous test regarding mental concepts, therefore, is possible only in the form of a thought experiment formulated in an abbreviated counterfactual conditional. This, I think, is clearly reflected in Scotus's formulation that the ISC means that a concept or *passio* would represent the same thing to the mind of whomsoever ("*apud cuiuscumque mentem fuerit, eandem rem se repraesentat*").[35] Interpreted in this way, "the assertion of the Philosopher," as the Conimbricenses noted with reference to Scotus, "is not absolute but conditioned in the following way. A concept is of such kind that in whosoever's mind it exists, it always represents the same thing." And they hasten to add that "for the truth of this, it makes no difference whether one person's concept can be transferred into the mind of another or not."[36]

A corresponding though somewhat different explanation of the ISC has been given by Petrus Rauledius (fl. 1519), who was obviously anxious to avoid the metaphysical problems involved in this fictional concept-transplantation.[37] But his own solution is problematic as well when he states that a certain concept, existing in the soul of someone, would still signify the very same thing even if it were formed by another intellect. The truth of this counterfactual conditional, however, Rauledius stresses, does not result from the antecedent being impossible according to the logical principle *ex impossibili sequitur quodlibet*. For, as he declares, he does not want to be understood as supposing that the very concept in one intellect could have been actually formed by another. What he is rather trying to express, I guess, is that the concept of $x$ may have been formed

---

35. See note 27. Cf. Johannes Dullaert, *Quaestiones super duos libros Peri Hermeneias Aristotelis* (Paris, 1515) fol. a 4va: "potest intelligi aliquam passionem eandem esse apud omnes in representando sic videlicet quod ipsa sit talis nature quod in quocunque intellectu ponatur semper idem representabit: et hoc pacto intelligenda est propositio philosophi. Et sic claret differentia vocum et passionum anime: non enim sunt sic voces eedem apud omnes dato quod coram multis proferatur hec vox homo non oportet quod idem omnibus representet. . . . Nec ex isto sequitur omnes esse eque scientes."

36. Conimbricenses (see note 26), 2.47: "respondetur iuxta mentem Scoti, propositionem Philosophi non esse absolutam, sed conditionatam: ad hunc modum. Conceptus eiusmodi est, ut in cuiusvis mente ponatur, idem semper repraesentet. Ad cuius veritatem nihil refert, an conceptus unius transferri possit in mentem alterius, nec ne."

37. In an objection against this way of spelling out the ISC the Conimbricenses point to the fact that "a concept formed by one person, since it is an accident, cannot migrate into the mind of another person" and argue, that, "even if it were to be transferred by God, it would not serve that other person any more, since, just as no one can live by the life of another, so neither can anyone understand by another's concept." Conimbricenses, ibid., 2.43: "conceptus ab uno formatus, cum sit accidens, nequit migrare in mentem alterius; ergo non potest alteri repraesentare. Imo tametsi transferretur a Deo, nihilo magis inserviret alteri ad cognitionem, quoniam, ut nemo vivere potest per alterius vitam, ita nec intelligere per alterius conceptum." The solution of this argument is unfortunately deferred to their—never written—commentary on Aristotle's *Metaphysics*. Cf. The Conimbricenses, *Some Questions on Signs*, trans. John P. Doyle (Milwaukee: Marquette University Press, 2001), 120 ff.

by whomsoever and is always apt to signify $x$ to whomsoever.[38] In other words: Any intellect, forming a concept of $x$, is forming it in such a way that this concept would signify $x$ in any other intellect, too. To this extent, Rauledius's way of explaining the meaning of the ISC agrees with what Scotus and Dullaert said. What they are after with their labored and seemingly strange way of spelling out the ISC-thesis is a formulation that, recognizing that conceptual signs are three term relations (a concept signifies ... to ...), provides a stronger version of sameness than the mere claim that any intellect, forming a concept of $x$, forms a concept that signifies $x$ (i.e., to the intellect forming it). For this would leave open the possibility that the concepts of $x$ in two distinct intellects A and B would be different from each other to such a degree that the concept produced by A would not be apt to function as a concept of $x$ for B and vice versa.

Interpreted along these lines, the ISC is reduced to sameness in reference, claiming that the concept of $x$ in intellect A is such that it would refer to $x$ in any other intellect. Nevertheless, this yields a rather weak version of the ISC-thesis, because it does not imply that all men are equal in knowledge (*aeque scientes*), having the same set of concepts such that for each and every concept in mind A there would exist a corresponding concept in mind B—many people, Scotus remarks, have knowledge about simple substances which others do not apprehend[39]—nor does it mean that all men conceive of the same things in the same way. For, as the Conimbricenses point out:

> Not only are diverse concepts formed by different men about the same thing, as can be seen in the case of a peasant and a mathematician, one of whom understands the sun to be greater than the whole earth, while the other thinks it less than the wheel of a wagon—not only do I say "diverse" but even opposite concepts [are formed], since about one proposition many may think opposite things.[40]

38. Petrus Rauledius (see note 26), fol. 33va: "Per passiones ... animae esse easdem non intelligimus esse easdem numero.... Sed intelligimus eas naturaliter proprie significare, quod est idem apud omnes designare, ad hunc sensum: quod si conceptus aliquis existens in anima alicuius fuisset formatus ab alio quovis intellectu idem penitus ei repraesentaret quod illi animae, cuius nunc est passio. Si dicas hoc verum esse: quia antecedens illius conditionalis est impossibile: Possibile siquidem non est saltem naturaliter conceptum sortis in anima platonis existentem fuisse formatum ab alio quovis intellectus, male me intelligis. Nolo enim dicere quod idem conceptus numero fuisset ab alio formatus. Sed si eiusdem rei conceptus formetur ab alio quovis intellectu non nisi illam rem significabit."

39. Scotus (see note 26), 191a: "multi ... sciunt aliqua simplicia, de quibus alij nihil apprehendunt."

40. Conimbricenses (see note 26), 2.43: "De eadem re non modo finguntur diversi conceptus a diversis hominibus, ut videre est in rustico, et Mathematico, quorum unus apprehendit solem maiorem tota terra, alter minorem rota plaustri, non modo inquam, diversi; sed etiam oppositi: cum de una propositione plerique contraria opinentur." The English translation is from J. P. Doyle (see note 37).

The ISC, therefore, does not entail conformity of opinions or convictions regarding the same things; it is nothing but sameness in reference, for Aristotle by no means wanted to claim that all men apprehend the same things in the same way.[41] However diverse the actual knowledge of different people about a certain object may be, the mental concept or mental image they form of the object in any case retains the same representation, that is, it is in itself apt to represent the same for all. In other words, intension does not determine extension. The simple concept, on this view, seems to be primarily, as it were, a referential kernel to which opinion and knowledge is or can be attached without changing its reference. This mainly Scotistic and Jesuit interpretation of the ISC, by emphasizing the sameness in reference or *extension*, diverges from the Thomistic position, which, on the basis of a different epistemological position regarding to the cognizability of substances,[42] tends to uphold the *intensional* sameness of concepts acquired in simple apprehension. Thus the Jesuit Balthazar Tellez (1595–1675) prefers the Scotistic way of spelling out the ISC, according to which mental concepts as natural signs represent the same object anywhere (*ubicumque ponantur, idem repraesentat*) over the Thomistic claim that all men form the same concept of the same thing (*omnes formant eosdem conceptus de eadem re*), because it frequently happens that different people, on hearing the same word, form totally diverse concepts (*diversis omnino conceptus*).[43] The Thomist Didacus Masius (1553–1608),

---

41. Ibid., 2.6: "non vult [sc. Aristoteles] omnes eodem modo apprehendere easdem res, nam alius perfectius, alius imperfectius eandem rem cognoscit. Sed ubicunque sit interna alicuius rei imago, qualiscunque illa formeretur retinere eandem repræsentationem, et secundum se æque aptam esse omnibus idem repraesentare."

42. See notes 71 ff.

43. Balthazar Tellez, *Summa universae philosophiae* (Lisbon, 1642), 100: "Cum Philosophus asserit, conceptus esse eosdem apud omnes, idem est ac dicere, conceptus esse signa naturalia, ita ut ubicumque ponantur, idem repraesentat; ita explicant Aristotelem nobiliores interpretes cum Scoto in hoc loco, q. 3 ut videre est apud patres Conimbricenses in Logica cap. 2 de Signis q. 4 art. 1. Quae interpretatio accomodatior videtur, quam ea, quae ab aliquibus affertur, qui asserunt, ideo dici conceptus eosdem apud omnes, quia omnes formant eosdem conceptus de eadem re, quod falsum est, nam audito eodem nomine, saepe diversis omnino conceptus formantur circa eadem rem, audito enim nomine 'Solis,' Mathematicus, et rusticus toto caelo diversi abeunt circa conceptus." This passage directly refers to the answer the Conimbricenses have given to the question "Utrum conceptus iidem sunt apud omnes." Cf. Conimbricenses; see note 26, 2.47: "ad argumentum initio articuli positum [challenging the ISC by pointing to the divergence of human opinions] respondet Boetius. Philosophum intelligere conceptus esse eosdem apud omnes priori modo: hoc est, omnes formare similes conceptus de una re. Quem D. Thomas exponit de conceptibus simplicibus; nam propositiones constat apud varios esse omnino discrepantes. Verum Scotus hic q. 3 [sic. actually it is q. 4] limitationem D. Thomae non admittit: et merito, ut ostendit impugnatio de conceptu solis in argumento posita: nisi D. Thomas intelligat ab omnibus formari eosdem conceptus simplices, si omnia sint paria; at hoc modo etiam propositiones sunt eaedem, quod impugnat. Quamobrem posteriori modo accipienda est mens Philosophi, videlicet conceptus natura sua habere vim significandi, ut ubicunque ponantur, idem repraesentent: quod non habent voces, et scripta, cum quibus Aristoteles conceptus comparavit." The Conimbricenses, in turn, are referring to

on the contrary, arguing in favor of the sameness in intension, answers the problem of the diversity of human opinions by drawing a distinction between a *conceptus certus* and a *conceptus opinativus et dubius*. Whereas, according to Masius, a concept formed in simple apprehension is a *conceptus certus* and therefore intersubjectively the same for all—people of all nations conceive a line as longitude without latitude—there can be a multiplicity of *conceptus opinativi*. The concept of quantity, for instance, is not the same for all in the sense that all would decide the question of whether or not quantity is distinct from the *res quanta* in the same way.[44] The variant interpretations of the meaning of the ISC are, thus, connected with different approaches to its rationale.

## THE RATIONALE OF THE ISC

It is but natural that the scholastic authors, seeking a justification of the ISC-thesis, tried to tease out the rationale of the ISC from the text in which it was stated. It has to be noted, however, that Aristotle in *De interpretatione*, unlike his scholastic commentators who explicitly posed questions like "*utrum passiones in anima sunt eaedem apud omnes,*"[45] "*utrum sit verum quod passiones*

---

Scotus's discussion of the ISC in quaestio 4 of his first commentary on *Peri hermeneias*, where he is—though without giving names—directly referring to Thomas's interpretation of the ISC, which, in his view, results in a too strong version of sameness. Presenting Thomas's position as an answer to the objection that from the ISC follows that all know the same things ("apud omnes sunt easdem res cognitae"), so that all are equal in knowledge ("omnes sunt aeque scientes"), he insists that the limitation Thomas is trying to make (by pointing out that the sameness only regards the mode of conceiving the *simplicia* but not the composition or division) is not practical for ruling out the problematic consequence of a sameness in knowledge. For it would still hold that all men were equally knowing in respect to the objects of simple apprehension, i.e., according to Thomistic epistemological assumptions, regarding to the definitions of simple substances. Cf. Scotus; see note 27, 190b: "ad primam rationem dicitur, quod licet omnes eodem modo simplicia concipiant, non tamen eodem modo componunt, et dividunt, unde 3. de Anima, context. 36. et 21 dicitur, quod intellectus circa quod quid est non decipitur nisi secundum accidens, et hoc est secundum ipsos, non in absoluta apprehensione, sed in componendo quod quid est cum altero. Contra, saltem sequitur, quod omnes erunt aeque scientes, quantum ad apprehensionem simplicium [191a], et ita erunt omnes aeque scientes definitive, quia definitio est via cognoscendi simpliciter; sed hoc manifeste est falsum, multi enim sciunt aliqua simplicia, de quibus alij nihil apprehendunt."—Scotus, finally, is referring to Thomas, *In lib. periherm*. I, lect. 2, n. 10. See note 68.

44. Cf. Didacus Masius, *Commentum in duos libros Aristotelis de interpretatione* (Valencia, 1592), 6b–7b: "conceptus de quantitate non est unus, et idem apud omnes... quidam enim concipiunt quantitatem distingui reipsa a re quanta, alii vero econtra concipiunt non distingui: ergo...[7b]...dicimus...duplicem esse conceptum, certum unum, alium vero opinativum: conceptus certus, qui praecipue fit in prima operatione intellectus, idem est apud omnes, nam quemadmodum Latini concipimus lineam esse longitudinem sine latitudine, ita et idipsum aliae gentes concipiunt: conceptus nihilominus opinativus et dubius non est idem, et ita cum hic conceptus, num scilicet quantitas distinguatur a re quanta sit conceptus opinativus, poterit esse multiplex et diversus."

45. Cf. Martinus Dacus (see note 26), 244; Conimbricenses (see note 2.42).

*animae sunt apud omnes eedem,*"[46] or "*quo sensu verum sit conceptus esse eosdem apud omnes,*"[47] does not introduce the ISC as something to be justified or proven. The ISC is rather taken as a matter of fact, providing an argument for the naturalness of mental concepts in contrast to the conventionality of spoken and written words.[48] For what is the same everywhere cannot be but natural.[49] However, even though Aristotle does not explicitly offer a proof of the ISC, the passage concerned seems to contain at least some hints as to how such a proof could be constructed. It is obvious that the ISC, in Aristotle's account of the matter, has something to do with the sameness of things,[50] so that the latter provides the reason for the former: Our concepts of things are

---

46. Cf. Gratiadei Esculanus (d'Ascoli), *Commentaria Gratiadei esculani Ordinis praedicatorum in totam artem veterem Aristotelis* (Venice, 1491) fol. 5ra; George of Brussels, *Quaestiones Georgii in logicam aristotelis* (Paris, 1493), fol. 40ra.

47. Conimbricenses (see note 26), 2.47; Franciscus Toletus (see note 26), 207a: "dubium posset esse, quomodo idem sint conceptus apud omnes, cum constet aliquem conceptum me habere hominis, alium habere Petrum, alium Ioannem?"

48. Cf. Thomas Aquinas, *In Libros Perihermeneias* I, lect. 2 n. 9: "quorum autem etc., ostendit passiones animae naturaliter esse, sicut et res, per hoc quod eaedem sunt apud omnes"; Richard of Campsall, *Quaestiones super librum Priorum Analeticorum*, ed. E. A. Synan (Toronto: Pontifical Institute of Mediaeval Studies, 1968) 2.18: "passiones significant a natura, quia sunt eedem apud omnes"; Conimbricenses (see note 26), 2.43: "idem esse apud omnes nihil est aliud, quam natura sua tale esse, non ex hominum arbitratu."

49. Cf. Boethius, *Commentarius in librum Aristoteles Perihermeneias*, ed. C. Meiser (Leipzig, 1877), 39: "Quod uero addidit: quorum autem haec primorum notae, eaedem omnibus passiones animae et quorum hae similitudines, res etiam eaedem ad hoc pertinet, ut naturales esse res intellectusque declaret." Boethius, *Commentarius in librum Aristoteles Perihermeneias*, secunda editio, ed. C. Meiser (Leipzig, 1880) 23: "dicendum est res et intellectus, quoniam apud omnes idem sunt, esse naturaliter constitutos."

50. Any attempt to explain the ISC by referring to the sameness of things is confronted with the problem that the sameness of things is no less in need of explanation than the ISC itself. For, as Ockham remarked, things are not the same for all in the sense that all would have the same things ("quascumque res habent aliqui habeant omnes alii." *Expositio in Librum Perihermenias Aristotelis*, ed. A. Gambatese and S. Brown, O.P. II, 372). The solution that Scotus has offered for this problem is based on the notion of signification as well. For just as the concepts are not in themselves (*in se*) the same for all, but only insofar as they are signs of things, so the things too are the same for all only insofar as they are signified by concepts: "res in quantum significantur per passionem, sunt eaedem apud omnes." Scotus (see note 27), 191a; cf. Antonius Andreae, *Scriptum super librum peryhermenias*, Venice, 1508, fol 63vb). Ockham explained that things are the same for all such that people using different languages call the specifically or numerically same things by different names ("sic sunt eaedem apud omnes quod diversi easdem res secundum speciem vel numerum vocant diversis nominibus"; *Expos. in Lib. Periherm.*, OP II, 372). If this sentence is to make any sense or give any information about the sameness of things it must be, I think, understood such that Ockham is trying to give account of the sameness of things by recourse to the extensional sameness of corresponding words in different languages (e.g., "man" and "homo," or "moon" and "luna," are of the same extension, that is, refer to the same things).

the same because the things of which they are concepts are the same.[51] This, however, as Abelard seems to have noticed, leaves open at least two ways of deducing the ISC from the sameness of things. For it can be deduced either *a simili* or *a causa*;[52] in other words, concepts can be said to be the same for all because of being either (1) *similitudines rerum*, that is, likenesses (*homoiomata*) of things, or (2) *passiones animae*, that is, affections of the soul (*pathemata*), caused or co-caused by the things. If the first option is chosen it might appear as if the underlying argument of Aristotle's remarks would go like this:

Things are the same for all.
Concepts are likenesses of things.
Therefore concepts are the same for all.

Such an argument, however (which Aristotle in fact does not explicitly offer) would hardly be conclusive, because from the bare facts that (1) a certain concept ($c_1$) in a certain intellect ($i_1$) is a likeness of a certain thing or kind of thing (r), and (2) that $c_2$ in $i_2$ is a likeness of r, too, it does not follow that $c_1$ and $c_2$ are "the same," viz. the "same likeness" (*eadem similitudo*).[53] For what is justified in the case of equality, namely, following Euclid, that "if two things are each equal to a third thing then they are equal to each other," does not hold for likeness, because it is well possible that there are two or more likenesses of a third, which are by no means similar to each other (as e.g. the floor plan and the perspectival image of a building). Thus, although, something more than mere likeness in an unspecified sense seems to be required for properly substantiating the ISC, this nevertheless seems to have been the prevalent way of reading the passage,[54] so that, as the Conimbricenses remark, the claim of con-

---

51. Cf. Peter Abelard, *Logica ingredientibus. Glossae . . . super Peri ermenias*, in *Peter Abaelards Philosophische Schriften*, ed. B. Geyer (Munster, 1927), 68: "dicit intellectus eosdem omnibus permanere et hoc per suprapositam rerum similitudinem ostendit, quia uidelicet quemadmodum res de quibus habentur intellectus, eaedem sunt, ita etiam intellectus"; Richard Brinkley (see note 26), 81: "Aristoteles . . . assignat causam quare conceptus sunt idem apud omnes, dicens quod conceptus sunt idem apud omnes quia res sunt eaedem apud omnes. Quae auctoritas aequivalet huic consequentiae: res sunt eaedem apud omnes, ergo conceptus rerum sunt idem apud omnes."

52. Cf. Peter Abelard (see note 51), 72: "Per identitatem rerum ostendit a simili vel a causa identitatem intellectuum."

53. For the formulation of "same likeness" see Siger of Courtrai, *In I Perihermeneias Zeger van Kortrijk, Commentator van Perihermeneias*, ed. C. Verhaak (Brussels: Paleis der Academien, 1964), 9 ff.: "passiones animae et res quarum similitudines sunt in anima, sunt eaedem apud omnes; eamdem enim similitudinem et conceptum rei apprehensae habet graecus et latinus." Cf. Nicolaus Tinctoris in the following note.

54. Cf. Peter Abelard, *Introductiones parvulorum*, in Pietro Abelardo: Scritti di logica, ed. Mario dal Pra (Florence: La Nuova Editrice, 1969), 74: "Passiones, id est intellectus, sunt iidem apud omnes et caeterae res sunt eaedem apud omnes, quorum, id est quarum rerum, hae passiones, id est intellectus, sunt similitudines, id est imaginationes, quia intellectu imaginamur esse rei sicuti est"; Aegidius Romanus, *Expositio in Artem veterem* (Venice, 1507) fol. 48ra:

cepts being images or likenesses of things is the principal argument by which the interpreters of Aristotle tried to prove the ISC.[55] This is especially the case where, as with Burley, the contextual invariance of an artificial image, always and anywhere representing the same object, is referred to in order to illustrate the ISC. For, as Menghus Blanchellus (ca. 1440–ca. 1520) noted, if something is a Caesar-picture, it will represent Caesar everywhere and not Caesar in one place and someone else in another.[56] And this, of course, also holds where concepts are compared to mirror images.[57]

---

"dicit (sc. Aristoteles) quod passiones in anima sunt eedem apud omnes. Nam idem est asinus apud nos et apud grecos: similiter et similitudo asini est eadem"; Menghus Blanchellus, *Commentum cum quaestiones super logicam Pauli Veneti* (1476) fol. a2vb: "causa quare terminus vocalis vel scriptus non significat idem apud omnes est quia non significat rem ex aliqua convenientia et similitudine quam habet cum rem quemadmodum terminus mentalis significat ex similitudine et convenientia cum re sed solum ex impositione primi impositoris"; Nicolaus Tinctoris, *Dicta super Summulas Petri hyspani* (Reutlingen, 1486), fol. Q5rb: "conceptus sive passiones animae sunt idem apud omnes. Eadem enim est similitudo naturalis repraesentans lapidem in mente greci et latini"; Johannes de Magistris, *Questiones subtiles et perutiles . . . super totum cursum logice* (Venice, 1490), fol. F5rb: "sicut res sunt eaedem apud omnes ita passiones animae quae sunt naturales similitudines rerum sunt eaedem apud omnes." Petrus Tartaretus, *Expositio super textu logices Aristotelis* (Paris, 1495), fol. 307ra: "sicut res ad extra sunt eedem apud omnes ita passiones anime seu conceptus qui sunt naturales similitudines rerum sunt eedem apud omnes"; B. Tellez (see note 43), 100: "conceptus sunt essentialiter imagines, quae transcendentaliter feruntur in obiecta, et quae repraesentant obiecta naturaliter: sed imagines naturales sunt eaedem semper apud omnes, ubicumque ponantur: ergo ubicumque ponantur conceptus, sunt ijsdem apud omnes."

55. Conimbricenses (see note 26), 2.43: "Ad explicationem huius dubitationis [sc. "quo sensu verum sit conceptus esse eosdem apud omnes"] est supponendum ex supra dictis conceptum perinde, ac speciem intelligibilem, esse imaginem ad vivum exprimentem suum obiectum; ad illudque referri transcendentaliter tanquam ad mensuram, et exemplar sui esse quae vero ita referuntur, per suammet essentiam et naturam tendunt in terminos: cum autem rerum essentiae mutari non possint, fit consequenter, ut huiusmodi conceptus ubique retineant suam repraesentationem, et per eam ducant potentiam in cognitionem obiecti. *Et haec est praecipua ratio, qua interpretes hoc loco probant conceptus esse eosdem apud omnes*" (italics mine).

56. Menghus Blanchellus (see note 54), fol a2rb: "terminus mentalis est similitudo rei in intellectu sive conceptus rem representans ad extra. . . . Cuius ratio est. similitudo (add. Venice 1492: ubique representat idem) sicut si esset imago Cesaris. illa ubique representaret Cesarem et non representaret in uno loco unum et in uno (1492: alio) loco alium. sic autem est de conceptibus et similitudinibus in anima"; cf. Chrysostomus Javellus, *Logicae compendium* (Venice, 1555), 17: "Terminus per se significativus naturaliter est ille, qui apud omnes homines idem ultra seipsum repraesentat intellectui, ut homo et animal in mente. est autem homo in mente species, sive similitudo, sive conceptus hominis. se habet enim huiusmodi similitudo sive conceptus ut vera imago, puta Caesaris, quae apud omnes ex sui natura repraesentat Caesarem."

57. Bonaventura Columbus, *Novus Cursus Philosophicus Scotistarum* (Lyons, 1669), 214a: "Conceptus rerum sunt idem apud omnes. Probatur . . . quia conceptus sunt naturales rerum imagines, ipsasque res naturaliter exprimentes, quarum sunt imagines, et similitudines naturales, et ubique servant suam naturalem repraesentationem, ut ad oculum cernitur, in imaginibus obiectorum per specula oblatis."

While, as Franciscus Toletus (1533?–1596) says, the same image will be an image of the king independently of whether it is located in Rome or in Mantua,[58] the ISC, in the view of others, requires a different explanation. According to Richard Brinkley (fl. 1365) it has to be illustrated, rather, that a man in Rome will naturally effect a concept which is specifically the same as the concept effected by a man elsewhere. This, of course, is a different story and results in a different approach to the ISC. For in this case, without making any direct reference to the notions of image or likeness, stress is laid on the fact that anything, just as it is one, naturally effects but one sign in respect to one cognitive power.[59] Even if, under the conditions of the *species*-theory, concepts are held to be caused (or at least co-caused) through species that are likenesses of things, these likenesses may be functionally irrelevant to the foundation of the ISC. For all that is needed is the regularity of the natural process by which the concepts are effected, because, as Martinus Dacus had already claimed in this context, any effect resulting from principles that are specifically the same for all will be specifically the same for all, too.[60] Still earlier, Albert the Great established the sameness of concepts on the grounds of their being generated by specifically identical things in intellective powers of the same nature. So, even though he is by no means denying that concepts are *similitudines rerum*, the argumentative function of their likeness to external objects is to explain the mode in which the latter are present to the mind rather than to support the ISC. For the sameness of concepts cannot rest on mere likeness but has to be substantiated by some sort of identity which Albert sees as given by the sameness of the external and internal conditions of their generation.[61]

58. Franciscus Toletus (see note 26), 207a: "dicitur eadem imago Regis, quae est Romae, et quae est Mantuae, quia sub eadem forma, et ratione idem significat: per sensus enim eadem re omnibus proposita omnes eundem conceptum eius in mente habebunt, si intelligant eam."

59. Richard Brinkley (see note 26), 81: "Voluit [sc. Aristoteles] ergo dicere quod sicut eadem est res in specie, ut sicut homo qui est Romae est idem in specie cum homine qui est hic, ita homo qui est Romae naturaliter est causativus conceptus, qui conceptus est eiusdem speciei cum conceptu hominis qui est hic. Consequentia Philosophi tenet per hoc medium quod 'quaelibet res sicut est una, ita naturaliter est tantum unius signi causativa respectu unius potentiae.' Quia causat aliud signum respectu potentiae intellectivae quam potentiae sensitivae vel signum quod eidem potentiae illam rem repraesentat."

60. Cf. Martinus Dacus (see note 26), 244 ff.: "dicendum, quod passiones animae sunt eaedem in specie apud omnes, et non numero.... nam passio ... est dispositio derelicta in passo ex impressione principii agentis. Cum igitur res per suam speciem agant in animam imprimendo suam cognitionem in ipsam, et illa impressio sit dispositio derelicta in passo, tunc oportet, cum res imprimentes sunt eaedem in specie apud omnes, quod passiones sunt eaedem [in] specie apud omnes ... [245] ... effectus in specie est idem apud omnes, cuius principia effectiva sunt eadem in specie apud omnes. Sed passio est effectus, res autem ipsae et animae rationales sunt principia effectiva, et illa sunt eadem apud omnes."

61. Cf. Albertus Magnus, *De interpretatione*, in *Opera Alberti Magni ad logicam pertinentia* (Venice, 1494), fol. 82rb: "conceptiones ... apud omnes eedem sunt: sicut anime passiones. quia *generata que unius forme habent generandi eadem* (fol. 82va) *sunt in forma et*

Though the production of a simple concept is always a particular act, it is not a subjective act (in the modern sense) but rather a process altogether natural, which, as with natural processes in general, always, given the same conditions, comes about in the same way and leads to results that are (in all their relevant aspects) the same. Under the condition of specifically identical cognitive faculties, it is, therefore, ultimately irrelevant for my concept to have been effected by my own intellect—for any other intellect would have formed it in a similar way.

It is possible and certainly illuminating to distinguish two fundamental scholastic models for explaining the form of concept acquisition, viz. a "formal causality model," paradigmatically represented by Thomas Aquinas, and an "efficient causality model," typically ascribed to Ockham.[62] While the former "is based on the idea that the natures informing the things of external reality, and making them to be what they are, are the very same natures that inform our minds when we have the concepts of these things," the latter is characterized by fixing "the relation of natural signification on the basis of natural laws systematically connecting causes with their effects."[63] Seen from the perspective of our topic, however, the historical situation is more complex than this distinction may suggest. For, on one hand, Ockham by no means renounces the idea that concepts are "likenesses" (*similitudines*) of things, but rather feels a need for a further notion to which he ascribes an important and indispensable epistemological function. General concepts of natural entities, he holds, are always caused by particular objects. In order for a certain concept of $x$ to signify not only that particular being by which it has been caused, but also (though confusedly) all individuals of the same kind, there must be something in the concept of $x$ which, being different from its merely being caused by $x$, makes it—under the condition of the normal course of nature—a concept or sign of all and only things of the same kind as $x$. And this "something" is such as to characterize the mental act or concept as "*similitudo obiecti*" and to render the concept suitable to fulfill semantic and logical functions in mental propositions.

---

*specie.* passiones sunt similitudines rerum in anima. Res vero se habent in anima per similitudinem generantis: cum ergo ubique et apud omnes sunt eedem, easdem in specie generabunt passiones. et ideo conceptiones ad omnes res recte concipiendas eedem sunt in specie. Et similiter etiam res apud omnes et ubique eedem sunt in specie, quarum passiones animae sunt notae quia rerum sunt similitudines in animabus a rebus generatae." Cf. ibid., fol. 83rb: "*passionum in anima generatio est ad modum naturae in hoc quod ad speciem moventis generatur in anima passio*: et res similiter non a nobis est sed a natura: ideo res et passiones manent eaedem apud omnes: *non eaedem numero vel proprio vel genere sed natura causante: vel extra vel in anima* et a voluntate hominis non diversificatae. Et quod dicitur quod non est una anima apud omnes: dicendum est quod hoc modo loquendi falsum est. Est enim una anima apud omnes unitate naturae producentis: sed non unitate numeri" (italics mine).

62. Cf. G. Klima, "Ontological Alternatives vs Alternative Semantics in Mediaeval Philosophy," *S. European Journal for Semiotic Studies* 3 (1991): 587–618.

63. Ibid.

For it is, as Ockham explicitly states, its being a likeness (*similitudo*) of the object that enables the concept to signify or to stand for things outside the mind, as well as to function as subject or predicate in a proposition, or to be a genus or species and so on.[64]

On the other hand, even within the Thomistic tradition, authors like Lambertus de Monte (1430/35–1499) or Johannes Versor (d. after 1482) have described the similitude of concepts to their objects in terms of concepts being natural effects of things.[65] Therefore, the difference between the two views seems to be more a difference in emphasis on the roles of formal and efficient causality than a clear-cut distinction between two alternative and mutually exclusive ways of characterizing the epistemological conceptions[66] underlying the modes of substantiating the ISC-thesis.

### THE ISC AND THE INFALLIBILITY OF SIMPLE APPREHENSION

Aristotle did not offer any explicit justification of the ISC in his *De interpretatione*. At the crucial point of his presentation, he rather referred to his *De anima* as the proper place for treating such issues. Even though no explicit discussion of the ISC is to be found in that text, the third book includes some epistemological remarks that could be—and, in fact, have been—read as arguments corroborating the ISC. Many authors, therefore, took Aristotle's reference to *De anima* as implying that he wanted to substantiate his assertion by claiming that the intellectual cognition of simple substances, just like sensory perception in grasping its proper object, is "never in error or admits the least possible amount of falsehood."

---

64. Cf. Ockham, *Quod.* IV, q. 35, ed. J. C. Wey, OT IX (1980), 474: "eo quod actus est similitudo obiecti, potest significare et supponere pro rebus extra, potest esse subiectum et praedicatum in propositione, potest esse genus, species etc."

65. Cf. Lambertus de Monte, *Copulata supra veterem artem Aristotelis secundum viam thomistarum* (Cologne, 1488), fol 136ra: "quod passiones animae naturaliter significant, patet quia *effectus naturale rei est naturale similitudo suae causae,* sed passiones in animae natura causantur per aliquam similitudinem impressam ab ipsis rebus modo naturae. ergo sunt ipsarum rerum naturales similitudines, et per consequens naturaliter significant"; Johannes Versor, *Quaestiones super totam veterem Artem Aristotelis* (Cologne, 1494), fol. 41ra: "passiones animae sunt ipsarum rerum extra animam existentium naturales similitudines naturaliter ipsas repraesentantes. Prima pars patet. quia passiones in anima nostra causantur ab ipsis rebus modo naturale. *Effectus autem naturalis rei alicuius est naturalis similitudo suae causae.* ergo ipsae passiones sunt ipsarum rerum naturales similitudines et per hoc patet secunda pars" (italics mine).

66. Both models, by the way, agree in that they are applicable only to a limited range of objects. Both lead to a "stones and trees" semantics, as it were, insuitable for giving an account of what Locke later has called "mixed modes." The limited explanatory value of taking concepts as either images or natural effects of what is conceived by them can be easily tested by asking in which sense the concepts corresponding to the nouns listed on any single dictionary's page (as, for example, "prayer," "preach," "preamble," "prebend," "precaution," "precedence," "precedent," "precentor," "precept," "preceptor," "precession," "preciosity," "precipe") could be characterized as images or effects of what they represent.

This way of endorsing the ISC goes back to Boethius's refutation of Aspasius, who, in the face of divergent views about the good and the just, wanted to limit the range of the ISC to the objects of sensory perception. Boethius, harshly rejecting this proposal, argued that whoever conceives what is good to be otherwise, may perhaps be said to have some *"passio animi"* but surely not to have an understanding of the good, for whoever opines the good to be bad cannot have a concept of the good that could be characterized as a likeness thereof.[67] In Thomas Aquinas's report, Boethius's argument sounds more concise: "Aristotle calls here the passions of the soul concepts of the intellect which is never deceived; and therefore its conceptions must be the same for all: for if someone deviates from the truth, he does not understand."[68]

Thomas points out, to be sure, that Aristotle's claim of undeceivability does not hold for the composing and dividing intellect but rather is confined to simple concepts corresponding to quidditative definitions. It is only with regard to these that the ISC-thesis is valid.[69] As we have seen, Scotus and some later Jesuits criticized the form of this limitation as insufficient to rule out the absurdity of all men being equal in knowledge.[70] Thomas, however, advocated a close analogy between the sense being informed by the likeness (i.e., *species*) of its proper object and the intellect being informed by the likeness of the essence of a thing, so that both cannot be deceived in the knowledge of their proper objects.[71] According to those who shared this view, simple concepts of

---

67. Boethius. *Comment. in lib. Arist. Perihermeneias* (see note 49), 41: "In hoc vero Aspasius permolestus est. Ait enim: qui fieri potest, ut eaedem apud omnes passiones animae sint, cum tam diuersa sententia de iusto ac bono sit? Arbitratur Aristotelem passiones animae non de rebus incorporalibus sed de his tantum quae sensibus capi possunt passiones animae dixisse. Quod perfalsum est. Neque enim intellexisse dicetur, qui fallitur, et fortasse quidem passionem animi habuisse dicetur, quicumque id quod est bonum non eodem modo quo est sed aliter arbitratur, intellexisse uero non dicitur. Aristoteles autem cum de similitudine loquitur, de intellectu pronuntiat. Neque enim fieri potest, ut qui quod bonum est malum esse arbitratur boni similitudinem mente conceperit. Neque enim intellexit rem subiectam."

68. "aristoteles hic nominat passiones animae conceptiones intellectus, qui numquam decipitur; et ita oportet eius conceptiones esse apud omnes easdem: quia, si quis a vero discordat, hic non intelligit." Thomas Aquinas, *Expositio libri Peryermenias* I, lect. 2, n. 10.

69. "sed quia etiam in intellectu potest esse falsum, secundum quod componit et dividit, non autem secundum quod cognoscit quod quid est, idest essentiam rei, ut dicitur in iii de anima; referendum est hoc ad simplices intellectus conceptiones (quas significant voces incomplexae), quae sunt eaedem apud omnes: quia, si quis vere intelligit quid est homo, quodcunque aliud aliquid, quam hominem apprehendat, non intelligit hominem. huiusmodi autem simplices conceptiones intellectus sunt, quas primo voces significant. unde dicitur in iv metaphysicae quod ratio, quam significat nomen, est definitio. " Ibid.

70. See note 43.

71. Thomas Aquinas, *STh* 1 q. 17 a. 3co: "sicut ... sensus informatur directe similitudine propriorum sensibilium, ita intellectus informatur similitudine quidditatis rei. unde circa quod quid est intellectus non decipitur, sicut neque sensus circa sensibilia propria."

essences or quiddities of things are therefore always true[72]—and thus the same for all.

Here, again, a fundamental difference between the Thomistic and Scotistic epistemology appears. While, according to Thomas, a cognitive faculty cannot fail in knowledge of a thing with the likeness of which it is informed ("*virtus cognoscitiva non deficit in cognoscendo respectu illius rei cuius similitudine informatur*"),[73] Scotus generally denies that the human intellect is informed by a proper species of substance ("*substantia non habet propriam speciem in intellectu possibili*"),[74] so that the intellect has immediate cognitive access only to the properties and accidents of substances but not to substances as such.[75] Many Jesuits adopted this view; Franciscus Suárez, for instance, fully accepted Scotus's doctrine of the human inability to know any substance directly ("*ratio Scoti est optima, quia non cognoscimus substantiam ut sic per propriam speciem*"),[76] taking it as a matter of fact, established by experience[77]—so that for these Jesuits, too, the direct object of intellectual apprehension is not substance in itself but rather its sensible accidents.[78]

In response to the objection that it may well be the case that different people differ in conceiving the same object ("*de eadem re diversi diversa concipiunt*"), the Thomist Gratiadei of Ascoli (fl. 1341) argues that, though they

---

72. Cf. Gaetanus de Thienis (1387–1465?), *Super libros de anima* (Venice 1493), fol 69ra: "non omnis intellectus est verus vel falsus. sed intellectus simplex qui est ipsius quid quod erat: secundum hoc quod aliquid erat esse idest ipsius quidditatis et essentie rei verus est, scilicet semper: sed intellectus compositus in quo aliquid dicitur de aliquo non semper est verus, sed est aliquando verus et aliquando falsus. Et hoc declarat per simile diciens: quod sicut videre respectu proprii obiecti visus semper est verus: sic intellectus simplex de ipso quod quid est semper est verus."

73. *STh* 1 q. 17 a. 3co.

74. Duns Scotus, *Lectura* I, 3, 1, q. 1, *Opera omnia*, 16, 265, 110.

75. Ibid. 266, 112. For the consequences on the account of the simplicity of mental concepts, see note 96.

76. Franciscus Suarez, *Disputationes metaphysicae*, disp. 35, sect. 3, n. 4, cf. Duns Scotus, 1 *Sent*. d. 3. q. 1.

77. F. Suarez, *Disp. met.* 35, 3, 5: "Nec censeo inconveniens concedere nullam substantiam cognosci a nobis quidditative in hac vita; quin potius existimo sufficienti experimento id notum esse. Quod enim a tantis philosophis et tanta adhibita diligentia compertum non est, satis verisimile est excedere naturalem facultatem ingenii humani; non video autem adhuc inventam esse hanc quidditativam cognitionem alicuius substantiae; quam enim maxime videmur cognoscere est humana species vel anima, et illamet cognitio tam est imperfecta, ut quidditativa dici non possit."

78. Cf. Antonius Rubius, S.J., *Commentaria in libros de anima* (Alcalá, 1611), 722: "accidens per se sensibile, et nihil aliud, est objectum per se adaequatum eius [sc. intellectus], tam motivum, quam terminativum. Nam licet substantiae corporeae, et rerum spiritualium formemus proprios conceptus, hoc est, illis solis, et non aliis convenientes cum eisque convertibiles, non tamen eas per se repraesentantes, sed illa tantum praedicata eis propria ex similitudine rerum per se sensibilium per discursum collecta; quare non dicuntur objecta per se et directe terminativa intellectus."

may have variable conceptions of one and the same thing in regard to its different aspects, it is impossible for them to have different concepts of the very same thing in the same respect (*"non tamen de una et eadem re et secundum idem possunt habere conceptionem nisi unam veram"*). Whoever, therefore, has a notion of man, necessarily conceives man in the very same way as being essentially composed of body and rational soul, whereas all those having a different concept do not have a false concept of man but rather do not have a concept of man at all.[79]

Among the Thomists we thus find two main arguments for the ISC: One grounding it in the alleged infallibility of simple apprehension with regard to its proper object, and another based on an axiom that may be termed the "bivalence principle of representation." Whereas the "classical" bivalence principle, referring to the second mental operation, says that any proposition is either true or false, the bivalence principle of representation says that, with regard to the first mental operation of simple apprehension, any mental concept either does or does not represent $x$. In the first case, it is a true image of $x$ while, in the latter, it is not a false image of $x$ but rather a true image of something different from $x$ and therefore simply not an image of $x$.

Whereas the first argument claims that simple apprehension is always true with regard to its proper object, that is, to simple essence, and thus leads to a strong version of the ISC, which has been criticized by Scotistic and Jesuit authors,[80] the second argument, which was accepted by most of them, simply claims that simple apprehension cannot be false, because every representation necessarily conforms to what it represents, for otherwise it would not represent it,[81] the

---

79. Gratiadei Esculanus (see note 46), fol. 5ra: "quaeramus, utrum sit verum quod passiones animae sunt apud omnes eedem. videtur enim quod non. Quia sicut modo diximus: passio animae sumitur pro ipso dicto intellectuali: quod nihil est aliud quam quaedam conceptio sapientis. sed de eadem re diversi diversa concipiunt. ergo non est verum quod animae passiones sint apud omnes eedem. Ad istam questionem est dicendum quod quamvis de [5rb] una et eadem re secundum diversa possint habere diversi homines varias conceptiones: non tamen de una et eadem re et secundum idem possunt habere conceptionem nisi unam veram. Cuius ratio est: quia res secundum unum et idem se habet uno et eodem modo. intellectus autem tunc est verus cum rem intelligit sicut se habet: qui autem ipsam intelligit aliter quam se habeat: non est verus intellectus sed falsus. Quia ergo res una secundum unum et idem uno et eodem modo se habet: et intellectus non est verus: nisi cum rem ut se habet ita concipit: necesse est ut omnes vere intelligentes de re una et eadem et secundum idem: unam et eadem conceptionem habeant. Quemadmodum patet manifeste in exemplo de homine quantum ad eius compositionem essentialem. Omnes enim homines vere hoc intelligentes concipiunt quod homo componitur essentialiter ex suis principijs quae sunt corpus et anima rationalis: Quicunque autem concipit aliter: talis non intelligit essentialem compositionem hominis."

80. See note 43.

81. Cf. Thomas Aquinas, *STh* 1, q. 17 a. 3 conc.: "in cognoscendo quidditates simplices non potest esse intellectus falsus, sed vel est verus, vel totaliter nihil intelligit." Cf. Conimbricenses (see note 26), 2.61: "Qui simpliciter cognoscit, vel rei naturam attingit, vel non: si attingit,

conformity to $x$ being the ground of its representing $x$.[82] This results in a weaker version of the ISC, amounting to nothing more than that those whose simple apprehension of $x$ conforms to $x$ do apprehend $x$ in the same way and therefore can be said to have the same concept of $x$. In other words: those who actually do have a concept of $x$ have the same concept of $x$, which, in turn, at least with the Jesuits and Scotists, may be interpreted as saying that they have concepts signifying the same object in the sense specified earlier.[83]

The issue of the ISC, thus, meets with another standard topic discussed in the scholastic textbooks: the so-called *veritas simplex*. The question under debate was whether and in what sense truth (or even falsity) may be ascribed to the first mental operation, that is, to simple apprehension.

## THE LATE SCHOLASTIC DEBATE ON INCOMPLEX TRUTH AND FALSITY

While it always was uncontroversial that truth and falsity, taken in the proper sense (*proprie*), formally (*formaliter*), simply (*simpliciter*), or "as such" (*absolute et secundum se*), are a matter of judgments or propositions, and therefore belong to the second mental operation, the operation of the composing and dividing intellect, there was a broad range of different views regarding the question of whether, and under what qualifications, truth and falsity may be ascribed to simple apprehension.

Those who preferred to restrict the notion of truth to its proper sense primarily referred to the authority of *De interpretatione* I, 1, 16a12–13 ("truth and falsity imply combination and separation") and *De anima* III, 6, 430b27–28 ("where the alternative of true or false applies, there we always find a putting together of objects of thought in a quasi-unity"), and built their argument on

---

conformatur obiecto, et est verus: si non attingit, non est falsus, sed ignorat illud, quod non percipit; quia non recte dicitur falso cognoscere id, quod re vera non cognoscit, sed illud ignorare." Cf. Petrus Hurtado de Mendoza, S.J., *Disputationes de universa philosophia* (Lyons, 1617), 823 ff.: "in apprehensione subiecti, vel praedicati solius nulla potest esse falsitas. . . . Probatur, quia actus ille repraesentat aliquid, hominem, v.g. aut animal: aut ergo repraesentat rationem hominis, vel animalis, aut non. Si primum: ergo conformatur cum obiecto: si secundum, ergo non apprehendit hominem, sed aliud obiectum, respectu cuius non erit falsus." Cf. Paulus Vallius, S.J., *Logica* (Lyons, 1622), 625a: "conceptus simplex vel est similis rei conceptae, vel non est. Si est similis, non est falsus, sed verus. Si vero non est similis, non est conceptus illius rei, sed alterius: ergo non potest esse difformitas inter simplicem conceptum et rem, cuius est ille conceptus."

82. It has to be noted, however, that in order to eliminate a too narrow interpretation of concepts being likenesses or images of things, there were several attempts in fifteenth- and sixteenth-century scholastic logic to reverse the foundational relation between likeness or image and representation; see S. Meier-Oeser, "Mental Language and Mental Representation in Late Scholastic Logic," in *John Buridan and Beyond*, ed. R. L. Friedman and S. Ebbesen (Copenhagen: C. A. Reitzel, 2004), 257 ff.

83. See note 35.

the correspondence between concepts and single words.[84] On the other side, the view that there is some kind of simple or incomplex truth (*veritas simplex, veritas incomplexa*), pertaining to the first operation of the mind, was primarily based on (1) the analogy between sensory perception of its proper object being always true, and the simple apprehension of the intellect, as it was mentioned by Aristotle in *De anima*, (2) Aristotle's explicit statement that the conception of the essence (i.e., the "*quod quid est*") of a thing is always true, and, last but not least, (3) the definition of truth as conformity of the intellect to its object.[85] Those who generally acknowledged the existence of some sort of truth on the level of simple apprehension—and this was the majority—subdivided truth of cognition (*veritas cognitionis*) regarding the two first operations into the simple truth (*veritas simplex*) of simple apprehensions and the complex truth (*veritas complexa*) of propositions.

The different accounts of simple truth, that is, of truth on the level of simple apprehension, are therefore to a certain extent governed by two paradigmatic models that had been underlying epistemological debates ever since antiquity: the propositional paradigm on one hand, and the pictorial paradigm on the other.[86] While the view that there can be neither truth nor falsity in simple apprehension—and therefore no *veritas simplex*—is based on the parallelism between simple concepts and single words, the view that there is, and always

---

84. Cf. Boethius, *Comment. in lib. Arist. Periherm.* (see note 49), 41 ff.: "similitudo est... quaedam inter se intellectuum [42] atque vocum: quemadmodum enim sunt quaedam simplicia quae ratione animi concipiuntur constitunuturque intellegentia mentis, in quibus neque veritas ulla neque falsitas invenitur, ita quoque in vocibus est. Simplex enim intellectus, ut verbi gratia hominis vel equi, neque falsitatem ullam retinet neque veritatem."

85. Cf. Radulphus Brito, *In lib. III De anima*, ed. Winfried Fauser, *Der Kommentar des Radulphus Brito zu Buch III De anima* (Munster, 1974), 266: "quaeritur, utrum circa intellectum componentem et dividentem solum sit veritas. (1) Arguitur quod non. Quia sensus respectu proprii sensibilis semper est verus. Ergo veritas habet esse circa apprehensionem sensus et pari ratione circa apprehensionem intellectus. Et ita non solum est circa compositionem et divisionem intellectus. (2) Item Philosophus dicit quod intellectus ipsius 'quod quid est' semper est verus. Et iste intellectus est simplex. Ergo circa simplicem apprehensionem intellectus consistit veritas. (3) Item veritas est quaedam conformitas ad rem. Sed intellectus apprehendens ita bene est conformis rei sicut intellectus componens. Ideo etc." For a detailed discussion of these arguments, see Gabriel Vazquez, S.J., *Commentariorum, ac disputationum in Primam partem S. Thomae t. 1*, disp. 75: "An veritas intellectus solum sit in compositione, et divisione" (Ingolstadt, 1609) 446a–452b.

86. According to these paradigms the two kinds of truth are characterized as adequateness of representation (*adaequatio repraesentationis*) or conformity "*per modum repraesentationis*" and as adequateness of saying (*adaequatio dictionis*) or conformity "*per modum dictionis*." Cf. Martin Smiglecius, S.J., *Logica* (1616), 103: "Veritas cognitionis...consistit in conformitate cognitionis cum re ipsa; estque duplex; alia simplex et incomplexa, absque ulla affirmatione et iudicio, alia complexa, hoc est cum affirmatione et illatione.... Prior veritas est conformitas cognitionis cum obiecto *per modum repraesentationis*: Posterior vero veritas est conformitas cognitionis cum obiecto non pure per modum repraesentationis sed *per modum dictionis*." Cf. Conimbriceses in the following note.

is, some kind of truth (i.e., *veritas simplex*) but no falsity in simple apprehension is motivated by the image-paradigm and the aforementioned bivalence principle of representation. For under the conditions that (1) mental concepts are taken to be mental images, (2) truth is defined, in the traditional manner, as adequation of intellect and its object and thus essentially characterized by conformity, and (3) the form of an image alone pins down what it is an image of, or, in other words, if intension determines extension, it is clear that images, and simple concepts as well insofar as they are seen as some kind of image, must always be true. For no image whatsoever can be dissimilar to its subject in that respect in which it is an image, because in case of its dissimilarity to $x$ it is not a false image of $x$ but rather is not an image of $x$.[87]

What would be conceded with regard to any material image, namely, that it conforms to its object in some respects while not so in several others, does not hold, according to this view, for simple concepts. For if it is taken as "simple," that is, as some kind of atomic, unanalyzable image[88] always referring to what it is a likeness of, any talk about nonconforming aspects is ruled out, so that the bivalence principle of representation is valid. Simple truth, thus, was guaranteed either by the alleged simplicity of mental concepts or by a sharpened notion of image, supposing something to be an image of its object only in those respects in which it conforms to it. Thus, any representation can be dissimilar to its object only in that respect in which it does not represent it (as for instance an image of Caesar, representing Caesar's colors and shape, though not his essence, is an image of Caesar in regard to his exterior figure but not so in regard to his essence), for, in general, to represent and to be represented are correlatives and thus always correspond to each other.[89]

87. See Conimbricenses (see note 26), 2.127: "non est praetermittendum insigne discrimen inter veritatem simplicem, et complexam; quamvis enim utraque posita sit in adaequatione intellectus ad rem, nihilominus veritas simplex primo, et per se consistit in adaequatione repraesentationis cum obiecto repraesentato. Unde oritur, ut nullam habeat oppositam falsitatem, quia nullius rei imago potest esse illi difformis, quoad ea, in quibus est illius imago... complexa autem veritas, etsi fiat per conceptus repraesentativos, non est posita primo in adaequatione repraesentationis, sed dictionis"; cf. P. Hurtado de Mendoza (see note 81), 823 ff.: "Dico primo, in apprehensione subiecti, vel praedicati solius nulla potest esse falsitas.... Probatur, quia actus illa repraesentat aliquid, hominem, v.g. aut animal: aut ergo repraesentat rationem hominis, vel animalis, aut non. Si primum: ergo conformatur cum obiecto: si secundum, ergo non apprehendit hominem, sed aliud obiectum, respectu cuius non erit falsus."

88. Cf. Suarez (see note 106).

89. M. Smiglecius (see note 86), 109 ff.: "sciendum est, primam operationem referri ad suum obiectum per modum repraesentationis: consistit enim apprehensio in sola repraesentatione obiecti absque ullo judicio: quare et conformitas ipsius vel difformitas cum obiecto est per [110] modum repraesentationis. Repraesentatio autem si referatur ad id obiectum quod repraesentatur, et quoad ea quae repraesentantur, semper est vera et conformis obiecto repraesentato; repraesentans enim et repraesentatum sibi correspondent. Quod si est dissimilitudo aliqua et difformitas inter ista, ea solum erit in iis quae non repraesentantur: Verbi gratia imago Caesaris repraesentat Caesarem in coloribus et forma exteriori, non in essentia, quocirca est conformis Caesarem in forma exteriori, difformis in essentia. Et universe loquendo. Imago

On the basis of arguments like this, most authors acknowledged the existence of simple truth (*veritas simplex*) on the level of first mental operation. Only a few, however, spoke in this context of truth in a proper sense, as Martin Smiglecius did with reference to the definition of truth in terms of conformity of knowledge to its object. For as any image is always a true image of what it represents, there is, without reference to any judgment, a representational conformity in the simple concept, being such *in repraesentando* as the thing represented is *in essendo*.[90] It was generally agreed that *veritas simplex* is truth only in a more or less improper sense. Incomplex truth, therefore, was terminologically distinguished from the formal truth of propositions by being characterized as virtual[91] or material truth.[92] However, the consequence that seems to follow from all this, namely, that there can be no room for falsity in regard to simple apprehension, was by no means universally accepted. Even if, again, there were only a very few authors who advocated the existence of falsity proper on the level of simple apprehension, many authors accepted, though under strict qualifications, the possibility of false concepts. This was partly motivated by the Scotistic view toward the human incapacity of knowing the substance of things.[93] Scotus had limited the claim that the intellect is always true regarding to the "*quod quid est*" to what he called the "*conceptus simpliciter simplices*," that is, the absolutely unanalyzable concepts of the highest genera and ultimate differences,[94] different from the notions of simple

---

in eo in quo est imago, est conformis ei cujus est imago, repraesentare enim et repraesentari sunt correlativa, et sibi correspondentia." Cf. F. Suarez, *Disp. met.* 9, 1, 15.

90. Ibid., 106sq.: "Dicendum . . . est dari in prima operatione veritatem incomplexam eamque esse proprie veritatem [107]. . . . probatur ratione. Veritas cognitionis est conformitas cognitionis cum re: atqui conformitas cognitionis cum obiecto potest esse simplex absque omni affirmatione et negatione . . . imago est vere imago ejus quem repraesentat. Ergo etiam similiter conceptus simplex erit verus conceptus rei. . . . Cum enim possit cognitio dupliciter conformari rei. Primo per repraesentationem, quia cognitio talis est in repraesentando, qualis est res in essendo. Secundo, per affirmationem quia affirmatur esse conformis, non sequitur si non est conformis per affirmationem quod non possit esse conformis per repraesentationem."

91. P. Hurtado de Mendoza (see note 81), 824: "simpliciter non est veritas, aut falsitas nisi in judicio, quia . . . communior usus vocis est pro veritate complexa. In specie impressa productiva iudicij reperitur veritas, aut falsitas, non formaliter, sed virtualiter, quia illa non est formalis, sed virtualis repraesentatio obiecti." See also note 96.

92. Cf. D. Masius (see note 44), 18a: "Veritas in actu exercito, materialiter, aut tamquam in subiecto, in sensibus reperiatur. . . . Haec eadem veritas reperitur in intellectu in prima illius apprehensione. . . . Confir. . . . intellectus in simplici rerum apprehensione est adaequatus, et conformis rebus cognitis, cum igitur veritas significet huiusmodi adaequationem, veritas proculdubio reperietur in prima functione intellectus. . . . [18b]: Veritas in actu signato, formaliter, et tanquam in cognoscente, in solo iudicio intellectus. . . ."

93. See notes 74–78.

94. Duns Scotus, *Quaestiones subtilissimae in Metaphysicorum libros Aristotelis* 6.3, in *B. Ioannis Duns Scoti opera philosophica*, ed. Girard J. Etzkorn et al. (St. Bonaventure, N.Y.: Franciscan Institute, 1997), vols. 3–4: "illud, De anima, quod intellectus circa 'quod quid est' semper est verus, sicut sensus circa proprium sensibile . . . est intelligendum praecise circa conceptum simpliciter simplicem."

substances.⁹⁵ Therefore, according to Scotus and his followers, the simple understanding (*intellectus simplex*) of any concept which is not "*simpliciter simplex*" can be, though not formally (*formaliter*) at least virtually false (*virtualiter falsus*) if the intellect apprehends it under inadequate determinations, that is, under determinations not pertaining to what the apprehension apprehends.⁹⁶ While "*veritas simplex*" is supported by the simplicity—or, as with Scotus, by the "simple simplicity"—of mental concepts, a further gateway for letting in the notion "*falsitas simplex*" was opened by considering that the actual form of mental life, the structure of mental operations—fortunately—is more complex than the clear-cut distinction of the first, second, and third operations of the mind may suggest. For the simple apprehension (*apprehensio simplex*) is not necessarily an apprehension of the simple (*apprehensio simplicium*), since propositions, too, can be objects of apprehension.⁹⁷ Furthermore, conceptions of simple objects are normally embedded in a more involute situational context of mental operations, such that in many cases a concept is not formed "*praecise et abstracte*"⁹⁸ but rather on the occasion of a certain object being present,⁹⁹ or with the intention to conceive a certain object,¹⁰⁰ or as providing the matter for judgment,¹⁰¹ so that there is, as already conceded by Thomas Aquinas, a

---

95. On Scotus's distinction between *conceptus simplices* and *conceptus simpliciter simplices*, see *Ordinatio* I d. 3 p. 1 q. 1–2, in *Opera omnia* (Vatican City: Typis Polyglottis Vaticanis, 1950), 3.49 n. 71: "conceptus 'simpliciter simplex' est qui non est resolubilis in plures conceptus, ut conceptus entis vel ultimae differentiae. Conceptum vero simplicem sed 'non-simpliciter simplicem' voco, quicumque potest concipi ab intellectu actu simplicis intelligentiae, licet posset resolvi in plures conceptus, seorsum conceptibiles." Cf. *Lectura* I d. 2 p. 1 q. 1–2 (*Opera omnia*, ed. Vaticana), 16.118–9 n. 24: "Ille est conceptus simpliciter simplex qui non reducitur in priorem aut simpliciorem, nec omnino in plures conceptus resolvitur, sicut est conceptus entis et conceptus ultimae differentiae. Conceptus autem non simpliciter simplex est ille qui licet apprehenditur sine affirmatione et negatione, tamen resolvitur in plures conceptus quorum unus potest concipi sine alio, ut est conceptus speciei in genus et differentiam resolubilis. . . .; sed non sic in simplicibus, quia vel totum ibi apprehenditur vel nihil."

96. Cf. Scotus (see note 94): "intellectus simplex circa conceptum non simpliciter simplicem, licet non possit esse formaliter falsus, potest tamen esse virtualiter falsus, apprehendendo aliquid sub determinatione sibi non convenienti"; cf. (nearly verbatim) Antonius Andreae, *Scriptum in arte veteri* (Venice, 1508) fol. 64r–v; cf. P. Hurtado de Mendoza (see note 91).

97. Cf. Raphael Aversa, *Logica institutionibus praevijs quaestionibus contexta* (Rome, 1623), 489: "Primus actus intellectivae cognitionis solet appellari Simplicium apprehensio. Sic etiam Aristoteles 3. de Anima text. 21 appellavit indivisibilium intellectionem. Verum quia simplicitas quae huius actui attribuitur, magis se tenet ex parte ipsius actus, quam obiecti; dicimus enim apprehendi etiam complexa et integras propositiones; simplici tamen actu"; see Suarez (note 133).

98. See Vallius, *Logica*, 625b.

99. Cf. Conimbricenses (see note 26), 2.62: "cognitio auri comparata occasione auricalchi praesentis habet pro obiecto aurum; et cum illo conformatur; cum aurichalcho vero, nec conformationem habet, nec difformitatem, quia illud non respicit."

100. See note 113.

101. See note 124.

certain accidental admixture of compositeness to the intellectual apprehension of the "*quod quid est*" and thus a possible, though accidental, falsity in the first mental operation. According to Thomas, this can take place in two ways: either by attributing to one thing the definition proper to another, wherefore the definition is false with regard to the object to which it is applied, or by composing a definition of parts that are mutually exclusive, so that the definition is false in itself (e.g., "a four-legged rational animal"). Because, however, falsity in this case results from adding a predicate which is incompossible with the particles of the essential definition, the infallibility of the intellect in its knowledge of simple essences, based on the bivalence principle of representation, as he sees it, is not compromised but rather supported by this.[102]

These two cases, namely, false ascription and incompossibility, have been taken as the main reasons for some kind of improper falsity in simple apprehension.[103] The notion of false ascription has been used to explain the common talk of "false images" and false simple concepts.[104] Just like Gottlob Frege, who later noted that "when we characterize an image as false, falsity does not properly pertain to the image itself but rather to our estimation of that image as being an image of this or that object, which it actually does not represent,"[105]

---

102. Thomas Aquinas, *STh* 1, q. 17 a. 3 conc. : "falsitas intellectus per se solum circa compositionem intellectus est, per accidens etiam in operatione intellectus qua cognoscit quod quid est, potest esse falsitas, inquantum ibi compositio intellectus admiscetur. quod potest esse dupliciter. uno modo, secundum quod intellectus definitionem unius attribuit alteri; ut si definitionem circuli attribuat homini. unde definitio unius rei est falsa de altera. alio modo, secundum quod partes definitionis componit ad invicem, quae simul sociari non possunt, sic enim definitio non est solum falsa respectu alicuius rei, sed est falsa in se. ut si formet talem definitionem, animal rationale quadrupes, falsus est intellectus sic definiendo, propterea quod falsus est in formando hanc compositionem, aliquod animal rationale est quadrupes. et propter hoc, in cognoscendo quidditates simplices non potest esse intellectus falsus, sed vel est verus, vel totaliter nihil intelligit."

103. Cf. Radulphus Brito (see note 85), 267, who stated that falsity of simple apprehension "non est aliud nisi quidam error et deceptio in apprehensione ipsius 'quod quid est'; quando aliquis componit 'quod quid est' alicuius rei ex partibus incompossibilibus sicut dicendo 'animal insensibile'; vel, ut dicunt alii, quando aliquis accipit 'quod quid est' alicuius rei cum alia re, sicut quando aliquis intelligit 'quod quid est' hominis est 'animal hinibile' vel aliquid huiusmodi. Hoc est error in apprehensione ipsius 'quod quid est' propter incompossibilitatem partium ipsius 'quod quid est' ad illud cui assignatur."

104. See, for instance, Isaac Watts, better known as the "father of English hymnody," who in his *Logic: or, the right use of reason in the inquiry after truth* (1725) states that "Our ideas are either true or false; for, an idea being the representation of a thing in the mind, it must be either a true or a false representation of it," and, after his discussion of some of the logical difficulties conjoined to this position, still holds that "since ideas are pictures of things, it can never be very improper to pronounce them to be true or false, according to their conformity or nonconformity to their exemplars."

105. Cf. Frege, *Logik*, 42 ff.: "Wenn wir ein Bild als 'falsch' kennzeichnen, dann liegt die Falschheit nicht eigentlich beim Bild selbst, sondern in unserer Bewertung dieses Bildes als ein Bild von dem und dem Gegenstand, den es faktisch gar nicht repräsentiert."

Suárez claimed that the alleged falsity of an image consists in our attributing the image to a subject it does not represent. And this falsity is not falsity proper but is only objectively in the intellect and denominated after the intellectual act.[106] The differentiation between a concept or idea in itself and the very same concept or idea insofar as it is ascribed to certain things is still effective in John Locke's claim of the falsity of our ideas of substances. While Locke, on the one hand, agrees with the propositional approach to truth and falsity, according to which "the ideas in our minds, being only so many perceptions or appearances there, none of them are false," because "truth or falsehood lying always in some affirmation or negation, mental or verbal, our ideas are not capable . . . of being false, till the mind passes some judgment on them,"[107] he concedes, on the other hand, that "ideas referred to anything extraneous to them may be true or false" or are at least are "capable to be called true or false." Referring ideas to what is extraneous to them is, as he sees it, by no means a marginal aspect of mental life. For the whole range of tacit assumptions of this kind covers the areas of other men's ideas, real existence, and real essences. While the former of these assumptions, by which "the mind supposes any idea it has conformable to that in other men's minds, called by the same common name,"[108] directly refers to the ISC, the latter, by which "the mind refers any of its ideas to that real constitution and essence of anything, whereon all its properties depend," refers to simple apprehensions of substance, as the scholastics took them. And in respect to these, Locke claims, "the greatest part, if not all our ideas of substances, are false."[109]

The works of post-Tridentine scholastic philosophy offer quite a number of variant accounts and terminological determinations of the falsity of simple apprehension in contradistinction to falsity in the proper sense. Paulus Vallius, referring to Thomas Aquinas, advocates an "accidental" truth or falsity based on the virtual composition that takes place when the intellect apprehends a thing not absolutely and abstractly but as falling under this or that species, as for instance when brass is apprehended as a kind of gold.[110] According to

---

106. F. Suarez, *Disp. met.* 9, 1, 15: "quando appellamus aliquam falsam imaginem, falsitas revera existit in attributione vel compositione nostra, quia scilicet attribuimus talem imaginem ei, quem non repraesentat, existimantes esse imaginem ejus et ita illa falsitas solum est objective in intellectu, seu denominative ab actu intellectus, eodem modo censendum est de simplicibus conceptibus seu actibus cognoscendi, quia ita se habent, sicut simplices imagines."

107. Locke, *An Essay Concerning Human Understanding* II, 34, 3.

108. Ibid., II, 34, 5.

109. Ibid.

110. Vallius, *Logica*, 625a–b: "Secunda pars conclusionis [i.e: "per accidens, possit esse veritas et falsitas"] probatur. Quia quamvis in prima operatione absolute, et secundum se nulla sit veritas intellectiva, et nulla falsitas, quatenus tamen in illa virtute est compositio, vel divisio, seu affirmatio aliqua, aut negatio, potest esse veritas vel falsitas aliqua intellectiva, immo etiam [625b] complexa. Quia . . . duobus modis possumus intelligere compositionem admisceri simplici apprehensioni. Primo formaliter, formando scilicet aliquam propositionem, qua affirmemus, vel negemus praedicatum de subiecto. Secundo, virtualiter, quia videlicet ex ipsa apprehensione apta est sequi propositio, et consequenter compositio, vel divisio. Quando

Franciscus Murcia de la Llana there is at least a "fundamental" falsity to be found in the first mental operation or definition.[111] Martin Smiglecius establishes the falsity of representation by distinguishing between the immediate and the ultimate object of mental concepts (*obiectum immediatum—obiectum ultimatum*), so that, for instance, the representation of a flying ass—even though it conforms to its immediate object, the flying ass—can be characterized as false because it does not conform to its ultimate object, the real ass.[112] Johannes Lalemandet acknowledges even the proper falsity of simple apprehension by pointing to the fact that the mental operation of apprehending something is regularly executed with the intention of apprehending some certain thing. If, therefore, "I intend to conceive man, but do not conceive him as he is, there is an inadequacy (*disconvenientia*) and therefore falsity."[113]

---

enim intellectus rem aliquam apprehendit, duobus modis potest se habere: Primo, praecise, et abstracte illam apprehendendo. Secundo, concipiendo sub aliqua compositione, ut concipiendo illam tanquam individuum, sub hac, vel illa specie contentum. V.g. quando obiicitur intellectum aurichalcus, potest primo concipere aurum abstracte omnino, et simpliciter; et tunc nulla est omnino compositio, vel divisio. Secundo, potest concipere aurichalcum tanquam individuum sub auro contentum, atque ideo concipere aurum tamquam speciem, vel genus aurichalci: quod est aliquo modo componere, quia quando intellectum conceptum auri per simplicem apprehensionem applicat huic individuo sibi subiecto, aliquo modo componit, quia concipit illud ut individuum auri, atque virtualiter affirmat aurum de illo; quod est vere, et proprie componere. Dicimus ergo, in simplici apprehensione, ratione huius virtualis compositionis, posse esse falsitatem, et veritatem propriam, et intellectivam, sed per accidens. Quia non sunt in illa, quatenus est formaliter simplex apprehensio, sed quatenus est virtualis compositio. Et hoc voluit indicare S. Thomas, quando dixit 1 par. q. 17 ar. 3 propterea intellectum formando hanc definitionem 'Animal rationale quadrupes' esse falsum, quia falsitas est formando hanc propositionem 'Aliquod animal rationale est quadrupes.'"

111. Franciscus Murcia de la Llana, *Selecta circa Aristotelis dialecticam subtilioris doctrinae quae in Complutensi academia versatur* (Ingolstadt, 1621), 392: "Veritas et falsitas solum reperiuntur in propositione, quae sit per secundam operationem intellectus, distinguo. Formaliter concedo. Fundamentaliter tamen reperiuntur in prima operatione intellectus, ad quam pertinet definitio (nam definitio non est propositio) et ad hoc, ut definitio dicatur vera aut falsa sufficit, quod in ea reperiatur veritas et falsitas fundamentaliter."

112. M. Smiglecius (see note 86), 110: "Veritas repraesentationis per se sumitur ex conformitate cum obiecto ut est in reipsa: si enim aliter sit in reipsa quam repraesentatur, repraesentatio erit simpliciter falsa: sic repraesentatio asini volantis est falsa, quia licet conceptus asini volantis sit conformis asino volanti, qui est obiectum immediatum: quia tamen non est conformis asino a parte rei qui est obiectum ultimatum, idcirco talis conceptus simpliciter non est conformis rei: obiectum enim immediatum refertur per conceptum ad obiectum ultimatum, et idcirco debet illi conforme. Quia igitur simplex apprehensio per se, et ratione repraesentationis potest esse difformis obiecto ultimato, ideo per se non per accidens convenit illis difformitas, et ex consequenti falsitas. Quod etiam a simili explicatur in secunda operatione. Nam cum affirmo hominem esse quadrupedem, talis affirmatio est quidem conformis obiecto immediato, nempe homini quadrupedi affirmato, quia tamen non est conformis homini a parte rei simpliciter et per se non vero per accidens est falsa."

113. Johannes Lalemandet, *Cursus philosophicus* (Lyons, 1656), 226a: "Ubi potest esse disconvenientia, et difformitas, ibi potest esse falsitas: sed in prima mentis operatione potest esse disconvenientia, seu difformitas, ergo et falsitas, maior patet ex definitione falsitatis,

Most scholastic authors, however, would deny *"falsitas simplex"* to be falsity proper. The Conimbricenses, for instance, characterize accidental falsity as a "radical and most improper falsity" resulting from "a sensation which is so confused that it gives an occasion to the internal sense or to the intellect to perceive one thing for another and to make a false judgment."[114]

### THE DESCARTES-ARNAULD DEBATE ON MATERIAL FALSITY

The issue of falsity on the level of simple apprehension has recently received more attention in the scholarly accounts of Descartes's position on the "material falsity" of adventitious ideas. As is well-known, Descartes in his Third Meditation holds that adventitious ideas, as for instance "heat and cold, . . . are not thought by me except very confusedly and obscurely, so that I do not even know if they are true or false, that is, whether the ideas, which I have of them, are ideas of particular things, or of non-things." Therefore, he says: "Although falsity properly speaking, or 'formal' falsity, cannot be found except in judgments . . . still there is . . . another 'material' falsity in ideas, when they represent a non-thing as a thing: thus, for example, the ideas I have of heat and cold are so far from being clear and distinct that from them I cannot say whether cold is just a privation of heat or heat a privation of cold, or both are real qualities, or neither."[115]

These remarks are the starting point of a prima facie puzzling debate with Antoine Arnauld on material falsity. This debate has been criticized, especially with regard to Descartes's contribution, as confused and incoherent by quite a number of contemporary commentators.[116] Already a short look at the aforementioned scholastic discussions on incomplex truth and falsity, however, will confirm Norman J. Wells's claim that "when Descartes' position on material falsity is understood in the light of late Scholastic sources, especially Suárez . . . the alleged confusion and incoherency vanishes."[117] For, the arguments exchanged in the Descartes-Arnauld debate on material falsity do indeed remain within the boundaries set by these discussions.

---

dicitur enim falsitas, difformitas aut disconvenientia quaedam: minor manifestatur, v.g. quando concipio hominem ut animal irrationale, nonne est disconvenientia et difformitas in illa cognitione de homine? Respondent non esse disconvenientiam, sed tantum ignorantiam, et nescientiam, sed esto sit ignorantia, ea tamen, ut ita dicam, est positiva, quia intendo concipere hominem, attamen non concipio ut est, ergo est disconvenientia, et proinde falsitas."

114. Conimbricenses (see note 26), 2.65: "est . . . aliquando sensatio adeo confusa, ut praebeat occasionem sensui interiori, vel intellectui percipiendi unum pro alio, et ferendi falsum iudicium, quod vocamus habere falsitatem per accidens."

115. Descartes, *Oeuvres*, 7.43,22–44,3.

116. For references to the various critical assessments on Descartes's position on 'material falsity' see the brilliant article of Norman J. Wells, "Material Falsity in Descartes, Arnauld, and Suarez," *Journal of the History of Philosophy* 22 (1984): 25–50, at 25–27. A good account of Descartes's position has been recently given by Lilli Alanen, *Descartes's Concept of Mind* (Cambridge, Mass.: Harvard University Press, 2003), 156–164.

117. Wells, "Material Falsity," 25–26.

While Arnauld advocates the position of those—predominantly Thomistic—authors who, on grounds of the bivalence principle of representation, claimed the truth of concepts but denied the possibility of any falsity on the level of simple apprehension, Descartes's position comes close to the position of those—predominantly Jesuit and Franciscan—authors who, on one hand, acknowledged truth and falsity proper exclusively as a matter of judgment, but, on the other hand, used terminological determinations like "virtual," "fundamental," or—as Suárez—"material" falsity in order to characterize certain defects of our simple concepts in their functional relation to the second mental operation of judgment. When Arnauld argues against Descartes by stating that "if cold is merely a privation, then there cannot be an idea of cold which represents it to me as a positive thing, and so our author here is confusing a judgment with an idea,"[118] he is in accordance with the commonly accepted scholastic position, supposing that any idea always conforms to what it represents,[119] so that, as Arnauld holds, "if cold is merely a privation, there cannot be a positive idea of it, and hence there cannot be an idea which is materially false."[120] For "the idea in question may perhaps not be the idea of cold, but it cannot be a false idea,"[121] so that the alleged falsity has to be explained in terms of false ascription: "But, you may reply, it is false precisely because it is not the idea of cold. No: it is your judgment that is false, if you judge that it is the idea of cold. The idea itself, within you, is completely true."[122]

Descartes's rejoinder makes clear that in this context he does not—like Arnauld—consider the idea in the formal sense as a representation of this or that object but rather "materially," that is, as an operation of the intellect insofar it is embedded in the complex framework of the different types of mental operations. The material falsity of ideas, as Wells has already pointed out, must therefore be seen "in terms of a relationship between the pre-judgmental level and the judgmental level wherein the former occasions, but does not cause, the shortcomings of the latter."[123] For such falsity is characterized by an idea's being so obscure and confused that it provides subject matter for error (*praebere materiam erroris*).[124] Thus, it closely corresponds to what Suárez considered the improper or denominative falsity or the imperfection of a simple apprehension

---

118. Descartes, *Oeuvres*, 7.206, 16–18.
119. See note 81.
120. Descartes, *Oeuvres*, 7.206, 22–24.
121. Ibid., 7.207, 9–10.
122. Ibid., 7.207, 11–13.
123. Wells, "Material Falsity," 45.
124. Descartes, *Oeuvres*, 7.232–233; cf. 7.234,13–18, where Descartes declares that his "only reason for calling the idea [of cold] 'materially false' is that, owing to the fact that it is obscure and confused, I am unable to judge whether or not what it represents to me is something positive which exists outside of my sensation. And hence I may be led to judge that it is something positive though in fact it may merely be a privation."

that occasions falsity of judgment[125]—and even more closely to what the Conimbricenses had said about the accidental falsity of a "sensation which is so confused that it gives an occasion to . . . the intellect to perceive one thing for another and to make a false judgment."[126]

In regard to material falsity, therefore, *pace* Arnauld, Descartes neither is in conflict with his epistemological-metaphysical principle that the idea of *x* is *x* itself as it is objectively in the intellect, nor does he confuse an idea with a judgment. For while he clearly acknowledges the difference between the material falsity of adventitious ideas and the proper falsity of judgments, his aforementioned principle (which, by the way, conforms to the older tradition in which a mental term signifying the same for all, was characterized as a natural objective likeness *"naturalis similitudo obiectiva,"* because of being such in the mode of a sign as the thing is in the mode of a significate,[127] or because of being such in representing as the thing represented is in being[128]) is valid only in regard to perfect ideas, that is, ideas which, according to Descartes—here again in agreement with the scholastic tradition[129]—are characterized as clear and distinct.[130]

---

125. Cf. F. Suarez, *Disp. Met.* 9, 1, 16, where he reads Thomas Aquinas's claim on the accidental fallibility of the intellect (see note 102) such that he "non intelligit falsitatem proprie sumptam in ipsa simplici apprehensione reperiri, sed esse in his apprehensionibus occasionem erroris et deceptionis et inde falsas nominari . . . quia sensus exterior movetur ab exteriori obiecto et apprehendit illud per modum intuitionis atque adeo per modum praesentis et existentis, ideo, quando apprehendit rem quae revera non est, vel non eo modo quo est, falli dicitur, quia discrepat ab illa re quam pro obiecto habere videtur, quamvis revera ad illam vel ad talem modum eius non terminetur eius apprehensio, et ideo non sit in eo propria falsitas sed imperfectio quaedam, quae est occasio falsitatis." Cf. ib. 9, 1, 19; 25, 319: "falsitas improprie dicta, quae rebus, vel simplicis conceptibus attribuitur, solum est denominatio extrinseca, vel signi, vel causae, seu occasionis."

126. See note 114.

127. Cf. Petrus a Spinosa, *Tractatus terminorum*, fol. 3v, see V. Muñoz Delgado, "Pedro de Espinosa y la logica en Salamanca hasta 1550," *Anuario filosofico* 16 (1983): 152: "Significare naturaliter proprie est esse noticiam anime quo modo soli termini mentales significant. Significant idem apud omnes. Terminus mentalis dicitur naturalis similitudo obiectiva. Notitia vocatur naturalis similitudo obiectiva, quia talis est in genere signi qualis res ad extra in genere significati."

128. M. Smiglecius (see note 86), 107.

129. Cf. R. Aversa (see note 96), 18: "Tunc [simplex apprehensio] est recta et perfecta, cum intellectus clare et explicite rem apprehendit: cum per se et distincte concipit et apprehendit ea quae in se distincta sunt. . . . Sic enim intellectus perficitur, ut clare res concipiat, et distincte, singulas sui proprias et essentiales rationes."

130. Cf. Descartes, *Oeuvres*, 7.233, 6–15: "Cùm autem ait Vir C. , *ideam frigoris esse frigus ipsum prout est objective in intellectu*, distinctione arbitror opus esse: hoc enim saepe contingit in ideis obscuris et confusis, inter quas hae caloris et frigoris sunt numerandæ, ut ad aliud quid referantur quàm ad id cujus revera ideae sunt. Ita, si frigus sit tantùm privatio, frigoris idea non est frigus ipsum, prout est objective in intellectu, sed aliud quid quod perperam pro istâ privatione sumitur; nempe est sensus quidam nullum habens esse extra intellectum." Descartes's position, however, sharply differs from the one maintained by the

While Descartes is surely right to claim that calling obscure and confused ideas materially false "does not in any way violate my fundamental principles," the question, however, remains whether his explicit terminological appeal to Suárez is justified when he maintains to have "found the word 'materially' used in an identical sense to my own in Suárez's *Metaphysical Disputations*, part 9, section 2, number 4."[131] For, at a first glance, it may seem that, in this rather intricate passage, Suárez is using the term "material falsity" in a somewhat different sense.

In the passage, Suárez, who generally argues in favor of a strict correlation between truth and falsity proper and judgment,[132] aims to give evidence that, even though there may be some sort of composition and division in the pre-judgmental apprehensive cognition of an assertive proposition representing a judgment, there is no falsity in the proper sense in it, but only an improper falsity "as in a sign" (*tamquam in signo*). No one, therefore, no matter how false the judgmental composition he apprehends may ever be, is to be held as erring or being deceived until he judges. And yet, just as it is possible to say that there is *"falsitas ut in signo"* in a mere composition of spoken words, it can be admitted that a nonjudgmental apprehension, too, includes falsity, though "as it were materially" (*quasi materialiter*) and in the mode of a sign that by itself signifies something false (*tamquam in signo quod secundum se falsum significat*).[133]

The doctrinal background for these remarks is this: Suárez, like many scholastic authors of the late sixteenth and early seventeenth centuries, adopted Gregory of Rimini's view on mental language,[134] according to which a mental proposition in the proper sense is seen as a simple mental act regularly including assent to what is asserted in a proposition. In other words: when we *think that x* we mentally *say that x* and do *mean that x*. This entails that for Gregory a mental representation of propositions regarding the truth value of which the intellect is undecided cannot be instantiated by mental propositions in the proper sense. Gregory's solution to the problem of how, then, the intellect represents propositions to which it has no definite propositional attitude (a commonly used

---

scholastic authors in his tendency to restrict the commendation of ideas as clear and distinct to the mind's innate ideas as well as in his denial of any immediate likeness between the sensory perception and its object.

131. Ibid., 7.235, 5–14.

132. F. Suarez, *Disp. Met.* 8, 4, 8: "omnis veritas cognitionis, eo modo quo est, in iudicio existit."

133. Ibid., 9, 2, 4: "Unde nemo censetur decipi seu errare donec iudicet, quantumvis falsas compositiones apprehendat. Quoniam autem apprehensio illa quae fit sine iudicio regulariter fit per conceptus vocum potius quam rerum, ut supra dixi, sicut in compositione vocum est falsitas sicut in signo, ita admitti potest in illa apprehensione, quamvis in ea sit quasi materialiter, id est, non tamquam in affirmante vel proferente falsum, sed tamquam in signo quod secundum se falsum significat."

134. Cf. S. Meier-Oeser, "Mental Language and Mental Representation."

example is the sentence "the number of stars is even") is such: in this case the mind is forming an *"enuntiatio mentalis improprie dicta,"* that is, it nonassertively entertains the proposition by internally representing the corresponding spoken utterance.

This is the point of reference of Suárez's claim for the existence of improper and "material" falsity on the level of simple apprehension.[135] The prejudgmental apprehension, for him, corresponds to a nonassertively entertained proposition. And here we regularly apprehend the concepts of the spoken words (*conceptus vocum*) rather than the concepts of the things (*conceptus rerum*), so that, just as falsity is commonly said to be in a spoken sentence as in a sign (*ut in signo*), it is justified to ascribe falsity, though not in the proper sense but *"tamquam in signo"* and *"materialiter,"* to a prejudgmental apprehension. In this context, therefore, the term *"materialiter"* is more than just a counternotion to *"formaliter"* in an unspecific sense, and does not simply indicate the improperness of the falsity in question. It rather seems to be motivated by and to allude to the semantic terminology of material supposition (*suppositio materialis*), as when Suárez compares the prejudgmental apprehension with a spoken proposition that is not used but mentioned (*materialiter prolata*).[136]

How can then Descartes claim that here the "word 'materially' is used in an identical sense to my own"? There is, of course, a general analogy in the way Descartes and Suárez both take the term to designate a kind of improper falsity in simple apprehension. But there is still another agreement, which, based on the reference to the concept of linguistic signs, leads deeper into the roots of Descartes's epistemology.[137] For Descartes, sharply rejecting the scholastic species-theory and its assumption that the relation of a sensory idea to its external object is determined by effective causality and likeness, refers to the model of arbitrary linguistic signification in order to give an account of the perception of external material reality.[138] Thus, just as Suárez holds that the mere apprehension of a false proposition is not formally false unless it is connected with assent, that is, unless it is judged as actually indicating what is the case, so too with Descartes, sense perceptions, though obscure and confused, are not formally—but rather

---

135. Cf. Suarez's remarks on prejudgmental apprehension in *Disp. Met.* 8, 4, 8.

136. The passage cited in note 133 continues: "Sicut est falsitas in hac propositione: Non est Deus, vel scripta vel materialiter prolata ab eo qui refert: Dixit insipiens in corde suo: Non est Deus; et ideo de huiusmodi falsitate eadem ratio est quae de falsitate quae est in compositione vocali, ut in signo."

137. For the function of the notion of sign for Descartes's theory of perception, see Jean-Luc Marion, *Sur la théologie blanche de Descartes* (Paris: Presses Universitaires de France, 1981) 253 ff.; J. W. Yolton, *Perceptual Acquaintance from Descartes to Reid* (Minneapolis: University of Minnesota Press, 1984), 22 ff.

138. Cf. S. Meier-Oeser, *Die Spur des Zeichens. Das Zeichen und seine Funktion in der Philosophie des Mittelalters und der frühen Neuzeit* (Berlin: De Gruyter, 1997), 354–360.

"materialiter"—false as far as they are not taken as signs indicating how things really are. "Material falsity" is thus, as the scholastics would say, a "virtual" falsity inscribed in the adventitious idea of sense perception that becomes effective by giving occasion to a formal or proper falsity, when the mind is induced by it to judge that things really are as the idea seems to indicate. In Descartes's view, however, it is not God, the originator of that "language" of perceptual signs of which the sensory ideas are elements, who is to blame for these shortcomings, but rather human misunderstanding of the cognitive function of perceptual signs and the resulting misinterpretation of them. For these are "given me by nature merely to signify to my mind what things are beneficial and hurtful to the composite whole of which it is a part . . . and are sufficiently clear and distinct for that purpose." If they are used, however, as "infallible rules by which to determine immediately the essence of the bodies that exist out of me, . . . they can of course afford me only the most obscure and confused knowledge"; for "this they signify only in a very obscure and confused way."[139]

It is clear that, differing from (at least parts of) the Aristotelian tradition, Descartes affirms that the alleged infallibility of sensory perception in regard to its proper object cannot function as a paradigmatic model for the truth or adequateness of intellectual apprehension. Intersubjective sameness alone by no means guarantees truth or adequateness in representing the nature and essence of things. For, as material falsity indicates, we all may easily err in the same way. While sensory perception, formerly regulated by the image paradigm, is now explained after the model of arbitrary linguistic signs (such having been considered originally as it were the antipodes of intersubjectively identical concepts), the image paradigm is still operative on the level of intellectual cognition. And here the doctrine of the innateness of clear and distinct ideas shows Descartes as standing in the long tradition of the ISC. For whenever Descartes appeals to the evidence of clear and distinct ideas and to the impossibility of thinking them otherwise, he is invoking a strong version of the ISC, not describing an actual state but rather a normative ideal, according to which the sameness of ideas, if these were only attentively considered, finally leads to a sameness of opinion about the objects represented.

With Descartes, the rationale of the ISC is not based on the sameness of things or on our cognitive contact with an external reality which is the same for all, but only on the truthfulness of its creator, who inscribed a certain set of fundamental ideas into the minds of men, or, in other words, provided them with the

---

139. Descartes, *Med.* VI, 15; *Oeuvres*, 7.83,14–23: "video me in his aliisque permultis ordinem naturae pervertere esse assuetum, quia nempe sensuum perceptionibus, quae proprie tantùm a naturâ datae sunt ad menti significandum quaenam composito, cujus pars est, commoda sint vel incommoda, et eatenus sunt satis clarae et distinctae, utor tanquam regulis certis ad immediate dignoscendum quaenam sit corporum extra nos positorum essentia, de quâ tamen nihil nisi valde obscure et confuse significant."

cognitive faculty they actually have.[140] With this, Descartes is still trying to give an account of the reason for the existence of the ISC, while for Locke, who discards the doctrine of innate ideas, the ISC is now reduced to the level of the most simple sensible ideas, and any abstract idea is nothing but a supposition we make, and perhaps—following some kind of "principle of charity"—*have to* make in order to be able to communicate successfully.

In any case, it is the medium of language alone on which we can rely in order to find out and test whether and how far the claim of the ISC is valid. And it is not unlikely that without this medium there would be very few concepts to be tested. But the issue of the ISC itself still seems far from sufficiently settled.

---

140. Cf. Descartes, *Notae in Programma quoddam, Oeuvres* 8/2.357: "Non . . . umquam scripsi vel judicavi, mentem indigere ideis innatis, quae sint aliquid diversum ab ejus facultate cogitandi."

# Mental Representations and Concepts in Medieval Philosophy

GYULA KLIMA

## THE "NOMENCLATURE" OF CONCEPTS

Talking about mental representations and concepts in medieval philosophy, one should probably start with clarifying these terms in the way medieval philosophers used and understood them. However, the phrase *repraesentatio mentalis* is rarely, if ever, used by medieval philosophers: "mental representation" is rather a term of art of modern philosophy of mind. Furthermore, although the term *conceptus* is widely used by medieval philosophers, its meaning and reference seem to vary widely among them, depending on their particular theories. Indeed, to complicate matters, many authors would use other terms, such as *intentio, intellectus, notitia,* or even *ratio* or *verbum mentis,* let alone *fictum* or *idolum mentis* or *conceptus obiectivus* or *species impressa,* on one hand, and *intellectio, conceptus mentalis, conceptus formalis,* or *species expressa* on the other, to designate what we would want to name "concept" and what other (or even the same) medieval authors would also be willing to call "*conceptus.*"

Having in this way successfully muddied the terminological waters, I should probably first clarify what *I* will mean by the English terms in the proposed title, and explain my understanding of the relevant Latin phrases as used by various medieval authors in relation to this meaning.

By talking about a "mental representation" in contemporary philosophy, we usually want to refer to something that represents something to a human cognitive subject as an integral part of the cognitive process of this subject. However, in the first place, using this phrase in relation to medieval philosophy, it will be useful to restrict its usage, in accordance with the medieval understanding of what constitutes *mental* phenomena, to *intellectual,* as opposed to *sensory,* representations. So, throughout this chapter, when I am talking about mental representations, I will mean representations that present something to us through our understanding, to the exclusion of sensory representations. In the second place, it should be noted that in the foregoing description of a mental representation as something that represents something to a human cognitive subject *as an integral part of the cognitive process of this subject,* the addition of this qualification is necessitated by the fact that, for example, a book I am reading is something that represents something to my understanding, but still we would not call the book, the physical object in my hand, *a mental representation of my mind*. By contrast, whatever I am intellectually conceiving on account of reading the book, *insofar as I am conceiving it*, is an integral part of my cognitive process.

And since I have just mentioned the act of conceiving, I can at once describe what I will mean by the term "concept" in this essay: a concept is either *that which* we can intellectually conceive, *insofar as it is conceived*, or that *by which* we conceive whatever it is we conceive. The significance of this disjunctive characterization is that both medieval and contemporary authors tend to use the term "concept" either as referring to the direct object of the verb "conceive," that is, as referring to *that which* is conceived, or to an indirect object that is somehow instrumental in conceiving the direct object, as that *by which* the direct object is conceived. Actually, there should be nothing surprising in this usage. After all, pretty much the same is the case with the word "sight" in English: it can either refer to *what* is seen (as in "The Hudson Palisades are a beautiful sight at sunrise") or to the power or act of seeing *by which* what is seen is seen (as in "My sight is no longer as sharp as it used to be" or in "An act of sight is an act of the visual power").

Obviously, these are not strict definitions, but rather somewhat vague characterizations of how I am going to use these terms here. Still, from these characterizations it might at once appear that concepts are just some sort of mental representations and mental representations are just some sort of concepts. At any rate, I hope these characterizations are clear enough to answer an important question concerning the relationship between concepts and mental representations, which will immediately take us to some intriguing medieval distinctions concerning both: Are *all* concepts mental representations and, vice versa, are *all* mental representations concepts?

The answer, perhaps, somewhat surprisingly, is "no" on both counts. In the first place, those medieval philosophers or theologians who contrasted *intelligible species* with concepts, most notably, but not exclusively, Aquinas and his followers, would take *intelligible species* to be mental representations in the sense described above, but still, they would sharply distinguish them from concepts. Thus, on their account, there would be mental representations that are not concepts. In the second place, Ockhamist nominalist philosophers would characterize certain concepts in a way that would not allow them to be regarded as mental representations in the sense described: in particular, *syncategorematic concepts* according to these philosophers would be nonrepresentative in themselves, but rather merely corepresentative with other, *categorematic concepts*.[1] Thus, for them, there are concepts that are not mental representations.

---

1. For a detailed discussion of the distinction, see G. Klima, "Syncategoremata," in *Elsevier's Encyclopedia of Language and Linguistics*, 2nd ed., ed. Keith Brown (Oxford: Elsevier, 2006), 12:353–356.

Now, whatever we may think of these answers at this point, they clearly demand a clarification of how one should identify and distinguish the items referred to here, such as intelligible species, concepts, and their various kinds. Thus, first of all, we need to delve a little bit into the ontology of mental representations and concepts: just what sorts of entities are they; well, if they are any sort of *entities* in the strict sense at all?

## THE ONTOLOGY OF CONCEPTS

Based on the foregoing, the answer depends on what sorts of concepts and mental representations we are referring to. For if we are referring to any sort of inherent mental representations, that is, mental acts inhering in a human mind as their subject, whether intelligible species or concepts, and whether per se representing (categorematic) concepts or per se nonrepresenting (syncategorematic) concepts, as those features of individual human minds *by which* these minds come to have some intellectual cognition of some things somehow, then we can say that they are regarded by medieval philosophers as individualized accidents (or modes) of these minds.[2] On the other hand, if we are talking about concepts as the *immediate objects* represented by such features of these minds, then they are taken by some medievals to be mere beings of reason, not entities in any real category. However, if we are talking about the *ultimate objects* of these mental acts insofar as they are denominated "concepts" from their being represented by these inherent features of the human mind, then these ultimate objects may be real entities to be classified in their respective real categories, whether as substances or as accidents.

To illustrate this somewhat strange scenario, we may first turn to a rather late description of what sorts of concepts we need to distinguish in this regard, coming from Francisco Suarez (1548–1617):

> We must first of all assume the common distinction between a formal and an objective concept. A formal concept is said to be the act itself, or (which is the same) the word [*verbum*] whereby the intellect conceives some thing or common definition [*ratio*], which is called a concept because it is, as it were, the offspring of the mind. It is called "formal" either because it is the ultimate form of the mind, or because it represents formally to the mind the thing that is known, or because it really is the intrinsic and formal term of the mental conception, thus differing from an objective concept, as I shall now explain. An *objective* concept is said to be the thing, or notion [*ratio*] which is strictly and immediately known or represented by means of the formal concept. For example, when we conceive of man, that act which we perform

---

2. For some details of the vexed history of modes as contrasted both with substances and accidents, see G. Klima, "Substance, Accident, Modes," in *Encyclopedia of Medieval Philosophy*, ed. H. Lagerlund (Dordrecht: Springer, 2011), 1219–1227.

in the mind in order to conceive of man is called a formal concept; but the man thus known and represented by that act is called the objective concept. As a concept, it is so called through a denomination that is extrinsic to the formal concept through which its object is said to be conceived; and hence it is rightly called "objective." For it is not a concept in the sense of a form intrinsically determining a conception, but in the sense of the object and subject matter around which the formal concept is deployed, and to which the mind's eye directly moves; in view of which it is called by some, following Averroes, the *intention formed by the intellect,* and by others the *objective relation*. From this we may gather the difference between the formal and objective concept, namely that the formal concept is always a true and positive thing, and a quality in created things inhering in the mind; but an objective concept is not always a true positive thing. For we conceive from time to time of privations and other items which are called "entities of reason," which have being only objectively in the intellect. Again, the formal concept is always a singular and individual thing, since it is a thing produced through the intellect and inhering in it; but an objective concept can indeed sometimes be a singular and individual thing, insofar as it can be presented to the mind and conceived by a formal act, but often it is something universal, or confused and common, such as "man," "substance," and so on.[3]

Somewhat earlier, Aquinas's famous commentator Thomas de Vio Cajetan (1469–1534) made the same distinction, being quite aware of the fact that that the way his authorities talk about concepts necessitates this distinction:

For an understanding of the terms, note that there are two sorts of concepts: formal and objective. A formal concept is some likeness which the possible intellect forms in itself and is objectively representative of the thing. Philosophers call it an intention or a concept and theologians call it a word. An objective concept, however, is that which, represented by the formal concept, terminates the act of knowing. For example, the formal concept of lion is that representation which the possible intellect forms of a leonine quiddity when we want to know it; the objective concept of the same thing is the leonine nature itself, represented and known. Nor should we think that when a term is said to signify a concept, it signifies only one of the two, for the term *lion* signifies both concepts, although in diverse ways. It is the sign of the formal concept as a means or that-by-which [it signifies], and it is the sign of the objective concept as of the end or that-which [it signifies].[4]

---

3. Disputation 2, section 1, §1; translation in R. Ariew, J. Cottingham, and T. Sorell, eds., *Descartes' Meditations: Background Source Materials* (Cambridge: Cambridge University Press, 1998), 33–34.

4. Cajetan, *Commentary on Being and Essence,* trans. L. H. Kendzierski and F. C. Wade (Milwaukee: Marquette University Press, 1964), c. 1, q. 2, 67–68 (translation slightly revised).

But lest we think this distinction is a late medieval invention, we might quote here Aquinas's student, Armandus de Bellovisu (d. ca. 1334), who discusses a distinction concerning the term *ratio*[5] that is quite the same, if not in terminology, at least in spirit, and which is, in fact, just a further elaboration of what we can find in Aquinas's own *Responsio ad fr. Joannem Vercellensem*.[6] And of course one might dig even further for precursors of this distinction under different terminologies in the early medieval or even the late ancient period. However, even without doing so here, one can quite confidently say that even if the terminology of the distinction between formal and objective concepts seems to have solidified in late medieval philosophy, it was merely the acknowledgment and further elaboration of a distinction entrenched much earlier in medieval thought about concepts. And the reason for this seems to be that, in general, any theory of concepts that characterizes concepts not only as inherent mental qualities, but also as what *we* may call the *information content* carried by these mental qualities, has to introduce this distinction, namely, the distinction between *formal concepts*, the inherent mental qualities by which this information is represented, and *objective concepts*, the *immediate, direct* objects of these formal concepts, the information content precisely as conceived and represented by these concepts *about* their ultimate objects.

Note, for instance, in Cajetan's example that the objective concept signified by the term "lion" is not any individual lion (although, of course Cajetan holds that the term, on account of signifying this concept, applies to individual lions), but rather leonine nature in general, conceived in abstraction from any individuating conditions, which is precisely the reason why *ultimately* it represents all possible lions. So, the objective concept of lions is just whatever we conceive by means of our formal concepts *about* leonine nature in general, which, however is still not any individual lion, but rather the information the formal concept carries about lions in general, *expressing the universal condition for something's qualifying as a lion* (whether this information actually provides *operative* distinguishing *criteria* or not, which is a further issue). But just because we can conceive of leonine nature in general in an abstract universal manner, it does not mean that there is an abstract, universal leonine nature in general that we can conceive of; in the same way as just because we can talk about a person in particular, using his proper name, or in general, providing a general description, it does not mean that we are talking once about a particular person, once about a general person; for there is no such a thing as a general person. So, if the objective concept is just the nature of individuals falling under this concept conceived in general, and what

---

5. Armandus de Bellovisu, *Explicationes Terminorum, Theologicorum, Philosophicorum et Logicorum* (Wittemberg: Typis Johannis Haken, 1623), cc. 208–209, 386–390.

6. *Responsio ad fr. Joannem Vercellensem*, Generalem Magistrum Ordinis Praedicatorum, de articulis CVIII ex opere Petri de Tarentasia. For a detailed analysis of Aquinas's passage, see G. Klima, "Theory of Language," in *The Oxford Handbook to Aquinas*, ed. B. Davies and E. Stump (Oxford: Oxford University Press, 2012), 371–389.

is thus conceived is neither the formal concept *by which* it is conceived, nor the individualized natures of the individuals that this objective concept is some general information *about*, nor any other really existing individual thing, then it has to be placed in a separate category of its own.

Accordingly, objective concepts, especially, objective, universal categorematic concepts, were found by authors providing this sort of analysis of their function to be dwelling in a separate ontological realm of *beings of reason*, that is, a realm of some "quasi-entities," whose *esse* may consist in nothing but their *being conceived* or *represented* by the formal concepts, being the immediate, direct objects of formal concepts in mere *esse obiectivum* (or *esse intentionale* or *esse repraesentativum*), although, perhaps, not lacking some "foundation in reality," namely, the individualized natures of individuals that the formal concept carries this general information about.[7]

To be sure, the immediate objects of our formal concepts were also accorded some *mind-independent* form of unity, namely, some less-than-numerical unity, by thinkers such as Scotus or Burleigh and their ilk. However, from our present perspective, this is just a further complication of the ontological picture (introducing certain further, perhaps "weird," modes of unity and being), leaving the *relations* of formal concepts and their immediate and ultimate objects basically unchanged.[8]

Given the ontological worries such conceptions naturally raise, no wonder there were several attempts to eliminate these quasi-entities. These ontological worries were most famously raised and resolved by William Ockham and the nominalist tradition engendered by his work. However, since the "nominalist resolution" of these ontological issues was done in terms of logical analysis, this consideration takes us from the issue of the *ontology* of concepts to their *logic*, or more specifically, their *logical semantics*.

### THE SEMANTICS OF CONCEPTS

As is well known, originally even Ockham subscribed to a theory of concepts involving entities in mere objective being, namely, the so-called *ficta*,[9] only to

---

7. For a detailed account of this "moderate realist" conception of beings of reason, contrasted with a typical nominalist account, see G. Klima, "The Changing Role of *Entia Rationis* in Medieval Philosophy: A Comparative Study with a Reconstruction," *Synthese* 96 (1993): 25–59. For an excellent, detailed study of later developments of the doctrine, see D. Novotný, *Ens rationis from Suárez to Caramuel: A Study in Scholasticism of the Baroque Era* (New York: Fordham University Press, 2013).

8. See Cajetan's excellent discussion of the issue of formal unity at 148–150, leading up to the detailed criticism of Scotus's conception of universals in q. 8, at 164–173, of his *Commentary on Being and Essence*. For an earlier Thomistic reaction to Scotus, it is very instructive to check Thomas Sutton. For the finer details of Burleigh, see Alessandro Conti, "Walter Burley," *The Stanford Encyclopedia of Philosophy* (Fall 2008 Edition), ed. Edward N. Zalta, http://plato.stanford.edu/archives/fall2008/entries/burley.

9. *Ordinatio*, d. 2, q. 8, 271–274.

be rejected by him later, partly persuaded by his confrere, Walter Chatton. However, despite this apparent ontological agreement, even already in his "*fictum*-period," Ockham seems to have had a conception of the *semantics* of concepts rather different from what we see in the writings of the authors mentioned earlier who endorsed concepts in mere objective being.

Therefore, since the role of Ockham's mature conception of concepts in his *ontological program* has been analyzed in great detail in the contemporary literature, especially by Claude Panaccio in his excellent monograph devoted to the topic,[10] and I have also analyzed the same issue at length concerning Buridan in my monograph,[11] instead of going into those details here, I would rather make a brief, *general contrast* between the role of concepts in *logical semantics* according to the nominalists and the same according to their realist counterparts.

The point of the contrast is that the decisive issue between nominalists and realists in this regard is not so much ontology as the *semantic function* they would attribute to concepts in their respective theories. This is a contrast anybody who ever compared nominalist and realist authors writing on these issues *feels* there is, but it is rather hard to articulate without conflating it with the different but, I would argue, merely coincidental contrast between their ontologies. So, first, by way of a preliminary, rough indication, I would say that what I take to be the main contrast here is that realists would endorse a view of concepts according to which they feature in logical semantics with their *intensions*, whereas nominalists would endorse a view according to which it is sufficient to take them into account in logical theory with their *extensions*.

Obviously, the terminology of "extension" and "intension" is borrowed from modern logical theory, and so ought to be used and understood with caution, indeed, with implicit quotation marks throughout the subsequent discussion. However, I think the transposition of this terminology from modern theories to medieval theories to characterize the distinction I am trying to make is not entirely unjustified, if we understand by the *intension* of a *formal* concept nothing but the corresponding *objective* concept, in line with the characterization of objective concepts I provided above in connection with Cajetan, and by the *extension* of a *formal* concept we understand all entities that the formal concept carries the information expressed by the objective concept about. For in the foregoing characterization of objective concepts, I said that they express some *universal condition of applicability* of the formal concept (and so of the linguistic expression signifying it) to their ultimate objects, which squares quite neatly with the contemporary intuitive understanding of the *intension of a term*. And, of course, it is customary to understand by the *extension* of a term all things that satisfy its intension.

Perhaps, a further justification for this usage may be taken from the following, rather difficult passage from Cajetan, in which he discusses Aquinas's remark

---

10. C. Panaccio, *Ockham on Concepts* (Aldershot: Ashgate, 2004).
11. G. Klima, *John Buridan* (Oxford: Oxford University Press, 2009).

that the concepts of the species and definition are somehow composed of the concepts of genus and difference:

> What we have said here, that the formal concept, namely, of species and definition, is composed from the formal concepts of genus and difference, can be understood in two ways: in one way, as concerning the mental concept; in another way, as concerning the objective concept taken formally. If taken in the first way, it can again be understood in two ways. In one way of the subjective being (*esse*) of the mental concept, or as what it is; in another way of its representative being (*esse*). The mental concept of species, according to what it is, is not composed from the mental concepts of genus and difference according to what they are, because they are all simple qualities, and cannot be distinguished into many constituent parts. For we must not imagine that when the intellect forms the concept of the definition of man, namely, of rational animal, that it forms many concepts; it forms only one, which is a kind of simple quality, and distinctly represents the singular parts, just as in things outside the mind, the thing defined has [what is signified in it by] the genus and the difference without a real composition. Thus, understood in this first way our statement is not true. Now the mental concept of species taken formally according to its representative being (*esse*) is composed of the mental concepts of genus and difference taken formally according to their representative being (*esse*), like an image which represents the whole by images of the parts. For man, existing in the mind, represents an aggregate of sensitive and intellectual perfections; while animal, existing in the mind, formally represents only the perfection of sense, and rational only the perfection of intellect. Then in this way our statement is verified. However, the objective concept of the species, since taken formally it is nothing but the formal significate of its mental concept, is of its very nature composed from the objective concepts of genus and difference taken formally; just as the formal significate of the species is of its very nature composed from the formal significata of genus and difference, as was shown above.[12] Thus when man is taken as the object of its specific mental concept, man is neither animal nor rational, but is composed from animal and rational, taking also animal and rational as the objects of their mental concepts. This is shown by the falsity of the proposition: *the specific formal object is the generic or differentiating formal object.* For man as such means something which is an aggregate of sensitive and intellectual perfection; animal as such means only one part of the aggregate, namely, the sensitive nature; rational as such means only the other part, namely, the intellectual perfection. But it is clear that the aggregate is not one

---

12. Here I had to change the translation significantly, changing the punctuation of the Latin text on which the translation is based, to make sense of this sentence: the comma after "*formale*" has to be moved after "*eiusdem*."

of the aggregating elements. Thus, understood in this way, our statement contains truth and is perfectly to the point.[13]

There are a number of important lessons to be drawn from this passage (and from several related passages that cannot be quoted here). In the first place, we should observe that although working out the details of a conception of mental language as constituting a compositional representational system of the human mind was the primary concern of nominalists (obviously motivated by the demands of their ontological program), the "realist" Cajetan here also addresses the issue of conceptual composition, which is one of the main requisites (indeed, I would say, the chief requisite) for a conception of mental language.[14] In the second place, in discussing conceptual composition, he rejects the idea that it would consist in forming some sort of aggregates of simple formal concepts: conceptual composition is not some process of putting together simple entities into a complex entity having the former as its integral parts. The formal concept expressing the quidditative definition of man is ontologically just as simple, a simple quality of the human mind, as are its "components." So, composition is rather a "functional composition," in the sense that the representational content of the complex concept is a function of the representational contents of the simple concepts, without those concepts entering into its ontological makeup.[15] That is to say, conceptual composition is done on the level of objective concepts considered formally, insofar as they are the expressed information contents of the formal concepts. Finally, and perhaps this is the most important from our present point of view, both the simple objective concepts and the complex objective concept specify the conditions of the applicability of the term signifying them, as it were, "making" these terms ultimately signify the "truth-makers" of their true predication of any individual (just as intensions in modern logic do).

In the logical-semantic tradition represented by Cajetan, what applies in this passage to complex mental terms, such as the quidditative definitions considered here, also applies to mental propositions resulting from the composition of mental terms by means of syncategorematic concepts, especially, the copula.[16] The resulting mental propositions, that is, simple qualities of the mind functionally dependent for their representational content on the representational contents of their "components," have as their direct objects some propositional states of

---

13. Cajetan, *Commentary on Being and Essence*, 122–123 (significantly revised).
14. On this issue, see also Joshua Hochschild's essay in this volume.
15. The same idea is very clearly expressed by earlier scholastic authors as well, in fact, authors as diverse as John Buridan (see G. Klima, *John Buridan* [Oxford: Oxford University Press, 2009], 38–47) and James of Viterbo (see Jacobi de Viterbio O.E.S.A., *Disputatio Prima de Quolibet* [Würzburg: Augustinus, 1968], esp. 8–9).
16. For an elaboration along these lines of Aquinas's scattered remarks on the function of the copula, see G. Klima, "Aquinas' Theory of the Copula and the Analogy of Being," *Logical Analysis and History of Philosophy* 5 (2002): 159–176.

affairs, variously referred to as *dicta, enuntiabilia, complexe significabilia*, or *real propositions*. To be sure, the actual presence of such a propositional state affairs, being the actual, immediate truth-maker of the entire proposition, is ultimately conditioned on the ways things ultimately signified by its terms are. But what specifies *which* state of affairs must obtain for this proposition to be true and, in turn, what ultimate extramental conditions are required for this state of affairs to obtain is the composition of the simple concepts signified by the parts of the proposition in question.

For Burley, for instance, the extramental condition for the existence of a *real proposition* signified by an affirmative spoken proposition is the cosupposition of the terms of the latter. But this cosupposition is secured by the coincidence of the forms ultimately signified by its subject and predicate in their *supposita*, i.e., the things actually having the forms signified by these terms (that is to say, the things actually satisfying the intensions of these terms). However, the forms signified by subject and predicate coinciding in these *supposita* are nothing but the direct objects of the mental concepts of the mind forming the mental proposition that has the real proposition as its direct and immediate object.[17] So, in the end, the truth-conditions of a proposition are determined by the intensions of the predicates, determining, in turn, the intension of the proposition. But less elaborate remarks indicate the presence of the same idea already in Aquinas, for instance, in passages where he explains the identity of the *supposita* of terms required for the truth of an affirmative proposition by the coincidence of the forms signified by its terms in the same *supposita*, which grounds the actuality of the *enuntiabile* signified by the whole proposition, identified on the basis of the composition of the concepts having these forms as their direct objects.[18] Therefore, if the task of a logical semantics is to provide a compositional specification of the truth-conditions of propositions in order to be able to provide a semantic definition of validity, then we may say that Cajetan's remarks here indicate that in the logical-semantic tradition represented by him, formal concepts were supposed to exercise their semantic functions by combining their *intensions* in determining the conditions of their true applicability to items of reality.

By contrast, the information content or intension of mental concepts does not have this logical role for Ockham and the nominalist tradition he initiated. Indeed, one may surmise that the reason why he had no qualms over giving up his *ficta* was precisely that he had no use for them in his logic. As is well known, what determines the truth-conditions of assertoric categorical propositions for Ockham is the cosupposition of their terms, which in turn is determined by the

---

17. See again Conti, "Walter Burley," esp. sect. 5.
18. For references and detailed elaboration of Aquinas's semantics along these lines, see G. Klima, "The Semantic Principles Underlying Saint Thomas Aquinas's Metaphysics of Being," *Medieval Philosophy and Theology* 5 (1996): 87–141.

emptiness or nonemptiness of the intersection of the sets of their actual ultimate significata (actual, that is, relative to the time connoted by the copula). And the ultimate significata of these terms are nothing but the individuals represented by the concepts to which these terms are subordinated.

However, and this is the crucial point here, the information content of these concepts has no role in determining the sets of these ultimate significata, in particular, it has *no role in specifying the conditions for the true applicability* of these concepts and the terms subordinated to them to individuals; and so, if the set of the ultimate significata of these terms can be called their extension, it has no role in determining the *extension* of these concepts. Indeed, for Ockham, the information content of a mental concept, whether it is "reified" by positing a *fictum* expressed by this concept or not, has nothing to do with the determination of its extension, which is determined simply by the natural causal mechanism of concept formation. In short, for Ockham, *the intensions of mental concepts do not determine their extensions,* and so they do not figure in specifying the truth conditions of the mental propositions resulting from their composition.[19]

Thus, we may say that while the realist logical-semantic tradition, despite all the differences among individual authors in finer, metaphysical details, is rather unanimous in endorsing a characterization of concepts that grounds an *intensionalist* logical semantics, the nominalist tradition stemming from Ockham's work abandons this characterization, endorsing a conception of concepts that grounds an *extensionalist* logical semantics.[20]

But then the question naturally arises: what *is* the role the information content of concepts for Ockham, if any? The answer to this question, however, leads us from the issue of the logic of concepts to the issue of their psychology and epistemology.

## THE PSYCHOLOGY AND EPISTEMOLOGY OF CONCEPTS

In his detailed discussion of Ockham's externalism, Claude Panaccio has argued that for Ockham this information content is but "a perceptual schema," helping the cognitive subject in recognizing members of the extension of a concept, but this perceptual schema does in no way determine this extension.[21] In fact, if we take a careful look at how Ockham characterizes his *ficta,* we can say that even those may be just some "quasi-reified" items somehow embodying the descriptive

---

19. See Claude Panaccio's excellent essay on this issue in the present volume.
20. For detailed expositions of the contrast indicated here, see G. Klima, "Nominalist Semantics," *The Cambridge History of Later Medieval Philosophy*, ed. R. Pasnau (Cambridge: Cambridge University Press, 2010), 159–172; G. Klima, "The Nominalist Semantics of Ockham and Buridan: A Rational Reconstruction," in *Handbook of the History of Logic,* ed. D. Gabbay and J. Woods (Amsterdam: North Holland, 2008), 389–431.
21. See again Panaccio's essay in the present volume.

content of a categorematic concept in the form of a nondistinctive mental image, which is therefore capable of indifferently representing a number of sufficiently similar individuals to the cognitive subject. So, for Ockham, a *fictum* seems to be just a sort of *psychological* factor explaining (1) why we can apply our universal terms to several, sufficiently similar individuals, or (2) what the quasi-objects of our awareness are when we are not considering any really existing object. However, once he realized that (1) he could attribute this indifferent mode of representation to the mental acts themselves and (2) that he could explain away "nonexistent objects" (the other main motivation for positing *ficta*) with reference to the representational features of complex mental acts without positing a realm of *ficta* "as if there were another world consisting of *impossibilia*, as there is one consisting of beings," he happily cut them out from his ontology.[22]

In any case, if *ficta* are just the "quasi-reified perceptual recognition schemata" of our universal mental concepts[23] accounting for the latter's indifferent representation, then, despite being posited in the same ontological realm, they have nothing to do with the objective concepts we encountered in Cajetan and the "realist" tradition he represents. For on this interpretation, *ficta* would be just these psychological factors, with no role in logic, whereas the objective concepts of the "realists" are the *par excellence* subject matter of *their* logic.[24] But whatever may be the case with *ficta*, the "perceptual schemata" of Ockham's intellective mental acts have certainly no role in his logic.

So, in conclusion, I would like to argue that with Ockham and his followers, there really is a big, "paradigmatic" shift in the conception of concepts, but perhaps not quite the kind commentators usually recognize. If I may be allowed to introduce one more piece of barbaric terminology, I would say that this "big shift" consists in the separation of what I would call the *phenomenal* and *semantic* contents of concepts, leading to a reinterpretation of their conditions of identity, which would then yield some serious epistemological implications, with far-reaching further consequences.

Talking about the identity-conditions of concepts, more specifically, of formal, mental concepts or mental acts, we need to take into account that they are two-faced entities. Insofar as they are real entities inherent in real, individual human minds, they have their own ontological characteristics distin-

---

22. See Ockham, *Summa Logicae*, ed. P. Boehner, G. Gál, and S. F. Brown (St. Bonaventure, N.Y.: Franciscan Institute, 1974), II, 14, 286–288.

23. Note that this is a radically different interpretation of *ficta* from that provided by Stephen Read, which assimilated *ficta* to Frege's (objective) concepts. See S. L. Read, "The Objective Being of Ockham's Ficta," *The Philosophical Quarterly* 27 (1977): 14–31.

24. See, e.g., R. W. Schmidt, *The Domain of Logic According to St. Thomas Aquinas* (The Hague: Martinus Nijhoff, 1966).

guishing them in kind and number, just as any other real entities do. But insofar as they are representations, they have representational characteristics, specifiable in terms of what they represent, how, and to whom. Exactly *what and how* they represent, whether their subject is actually aware of this or not, is what I would call their *semantic content*. (In case this sounds doubtful, we should note that of course, we can have all sorts of representations in our cognitive apparatus that objectively represent something, but of which we are actually unaware, ranging from unnoticed sights to suppressed memories to future singulars our universal concepts represent without our being quite aware of them.) But what I would call the *phenomenal content* of our concepts is *precisely* what they make us aware of or what their represented objects *appear to us as*, on account of having these concepts; or, in short, the phenomenal content of a concept is the content of our consciousness we have on account of entertaining that concept.

Accepting Claude Panaccio's intriguing suggestion about Ockham leads then to the conclusion that for Ockham, the phenomenal content of a simple categorematic concept may on occasion radically mismatch its semantic content. Its semantic content is simply its extension: the set of its *significata* (and *connotata*, as the case may be, provided there are simple connotative concepts, as Panaccio also contends). But what these significata appear to the subject having these concepts *as*, i.e., what the subject becomes aware of on account of entertaining this concept, is but the "perceptual recognition schema" of this concept, the descriptive characteristics on the basis of which we would normally identify individuals as falling under this concept. However, since these characteristics are just sensible accidents of this kind of objects, and so objects of this kind may not exhibit them, whereas objects of another kind may, we can, and often do, misclassify objects on the basis of their appearances, i.e., we are deceived. To be sure, this need not lead to skepticism; after all, under normal circumstances we have sufficiently reliable procedures to correct mistakes of this sort. And this is not even the point here. The point rather is that *the mere possibility* of this mismatch radically distinguishes Ockham's and his followers' theory of concepts from the tradition represented here by Cajetan, *quite independently from ontological considerations* concerning the "mysterious" *esse obiectivum* of whether *objective concepts* or *ficta*.

For if we go back to Cajetan's characterization of objective concepts, as the direct, immediate objects of our formal concepts, we can see that these are the *essential natures* of the individuals falling under these concepts conceived of in abstraction from their individuating conditions. The phenomenal appearance of these individuals does not even figure into the specification of the objective concept. Thus, the objective concept, being at the same time the intension of the formal concept accounting for its objective applicability to the individuals that have the natures represented by it *and* that item on account of which we are aware of this nature, is *both* the semantic and the phenomenal content of the same formal concept. Therefore, on this conception, the semantic and phenomenal contents of a formal concept, being the same, are inseparable; indeed, so much so that the item in which they coincide, namely, the objective concept, is precisely the characteristic of a formal concept in terms of which it is identified and distinguished from others, rather than its ontological, real properties, whatever those are. So, to make the contrast even sharper, we may say that while for Ockham the *phenomenal content* of a concept is just a somewhat vague snapshot of the typical sensible characteristics of an individual of a certain kind (whether this snapshot is "projected" into a *fictum* or not), whereas its *semantic content* is the individual's kind, for Cajetan and his ilk, both the phenomenal and the semantic contents of a formal concept are the objective concept, representing the information encoded by the formal concept about the nature of individuals falling under this concept, identifying *this* concept as opposed to any other.

Aside from usual ontological worries about objective being and universals, objective concepts and in general any "intermediaries" between cognitive acts and their ultimate objects tend to be rejected for the *epistemological* reason that the "representationalism" embodied in positing such intermediary representations has to lead to skepticism, as opposed to the "direct realism" that eliminates such intermediaries. In fact, already Walter Chatton used this sort of argument against Henry of Harclay and Peter Aureol, which then Ockham picked up in his later theory of concepts as a justification for abandoning his own *ficta*.[25]

However, as I have argued on numerous occasions,[26] the *kind of representationalism* which posits intermediaries that are part and parcel of the identity conditions of formal concepts through specifying what is both their *phenomenal* and *semantic* content (i.e., their intension) is not susceptible to these skeptical worries, whereas quite paradoxically, the *kind of direct realism* which allows a merely *contingent* relationship between formal concepts (along with their phenomenal content, i.e., their intension) and their semantic content (i.e., their extension) is susceptible at least to *the possibility* of the kind of radical skepticism

---

25. See Adams, *William Ockham*, I, 85.
26. See G. Klima, "Intentional Transfer in Averroes, Indifference of Nature in Avicenna, and the Representationalism of Aquinas," in *Universal Representation, and the Ontology of Individuation*, ed. G. Klima and A. Hall (Newcastle upon Tyne: Cambridge Scholars Publishing, 2011), 45–54; "The Anti-Skepticism of John Buridan and Thomas Aquinas: Putting Skeptics in Their Place vs. Stopping Them in Their Tracks," in *Rethinking the History of Skepticism*, ed. H. Lagerlund (Leiden: Brill, 2010), 143–166; and G. Klima and A. Hall, eds., *The Demonic Temptations of Medieval Nominalism* (Newcastle upon Tyne: Cambridge Scholars Publishing, 2011), esp. 83–128, containing my exchange with Claude Panaccio on the issue.

we find cropping up in late medieval considerations about a possibly deceptive God, which would eventually turn into the starting point of an entirely new epistemological program in Descartes's Demon.[27]

---

27. A particularly illuminating exchange I recently had with Elizabeth Karger over her contribution to this volume showed me, however, that besides the shift in the conception of the identity conditions for concepts discussed here and in my papers referred to in the previous note, something else is also required for "full blown" Cartesian Demon skepticism (the kind that would call into doubt even pure truths of reason), namely, a new modal conception, one that denies what we would call "S5 modal principles." For it is only with the denial that what is possible is necessarily possible, i.e., with the affirmation that something that is actually possible (or conceivable) may in another creation be impossible (or inconceivable), that the kind of total cognitive isolation required by the Demon scenario becomes a logical possibility. (Here I do not want to conflate the distinct notions of possibility and conceivability, but I do want to indicate that both have an important role to play in the relevant developments.) Adam Wodeham, for instance, would not have bought into this modal conception. But for Descartes, this conception is apparently plausible enough to entertain the genuine logical possibility of the total cognitive isolation of an intelligent subject from external reality even concerning what is intellectually conceivable by it of that reality. Dealing with this conceptual development properly, however, would take another volume.

# BIBLIOGRAPHY

Ackrill, J. L. "Aristotle's Distinction between *Energeia* and *Kinesis*." In *New Essays on Plato and Aristotle*, edited by R. Bambrough, 121–141. New York: Routledge, 1965.
Adams, Marilyn M. *William Ockham*. Notre Dame, Ind.: Notre Dame University Press, 1987.
Aegidius Romanus (Giles of Rome). *Quodlibeta*. Louvain, 1646.
Albert of Saxony. *Perutilis Logica*. Hildesheim: Georg Olms, 1974.
Amerini, F. "Realism and Intentionality: Hervaeus Natalis, Peter Aureoli, and William Ockham in Discussion." In *Philosophical Debates at Paris in the Early Fourteenth Century*, edited by Stephen F. Brown, Thomas Dewender, and Theo Kobusch, 239–260. Leiden: Brill, 2009.
Aquinas, T. *De ente et essentia*. Cura et studio Fratrum Praedicatorum. In *Opera omnia* XLIII, 369–381. Rome: Editori di san Tommaso, 1976.
———. *De Potentia*. Edited by P. M. Pession. In *Quaestiones disputatae* II. Turin: Marietti, 1965.
———. *Expositio libri Peryermeneias*. Cura et studio Fratrum Praedicatorum. In *Opera omnia* I* 1. Rome/Paris: Editori di san Tommaso/Vrin, 1989.
———. *Expositio libri Posteriorum*. Cura et studio Fratrum Praedicatorum. In *Opera omnia* I* 2. Rome/Paris: Editori di san Tommaso/Vrin, 1989.
———. *In duodecim libros Metaphysicorum Expositio*. Edited by M.-R. Cathala and R. M. Spiazzi. Turin: Marietti, 1964.
———. *In octo libros Physocorum Aristotelis Expositio*. Edited by M. Maggiolo. Turin: Marietti, 1965.
———. *Liber de Veritate Catholicae Fidei contra errores Infidelium seu Summa contra Gentiles*. 3 vols. Edited by C. Pera, P. Marc, and P. Caramello. Turin: Marietti, 1961.
———. *Opera omnia*. Rome: Commissio Leonina, 1882ff.
———. *Quaestiones de quolibet*. Cura et studio Fratrum Praedicatorum. In *Opera Omnia* XXV, 1–2. Rome/Paris: Commissio Leonina/Vrin, 1996.
———. *Quaestiones disputatae de potentia Dei*. Ed. M. Pession. Rome, 1953.
———. *Quaestiones disputatae de Veritate*. Curo et studio Fratrum Praedicatorum. In *Opera omnia* XXII, 1–3. Rome: Editori di San Tommaso, 1972.
———. "*Quaestiones disputatae de Veritate*." In *Opera Omnia* (Leonine Edition), vol. 23. Rome, 1970–1976.
———. *Responsio ad fr. Joannem Vercellensem*. Generalem Magistrum Ordinis Praedicatorum, de articulis CVIII ex opere Petri de Tarentasia. Turin: Marietti, 1954.
———. *Scripta super libros Sententiarum*, 2 vols. Ed. P. Mandonnet. Paris: Lethielleux, 1929.
———. *Scriptum super librum Sententiarum magistri Petri Lombardi*. Edited by P. Mandonnet. Paris: Lethellieux, 1929.
———. *Scriptum super secundum librum Sententiarum magistri Petri Lombardi*. Edited by P. Mandonnet. Paris: Lethellieux, 1929.

———. *Sentencia libri de anima*. Cura et studio Fratrum Praedicatorum. In *Opera omnia* XLV, 1. Rome/Paris: Commissio Leonina/Vrin 1984.

———. "Summa Contra Gentile." In *Opera Omnia* (Leonine Edition), vols. 13–15. Rome, 1918–1930.

———. "Summa Theologiae." In *Opera Omnia* (Leonine Edition), vols. 4–12. Rome, 1888–1906.

———. *Summa Theologiae*. Cinisello Balsamo: Edizioni San Paolo, 1988.

———. *Super Evangelium S. Ioannis Lectura*. Edited by R. Cai. Turin: Marietti, 1952.

———. *Scriptum super Sententiis*. Edited by P. Mandonnet and M. F. Moos. 3 vols. Paris: Lethielleux, 1929–1947.

Ariew, R., J. Cottingham, and T. Sorell, eds. *Descartes' Meditations: Background Source Materials*. Cambridge: Cambridge University Press, 1998.

Aristotle. *Categoriae*. Edited by L. Minio-Paluello. Oxford: Clarendon Press, 1959.

———. *De anima*. Edited by W. D. Ross. Oxford: Clarendon Press, 1956.

———. *De anima: Books II and III (with Passages from Book I)*. Translated by D. W. Hamlyn. Oxford: Clarendon Press, 1968/1993.

———. *De generatione et corruptione*. Edited by H. H. Joachim. Oxford: Clarendon Press, 1922.

———. *Metaphysica*. Edited by W. Jaeger. Oxford: Clarendon Press, 1957.

———. *Metaphysics. Book*. Translated with an Introduction and Commentary by S. Makin. Oxford: Clarendon Press, 2006.

———. *Physica*. Edited by W. D. Ross. Oxford: Clarendon Press, 1950.

———. *Topica*. Edited by W. D. Ross. Oxford: Clarendon Press 1958.

Armandus de Bellovisu. *Explicationes Terminorum, Theologicorum, Philosophicorum et Logicorum*. Wittenberg: Typis Johannis Haken, 1623.

Ashworth, E. J. "'Can I Speak More Clearly than I Understand?': A Problem of Religious Language in Henry of Ghent, Duns Scotus, and Ockham." *Historiographia Linguistica* 7 (1980): 29–38.

———. "Jacobus Naveros (fl. ca. 1533) on the question: 'Do spoken words signify concepts or things?'" In *Logos and Pragma*, edited by L.M. De Rijk and H. Braakhuis, 189–214. Nijmegen: Ingenium, 1987.

———. "Medieval Theories of Singular Terms." In *The Stanford Encyclopedia of Philosophy* (Winter Edition), edited by Edward N. Zalta, http://plato.stanford.edu/archives/win2003/entries/singular-terms -medieval.

———. "Singular Terms and Singular Concepts: From Buridan to the Early Sixteenth Century." In *John Buridan and Beyond*, edited by R. Friedman and S. Ebbesen, 121–152. Viborg: Royal Danish Academy of Science and Letters, 2003.

Augustine. *De Doctrina Christiana*. Edited by R. P. H. Green. Oxford: Clarendon Press, 1995.

———. *De Trinitate libri XV (Libri I–XII)*. Edited by W. J. Mountain. CCSL, L, pars XVI, 1. Turnhout: Brépols, 1968.

———. *On the Trinity*. Edited by Gareth Matthews. Cambridge: Cambridge University Press, 2002.

———. *The Literal Meaning of Genesis*. Trans. J. H. Taylor. Mahwah, N.J.: Paulist Press, 1982.

Autrecourt, N. "Exigit ordo." In J. R. O'Donnell, "Nicholas of Autrecourt." *Medieval Studies* 1 (1939): 179–266.

———. "Quaestio de qua respondet magister Nicolaus de Ultricuria." In ibid., 268–280.

———. *The Universal Treatise of Nicholas of Autrecourt*. Trans. L. A. Kennedy, R. E. Arnold, and A. E. Millward. Milwaukee: Marquette University Press, 1971.

Averroes. *Commentarium magnum in Aristotelis De anima lib. III, com. 5*. Edited by F. Stuart Crawford. Cambridge, Mass.: Medieval Academy of America, 1953.

Avicenna Latinus. *Liber de anima seu Sextus de naturalibus*. IV–V. Edited by S. Van Riet. Louvain/Leiden: Éditions Orientalistes/Brill, 1968.

Aydede, M. "The Language of Thought Hypothesis," *The Stanford Encyclopedia of Philosophy* (Fall 2004 Edition), edited by Edward N. Zalta, http://plato.stanford.edu/archives/fall2004/entries/language-thou ght.

Bakker, P. J. J. M. "La raison et le miracle. Les doctrines eucharistiques (c. 1250–c. 1400). Contribution à l'étude des rapports entre philosophie et théologie." PhD dissertation, Nijmegen, 1999.

Barnes, J., ed. *The Complete Works of Aristotle*. Princeton: Princeton University Press, 1984.

Baudry, Léon. "Gauthier de Chatton et son commentaire des Sentences." Archives d'historie doctrinale et littéraire du moyen age 14 (1943–45): 337–369.

Bérubé, Camille. *La connaissance de l'individuel au Moyen Âge*. Montreal: Presses Universitaires de France, 1964.

Bettoni, E. *Il processo astrattivo nella concezione di Enrico di Gand*. Milan: Vita e Pensiero, 1954.

Biard, J. "Intention and Presence: The Notion of *Presentialitas* in the Fourteenth Century." In *Consciousness: From Perception to Reflection in the History of Philosophy*, Studies in the History of Philosophy of Mind, 4, edited by Sara Heinämaa, Vili Lähteenmäki, and Paulina Remes, 123–140. Dordrecht: Springer, 2007.

———. "Intention et présence: la notion de *presentialitas* au XIV$^e$ siècle." In *Ancient and Medieval Theories of Intentionality*, edited by Dominik Perler, 256–282. Leiden: Brill, 2001.

———. *Logique et théorie du signe au XIV$^e$ siècle*. Paris: Librairie Philosophique, 1989.

*Biblia Sacra: Vulgatae Editionis Sixti Quinti Pontificis Maximi jussu recognita et Clementis viii auctoritate edita*. Tournai, 1901.

Biel, G. *Collectorium circa quattuor libros sententiarum*. Edited by W. Werbeck and U. Hofmann. Tübingen: J. C. B. Mohr (Paul Siebeck), 1973–84.

Black, D. L. "Conjunction and Identity of Knower and Known in Averroes." *American Catholic Philosophical Quarterly* 73 (1999): 159–184.

Blackburn, S. *The Oxford Dictionary of Philosophy*. New York: Oxford University Press, 1994.

———. *Spreading the Word*. Oxford: Clarendon Press, 1984.

Boehner, P. "The Realistic Conceptualism of William of Ockham." Traditio 4 (1946): 303–336.

Boethius, A. M. S. *Commentarii in librum Aristotelis Peri Hermeneias: Editio Prima*. Edited by C. Meiser. Leipzig: Teubner, 1877.

———. *Commentarii in librum Aristotelis Peri Hermeneias: Editio Secunda*. Edited by C. Meiser. Leipzig: Teubner, 1880.

Boler, J. "Intuitive and Abstractive Cognition." In *The Cambridge History of Later Medieval Philosophy*, edited by Norman Kretzmann, 460–478. Cambridge: Cambridge University Press, 1982.

Bos, E. P. *Logica modernorum in Prague about 1400*. Leiden: Brill, 2004.

Bos, E. P., and S. Read. *Concepts: The Treatises of Thomas of Cleves and Paul of Gelria*. Leuven: Peeters, 2001.

Braine, D. "The Active and Potential Intellects: Aquinas as a Philosopher in His Own Right." In *Mind, Metaphysics, and Value in the Thomistic and Analytical*

*Traditions*, edited by John Haldane, 18–35. Notre Dame, Ind.: University of Notre Dame Press, 2002.

Brentano, F. *Psychologie von empirischen Standpunkt*. Edited by O. Kraus. Hamburg: Duncker & Humblot, 1973.

———. *Psychology from an Empirical Standpoint*. Edited by Linda L. McAlister. London: Routledge & Kegan Paul–Humanities Press, 1973.

Bridoux, A., ed. *Descartes. Oeuvres et lettres*, Paris: Pléiade, 1953.

Brower, J. E., and S. Brower-Toland. "Aquinas on Mental Representation: Concepts and Intentionality." *The Philosophical Review* 117 (2008): 193–243.

Brower-Toland, S. "Can God Know More? A Case Study in the Late Medieval Debate about Propositions." In *Later Medieval Metaphysics: Ontology, Language & Logic*, ed. R. Keele and C. Bolyard, 161–187. New York: Fordham University Press, 2013.

———. "Facts vs. Things: Adam Wodeham and the Later Medieval Debate About Objects of Judgment." *Review of Metaphysics* 60 (2006): 597–642.

———. "Intuition, Externalism, and Direct Reference in Ockham," *History of Philosophy Quarterly* 24 (2007): 317–335.

———. "Later Medieval Theories of Propositions: Ockham and the 14th Century Debate at Oxford over Objects of Judgment." PhD dissertation, Cornell University, 2002.

———. "Ockham on Judgment, Concepts, and the Problem of Intentionality." *Canadian Journal of Philosophy* 37 (2007): 67–110.

Brown, J. V. "Intellect and Knowing in Henry of Ghent." *Tijdschrift voor Filosofie* 37 (1975): 490–512, 692–710.

———. "Sensation in Henry of Ghent: A Late Mediaeval Aristotelian-Augustinian Synthesis." *Archiv für Geschichte der Philosophie* 53 (1971): 238–266.

Brown, S. F. "Walter Chatton's Lectura and William of Ockham's Quaestiones in libros Physicorum Aristotelis." In *Essays Honoring Allan B. Wolter*, edited by W. A. Frank and G. J. Etzkorn, 82–115. St. Bonaventure, N.Y.: Franciscan Institute, 1985.

Brown, S. F., Thomas Dewender, and Theo Kobusch, eds. *Philosophical Debates at Paris in the Early Fourteenth Century*. Leiden: Brill, 2009.

Burge, T. "Reply to Normore." In *Reflections and Replies: Essays on the Philosophy of Tyler Burge*, edited by Martin Hahn and B. Ramberg, 291–334. Cambridge, Mass.: MIT Press, 2003.

Buridan, J. *In Metaphysicen Aristotelis Questiones argutissimae*. Paris, 1588. Reprinted in *Kommentar zur Aristotelischen Metaphysik*. Frankfurt: Minerva, 1964.

———. *Quaestiones in Isagogen Porphyrii*, in Ryszard Tatarzynski, "Jan Buridan, Kommentarz do Isagogi Porfiriusza," *Przeglad Tomistyczny* 2 (1986): 111–195.

———. *Quaestiones in Metaphysicen Aristotelis*. Paris, 1518. Reprinted in ibid.

———. *Quaestiones super decem libros Ethicorum Aristotelis ad Nicomachum*. Paris, 1513. Reprinted as *Super decem libros Ethicorum*. Frankfurt: Minerva, 1968.

———. *Questions on Aristotle's De anima*. In Jack Zupko, "John Buridan's Philosophy of Mind." PhD dissertation, Cornell University, 1989.

———. *Sophismata*. Edited by T. K. Scott. Stuttgart: Fromann-Holzboog, 1977.

———. *Subtilissimae Quaestiones super octo Physicorum libros Aristotelis*. Paris, 1509. Reprinted in *Kommentar zur Aristotelischen Physik*.

———. *Summulae de dialectica*. Translation and introduction by G. Klima. New Haven: Yale University Press, 2002.

———. *Summulae de Suppositionibus*. Edited by R. van der Lecq. Nijmegen: Ingenium, 1998.

———. *Tractatus de differentia universalis ad individuum*, in Slawomir Szyller, "Johannis Buridani, Tractatus de differentia universalis ad individuum," *Przeglad Tomistyczny* 3 (1987): 137–178.
Burnyeat, M. F. "Aquinas on 'Spiritual Change' in Perception." In *Ancient and Medieval Theories of Intentionality*, edited by Dominik Perler, 129–201. Leiden: Brill, 2001.
———. "De anima II.5." *Phronesis* 47 (2002): 28–90.
———. "*Kinesis* vs. *Energeia*: A Much-Read Passage in (but not of) Aristotle's Metaphysics." *Oxford Studies in Ancient Philosophy* 34 (2008): 219–292.
Cajetan, T. de Vio. *Commentaria in De Ente et Essentia*. Edited by M. H. Laurent. Turin: Marietti, 1934.
———. *Commentary on Being and Essence*. Edited by L. H. Kendzierski and F. C. Wade. Milwaukee: Marquette University Press, 1964.
Caroti, S. "'Or i est or n'i est une,' Nicolas d'Autrécourt et le 'ludus baterellorum' ou de la génération et de la corruption." In *Chemins de la pensée médiévale. Etudes offertes à Zénon Kaluza*, edited by P. Bakker et al., 135–168. Turnhout: Brépols, 2003.
Caston, V. "Towards a History of the Problem of Intentionality among the Greeks." In *Proceedings of the Boston Area Colloquium in Ancient Philosophy* IX, edited by John J. Cleary and William Wians, 213–245. Lanham, Md.: University Press of America, 1993.
Cesalli, L. "Some Fourteenth Century Realist Theories of the Proposition: A Historical and Speculative Study." In *Signification in Language and Culture*, edited by H. S. Gill, 83–118. Shimla: Indian Institute of Advanced Study, 2002.
Chalmers, D. *The Conscious Mind: In Search of a Fundamental Theory*. Oxford: Oxford University Press, 1996.
———. "Is There Synonymy in Ockham's Mental Language?" In *The Cambridge Companion to Ockham*, edited by Paul Vincent Spade, 76–99. Cambridge: Cambridge University Press, 1999.
Chatton, W. *Reportatio et Lectura Super Sententias: Collatio ad librum Primum et Prologus*. Edited by J. C. Wey. Toronto: Pontifical Institute of Mediaeval Studies, 1989.
———. *Reportatio super Sententias*. Edited by Joseph C. Wey and Girard J. Etzkorn. Toronto: Pontifical Institute of Mediaeval Studies, 2002–2005.
Conti, A. "Complexe Significabile and Truth in Gregory of Rimini and Paul of Venice." In *Medieval Theories on Assertive and Non-Assertive Language*, edited by A. Maierù and L. Valente, 473–494. Florence: Olschki, 2004.
———. "Walter Burley." In *The Stanford Encyclopedia of Philosophy* (Fall 2008 Edition), edited by Edward N. Zalta, http://plato.stanford.edu/archives/fall2008/entries/burley.
Coope, U. "Aristotle's Account of Agency in *Physics* III 3." *Proceedings of the Boston Area Colloquium in Ancient Philosophy* 20 (2004): 201–221.
———. "Aristotle on Action." *Proceedings of the Aristotelian Society Supplementary Volume* 81 (2007): 109–137.
Courtenay, W. "Ockham, Chatton, and the London Studium: Observation on Recent Changes to Ockham's Biography." In *Gegenwart Ockhams*, edited by W. Vossenkuhl and R. Schönberger, 327–337. Weinheim: VCH-Verlagsgesellschaft, Acta Humaniora, 1990.
———. "The Reception of Ockham's Thought at the University of Paris." In *Logique, Ontologie et Théologie au XIVe siècle: Preuves et raisons à l'Université de Paris*, edited by Z. Kaluza and P. Vignaux, 43–64. Paris: Vrin, 1984.
Cova, L. "L'unità della scienza teologica nella polemica di Walter Chatton con Guglielmo D'Ockham." *Franciscan Studies* 45 (1985): 189–230.

Crane, T. "Intentionality." In *The Oxford Companion to Philosophy*, 2nd ed., edited by Ted Honderich, 438–439. Oxford: Oxford University Press, 2005.

Crathorn, W. *In primum librum Sententiarum*. Edited by F. Hoffmann. Munster: Aschendorff, 1988.

———. "Quaestiones super librum sententiarum." In *Questionen Zum ersten Sentenzenbuch*. Edited by F. Hoffmann. Munster: Aschendorff, 1988.

Davidson, H. A. *Alfarabi, Avicenna, and Averroes on Intellect: Their Cosmologies, Theories of the Active Intellect, and Theories of Human Intellect*. New York: Oxford University Press, 1992.

Day, S. *Intuitive Cognition: A Key to the Significance of the Later Scholastics*. St. Bonaventure, N.Y.: Franciscan Institute Press, 1947.

Delorme, F.M. "Le cardinal Vital du Four. Huit questions disputés sur le problème de la connaissance." *Archives d'histoire doctrinale et litteraire du Moyen Age* 2 (1927): 151–337.

Denery, D. G. "Nicholas of Autrecourt on Saving the Appearances." In *Nicolas d'Autrécourt philosophe*, edited by S. Caroti and C. Grellard, 65–84. Cesena: Stilgraf editrice, 2006.

———. *Seeing and Being Seen in the Later Medieval World*. Cambridge: Cambridge University Press, 2005.

de Rijk, L. M. *Giraldus Odonis O.F.M. Opera Philosophica. Vol. II: De intentionibus. Critical Edition with a Study on the Medieval Intentionality Debate up to ca. 1350.* Leiden: Brill, 2005.

———. "On Buridan's View of Accidental Being." In *John Buridan: A Master of Arts. Some Aspects of His Philosophy: Acts of the Second Symposium Organized by the Dutch Society for Medieval Philosophy Medium Aevum on the Occasion of Its 15th Anniversary*, edited by E. P. Bos and Henri Krop, 41–51. Leiden-Amsterdam (Vrije Universiteit), 20–21 June 1991. Nijmegen: Ingenium Publishers, 1993.

Descartes, R. *Oeuvres et lettres*. Edited by Andre Bridoux. Paris: Pléiade, 1953.

———. *The Philosophical Writings of Descartes*, volume II. Translated and edited by J. Cottingham, R. Stoothoff, and D. Murdoch. Cambridge: Cambridge University Press, 1984.

Dewan, L. "St. Thomas and Pre-Conceptual Intellection." *Études Maritainiennes/Maritain Studies* 11 (1995): 220–233.

Dorp, J. *Perutile Compendium totius logicae Joannis Buridani cum praeclarissima solertissimi viri Joannis Dorp expositione*. Venice, 1499. Frankfurt: Minerva, 1965.

Dufresne, C. (Dominus Du Cange). *Glossarium novum ad scriptores mediae aevi*. Paris, 1766.

Dumont, S. "The Scientific Character of Theology and the Origin of Duns Scotus's Distinction Between Intuitive and Abstractive Cognition." *Speculum* 64 (1989): 579–599.

Dunbabin, J. "The Two Commentaries of Albertus Magnus on the *Nicomachean Ethics*." *Recherches de Théologie Ancienne et Médiévale* 30 (1963): 232–250.

Duns Scotus, J. *Lectura*. Vatican City: Typis Polyglottis Vaticanis, 1960–2007.

———. *Opera Omnia III*. Vatican City: Typis Polyglottis Vaticanis, 1954.

———. *Opera omnia XVI*. Vatican City: Typis Polyglottis Vaticanis, 1960.

———. *Ordinatio*. Edited by C. Balic. Vatican City: Typis Polyglottis Vaticanis, 1954–63.

———. *Quaestiones subtilissimae super libros Metaphysicos Aristotelis*. (*Opera Omnia*, vol. 7) Paris: Vivès, 1893.

———. *Quaestiones super libros Metaphysicorum Aristotelis. Libri VI–IX*. Edited by R. Andrews et al. In *Opera philosophica* IV. St. Bonaventure, N.Y.: Franciscan Institute Publications, 1997.

———. *Questions on the Metaphysics of Aristotle*, 2 vols. Translation by G. Etzkorn and A. Wolter. St. Bonaventure, NY: Franciscan Inst. Publ., 1997–1998.

———. *Quodlibet*, q. 13. In *Opera omnia* XXV, 507–586. Vivès: Paris: 1891.

———. *Reportatio I-A*. Edited by A. W. Wolter and O. V. Bychknov. St. Bonaventure, N.Y.: The Franciscan Institute Publications, 2004.

———. *Theoremata*. Edited by M. Dreyer, H. Möhle, and G. Krieger. In *Opera Philosophica* II, 567–721. St. Bonaventure, N.Y.: Franciscan Institute, 2004.

Fitzpatrick, Noel A. "Walter Chatton on the Univocity of Being: A Reaction to Peter Aureoli and William Ockham." Franciscan Studies 31 (1971): 88–177.

Floucat, Y. *L'intimé fecondité de l'intelligence: Le verbe mental selon saint Thomas d'Aquin*. Paris: Téqui, 2001.

Fodor, J. *Concepts: Where Cognitive Science Went Wrong*. Oxford: Oxford University Press, 1998.

———. *The Language of Thought*. Cambridge, Mass.: Harvard University Press, 1975.

Fraser, A. C. *John Locke: An Essay Concerning Human Understanding*. 2 volumes. New York: Dover, 1959.

Fredborg, K. M., N. J. Green-Pedersen, L. Nielsen, and J. Pinborg. "The Commentary on 'Priscianus Maior' Ascribed to Robert Kilwardby." *Cahiers de l'Institut du Moyen-Age Grec et Latin* 15 (1975): 56–65.

———. "An Inedited Part of Roger Bacon's *Opus maius: De signis*." *Traditio* 34 (1978): 75–136.

Freddoso, A. J., and Kelley, F. E., trans. *William of Ockham. Quodlibetal Questions*. 2 volumes. New Haven: Yale University Press, 1991.

Frede, M. "La théorie aristotélicienne de l'intellect agent." In *Corps et âme: sur le De Anima d'Aristote*, edited by G. Romeyer Dherbey and C. Viano, 377–390. Paris: Vrin, 1996.

Friedman, R. L. "On the Trail of a Philosophical Debate: Durandus of St. Pourçain vs. Thomas Wylton on Simultaneous Acts in the Intellect." In *Philosophical Debates at Paris in the Early Fourteenth Century*, edited by Stephen Brown, Thomas Dewender, and Theo Kobusch, 431–461. Leiden: Brill, 2009.

———. "Peter Auriol." In *The Stanford Encyclopedia of Philosophy* (Fall 2009 Edition), edited by Edward N. Zalta, http://plato.stanford.edu/archives/fall2009/entries/auriol.

———. "Peter Auriol versus Durand of St. Pourçain on Intellectual Cognition." *Recherches de Théologie et Philosophie Médiévales/Studies in Medieval Theology and Philosophy/Forschungen zur Theologie und Philosophie des Mittelalters*, 2014.

Gál, G. "Adam of Wodeham's Question on the 'complexe significabile' as the Immediate Object of Scientific Knowledge." *Franciscan Studies* 37 (1977): 66–102.

———. "Gualteri de Chatton et Guillelmi de Ockham controversia de natura conceptus universalis." *Franciscan Studies* 27 (1967): 191–212.

Gál, G., and S. Brown. Introduction to *Summa Logicae* (*Opera Philosophica* I). Edited by P. Boehner, G. Gál, and S. Brown, 7–73. St. Bonaventure, N.Y.: St. Bonaventure University Press, 1967.

Gaskin, R. "Bradley's Regress, the Copula and the Unity of the Proposition." *The Philosophical Quarterly* 45 (1995): 161–180.

———. "*Complexe Significabilia* and Aristotle's Categories." In *La tradition médiévale des categories (XII<sup>e</sup>–XV<sup>e</sup> siècles)*, edited by J. Biard and I. Rosier-Catach, 187–205. Louvain: Éditions Peeters. 2003.

Gauthier, R.-A. *Saint Thomas d'Aquin, Somme contre les gentils*. Paris: Éditions Universitaires, 1993.

Geiger, L.-B. "Les rédactions successives de *Contra Gentiles* I, 53, d'après l'autographe." In *Saint Thomas d'Aquin aujourd'hui*, 221–240. Paris: Desclée de Brouwer, 1963.

Glorieux, P. ed. *Les premières polémiques thomists*. Volume 1: *Le Correctorium corruptorii "Quare."* Le Saulchoir: Kain, 1927.

Godfrey of Fontaines. *Quodlibet V, q. 10*. Edited by M. De Wulf and J. Hoffmans. Louvain, 1914.

Goehring, B. "Henry of Ghent's Use of Aristotle's *De anima* in Developing his Theory of Cognition," in *Medieval Perspectives on Aristotle's De anima*, edited by R. L. Friedman and J.-M. Counet, 61–99. Leuven: Peeters, 2013.

Goris, W., and M. Pickavé. "Von der Erkenntnis der Engel. Der Streit um die *species intelligibilis* und eine *quaestio* aus dem anonymen Sentenzenkommentar in ms. Brügge, Stadsbibliotheek 491." In *Nach der Verurteilung von 1277: Philosophie und Theologie an der Universität von Paris im letzten Viertel des 13. Jahrhunderts*, edited by J. A. Aertsen. K. Emery, and A. Speer, 124–177. Berlin: W. de Gruyter, 2001.

Grassi, Onorato. "The Object of Scientific Knowledge in Some Authors of the Fourteenth Century." In *Knowledge and the Sciences in Medieval Philosophy. Proceedings of the Eighth International Congress of Medieval Philosophy*, edited by S. Knuuttila, R. Tyorinoja, and S. Ebbesen, 180–189. Helsinki: Luther-Agricola Society, 1990.

Gregory of Rimini. *Super Primum et Secundum Sententiarum*. Venice, 1522. St. Bonaventure, N.Y.: Franciscan Institute, 1955.

Grellard, C. *Croire et savoir. Les principes de la connaissance selon Nicolas d'Autrécourt*. Paris: Vrin, 2005.

———. "La causalité chez Nicolas d'Autrécourt." *Quaestio* 2 (2002): 267–289.

———. "L'usage des nouveaux langages d'analyse dans la *Quaestio* de Nicolas d'Autrécourt. Contribution à la théorie autrécurienne de la connaissance." In *Quia inter doctores est magna dissensio. Les débats de philosophie naturelle à Paris au xive siècle*, edited by S. Caroti & J. Celeyrette, 69–95. Florence: L. Olschki, 2004.

———. "Nicholas of Autrecourt's Atomistic Physics." In *Atomism and Its Place in Late Medieval Philosophy*, edited by C. Grellard and A. Robert, 107–126. Leiden: Brill, 2009.

———. "Nicholas of Autrecourt's Skepticism: The Ambivalence of Medieval Epistemology." In *Rethinking the History of Skepticism: The Missing Medieval Background*, edited by H. Lagerlund, 119–144. Leiden: Brill, 2010.

———. "*Sicut specula sine macula*. La perception et son objet chez Nicolas d'Autrécourt." In *Image et représentation dans la pensée médiévale, Chôra. Revue d'études anciennes et médiévales* 3–4 (2005–2006): 229–250.

Guillelmus de Wara (William of Ware). *I Sent. d. XXVII q. 3* (= *Sent.* I, d. 27, q. 3). In *De Liber propugnatorius des Thomas Anglicus und die Lehrunderschiede zwischen Thomas Aquin und Duns Scotus*, edited by M. Schmaus, 2:253–271. Munster: Aschendorff, 1930.

Haase, D. N. *Avicenna's De Anima in the Latin West: The Formation of a Peripatetic Philosophy of the Soul, 1160–1300*. London and Turin: Warburg Institute/Nino Aragno Editore, 2004.

Hahn, M., and B. Ramberg, eds. *Reflections and Replies: Essays on the Philosophy of Tyler Burge*. Cambridge, Mass.: MIT Press, 2003.

Heinämaa, Sara, Vili Lähteenmäki, and Paulina Remes, eds. *Consciousness: From Perception to Reflection in the History of Philosophy*. Dordrecht: Springer, 2007.

Henninger, M. G. *Relations. Medieval Theories 1250–1325*. Oxford: Clarendon Press, 1989.

Henry of Ghent. *Quodlibeta*, 2 volumes. Edited by J. Badius Ascensius. Paris, 1518. Leuven: Bibliothèque S.J., 1961.

Herrera, Max. "Understanding Similitudes in Aquinas with the Help of Avicenna and Averroes." In *Universal Representation, and the Ontology of Individuation*, edited by

G. Klima and A. Hall, 5–23. Newcastle upon Tyne: Cambridge Scholars Publishing, 2011.
Hickerson, R. *The History of Intentionality: Theories of Consciousness from Brentano to Husserl*. New York: Continuum, 2007.
Hoffmann, T. ed. *A Companion on Angels in Medieval Philosophy*. Leiden: Brill, 2012.
Holcot, R. Quaestiones quodlibetales. In W. J. Courtenay, "A Revised Text of Robert Holcot's Quodlibetal Dispute on Whether God is Able to Know More Than He Knows." Archiv für Geschichte der Philosophie 53 *(1971)*: 1–21.
Hubien, H. ed. *Iohannis Buridani Quaestiones in duos libros Aristotelis Posteriorum Analyticorum*. Unpublished typescript.
Jacobi de Viterbio O.E.S.A. *Disputatio Prima De Quolibet*. Würzburg: Augustinus, 1968.
John of Holland. *Four Tracts on Logic*. Edited by E. P. Bos. Nijmegen: Ingenium, 1985.
Kahn, C. "Aristotle on Thinking." In *Essays on Aristotle's De Anima*, edited by M. C. Nussbaum and A. O. Rorty, 359–379. Oxford: Clarendon Press, 1992.
Kaluza, Z. "Les catégories dans l'*Exigit ordo*. Etude de l'ontologie formelle de Nicolas d'Autrécourt." *Studia Mediewistyczne* 33 (1998): 97–124.
———. *Nicolas d'Autrécourt, ami de la vérité*. Paris: Histoire littéraire de la France, 1995.
Kann, C. *Die Eigenschaften der Termini*. Leiden: Brill, 1994.
Karger, E. "Adam Wodeham on the Intentionality of Cognitions." In *Ancient and Medieval Theories of Intentionality*, edited by D. Perler, 283–300. Leiden: Brill, 2001.
———. "Ockham and Wodeham on Divine Deception as a Skeptical Hypothesis," *Vivarium* 42 (2004): 225–236.
———. "Ockham's Misunderstood Doctrine of Intuitive and Abstractive Cognition." In *The Cambridge Companion to William of Ockham*, edited by Paul Vincent Spade, 204–226. Cambridge: Cambridge University Press, 1999.
———. "William of Ockham, Walter Chatton, and Adam Wodeham on the Objects of Knowledge and Belief." *Vivarium* 33 (1995): 171–186.
Keele, R. "Can God Make a Picasso? William Ockham and Walter Chatton on Divine Power and Real Relations." *Journal of the History of Philosophy* 45 (2007): 395–411.
———. "Oxford Quodlibeta from Ockham to Holcot." In *Theological Quodlibeta in the Middle Ages*, edited by Christopher Schabel, 651–692. Leiden: Brill, 2007.
———. "The So-Called Res Theory of Walter Chatton." *Franciscan Studies* 61 (2003): 37–53.
Kelley, F. E. "Walter Chatton vs. Aureoli and Ockham Regarding the Universal Concept." *Franciscan Studies* 41 (1981): 222–249.
Kilcullen, R. J., ed. "Buridan, On Aristotle's *Ethics*, Book X." (1996). Online edition available from www.humanities.mq.edu.au/Ockham/wburlat.html.
King, Peter. "Abelard on Mental Language." *American Catholic Philosophical Quarterly* 81 (2007): 169–187.
———. "Duns Scotus on Singular Essences." *Medioevo* 30 (2005): 111–137.
———. "Le rôle des concepts selon Ockham." *Philosophiques* 32 (2005): 435–447.
———. "Rethinking Representation in the Middle Ages: A Vade-Mecum to Medieval Theories of Mental Representation." In *Representation and Objects of Thought in Medieval Philosophy*, edited by Henrik Lagerlund, 81–100. Ashgate: Aldershot, 2007.
———. "Scholasticism and the Philosophy of Mind: The Failure of Aristotelian Psychology." In *Scientific Failure*, edited by T. Horowitz and A. I. Janis, 109–138. Lanham, Md.: Rowman & Littlefield, 1994.
———. "Scotus on Mental Content." In *Duns Scot à Paris, 1302–2002*, edited by O. Boulnois et al., 65–88. Turnhout: Brépols, 2004.

———. "Scotus on Metaphysics." In *The Cambridge Companion to Duns Scotus*, edited by T. Williams, 15–68. Cambridge: Cambridge University Press, 2003.
———. "Two Conceptions of Experience." *Medieval Philosophy and Theology* 11 (2004): 1–24.
Klima, G. "The Anti-Skepticism of John Buridan and Thomas Aquinas: Putting Skeptics in Their Place vs. Stopping Them in Their Tracks." In *Rethinking the History of Skepticism*, edited by H. Lagerlund, 143–166. Leiden: Brill, 2010.
———. "Aquinas' Theory of the Copula and the Analogy of Being." *Logical Analysis and History of Philosophy* 5 (2002): 159–176.
———. "The Changing Role of *Entia Rationis* in Medieval Philosophy: A Comparative Study with a Reconstruction." *Synthese* 96 (1993): 25–59.
———. "Intentional Transfer in Averroes, Indifference of Nature in Avicenna, and the Representationalism of Aquinas." In *Universal Representation and the Ontology of Individuation*, edited by G. Klima and A. Hall, 45–51. Newcastle upon Tyne: Cambridge Scholars Publishing, 2011.
———. "John Buridan on the Acquisition of Simple Substantial Concepts." In *John Buridan and Beyond: Topics in the Language Sciences 1300–1700*, edited by R. L. Friedmann and S. Ebbesen, 17–32. Copenhagen: Royal Danish Academy of Sciences and Letters, 2004.
———. "Nominalist Semantics." In *The Cambridge History of Later Medieval Philosophy*, edited by R. Pasnau, 159–172. Cambridge: Cambridge University Press, 2010.
———. "The Nominalist Semantics of Ockham and Buridan: A Rational Reconstruction." In *Handbook of the History of Logic*, edited by D. Gabbay and J. Woods, 389–431. Amsterdam: North Holland, 2008.
———. "*Nulla virtus cognoscitiva circa proprium obiectum decipitur.*" http://faculty.fordham.edu/klima/APA.htm.
———. "Ockham's Semantics and Metaphysics of the Categories." In *The Cambridge Companion to Ockham*, edited by P. V. Spade, 118–142. Cambridge: Cambridge University Press, 1999.
———. "Ontological Alternatives vs. Alternative Semantics in Medieval Philosophy." *S. European Journal for Semiotic Studies* 3 (1991): 587–618.
———. "Ontological Reduction by Logical Analysis and the Primitive Vocabulary of Mentalese." *American Catholic Philosophical Quarterly* 86 (2012): 303–414.
———. "The Semantic Principles Underlying Saint Thomas Aquinas's Metaphysics of Being." *Medieval Philosophy and Theology* 5 (1996): 87–141.
———. "Substance, Accident, Modes." In *Encyclopedia of Medieval Philosophy*, edited by H. Lagerlund, 1219–1227. Springer: Dordrecht, 2011.
———. "Syncategoremata." In *Elsevier's Encyclopedia of Language and Linguistics*, 2nd ed., edited by Keith Brown, 12:353–356. Elsevier: Oxford, 2006.
———. "Three Myths of Intentionality vs. Some Medieval Philosophers." *International Journal of Philosophical Studies* 21 (2013): 359–376.
———. "Tradition and Innovation in Medieval Theories of Mental Representation." In *Mental Representation*, edited by G. Klima and A. Hall, 7–16. Newcastle upon Tyne: Cambridge Scholars Publishing, 2011.
———. "William of Ockham: Summa Logicae." In *Central Works of Philosophy*, edited by John Shand, 1:242–269. Chesham: Acumen, 2005.
Klima, G., and A. Hall, eds. *The Demonic Temptations of Medieval Nominalism*. Newcastle upon Tyne: Cambridge Scholars Publishing, 2011.

Koch, J., ed. *Durandi de S. Porciano O.P Quaestio de natura cognitonis et Disputatio cum anonymo quodam necnon Determinatio Hervei Natalis O.P.* Munster: Aschendorff, 1929.

Kosman, L. A. "Perceiving That We Perceive: On the Soul III, 2." *The Philosophical Review* 84 (1975): 499–519.

Kretzman, N., A. Kenny, and J. Pinborg, eds. *The Cambridge History of Later Medieval Philosophy.* Cambridge: Cambridge University Press, 1982.

Lagerlund, H. "John Buridan and the Problems of Dualism in the Early Fourteenth Century." *Journal of the History of Philosophy* 42 (2004): 369–387.

———. "Representations, Concepts and Words: Peter of Ailly on Semantics and Psychology." In *Knowledge, Mental Language, and Free Will*, edited by G. Klima and A. Hall, 19–46. Newcastle upon Tyne: Cambridge Scholars Publishing, 2011.

———. "What Is Singular Thought? Ockham and Buridan on Singular Terms in the Language of Thought." In *Mind and Modality: Studies in the History of Philosophy in Honour of Simo Knuuttila*, edited by V. Hirvonen, T. Holopainen, and M. Touminen, 217–237. Leiden: Brill, 2006.

Lagerlund, H. ed. *Rethinking the History of Skepticism: The Missing Medieval Background.* Leiden: Brill, 2010.

Lambert. *Logica (Summa Lamberti).* Edited by F. Alessio. Florence: La Nuova Italia, 1971.

Lee, R. *Science, the Singular, and the Question of Theology.* London: Palgrave Macmillan, 2002.

Leff, G. *William of Ockham: The Metamorphosis of Scholastic Discourse.* Manchester: Manchester University Press, 1975.

Lewis, D. and R. Langton. "Defining 'Intrinsic.'" *Philosophy and Phenomenological Research* 58 (1998): 333–345.

Lisska, A. "Medieval Theories of Intentionality: From Aquinas to Brentano and Beyond." In *Analytical Thomism: Traditions in Dialogue*, edited by Craig Patterson and Matthew S. Pugh, 147–169. Burlington: Ashgate, 2006.

Lonergan, B. *Verbum: Word and Idea in Aquinas* (Notre Dame: University of Notre Dame Press, 1967). Edited by Frederick E. Crowe and Robert M. Doran. Toronto: Lonergan Research Institute, 1997.

Loux, M. J. *Ockham's Theory of Terms. Part I of the Summa Logicae.* Notre Dame, Ind.: University of Notre Dame Press, 1974.

Lycan, W. G. "Philosophy of Mind." In *The Blackwell Companion to Philosophy*, 2nd ed., edited by Nicholas Bunnin and E. P. Tsui-James, 173–201. Malden, Mass.: Blackwell, 2003.

Lynch, J. *The Theory of Knowledge of Vital du Four.* St. Bonaventure, N.Y.: Franciscan Institute Press, 1972.

MacIntyre, A. "Which God Ought We to Obey, and Why?" *Faith and Philosophy* 3 (1986): 359–371.

Margolis, J. "Reflections on Intentionality." In *The Cambridge Companion to Brentano*, edited by Dale Jacquette, 131–148. Cambridge: Cambridge University Press, 2004.

Marshall, P. "Nicole Oresme's *Questiones super libros Aristotelis De anima*: a critical edition with introduction and commentary." PhD dissertation, Cornell University, 1980.

Marsilius of Inghen. *Quaestiones super Quattuor libros Sententiarum I–II.* Edited by M. Santos Noya. Leiden: Brill, 2000.

———. *Treatises on the Properties of Terms.* Edited and translated by E. P. Bos. Dordrecht: Reidel, 1983.

Marston, Roger. *Quaestiones disputatae de anima.* Edited by the Collegium S. Bonaventurae. Quarrachi: Collegium S. Bonaventurae, 1932.

Maurer, A. "Ockham's Razor and Chatton's Anti-Razor." *Mediaeval Studies* 46 (1984): 463–475.

McGinn, C. "Can We Solve the Mind-Body Problem?" *Mind* 98 (1989): 349–366.

———. *Mental Content.* Oxford: Blackwell, 1989.

Meier-Oeser, S. "Medieval, Renaissance, and Reformation Angels: A Comparison." In *Angels in Medieval Philosophical Inquiry: Their Function and Their Significance,* edited by I. Iribarren and M. Lenz, 187–200. Aldershot: Ashgate, 2008.

Meissner, W. W. "Some Aspects of the *Verbum* in the Texts of St. Thomas." *The Modern Schoolman* 36 (1958): 1–30.

Michael, B. "Johannes Buridan: Studien zu seinem Leben, seinen Werken und zu Rezeption seiner Theorien im Europa des späten Mittelalters. Vols. 1–2." PhD dissertation, University of Berlin, 1985.

Millikan, R. G. *White Queen Psychology and Other Essays for Alice.* Cambridge, Mass.: MIT Press, 1993.

Nivard of Ghent. *Ysengrimus.* Edited and translated by Jill Mann. Leiden: Brill, 1987.

Normore, C. "Burge, Descartes, and Us." In *Reflections and Replies. Essays on the Philosophy of Tyler Burge,* edited by Martin Hahn and B. Ramberg, 1–14. Cambridge, Mass.: MIT Press, 2003.

———. "The Invention of Singular Thought." In *Forming the Mind,* edited by Henrik Lagerlund, 109–128. Dordrecht: Springer, 2007.

———. "Some Aspects of Ockham's Logic." In *The Cambridge Companion to Ockham,* edited by Paul Vincent Spade, 31–52. Cambridge: Cambridge University Press, 1999.

Novotny, D. *Ens rationis from Suárez to Caramuel: A Study in Scholasticism of the Baroque Era.* New York: Fordham University Press, 2013.

Nuchelmans, G. *Late Scholastic and Humanist Theories of the Proposition.* Amsterdam: North Holland, 1980.

———. *Theories of the Proposition: Ancient and Medieval Conceptions of the Bearers of Truth and Falsity.* Amsterdam: North Holland, 1973.

Nys, T. *De werking van het menselijke verstand volgens Hendrik van Gent.* Leuven: Nauwelaerts, 1949.

O'Callaghan, J. J. "The Second Question of the Prologue to Walter Catton's Commentary on the Sentences on Intuitive and Abstractive Knowledge." In *Nine Mediaeval Thinkers,* edited by J. R. O'Donnell, 233–269. Toronto: Pontifical Institute of Mediaeval Studies, 1955.

O'Callaghan, J. P. "Aquinas, Cognitive Theory, and Analogy: A Propos of Robert Pasnau's *Theories of Cognition in the Later Middle Ages.*" *American Catholic Philosophical Quarterly* 76 (2002): 451–482.

———. *Thomist Realism and the Linguistic Turn: Toward a More Perfect Form of Existence.* Notre Dame, Ind.: University of Notre Dame Press, 2003.

———. "*Verbum Mentis*: Philosophical or Theological Doctrine in Aquinas?" *Proceedings of the American Catholic Philosophical Association* 74 (2000): 103–119.

Ockham, W. *Opera philosophica (OPh) and Opera theological (OTh).* Edited by P. Boehner et al. St. Bonaventure, N.Y.: Franciscan Institute, 1967–1988.

———. *Opera Theologica.* 10 vols. St. Bonaventure, N.Y.: Franciscan Institute, 1967–1988.

———. *Quodlibeta Septem.* Edited by J. Wey. St. Bonaventure, N.Y.: Franciscan Institute, 1980.

———. *Scriptum in primum librum Sententiarum: Ordinatio (Dist. XIX–XLVIII).* In *Opera theologica* IV. St. Bonaventure, N.Y.: Franciscan Institute, 1979.

———. *Summa Logicae*. Edited by P. Boehner, G. Gal, and S. F. Brown. St. Bonaventure, N.Y.: Franciscan Institute, 1974.
Olivi, Peter John. *Quaestiones in secundum librum Sententiarum*, 3 vols. Edited by B. Jansen. Quaracchi: Collegium S. Bonaventurae, 1922–1926.
Oresme, N. *Nicolai Oresme Expositio et Quaestiones in Aristotelis De anima*. Edited by B. Patar. Louvain: Éditions Peeters, 1995.
Ovid. *Heroides*. Edited by H. S. Sedlmayer. Vienna: Konegen, 1886.
———. *Tristia*. Edited by S. G. Owen. Oxford: Oxford University Press, 1922–24.
Owens, J. "Aristotle: Cognition, a Way of Being." *Canadian Journal of Philosophy* 6 (1976): 1–11.
———. *Cognition: An Epistemological Inquiry*. Houston: Center for Thomistic Studies, 1992.
Paissac, Henri. *Théologie du verbe*. Paris: Cerf, 1951.
Panaccio, Claude. "Aquinas on Intellectual Representation." In *Ancient and Medieval Theories of Intentionality*, edited by D. Perler, 185–201. Leiden: Brill, 2001.
———. "From Mental Word to Mental Language." *Philosophical Topics* 20 (1992): 125–147.
———. *Le discours intérieur de Platon à Guillaume d'Ockham*. Paris: Éditions de Seuil, 1999.
———. "Mental Language and Predication: Ockham and Abelard." *Analytica* 14 no. 2 (2010): 183–194.
———. *Ockham on Concepts*. London: Ashgate, 2004.
———. "Réponses à mes critiques." *Philosophiques* 32 no. 2 (2005): 449–457.
Panaccio, C., and Perini-Santos, E. "Guillaume d'Ockham et la *suppositio materialis*." *Vivarium* 42 (2004): 202–224.
Pasnau, R. "Aquinas on Thought's Linguistic Nature." *Monist* 80 (1997): 558–575.
———. "Cognition." In *The Cambridge Companion to Duns Scotus*, edited by Thomas Williams, 285–311. Cambridge: Cambridge University Press, 2003.
———. "Henry of Ghent and the Twilight of Divine Illumination." *The Review of Metaphysics* 49 (1995): 49–75.
———. *Theories of Cognition in the Later Middle Ages*. Cambridge: Cambridge University Press, 1997.
———. *Thomas Aquinas on Human Nature: A Philosophical Study of* Summa theologiae Ia 75–89. Cambridge: Cambridge University Press, 2002.
———. "What Is Cognition? A Reply to Some Critics." *American Catholic Philosophical Quarterly* 76 (2002): 483–90.
Pasnau, R., ed. *The Cambridge Translations of Medieval Philosophical Texts*. Volume 3: *Mind and Knowledge*. Cambridge: Cambridge University Press, 2002.
Peacocke, C. *Sense and Content*. Oxford: Oxford University Press, 1983.
Perler, D. "Essentialism and Direct Realism: Some Late Medieval Perspectives." *Topoi* 19 (2000): 111–122.
———."Late Medieval Ontologies of Facts." *The Monist* 77 (1994): 149–169.
———. "Peter Aureol vs. Hervaeus Natalis on Intentionality: A Text Edition with Introductory Remarks." *Archives d'histoire doctrinale et littéraire du Moyen Age* 61 (1994): 227–262.
———. *Theorien der Intentionalität im Mittelalter*. Frankfurt: Klostermann, 2002.
———. *Théories de l'intentionnalité au moyen âge*. Paris: Vrin, 2003.
———. "What Are Intentional Objects? A Controversy among Early Scotists." In *Ancient and Medieval Theories of Intentionality*, edited by D. Perler, 203–226. Leiden: Brill, 2001.

Perler, D., ed. *Ancient and Medieval Theories of Intentionality*. Leiden: Brill, 2001.
Peter of Ailly. *Conceptus et insolubilia*. Paris, 1500.
———. *Tractatus de anima*. Edited by O. Pluta. Amsterdam: Verlag B. R. Grüner, 1987.
Pickavé, M. *Heinrich von Gent über Metaphysik als erste Wissenschaft*. Brill: Leiden, 2007.
Pinborg, J. "The *Summulae*, *Tractatus I De Introductionibus*." In *The Logic of John Buridan*, edited by J. Pinborg, 71–90. Copenhagen: Opuscula graeco-latina, 1975.
Pini, G. "Il dibattito sulle specie intelligibili nel tredicesimo secolo." *Medioevo* 29 (2004): 267–306.
Prezioso, F. *La "species" medievale e i prodomi del fenomenismo moderno*. Padua: CEDAM, 1963.
Ps.-Buridan, J. *Quaestiones in tres libros De Anima Aristotelis*, in *Le traité de l'âme de Jean Buridan (De Prima Lectura). Édition, Étude Critique et Doctrinale*, edited by Benoît Patar. Paris: Éditions de l'Institut Supérieur de Philosophie, 1991.
Pylyshyn, Z. *Computation and Cognition*. Cambridge, Mass.: MIT Press, 1984.
Read, S. L. "How Is Material Supposition Possible?" *Medieval Philosophy and Theology* 8 (1999): 1–20.
———. "The Objective Being of Ockham's Ficta." *The Philosophical Quarterly*, 27 (1977): 14–31.
Reina, Maria Elena. "La prima questione del Prologo del 'Commento Sentenze di Walter Catton.'" *Rivista critica di storia della filosofia* 25 (1970): 48–74, 290–314.
Rombeiro, M. E. "Intelligible Species in Some Late Thirteenth-Century Theories of Cognition." *Journal of the History of Philosophy* 49 (2011): 181–220.
Schabel, C. "Oxford Franciscans After Ockham: Walter Chatton and Adam Wodeham." In Commentaries on Peter Lombard's Sentences, edited by G. P. Evans, 359–377. Leiden: Brill, 2000.
Schmidt, R. W. *The Domain of Logic According to Saint Thomas Aquinas*. The Hague: Nijhoff, 1966.
Scott, F., and S. Herman, eds. "John Buridan's *De motibus animalium*." *Isis* 58 (1967): 533–552.
Searle, J. R. *Intentionality: An Essay in the Philosophy of Mind*. Cambridge: Cambridge University Press, 1983.
Sebti, M. *Avicenne. L'âme humaine*. Paris: Presses Universitaires de France, 2000.
Serene, E. "Demonstrative Science." In *The Cambridge History of Later Medieval Philosophy*, edited by N. Kretzmann, A. Kenny, and J. Pinborg, 496–518. Cambridge: Cambridge University Press, 1982.
Shields, C. *Aristotle*. New York: Routledge, 2007.
———. "Intentionality and Isomorphism in Aristotle." *Proceedings of the Boston Area Colloquium in Ancient Philosophy* 11 (1995): 307–330.
———. "The Peculiar Motion of Aristotelian Souls." *Proceedings of the Aristotelian Society. Supplementary Volume* 81 (2007): 139–161.
Simons, P. "Brentano." In *A Companion to the Philosophers*, edited by Robert L. Arrington, 179–81. Malden, Mass.: Blackwell, 1999.
Sobol, P. G. "John Buridan on the Soul and Sensation." PhD dissertation, Indiana University, 1984.
Sorabji, R. "From Aristotle to Brentano: The Development of the Concept of Intentionality." In *Aristotle and the Later Tradition*, edited by Henry Blumenthal and Howard Robinson, 227–259. Oxford: Clarendon Press, 1991.
———. "Intentionality and Physiological Processes: Aristotle's Theory of Sense-Perception." In *Essays on Aristotle's De Anima*, edited by M. C. Nussbaum and A. O. Rorty, 195–225. Oxford: Clarendon Press, 1992.

Spade, P. "Ockham's Nominalist Metaphysics: Some Main Themes." In *The Cambridge Companion to Ockham*, edited by Paul Vincent Spade, 100–117. Cambridge: Cambridge University Press, 1999.

———. *Thoughts, Words, and Things: An Introduction to Late Medieval Logic and Semantic Theory* (1996). http://pvspade.com/Logic.

Spade, P., ed. *The Cambridge Companion to Ockham*. Cambridge: Cambridge University Press, 1999.

Spruit, L. *Species intelligibilis: From Perception to Knowledge*. Volume 1, *Classical Roots and Medieval Discussions*. Leiden: Brill, 1994.

Stump, E. *Aquinas*. New York: Routledge, 2003.

———. "Aquinas's Account of the Mechanisms of Intellective Cognition." *Revue internationale de philosophie* 52 (1998): 287–307.

———. "The Mechanisms of Cognition: Ockham on Mediating Species." In *The Cambridge Companion to Ockham*, edited by Paul Vincent Spade, 168–203. Cambridge: Cambridge University Press, 1999.

Suarez-Nani, T. *Connaissance et langage des anges selon Thomas d'Aquin et Gilles de Rome*. Paris: Vrin, 2002.

Szyller, S. ed. "Johannis Buridani, *Tractatus de differentia universalis ad individuum*." *Przeglad Tomistyczny* 3 (1987): 137–178.

Tachau, K. *Vision and Certitude in the Age of Ockham: Optics, Epistemology and the Foundations of Semantics 1250–1345*. Leiden: Brill, 1988.

———. "Wodeham, Crathorn and Holcot: The Development of the *Complexe Significabile*." In *Logos et Pragma: Essays on Philosophy of Language in Honor of Professor Gabriel Nuchelmanss*, edited by L. M. de Rijk and H. A. G. Braakhuis, 161–187. Nijmegen: Ingenium, 1987.

Taylor, John Hammond, trans. *St. Augustine, The Literal Meaning of Genesis*. 2 volumes. New York: Paulist Press, 1982.

Thijssen, J. M. M. H. "The Quest for Certain Knowledge in the Fourteenth Century: Nicholas of Autrecourt against the Academics." *Acta Philosophica Fennica* 66 (2000): 199–223.

Thijssen, J. M. M. H., and J. Zupko, eds. *The Metaphysics and Natural Philosophy of John Buridan*. Leiden: Brill, 2001.

Torrell, J.-P. "La vision de Dieu *per essentiam* selon Thomas d'Aquin." *Micrologus* 5 (1997): 43–68.

Trentman, J. "Ockham on Mental." *Mind* 79 (1970): 586–590.

van der Lecq, R., ed. *Johannes Buridanus, Questiones longe super librum Perihermeneias*. Nijmegen: Ingenium, 1983.

van der Lecq, Ria, and H. A. G. Braakhuis, eds. *Johannes Buridanus, Questiones Elencorum*. Nijmegen: Ingenium, 1994.

Waim, Gervasius. *Tractatus noticiarum*. Paris: Conrad Resch, 1519.

Waszink, J. H., ed. *Timaeus a Calcidio Translatus Commentarioque Instructus*. London/Leiden: Warburg Institute/Brill, 1962.

Weidemann, H. "Sache, Satz und Satzverhalt: Zur Diskussion über das Objekt des Wissens im Spätmittelalter." *Vivarium* 29 (1991): 129–147.

Wey, J. C. Introduction to *Quodlibeta Septem*. (*Opera Theologica* IX, 7–41). Edited by J. C. Wey. St. Bonaventure, N.Y.: St. Bonaventure University Press, 1980.

———. Introduction to Reportatio et Lectura super Sententias: Collatio ad Librum Primum et Prologus, 1–8. Edited by J. C. Wey. Toronto: Pontifical Institute of Medieval Studies, 1989.

Witt, C. *Substance and Essence in Aristotle: An Interpretation of* Metaphysics *VII–IX*. Ithaca, N.Y.: Cornell University Press, 1989.

Wodeham, A. *Adam Goddam super quatuor libros Sententiarum, (the so-called "Abbreviatio") made by Henry Totting de Oyta from Wodeham's Oxford commentary on the four books of the Peter Lombard's Sentences.* Edited by J. Major. Paris, 1512.

———. *Lectura secunda in librum primum Sententiarum.* Edited by R. Wood and G. Gál St. Bonaventure, N.Y.: Franciscan Institute, 1990.

———. *Tractatus de indivisibilibus.* Edited by R. Wood. Dordrecht: Kluwer, 1988.

Zupko, J. "How It Played in the rue de Fouarre: Reception of Adam Wodeham's Theory of the Complexe Significabile in the Arts Faculty at Paris in the Mid–Fourteenth Century." *Franciscan Studies* 54 (1994): 211–225.

———. *John Buridan: Portrait of a Fourteenth-Century Arts Master.* Notre Dame, Ind.: University Press, 2003.

———. "John Buridan's Philosophy of Mind." PhD dissertation, Cornell University, 1989.

# CONTRIBUTORS

SUSAN BROWER-TOLAND is associate professor of philosophy at Saint Louis University. Her work in medieval philosophy focuses primarily on issues at the intersection of philosophy of mind, language, and metaphysics. Her papers have been published in journals such as *The Philosophical Review*, *Philosophers Imprint*, *Oxford Studies in Medieval Philosophy*, and the *Journal of the History of Philosophy*.

RUSSELL L. FRIEDMAN is professor of philosophy at the University of Leuven in Belgium. His work focuses on medieval theories of cognition and philosophical theology. His publications include *Intellectual Traditions at the Medieval University: The Use of Philosophical Psychology in Trinitarian Theology among the Franciscans and Dominicans, 1250–1350* (2013).

CHRISTOPHE GRELLARD is associate professor of philosophy at the University of Paris 1 Panthéon-Sorbonne and a junior fellow of the Institut Universitaire de France. His recent publications include *Jean de Salisbury et la renaissance médiévale du scepticisme* (2013) and *De la certitude volontaire. Débats nominalistes sur la foi à la fin du Moyen Âge* (2014).

JOSHUA P. HOCHSCHILD is dean of the College of Liberal Arts and associate professor of philosophy at Mount St. Mary's University in Emmitsburg, Maryland. A founding member of the Society for Medieval Logic and Metaphysics, he is the author of *The Semantics of Analogy: Rereading Cajetan's De Nominum Analogia* (2010).

ELIZABETH KARGER, now retired, was affiliated with the Centre National de la Recherche Scientifique in Paris. She is the author of numerous articles on medieval philosophy, especially on late medieval logic, epistemology, and theory of mind.

PETER KING is professor of philosophy and of medieval studies at the University of Toronto. He is the author of numerous articles on medieval philosophy and has published translations of Augustine and Buridan.

GYULA KLIMA is professor of philosophy at Fordham University, Doctor of the Hungarian Academy of Sciences, director of the Society for Medieval Logic and Metaphysics, and editor of the society's proceedings. Among his books is *John Buridan* (2008).

HENRIK LAGERLUND is professor and chair of the Department of Philosophy at the University of Western Ontario. He has published extensively on medieval philosophy, including the monograph *Modal Syllogistics in the Middle Ages* (2000). Among his edited books are *Rethinking the History of Skepticism* (2010) and *The Philosophy of Francisco Suarez* (2012). He is also the editor-in-chief of the *Encyclopedia of Medieval Philosophy* (2011).

STEPHAN MEIER-OESER is *Privatdozent* of philosophy at the University of Münster and editor-in-chief of the philosophical writings and letters of G. W. Leibniz at the Leibniz-Forschungsstelle Münster (Akademie-Ausgabe).

CLAUDE PANACCIO holds the Canada Research Chair in the Theory of Knowledge at the University of Quebec in Montreal and is a fellow of the Royal Canadian Society. His books in the field of medieval philosophy include *Le Discours intérieur. De Platon à Guillaume d'Ockham* (1999) and *Ockham on Concepts* (2004).

MARTIN PICKAVÉ is Canada Research Chair in Medieval Philosophy at the University of Toronto. He specializes in later medieval philosophy of mind and metaphysics and is currently working on a monograph on medieval theories of the emotions. His most recent book, coedited with Lisa Shapiro, is *Emotion and Cognitive Life in Medieval and Early Modern Philosophy* (2013).

GIORGIO PINI is associate professor of philosophy at Fordham University. He held visiting positions at Leuven University, Cornell University, and All Souls College. He has recently published articles in the *Journal of the History of Philosophy* and *Oxford Studies in Medieval Philosophy*, among other scholarly journals.

OLAF PLUTA has been associated with Ruhr-Universität Bochum, Radboud Universiteit Nijmegen, Harvard University, the University of California at Los Angeles, and the Centre Pierre Abélard de la Sorbonne in Paris. He is an editor of *Bochumer Studien zur Philosophie* and *Bochumer Philosophisches Jahrbuch für Antike und Mittelalter* and the creator of Abbreviationes, the first database of Medieval Latin abbreviations.

STEPHEN READ is honorary professor of history and philosophy of logic at the Arché Research Centre for Logic, Language, Metaphysics and Epistemology at the University of St. Andrews, Scotland. He edited and translated Thomas Bradwardine's *Insolubilia* (2010) and is the translator of a new edition of John Buridan's *Treatise on Consequences* (2014).

JACK ZUPKO is professor and chair of the Philosophy Department at the University of Alberta. He is the author of *John Buridan: Portrait of a 14th-Century Arts Master* (2003) and, with Edward Buckner, of *Time and Existence: Duns Scotus' Commentaries on Aristotle's "Perihermenias"* (2014).

# INDEX

absolute of intellection, 153–154, 163
abstraction, 9, 11, 13, 18, 32, 64, 66, 85, 88–89, 93–96, 109, 129, 137–139, 248, 278–279, 327, 335
act of thought. *See* intellection
agent intellect, 32, 64–67, 85–86, 93–96, 107–108, 110, 118, 159, 162
assimilation, 76–77, 79, 119, 125, 153–154, 174, 303–304, 320
attention, 156–157, 162, 215, 224, 242

being: apparent, 4, 144–145, 147, 150–153, 155, 157; diminished, 144, 151–152, 156; intentional, 4, 142, 144–145, 147, 149–151, 154; modes of, 144, 164, 211, 251, 259–260, 279; objective, 6, 135, 139–140, 144, 162–163, 236, 244–250, 328–329; real, 4, 6, 144, 151, 158; of reason, 164, 328; representative, 328–330

causality, 39, 46, 49, 51, 92, 105, 119, 155, 173
cogitative power, 9, 256
cognition: abstractive, 94–95, 101–102, 111–114, 117, 123, 124, 126, 128, 137–138, 186, 194–203; act of, 4, 11–13, 26–27, 49–50, 63, 122, 125, 134, 247; angelic, 48–51, 70–76; evident, 182–183; intellectual, 3–4, 31–32, 37, 46–47, 63–65, 68–69, 74–76, 78–79, 81, 85–86, 94, 108, 110, 114, 137, 141–142, 148–150, 153–154, 156, 158, 161–162, 304, 321, 325; intuitive, 3, 82, 101, 111–120, 123–128, 133–138, 170, 173–175, 183–184, 186, 194–203, 246; sensitive (sensory), 9, 60, 67, 74, 86, 106–108, 123, 132, 136–137, 173, 237; singular, 110, 127–129, 135–136; universal, 7, 112, 136, 279

cognitive act, 4, 48–50, 77, 94, 117, 164, 231, 265, 336
cognitive faculties, 4, 113, 145, 240, 303, 306, 322
cognitive powers, 9, 25, 32, 45, 71, 73, 77–79, 142, 145, 148–151, 160, 164, 245–248, 262, 279, 302
cognitive science, 12–13, 105
common sense, 9, 136
common sensible, 23, 106
complex idea, 288–289
*complexe significabile*, 21, 190–191, 228–229, 332
compositionality, 41–44, 117, 140
concepts: absolute *versus* connotative, 130–131, 134, 138, 170, 175–178, 180, 335; acquisition of, 13–14, 113, 138, 180, 303; bare, 175–177; categorematic, 10, 21, 325, 328, 334–335; combination of concepts, 21, 36, 40–45, 108, 207, 238, 308; content of, 5, 12, 43, 138–139, 188–190, 334–336; conventional, 173, 178–180; hyperintensionality of, 10; objective *versus* formal, 33, 40, 42–45, 290, 325–331, 334–336; simple *versus* complex, 8, 19, 21, 36, 39, 42, 132, 134, 137, 175, 177, 266, 297, 303, 305, 309–311, 313, 317, 331–332, 345; singular, 4, 104, 113, 122–124, 131, 133, 138–139, 271; syn/categorematic, 21, 178, 324, 328, 331, 334–335; transcendental, 195–198, 251; universal, 7, 129, 205, 210, 278, 280, 335; vague, 122, 128, 132–135, 139
consciousness, 3, 5, 141–143, 145, 150, 157, 163–164, 221, 272, 286, 335
content of concepts, 12, 175; phenomenal/semantic, 5, 335–336
content of thoughts, 4–5, 188–190

357

*dictio*, 10, 150–151, 155, 162
direct realism, 6, 33–34, 77–78, 117, 191, 235–239, 242, 244, 249–250, 336
Divine Word (*Verbum*), 36–40

estimative power, 9, 266
expressed species. *See* impressed/expressed species
extension: bodily, 64, 260–261; in semantics, 175–180, 184, 297, 299, 310, 329, 333, 335–336
extensional(ist) (semantics), 8, 19, 299, 333
externalism, 3–5, 104, 117, 120, 166–168, 172–173, 175, 177–178, 180–181, 184–185, 203, 333
externalist(ic), 3–5, 31, 118, 120, 166, 173–175, 177, 181, 183–185, 186, 202–203

*ficta*, 176, 210–211, 213, 323, 328–329, 332–336

habitus, 50, 76, 89, 100, 118, 137, 160, 188, 202, 260–262
haecceity, 115–116

identity, 22, 82, 114–116, 119–120, 276, 302, 332; formal, 41, 84; intentional, 6; mental, 19; numerical, 84, 292
illumination (divine), 110
imagination, 1, 4, 32, 56, 63–66, 78, 86, 106, 161–164, 245, 256, 262, 300
imposition (*impositio*), 9, 15, 38–39, 168–172, 180–185, 263, 293, 301
impressed/expressed species, 2, 49–51, 60, 62, 67–78, 106, 323
impression, 14–15, 18, 55, 57, 67, 69–72, 74, 85, 105, 119–120, 168, 302
in a cognizer *versus* in a subject, 16, 67–68, 79
intellection (act of thought), 34, 64, 81, 95, 97–98, 110, 125–126, 137, 142–143, 150–163, 167, 171, 173, 186, 190–195, 245, 323
intelligible species, 2–3, 32–35, 44, 46–50, 66–72, 74–79, 83–86, 88–96, 99, 108–110, 116, 118, 157–150, 163, 261, 266, 324–325
intension (and remission), 246–247

intension(al/ity in semantics), 8, 19, 254, 297298, 310, 329, 331–336
intention (*intentio*), 6, 17, 34–37, 59, 90, 119, 144, 168–169, 254–257, 260–262, 267, 271; second intention, 178, 262–266, 268–272, 312, 315, 326
intentional action, 148, 157
intentional being. *See* being: intentional
intentional inexistence, 251, 270
intentional object, 6, 142, 150–154, 162, 164, 211, 235–237, 249–250, 268
intentional reception, 35, 55–56, 60, 67. *See also* spiritual/intentional change
intentionality, 1, 3–6, 11–12, 24, 62–63, 73, 79, 81–83, 90–94, 100–103, 141–145, 150, 267–272
interior/internal senses, 107, 256, 316
internalism, 3, 104, 167, 172, 181, 203
intrinsic, 1, 5, 61–62, 75–79, 144, 184 197–199, 203, 232, 325–326

life force/vital force, 146–148
likeness (*similitudo*), 15, 25, 28, 30, 35, 48–49, 51, 75, 84, 92, 101, 119, 122, 124–125, 127, 147–148, 152, 158–159, 164, 173, 176, 190, 262, 293, 300–304, 309–310, 313

material falsity, 316–321
memory, 56–57, 117, 137, 271; intellectual, 108, 149, 159–161; sensory, 4, 106, 147–148, 262, 276–277, 280–282
mental language, 2, 6, 10, 13, 18–20, 29–31, 41–45, 120, 122, 134–135, 139–140, 179, 207–211, 217–220, 225, 319, 331
mental proposition, 10–11, 18–23, 42, 44, 179–181, 191, 194, 303, 319, 319–333
mental qualities, 82, 188–199, 260–263, 290, 292, 327
mental word, 2, 18–19, 36, 38–45, 150. *See also verbum mentis*
mode of existence. *See* being: modes of
*modus essendi*. *See* being: modes of

narrow content, 104
natural *versus* cognitive change, 2, 58, 73, 103. *See also* spiritual/intentional change

neo-Aristotelian synthesis, 106, 108, 110, 113, 117–118, 121
nominalism, 2, 5, 8, 11, 13, 29–30, 33–34, 41, 45, 132, 139, 209, 227, 260, 264, 324, 328–329, 331–333, 336

object (immediate/ultimate), 21, 134, 209–210, 215, 225, 228, 315, 325, 327–329, 332, 335–336
objective being. *See* being: objective

passivity of the intellect, 73
*phantasia*, 125, 157, 162–163, 256. *See also* imagination
phantasm, 4, 32, 35, 47, 63–68, 74, 76–78, 85, 89–90, 96, 106, 108–110, 126, 137, 159–162
Platonism, 5, 13, 244, 250, 291
possible intellect, 32, 44, 65, 85–88, 90, 93–96, 107–110, 118, 159, 164, 326
possible things, 195–199, 203
potency, accidental/essential, 98, 112, 160–161

realism, 11, 41, 45, 82, 143, 244
representationalism, 31, 33–36, 117, 336
rigid designator, 134
real proposition, 332
reverse subordination, 178–180. *See also* subordination

sense (sensory) organ, 54–55, 58–61, 79, 105–107, 200
sense (sensory) perception, 51–54, 64, 67, 70, 74, 79–80, 272, 288–289, 304–305, 309, 319–321
sensible species, 63, 71, 75, 147, 200
sensitive (sensory) powers, 32, 51–61, 63–64, 67, 76, 79
sign: conventional, 2, 10, 16, 22, 24–25, 134, 261, 288; natural, 10–11, 18, 22–25, 41, 44–45, 168, 173, 175, 179, 293–294, 297, 303, 319
signification, 9–11, 14–28; immediate, 10, 172, 216, 258, 288; ultimate, 10, 24–28, 257–258, 331–333

similitude. *See* likeness
simple apprehension, 6, 8, 82, 132, 288, 297–298, 304, 307–317, 320
simple idea, 288–289
singular concept. *See* concepts: singular
singular thought, 3–4, 83, 104, 109–121, 123–124
soul: intellective, 7, 107–109, 123, 126, 134, 187, 278; sensitive, 108, 123, 151
*species impressa/expressa*. *See* impressed/expressed species
species in the medium, 35, 54–55, 105
species reception, 54, 56–63, 67
spiritual/intentional change, 55, 58–60. *See also* natural *versus* cognitive change
supposition (*suppositio*), 26, 128, 132, 179, 320, 332
states of affairs, 186, 189–190, 193–194, 209, 332
subordination, 10, 18–19, 21, 26, 39, 168–173, 178–180, 184–185, 192, 259, 294, 333
subpersonal, 105, 117–118, 120

term: mental, 19, 21, 24–26, 124, 134–135, 180, 318, 331; singular, 4, 104, 120, 123–128, 256 (*see also* concepts: singular); universal, 256, 334 (*see also* concepts: universal)
thinker's gaze, 148–149, 156–157
transduction, 108

universal. *See* concepts: universal; *see also* abstraction

vague concepts. *See* concepts: vague
*verbum mentis*, 34, 36–40, 88, 92. *See also* mental word
veridical(ity), 236–237, 240, 245, 272
*veritas simplex/complexa*, 8, 308–312
*Vorstellung*, 252, 287, 290, 292

wide content, 104

# MEDIEVAL PHILOSOPHY: TEXTS AND STUDIES

Ronald E. Pepin, *The Vatican Mythographers*

Paul Thom, *The Logic of the Trinity: Augustine to Ockham*

Charles Bolyard and Rondo Keele (eds.), *Later Medieval Metaphysics: Ontology, Language, and Logic*

Daniel D. Novotný, *Ens rationis from Suárez to Caramuel: A Study in Scholasticism of the Baroque Era*

John Buridan, *Treatise on Consequences*. Translated and with an Introduction by Stephen Read; Editorial Introduction by Hubert Hubien

Gyula Klima (ed.), *Intentionality, Cognition, and Mental Representation in Medieval Philosophy*

www.ingramcontent.com/pod-product-compliance
Lightning Source LLC
Chambersburg PA
CBHW022027290426
44109CB00014B/775